Barbara
Newhall Follett
| A LIFE IN LETTERS |

Barbara
Newhall Follett
| A LIFE IN LETTERS |

Edited by Stefan Cooke

farksolia

Barbara Newhall Follett: A Life in Letters
Copyright © 2015 Stefan William Follett Cooke

All rights reserved. Printed in the United States of America.
No part of this book may be used or reproduced without written
permission except in the case of brief quotations for articles
or reviews.

Cover design by Resa Blatman · www.blatmandesign.com

For more BNF visit farksolia.org

ISBN: 978-0-9962431-1-7 (softcover)

First edition August 2015

For Barbara and her sisters

My heartfelt thanks to my wife, Resa Blatman, for her love and support; to Grizzly, Minx & Little Mouse for furry distraction; to Columbia University's Rare Book & Manuscript Library; to the Literary Trustees of Walter de la Mare and The Society of Authors as their representative; and to all who keep Barbara's flame flickering.

Introduction

Three years ago I visited the archive of Barbara Newhall Follett, my mother's half-sister, at Columbia University in New York. I had little idea of what I would find, and the amount of material left me very happy indeed. Hundreds of letters, stories and essays long and short, poems, photographs, watercolors, press clippings, galley proofs, an account of Farksolia (Barbara's imaginary world) and a lexicon of Farksoo (its language), *Lost Island* (a lost novel). I had only a few hours with this treasure and speed-read as much as I could, photographing the pages I wanted more time with. I returned a couple of months later and spent several leisurely days with Barbara and her mother, Helen, whose archive is also at Columbia.

The papers in Barbara's and Helen's fourteen boxes are organized by broad category and much of the material is undated and/or unidentified. Many pages are brittle and crumbling—some repaired with Scotch tape brown with age. No matter how careful I was, my table in Butler Library was covered with confetti. I couldn't let Barbara disintegrate like this: I photographed almost everything. When the library closed I wandered the streets of the neighborhood nearby where Helen, Barbara, and her sister, Sabra, had lived eighty years earlier. I sat in the little park near Grant's Tomb that two of their apartments had overlooked, trying to imagine what things were like back then.

Back at home I sorted through my thousands of digital photographs. The more I read, the more I fell in love with Barbara and the more I wanted to share her remarkable writing and life. I wrote a short biography and transcribed some of her stories and *Lost Island* for a website I had made, Farksolia. I posted a few letters and photos and some other bits and pieces, but soon realized that what I really wanted was a big book of Barbara on my shelf next to *The House Without Windows*, *The Voyage of the Norman D.*, *Magic Portholes*, *Stars to Steer By*, and *Barbara: The Unconscious Autobiography of a Child Genius*. Her letters are so vibrant and generous—and her philosophy and yearning and lust for life so timeless—that I knew the best way to tell her story was through her own words. So I transcribed all of her letters and many of those of her correspondents, and did more research. And here—101 years after Barbara was born—is her big book.

A note about the editing. To borrow from my grandfather's Historical Note in *The House Without Windows*, "Barbara, whose spelling and grammar happen to be very reliable, would want us to straighten them out for her if they weren't." Likewise I've fixed a few of Barbara's very rare mistakes for readability's sake, as I think she would have liked. I've retained her preference for British over American spelling, although you'll find that that preference tended to waver. I've also given her underlined words italics, and changed her double-hyphens to em dashes.

You'll notice that several of Barbara's earlier letters are unsigned. She often typed a draft, edited it by hand, then typed a clean copy for her correspondent. These drafts made their way into the Columbia archive many years later, while many of the signed letters were forwarded to Helen in the 1940s and '50s, their recipients rightly thinking them worth keeping.

1

HERE (1914-1922)

Barbara Newhall Follett was born on March 4, 1914, in Hanover, New Hampshire. Her father (my grandfather), Roy Wilson Follett (1887-1963), was teaching English at Dartmouth College while her mother, Helen Thomas Follett (1883-1970), a former school teacher, stayed at home with Barbara and Helen's mother—Lizzie Humphrey Newhall Thomas (1850-1934)—or "Ding" for short.

Barbara's parents kept a diary for her early years. Several of the entries follow—almost all of them by her mother, but the first is Wilson's.

11 August 1914
Blessed Barbaretta:

Do you mind if your daddy—an insufficient substitute in any case—scribbles you off a wee bit of a letter *in propria persona*, in lieu of diary? The fact, the persistent and inescapable fact, is that you're a mystery to me. I watch you lovingly and lingeringly, by hours and multiples of hours; I hang on the queer motions of your hands; my spirit dissolves in ecstasies over the inscrutable things you do with your dimpled feet; I marvel over your limpid baby-eyes that grow browner and browner; and everlastingly I speculate about what you mean by all these things. But I do not understand. I can do everything except that. You are not a reticent nature; I do not think your most unsparing critic could accuse you of being uncommunicative. And beyond doubt your naive and charming disclosures have a sweet clarity of their own—are, in fine, models of expository self-revelation. Only—one does not know the language! One cannot know it; one can find no way to the obscure code of your choosing. And so this whole period of your unfolding (a period that you yourself are going to forget while you are still only on the verge of understanding it in our crass and arbitrary terms) baffles and must baffle us. We admire, we gloat, we adore, we worship—but O! how we want to understand! Perhaps you are the sole being in our cosmos whom to understand perfectly would be not to love less.

Well, we watch you. Our eyes widen in wonder as we watch; all the unassuming and spontaneous tricks of your development (and there is a new trick every day) are the historic, breath-bereaving events of our state. Today, it seemed a memorable thing that you should have come, at some appalling hour hard after midnight, out of angelic sleep into a stratum of rubbing your eyes open and murmuring silken murmurs. Later on, you paid by sleeping until half-past six, instead of waking on the hour and clucking to the mother whose eyes are so quick to open at your call—and that too seemed momentous. Those, perhaps, are things you have done before; things not unprecedented, but only faint departures from your charming amenable personality. Yet they stirred us momentarily. Judge, then, how we—your mother Helen, your ecstatic grandmother, your acquired Aunt Belle, and your daddy who manages the type-machine better than the pen—passed into a delirium of joy when, kicking solemnly in your bath, you twisted with one alarming lurch out of your mother's arms and turned clean over on your cherubic belly, there to seize the rim of your insufficient tub in two dimpled fists (four dimples each!) and hold fast, smiling at Europe! That was a great moment in your life—in this first of your lives, this serene and limpid shadow-existence across an impenetrable barrier from us who love and watch and—wait... This afternoon, as you lay supine on the many-times-folded comforter, and wrestled to turn over, were you re-living that triumph of the morning, touching again in some dim reflex way the attitude of that first thrilling experience? I suspect you were; I suspect you were, in your own devious and inexplicable way, remembering. Certainly, when I gave you a finger to clutch in the baby-fist of unbelievable softness and so supported just the needed half-ounce of propulsion, you gave me the same smile. Doubtless you thought you had done it all yourself—and spiritually you had! Spiritually, you were an explorer in unknown lands, a voyager in uncharted seas. You were great; you were coping with the world, unafraid and radiant with hope. And I think you were remembering. But that is another of the things we can't know. All we can know is, that I gave you a finger that knew its strength and your weakness, and so turned you over.

Just now, you lie up there, a tiny in a vastness of crib and coverlet, three hours deep in your own slumber-world of fairies and moonshine—looking so rare and radiant and beyond everything so beautiful that it's only a wild surmise your being there at all a few minutes hence, when arms go out to you for the last meal and the goodnight. For you're so precious a thing one doesn't see how this world can hold you. Never, surely, did any being stay in it with so sweet a condescension, so absolute a sense of probation, so clear a conviction of being able to leave it at will. It isn't really so: you can't go if you will. You tried this afternoon, when it was hot and sticky, and you didn't approve of things; you protested with wails, and tried your hardest to leave us. You were a material baby then, aetas five months, weight fourteen eleven. But now you are an age-long, ageless incarnation of the spirit, the rarefied essence, of Baby, a creature of dream and desire, and we know you could dissolve into a wish, and become only a dream-that-was-too-beautiful. And we don't want you to go; we want, O how we want! you to stay...

20 August *[1914]*
My Lassie:

Your Helen-Mother is alone tonight, alone she has been since the very early and very foggy hours of Tuesday last. For it was then that your Daddy with pack on his back, tremendous shoes on his feet, and joy in his heart started forth to seek the freshness of the mountain. Not alone but with a sturdy camp companion (by name, Myron Fisher). He was glad to go, happy in the quest of fresh truth, new thoughts, and he knew that the mountains would give him both. A tired Daddy. Tonight I am thinking of him so hard. You, Blessed, are asleep in your big dream bed, and not even the thunder bolts disturb you or chase away the fairy moonbeams that surround you. Yes, you are very safe; but where is your daddy? Is he rolled up in his warm blanket, dreaming of us whom he sees in the stars, or is he seeking shelter somewhere from the cold winds and rains? How can we know? But we do know that he is with us—spiritually, that whether he is by his camp fire in a wild and strange wilderness, or whether he is sleeping rolled up in blanket and rain-coverings, he is thinking of his babe and her mother. We know that, and we are happy in the knowing.

Barbara in her carriage

Are you missing your daddy, I wonder? You have been such a sleepless, restless, high-kicking lassie all day. But a twenty minutes snooze have you taken since you first began your chuckling at six o'clock this morning. You refuse with a very strong back-bone to lie on your back as much as you ought; in your carriage yesterday, you seized the rungs on each side and mighty near pulled yourself way up straight! And a finger held out to you is all you need, and up you came, smiles all over your chubby face.

And you were as funny tonight and clever too! As you lay on the soft covering on the floor drinking, you noticed the little white tassels on your blue socks. (You were wearing them because it was so cold today) and you seized and pulled and pulled, and still pulling you brought your little feet up very near your head, and then what seemed one more tremendous pull you rolled over and up you came on your little belly, smiling, nay, grinning. And you repeated the trick. Daddy's finger was not there, but the string was! And that was what you needed!

O blessed little heart-joy asleep in your world of Brown-birds and fairies! How my arms ache for you now, how I long for the last meal hour (at ten) to come, that I may again feel the baby body, kiss the baby head, and tuck away the lassie for the long night. Do you know the tenderness that covers you? Do you know how a mother's hands smoothes out the cover over you, how tenderly, reverently? You will never know till some day the magic time comes for you, my Blessed, to be even as I am now, a Mother.

In September the family moved to Providence, Rhode Island, where Wilson had a new job teaching English at Brown University.

12 October 1914
My Lassie:
You have been our greatest joy during all the weeks when time pressed us and when courage failed us. These were days of packing in Hanover during the first week of September and there were days of waiting in good friends' rooms while your Daddy was nest-hunting in Providence; and then there was one great day when we three (Grandmother, you and I) came south in your first train (this was September 16) (and you were a sweet babe and a happy, playful one all the way down); and there was one greatest meeting with our Daddy at Providence (about 6:30 the same 16 Sept.); then came our first cab ride (and you snuggled up close in my arms, your eyes bright, big, wonderful) and we arrived! O that arrival at the new little cottage which our Daddy had found for us! How hard he had worked for us, and how lovely it looked. You, Blessed, knew you were home again,

for you slept—O how you slept!—and the next day, and each succeeding day you were feeling tip-top; no more wakeful nights—for you were home again. And every day saw you grow more beautiful, more full of delightful capers. Then of a sudden came a *[?]* upon us all—on the 23 day of September your only Aunty—Aunty Belle died. I can scarcely believe now what I am writing. Your dear, dear Aunty whom we all loved, who loved you above all babes. You shall hear of her some day when you are bigger; I shall tell you things about her that will make you love her. But, Little One of Ones, no sorrow has come to you yet, no sorrow, no sickness, not a day's worth. Just sunshine, joy, laughter, the Brown-Bird twitterings, and love, much love—these things are yours. And they shall be yours, my Precious, just so long as we can help and keep them yours.

Your mischievous capers are growing in number so fast that 'tis almost impossible to keep up with them. You roll and tumble about in your pen in a wondrous fashion; quick as a flash you are over now, first on your back, then on your belly and you hitch along at a pretty brisk rate. You do creep sometimes—you lift your body entirely off the floor—and then you almost leap forward. Strings are still your most happy playthings; little celluloid balls on a ribbon, Grandmother's watch chain, the strap of your carriage: you love these very much. It happened when you were hardly 7 months old that you made the discovery of producing a noise by hitting two things together, and you (from that time) have been delighting us all with your whackings.

And today (one week later) you whacked your daddy with a very hard darning ball, you grasping the handle in your own chubby hand. You hit him hard on his face, and it hurt! But he invited it, for he had unrolled his long self in your 4x4 pen, and immediately he had become one of your playthings to do with as you liked. O that play hour for babes and grown-ups! From 5-6 each afternoon is your daddy's most blessed luxurious time of the whole day. That hour is yours, my Darling, and only rarely does anything keep us away from you then. We watch you, and adore you. Tonight, when your Mother was about to offer you your usual water from your spoon, your little hands came forth and took the spoon, and into your mouth it went—water and all! And each time after that, you insisted upon feeding yourself with water. We called your Grandmother to witness! And she, of course, said something very silly about you!!

4 August *[1915]*

And this is 4 August! Babbie is seventeen months old. Where has the time gone; and why have I not written a word about my Babs, her tricks, her games and—her curls. The months have passed too swiftly; the little cottage at 68 Hazard Avenue has been so packed with busyness. Babbie's father has spent his days (all out of college) and far too many nights at The Desk, the only desk—and the only at all comfortable place in the over-crowded (with people and things) house. O yes! There was lots to write about—which indeed was just the trouble. Babbie's tricks multiplied with much speed; her outrageously roguish capers changed so during the hours of the day that a line or two, a word here and there would never have answered. Never.

And here it is 4 August. On the first day we moved up to the white house at 42 Hazard Avenue, and we have all been happily rushing from cellar to bed-rooms. From carpet hunting to picture hanging. And Babs has been supremely content through all. She loved her room on first sight; and when she woke up after her first nap, she said over and over again, "Fwower." And indeed the paper on the wall is blossoming with small flowers. She loved the great hall upstairs. O what a run was there! And how she did poke into closets (huge ones) and squeal. Just plain joy and fun in her discoveries.

November 19 *[1915]*

A terrifically rainy and windy day. Miller's house started on its journey yesterday; today it is in the field. Babbie looks at the cellar hole and says in her most tragic manner: "Hool-how (house) gone, Mil how (Miller's house)." I reckon the little lass is convinced that her own house or that of anyone else's may walk away at any time.

Tonight she played with Mater's waste basket a long time, hiding in closets and then hunting for it. I said, "Why don't you put it on your head, Babbie?" Immediately she stuck it on. Her head was entirely out of sight; and with that thing on she paraded round, waving her arms and giggling. One of the funniest things she ever did. And she knew it was funny! She's only 20 months old!

Two months later, 16 January, 1916

A lot of things have piled up during these last two months, months so full of baby activity, baby growth development and change.

1. Just when Babs began to insist upon knowing her letters, I can't remember. I do remember, however, that she did insist, and that she would put her finger upon a letter and come to me. I told her, and that was the end of it for the nonce. Today *she knows every letter in the alphabet.* Yesterday she was confused over V calling it A. Today she knows the difference.

2. When she began to want to count, I don't remember; some weeks ago, however, she imitated her Grandmother who said, 1, 2, 3 and at 3 dropped her little bunny into the waste paper basket. Well,

today and yesterday she counted up to 10 quite correctly.

3. Her love for books began quite distinctly when she was a year old. Now books are her passion. She knows all her nursery rhymes, filling in words anywhere; she knows and adores (thus showing her good taste) *The House That Jack Built, The Two Bad Mice,* Curly Locks book and—two oddities in juvenile fiction at any rate she loves: one is a small paper leaflet called *A Grammar for Thinkers* (!) and the other a catalog of Harvard College (!). Her love for *[A Grammar...]* comes from her love for *commas,* and *periods*! (Ridiculous!) The Lady Babs brought the book to me, and with her tiny (not so very, though) forefinger pointing out the curious marks, asked me what they were. We made commas on paper, I guiding the pencil held in the small hand. "More commas," she cried. And on we went, making commas and periods and various letters.

4 March and thereabouts *[1916]*

Babs now makes herself clear upon nearly all subjects relating to her desires and needs. Her expression is not clear in all cases: S is still hard; and she has a tendency of compressing all words of more than one syllable into *one* syllable: handkerchief is hank; Hattie is Hat; Mother is Mire; bottle is bot; potato is tate; etc. When she does use two syllables, she invariably accents the second: papū; Dedée. We noticed that nouns come first, verbs second, then adjectives and their prepositions. Now she says easily: "Mère plee get book on table," and when asked: "Can you see it?" Babs answers: "I can see it." When asked, "What can you see?" she begins like this: "I can see table; I can see book; I can see lamp; I can see kim (chimney out the window; I can see (s)moke." Etc.

She knows all her letters (and has for some time), and is delighted to read them over sign boards, books, what-not—even sees them when they don't exist, as for example—in certain accumulations of dust on the ceiling! She sees A's in the angle created by a door open letting in either sunlight on the ceiling, or light from the electric lamp in the hall.

She knows *The House that Jack Built,* from the end to the beginning, with only a "that" interpolated by someone. And, of course, she has known for some time her Mother Goose rhymes. She still adores books of letters (large ones) and bristling with commas and periods and question marks.

Her associative imagination is vivid. For instance, a goose girl given to her at Christmas time (a goose girl with stick in hand, driving two geese—mechanical) has given her all sorts of ideas about wheels. She called the egg-beater, "goo-girl"!

August 21, 1916

Barbara *playing* on the piano: as she strikes some bass notes she says: "Sounds like a punder tower (thunder shower) down there."

20 October 1916

Ding playing *Pussy can sit by the fire* with one hand, and humming the air; Bar rocking in the brown chair. When Ding gets through, Bar says: "Pretty good for *Granma!*"

Barbara reading with her father

8 December 1916 *[by Wilson]*

Bar, sitting astraddle of Daddy's knee, in Mère's room. Two lighted candles on the bureau, throwing shadows. "Two daddies on the wall, and (laying a delicate forefinger on Daddy's nose) one Daddy in the green chair, and that makes *free* of 'em.

Sunday, 25 March *[1917]*

Eleven or twelve people in library, drinking tea, talking war; Barbara peeking in at dining room door then running away again. "Oh! I am so frightened!" Barbara upstairs to Ding: "Now I'm going downstairs to be frightened again!"

5 April 1917

Barbara, 3 years 1 month old (Apr. 4). She recognizes instantly the following words, learned from her Primer (Aldine Method): 1. come 2. away 3. and 4. play 5. run 6. rain 7. ring 8. some

These words she knows anywhere either in caps. or small letters. We prophecy that in 3 months she will know how to read almost anything in the book.

6 April 1917

Several new words recently added to B's vocabulary: *protect disturb muddy*

She learned the word "protect" when she was told that the jacket of her pussy willow *protects* it. Then she used the word in this way: "The wires *protect* the little trees from the dogs and horses, don't they Mother?"

20 April 1917

Barbara on her stool being dressed in the bathroom, and playing with a tooth brush which she held up to the faucet, pressing it tightly so that the water spatters delightfully. "See Mother, the water is butterflying!" She calls that brush her butterfly brush, the other brush her "swigging" brush.

September 1917

This book is dusty. I find trouble in settling down to write anything; for some time it has been an impossible thing to finish any definite task. War, I suppose, has made us all restless, has made us more aware than ever of the littleness of each of us, of the futility of all things that are.

Barbara is 3 1/2 years old; a splendid and beautiful creature, well, keen, acquisitive, unfathomable, and inexplicable. She is now using the Corona typewriter intelligently: she has discovered the way of rolling in the paper, of turning the roll and spacing and she knows all about the little bell and what one is supposed to do on hearing it. She writes letters over and over again, and three or four words: to, come, away, bluebird. I have an idea the typewriter will interest her more in words and spelling than anything else.

[ca. November 4, 1917]

Barbara at 3 1/2 years and two months old.

In these past two months she has caught on to the reading game with (to us) astounding rapidity and never ceasing eagerness. She has almost finished her first Primer. I am using the Aldine Primer and like it immensely; and I can truthfully say and bring witness to court that B. can read anything in the book through the snowflake story, which is, I believe, the next to the last story in the book. And the words she has learned in this book she recognizes wherever she sees them and in any context whatever.

In counting she can easily reach 100 and has got on to the scheme of the counting business after 100. Addition and subtraction from

1-10 are perfectly easy for her.

One of her favorite games and the one we (B. and I) most frequently resort to as we loiter our way across the field is the "rhyming game." "What rhymes with 'girl'?" But Bar will not only say: curl, pearl, and others but will make up words which if they don't mean anything at least show that she understands perfectly the rhyming scheme.

"Motor, motor come along
Linger, binger, dinger dong"

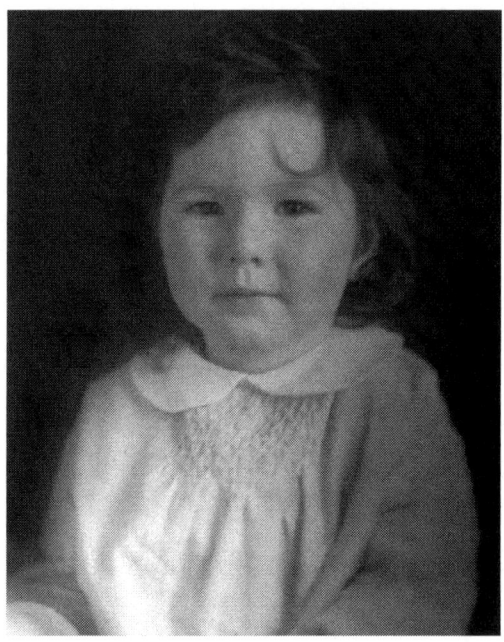

As is shown by the above which we call Bar's first poem and which filtered down to us (just as I have written it) from her crib when she composed the thing during her rest hour or two.

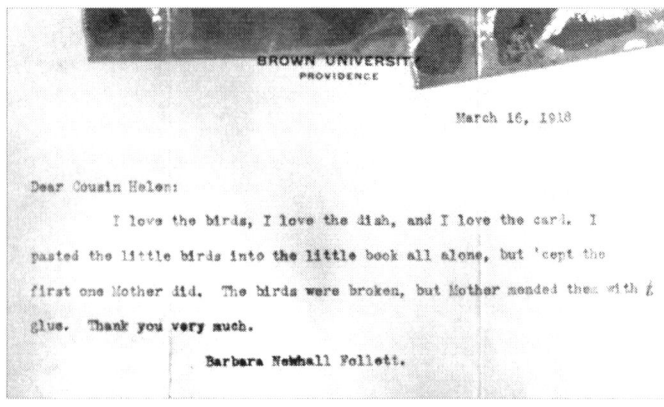

According to Wilson's essay Schooling without the School *(Harper's Monthly Magazine, October 1919), Barbara's first typewritten letter was to Cousin Helen in June 1917. The first letter in the archives at Columbia, however, is the following from 1918. Helen's accompanying note suggests that this was in fact her first letter on the typewriter. Wilson was almost a year off.*

Helen's note reads: "This is to tell you something that may surprise you—that Barbara really wrote every word of the enclosed letter(!), and also addressed the envelope. Of course, I dictated the spelling, but the actual writing, she did, including commas and periods and capitals. No mean accomplishment for a not quite four year old typewriter-lady!"

March 16, 1918

Dear Cousin Helen:

I love the birds, I love the dish, and I love the card. I pasted the little birds into the little book all alone, but 'cept the first one Mother did. The birds were broken, but Mother mended them with glue. Thank you very much.

        Barbara Newhall Follett.

March 22, 1918

Yesterday was Barbara's Daddy's birthday—31. He is out of the draft age now, which, of course, will make no difference. He said he'd like to get into the motor-truck driving for the Red Cross—carrying supplies from the wharves to the store-house. If he desires to, he may. Provided, of course, he can get me out of this financial snarl first. Once on my feet, I shall, I think, be all right; but I don't like the idea of carrying too much all at once.

Barbara has had her flower birthday, on the fourth. A pot of yellow daffodils tied with silver and yellow; four groups of four small candles on the four sides of the table; two larger candles on her bureau, and that is all. But it was very pretty; and the little fairy-yellow girl was the most beautiful of all.

Barbara has a little girl (her favorite, I think, of 29) named Bunny. Last night Bunny was put to bed on Ding's couch, covered with Ding's yellow shawl and Barbara's own brown blanket, which she has over her every night. Now, it grew colder during the night, and I didn't like to leave Barbara without her blanket. So before I went to bed, I took away from Bunny the brown blanket, and put it over Barbara. Was 12 midnight when a baby cry came and woke me: "She'll be cold! She'll be cold." I had to go to Bar, and actually take off that brown blanket, carry [it] down into Ding's room (Ding, being sound asleep) and put it back on the couch where there was literally nothing, but imaginatively, Bunny.

By a great deal of skillful planning (it was skillful, if one takes in mind that I was waked out of a sound sleep for all this) I persuaded Bar to let me put her pink puff on Bunny, and bring back the brown blanket.

Things are at this point now. Barbara is calling, she wants to get up.

In 1919 Wilson swapped teaching for editing. He got a job at Yale University Press and the family rented a house in Cheshire, a few miles north of New Haven, Connecticut.

Barbara was home-schooled with assignments provided by her mother. Writing letters was always part of the curriculum, and over the years she had several regular correspondents—the first being Holdo Teodor Oberg, who ran an antique restoration shop in the Hoppin-Homestead building at 357 Westminster Street in Providence. Mr. Oberg was born in Sweden in 1855, came to the United States when he was two, and became a citizen in 1920. Barbara loved his shop because of all his ticking clocks—at the time her favorite things.

Cheshire, Connecticut
11 March, 1919

Dear Mr. Oberg:

I love Mrs. Clock a thousand-millions. She is up on my book-case and wakes me every morning at seven o'clock. But Mr. Clock is on the dining-room shelf and I don't like him so well as I used to because he stops very often.

I thank you very very much.

    Your little friend
    Barbara.

Cheshire, Connecticut
June 14, 1919

Dear Mr. Oberg:

Thank you for the little picture of the roosters and the rabbits; I love it very much. I am going to put a little hinge on it so I can see the pictures and read the letter; I am going to paste it in my scrap-book.

    Your little friend,
    Barbara Newhall Follett

Cheshire, Connecticut
13 July, 1919

Dear Mr. Oberg:

The goldfinches come every afternoon and eat their supper on the clump of bachelor's-buttons right on the left-hand side of the path that leads from the back door to our road. There are ten goldfinches, five males and five females. Before they eat their suppers, they sit on the clothes-line and swing in the breeze. I wish you could be here to see them.

Day before yesterday Daddy killed a snake in the potato-patch; then he threw the snake away with a stick, and then he threw away the stick. The next day Ding and I went down Ridgeview Place, and there were the snake and the stick. The snake was about three feet long.

Grandfather Bunny has lost his right eye, and I stuck in a black and blue pin.

One day last week Ding and I went down to the orchard and sat among the brown-eyed Susans and had a picnic. I took two Bolivar cookies and some bread-and-butter sandwiches in my lunch-basket.

We have some enormous pink hollyhocks in the flower-garden, and lots of white ones. A few of the flowers have gone to seed, but new ones are coming all the time.

   Barbara.

Cheshire, Connecticut
28 September, 1919

Dear Mr. Oberg:

Please come back with Mother and Daddy.

Thank you very much for Peter, the painting-book, and the little animal eyes for Grandfather Bunny and Peter.

   Love from
   Barbara

An excerpt from my grandfather's Schooling without the School, *mentioned above.*

She will sit for a whole afternoon, if the day be warm, on the thick velvet turn of the drying lawn, her crowd of toy animals surrounding her; and when she comes in she will go in sober silence to the typewriter and set down the home-made lyric which has been evolving in her head all that time:

The animals walk in the animal-patch,
   Sometimes the whole day through.
And whenever any strange thing comes along
   They frighten it away.
     The rabbits are the best of all.
     They néver bite ánybod´y at áll.

And then she will come to me with music-paper and insist that I write down the home-made tune as she hums it; after which she will copy in the words under the proper notes and pick out the melody on the piano from the notes. Who will say that the "animal-patch" does not mean more to her that day because she knows she is going to signalize it, to her own liking, in song, and more the next day because she has so signalized it the day before?

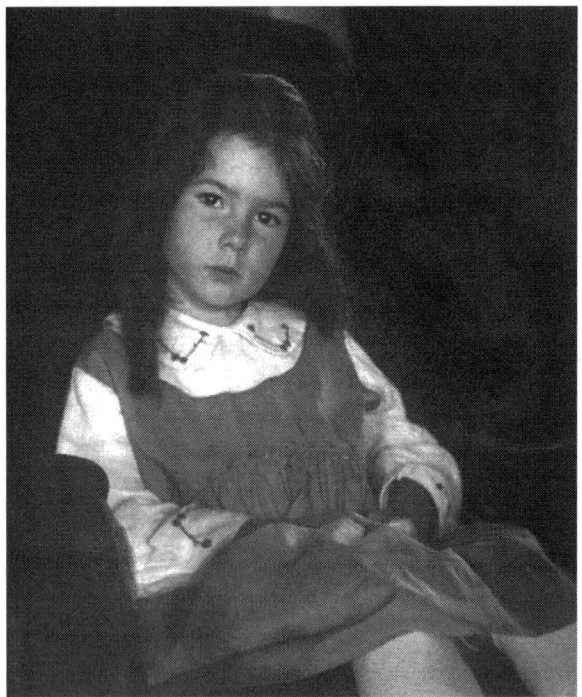

Mr. Oberg's portrait of Barbara, 1919

Cheshire, Connecticut
February 15, 1920

My dear Mr. Oberg:

Nonillion happiness from Barbara that you've got an old-fashioned spinning wheel; I can hardly wait for it to come, I am so anxious to play great-great-grandmother.

And, Mr. Oberg, I have a surprise that I got for Christmas, and we've got to go all through this performance for you to see it—you'll see when the time comes.

One day I tried to make a dress for Grandfather Bunny out of green cloth but I could not make it; so finally we discovered a dress of red velvet. Now he has three petticoats, one to wear in the winter and two to wear in the summer—the red velvet dress, and a white collar that he wears with it.

> From your little friend
> Barbara

Cheshire, Connecticut
March 5, 1920

My dear Mr. Oberg:

Nonillion thanks to you, Mr. Oberg, for the letter in poetry about the little yellow chair, the dear little pictures that go with it, and the chair itself.

I will now tell you how Daddy and I got the chair. As it happened, the box was hidden in the Post-Office; Daddy took me out on my sled, and he, himself, went on skiis. When we started home Daddy put the box on the sled and me on the box.

When we got home the box was opened in the living-room, as we call it, and we all stood around. Grandfather Bunny sat on the top of the box! Pretty soon the box was open, and there in it was the BEAU-TIFULLEST yellow chair in the world!

There was *one* thing that was missing: it was you, YOURSELF.

> Love to the "little boy" from
> Barbara

[March 20, 1920]
My dear Mr. Oberg:

You asked me if Grandfather Bunny's pink eyes were both there, and so I will tell you: they are.

The surprise that you wondered about is a giraffe, at least I think it is; but he is a funny giraffe, for his neck is short, and he isn't spotted like most giraffes but is brown all over. He has short ears, and so I think he might possibly be a brown lop-eared rabbit.

> Love from
> Barbara

April 26, 1920

My dear Mr. Oberg:

Thank you very, very, *very* much for the little card with the picture of the three rabbits on it, and the little song that you made up for it.

Now that the snow has melted and the skiis and snowshoes are put away, I am climbing trees and bushes, digging holes with sticks, picking ferns and other things such as maple blossoms, and that's about all.

Love from the little girl to the little boy.

   Barbara

Cheshire, Connecticut
May 7, 1920

Dear Ding:

Thank you very much for the little May baskets; they are lovely, and I'm going to put flowers in them.

I'm now going to tell you something that will make you *very* happy: The bluets are in blossom, and the violets and dandylions are beginning to blossom.

The butterflies are coming fast now. Sometimes I sit down in a chair and suddenly I see a white Butterfly fly in circles about the potato patch; and I jump from my seat and run after it and see it alight and I tiptoe up to it, and I am just about to open my fingers to take it by the wing when away it would fly.

I miss you terribly. I hope you will be back before the buttercups come because I want you to see every one of them.

A week ago Daddy and I went into the woods and found some yellow Adders tongue and some anemones.

The maple blossoms have come and gone, and the trees are light green with leaves now. I think by the time you come home the trees will be dark green with leaves and that you can't see Mrs. Woodbury's house because the trees will be so thickly covered with leaves.

   Love from
   Barbara

Friday night,
14 May, 1920

Dear Barbara:

I am extremely sorry to be obliged to tell you that it is impossible to take the wheels off the bear without taking him completely apart; and if I did that, I am afraid I might spoil him so that he would never be the same bear again. Perhaps when Mr. Oberg comes to see us he can do something about it; but for my part I am afraid to try, because it would be dreadful if I should ruin the distinguished appearance of so splendid an animal. I am sure you will be patient about it, even if you *are* a trifle disappointed.

>Your
>Daddy.

Cheshire, Connecticut
June 23, 1920

Dear Fox:
Thank you very much for the little ivory elephant and for the little Japanese book. I like them both very much.

You should come and see my new animals. One of them is a little brown squirrel with a strip of white running down his front. Her head turns, her arms turn, her tail turns, and her feet turn. Her real name is Frisk Squirrel, but she is Grandfather Bunny's little sister and so I shall call her Little Sister.

[Oct. 19, 1920]
Observatory Place,
New Haven,
Connecticut.

Dear Mr. Oberg:
We are now living in the new house, and I should like ever so much to have you come to see me.

>Barbara

At four chapters and thirteen pages, The Life of the Spinning-Wheel, the Rocking-Horse, and the Rabbit *was Barbara's first substantial story. She completed a sequel, the sixteen-page* Mrs. Spinning-Wheel, Mr. Rocking-Horse, and Mr. Rabbit Go Traveling, *on June 21, 1921.*

Observatory Place
New Haven, Conn.
March 30, 1921

My dear Mr. Oberg:
As you wanted me to tell you the flowers are coming very fast, and now I suppose the wild flowers will begin to come. But I don't think we shall find many buttercups and daisies because they like the open places, and we have the woods—but still we may find a few

in the fields across the roads. I think we shall find some violets, and the wood flowers will be very thick.

The crocuses and snowdrops have even gone by. The yellow forsythia is on its way out, just as the little brook is on its way to join the big river.

You have read the Spinning Wheel, the Rocking-Horse, and the Rabbit, haven't you? Well, I am beginning a new adventure of how they got traveling to China. If you will come to see me I will read it to you.

Many thanks for the beautiful card you sent me.

With love from Barbara to Mr. Oberg.

Margaret (Peggy) Tilson (1912-2004) was the daughter of John Q. Tilson, Connecticut representative in Congress (and future House Majority Leader), and his wife, Marguerite. The Tilsons owned property on Lake Sunapee in New Hampshire—a place that will become very special to Barbara.

Observatory Place
New Haven, Connecticut
July 25, 1921

My dear Peggy:

This morning I made a house, and I think you would like to hear about it. It was a nice big house because I used all the front piazza to make it. Do you remember that the smaller of the two piazza rugs was right in front of the front door? Well, I moved that rug over to the right hand side of the piazza, and there I put the dining-room table and chairs. The table was a stool, and the chairs were just two chairs.

On the big rug I had the bedroom with two beds in it. One was intended for Ding because she said she would play, but she didn't, and the bed is still there. The beds are made on one rocking chair for each. Each bed has two pillows, one to sit on, and the other to put your head on. One bed has three blankets and one towel for covers, and the other bed has only one rug for both a blanket and spread.

I now have the ice-chest to describe. Do you know the hole around the corner of the piazza? Well, I pretend that that is my ice-chest, and that there is a string sticking out of it. On that string there are the names of anything that anybody would keep in an ice-chest. If you want anything out of the ice-chest you pull the string until the word comes up that is the name of the thing you want; for instance, if you want the pudding you pull the string until the word 'pudding' comes up (of course you would keep pudding in an ice-chest); when you see the word 'pudding' you take hold of it with your thumb and fore-finger and pull, and if the pudding doesn't come up first there is something wrong with the ice-chest. While you are pulling on the string, looking for the word that is the name of the thing you want, the things inside are churning round and forming a line that will let what you want come up first. Don't you think that is a remarkable ice-chest inside of a nice house, Peggy?

I hope you will be home on the twenty-eighth as you said in your secret. Thank you for the letter you wrote me, and such a nice one, too.

    Barbara Follett

Observatory Place
New Haven, Connecticut
August 20, 1921

My dear Mr. Oberg:

The Beads you sent me are very beautiful, and I send you ever so many thanks for them. I think it was awfully nice of you to buy them and send them with Mother's ring. I wonder if the silver-colored beads with the red tassel at the end of them are silver, or steel, or lead, or what? The three little shells are sweet, and I think they are just as beautiful as the beads. I thank you for them, also. The chain of tiny fragile beads is so beautiful that I shall probably hang them on the Christmas Tree next Christmas.

We have been going down to a certain beach called Indian Neck every Wednesday, and I have learned to swim the Dog Paddle. Once the tide was low enough for me to go out to the raft. I went out and jumped off and I bounced on the sand the way a tennis ball would bounce on the sidewalk; I wasn't afraid to jump off because the salt water was only up to my neck.

Now, we can't go down to the beach any more because we are going off camping either Tuesday or Wednesday. We are going to camp on the Tilson's land in a big 12 x 14 that Daddy bought. We are going to sleep on three folding cots which are even more comfortable than Cousin Hattie's beach beds which I slept in once on a visit.

The eagle story which you translated for me is so interesting that I am going to take it away with me to read to the children, and to myself. A million thank-yous for taking that trouble to translate it. I like especially the part where Truls rescued the princess from the giant.

    Over the hills for
      columbine,
    The flower is red

>   It is yours; it is mine
>   The sweet
>   columbine. *[The letter at Columbia ends here.]*

Observatory Place
New Haven, Connecticut
November 29, 1921

My dear Mr. Oberg:

This is Barbara Newhall Follett speaking through the telephone that goes from New Haven to Providence.

I want to tell you about what I did Monday. My dancing teacher gave a lecture at the Westville club-house, and she had some of the children dance for her. I danced The Seven Jumps and The Crested Hen in little Swedish costumes. First I will describe the costume I wore to the club-house: It consisted of a little red jacket embroidered with worsted work, a little red frontpiece with a strip of black velvet across the top and a patch of beads on the front, a little black skirt with three red strips of cloth on the bottom, a little red belt with beads sewed in the shape of flowers and stars on it, and a little red cap covered with beads also sewed in the shape of flowers and stars. I wore all of that in The Crested Hen except the skirt, which was too short to wear in the dance. The Seven Jumps costume consisted of a pair of black pants, a stocking cap with a tassel at the end, and a white vest with yellow and black stripes on it. It was the first time I ever danced before so big an audience.

I should love to see your new cat, but I am too far away to come today. The name of your cat is about right, but there is no q u in our cat's name. Our cat's name is just Booskey. I thank you very much for the postage stamps. Goodbye Mr. Oberg.

And now Barbara Newhall Follett hangs up the receiver.

>   With love from
>   Barbara Newhall Follett
>   to her most loving friend
>   Mr. Oberg

Observatory Place
New Haven, Connecticut
December 28, 1921

Dear Mrs. Day:

Thank you ever so much for the lovely orange-colored bag you sent me. It is exquisite and the nuts in it are very good. I shall keep them in it until it is empty, and then I shall go down town with a piece of sunshine in my hand. I think it is too beautiful to keep money in, so I'll carry it only for beauty and keep money in something else. I think it would be wonderfully beautiful with my Tarantella costume, which is all lovely blue and gold. The Tarantella costume was also one of my Christmas presents. Grandmother made it out of material sent by my dancing teacher, Mrs. Wallace.

Just now I am quite interested in the orchestra. When I was dancing into the Christmas room, Christmas Morning, I heard four faint tinkles. I was very curious to know what they were, but I didn't say anything for quite a while; in fact, I didn't say anything about it until my dance was over. And then Mother said: "Did you hear any tinkling while you were out in the hall?" And I said: "I did, only I didn't know exactly what it was." Then I went round shaking everything on the tree, to see if it made a tinkle like the one I had heard. At last Mother said: "What would it be in an orchestra?" And I jumped up and down shouting: "Triangle! Triangle! Let me see the Triangle!" And that was one of my Christmas presents.

Pretty soon, when we were settling down a little, Mother said something about a Tooter; I think it was: "I forgot the Tooter." Of course I was very busy playing with my triangle, and I didn't notice what was going on. After a while I began to walk round again and saw something black, with something ivory sticking out of one end of it, and it made a musical note; and I shouted: "Flute! Flute! Is it a Flute? Tell me!" And Daddy said: "No, it's a Flageolet."

So we have got two instruments in the house, one of percussion and the other of wood-wind. That will make a better orchestra (if we ever do have an orchestra) than a mandolin and a piano and a very poorly behaving phonograph.

I hope you have had a Merry Christmas and will have a Happy New Year.

    Love to Mrs. Day
    from Barbara

Observatory Place
New Haven, Connecticut
January 12, 1922

Dear Mr. Oberg:

Saturday I had a show, and I wish you could have been here to see it. It was a dance, and I danced in tinsel costumes. I will describe the costumes to you. For one costume, I had on a white dress, a tinsel band around my forehead, a band of tinsel around the bottom of my dress, a little circle of tinsel hanging every little way from the band of tinsel around the bottom of my dress, a tinsel belt, a band of tinsel around my cuffs, and a band of tinsel sewed around the neck of my dress. That is all of that costume, and now I will describe another costume to you. For the second costume I had on another white dress. The costume was: a pink ribbon for a belt, and sewed on to the right-hand side of my belt was a pink artificial rose; around my forehead was the same band of tinsel, as in the first costume, and in my hair were some more artificial flowers. I gave six dances—two dances in each costume. The third costume was the one I described to you in the other letter. I will now describe Peggy's dance. She gave one dance, and that one came after mine. I had on in that dance a little yellow dress made out of material that shows all your underclothes, and by mistake the flowers stayed in my hair.

I don't think I will tell you anything more about my show, but I want to tell you about some friends of mine that I pretend. I pretend that Beethoven, the Two Strausses, Wagner, and the rest of the composers are still living, and they go skating with me, and when I invite them to dinner, a place has to be set for them; and when I have so many that the table won't hold them all, I make my family sit on one side of their chair to make room for them. My abbreviation for the Two Strausses is the Two S's. Beethoven, Wagner, and the Two S's have maids; Beethoven's maid's name is Katherine Velvet, Wagner's maid's name is Katherine Loureena (she got the name Loureena when she was a little bit of a girl because she loved to skate in the Arena), and Strauss's maid's name is Sexo Crimanz... Now I am going to tell you about a funny accident that Wagner had. One morning when I had two chairs set out, one for Beethoven and the other for Wagner, I hadn't pretended long enough to get my family used to them, and Daddy suddenly grabbed the chair that Wagner was sitting in, but I held on to it squealing: "Hey, that's Wagner's chair!" Then he went around to Beethoven, and I was looking suspiciously at him all the time. But he turned around again and didn't bother Beethoven. I suppose that when he got around there, he thought that Beethoven was there.

Did I tell you in the letter about the Triangle and the Flageolet, that you can take off a piece of the Flageolet and put on something else and make a Piccolo? I don't think I did, because I don't seem to remember the word Piccolo. I can play it pretty well, but not so well as the Flageolet, because with the Piccolo one has to force one's bottom lip against the bottom row of teeth, and one has to let one's upper lip hang over the hole in the side of the Piccolo, not quite touching it. Of course the end of the Piccolo is pointed to the right-hand side, and when you play it, your lips mustn't touch the side that is opposite to the regular position of the Piccolo.

I have told you so far, counting both letters, quite a little about the family orchestra. Well, I have got something more to tell you about it. Of course everybody had a little more fun than they used to, and a little later on I went to an orchestra rehearsal, and there was quite a lot of percussion in two of the things they played. Now, in one of these things I got very much interested in the cymbals, so at last we bought a pair of cymbals, and now we have more fun than we ever had in all our lives. I pretend that I am the percussion man in the orchestra, and I have a bag to keep all my instruments in. I strap up the bag and go to the orchestra, and when I get there I take out my percussion, and Mother plays the piano, and I have a time. Then when the rehearsal is over I strap up my bag again and go home.

I got the handle of the Bunny and Tortoise top without looking for it. Mother was just pulling out things in a box, and she pulled out that without looking for it.

The verses that I spoke about in the other letter, came from the little calendar that you sent in the big box.

Thank you very much for the chocolate and the dates and the raisins, that you sent in Ding's bag. The Ali Baba dates interested me very much, because I had read a story of Ali Baba a few weeks ago.

February 25. You see it is a long time ago that I wrote this letter to you, or, at least started it, but all kinds of things got in my way to prevent my finishing it.

Don't forget that my birthday is the fourth of March, and that you said that you might be able to get down to see me then. Please do if you can.

I believe "Aunt" Mildred Kennedy was the daughter of George Golding Kennedy, a prominent Boston physician who died in 1918.

Barbara's violin teacher, Hildegarde Donaldson (1898-1948), was the wife of Norman Donaldson (1899-1964), an editor at Yale University Press. Norman will become Barbara's friend and correspondent (and namesake for her second book, The Voyage of the Norman D.*)*

Observatory Place
New Haven, Connecticut
March 7, 1922

Dear Mr. Oberg:

Thank you ever and ever so much for the exquisite little box you sent, and also for the amber beads you sent with the box. The box is so beautiful that it seems impossible, and I don't see how any man could take thousands and thousands of those little chips of wood and just put them in one at a time, and make it come out an exquisite box. I just don't see how it can be done. It is all right to say it is beautiful, but I don't see how it is done, that's all. The beads we first thought were amber, then we decided that they weren't, and then we knew that they were. I like them for three reasons: the first is because I love the colour, the second is because I love the little odds and ends of big beads and the tassel at the end, and the third is because they cast a wonderful piece of yellow light onto my dress right where each bead is.

You know how much I have wanted a violin, and you know that I have wanted one for a long time. Well, after dinner, we all went to search what there was to search for. Then we went into the library and saw this big bundle on the sofa. We all thought surely that was Mr. Oberg's bundle, and then we all though it was peanuts as usual, but I didn't think that peanuts would come in a box that looked like the shape of a violin. Well, I didn't want to say that it was a violin because I knew that a violin was ever so much smaller than that. Daddy undid the string and I just lifted up the corner of the paper, and saw something black. I knew it was a violin case, but I didn't want to say so. I went back in the room and let Daddy undo the paper. He undid it, and then he told me to lift the cover of the case up. I did so and saw the violin wrapped up in purple oil-silk; I said: "I have done what you asked me to, I have lifted up the top of the case, now you do what ever you want to." Daddy unwrapped the violin and brought out the most beautiful one that anybody ever saw, for a small violin. There was, at the end of the case, a little box, and I lifted the cover up. Inside were all sorts of little odds and ends needed on the violin, such as rosin, another E string, and the only thing that mother said she could play out of that outfit, was a violin tuner. It was a little thing that had marked on it the strings of the violin, G, D, A, E, to tune the violin by.

The violin was exquisite, the G string was gut wound with wire, the D string was gut, the A string was gut also, and the E string was metal. The back of the violin was made of pretty dark wood mottled with darker wood, and the front of it had on it little marks of age. Also the underneath part of the neck was very light wood mottled with darker wood, and also the outer part of the part of the violin between the back and the front was the same as the back, light wood mottled with darker wood. The part of it that comes down under the strings over the front of the violin was black and the dainty little strings stretched over it added to its beauty.

This exquisite noun was brought to me by Aunt Mildred Kennedy, and with it were several books to play from, and a stand. The lessons have just begun, every day for two weeks, by Mrs. Donaldson.

Let me thank you once more for the exquisite noun sent by you, and remember it was very much appreciated by all the members of the family, young and old and medium.

Good-bye.

>Love to Mr. Oberg
>from Barbara

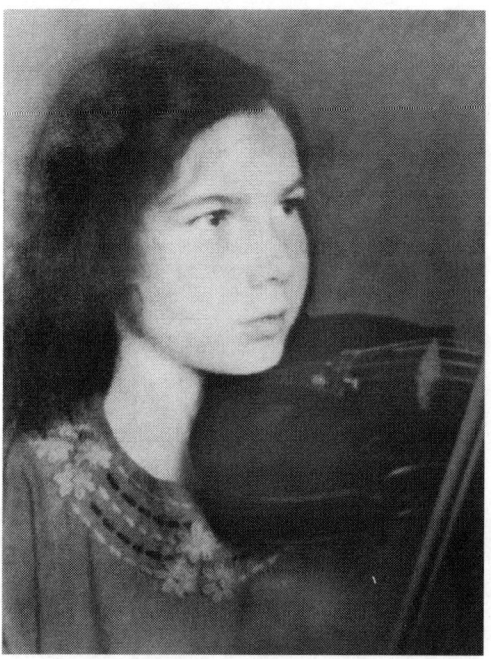

Observatory Place
New Haven, Connecticut
April 23, 1922

Dear Cousin Helen:

I am extremely sorry that this letter has been delayed so long, but it is because there have been so many other things to do that I haven't been able to find a minute to do it in.

Nothing has delayed spring this year. The flowers are everywhere, the green things are everywhere, the birds are everywhere, and a few butterflies' wings are lending the beauty to the year. I have seen bluets, squills, one violet, blood-root, dandelions, daffodils, and the crocuses and snowdrops have gone. For birds I have seen robins, sparrows, blackbirds, bluejays, and I think a few starlings. Some of the birds that I have named have stayed all winter, but I haven't seen any. I have heard many other songs from the birds, but I haven't known what birds they were from. I have also seen loads of forsythia, and a few pansies. We have decided to get some cosmos, poppies, and some pansies.

I have a little tiger kitten who is a little over half a year old. He was half a year about my birthday, and now, oh dear! He is getting rather big, but he still plays a lot. He bothers the big cat Booskey almost to death. This year he almost caught a robin this way: One day a flock of robins were out on the front lawn, and the kitten, Citronella, crouched ready to spring, but I warned them. I thought the flock had flown away, but evidently they settled somewhere else. I saw the kitten getting ready, and I looked about for the birds, but I couldn't find them. Citronella did, though. Then she ran a few steps and looked about. She kept this up for some time and at last she leaped. Then I screamed and the birds flew away, but Citronella almost caught one.

Thank you for everything that you have sent me and especially the photograph of Beethoven that you sent on my Birthday.

        Love to Cousin Helen
        from Barbara Newhall Follett

Now eight, Barbara's imagination turned to princesses and fairies and the magical landscapes that would evolve into Eepersip and Farksolia. The Fairy's Nest is missing from the Columbia archive, but there is a lot of material available from this productive period, including The Forbidden Forest *(a play),* The Fairy Orchestra, Mermaids, *and* Fairicter *(a compendium of fairy types).*

Observatory Place
New Haven, Connecticut
May 2, 1922

Dear Miss Deane:

Thank you ever and ever so much for the trailing arbutus that you sent me. I appreciate your kindness very much in thinking to send it to me.

The eighth of May I may go off with Daddy into the woods to find and pick some trailing arbutus. We mean to find two little glades, one with ever-green trees around it, with the needles scattered over moss, and the other full of flowers where we can pick all we want to; we are going to have luncheon in the woods and have a whole day to ourselves. The year before last we went into the woods together, and for the first time I saw some yellow adder's-tongue and also some anemones. When I saw the yellow adder's-tongue I didn't know what it was at first, but after a while I told Daddy that I had once seen in the wild-flower book a picture of a flower that looked something like that one, and that they called it yellow adder's-tongue. Every one that we found had two narrow pointed leaves near the bottom and a long smooth stem; we pulled the flower right above the leaves and the stem slipped out from between them, so that no leaves were picked with the flower.

We have had for flowers squills, violets, bluets, and daffodils, and the crocuses and snowdrops have gone long ago. For birds we have had crows, blackbirds, I think some starlings, bluejays, and we have seen one flicker; we have also seen some little gray birds that we couldn't see well enough to know what they were. Some of the birds that I have named stay all winter, but I haven't seen any birds all winter.

Yesterday I started writing a fairy play. There are three fairies in it, Viren, Raindu, and Rondaintu, and they all have very important parts. The play is called *The Fairy's Nest*, because the fairies all make a little nest on a big rock covered with vines. There is also a goblin in the play, who is the worst enemy of the fairies. The fairy parts are written in poetry, but the goblin part isn't. It may have four acts, or the third and fourth may be put together; I'm sure I don't know. It may even turn out to be a one-act play.

I have also written a bird book that has got in it eighteen imaginary birds, with a description of their songs, calls, nests, and eggs. It really is very interesting, but the most interesting birds are the fisheens and the finourios. I am going to have a book published full of my stories, and some of my birds will be put in it, and then you can read about them and their wonderful habits and ideas.

I am making a china collection of every piece of broken china with a color on it. I have not time to describe it now, but I hope that sometime you can visit me, and then you can see it for yourself.

    Love to Miss Deane
    from Barbara

Dorothy Pulis Lathrop (1891-1980) was a writer and illustrator of children's books, including one of Barbara's favorites—Walter de la Mare's Down A-Down Derry. *Dorothy's mother, Ida (1859-1937), painted Barbara's portrait in the summer of 1922 while both families were at Sunapee. At about the same time her sister Gertrude (1896-1986) took a few photo portraits.*

Verbiny and Her Kittens *was the first in a series, followed by* Verbiny and Her Butterflies *and* Verbiny and Her Birds.

Portraits by Ida and Gertrude Lathrop, 1922

Observatory Place
New Haven, Connecticut
May 12, 1922

Dear Miss Lathrop:

Thank you ever and ever and ever so much for sending me a copy of Walter de la Mare's Down A-Down Derry. I think the pictures are wonderful and especially the frontispiece is a wonderful illustration of a fairy. I also love the poem that goes with that picture. I think it is perfectly wonderful the whole business.

I have now started a story about kittens, and the most important character is Verbiny the princess who found the mother-cat in the woods, caught her, and tamed her. One of the four kittens has a black back arched up like a kangaroo rat's, and at the top of each white stocking was a band of yellow. All the kittens catch little crickets and grasshoppers, and one of the kittens catches a bay mouse, and a kitten named Citrolane catches two sparrows, one with each paw. But just a little while after the kittens are born they want so much to see what is on the other side of the fence that fenced in their property that they climb up over it and jump down and almost land on a porcupine, but he good-naturedly steps aside in time. In a chapter called Springtime I have written down a little poem in a secret language that Verbiny called Farksoo. In the secret language it was this:

> Ar peen maiburs barge craik coo
> Peen yars fis farled cray pern.
> Peen darndeon flar fooloos lart ain birdream.
> Afee lart ain caireen ien tu cresteen der tuee,
> Darnceen craik peen bune.

I will now translate it as best I can.

> As the (and *maiburs* means a flower that comes in May) begin to come,
> The air is filled with perfume.
> The dandelion fluff floats like a (and *birdream* means something very beautiful).
> Also like a fairy in her dress of gold,
> Dancing to the wind.

But the most interesting thing about these kittens is the way they are taught to use their noses and eyes well. I will copy that chapter if you want me to.

[Here Barbara typed several paragraphs from Verbiny.]

The next chapter is interesting too because Rosack becomes acquainted with a kangaroo rat and spends nights there, but he doesn't spend days there because Verbiny discovered him, and he didn't dare run away. But he spent every night there. Sometimes perhaps I can read it to you, and I think you will like it.

Thank you again for the wonderful book of poems that you sent me, with the wonderful pictures.

                Love from Barbara
                To Miss Lathrop

Observatory Place
New Haven, Connecticut
May 22, 1922

Dear Mr. Oberg:

I am very sorry that I haven't found time enough to write a letter to you, but, in the midst of all the things that I have to do, I have first forgotten about it and then there have been too many other things that I had to do first.

Thank you very much for the little basket with the Easter eggs that you sent me. They are all gone, but they were so good that I couldn't help eating three or so a day. I like all the flavors, but the oranges are my favorites. I have been wondering whether you made the little basket or not; I think it is dear whoever made it, but I think that you did.

Talking of eggs reminds me of the makeup birds that I have been writing about. There are eighteen of them and I think they are all quite interesting, but the most interesting ones are the six finourios and the four fisheens. The finourios are all very pretty, but the knowraino finourio has the power to change his coat and also his song before it rains. The fisheens also are quite pretty, and they are the birds that sit on rocks sticking out of the water, and catch fish as they come by. But the short-billed fisheen has to duck his head under water to catch the fish. The total length of the fresh-water fisheen's bill is six inches; the total length of the salt-water fisheen's bill is four inches; the total length of the short-billed fisheen's bill is one and a half inches; and the total length of the silvery fisheen's bill is four and two eighths inches. When you come to see me I will read the rest of the birds to you.

In June I am going to Lake Sunapee, at least I think I am; but instead of camping we are going to live in the Tilsons' cottage while they are in Europe. When we come home we shall stop in Providence for you and then you will be coming in an automobile instead of in an old stuffy train.

    Love to Mr. Oberg
    from Barbara

The Tilsons owned Timberlost *on Lake Sunapee, and they may also have owned property on nearby Little Sunapee Lake (a.k.a. Little Lake Sunapee), where the Folletts rented a cottage for the next several summers.*

The Cottage in the Woods
August 8, 1922

Dear Daddy:

If you had only waited till today to go home you would not have missed a wonderful sight. Late in the afternoon I went out for a little row in the boat. It began to sprinkle and so I came back. A few moments after I had reached the house the sprinkling changed to pelting, and a storm arose over the lake. I certainly think that some other people got it worse than we did. The wind blew the rain and part of the surface of the lake eastward, sometimes blowing them a foot or so above the water, and sometimes rolling them on the water. The wind did not let the rain fall where it wanted to, but blew it along a few feet beyond the spot. It was certainly wonderful to watch!

You know that I have put the baby lizard in the minnow pail. Of course there was no other place to put the tadpoles but in the lake. So I left the tin in the water by the boat tied to one of the oar-locks, and I kept thinking that they weren't safe and worrying about them part of the night. In the morning I came down to see how they were and the tin was on its side and the cover was slit open, but there was not a tadpole there. But I don't care much for I know they are safe and sound in Little Sunapee Lake. And besides I think that they will live better.

The baby lizard is so little that I have some trouble to find him when I want him, but I am sure he is all right in that great pail. The hurt lizard hasn't died yet and I think he will be all right sooner or later. I hope so, don't you?

    Love and kisses from Barbara
    to Dear Daddy-Dog

The Cottage in the Woods
August 15, 1922

Dear Daddy:

As you said in the second letter that I got from you, I will say the same. It *is* too bad that you are not getting my letters; I have written seven or eight so far and I have only two from you. I have been writing two times a day almost always, and often I have written three a day. I only remember once that I wrote once.

I am getting on very well with the violin; I have tried almost everything; it was only where Mrs. Donaldson gave a page and a half of finger exercises that I haven't tried all of the exercises. There was another page and a half of exercises in sixteenths where I hadn't done all of the exercises. So you see I have tried almost all the things.

This morning I rowed over to the Lathrops' with Mother, and I left the baby lizard in care of them, thinking that they could take much better care of him than I could. I certainly think he is turning into a land lizard. He has turned much redder and almost always keeps his head out of water, often climbing on a stone that I put in the pail for him. This morning I found him in a comical position: he was clinging with his legs to the side of the pail with the whole length of his body out of water.

Today I saw a little fish and tried to catch it with my net, not succeeding. It was about the size of a small sunfish looking much smaller swimming swiftly. It was white with a faint tinge of green in it with micary scales of the same color all over its body, only they didn't sparkle like mica, and its tail was tipped with black.

Along with the aquarium books and the flowers books that you said that you would send, I wish you would please send up *The Princess and the Goblin* and *The Princess and Curdie* because I have wanted to read something for a long time besides *The Water Babies* (which I read over) and *The Light Princess*.

> Love from Barbara
> to Daddy-Dog

A keen outdoorsman and naturalist, Edward Porter St. John (1866-1953) was Dean of the Theological Seminary in Auburn, New York. After meeting Barbara at Sunapee, he became her second important correspondent.

October 22, 1922
708 Orange Street
New Haven, Connecticut

Dear Mr. St. John:

I was very much pleased to get a letter from you so soon, but I am very sorry that I haven't answered it any sooner than this. The shell which you sent to me I thought was very beautiful, and when it is held up to the light there are many curving and twisting streaks in it that can't be seen otherwise.

Up at Sunapee I had two adventures with red squirrels that I think you would like to hear about, since you are so much interested in the wild folk. The first one happened this way. I was playing in the woods, and I heard a lot of red squirrels chattering together. I walked toward the sound, until I came to a little clearing, carpeted with the leaves of the clintonia, the berries gone, and there I sat down to watch. I kept so still that before long a red squirrel came out of the underbrush and peered at me. Then with a frightened shriek he scurried away. He only went as far as a tree five or six feet back into the woods. Then he turned around and came back to peer at me again. Then with another shriek he went back to the tree. It was mere curiosity. He came, peered, and went, five or six times, with a little shriek each time he went, until finally with a bound he scurried away perhaps to tell the other squirrels the news. Then, before many minutes had passed, another smaller red squirrel came galloping across the clearing with a nut in his mouth. On the right of where I was sitting was a mound of earth with a couple of trees growing on it, and the red squirrel went behind the two trees, came around, peered at me for a minute, and went into a small hole that I hadn't noticed before, and after he had deposited the nut, came out for another one, as the clearing was near some beech-trees. In this way seven or eight nuts were put in the hole before I went home.

The second adventure happened this way. Before we went home the stretch of beach that goes around to the other little beach where I caught the minnows, was there to go around on, for the water had gone down and left it. One day as I was coming home from the minnow beach that way, I heard a rustle in the woods, and kept very still because I wanted to understand whatever it meant. Pretty soon a red squirrel came out of the woods in back of the beach, peered at me for a second or two, went back into the woods and came out again farther down the beach. Then he went down to the water and took a drink. His little pink tongue lapped the water much the way a cat's tongue does. Have you ever seen a red squirrel do that? I presume you have, but Daddy said he never had.

And now I will tell you about something else. I have found many varieties of aquatic plants, most of them very beautiful. I found two especially beautiful ones, one with eight or nine narrow leaves pointed at the top, about two and a half inches long, dark green at the top, and orange coloured at the roots; and the other was a long slender grass, with little brown buds on it, one having a white blossom so small that it could just be seen.

And now for the salamanders. I had been trying desperately to keep them in deep pails, but I never succeeded because they climbed right out. So finally I said to Daddy: "Can you tell me how to keep those lizards *in* and happy?" And he got a wooden box, asked me to make a garden of mosses and ferns in it, and then he nailed some wire netting over the top of it, cut a rectangular hole in it, and put the lizards in. Once Daddy went up Burpee Hill to get the car, and he brought back to me a lizard about an inch and a quarter long, under the seat. I put it in a dish with some moss in it while I went to ride, and when I came back he was gone. For this was before Daddy had made the cage. Another time before we had fixed the box up, I found another one smaller than that, and I kept him longer. Once I took him out and showed him to Daddy who said: "There ain't no such animal." But alas, one day he got out, and I had the box that he was in on the piazza. I'm glad that I didn't have the other baby on the piazza, which is really the most treacherous place for a lizard because it is full of cracks and crevices. But happily I found a lizard smaller than the last, and had the box to put him in. I saw him every day with a lot of other salamanders, and when I left the box out in the rain some nights they would all be out from under the moss the next morning. When we went home I let the lizards go, and I took them out one by one to find the little one, but though I found some pretty small ones, I didn't find the tiny one. I have a strong suspicion, however, that he had grown to be one of these.

I am sending you a bit of prose about October in Sunapee, for you weren't there to see how beautiful it was.

Thank you ever so much for your nice letter, and the box turtle shell, and let us hope that before very long we shall meet again. But remember if you ever come to New Haven, Connecticut for anything please call on us.

> Love to Mr. St. John
> from Barbara Follett

OCTOBER

In the radiant sunshine of October the trees on Lake Sunapee are crimson, gold, and red. The reflection of them in the lake is nearly as clear as the trees themselves. Canoeing to one of the crimson shores will mean paddling in painted water, vivid and quivering. One can think of water flowers growing in the painted water and turning red. Only the evergreens stay green, and there on a point of evergreens bordered with crimson maples dance the nymphs night and day, in dresses of red and green. They are gay little fairies, dancing and flying, whispering and talking to one another, in voices clear as bells, catching butterflies and talking to them, and singing with the birds, and having concerts with them. O then the life is of happiness and freedom, until one day the radiant leaves fall, and winter draws near.

2

THE COTTAGE IN THE WOODS (1923-1926)

708 Orange Street
New Haven, Connecticut
January 5, 1923

Dear Mr. Oberg:

I am extremely sorry that you have written two letters in succession to me and that I have not written any letters at all. However, here is my chance—early in the morning, before anybody is up.

I had the time of my life with your Christmas box, and I thank you very much for everything that was in it: buds, peanuts, apples, and a lovely cornucopia full of hard candy. I thank you especially for my jewels: the "throw" (which you fixed with great success), the pearls (which you also fixed with great success), and the lovely little butterfly locket with its gold chain. *That*, I thought, was the loveliest thing you sent, though everything was so perfectly beautiful, that I can't decide which I liked best.

I wonder whether the winged insects on the locket are both butterflies, both moths, or the open winged one a butterfly and the other a moth, or just opposite. It seems to me that they are both butterflies, but I will leave it to you, entirely.

I will here go on and tell more about my Christmas. I have been wanting for some time something alive in the house. Some friends of mine gave me two beautiful fan-tail goldfish, one with a round short body and a single tail, and the other a much more graceful shape, of a much more delicate and pale gold, with a double tail. Indeed the single tail, which is much larger than the double tail, is of a very rich, deep, and red gold, while the double tail is of such a delicate color that in some lights he is transparent. I give them food and change their water every day, and they are now in fine condition.

I will here thank you for the coin and the camel very much.

We didn't have a very large Christmas tree, but as we put less and less decorations on it each year, it gets more and more beautiful. We didn't have all our lovely beads this time, but only balls and tinsel. But it was as nice as any Christmas I have ever had, and I thank you again for all that you did to make it nicer.

I am enclosing some of my make-up butterflies for you to copy by way of water-colors.

Now I must again thank you for all the lovely things you send, and close, but we'll hope that I can open again by and by. Remember to write to me before very long, but I should rather have you visit me.

      Love from Barbara

708 Orange Street
New Haven, Connecticut
January 8, 1923

Dear Mr. St. John:

I am extremely sorry that you have been ill, but extremely glad that you have had a chance to climb the mountains of West Virginia.

I had a very merry Christmas, and beautiful presents. We didn't have such a large Christmas tree as we have sometimes, but as we put less and less decoration on it (as we do each year), the tree grows more and more beautiful. Some friends of mine gave me two beautiful fan-tail goldfish, one with a short body, with a deep, rich, red gold and a long single tail, and the other of a much more graceful shape, of a much more pale and delicate color, with a shorter double tail. It says in my Aquarium book that very good fishes have the tips of the fins wavy, and as to me my fishes' tails are wavy, I suppose that they are good fishes. I shouldn't believe that they are the same kind of fish—they are so different. The single tail I named Simplex, and the double tail Douplex—Simp and Doupe, as Mother says.

I thought the pictures that you sent me with your letter were perfectly beautiful—especially the one on Mount Chocorua; that and the one of the river from the lawn at Rivernook I thought were the nicest of them all. I also loved the picture of Shawondasee in summer. How I should adore being on Chocorua this very minute! When *you* get talking about mountains you make me feel as if I could get all packed up and go with you tomorrow. I hope I shall do that sometime—just go all alone with you—Shouldn't we have a good time? But that cannot be for a while now.

I thought the background of the picture of myself was very pretty—it is green and luxurious, and very summerlike.

Oh how I should like to be in the pine grove with the birds singing above my head, and all the green summer things about. Though I don't believe that I should like it very much now—I only wish it were summer.

When I *do* go up there Daddy and I are going to make a map of all my secret twisting and turning paths. This will be made on a large sheet of paper, and every summer as I make new paths, the new ones shall be added on. When I get to the end of the paper on all sides, I shall take four more pieces, and continue my ground North, South, East, and West.

I am so anxious to know whether the frost has splintered my shells that are buried in my treasure cave, near the shore of the lake. They are common mussel shells, but beautiful beyond words. They have beautiful brown backs and are lined with iridescent purple. If they have been splintered I shall feel rather sorry, though I can get plenty more. I took home two very fragile shells, not daring to leave them up there. *They* break with the slightest knock, and I gave them to Daddy for a Christmas present. They are light yellow on the backs with brown stripes, and inside they are lined with pale iridescent colors. They are not so common, and I didn't see many of them there.

I am very anxious to see the red salamanders and enjoy them with you. I think they are the most beautiful small things on the lake.

I am also anxious to see if the minnows are still at the minnow beach, and if they aren't I should like to find out where they are. Probably they are not there any longer, and yet I suppose they might be. If they aren't I should like to find some other minnows. They are so pretty with their gleaming silver scales.

Everything I am anxious to see, and I hope with all my heart that you can come to Sunapee to see them with me.

> With much love,
> from your friend,
> Barbara.

708 Orange Street
New Haven, Connecticut
January 8, 1923

Dear Mrs. Coleman:

I am very sorry that I haven't written to you before this, but various things made me postpone reading *Peter and Wendy*, and therefore I couldn't write to you to tell you how glad I was to get it. I will now thank you a thousand times for one of the loveliest books that I have ever read.

I don't see how you knew just exactly what I liked—I have always wanted to fly, myself, and some one of these days, I am going to have a flying club, and invite all my smart friends to try to think out a way to manage *artificial* flying. If you are interested (I suppose you are) I will invite you, too.

I have been always fond of flying things: birds, butterflies, moths, and dragonflies; and I have always liked to notice in my walks in the fields what butterflies flew with long, beautiful, and graceful strokes, and what butterflies just fluttered. I also like to notice the way bees move their wings so fast that it seems, unless you look carefully, that the wings are not moving at all. It is very pleasant to me to watch all these things, for I am so interested in wild things. Probably Peter and Wendy flew more like birds.

Thank you again for sending me the pretty tale about Peter and Wendy and all about how they visited the Neverlands.

        Love to Mrs. Coleman
        from Barbara

708 Orange Street
New Haven, Connecticut
January 23, 1923

Dear Mr. St. John:

I am crazy about the cocoons you sent me, and I, in spite of the fact that you told me a lot about them, have quite a lot to ask you about them. In the first place I want to ask whether it would be best to keep them in a warm place. Daddy thinks that to keep them in a cold place would be the best idea, so that when the moths got developed we could take them off and let them go without freezing them. Daddy is in great doubt about keeping them after they have come out of the cocoon, unless we could "scrape acquaintance" with a man who has a hot-house. But I really think that the best thing to do is to let them go after they have come out, and we have had the fun of seeing them come.

Do you know what food they eat? If you do I might arrange a cage for them with their natural surroundings and keep them a while. What do you think about that?

I know *Luna*. Daddy brought her home from Cheshire Connecticut, one day, and then we let her go again. She is the one with the long "feet," as I call them. I also call them "tails" sometimes. I know that they curve out slightly like little crescents. *Luna* is a beauty, and I am very glad that one of the cocoons may turn out to be she.

I wish you would tell me something about the way moths and butterflies mate. Suppose I ask you some questions about it and you answer them in your next letter:

Does the moth or butterfly, after coming out of the cocoon, find a mate, or does the mate come out with him? Does the moth or butterfly stick near his mate, or are they two independent creatures? Are the moths or butterflies just out of the cocoon very weak and unable to fly at first, or are they as strong and vigorous as ever? Are the moths or butterflies just out of the cocoon their full color, or does that come afterwards?

I suspect that after trying to answer all these questions you are very tired. I shall have to try you a little more with a new subject now, that will take centuries to straighten out—really a great subject—that, besides writing to you my feeling, I will discuss with you when I see you in New Hampshire, or Lake Sunapee.

Everything is now (except human beings) just as Nature has planned it. Nature did not plan her children to be killed, except sometimes by one another, but she planned them to live and enjoy the earth—the sunlight, the flowers, the trees, and all Nature's beauties. If only we mortals will wake up and learn a lesson, here is a lesson for us to learn. As Nature has *not* planned her children to be killed, why do we kill them? Who can answer this question? Nature has trusted to us, animals' big brothers and sisters, to leave her babies alone. If only some of us could wake up and be brought to see the right side of this very complicated subject, they would think, the way I do, of the person who gets wounded, what he feels like, and how his feelings are hurt. Why do we kill pigs for pork or ham? why do we kill cows for beef? or lambs for their meat? When we kill the animals we are not doing what Nature has planned; whereas the animals do what Nature has planned, no matter what this may be.

Volcanoes that spout up ash and kill plants near by cannot help it, for Nature has planned it; worms we hate because they are ugly— they do nobody any harm, and they cannot help how they look, for Nature has planned it; and the plants they kill we needn't blame them for, for Nature has planned it; eagles, falcons, and hawks cannot help killing and eating smaller birds, for that is their nature, and that is what the real Nature has put in them. Old Mother Nature must have some bad animals as well as good ones, or the world would never get along. But I don't think she needs us. For my part I think that we mortals should be cleared off the earth entirely—I shouldn't mind being cleared off, because I know what harm we do.

How one can look at the fuzzy yellow ball of a little chicken and then want to kill it is more than I can see—even for Easter, which some people think is more important than the lives of chickens. The chicken never did anybody any harm; it is human greed that makes us kill them. I could never see how anyone can do such a thing. How one can look into the gentle loving eyes of a deer and then want to kill him, I can't understand. Perhaps it would be all right to kill a few, for the earth would soon be overrun with them if we didn't, but why should North America all over have the same seasons for killing deer? You know in some places this season comes in the mating time. My idea is that every different climate should have an open season that doesn't come in the mating time. How one can want to shoot ducks is also more than I can see, even for the good meat. They never did anybody any harm, and probably never will. It is *only* human greed.

Now animals like horses, cows, donkeys, and bees are meant to serve man: the horses and donkeys to carry burdens, the cows to give us milk, and the bees to give us honey. But if man could only be *contented* with all these luxuries! It doesn't hurt these slaves of ours to serve us, for that is what Nature has planned, but Nature has not planned minks, beavers, seals, bears, skunks, and muskrats to serve us, and, therefore, it hurts them. For we take their skins.

Nature has not planned naughty boys to throw stones at chipmunks, squirrels, and birds; Nature has not planned us to catch fishes and eat them (something which even I do); Nature has not planned naughty boys to catch lizards or salamanders with crooked pins (something which I cannot bear to think about).

Now about butterflies. If we *could* only be brought to see as I do. Why do people have to know exactly where every spot on a butterfly's wing is? There is no need to make collections of butterflies, for why *do* we have to know just exactly about them? I think that it is much better not to catch them and put them in a sieve and describe them. I think that it is much better not to get their description exact and to let the butterfly live on, in its lovely life, than to kill and get everything exact. This is what I do, and I hope that you think it is better as well as I. Butterflies live such lovely lives and are such lovely things that I couldn't think of killing them. I simply love them!

Now again, I can't understand how a boy with any heart at all can bear to take little birds out of their nest. Jays and crows that steal the nests we hate, but it is their nature and they can *not* help it.

Now again I don't see how anyone can bear to see flowers die in the heat of a train—I'm sure I can't.

In other words I am a friend of all Nature save human beings, and for this reason can be brought to see the right side of things.

I, when I see you again, will talk over this subject with you thoroughly, for to me it is very important.

Now about mountains. Do you know the feeling that volcanoes and other mountains are alive and have a sensation like other things? I adore mountains, and hope that when I grow up I shall be strong and able to climb the big fellows. I know that you are going to be my most intimate travel mate, and I hope to travel with you a lot.

Mother has now told me to tell you about The Valley of Ten Thousand Smokes. This is a book by Robert F. Griggs, about the National Geographic Society exhibition, exploring the district of Katmai Volcano, continuing for five years starting in 1915 and ending in 1919. It was after the eruption of Katmai Volcano in Alaska—the eruption of 1912. The author was a member of the party. I haven't finished the book yet, but I advise you to get it and read it. I have only just got to the Ten Thousand Smokes part of it (though most of it is about various things that happened before they discover the Valley). Here (in the Valley) the ground is fissured everywhere all around, and from these fissures columns of steam rise up. They are of different varieties: big fissures, small steams; small fissures, big steams, continuing in that peculiar order for a long time.

I have forgotten whether or not you saw the fish pen that Daddy made for me, in which I kept numbers of perch, bass, and sunfish. If you never saw that, write to me and I will tell you about it. The fishes in it all died, and Daddy said that he would try it again next summer. But I am going to tell him that the aquarium is better free, like the menagerie.

> From your best friend and playmate,
> Barbara

708 Orange Street
New Haven, Connecticut
February 4, 1923

Dear Mr. St. John:

I hope you had a lovely time exploring the mountains of Virginia. I wish you would tell me all about it. As I said before I am perfectly wild to do it with you.

My cocoons have not developed yet, but it seems to me the big one has got fatter, though I don't quite see how it could be. One wouldn't think that they could be so heavy, especially as they are so small, and besides I never noticed that they were heavy until just a few days ago. I think that probably the moths will be out pretty soon. I shall be crazy to see them!

A few days ago I asked Daddy what other mountains I could climb next summer besides Cube, which, you know, is north of Hanover. Daddy said that I could climb Chocorua, and possibly Moosilauke, though probably not. If I can climb Chocorua I will do it with you, so we shan't have to wait so very long, shall we? If you are coming to New Hampshire to see me next summer, I want you to stay longer than you did last summer, so that we can do lots more things.

As I am so crazy to go to Sunapee Mother once said that we should try to go the first of July, but I simply cannot wait that long in this vile place, and I am thinking about the first of June. You see after February, which is a short month, there would be only March, April, and May to wait, whereas the first of July would leave June, too. Though it was in January that I said it with more eagerness: "Mother, if we went then after January had gone (it was early in January) we should have to wait five months, and I cannot wait as long as that." But I am now saying it in February, which takes away one month. I am now not thinking of the time to wait, for it goes so quickly, but I am thinking of the time that I am to stay there. I want as long as possible in that green, fairylike, woodsy, animal-filled, watery, luxuriant, butterfly-painted, moth-dotted, dragonfly-blotched, bird-filled, salamandous, mossy, ferny, sunshiny, moonshiny, long-dayful, short-nightful land, oh that fishy, froggy, tadpoly, shelly, lizard-filled lake—on, no end of lovely things to say about that place, and I am mad to get there. I want as short a time as possible in this vile apartment house—oh, anywhere, everywhere except here!

Did you know that I have been writing a story, started long, long ago? I will tell you about it. It is about a little girl named Eepersip who lived on top of a mountain, Mount Varcrobis, and was so lonely that she went away to live wild. She talked to the animals, and led a sweet lovely life with them—just the kind of life that I should like to lead. Her parents all tried to catch her, with some friends of theirs, and every time she escaped in some way or other. Toward where I am working now, Eepersip's ways of escaping grow more and more foxy, though now they have given up trying to catch her, but for the first few times she saved herself by way of the deer which grazed in the meadow where Eepersip lived. She loved the flowers, trees, animals, and all Nature's wonders as much as you or I do, or even more. She played games with butterflies! If she didn't like Nature's wonders as well as you or I, she understood them better, for who ever heard of a person playing a game with butterflies? She often thought that she was going to learn from end to beginning butterfly history.

Have you read the Valley of Ten Thousand Smokes, by Robert F. Griggs, yet—the book that I mentioned in the other letter? I have now got well into the Ten Thousand Smokes part of it. I will copy one of the funniest passages in the book. The party was trying to find the best place to hold a pan of bacon as they fried it in a fumarole of the Valley:

> While experimenting to find the best place to hold the pan, we tried pushing it down into the cavern below the orifice, but immediately it was caught by the back draft and—piff!

the bacon was whisked out of the pan, flying through the air in every direction, to be eagerly caught and devoured by the spectators, who howled with delight at this sudden turn of events. Discovered accidentally, this trick was repeated again and again till we tired of chasing the flying slices.

But really all this will give no idea of how it is in the story, and the best way is to read the book for yourself.

February 8.

I was extremely glad to receive your lovely letter, the last one you wrote. I was especially glad to have you answer those rather difficult questions. I was glad to have them answered, for I have wondered about them for a long time. I think that what you told me about the female moths is perfectly fascinating, and I am glad that you agreed with me in the big subject. I hope you think it is "big."

I can easily answer your question, did I do the typewriting myself? I do all my letters myself both the composing and the typewriting; then if there are any big errors Daddy or Mother corrects them and I copy the letter.

I think the "double" picture is the most amusing photograph I ever saw. Both the "parts" of it are very lovely, though the combination is not so excellent. At first I thought that it was all one, without noticing the figures, and it looked to me like a rock on the shore of the lake. I myself was looking for the photograph of Mother and myself last Christmas, but forgot to ask about it. I think Mother is sorry that she spoiled two pictures for you. She will pay for them. How many quarts of blueberries equal one film? Mother doesn't agree that they are spoiled, for she thinks they're very interesting, but for heaven's sake you don't want figures in a landscape picture.

I want more and more to go to—of course you know where. I am thinking even now of how lovely the first night is going to seem—I can just imagine the first night—oh, it will be great if it is a nice night. Do you know the feeling that sometimes, when you want especially to do a thing, it is good that it seems impossible, and you can't believe your eyes when you at last do it? I know that I shall have the feeling when I go to Sunapee, and I really fear that the first morning that I spend there I shall be so full and bubbling over with happiness and joy and merriment that I shall really explode! Oh dear—and now, even now, I am almost exploding even when it is so far off. Please excuse all the dashes. I really forget my grammar when I begin to think about Sunapee. I am thinking now about my first morning there. I shall get up early, say six o'clock, and get my breakfast, consisting of Shredded Wheat; I shall run outdoors in the early morning light before anybody is up, and I shall run to my treasure chest and hurry out all my buried shells and pebbles; I shall dash up into the woods, exploding all the time, to my lovely little playhouse; I shall dash at full speed, nearly falling from more explodements, to the sun-laden pine grove; I shall talk to the nymphs and fairies; and when Mother gets up I shall dash around harder than ever at all my stocks and stores. I shall run over to my playhouse again to see if my moss seats are still there, I shall fly over to the woods on the other side of the lane and see my old friends the red squirrels, I shall run back again to see if my precious chipmunk hole is still by the side of the cottage. But maybe I shall be too tired from the trip to do all these things. If I am not too tired I shall do a lot more things than those just mentioned. I shall go to the Magic Perch of the Nymphs, a rock off one end of the pine grove, which can be got to by way of other rocks, and see if the water is low enough to get to it; I shall sit on the beach in front of the cottage and watch the little spotted sandpipers run along the beach; I shall go to the minnow beach and see if there are still any minnows there—oh dear, I am giving out now. I shall do a lot more things, but it is not worth mentioning them. But shan't we really have fun when we meet again? We'll find red salamanders, we'll go fishing (oh dear, there I am again), we'll find baby lizards in the lake, we'll sit in the pine grove and talk over various things, and above all we'll climb mountains. A little girl, a friend of mine, who has a summer home on Big Lake Sunapee is also crazy to get there as well as her Mother and sister. We have a great game together, and there are nice places to play both at her summer home and at mine. We shall have great fun, and that is one of the things that I am looking forward to, though I forget it when I think of climbing mountains with you. But there is no use in talking about it any more. We can see in time, and it will save a lot of breath.

    I have now written a long letter and must close. I really think that we have so many things to talk about that it is not worth writing them all down and that it would be better really to see each other. However, I will write to you some of the littler things. A letter, you see, is only a "false visit"—a real visit is much better.

    I made a mistake about writing on this paper, for it won't take ink; therefore I cannot sign my name with ink.

        With much love from your friend,
        Barbara.

Bruce T. Simonds (1896-1989), a concert pianist and Barbara's piano teacher, taught music at Yale for five decades. From 1941-1954 he was Dean of the School of Music.

THE COTTAGE IN THE WOODS (1923–1926)

708 Orange Street
New Haven, Connecticut
March 19, 1923

My dear, *dear* Mr. Oberg:

Thank you ever and ever so much without getting to the end of the thanks for the two sweet little pictures for my little house. They are very lovely, and I think that they will look charming in my little living-room. Thank you also for the poem you composed about "The Nymph of Sunapee." You always send something funny at Christmas and something lovely on my Birthday.

I went to the exhibition at the Paint and Clay Club yesterday, and I saw Mrs. Lathrop's portrait of myself. It is the one she painted of me last summer at Sunapee, and Mother and Daddy like it very much. But I like *Herring Gulls* by Henry H. Townshend the best. I liked also *On the Connecticut River* by Elizabeth S. Pitman; *The Enchanted Pool* and *Morning Mist in California* by Henry J. Albright.

I had a half nice and half unnice birthday, being sick in bed with the Grippe, but I never got such presents. Marion Peasley of Cheshire gave me a tiny ivory box with a little flower and leaves of Mother-of-Pearl, which I loved enough to take to bed with me. It wasn't intended to be a *Birthday* present though. But it was so near to my birthday that I called it one. Then my third cousin, Cousin Helen, sent me a Japanese Lacquer black box, in which I keep some of my treasures. My violin teacher gave me a lovely picture of Wagner, the composer, which I highly prize. From Bruce Simonds came *Scenes from Childhood*, some pieces of music by Schumann. Mother also gave me a lovely English edition of a book of Beethoven Sonatas, which I just love. She also gave me a nice music case. Ding made me six doilies for my little house. Mrs. Patterson, whom I don't know, gave me *Undine*, a poem by herself, which I like enough to read nearly ever day.

Dorothy Lathrop, the daughter of the one who painted my portrait, came to see us Saturday and gave me a little German rabbit of china and I carry him about with me all the time. I also got for my birthday from Mrs. Tilson a little German napkin-ring which I keep in my Japanese Lacquer box.

Every day I perform magical operations with my treasures, but I cannot explain to you now about them. When you come to see me I will.

I am enclosing a sheet of the size paper that you are to put the painting of my make-up butterflies on. Some other time I will send some more for you to paint.

        Love from your friend,
        Barbara

708 Orange Street
New Haven, Connecticut
March 19, 1923

My dear Mr. St. John:

I was extremely glad to receive your letter and your little book of game birds. You described everything so carefully in your letter that I was nearly with you. The rabbit that you saw trying to get up the bank must have been dreadfully funny; he makes me laugh even now. Seems to me it's dreadfully early for spring flowers, the snow not being gone. I should have liked to have been with you when you saw the five species of ducks. They must have been very interesting.

A friend of mine came down to see us from Albany telling me that her Mother, Mrs. Lathrop, who painted a portrait of me, had taught four red salamanders to stand on their hind legs and wave their front paws in the air. She asked me for four names for them and I have them made up now. But you should hear her talk about her livestock in the house! They have three dogs, a greyhound, a pekingese, and a collie; you should hear her talk about the greyhound stuffing himself on a loaf of bread and his sides bulging out!

I myself am thinking about what kind of a dog to have in the new house (when we have it). Mother now thinks a collie or a setter, but I like a Chow. I have only seen one, and even then never got acquainted with him, but I have read about them. A good many of my friends like airedales. An airedale is a one-man dog as well as a Chow, but I don't like them. One friend of mine who has an airedale says that a Great Dane is the one-man dog (she dislikes Chows, and says that they're a step better than a Pekingese) but a Great Dane is altogether too fierce and treacherous. There is nothing that strikes me more than a Chow. What do you think? Please tell me in your next letter.

I am also thinking about how to make birds feel happy on our new house lot. I want to attract small birds, especially humming-birds and wrens. I want plenty of lilac trees and rhododendrons for the humming-birds. In the winter I want to have luxury on hand for the darling little snow buntings. I am not going to have any cats, and I hope with all my might that the neighbors' cats (if they have any) will keep away. In the summer I want especially thrushes, goldfinches, song sparrows, orioles, and possibly redstarts. Do you know how I can make them comfortable?

Now I must close, only to open again by and by.

        With much love, from your friend,
        Barbara

P. S. March 26: I just received your post card and should be delighted to visit you if it's possible. B. N. F.

708 Orange Street
New Haven, Connecticut
April 10, 1923

My very dear Mr. O:

I am now writing to send you a few more of those make-up butterflies that you said you'd make illustrations of.

I shall skip a few of the butterfly's habits in my copy, but leave the description:

The Oreecler

The upper side is a beautiful orange with green and black threads on it crossing and recrossing themselves, but not so thick that the orange is hidden from sight. The under side is dark blue, with white circles, bands, and spots on it.

The female is amber colored on the upper side, with lines, threads, spots, and blotches of darker amber. The under side is white with amber streaks through it.

The total width is two and one half inches.

The Frillerteena

The upper side is white, with a large yellow spot in the upper corner of each upper wing. Around the head is a little necklace of yellow spots. He cannot see in the dark, but he carries two little lights with him. At the end of each feeler is a little gold ball, and somehow he can turn on a little light inside and then he can see. The under side is plain gold. Strange to say this little butterfly has no mate.

The total width is three quarters of an inch.

Please, what were the butterflies that I sent the first time? I should like to know, in order to know what to send next.

Sometime I will write and tell you the news.

> With fifty million ocean steamers all *loaded* with love, embracery, and kisses.
> Barbara.

Sunday, April 15, 1923

Dear Mr. Lewis:

We have had a most wonderful time at the *House of Unexpectedness* (I call it that, for everything is so unexpected, everything is just what you don't expect), staying in and going out, taking walks and playing cards with *Toots and Tabby*, the cat-and-dog cards (I suppose you know what I mean).

I certainly love the way roosters get into conversation. In the morning and sometimes at night I hear the rooster here, and then from way off (another farm) comes the faint answer of the rooster there.

We are going home this afternoon, though of course I don't want to. As I said before, we had a wonderful time, and much appreciate your kindness in inviting us.

      With love,
      Barbara.

708 Orange Street
New Haven, Connecticut
April 16, 1923

My extraordinarily dear Mr. St. John:
Excuse me for not writing sooner after I had received the clay tablets. As a matter of fact we have been to Farmington for three days where Daddy had gone to work since April 3rd. Also, we only came home yesterday afternoon, though, of course, much against our will. It was the house of Mr. Lewis, a friend, who had gone to California, leaving a colored man and his wife to take care of the house. So you see we were in luxury, not having to cook or clear up. The house I call *The House of Unexpectedness*, as everything is just what one doesn't expect; for instance, the dining room is in the place where you would expect a *hall* to be. There are hens there, and the loveliest fields to play in.

But now comes still more interesting news! What do you think? A few days ago a Promethea came out of her cocoon, and was discovered as I was going to bed one night. It fluttered about so fast that until it settled down I thought that it was a small bat; and Daddy wasn't here to decide. Then she hid away, and we didn't find her until yesterday, when we came back from Farmington. I can't decide which cocoon she came out of.

I have another question to ask. Some people say that butterflies and moths live only a day; some say that butterflies live a week, and that moths live a day, and other things like that. I want to find out straight from you, and get that off my mind. I mean, of course, butterflies that are not caught and—oh! how I hate these words—chloroformed or pinned. Speaking of that makes me say again that I don't see why people have to know exactly. Don't you agree with me that it's much better not to get the description exact and let the poor thing live? I know you've agreed with me once, but I want to be reassured, for the matter is never out of my mind.

Won't it be nice when we have a Luna moth around? I do so hope that the big cocoon *is* a Luna as you said it might be.

I am sending you one of my little cards. Mes. is abbreviation for Messenger.

I think that the clay tablets are awfully interesting and also hope that sometime when you write you will tell me all about them. Did you scratch the face on the "baby"? It looks to me as if somebody did. The arrow head is also very interesting.

> I send love from each little flower, leaf,
> tree, and from each little fairy of the woods we
> so much love.
> Barbara.

708 Orange Street
New Haven, Connecticut
April 28, 1923

My very dear Mr. St. John:

That which we have waited for so long has surely come. Spring! Yesterday I saw eleven white butterflies two of which were bumping and biffing one another, whirling round and round, cutting up all sorts of antics, first one on top and then the other, and whirring round and round across somebody's lawn. The day before I saw a yellow one. Last winter I was afraid that the flowers were never coming, but now the crocuses have gone by with the tiny blue squills, and nearly every house has a yellow fringe of daffodils around it. As for bush flowers, forsythia is at its best, and the delicate blossoms of the magnolias are lending perfume to the air. Lawns, nearly all the lawns are dotted with bluets and dandelions.

A few days ago the second moth came out of her cocoon, Cecropia. A friend of ours showed us some very remarkable things about him. I didn't know that moths ever got up a temper, but when she took him out of his box on a little twig he actually got furious and afraid, also. We didn't let this moth stay half so long in confinement, letting him go the day after he came out. He was simply lovely.

You said that my big cocoon was either a Luna or a something else, I can't remember the name. A few days ago I drew and painted a Luna moth, from my Holland moth book, and it really looks like a moth. They are harder to draw than you think. First I got the tails too short, and then I got them much too long, then I got them too narrow, and then too broad, and then too round and then too straight, but finally I got them just right. I will send it to you.

As for birds I have only seen sparrows, robins, starlings, grackles, and one bluejay. To be sure the sparrows stay all winter, but I count them just the same. Squirrels skip up and down the trees and across the roads and sidewalks; the maple buds are red; and truly Spring has come!

This is only a little letter, but soon I will write a longer one.

>With much love, your friend,
>Barbara.

[Barbara included a poem for Mr. St. John]

FOR YOU
   When the tracery of leaves on the trees begins,
     When the sky turns blue, and the days grow long,
   And the bluebirds and song sparrows warble their notes,
     All these things make me think of a far-away song.
   When the buttercup nods to and fro on the grass,
     (I don't know why it is true);
   But the mountains and trees, the rivers and brooks
     All make me think of you.

708 Orange Street
New Haven, Connecticut
May 5, 1923

My dear, *dear* Mr. St. John:

More and more signs of Spring have come! Forsythia is dropping, and cherry blossoms of the loveliest fragrance are coming. I have stopped keeping count of the butterflies that I have seen. I saw one mourning-cloak a few days ago, and see lots of blue ones. There is more variety of flowers now. Tulips and pansies are at their best. But the wild flowers! I will save them for a later part of this letter.

Yesterday Daddy, Mother, a friend, and I went to Woodbridge to look for arbutus. We passed a reservoir on the shore of which we were to meet our goal. We stopped at an open field where there were violets, five-finger or cinquefoil, and bluets in bloom. Then we started down a lane toward the reservoir. Violets, white and purple and blue, and strawberry blooms were sprinkled across the path. We transplanted some white violets. In the woods on our right were the mottled leaves of snakeweed and yellow adder's-tongue, and everywhere were purple trilliums and anemones, of which we found a blue one. Farther on we turned into the woods to a narrow gorge down which a brook ran in the prettiest of falls, large and small, here pouring down over a mossy ledge of rock, there rushing away to break up into ripplets and eddies and whirls. On the very steep banks grew mountain laurel. We strammed down on the narrow banks, where every minute we expected to fall in. (Mother had stayed in the car.) But the hard task was over at last, and we found ourselves on a very steep mossy bank—oh, such soft moss!—where there were rocks here and there, and we found ourselves shrieking with delight at the fragrant masses of arbutus.

Here we were on the shores of the Reservoir, which we had wanted so much to get to. The easiest way of getting around on the soft, delicious, slippery moss when going down was to slide. This was much quicker, easier, and safer than to scramble. Only, to be sure, no way was actually safe here. I found that there were plenty of rocks to use as brakes. But even then we were never *sure* that we were not going to fall in.

Just then I made a discovery—some small blue flowers, liverwort, which I later found were the same as the hepatica which you mentioned. Farther eastward I found a tiny portion of the banking covered with it. There were white, pale pink, deeper pink, lavender, and more of the heavenly blue of that which I first discovered. Still farther eastward, where the moss was even more luxuriant, it was a perfect Fairyland. Wood anemones peeped at me from behind the logs and the trees behind us, peeping like little gnomes and fairies; up a tiny trickle of a brook marched stately yellow adder's-tongue, forming a fairy passage-way; back farther in the woods were the tremendously interesting purple trilliums; on the shores of another brook were skunk cabbages; the liverwort was scattered in symphonies of color; clinging around on the rocks were the fairy-like arbutus, our hearts' end and aim; and everywhere was cool, soft moss. You would have liked to be with me then!

While Daddy and the friend sat at rest after having picked quantities of arbutus, I played nymph and decorated them with flowers. Then I did them a good turn by having curiosity. I rambled on still farther eastward (I had to cling with all my strength to the moss to keep from falling) and finally came out to a place where arbutus was everywhere. Then, of course, I had to call to the others to come, too. It was hard work getting there, but it was worth it.

I never had such a day, and I'm not sure that it was not a dream. But I still have a right middle finger with a mighty sore edge from picking, to prove it. I wish with all my heart, and I guess you do too, that you had been there. Perhaps you don't quite believe me about all this. But if I'm real at all, if my whole life *isn't* a dream, every word of it is true. Perhaps I'm asleep now and dreaming, and when

I mention yesterday Mother or Daddy will correct me that it was a dream. Perhaps when I wake up I shall have no sore middle finger to prove that it *was* true.

It was very lovely, anyhow.

>Good-bye.
>Barbara.

Walter de la Mare (1873-1956) was an English writer best known for his children's stories. His books were among Barbara's favorites. He was interested in how a child's imagination developed and must have been quite intrigued by Barbara. He would be quoted widely in the British press when The House Without Windows *was published by Alfred A. Knopf in London.*

I am very grateful to the Bodleian Library in Oxford for sending me a copy of the following letter.

708 Orange Street
New Haven, Connecticut
May 6, 1923

My very dear Mr. de la Mare:

It is impossible to describe how much I have enjoyed a morsel from Peacock Pie every little while. I knew the book and all the poems practically by heart, but it was only an American edition, and I like the one you sent me ever so much better. I like especially the poems Some One, The Ship of Rio, The Cupboard, and best of all the Three Queer Tales. I also like fully as well your new volume of poems, Down-adown-Derry, and I love the poem called The Stranger.

Of course I simply adore The Three Mulla-Mulgars. I have practically lived on it ever since our friend Mr. Knopf published it, which was when I was five years old. It is exactly the most superb thing in my library. I have read the Mullas so many times that the first copy I had was simply read out—not soiled, but just read to pieces—and I had to have a new one. Please remember your promise and write the *second* adventure of the three Mulla-Mulgars—

> "All that befell these brothers dear
> In Tishnar's lovely Valleys."

I have been waiting dreadfully long and *very* impatiently, and I should be so happy if you would hurry up and start it!

Dorothy Lathrop is one of my best friends. We spend our summers in the same place, Lake Sunapee in New Hampshire, and we see a lot of each other, for we are only a mile apart and are always rowing back and forth. Gertrude, her younger sister, is a sculptress, and last summer she did her saddle-horse, Nelshon (I'm not sure how to spell this), and also a three-day-old calf which she saw up in Quebec. This piece of work is now mine, a Christmas present from Mother. Mrs. Lathrop, her mother, painted a most lovely outdoor portrait of me, which was exhibited here in New Haven at the Paint and Clay Club this winter. The Lathrops love the woods and all its little creatures just the way I do, and Dorothy and I have found many of the little red lizards up at Sunapee, creeping and burrowing in the moss. (There is one of them in the frontispiece of Down-adown-Derry.)

The last story I wrote is about just what I should like to be—a little girl, Eepersip, who ran off to live wild, with her animal and butterfly friends. Presently she turned into a fairy. (Daddy says I ought to tell you that the story is about 30,000 words long.) On my birthday I gave Mother a book of poems; the first one was about our summer vacation place on Lake Sunapee. I also did some illustrations for them. And on Daddy's birthday I gave him a book of sixteen poems, with my illustrations. I am very fond of writing about butterflies and moths, and the first poem in his book was a sort of Ode to a Butterfly. Near the end I also wrote a Song to a Frog. When I write seriously I like to interrupt my seriousness by something amusing.

Perhaps it would interest you to know that a friend of mine sent me some cocoons this winter. A Promethea came out of one of them last month, and a little while ago a Cecropia came out of another one. The Promethea I let fly around in the house for quite a while, but the Cecropia I let go in the woods the very next day, when it was strong enough to fly. The Promethea was very lovely; but the Cecropia was the most gorgeous creature I ever saw. One of my cocoons is either a Luna moth or something else. I do hope it is a Luna, because I love Lunas so. When I write about moths I usually write about green ones, and a Luna is such a beautiful Nile green.

I love the sound of your make-up words in the Mullas, and also the monkey talk. This must have been the cause of my making up a language called Farksoo. I once made two poems in it; I will enclose one of them. Nobody can decide what language mine sounds like. Here is an example: Peen flitterveen fis fithic soocun peen urnees. It means: The butterfly is flying over the meadows. "Flitterveen" is the word for butterfly. "Veenic" is the word for beautiful. It comes from Venus, the goddess of beauty, and "flitterveen" simply means a beautiful flitter. I use Farksoo in my books of imaginary creatures, like a scientific language such as Latin. I have written make-up Inhabitants of the Make-up Aquarium, Make-up Butterflies, and

Make-up Birds and Animals; and I am writing a book of all the different kinds of fairies that I imagine. Another thing I like to do, once in a while, is to draw or paint a make-up map of a part of a make-up land, naming the places in Farksoo. I pretend that there are millions of different branches of Fairyland. I do this because everybody has his own idea of Fairyland, and it can't be settled who is right.

I also write butterfly diaries. I catch the butterfly with my net, put him in a sieve, describe him, and then let him go. I would never think of collecting—I am too much a friend of Nature to do that. Some of the names of my imaginary butterflies are Pearleetue, Oreecler, Blueetue, Frillerteena, and Perpander. A few of my imaginary birds are Ashlaroo, Ositeroo, Orine, and several varieties of Finourio.

But above all the things I have told you I *love* the woods. I long to get away from the city street which we live on, to my summer vacation place. I love to dance out on a small peninsula of woods, on which there is a gorgeous pine grove. I love to play that I'm a nymph—to dress my hair up with ferns and berries—yes, yes, I love to pretend that I'm afraid of everybody except my nymph friends, and that people have to keep very quiet in order to make me appear.

At Sunapee last summer I had some wonderful adventures with red squirrels. Wandering about in the woods at the time when the red squirrels were storing away nuts for the winter, I heard a chattering and a chirring, and, as I don't like to miss any chances of seeing wild folk, I went toward the sound. Coming to a little open glade, I sat down to watch. In a little while a red squirrel came out from the beech trees on the left side of where I was sitting. He poked his head through the bushes and stared at me. Then with a frightened whirring noise he went scampering off. All the time I was sitting as still as I could. In a little while, from mere curiosity, he came back and did the same thing over. The operation was repeated several times, and then off he went to tell the news. Before many minutes had passed a smaller red squirrel galloped across the glade to the right hand side of me and went into a small hole with a nut in his mouth. Then out he came and back for another. He buried many nuts. Then I went home, and that was all of the first adventure.

The remembrance of the second I treasure carefully, because I saw something that a friend of mine—a person who is as fond of the woods as I am, and who has seen foxes and fox cubs and can read all sorts of stories in the snow—has never seen. I was walking along on some stones close to the water. Above me was a little banking on top of which were the woods. All of a sudden I heard a rustling in the leaves. I stood still, for, although I thought that it might be a red squirrel, I wanted to see it. Finally a little head with its pair of mischievous-looking black beady eyes popped out of the bushes. After he had looked at me for a few minutes he scampered, but still I waited. In a minute he came out of the woods down on to the stones. Then he drank from the lake, exactly like a kitten. His little red tongue lapped the water just as a kitten drinks milk. I shall always remember these two interesting adventures.

Thank you again and again, without ever coming to the end of the thank-you's, for Peacock Pie. I think you would also like to know that every time I read that incomparable thing, The Three Mulla-Mulgars, it starts me on a new story of my own.

>With joy and love,
>Your friend,
>Barbara Follett.

708 Orange Street
New Haven, Connecticut
May 10, 1923

My dear Mr. O:

I am sending you a small box the contents of which you may think are very peculiar, but now I will explain. First, you will find some cotton; then you will see a little red box. Inside you will find a bottle of liquid. It is the ingredients of a very precious charm. Next comes some more cotton and then you will see some amber-colored beads off a lamp and a little roll of string. The beads you must put across the back of your hand so that one end dangles on each side of your wrist; tie the two ends together with the string. I forgot to say it is to be your left hand. Next put on the palm of the same hand some wood shavings from your shop, and then pour the contents of the little bottle over them and with your other hand rub them off. The charm will then be completed and you will be happy.

I am getting crazy over magic of different kinds, and when you come down this fall I will teach you my best charms and spells. At least if you are for good magic, magic of badness and magic of mystery I know nothing about. I have a way of making a healthy-happy summer, happier than any of the preceding summers; I have a way of making a happy winter, but it takes all summer to gather the charm. I have started a winter charm now; I have another charm that I have not yet experienced; it is a charm of good effect on everything; I possess magic over my treasure, the key of my jewel box is kept in such a place that nobody can find it, and even if they poked right into its very box they couldn't find it. I have to pronounce two magic words when I open the box and two when I turn the key. I have also a charm of making other people happy; this charm affects different people in different ways: one friend of mine went up to the ceiling, Daddy turned into a wild kangaroo for jumping, but Mother I was disappointed in. I have still another charm of good effect for the outdoors, a charm something like the one which I told you before that I hadn't experienced a charm of good effect only yesterday I did it. The first charm of good effect is a charm of the spring, a charm of:—

> Snowdrops and the blue-eyed squill,
> Of violet and daffodil.

I have also many keys which unlock the gateways of towns and cities.

When I have the new house, the idea of which is getting hopeful, I shall have a little house of my own to produce my charms in. When I'm doing magic (then I'm mighty serious) I shall keep my door locked.

In my mind I have the idea of a garden, a little old-fashioned garden shaped like a butterfly with a triangular wing on each side of a path which will be his body. But of course one can't really tell about a garden until the house is built.

Your correction of my butterflies was quite right and hereafter I will call it the width. Are you ready for some more butterflies? Are you still interested in them? However I will send you some more.

The Daylight Fuzzywing.

These butterflies are very common and very well known. They are never very large, and the wings are never too long for the width but are always the regular shape. The wings are very fuzzy, hence the name. They are often so fuzzy that people call them fur-butterflies, but fuzzywing is the best name. The upper side is mostly white, but there is a band of orange around the wings with a row of six silver spots set in the band like precious stones, six of them on the upper wing, and four on the lower one. The under side is light blue with a band of orange around the wings, and there are six white spots set in the band of the upper wings and four on the lower ones. This is the *male*. The *female* is plain white and curiously marked on the upper side with a nile green band around her neck, down on the part of the wing near the body, around in a curve, crossing itself, and touching her waist on each side, like this: *[rough drawing in pencil here]*. The female is so different from the male that some people think it is a different species of butterfly, and call it the ribbon-butterfly, but it is really the female daylight fuzzywing.

Total width is two inches.

The Midnight Fuzzywing.

Unlike the daylight fuzzywing these butterflies are not common, and very few people have a chance to know them. This is because they will not go where there is any light, and they stay in such a dark place that nobody ever visits them. Some people chase them with lanterns and flashlights, but even at so much light they will soar way, way up, and fly to the darkest place in a dark forest, and nobody can catch them. The young can stand light and the people who do know them are the ones that have been as skillful as to find a nest of the babies. The upper side is a beautiful shiny white that shows in the darkest night with a border of gold just as showy around the wing. The under side is plain gold very dazzling to the eyes. This is the male. The female is pure white on the upper side with a band of blue around the wings. The under side is brown with a band of silver around the wings.

The total width is eighteen inches. (You can draw on scale.)

This is the first copy of the letter and I hope that you will excuse the mistakes, for I didn't have time to copy it.

> With much love,
> your friend,
> Barbara

Pearlectia

Columbia has twelve of the butterflies Mr. Oberg drew for Barbara.
Above are the male and female Pearleetue and Blueetue.

708 Orange Street
New Haven, Connecticut
June 12, 1923

My very dear Mr. Oberg:

Oh, how I love those butterflies! They are so lovely that I don't know what to say about them. There is nothing wrong with any of them, and they are just what I intended by my descriptions. But what materials did you use to make them? They look to me like a mixture of crayon, oil paint, watercolors, and some kind of varnish. Whatever they are made of, we are all perfectly crazy about them, and all the friends that I show them to say the same thing. I am also glad that you find it pleasant work, for I was afraid that it bothered you.

So that you won't beat me in charms I am sending you still another one. In an envelope, which I am sending in a separate package, and which also has one corner turned over, is some magic pink powder, which you must throw into a basin of water. Then you must say: "Pink Rose, come hither; Wild Winds, come to my summer." A fairy whom you cannot see will touch you with the tip of her wand, and those words will be granted. During July Pink Rose and Wild Winds will come to you.

Your charm worked beautifully. I see that you are a magician too. Well then, you practice, and I'll practice, and this fall when I see you again we'll have a contest.

If any of the contents of the magic envelope fall into the box in which the envelope is, you can just empty the box into the water, too.

Once more I thank you again and again for those precious butterflies.

> With much love,
> from Barbara.

Barbara's mother didn't go to Sunapee in 1923 due to baby Sabra's imminent arrival, so Barbara went with Bruce Simonds, his wife Rosalind, and his sister Helen.

The Cottage in the Woods
July 19, 1923

Dear Mother:

I am beginning to feel a bit lonely now and have written to Daddy begging him to come up. You see, the Bruces never go off anywhere on trips and adventures. And Bruce doesn't much like to explore. I like to explore alone, but sometimes I like to have someone with me. I never get that person. I had a far happier time with Daddy and Raymond than I ever can have with the Bruces. So I wish we could change round again.

The place seems to have lost a third of its beautiful atmosphere. For now I feel rather tired of it. It would be all right if Daddy were here. I feel as though I wanted to go somewhere else next summer.

Bruce is now learning to swim, but he never goes to the bathing beach. He will stay on this rocky shore, even when there is not a soul at the bathing beach.

Every day now there are turtles on the rocks which fall splashing off as the tub approaches (sometimes I row over there). Once indeed when Norman and Hildegarde and her sister came over to see us, Norman and I managed to come quite close.

I'm afraid this is a letter of loud complaints, but that's all there is.

> With love,
> Barbara.

Sabra Wyman Follett was born on July 27, 1923.

The Cottage in the Woods
July 30, 1923

My dear Mr. Oberg:

I am very sorry that I have neglected for so long to write to you, but you see I am in Sunapee now and there is hardly time for writing any more letters than the ones that I write to Mother and Daddy. It is very lovely here, and I wish you could be here. I will now tell you how Mother and Daddy didn't come to Sunapee. First Daddy and I went to Hartford where we picked up a friend and came here. We stayed a week, then Daddy and the friend went back and Mr. Simonds, Mrs. Simonds, and Miss Simonds all came up in their stead. Mother was unable to come.

We see minks around here, and a little while ago the place was a Paradise with birds. They don't seem to sing so much now, and we don't see as many as we used to. When I wade around among the rocks I see all sorts of little fishes: minnows, with their silvery scales; bass, with their black tail-tips; and pickerel, with their many-colored scales. The minnows keep together in schools; often they are quite large. Sometimes a little fish will turn over and there will be a flash of silver which is his silver belly. The pickerel will dart out from where they have been hiding as quick as lightning, then will stay perfectly still until they are started up again. Most of them are about four inches long though I saw one that was about two inches. They are very pretty.

One can find some very beautiful shellbeds in which one can find heavenly shells. They shine with all the colors of the rainbow always being more beautiful when wet.

Sometimes I see wild ducks swimming around, but mostly early in the morning. Mr. Simonds and I once saw two flying over the lake. One morning before anybody else was up I saw one swimming about in front of the cottage. One morning I also saw one, two, three, swimming around, not directly in front of the cottage, but quite near.

Best of all I now have a little *B A B Y   S I S T E R* born the twenty-seventh of July, and though I haven't seen her yet, they tell me she is a lovely baby. She isn't named yet, but I am deciding slowly. Isn't that joyful?

One day, during the days that Daddy was up here, I was playing around when Daddy whistled for me and I came bounding to the cottage to see. Daddy had a little baby woodmouse in a pail. How he got there Daddy told me he didn't know—he just found him there, and he couldn't get out. So we fed him and kept him in the pail until the day came when Daddy had time to make a cage for it. I have him now—Heather is his name, and a very lively sprite he is, though he comes out only when it is dark. There is a woodmouse family living round here and one night when Daddy was here we had quite a merry adventure with them. I was undressed and all ready for bed when

Daddy called me down. I found that Daddy had the lantern lighted and was following a little baby mouse that was running wildly round among the beams. The little fellow had just lost his head. In a moment more the mother woodmouse came from her hiding place and, taking the little one by the scruff of his neck she carried him down to a tiny hole in the floor and backing down pulled him in after her. But that is not all. I had gone back to bed and was half asleep when I heard another call. I got up and went downstairs. Daddy said that before I came down the mother had come from her old home (she had another nest up among the beams and was now moving her family) with two little ones in her mouth. He said that while she put one down the hole the other had got away. Now in a minute the mother came out of the hole and took the other little one in her mouth and stuffed him into that hole as if he had been a pillow and the hole a pillow-case. It was very amusing.

   With heaps of love,
   Barbara.

The Cottage in the Woods
July 31, 1923

My dear Mr. St. John:

 I am very sorry that I have neglected to write you this summer, but you see I am in Sunapee now, and have hardly time to write letters. I wish you were camping in the cut now because there are so many things for us to see and do.

 One morning I was playing around when I heard Daddy whistle. I came running back to the cottage and saw that he had a little baby woodmouse in a pail. How he got there we don't know. Well, I kept him in the pail and fed him on crumbs until Daddy had time to make a cage for him. I named him Heather, and he is the sweetest pet I ever had.

 Now for the best news. My little baby was born the twenty-seventh of July. I haven't seen it yet. But they tell me it is a lovely baby. It is a sister.

 There is something wrong with the typewriter and so I have to handwrite. I hope you will excuse my vile writing. I don't have much practice.

   Heaps of love,
   From Barbara.

A Cottage you know
August 16, 1923

Dearest Mother:

I am just wild to see you and Sabra but please don't come up until you hear from me that I am all well, for, you know, I wouldn't have that baby catch the whooping cough for anything. I am really crazy to see you, but must wait patiently. It is rather hard, especially as there is a new baby in the family, but worse shall have to be done in the course of time.

I want you to see Heather very much. You would love him at the first look.

You would also love to walk in the woods and see the chickadees chickadeeing about your head.

Well goodbye for now, Mother dear.

>With barrels of love,
>Barbara.

The Folletts returned to New Haven in October. Within twenty-four hours the kerosene burner attached to the kitchen stove in their rented house on Orange Street exploded. The building and its contents were destroyed, including Barbara's Eepersip manuscript, her stuffed animals and violin, and other treasures. The family was lucky to survive unharmed.

Professor George Hendrickson (1865-1963), Latin teacher and chair of Classics at Yale, put them up while construction of a house on Armory Street, which had begun earlier in the year, continued apace.

461 Humphrey Street
New Haven, Connecticut
November 12, 1923

My dear Mr. Oberg:

After my books had arrived at the house that we were taken into through kindness we discovered that Eepersip, my long story, had been destroyed in the fire. For many days I tried to rewrite it and could not, but after a while I got a sudden inspiration, and I am now working on it like fire. Every little while I think of rewriting all those exciting adventures, seventy-two pages of them, and when I think of that I almost give it up again. But, as Daddy thought before I began, it is going to be a much better story than the first one and that is partly what keeps me going on it. Before I had this inspiration I had started on a new story, an entirely different one, and I had gotten far ahead in that one. But now Eepersip seems to me far more important now and so stopped *The Great Labyrinth of Sarbea,* as I call my new story, and have gotten Eepersip still longer. I am also working on a sort of dictionary of my made-up Farksoo language and that is also fun. I have arranged the words that I had before in an alphabetical order and am now adding words. To be sure, we are not as well off as before, but in the midst of it all we grin to see the new house going up.

They have now nearly finished putting on the finish coat of plaster, and pretty soon I suppose they will do the windows, the woodwork, and the cement of the cellar. The house looks very old and beautiful now that they have got all four of those strange ornaments called wasps' nests on and painted. Before it looked as if it boomed up, but the wasps' nests in a way drag the second story down. We saw the difference when only one was on. We have had the beautiful arch of the chimney, which was filled up with plaster, cut open again and though it's not as good as it would be if they hadn't plastered the wall around it all it is a lot better than to have it filled up and so we feel quite pleased. Another great addition to the house is the thought of using the room on the top floor which we were going to have for a storage room made into a playroom for little Sabra when she is older. It is, you know, an enormous room and Sabra will have great fun running in and out of the big arch, we think.

Sabra is well and beautiful. She is getting very much interested in the curious world around her and grins and smiles all over herself. She tries to talk, too. Sometimes she makes a queer little coughing noise that sounds as if she was trying to swallow her tongue, and sometimes she makes cry-noises and we think she is going to cry, but, we found that she is only trying to talk. We think that perhaps she is trying to say: "I should like it very well if I could only talk." Perhaps that is just it.

I hope with all my heart that you will be here for Thanksgiving or, at least, Christmas, and I wish you could have been here for Halloween, for Miss Ralph, the nurse, while Mother and I were away, decorated the dining room table with all sorts of things, grapes, candles, pears, oranges, dried leaves, worthless ears of corn, and Jack in the middle of it all. It was very beautiful indeed.

>With sweet love,
>from Barbara.

I believe Barbara left The Great Labyrinth of Sarbea *unfinished at nineteen pages.*

461 Humphrey Street
New Haven, Connecticut
November 24, 1923

My own dear Ding:

After we had the fire all my hopes were concentrated on the remaining chance that Eepersip was to come by express with my books. But that chance, too, disappeared mercilessly. Eepersip was lost! One day I tried very hard to rewrite, but I couldn't get more than half a page done. So I gave it up and started an entirely new story called *The Great Labyrinth of Sarbea*. Sarbea is the hero of the story—he is the son of a poor couple that lived by the sea. They had in their possession a great blue pearl about the size of a hen's egg. When they died they handed it over to Sarbea, who, with the aid of the queen of the country, found his way to an uninhabited island and built for its keeping a great labyrinth all doors, doors, rooms, large and small, and a great tangle of passages, long and short. Sarbea found an enchantress who got for him some great dragons who guarded the labyrinth, a dragon standing at all of the entrances and nearly all of the main passages inside. Many folks from neighboring islands strove for the pearl, but always at a great loss. After the labyrinth was built Sarbea returned from the island to his own land and, also with the aid of the queen, and at the same time against the will of the king, married the beautiful princess, Chrysothemis. Then husband and wife returned to the uninhabited island where they built a little cottage and where Chrysothemis worked very diligently in a beautiful garden she was making every day.

In the middle of this new story I had an inspiration, a very sudden inspiration, it came to me while I was working on *The Great Labyrinth of Sarbea*, and I turned the page out quick as a wink, put in a fresh one and wrote on the top of it: *The Adventures of Eepersip*, and worked on it like fire for four pages. It is turning out to be a much better story than the first with lots of things taken out and more put in. I think you may remember that in my first Eepersip some of the plans the family made to catch Eepersip were too fancy and ingenious, these plans are much more simple and I think more to the interest of the reader. The two stories now have about the same number of pages; I think it is nineteen to nineteen now, but possibly Sarbea has one page more than Eepersip.

A few days ago my friend Miss Jessup came around to see me and showed me how to draw trees and many other things. So of course, I am so easy to get inspired with new inspirations just at present, she got me inspired with the art of drawing and painting. Before she showed up I had been painting quite a little, but she started me on a fresh outburst. I am sending you a picture with this letter.

How are you, Ding? Are the waves at Sound Beach rolling and thundering on the shore? I should certainly like to see them if they are, for one of my greatest desires just now is to see the sea. Oh, I love it so! with its thunder and lightning, storms and bays, waves, and ripples. Have you seen any of the beautiful white gulls with their long narrow wings sweeping and swirling? When you got to Sound Beach had all the birds gone or did you see any of the birds that you used to? I am so anxious to know! I love them all so much!

Well Ding I'm sure that you would now be perfectly delighted to see Sabra, for, though she grinned a little when you last saw her she grins all over herself now. She even talks a little. She makes curious little coughing noises and sounds exactly as if she was trying to swallow her tongue. She makes another little noise which I think she does by letting out all her breath and then drawing it in again fast and suddenly. When she grins she opens her mouth so wide that I should think that she would choke. The scales which we are weighing her on broke and when they broke she weighed eleven pounds, twelve ounces. Yesterday Daddy fixed the scales and this morning when she was weighed it was exactly twelve pounds. But that is no extraordinary weight for it was a long time ago that the scales broke.

The new house—I suppose you have almost forgotten that we had a new house—is coming along famously. You know, they put on two coats of plaster and now the second coat is all on. The windows are all sealed up with white cloth so that the plaster will dry. But when you try to look from the inside of the house out through the white cloth you can't see a thing if you knock your eyes into it ever so much. All the windows now aren't sealed up with white cloth, for they have now put on a good many of the casements and for all I know they may have all the casements in now, for I haven't seen the house for quite a while.

My, I had almost forgotten to tell you about the Simonds' baby which will be a month old on the twenty-sixth of this month. She is a very nice baby, but I like this baby a lot better. They play with her a lot and dandle her around, and sing to her so that between Bruce, Rosalind, and Miss Head, the nurse, they are rather spoiling her. But she is very nice, just the same and her name is Elizabeth Treat Simonds.

Well, Ding, goodbye for now.

With love from
Barbara.

461 Humphrey Street
New Haven, Connecticut
16 December, 1923

Dear Mr. St. John:

Your letter to Barbara was very, very welcome to all of us. I am writing this brief note to you that you may understand why Barbara hasn't written to you since she last saw you; and it may also explain the delay now, should there be one. Twenty-four hours after leaving Sunapee we were burned out of the little house we had taken out of New Haven for a few months, burned out so dreadfully and so completely that nothing has remained of the horror. Nothing, that is, of the things which were precious to us beyond words—Barbara's violin, her manuscripts, and a thousand dear treasures including your letters and the pictures you had sent her during the summer. Our loss was total and complete as regards clothes, and all the intimate things one takes [with] him, things too choice to leave behind, and too valuable to trust even to the express companies. As devastating as it all was, and as horrible a financial setback as it was, we can easily contemplate the catastrophe when we look at our glorious baby, for she, herself, came within two minutes of being exploded. It is a great miracle that we are all alive, free of burns, and still in possession of our arms and legs. You see, the stove in the kitchen, fitted with a kerosene burner exploded, and within five minutes the whole house was in the cellar. Nothing was recovered. And we had not transferred our insurance!

Barbara has been a brick about it all; she has suffered as only a sensitive person can suffer, but she has been absolutely silent about it. She became immediately absorbed in Shelley, and has gone quite wild over his poems. The only thing she wants for Christmas is a trip to the sea, a whole day at the sea where it is particularly lonesome and wild. This she wants to do as a sort of memorial to Shelley! I am trying to find a print of him for her. As to the fire, she never speaks of it, and she has avoided writing to any one, I think because she didn't want to refer to it, and yet was too full of it to be able to speak of anything else.

We are staying here with Professor Hendrickson until our house is ready to go into, that is, if we can hold on to the house at all now. Mr. Follett has been working sixteen hours a day until today when he came down with tonsillitis, and I have been doing more editorial work for him and for the Press. We have the need, and the desire, if we only have the strength.

How are you and Mrs. St. John? We should love to see you, and just take it for granted that you won't skip us, if by any chance you come through New Haven on your way Anywhere!

Our Greetings go to you with this note, that you and Mrs. St. John may have a very lovely Christmas, and that you may have the best kind of a southern trip.

>Yours sincerely,
>Helen Thomas Follett

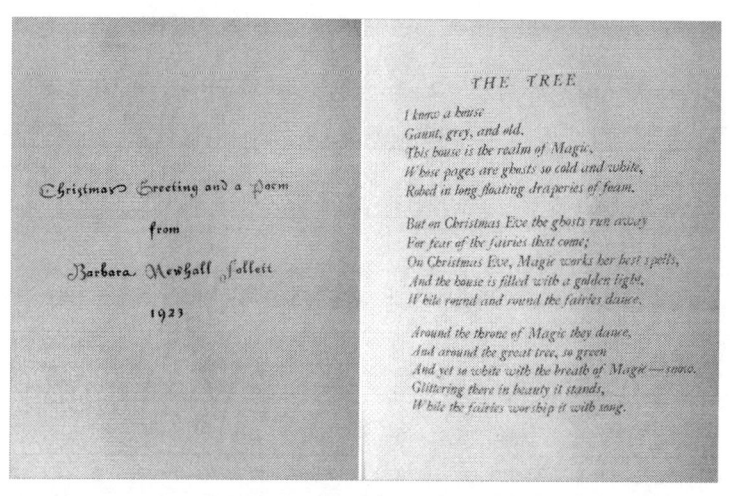

For the next three Christmases Barbara designed cards for her friends and family. In 1923 she composed a poem, laid out the type and, with her father's help, ran the press.

>THE TREE
>I know a house
>Gaunt, grey, and old.
>This house is the realm of Magic,
>Whose pages are ghosts so cold and white,
>Robed in long floating draperies of foam.
>
>But on Christmas Eve the ghosts run away
>For fear of the fairies that come;
>On Christmas Eve, Magic works her best spells,
>And the house is filled with a golden light,
>While round and round the fairies dance.
>
>Around the throne of Magic they dance,
>And around the great tree, so green
>And yet so white with the breath of Magic—snow.
>Glittering there in beauty it stands,
>While the fairies worship it with song.

461 Humphrey Street
New Haven, Connecticut
January 3, 1924

Dear Mr. Oberg:

I am writing to express the thanks and enthusiasm of the family over the Christmas box that always comes in some form. I think this form was just about the best so far. I simply adore the beautiful painted feather fan and the little ivory one that you repaired for me. The apples were delicious, juicy and sweet. We would eat handfuls of peanuts, morning and evening. You should have seen the fireplace, littered with peanut shells. I thank you again for all that you have done for us.

We hope to be in the new house in a little more than a month from now, and, of course, are looking forward to the day when we shall move eagerly. We want to be in there as quickly as possible so that we shall have a place for you. I want to see you any time, but I fear that we couldn't keep you here. You know, we are living in about three rooms all jammed together.

I wish to see you on my birthday anyway, even if I don't see you before, which, of course, I would love. I am so crazy to see you and the things that you have been doing for us, in the way of furniture. I have heard so much about the desks and the Grandfather Clock that I am as eager to see them as ten lions after ten hares.

Goodbye, now, and I thank you once more for the things you have sent to us and also for the things that you are doing for us that we haven't seen yet.

> With love,
> Barbara.

From Michael A. Morrison's book, John Barrymore, Shakespearean Actor: *"On 15 December [1923], Barrymore played his final Hamlet in New York, and the next week began his first trip into the provinces in five years. The first week was divided between New Haven and Hartford. Barrymore commuted back to New York every evening. According to [Lark] Taylor, he hurried through the play to make his train, 'shortening the performance almost an hour, to its great improvement'." As you'll see, Barbara named the animals she received for Christmas after characters in* Hamlet.

461 Humphrey Street
New Haven, Connecticut
January 3, 1924

My dear Mr. St. John:

You may think I have neglected you in the way of letters, and really I think I have, but we have been very excited in the place that we are living in now, and I really must confess that I haven't had much time. But I have been perfectly delighted to get long letters from you so often, dear friend.

I don't believe I ever had such a Merry Christmas before. I had a perfectly delightful stocking. I will skip most of the things in the stocking and tell you about the two most important things. A few days ago, well longer than a few days ago, John Barrymore, as Hamlet, came to New Haven, and we went. Now when we heard that he was coming I made haste to read the play, and I was never so crazy about anything else that I read. I was more crazy about the acting and, even if John Barrymore is a great actor, I certainly don't see how he can remember all Hamlet's parts, even if he has studied years and years. Then I wanted to have the play with me all the time, and I didn't have small enough books to put in my pocket. I had the Temple edition which, I suppose you know, is pretty small, but it wasn't small enough to satisfy me. Miss Ralph, the nurse, who is also our best friend in every way, found out from me that I wanted a little Hamlet, about three inches long, and, without my knowledge the family went down town to try to secure it for me, but when we found one just right, we found from the dealer that it belonged to a little set of all the plays and he didn't wish to break the set up. They argued and argued, but to no purpose. Then Marion Hendrickson, the daughter of Professor Hendrickson, our landlord, went in town and argued and argued with the dealer, and finally she got the little book and I found it in the toe of my stocking. Then I also got in my stocking a little red pen-knife with two blades, a long one and a short one.

But before I opened my stocking I had another great pleasure, almost the greatest of my Christmas. About a week before Christmas Mother and I went in town shopping and deciding what to get for Daddy. We decided on a nice, warm, fuzzy bathrobe, which Daddy has been miserable without when he gets up in the morning. We also got a box holding ten or twelve packages of Lucky Strike cigarettes, the kind that Daddy smokes. And also we got two packages of Neccos, and a bag of caramels. The things we put in the huge pockets of the bathrobe, together with a green tie with blue stripes in it, which Daddy now considers the handsomest one he has. All these things I put together in paper and a box with about three tags on it and, early Christmas Morning, I crept downstairs from the third floor, where I sleep, and laid the box on Daddy's bed. I had some adventures before I got downstairs, though. The stairs from the third floor come down to a hall, then this hall turns to right angles and right there there is a door. In fact the hall turns two right angles, for the rest of it turns right angles on the other side of the main hall and leads to an upstairs living room, which we use. Well, I came down the stairs, crept along the hall to the door, put the box down, opened the door, and then decided that it would be better to shut the door before I opened the next door that led into the bedroom so that sudden light wouldn't come from the main hall into the bedroom and wake Mother and Daddy up, for there was a light going in the main hall. So I had to pick the box up, go through the hall door, put the box down, shut the door, take the box up, come to the bedroom door, put the box down again, and begin to open the bedroom door, very softly. Then I felt the door beginning to stick and I knew that it would creak if I pushed it any more. The slit that I had made was just the size for me to go through, but, how about the box? That was the question. Well, anyhow I took the box up and instead of holding it horizontally I held it vertically and managed to slip it through. The rest was easy. I put my heavy burden down on Daddy's bed. Then I crept away relieved of quite a heavy load.

Immediately after breakfast we went into the *room*, which Daddy and Mother had arranged surprisingly beautifully overnight. Last Christmas the first thing I saw when I came into the *room* was the globe with the two beautiful gold-fish in it. The two beautiful ill-fated gold-fish. It was the same way this Christmas. The first thing I saw wasn't the tree, it was a large tank with seven gold-fish, one tad-pole, and two snails in it. The tad-pole is Polonius, a great gold beauty with tail and fins tipped with black is Claudius, a small brilliant one with a long tail is Gertrude, a small rather ordinary looking fish with yellow underneath and dark brown or maybe black on the back on the back, which, they say, is going to turn silver, is Reynaldo, and a rather large very brilliant fish with a short tail is Horatio. The live-stock has been added to since Christmas, though. There is now a beautiful silver fish, with a double tail, Ophelia; a smaller tad-pole, Laertes; and two more snails.

Then all sorts of lovely gifts were delivered, not forgetting the book of Irish Fairy Tales, which I wish to thank you for. I love them. I have read a lot of them already and think they are lovely stories. Then I also got a Brownie camera, and have already taken three pictures of the new house from various angles.

THE COTTAGE IN THE WOODS (1923–1926)

Speaking of the new house, I must tell you how beautifully it is coming on. We have decided to paint the third floor instead of wall-papering it, and we are painting Daddy's study a beautiful blue, and the room intended for the maid, which has now come to my possession, a beautiful green. Won't it be fun to sleep on the top floor? Will you come and sleep up there with me? You see the house is coming famously.

Sabra, my sweet sister, is growing more lively every day. She loves to look at her own tiny pink hands. She moves them unconsciously, but you can see her following their rather jerky motions with her little bright brown eyes, with a little silver star in each. But she has lately learned a new trick. Miss Ralph sits her up straight (for some peculiar reason she likes that position) and she seemed as if she was seized with a sudden rage, for she worked her arms up and down, one after the other. It was very funny, but very cunning. Probably she will discover something new almost every day.

I wonder if I ever showed you or told you about the language that I made up. I can't seem to remember. It is called Farksoo. I had it on a rough and tumble manuscript, but I decided that I would arrange the various words on cards alphabetically. So I started out to do it and now I have two indices, one of Farksoo-English and the other of English-Farksoo. The language is interesting but the history of Farksolia is more interesting. Farksolia is the land where the Farksoo language is spoken. It is a separate planet from the Earth, and I think it is really more interesting than the Earth. There were eleven great queens over Farksolia and they are in order: Queen Bruwanderine, Queen Lacee, Queen Ibirio, Queen Flitterveen, Queen Rooeetu, Queen Liassa, Queen Atee, Queen Lazade, Queen Herazade, Queen Chrysothemis, and Queen Perazade. Queen Atee, the seventh, was chosen because of her beauty, and when she got to ruling she seemed too harsh for the people. So they waged the great Farksolian war against her and her friends. During this war the Farksolians were extinguished down to two families. One family has a little boy, and the other a little girl. The boy is about six years old, and the girl about six months. I hope that when they grow up they will marry and breed the race again.

Sheheritzade is the big city where all the Farksolians lived together. They all agreed that living in one big, beautiful city like that their planet was much more beautiful because the woodlands were not spoiled by houses. During the reign of Queen Bruwanderine, the first, the people were a little bit lower in their life than we are now. But they became better much faster than we did and during the reign of Queen Liassa, the sixth, they looked back upon themselves as savages. During the reign of Liassa they were much higher than we are now, so it is hard to imagine what they were like.

About two thousand miles from Sheheritzade there is a great sea called the Farksolian Sea. It is at least twice as broad as the Pacific Ocean. But oh, what a wonderful sea it is! Bluer than any sea here, and when you look off into it sunlight sparkles and dances on the horizon, and the sunlight makes it appear blue and gold and green. Oh, what marvelous colors can be seen on that sea! What wonderful fishes marked to match the sun and the sea marked with bands of blue and gold! Oh, what wonderful white sand there is there, and what beautiful lacy sea-weeds are brought up on the sand by the billowing waves, capped with sparkling white foam. These sea-weeds are of marvelously beautiful colours—greens, browns, and even reds. The beaches there are beautiful but I think the rocks may be more beautiful. Great towering rocks, jagged and precipitous, towering into the blueness of the great sky. This sea surely is wonderful, but so is the great plain which borders the great sea on the other side. On it are about two habited houses, and even those are very inconspicuous. Over this great plain run strange little brown animals; over it fly strange but very beautiful little birds and butterflies. All around this plain are woodlands, rich and green, and purple and green mottled mountains, and in these wonderful places there are also strange little creatures and flowers, of unusual colors, red and white together.

But now let us return to beautiful Sheheritzade. Around the city are great green and purple mountains, the Farksolian range, but one mountain, the highest and also the nearest to the city, is called the Sheheritzadian Mountain. These mountains are very sacred.

There is a very strange fact about the snows of Farksolia. Where the snow falls on the mountains it just melts away from the warmth of the spreading boughs of the trees over the ground. And also snow cannot rest on the little twigs and shoots of the trees, because the sap of the Farksolian trees is very warm and it melts the snow almost as soon as the snow touches the branches. Therefore the mountains look a lot greener, though, of course, not as green as they do in summer. But, of course, on the plains and where there are not so many trees the snow lies thick; indeed sometimes the level on the great plain rises to twenty feet.

Don't you think that the history of Farksolia is interesting? Here is a little poem in the Farksoo language which I will say 'goodbye' with:

    Ar peen maiburs barge craik coo,
    Peen yar fis farled cray pern.
    Peen darndeon flar fooloos lart ain birdream.

> Avee lart ain caireen
> Ien tu cresteen de tuee,
> Darnceen craik peen bune.

This poem is very famous in Farksolia, or, at least, it was, and also very old, and the old Farksoo is quite different from the new. But still this poem is not so different from the new Farksoo as another poem is which I will also send you:

> Flitterveens, flitterveens, veenic flitterveens,
> Cobreebering soocun peen urnees.
> Flitterveens, flitterveens, marlershoo flitterveens,
> Fithic soocun peen paperteebruee.
>
> Soocun peen fileshay,
> Soocun peen paperteebruee,
> Soocun peen urnees fith peen flitterveens,
> Cobreebering, fithic soocun peen bines—
> Veenic, marlershoo flitterveens.

This poem has much more of the old language in it even if it isn't as old as the first one. I will now translate them for you.

The first runs this way:
> As the (maibur is a flower that comes in May,
>   and the plural is maiburs) begin to come,
> The air is filled with perfume;
> The dandelion fluff floats like a (birdream is
>   something very lovely).
> Also like a fairy in her dress of gold,
> Dancing to the wind.

The second poem translated runs thus:
> Butterflies, butterflies, beautiful butterflies,
> (Cobreebering is to flap the wings making
>   no progress in the air) over the meadow.
> Butterflies, butterflies, exquisite butterflies
> Flying over the brook.
>
> Over the mountain,
> Over the brook
> Over the meadow fly the butterflies,
> Cobreebering, flying over the trees,
> Beautiful, exquisite butterflies.

Both of these little poems have lovely little tunes which, alas, I must see you to sing.

Well, goodbye, dear friend, until some other time, when I hope I can entertain you in the new house.

> May a ship reach your port full of love and kisses,
> from your true friend ever,
> Barbara.

The Columbia archive has several assignments that Helen typed up for Barbara's morning lessons.

Saturday, 5 January 1924
1. Finish up your letter to Mr. St. John, and mail it.
2. Violin — a good forty minutes.
3. Hamlet: Act I, scene 2. Read the notes and glossary carefully, and use your dictionary.
4. Piano — a good forty minutes.
5. Arithmetic: review Percentage by doing the examples on page 69; then select those you can do on page 71.
6. Read *Le Poisson D'Or [an 1878 novel by Paul Féval]*
7. More violin, and more piano. Try to do an hour of each each day.

Sunday, 6 January *[1924]*
1. Try to write a letter—not necessarily a long one—to Mr. and Mrs. Knopf, to thank them for *Come Hither*.
2. Violin — a good long session.
3. Water-colors. See how good a copy you can make of the little picture in a gold frame just to the left of the west window (that's the window nearest the goldfish bowl). Enlarge the picture if you want to.
4. If you take a walk with Miss Ralph, carry your Brownie and see if you can't find something worth using the rest of the film on. Don't forget to turn the film along after each exposure.
5. Piano — I should think you might do an hour without hurting yourself.
6. Read, in Miss Dean's Keats:
   Ode to a Nightingale
   Ode on a Grecian Urn
   Ode to Autumn
   On First Looking into Chapman's Homer
   Last Sonnet ("Bright Start, would," etc.)

461 Humphrey Street
New Haven, Connecticut
January 15, 1924

Dear Mrs. Day:

I am writing to thank you a million times for the sweet little jar of ginger that you sent me. The jar itself was sweet, but the way it was done up gave me beautiful ideas. It made me think of Sunapee, and the pine trees, and the little bottles of flowers. And it looked as though it had been taken from Sunapee, and I nearly cried to think how beautiful it was up there and how we might go up this summer, but that the winter couldn't pass quickly enough. Even if we were going next week I couldn't wait. It seems when you are anticipating a thing, that it can't come. If we were going to Sunapee tomorrow, tomorrow I would think, "Well, it's tomorrow that we go." I could never quite get to tomorrow; it would never be tomorrow—always tomorrow would be one day off. It is that way when a kitten chases her tail or when you try to step on your shadow.

But I am going far off the subject of the sweet package. I never ate preserved ginger, but I fancy that I shall like it very much. If I don't I can give the ginger to Ding, my grandmother, who is very fond of it. Anyhow, the bottle is sweet and it was very sweet of you to send it to me. I thank you again very, very much.

       Love from
       Barbara.

This letter was to the Lathrop sisters.

461 Humphrey Street
New Haven, Connecticut
January 29, 1924

Dear Gertrude and Dorothy:

I want to express the feeling of thanks which I have toward you for the adorable little box from India. It fills me with beautiful ideas of beautiful things. It reminds me of a deep dark woods containing one blazing brilliant bush, covered with wild flowers of fantastic shapes and strange colors. It makes me think of Fairyland and a black woods streaked with gold growing marvelously beautiful bushes. Or it makes me think of Queen Atee, who was so beautiful and yet harsh. Or maybe of Queen Flitterveen who was very loving. It makes me think also of a dark green meadow with one flaming bush on which there are strange birds and beautiful butterflies lighting on it. It makes me think of looking over that colored bush in miles and stretches of gold and black woods in Fairyland. It is not only beautiful but it is useful. We keep clips and pens in it all the time.

    Lovingly,

[Enclosed on a separate sheet dated January 30, 1924]

For Gertrude and Dorothy:
    Ideas flow through my mind of marvelous and
        beautiful things,
    Of the box which you have sent me.
    It is a congregation of fairies
    Dancing round a solitary blazing bush
    In the center of a deep black wood
    Where roam the ghosts
    Whose footsteps pave the wood with pearls and foam.
    But the golden-robed fairies frighten the ghosts away;
    And on silent golden wings the butterflies soar in the blue
        of a sapphire day.
    The leaves of the magical bush glimmer like emeralds
    And in the entrancingness of the fairy wood
    Is heard a wondrous song.
    It rings and rises through the woodland green and gold.
    The fairies feast around the bush
    On emerald and ruby drops of dew.
    And still the magic music sounds
    And the butterflies flying overhead
    Soar up and up into the beauty and the stillness of the
        Sapphire sky.

    Lovingly,

461 Humphrey Street
New Haven, Connecticut
January 31, 1924

My dear Mr. Paul:

Thank you ever and ever so much for the beautiful print of Beethoven that you sent. It was lovely in you to have the intention of sending it to replace my other ones if they were lost in the fire. This winter I am taking piano lessons of Bruce Simonds, and you may remember that I took them of Rosalind last winter. We are working on the two Sonatas of Opus 49, numbers 1 and 2. Then we are also working on the Andante of Opus 79. It is a great pleasure. Thank you very much for the picture, anyway.

The new house is coming on famously, and we are thinking seriously of moving in soon. Probably we shan't move with our things; we may remain here for two or three days after the furniture goes in, but I am thinking how delicious it would be if we spent a night there Wednesday which we are thinking of doing. They have put on the wainscoting in the living-room; the wall-paper in several of the bedrooms; they have put on the linoleum in the kitchen and bathrooms. We hope that very soon we can entertain you there.

Sabra is growing sweeter every day. She is flourishing beautifully and weighs 14 lb. 8 oz. She was six months old the 27th. Every afternoon she is taken up to play till six o'clock and her bottle time. She has all manner of amusing tricks but I cannot stop to tell about them all now.

       Your friend

461 Humphrey Street
New Haven, Connecticut
February 5, 1924.

My dear Mr. St. John:

Thank you very very much indeed for the box of persimmons that you sent me from Virginia. They had the strangest flavor that I ever tasted, but they were perfectly delicious. I showed them to all the people in this house to find out if they knew what they were. Several of them didn't. I thought it was quite a joke. Thank you very much for sending them to me, anyway.

The new house is coming along famously. We hope to be in very soon now. We are having the men put on wall-paper. My little study has a very beautiful paper with little gold and bronze-colored birds sitting on little gold and bronze-colored leaves and branches. For Sabra's room they have put on a paper with all sorts of lovely flowers twining all over it. For my grandmother's room a rather simple paper simply showing red and pink flowers twining around greenish stalks. For the guest room they have put on a paper showing little streams with bridges over them and swans swimming under the bridges. For Mother's room they have put on a true Jacobean paper which fits the house in every way. It simply shows lovely green leaves of queer shapes twining up and up on slender stalks.

I know that I shall feel like this odd little poem when I get to Armory Street:

> Ah, silken amber-winged butterfly
> Your wings are silent and golden,
> You are borne by the wind on those silent amber wings.
> There you go into the sapphire sky

> And over the sapphire lake
> Whose drowsy ripples
> Make me feel like you
> Silken-winged insect;
> Borne by the wind on silent golden wings
> Through the blue of a sapphire sky.

It *is* an odd little poem I know, but it expresses a certain feeling that I sometimes have when I think that everything that is odd is beautiful. I wrote it when I felt that way. That is why it is odd. Here is another rather odd snatch of verse:

> *Apollo's Arrows*
> The sky is ultramarine,
> The sun and moon have gone to rest,
> The stars are shining brightly.
>
> Blue Vega in the zenith,
> Orange Arcturus in the west
> White-eyed Capella rising in the east.
>
> Then there comes a golden arrow swiftly gliding
> Through the silent bed of the sky
> And through the noisy feast of the stars.

That is one of my oddest bits of verse, but I can't help liking it just the same. It refers to a shooting star, and I can remember how entranced I was when I first saw a shooting star. I have a few more odd little bits of song-like verse:

> *The Winter in Fairyland*
> It is a mountain
> Covered with snow
> There are pear-shaped flames there
> Dancing in purple and blue.
> It is a gorgeous garden
> Each petal is white and silver.
> The sapphire sky floats overhead
> And in it is no sun nor moon nor stars.
> It is not night or day.

I am really surprised how odd it seems, but I think I like all three very much just because they are odd, don't you? I think this is an odd letter but that is because I am writing it while I am in that odd state of mind.

>> Very lovingly,
>> Barbara.

THE COTTAGE IN THE WOODS (1923–1926)

Mr. St. John wrote a poem for Barbara in February 1924.

> Eepersip, Eepersip, where are you hiding?
>   Come from your lurking place in the deep wood;
> Play with me, stay with me, nestle beside me:
>   I am your henchman, the slave of your mood.
>
> I am your travel-mate; we will go journeying,
>   Wandering, wondering, under the trees,
> Trailing the rivers and climbing the mountains,
>   Gay as the sunlight and free as the breeze.
>
> Eepersip, Eepersip, child of enchantment,
>   I will make magic to draw you to me:
> I will blend bird notes with play of young foxes,
>   Flavor of beechnuts, and strength of the sea.
>
> Grace of a fern leaf, tinkle of fountains,
>   Sparkle and darkle of moonlight on dew,
> Odors of wild grapes and quaintness of orchids—
>   These, and your name, will I put in the brew.
>
> Eepersip, Eepersip, why do you run from me,
>   Hurrying, scurrying, through the dry leaves?
> Down by the brookside I hear your light laughter:
>   Do you not care that your comrade grieves?

461 Humphrey Street
New Haven, Connecticut
February 9, 1924

Dear Mr. Oberg:

   I am looking forward for the house to be finished not only so that we can be in it, but also because we can't have the pleasure of being together until the house is finished. It is very nearly finished though. For several of the rooms we have picked lovely wall-papers and they have been put on. Isn't that great. You see, we may be together very soon now.
   F A R K S O O ! F A R K S O L I A ! H a r r a h ! Would that the greatest people in the universe would let down their mighty mchine which will take them to other planets and take us to their planet Farksolia. Ah, wouldn't that be wonderful? I wonder how you would like it, for though it is beautiful it is very peculiar and strange in almost every way. It is

> Where the skies are bluest,
> Where the leaves are green,

Where the white-capped wavelets
Glisten with shimmery sheen.

Where the waves come rolling in,
Where a song of the sea is heard,
Where the goddess Virodine
Leaps to the song of a bird.

Where the skies are black and blue,
Where the stars are shining white,
Where the blackened billows
Thunder with terrible might.

Where the grass is soft and green
Where the flowers bloom;
Where the billows blue once more
Mightily do boom.
Where the flower stars are shining,
Where the wind-borne butterflies
Do silently sail
Through the sapphire skies.

    This is like Farksolia with a sea more wonderful than any Earthen thing, and where more lovely butterflies than ever dreamed of on Earth sail wind-borne through sapphire skies. Ah, Farksolia is surely a wonderful place with its booming billows thundering against high cliffs. I should like a little ship with white fluttering sails to come for me loaded with my Farksoo friends, for I have some friends of Farksoo and they love me dearly. They, if they could, would come for me in the ship that I want. It has a green ship part and the rest would be fluttering sails. They would come for me if they could, and I would gather my precious belongings and then we would be off! Through the waves of our sea we would gently glide and then we would reach an unknown land where the other Farksolians would be waiting for us with that powerful machine and then we would be off for Farksolia! Through the foaming dashing waves we would go with a silent gliding motion and when we got to the unknown land we would be off for Farksolia! And if I ever come back, which would be doubtful, I would never be contented with the Earth again. Don't you think that it sounds like a very wonderful place and wouldn't you love to go there?

    Thank you very much indeed for the lovely poems that you sent us. I just know what patience you must have had over it and what great care you must have taken. They were very lovely anyhow and I thank you again for sending them to me.

I wonder if you are still working on make-up butterflies. If you have done all that I have sent you tell me and I will send some more, but also if you need more send me a list to keep of those that I have already sent you. But don't trouble to do that unless you need more descriptions. I am now telling you more or less about what the cover will be like. You see the Farksolian butterflies are about to be one section of a large book on Farksolia. This book will be divided into several divisions on Farksolia. One will be of the main plans and maps of Farksolia; one will be of Farksolian Birds and Butterflies; and one will be of the water creatures of Farksolia and about all that lives under water. Then there will be a section on not only a little detail of the place, but about the Farksolians' habits, workmanships, inventions, and about what is found in the planet and what kind of fruits are grown, and what kind of foods are gathered, and a good many such details. You may think I expect too much of you when I invite you to draw the Farksolian Birds also! If you do, do not by any means accept this invitation. Come down as soon as you can and we will talk it over anyhow.

    Love from
    Barbara.

461 Humphrey Street
New Haven, Connecticut
February 9, 1924

My best and dearest friend [Mr. St. John]:
 I would like a little ship to come for me, a little dark green ship with fluttering white sails, laden with my Farksolian friends, for I have some friends of Farksoo and they love me dearly. If they could, they would come for me in the ship that I want. When they got here I would gather up my most precious belongings, and you, dear friend, for you are my best belonging and my most precious. Then we would sail across our ocean and reach an unknown land where some more of my Farksolian friends would be waiting for me with their powerful machine which takes them from one planet to another. Then we would be off for a separate planet. Ah, how wonderful that would be! I wonder what would be the first thing that we should do. I think that the first thing I would do would be to stare all around me for ten whole minutes; then I should fall unconsciously on the ground and would be sick for about twenty-four hours which is not the whole of a Farksolian day. I would be sick from breathing the air of the Farksolians', for the air is so different from ours. It is so easy to breathe that an Earthen going to Farksolia would breathe in too

much at a time. That is why I should be sick, and I think you would be sick, too. Then I would take you and grip you as though I were afraid of losing you, and we would wander out from the city of Sheheritzade into the open fields. Then we would lie down together and gaze from the soft green emerald grass to the sapphire sky, where we should see the swallow-like birds circling. Then I should look a little lower and would see the butterflies. Then I would look down in the grass around me and would see the dear little busy insects visiting first one flower, then another. We would watch the golden butterflies going everywhere on soft, silent, golden wings. The wind would bear them through the sapphire sky over us, and under us would be the rich brown earth of Farksolia. I would feel the soft green grass all up my back and would smell of all the flowers coming within reach of my happy nostrils. We would breathe in great breaths of the warm scented air. How happy we would be. I think that we would be perfectly contented to stay there all day without eating a morsel. Then when dusk came on we would wander into the city again and dine on silvery fruits of marvelous tastes. Then at night we would gaze from the meadow again into the wonderful night sky of a mixture of ultramarine and black. We would see the constellation called "Peen Flitterveen." It has this name because it is shaped exactly like a big butterfly with beautiful curving lines of stars for the feelers. And a curious thing about this constellation is that all the stars in it are of a golden color. Then we would also see the other important constellation, called "Peen Farksiades." That constellation hasn't a very remarkable pattern, but the stars! They are remarkable because they are black, little black stars! Oh, how lovely they are, though they are very inconspicuous against the ultramarine and black night sky! My, but they are lovely! Then we should also see the two moons of Farksolia and their names are Vaireen and Seeven. Vaireen is rather like our moon in coloring, but Seeven is very inconspicuous for it is nearly the color of the day sky in the day and the night sky at night. But both moons are very lovely. Do you think that this is a very true description of what we would do if we went to Farksolia? I do.

      Very lovingly,
      Barbara.

To George Hendrickson's daughter, Marion, from an undated draft (circa February 1924).

Dear Marion:
>In the depths of a woodland shady and green
>Where the flitterveens fly and caireens sing
>In one ecstasy of beauty and wonder
>There is a fairylike pool.
>Around it grows the sweetest, softest and the greenest grass
>And tiny blue flowers there blossom
>The bottom of the pool is clearest sand, crystal and white,
>And over it swim tiny white fishes.
>Over the pool hangs a woodland bough
>With the dark green leaves and golden fairy fruits,
>And by the pool fair Flitterveen, baby, two years old,
>   is sitting!
>Her silken golden hair is like the sunbeams
>Which now do float in, there.
>Around that hair so golden is a wreath which the fairies
>   have crowned her with.
>She is gazing at the silvery fishes
>Swimming over the sparkling silver sand.
>In that wild but too beautiful forest place.
>Her fair blue eyes shine like stars of heaven,
>Beauty found only in that heavenly place.
>Fairy baby, she is more beautiful than ever here.

It is true! The highest compliment that I can possibly pay to the picture that stands on your father's bureau is that you look more like a Farksolian baby than any Earthen baby. Indeed, you do not look at all like an Earthen baby; you look absolutely and from all my points of view like a Farksolian baby. You look in the picture like almost any Farksolian baby, but mostly like Queen Flitterveen when she ran away and sat by the pool looking at the fishes, in the softest green grass with a wreath of dark leaves around her silken golden hair and when the people looking for her saw a baby two years old they were entranced with the beauty of the fairy place. Think of it, Marion! A baby two years old actually entranced with beauty! I know I ought to be able to pay the picture still higher compliments, but it *is* a high compliment to be told that you looked like a Farksolian baby. Don't you think so? Even if I cannot express my feelings any higher I *can* say that I think the picture is beautiful, the loveliest one *I* ever saw and that I come into your father's room every day and look at it.

I wonder if my card catalogue drawers came while you were still here. I don't think they did. Anyhow, Daddy sent to Boston for two card catalogue drawers with small rods to put the cards on (though the cards have to have holes in them). Well, I made quite a long job of punching through my Farksoo cards. I had two catalogue drawers, one to keep the Farksoo-English cards in, and the other to keep the English-Farksoo cards in. Now, my Farksoo is not such a job because I have now no great groups to punch. When I get six or eight cards written on I punch them right then and there so that I don't accumulate a great bunch, like the bunch that I had before the drawers and the punch came. It is great fun!

We are now seriously thinking of "moving in" soon. The house really is nearly finished. They have put the paper on four of the rooms and maybe they have finished the fifth, but the last thing I heard was that they were putting it on in Mother's big room, and I really don't believe they have finished yet. For Sabra's room they have put on a wall-paper with little flowers on it which has the appearance of black and white but which has many other colors on it. For my little study they have put on a wall-paper with long, pointed leaves, and little birds sitting on twigs all in gold and bronze and brown. For my grand-mother's room an old-looking paper with just a little pink and red flowers twining up it. For the guest room they have put on a paper with a very complicated pattern: it shows little bridges and streams and swans swimming; then it also shows windmills, and groups of tall trees which look rather like poplar trees; then around and all over there are vines of lovely green leaves. For Mother's big room they are putting on a true Jacobean paper. It has green leaves twining up and up on twisty and gracefully curving stalks. It is very nice. So you see we are nearly finished, and the speed depends a good deal on us, for they can't put on wall-paper until we choose and we are having a rather difficult time choosing it. Anyhow we hope to be in ourselves in two weeks or maybe before that, and our furniture may go in in a very short time.

Sabra is perfectly beautiful. She is getting to the point where she can imitate quite a few things that she sees other people do. For instance, sometimes if you say sssssssssssssssssss to her she will imitate that noise. But the funniest thing that has happened yet was once when Daddy was shaking his head at her to keep her from crying she began too, and shook her head like mad. She finds out new things and has new tricks every day. She is dear and we hope she will have a good time in the house, running around the big straddle chimney and chasing herself and other people in the big playroom.

    With love from,
    Barbara

THE COTTAGE IN THE WOODS (1923–1926)

Transcribed from a draft to an unknown recipient whom Barbara had met recently. This may be her first letter from the new house.

176 Armory Street
New Haven, Connecticut
March 5, 1924

My dear friend:

I was very glad to hear from you so soon after I had made your acquaintance and I myself would have written sooner if it hadn't been for the hustle and bustle of moving, for we have moved into the new house that we showed you. Of course most of the bustle is not through with so that there isn't really much pleasure yet, but I can see that it is going to be ideal living. I know how beautiful the woods are going to be in the springtime with the little squirrels playing around in the leaves. I think that there are going to be some beautiful birds here, too, but now there are only sparrows, jays, and crows. I haven't seen any chickadees, much to my surprise, for I am pretty sure that I have seen chickadees before in the woods in the winter.

Last night a very exciting thing happened. I was going to bed, and Daddy was leaning way out of the window of my room. He was looking down where the kitchen light lighted up a small area outside the kitchen door. And Daddy saw a great big yellow tom-cat in the circle of light. He sneaked and sneaked into the dark where we couldn't see him and presently we heard the cover of the garbage-can fall off with the rattle. That was all we saw of him, but after I was in bed I heard some rustles in the leaves, and I fell asleep thinking of that big cat sneaking and sneaking!

A few days ago there were many dogs out in the back yard and all we saw all day were dogs and dogs. In the evening the dogs continued to go back and forth, and the faint light would sometimes show their colors all in black. But there was one dog that was sneakier and blacker and more mysterious than any of the others; and we thought of wolves, wolves out in the back yard. And then I thought how amusing a picture it would be if there really were a pack of black wolves out in the back yard showing black against the outline of the silent house, and against the outline of the dark night sky with stars and stars in it and the great warrior Orion amongst them with his glittering silver armor. Then from inside we might hear them and see them lifting up their dark heads with golden eyes and barking. How thrilling to see those wolves, out in the back yard!

Thank you very much for sending me that lovely photograph of the little pond which you discovered. And to think of discovering it! The thrill of discovering a thing which no one else has ever seen!

Isn't it a wonderful thrill? That you must tell me for I have never discovered a thing. Isn't it wonderful to go and struggle through the thick woods, bushes, and briars, and then suddenly come upon an open space with a valley and a range of mountains before you, and—in the valley is a little secret pond which is yours. If I discovered a thing like that I would think of Eepersip. She also discovered many little pools and lakelets. And Eepersip, you may remember, is the character of my story. Have I told you about Eepersip?

I wonder which kind of mountain you like the best, the low woodsy kind rich and green, or the tremendously high kind with great precipices and the tops bare solid rock with eagles flying over them. Don't you think it would be nice to climb suddenly on to the bare rock out from the deepest woods and see in the mountain sky a great eagle with mottle brown and white wings outspread, sailing down the still sky. Close to the ground there might be no wind, but where the eagle was there would be a strong wind blowing and the eagle would sail and sail. And then you would go back into the woods to your little log cabin and sleep and in your dreams you would see the blue sky with only one thing in it, the great brown and white eagle with wings outspread.

Please come to see me here sometime pretty soon, the sooner the better. We can have great fun watching the chipmunks and squirrels and the lovely golden butterflies fluttering amid spring-laden flowers and trees.

    Yours lovingly,

Transcribed from a draft to Mildred Kennedy with "Armory St. '24" noted on it by Helen. Barbara probably wrote it soon after her tenth birthday.

Dearest Aunt Mildred:

Thank you ever and ever so much for the dear little bag that you sent me. It is perfectly sweet and I know I shall use it a lot.

I wonder if you would come and see me here in the new house some time. I should be tremendously glad to have you, because I have so many things to tell you about and because I also think that you would love it here. You know I was very much disappointed when you didn't come the day that you said you would.

I want to tell you all about Farksolia: Farksolia is a land, in fact, a planet, and a separate planet from Earth. Farksolia is my imaginary land, and I can introduce its history by telling you that I love it much more than any land here and I have a good right to. I hope you will love it the way I do. First, let me tell about its past history.

Now the planet wasn't so large as Jupiter, but it was bigger than the Earth; and there were very few people living on it in proportion to the size of it. They all loved the woods and wanted some arrangement so that they could prevent the woods from being cut up into little choppy villages. So they decided to live in one big city together, and the name of the city is Sheheritzade. Now Farksolia had eleven queens in succession to rule over it and in order their names are: Bruwanderine, Lacee, Ibirio, Flitterveen (which means butterfly), Rooeetu (which means bird), Liassa, Atee, — Lazade, Herazade, — Creesotheemis, Perizade. Now where I have made the first dash is where the Farksolians stopped their peaceable living and changed it to a war against Queen Atee and her friends. During the reigns of Lazade and Herazade the war lasted. Then where the second dash comes is where the friends of Atee were extinguished and where, during the reigns of Creesotheemis and Perizade, they lived peaceably again. During this war some people from Sheheritzade went across the great Farksolian ocean (about which I will tell you more later) and made themselves a little village on the other side (about which I will also tell you more later) to escape the war. After the last queen mentioned died, there were only two families living in Sheheritzade. I don't know why this was or why the people after Perizade suddenly began to die quickly and quietly. Anyhow there were only two families left in a short time. One family had a little girl and the other family a little boy, and we thought that the life of the planet depended upon their marriage and breeding of the race again. Well, we had quite forgotten about the few people who were on the other side of the ocean—and a few days ago back they came to Sheheritzade, and amongst them was the lovely daughter of the last queen Perizade whose name was Perizade Juliet. A few days ago she was crowned as the twelfth queen of Farksolia.

And now to the sea of Farksolia which I mentioned before. Never was a more wonderful sea seen than that of Farksolia. The sun shines on it and makes it sparkle and quiver; altogether it is the most beautiful thing on the planet. On the other side there is a great long plain which extends all up and down the coast. Strange little brown animals run amongst the curling ferns and the beams of golden sunlight which stream down. Then also on the other side there is a marvelous forest. It is very deep and dark and choked up with dark green leaves broad and flat. Amongst this forest are strange curling ferns and strangely leaved trees bearing bright red fruit. Oh, what strange fruits grow in this forest, this deep forest where not a sunbeam penetrates. And yet there is not a bramble there. My what a marvelous forest this is!

The Farksolian food consists largely of fruits and wild plants. Hardly any cooking is done. They have beautiful fruits of all colors. One plant is very much like our celery in looks. A person going there would say: "Pooh, this is only celery, I expected to have something marvelous." Biting into it he would find the stalk filled with a red and purple juice in which flow little golden seeds.

Now I'll tell you more about the eleven queens. Queen Bruwanderine was very dark-haired; Lacee was with snowy hair; Ibirio had pale gold; Flitterveen, deeper gold; Rooeetu—nobody here is certain about her. Liassa had dark hair, so had Atee, Lazade, and Herazade; but Creesotheemis again had snowy white hair; and Perizade had the most beautiful hair of all, dazzling gold. During the reign of Liassa, which reign was the reign in which a census of the people was taken, it was calculated that there were about 40 people with black hair, 145 with auburn hair, and about 500 with golden heads. A good many of the golden-heads had very dark eyes, which point added a great deal to their beauty. Perizade did, she had very dark eyes, and I told you that she had golden hair.

Liassa was a peculiar queen. Maybe it was because she was the queen before the war and because she felt the war brewing in the air. She loved dark colors. She always dressed in black or very dark brown velvet. Her handmaidens wore uniformly neat little white dresses with a huge brown gauze shawl tied round the head with a black band sweeping down at the sides and round the front so that there was very little to be seen of the white dress.

Creesotheemis was just the opposite. In her palace everything must be white and delicate gold. The dress of the queen was sometimes of black velvet (opposite to what I have just said) on which her snowy hair shone out beautifully. This was very rare though. Usually she wore a white and very delicate gold dress hung with white beads which gave it a rather milky appearance. When Creesotheemis felt very dressy she wore a sparkling golden dress. Because of the difference between Liassa and Creesotheemis the Farksolians sometimes spoke of night and day as Liassa and Creesotheemis.

The beautiful queen Lacee wore a white dress of beautiful shiny material trimmed with light but sparkling gold beads. Lazade, on the other hand, wore black or brown and, during the reign of Lazade, some people wore strange bead ornaments on their foreheads with loops or strings of two contrasting colors, beads like black and white coming down over their eyes. They must have tickled and felt funny certainly! Herazade was much the same. Queen Flitterveen's palace was about the gayest, for it was decked out with gold and green and those were the colors of almost all the dresses. About the costume of Queen Rooeetu we know little, but we know well that her handmaidens dressed in long dresses of green with a sort of Arabs' headdress arrangement of bright red or lavender shading off into almost white like the scarf that you sent Mother. A very picturesque combination of color!

Beautiful Queen Atee, for whom the war was waged, had pitch-black hair and sometimes wore a milky blue dress looped with white beads which was a marvelous background for her hair. Perizade usually wore a blue dress with a few twining patterns like clover leaves in white-gray. She wore a crown of bluish leaves held in place by a golden band. On her lovely robes her golden hair looked like, ah! I cannot express in words the beauty of that golden hair on the dress. Her colors were gold and blue. Of blue and velvet was her throne, and her handmaidens were dressed in robes of silver. Perizade's beautiful sister, also Perizade, was quite different from the queen. She had black hair and very dark eyes and in her dark hair she wore a wreath of golden leaves. Her dress was of silver, long and not full, and she had beautiful arm-droops of gold cloth. Indeed some people preferred Perizade's sister to Perizade as for beauty. I did indeed mention the queen's beauty, but as I think it over I think maybe I prefer Perizade's sister.

Perizade's fairer sister had a palace of her own. It was adjoining to her sister's palace. The sister loved the woods near Sheheritzade. She often went to the forests, and one could see her in her gold and silver dress standing out clearly with a back-ground of dark green leaves and glossy red berries. Now I must tell you that about six miles from Sheheritzade there was a beautiful grove of trees bearing beautiful blossoms of pink and white with very slight tints of blue. Here was the favorite haunt of the dark-haired Perizade. During the fourth and fifth of the eight seasons (of which I will you more about) the lovely blossoms grew; and during the sixth, lovely smooth-skinned golden fruits hung like lanterns overhead. This grove was famed for its intense beauty throughout the Farksolian world.

These seasons of which I was speaking are eight in number. During the first and second the snow melts, during the third buds begin to come, during the fourth birds and butterflies come. Then the fifth is the loveliest. The fifth bears blossoms and rather pale greens. The sixth brings the fruits and still deeper green grass with hotter weather. The seventh turns very rapidly to first snows, birds and butterflies vanishing, buds and blossoms withering, leaves slowly falling and bare winter. The eighth, first, and second seasons are the only months of cold weather. If the snow does begin to come in the seventh season the weather is still quite warm. In the middle of the second the snows go tremendously quickly, and in the third it is a little like our April and May.

The fishes of the Farksolian Ocean are very beautiful and very strange indeed. There is one little fish striped with alternating bands of blue and gold, another all gold, and another all silver. The silver one likes shelter in the rocks, long windy passages in the rocks lined with sea-plants and shells, some of which are very lovely. The blue and gold one wants almost bottomless depths and no rocks, just "plain water" as one might say. The gold one is at home in a deep slime-lined green grotto in the rocks or on a narrow sandy beach place. When you see it swim all you see is a flash of gold. Then it stays still a minute and then darts swifter than a golden arrow again. Then it stops, pivots on still flipping fins of sparkling gold, then rushes on again. Some of the marvelous fishes love the twisty gardens of plants. There are little hard miniature tree effects of white and red which stick very tightly to the rocks or pebbles.

If one could only see the Farksolian sunsets in the evening, or "Sarabeeine" in their language. They are marvelously red and if there are little clouds they are no longer white but dull gray outlined with crimson. From the very red near the ball of the sun the colors shade off through orange, purple, and yellow, to a dull gray outlined with orange and then the dull blue color of the evening sky. The sunset is all the more wonderful when seen reflected in the sea. The evening or even midnight sky is not the dull gray-blue of our skies; it is just blue, a deep blue yet a bright blue, but not at all gray. On this background the stars are marvelous.

I will now say some more about the stars. One of the most beautiful constellations is "Peen Flitterveen" or in our language, "The Butterfly." It consists of rows of golden stars arranged in such a manner as to form a perfect butterfly all in golden stars. Another constellation, a very odd constellation, is "Peen Farksiades." That consists of a small pattern in the form of interlacing rings of quite black stars. But they certainly are bright and don't they show up well? The Farksolians have two moons, by names Vaireen and Seeven. Vaireen is very inconspicuous, for it is almost the color of the sky, but Seeven! Seeven is bright silver, a gorgeous moon.

I told you, I think, about the great joy of Perizade Juliet coming across the ocean. She has now two little children both also Perizades, Perizade Creeso and Perizade Bruwine. They are called Creeso and Bruwine. Now they are twins, only four years old, but we think that they are going to look like their great-aunt, the first Perizade's fairer sister that we were talking about not long ago. We will talk about her some more now.

Now Perizade's sister was a queen too! She helped her sister rule. Her palace was connected to her sister's by means of a passageway, but for the most part the passageway was not used. Perizade's sister's palace was more beautiful than her sister's, and her throne was of blue velvet. One handmaiden sat on either side of the queen all the time on cushions of blue and gold velvet. These handmaidens wore beautiful dresses of green and purple gauze. The chief maiden who had charge of the costumes and the dresses dressed in a straight dress of purple velvet trimmed with a braid of brilliant silver. Some of her maidens wore neat little dresses of pale yellow, others wore flouncy dresses of silver braid. Still others wore sweet little dresses of yellow and white trimmed with little sparkling gold beads. Her messengers wore little dresses of yellow covered quite with sparkling golden braid. Still other maidens wore flouncy dresses of white all covered with delicate white beads. More maidens wore plain dresses of yellow and white, and still others of milky blue. Some maidens wore straight skirts of green stuff covered with a thick skirt of gauze. One of the queen's pet maidens wore a sleeveless dress with a tightish waist of pink and a skirt of pink with a more flouncy skirt of pink gauze over it with the bottom trimmed with little rosettes of pink gauze also. Another chief maiden wore a dress of the same kind with some sparkling golden beads on it. One maiden again wore a flouncy skirt of green gauze with a lot of golden beads sparkling in the waist. The feast bearer wore a flowing beautiful dress of bright carmine with some silver and gold beads which whitened off the rather alarming color. The pretty girl who scattered the flowers wore a long, slim dress of pale yellow and blue. The maiden that took care of the queen's jewels wore also a dress of carmine, but of paler carmine than that which the feast-bearer wore.

In the midst of all this splendor so sat the queen. The walls of the palace were all hung from top to bottom with gauze of a mixture of pale green, purple, and yellow. The window near where the queen sat looked out on to a garden of pink flowers. From the ceiling there hung a light decked with gold braid which cast a marvelous gold light over all the splendor. This light was kept burning all night, but not at day.

Now for the queen's chamber! It had an arched ceiling of pure white material. The bed was made of silver and draped with gold. On it was a pink puff. The walls of the room were of silver ornamented with a great variety of precious stones. A little maiden dressed in blue and yellow was waiting for the queen to go to bed. She pulled open the bed, took out the roses which had lain there a while to keep the bed smelling sweetly; then the maiden pulled off the golden light and went out. At the dawn the same little maiden was in the chamber again helping the queen to dress and also to straighten the bed. Then the queen would walk down the hall to the throne-room and there she would order the breakfast. After breakfast every morning the queen gave her orders and mysteriously disappeared, nobody knew where. But we know well that she went to the woods to gather marvelous golden fruits, and sometimes she went to the shore of the little lake which was there near the palace.

Maybe we have worn out Perizade's sister. Let us turn to something else besides just queens and costumes. What else is there? Oh, I haven't told about the writing and mailing arrangement they have there.

In somewhere about the middle of the city there is an electric mail station. There runs from this mail station underground tunnels to every house. The person from the house places the letter or package on an electric slide in the tunnel, pushes a little button and shoots the package along the slide to the mail station. There the man takes out the letters and packages, reads the addresses, and sends them through the tunnels that lead to the house to which it is addressed. Now the writing materials that they have are very peculiar. The pen is of wood sharpened into a very sharp point, and it is hollow. Just above the point there is a very tiny little hold. Now the writing fluid is placed inside the pen and to wet the point you press a little rubber button near the end and it trickles down out the hole and over the point; when it gets dry you do the same thing again. The writing fluid is composed of the sap of a certain tree which is dark green in color. But of course it goes through several operations before it can be used.

Now I would like to turn back to queens and costumes again, because of a sudden I have thought that you might be interested in the lovely queen Ibirio. She had very pale golden hair and very dark eyes. She usually wore a pale blue velvet dress sometimes plain and sometimes trimmed with silver or gold braid. She wore blue velvet slippers to match with golden buckles. She occasionally wore a dress with a brown velvet waist and a skirt of satin covered with another skirt of brown gauze. Her handmaidens wore very flouncy skirts of green gauze trimmed with gold or silver braid and sometimes with gold beads. Indeed sometimes they were left plain. The walls of Ibirio's palace were of some amber-colored material, which spickled and speckled and glimmed with all the possible shades of amber.

The chamber of Ibirio had sparkling blue walls hung with golden drapes. Two cherubim of coral stood one on either side of the mantle-piece. On the bed there was a great blue and pink puff. On all the floor there was a great fleecy white rug. This chamber I think is almost as beautiful as Perizade's sister's. Ibirio's chief waiting-maid wore a long flowing pink dress with a little artificial pink flower in the belt.

Now I will give you a sample of the characters of the Farksolians' lettering.

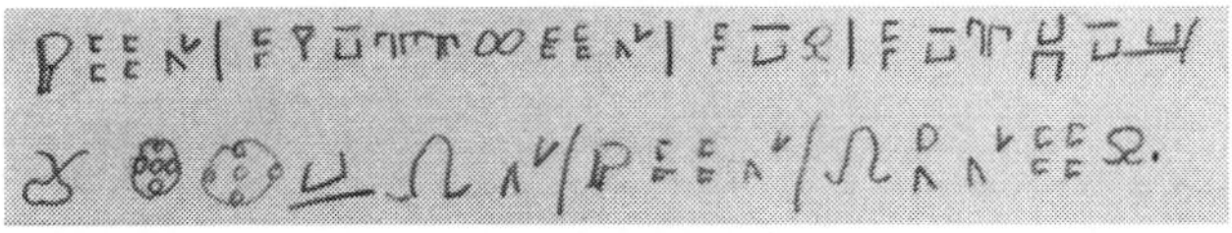

[handwritten Farksolian script]

Now that means: Peen Flitterveen fis fithic soocun peen urnees. And that means: The Butterfly is flying over the meadow. You must perceive that I do not write well in it, for as you see I cannot keep those unfamiliar letters of the same size.

The Farksolians believed that there were real mermaids in the sea and that they had gold but not glittering hair. They had dresses of that pulpy sea-weed that hung down straight by their sides. They played on very sweet-sounding, strange-appearing instruments. They believed quite truthfully in these mermaids, and I as a favor to the Farksolians believe in them quite as truthfully.

The Farksolians had one goddess, Virodine, who had charge of all Nature. In fact she was Nature. She took the same place as Nature does on our planet. On the range of mountains around Sheheritzade they worshipped her. Ah, how they loved her.

I have one more costume arrangement to tell about before I leave off. It is of Queen Bruwanderine, the first. She wore a bright blue dress with gray trimming and long gray sleeves and on the dress were gray in all sorts of twisting leaf-pattern effects on the blue. It had a belt of deep blue satin. Queen Bruwanderine sometimes wore a band of blue leaves held in place by a golden band. On other occasions she wore a black velvet band around her head and on it a strange brilliant red flower. She had auburn hair.

Now I think that I will leave off about Farksolia for a while, because I fear that at this rate it will get tiresome. I will say a little about how happy we are in our new house. Extremely happy—except for one thing. Mother's siege of boils. They began up in Sunapee and she has held out against them bravely for the past eight months! The one she is having now she has almost given before [sic], she has had one hurting, paining, fussing, tinkering, puttering doctor in to see her two or three times a day for a week now. That is why she hasn't written. But when that is through with I think we shall be very happy indeed here, all surrounded with the happy laughing woods and the gay frisky little squirrels, and the flitting, fluttering little birds and butterflies. I have been a nymph in these woods many a time and I never in any place found so many hiding-places, lurking-places, peeking-places, peering-places, in my life. My it is great fun, and I earnestly hope that soon you will be here to enjoy it with me.

Very lovingly,

Two more of Barbara's school assignments.

Thursday, 6 March [1924]

I. Practice on the piano. You must have a good lesson for Bruce. See if an hour of practicing is too much. Remember that the other children in school don't have this chance of getting in some good music during the early part of the day.

II. At 10 o'clock begin the following French: Review lesson 28, see if you can write the forms of the verb given in that lesson. Review the vocabulary in that lesson. On page 43 write the short sentences under Oral Drill. These sentences are very good practice for your verb forms. Review the poem you memorized, and try writing it. Then learn the vocabulary under lesson 29. This will get you ready for me to take up lesson 29 with you. Time yourself in doing this French. Use every moment hard.

III. At about 11 o'clock begin your violin. Time this also, and tell me exactly how long you can keep at it well. I imagine that an hour on the piano would not be too much, but that an hour on the violin would be.

IV. Page 89 of your Arithmetic book do over again examples 17, 20, 21, 23, 24, 26, 27. I am anxious to get through with this commission business and get into interest with you—banking, etc. But we can't get alone until you have got the idea of discounts and commissions.

V. This is a good morning's work. See that the work you do is neat enough to show Mr. Oberg. Let him see what kind of lessons we can do when we get started. This afternoon is your play-class, remember.

Thursday, 27 March, 1924

Violin

Science: Write for me an account of what you read yesterday. I have kept all your science sheets, and they make a very good condensed version of the book.

Piano: Do some good work for Bruce this week. Really get somewhere with your practicing. You can work at least forty minutes at a time now.

French: Page 45 in your Grammar. Write in French the sentences at the top of the page. Write from memory the following phrases: (1) What is that? (2) That is... (3) How is the...? (4) What is ... ? Then turn to page 11 in *Easy Lessons in French* and fill in the blank spaces in the exercise at the top of the page. Do the same to the sentences at the top of page 12. You had better write all these sentences and not mark up your book. Review *Les Trois Souhaits* and look carefully at the constructions as you go along so that you can answer simple questions.

Read: Take the National Geographic and look at the pictures of *Geography and Some Explorers*; then read the article what ever interests you, but especially read beginning on page 272 through to the end.

Arithmetic: Page 92, do ten examples beginning with example 8.
Piano

Write me a page of description. Make it a page of Sunapee if you like; or make it up entirely out of your imagination. Make it either poetry or prose. And give a title to it.

After these things are done, then do what you like with Eepersip or read whatever you like.

A letter to Mr. St. John from about March or April 1924.

My dearest friend:

I have been intending to write to you for some time, and tell you how sorry I was that Mrs. St. John has had an accident, but this and that have prevented me. I hope you will tell her for me how terribly sorry I am.

I remember I wrote you one letter on Farksolia, but now I would like to tell you a little about how my story, The Adventures of Eepersip, is coming along. Of course, you know about how she ran off to live wild on the great meadow, but I don't believe I ever told you about how she got a little bit tired of the meadow and one evening saw the sea from a high peak and went there, to the sea. Well, that is what she did in the fourth summer that she had spent wild. And there she spent her time playing with the waves and the sea-gulls, being in the water probably a third of her time. She spent five summers doing this kind of thing all the time and in the spring of the sixth summer that she had spent at the sea and the tenth summer that she had spent wild she went to a great pasture where the "steeple-bush made the air golden" and where it was fresh and beautiful with the scent of sweet fern. This is what I wrote about this pasture. "There were lovely ferns and nodding golden flowers and the air was scented with the intoxicating fragrance of steeple-bush, the steeple-bush which makes the air golden with smells." To quote actually that is what I wrote. And there Eepersip got so wild that she could receive messages from the fairies, and one day they came to her clutching her dress and kneeling before her and telling her that she had a sister, five years old, and her name was Eeverine. And Eepersip went back to her old house and without mercy on the parents she took Eeverine away, to live wild with her! And oh! I love Eepersip so! I have suddenly been having quite an outburst of Eepersip all of a sudden.

And do tell Mrs. St. John how sorry I am, won't you?

> With love and full of wishes that we meet soon,
> goodbye, dear friend.
> Barbara.

[On a separate sheet attached to the above]

To My Dearest Friend

The poem I send to you, my friend, is from the land of water-nymphs, robed in waterlilies and soft green.

> May every single butterfly
> And every single bird,
> Bring you my love unbounded,
> Like a vast—vast sea.

> May every single bird that chirps
> Sing love from me to you,
> May every ripple of every river
> Bring you happiness and joy.

> May every silver rain-drop
> Bring you tidings from the water-nymphs,
> The water-nymphs so beautiful,
> The water-nymphs I live among.

> May nothing harsh or ugly
> Enter into your life, my friend,
> May everything bright and beautiful
> Come flocking with love to you.
> May your life be like an appleblossom
> Or a wild rose bud.

> May a ship loaded with butterflies
> Of blue and fairy golden,
> Come sailing to your port someday
> Each bearing love to you.

THE COTTAGE IN THE WOODS (1923–1926)

A plea from Barbara to her parents. ("Armory Street about 1923," Helen wrote on it, but if Armory Street it would be March 1924 or later.)

Talk about something! Get rid of your female friends who talk about nothing but their children and your gentlemen friends who talk about nothing but books and colleges and automobiles. Or, if you can't get rid of them, make them talk about something really worth while. The worst part of this dull talk is that the listeners are interested! Instead of listening intently and gossiping about everybody with your female friend, Bess Sheldon, why don't you say: "I'm not interested, can't you talk about anything but other people's affairs?" (I don't mean that you should be really rude, though.) Now think what an effect that would have. You might be able to make your friends *real* friends instead of *pretend* friends. Now, why under the sun does Daddy listen so intently when everybody talks about books, books, books with never a moment's rest. Sometimes they do talk a little about automobiles, but these authors are made of books anyhow and they can't talk about anything else, even if they tried. Make them! Get it into them that they must talk about something else. You say you have business to do—well do it! You could get it through with in five minutes if you really tried. But you string it out to the last possible detail, as if you really enjoyed it. I can't believe that you do enjoy it, it is so stupid. Now if I were leading a conversation, I would first say a good deal about Farksolia, but before my audience got tired of it I would say something about how vile the slaughter of trees is getting. Then I would go back into Farksolia a minute and mention how disgusted a Farksolian would be with this slaughter. Then I would say a little about the gorgeous swallowtail that I saw resting so long amid the green leaves before he flew away. I would ask this one what kind of flower this was, and if he knew anything about this variety of bird, and I would say a little about books and poetry. Not that I am putting an abuse on the books. I love books, but this everlasting talk about them all the time (and mostly not interesting ones at that) drives a sensible fellow mad. At least I should think it would.

If you try the plan I have adopted I think you would get many more friends, and more interesting friends at that. There should be nothing to make a man or a woman happier than a pack of real, honest-to-goodness friends, who will always stand by you in your troubles of which you are sure to have many. Make your talk really bright and interesting. Have you ever known—could you ever imagine Helen Winternitz to come in saying: "I saw the loveliest butterfly yesterday," or "I found a marvellously dainty little bird's nest as I was coming along to your house."

This page and a half that I have written can be expressed in just a few words: *Make your talk more interesting.* Just try this and see if it doesn't work. Of course if it doesn't work you needn't keep it up, but I think it will.

Barbara's other grandmother, Cordelia Adelaide (White) Follett (1859-1952), lived in North Attleboro, Massachusetts, with her husband Charles (1855-1928) and granddaughter Grace (1911-1995). Grace was Wilson's daughter from his first marriage, to Grace Huntington Parker, who died two days after her baby was born.

[undated, but early April 1924]
176 Armory Street
New Haven, Connecticut

Dear Grandmother Follett:

You know that at present that there is no delivery here, and some of our mail is sent to Daddy at the Press and some just stays at the post-office. Your lovely package of cookies was among the unfortunates, I am sorry to say, for, by the time I received them, April 2, the doughnuts were a little too hard to be eaten, but the cookies were still delicious. I felt dreadfully at the thought of all that care of putting them up going for nothing, but there was nothing I could do about it. The cookies however were perfectly delicious. They make me think a little of tarts, they are so rich and filling! I was very glad to get the box anyhow.

I do so much want to see you. It seems as if I couldn't wait any longer. We have a wonderful place here and I am sure that if you came you would enjoy it thoroughly. Especially Sabra. Sabra Wyman Follett, my cherub of a sister. She gets one more trick every day and sometimes two. She is eight months old now, but she is not creeping or even sitting up. She adores the sitting posture, however, and I think she will be sitting by the time she is nine months. If you are fond of babies at all you would be fond of her. She is—well, you couldn't have anything better as far as health is concerned. She is outdoors in the back piazza all day when it is pleasant, breathing fresh, woodsy air. When she comes in her dark brown eyes shine and her cheeks are fiery red. She is beginning to do her first plays in the bath-tub. For a long time past she has been kicking on the bed, but she has just begun to play in the bath-tub. She is lovely.

I have so many things to tell you about when you come to see me, you will be bothered to death with my talking, because when I have a lot to say my tongue runs fast—so be prepared for it. For I have ever so much to tell you about my delightful ideas of Eepersip and Farksolia.

 Lovingly,

A letter to Mr. Oberg. Grant Showerman (1870-1935) was a Classics teacher at the University of Wisconsin.

June 19, 1924
New Haven

Dear Friend:

 I know how shameful it is that I haven't written to you, but I think you know how it is when one is so busy that one doesn't know where or how to begin. I am now a lot freer than I was before, because tomorrow is my last piano lesson and I have already finished for the summer my violin. I have been lazy at getting Eepersip going again (for a few days ago I let up again), but now I have had another outburst. I wonder if I made [it] up [to] this point when I saw you last. The fairies told Eepersip that she had a little sister, and Eepersip went home from the sea, miles and miles it was, and she took her sister (whose name is either Eeverine or Belldina) away to live wild with her. You see, Eepersip was rather hard on the parents. Now the Igleens (the parents, of course) loved Eeverine (I shall call her Eeverine, *not* Belldina in this letter) more than they had ever loved Eepersip, but they said nothing about Eepersip to her for fear that she would run away, too. That would have succeeded if it hadn't been for Eepersip's knowledge of her sister. If Eepersip hadn't known that she had a sister of course, she wouldn't have come home to take her. The Igleens were more determined to take back Eeverine than they were Eepersip but, though there were many clever tricks, Eepersip's slyness avoided them all. And Eepersip loved Eeverine dearly, and wove dresses of ferns for her, as she had for herself. And Eepersip now had a gift from the fairies, and it was this: that flowers that she wore would live, no matter how long they remained on her dress or in her hair, and also Eepersip had that power over the flowers on the dress or in the hair of any person she wished. So, of course, Eeverine's flowers lived as well as Eepersip's.

 But now, the Igleens, finding that they could not catch either Eepersip or Eeverine, had another child, and her name was Fleuriss. Now Eeverine and Eepersip both had auburn and golden-brown hair mixed, but Fleuriss had the loveliest black hair, which was adorable when she wore a wreath of yellow flowers. The Igleens *told* Fleuriss about Eepersip and Eeverine, thinking to persuade her *not* to go. But she went all the same, and I am telling about an adventure in a marvelous place of her own. Eepersip had not stolen her away; she went quite of her own accord. But there is no use in my describing the place she went to, for it is copied from a really true place where I go very often! Instead of telling you about Fleuriss' adventures there, I will tell you about *my* adventures there, and it will be about the same.

Two or three days ago a friend of Daddy's whose name was Grant Showerman came to lunch and supper to see Daddy. He was a very interesting person, and when he had done his business with Daddy he wanted to go for a walk with me. So we went down the street a little way and then turned under the tall fence, where it was broken down to build the houses, to where we went to take a picture of the house. But we weren't content to stop there (I had been to this place many times before, but this is the most exciting adventure I have ever had there). We went on through bushes and briars and up terrible rocks and cliffs (I must add that this gentleman is a mountain-climber), and finally got to the top. And there was the great, round ogre's castle (the water tower), and we were bold enough to go up and knock on the great door, and it sounded hollow. I don't think the ogre was at home. Well, we went on and such a lovely place it was! There was every kind of land possible. There were bright shiny patches of deliciously soft grass, and then there were hard patches of rocks and disagreeable brambles, choking vines and such. Well, we went on towards the house on top, and as we approached it it looked a little more landscaped as there was a neatly graveled road bordered with roses, and a bright, beautiful *[missing word]* also bordered with them. We went a long way until we saw the house, but we didn't look there long—our attention was too much distracted by the place itself. There were the loveliest flower beds one could imagine, but we didn't stay there long, for we had been too long in the wild part of the place, and the folks at home must have wondered where we were. But there was no hard rock climbing on the way down; we walked slowly down a little winding path, a very easy way out, and we were rewarded for all our trouble to get up.

Little Fleuriss had the same adventures, except that she didn't come down. No sir, she stayed for a long time. I have now left my story at a very exciting point: Eeverine captured, and Fleuriss there. I think that in the end they are all united again, for now there are three and yet none of them are together, because Fleuriss is far from Eepersip, and Eeverine is also far from Eepersip, in a cage, and Eepersip doesn't know where. But, by a chance shot of Nature they are going to be united again, more happy than Eepersip ever was. The going to be united again, more happy than Eepersip ever was. The question is: shall they meet at Eepersip's place, or at Fleuriss's? Of course, not at Eeverine's, the farther away from there the better. I think I shall make it Fleuriss's because Fleuriss's is the loveliest of all the places in the story, much lovelier than the places Eepersip found with Eeverine.

Now let me say a little about Sabra. She is terribly funny. She gets funnier every day. This morning especially so. She now kneels in her crib when she takes her cereal, and instead of kneeling she sometimes stands, holding on to the bars, of course. This morning she exaggerated this a little, going so far as to do it in her little bathtub.

Thank you ever and ever so much for everything, the pictures, the drawings, and the pencil, that especially. I have reloaded it a lot for the practice, and I succeeded beautifully. I love it very much. And thank you again ever and ever so much.

Very lovingly I sign my name with the pencil I love it so

>from your dear friend, Barbara.

Helen, Barbara, and Sabra went to Sunapee for the summer. Wilson joined them about a week after writing this letter.

176 Armory Street
New Haven, Connecticut
18 July, 1924
(Friday night)

My dearest Barbara:

It was terribly nice to get your letter at the Press this morning—your little note about the warblers and the silvery minnows and the perch with a grin on his face. You will have the books in a few days, and a paper supply along with them. And me not many days after that!

It is frightfully lonesome here, living alone as I do, and you can have no idea how I miss Mother and you and the Brat.

The goldfish are all right and seem to be thriving; I am sure I have given them enough to eat, and I only hope I shan't kill them with kindness. Also, there is a flock of quail living in the woods just west of us, and they are so tame that I almost run over them with the Pierce when I drive in by the cartpath from Prospect Street.

One week from to-morrow! Won't it be grand!

>Daddy.

An incomplete letter typed on three index cards (I suppose the paper supply hadn't arrived).

From the Woods
July 23, 1924

Dearest Friend:

I suppose you know that I am now in the most beautiful place in the world. The home of nymphs and fairies, gnomes and elves, birds and butterflies, bees and dragonflies, moths and flowers, fishes and frogs. It is not only the home of all these things and more, but it is the home of Nature and Beauty. You know all that.

I wonder if you have ever stood on a beach throwing crackers to a merry, happy little school of silvery minnows. I do almost every day. The minute the piece of cracker lands among them they all rush at it, and for the next several seconds the water is solid with the lively little fishes. Finally, when the cracker is small enough for one fish to seize it, the one fish does, and then, unless he wants to lose his prize, he has to do a very breathless deed: swim as fast as he can and eat at the same time. I have never tried that, but I can guess that it is sort of tiring. It is all very amusing.

Last night a handsome visitor came to our garbage box, all dressed in black and white. In the morning we knew he had been there. There were two reasons. The most prominent of them was that our friend had got angry with some mischievous animal that was foolish enough to come near him, and had gone away, wiser and smellier. The other reason was that a piece of bacon rind which Ding was watching had disappeared.

Also typed on three index cards and unfinished.

From the Woods
July 25, 1924

Dearest Friend:

I wonder if you know, by any chance, that I am now in the home of Beauty and Nature. This is where nymphs, fairies, gnomes, elves, live. Nowhere in the world, I believe, is there a place so fertile and luxuriant. On the sand-bars and shallows of Sunapee are minnows which can be reckoned only by hundreds. These minnows gleam like the jewels in the crown of Creesotheemis. (Creesotheemis is one of the queens of my imaginary land, Farksolia.) Beautiful dragonflies, their wings gleaming like shimmering opals and moonstones, glide through the air, swerving with a speed which seems impossible for such small flimsy wings. Great orange butterflies go flittering through the air, on those noiseless wings, which seem to have gathered an unimaginable beauty and mystery.

It is a windy day. The silvery white-caps bring me tidings from Nature, tidings from the mermaids. For this is the kind of day that one hears the wondrous and mysterious songs, sung in praise of the goddess of the lake, in those soft, round voices, which thrill every heart with their silvery music.

I have never experienced any such evenings as those we have here. The mystery which is part of the evening is not interrupted even when the silvery tones of that incomparable singer, the woodthrush, break that indescribable stillness.

From the Woods
July 31, 1924

Dear Mr. Oberg:

Needless to say, I am now in the land which Nature loves so much. It is the land of the lake of beauty unsurpassed, it is the land of the little shy nymphs and fairies, that here one sees all the time. Of course, it is Sunapee! Sunapee, the loveliest land in the world! Now of course, that isn't saying very much, for I have not seen the whole world. I have not even seen the whole of the New England States. There may be lands which are more beautiful in scenery which is always the outside of a land, but there is no land equal to it when you take it from the inside. Now no one really knows what the inside of a land is, but, even if you don't know, you can always be sure that it is the inside of a land that counts, not the outside. Also, even if one doesn't know what the inside of a land is, one can usually tell by magical signs whether the inside of one land is better than the inside of another. But that is not of importance. I think Sunapee is the nicest land in the world, let that suffice.

I am swimming so much better than I did last summer, that I really [believe] that there must be some magic concerned in it. The first time I was in the water this summer I swam much better than last summer. The puzzle is this: that peculiar change didn't come gradually, it came over the winter, and, of course, I had not been in at all in the winter. Yesterday, for the first time, I had the nerve to go in head-first. Then I did several other times in rapid succession! I guess I dived twelve or fifteen times, and only two were bad, and then, not so very bad. I thought that I wouldn't like the sensation of going in head-first, but oh! I do! Daddy persuaded me all the time to open my eyes under water and see things, so I've decided that I will the next time I dive. The children that play out at the raft jump off feet first and feel around when *[they]* want to bring up some of the fresh-water clams, that are so common there, but, when I get to bringing up clams, I'm going to dive and look for them with my eyes open. Helen Stanley always dives when she goes for clams, but I think she feels about for them. Eunice Stanley jumps off and stoops over to pick them up.

Barbara and Sabra at Sunapee, 1924

If you could see Sabra, you'd certainly see something that would make you feel happy. She loves Sunapee, especially in the morning and afternoon when Mother turns her loose with Ding or me in the sand. She likes to feel the nice sand run through her rose-bud fingers. She is a little apple-blossom. Thank you very very much for the dear little cards you sent her. I'm sure that when she gets *[to be]* three or four and I show them to her and tell her that they were her one-year-old birthday cards she will be highly pleased. I'm going to keep them very carefully until that time.

> May a great, big ship, with jeweled sails and mast
> of gold reach your lonesome port loaded high
> with love and kisses, from your loving friend,
> Barbara

To Mr. St. John.

From the Woods
August 6, 1924

Dearest Friend:

I was very glad to get your letter, the picture of the silver fox, your account of your search for orchids, and what you are going to do at Shawandasee. Then, of course, I was glad to hear about Mr. 'Coon. I like them very much: they are so pretty with their black masks, their dainty little feet, and their gorgeous tails.

I would like to tell you about an adventure I had this morning with one of our feathered friends. I was over at the Secret Beach—I had been watching the pretty sparkling minnows, the little golden-colored perch, and the sometimes solitary, sometimes in school, bass. The three kinds of fish sometimes mingle together, the ones at the Secret Beach being about the same size. As I said before, I was over at the Secret Beach watching them all, when a great flapping of mighty wings reached my ears. I looked up and saw a great bird fly to a tree and alight on one of the limbs. He looked like a great dark splotch, but, as I had seen him alight there, I knew it was he. I crept along through the bushes stealthily (afterwards I discovered that there was no need of being stealthy) until I got out on the path over which passed the limb on which he sat. One leg he held tightly against his bluish grey breast of a very pale color. He was all pale grey-blue with some brown mottling on his back and throat. His under tail parts were almost white. I bet he's still sitting there on the limb. The whole family has seen him—and he just sits there and looks at what is going on around him. I don't know what kind of bird he is.

I hope very much that on the way to Passaconaway you will stop in the Gravel Cut.

> With ships, with fluttering sails and jeweled masts, of love in baskets woven and embroidered with flowers,
> from Barbara

From Sunapee
August 14, 1924

Dear Rappe:

Thank you ever and ever so much for sending me the Herbarium. As you wish I certainly shall try to start a collection here, the way I did ferns last year.

Daddy and I are planning to make a big net of some kind like a seine to catch a whole big school of minnows in and transfer them to the Secret Beach. In the school there are two or three that gleam with a strange-beautiful green light. I think they must be the daughters of the mighty leader.

> Thank you again for the Herbarium.
> Yours,
> "The Spirit of the Brown-Tailed Moth."

A letter to Mr. St. John describing Barbara's first extended expedition into the wilderness—a weeklong canoeing trip with her father ending in an overnight stay on Mount Chocorua, one of New Hampshire's finest peaks.

October 5, 1924
176 Armory Street
New Haven, Connecticut

Dearest friend:

Dear me, here it is October and I haven't written to you since August I think, and then it wasn't really a letter. I was very glad to get your nice letter, telling me so much about the things you've seen and done. I know all the flowers you mentioned I think, except the Cardinal Flower, and that I've heard of but never seen. I know the witch hazel, and have heard about its popping across the room, but never have happened to see the last.

I have not been writing about Eepersip and Eeverine, Mirodine, as I have renamed her. I can imagine them dancing away happily in that fairy-like spot amid the stalks of the Cardinal Flower, which, I hope, has golden seeds.

The best event of this hectic summer was—a week's camping trip alone with Daddy. I hope you won't feel hurt when I tell you that I really couldn't wait—to do the long-looked-for climb with you—and so I did it with Daddy, the last thing in the trip. But I shouldn't mind doing it again with you, in fact I would love to, so I hope we can manage it or some other trip *next summer*.

We too were very much disappointed not to go up to your place at Passaconaway. I hope that we can do that too next summer, amid many, many other things we have postponed time and time again.

Sabra simply adored it up in Sunapee, and simply adores it here, except that she hasn't got a beach to creep on. Up at Sunapee she was just beginning to walk quite rapidly when one held on to her, and two or three steps alone, but the climax so far came today. In the morning she walked eleven steps alone, and so I thought she wouldn't be long then. But this afternoon, when we partly undressed her and put her on the floor of Mother's room to creep as usual, she didn't creep at all—she walked! Every few steps she would sit down hard, but only to get up and try again. I am thankful, and shall be more so, when the creeping stage is over. Perhaps it is the cunningest stage of all, but she gets so dirty. And, though it was better in Sunapee of course, here there really is no very nice place to let her do it out-doors. Well, I certainly wish you could see her.

Now as to the long camping trip I told you about. I feel sure you would be interested to hear about it, so I will now begin. Daddy and I started north-ward with the canoe firmly lashed on to a trailer we borrowed, and the tonneau of the old Pierce Arrow loaded with things such as we needed. That afternoon we arrived at the little town of West Ossipee, which, perhaps, you have heard of. That afternoon we took the canoe off the trailer, loaded it with the things in the tonneau and put in at the small Bear Camp River which flows under the bridge at West Ossipee. That evening we camped on an island. But before that I experienced the real thrill of the river—somehow the rushing current, still unusually high from the big two-day rain, the treacherous snags and golden sparkling quicksands held an almost endless fascination for me. Before that I had experienced another fascination, that of pausing a moment to watch before a large bay of Winnipesaukee far, far off, the last thing visible—part of the Sandwich range, faintly outlined in the blue immensity of space. But then, they were outlined in pale misty blue, and I never dreamed they were topped with the white granite that they really are.

Well, to go on with what I was saying. We camped on this island—that night made an island only by the fact that the big rain had caused a back-channel around the part that was once mainland making it therefore an island—for the most part an open meadow, swampy in places. After we had put up our big tent, our two army cots, and piled our stuff in a neat corner of the tent, we set out to find a house with some water, for we hardly liked to use the river water, as it *did* come out of West Ossipee. I had a couple of canteens and Daddy a cloth water-bucket.

We paddled across the river and landed at a steep mud-bank on the other side. Through a thick border of bushes we pushed out into the open meadow, where I thought every shadow was a rain-pool on the grass. Directly ahead there was a big double maple and by this we land-marked the place where the canoe was. Finally we came out on the street where we looked first down one way and then the other, and at last we spied a house, and briskly set out towards it. A very kind old farmer welcomed us, filled our canteens and bucket, took fifteen cents for a half dozen ears of corn which we were to take in the morning together with two hills of potatoes, only he said to take eight or nine ears.

At last we got back, getting supper and *Bed* quickly. The several fascinations and charming visions had got me nervously excited, consequently I did not sleep very well but hoped to do better after I got used to it. It was very difficult to get up in the morning, but I did, and was mightily glad I had, for I had a grand time skipping here, there, down to the river, back, going down on the beach to wash hands and face and dishes! As I was washing the breakfast dishes I spied several shoals of the tiniest fishes I ever saw. Oh, they were darlings!

After breakfast we broke camp very neatly and quickly, considering that that was the first time we had done it, loaded our stuff into the old canoe again and pushed off. Across the river we went to get our corn and potatoes, and, having collected them, we started off for Ossipee Lake into which the Bear Camp flows. That morning we got there and it answered my dearest hopes. It was a great round lake with not any coves to speak of in it and no islands either. We had dinner on a beach there, composed of sand which looked as if it might make good Wheatena if poured into boiling water. After dinner we started towards the spot where a very inaccurate map told us The Narrows were.

But we had an adventure before that; in fact we had it as soon as we entered the lake. Those wonderful mountains again revealed themselves, but now we saw them quite near and the sun flashing on those pure white granite peaks and we looked at them long and longingly and then—we dipped our paddles into the blue of the lovely lake and sped on.

Now the Narrows, or, as we found afterward, Lake Paugus would have been the beginning of the Ossipee River except for a dam a few miles below which caused this part of the river to overflow, making swampy luscious ground in through there, a perfect labyrinth of coves and islands, indescribably lovely and enchanting. And as I passed through there, gliding gently onwards, so entranced that I could paddle only two or three strokes and then stop, for a long time, everything seemed bewitched. It was there that we saw the first loon of the expedition, though altogether we must have seen several, for later we saw that one joined by another, and later still we saw two others scouting round on the other side of the lake, and after that we saw several at various times.

After having visited several camping sites we decided upon a moderate-sized island, but quite different from the other. For the other, as I said before, was an open meadow, and this second one all strangled with bushes and saplings, a good part of which were poplars. The next thing after pitching our tent was, of course, supper, and—goodness, there goes the top of the ribbon-spool on my type-writer—hot cocoa, big hunks of cheese and slabs of Mother's excellent nut-bread tasted mighty good. Then we went to bed and there we chattered together for ten or fifteen minutes, and every little while we would say in the midst of our chatter, "There goes another loon!" and would listen while the strange cry would echo again and again in our ears. After a few moments of happy chatter we told each other we wanted to go to sleep and so we rolled over and went quicker than before.

The next morning Daddy was up before I was. He went out to see what was to be seen and called me, telling me to slap something on my feet and come. I went out quickly and looked to where he pointed, and there rose Chocorua, that long-hoped-for peak with the sun shining all over it making the whole thing, not only the top peak, that same unhuman dazzling lightning white. And all morning with the sun on it the mountain kept changing—sometimes only the peak would be shining, the rest in wonderful shades of black, green, and blue. It was then that we named the peak Arakaboa, the Dream Mountain. And the lake, Lake Solitude.

Soon we started off for Effingham Falls where the dam was, but without breaking camp this time, for, you see, we had planned to come back there, collect our things and go back. But ill-luck had also been planning, and had been planning otherwise. For, we came back from Effingham Falls in a smart little shower, turning to a constant drizzle all afternoon. So we stayed there in the tent on the lonely little island, laughing, chattering, playing games, and listening to the lapping of the wavelets and the strange, weird cries of the loons playing in the rain.

That was surely a lazy day. But I was glad of the afternoon rest because next day there was to be harder work than we had bargained for. The next morning Daddy was up early, in fact at dawn, and he got the cocoa on the little gasoline stove, the very lighting of which takes quite a while, and when breakfast was almost ready he hauled me out of bed, still storing soundly. We had breakfast, then we broke camp and started about the time we had risen before. We paddled the five or six miles back to Lake Ossipee and, as we went around the last bend of the Narrows, we saw great breakers topped with white spray come rolling in.

Then, as we went around the bend we saw Ossipee in the sharpest gale I had ever seen, even on the ocean. We landed on a sandbar, drew up the canoe to get a couple of photographs and consider things. Daddy said that, as the next mile or so across the lake was a continuous sand-bar, where it was only about to Daddy's shoulders, most of the worst would be right there, because of the shallowness, therefore from that we could determine whether or not we could do the rest of it. So we dug in and tried. We made famous progress considering the circumstances, a heavily loaded boat, a canoe at that, only one really strong paddler, not to speak of the wind and the breakers and squalls. Well, we managed it very well, neither of us missed a stroke, and we didn't ship enough water to unload and turn over the canoe for—and, to our surprise, the canoe carpet soaked it up very well. It really didn't seem very long, I thought about an hour, but the terrific labor made it seem years. Daddy said it was probably a two-and-a-half or three-hour job. Well at last we got across and there we experienced the utter happiness in stretching out in the sun, for it was very sunny, resting and relaxing every tired muscle, and drying out, for I was wet up to my elbows.

We had dinner there, and we saw three ducks, swimming around the little point where it was quite calm, and out into the magnificent gale, which was still raging. After dinner we went to the mouth of the Bear Camp, whose current was still fiercely raging and paddled all the way back to West Ossipee that afternoon. Whereas before, with an even stronger current helping us we had done it in almost an afternoon and a morning. Then we got the bus and the trailer, unloaded the canoe, put it on the trailer, and loaded the tonneau of the old Pierce.

And now comes an event which may amuse you. Daddy intended to camp on the shores of Chocorua Lakes, so that we should be near Chocorua for climbing purposes next morning. We started on the road towards Chocorua Lakes, only instead of turning left on the road that went to the lakes in a few miles he went straight on over Washington Hill, and on and on until the signs told us we were coming out near Silver Lake, in quite the other direction from where we wanted to be. So we stopped, and hand in hand, we walked up to a square house with a glassed-in porch on two sides of it, perhaps three. Daddy walked around to where he thought the back door was, but there was no back door to be seen. Then we walked around farther still to where we thought there might be a side door, but there was no side door to be seen either. There was a door on to the glassed-in porch all right, all right, but there simply wasn't any door into the house. So we christened it: "The house without an entrance," and moved on to the next house, where there was an entrance, a very nice little old lady, a Canada lynx, beautifully stuffed and mounted, on the piano, a nice pet of a collie dog, and lots of information.

So we merrily go back to Chocorua Lakes, and pitched our tent in the same place where Daddy and Leo Meyette, a friend of ours in Sunapee, once rolled up in the bushes on a mountain trip.

The next morning we had breakfast, fairly late, and broke camp, together with something additional—packing our packs for the spend-the-night. Three blankets were all we could conveniently carry for bed-clothes, only Daddy planned to keep a noble fire going all night. Then off we drove for Clement Inn, at the foot of Chocorua. When we got there, we left the car, put on our packs, and started up the Piper Trail. It was not steep at all at first, indeed it was almost level, but up above Chocorua Brook a slight change began. Still farther there was quite an abrupt change, and the hard climbing began. Then we were I think about half a mile from the cabins. We began to get tired, and our discomforting packs pulled back our shoulders, and tried their best to make our feet fly out from under us. At last we got to the cabins—Camp Penacook and Camp Upweekis. We visited them both, but found Penacook much the preferable. The view from Camp Penacook was the picture you sent me from Chocorua—I recognized it as soon as I looked down from the camp.

After we had rested and deposited our packs we went on towards the summit, intending, you see, to come back to the cabins that afternoon and spend the night. I was pretty well done for after the climb to the cabins, and Daddy had his doubts about my getting up to the summit that afternoon, but, strange enough, after I was freed from the heavy burden of my pack Daddy couldn't keep me in sight all the way. I ran up precipices of granite, and caught up to and even led some people who, a long time ago, near the foot of the mountain had passed us while we were resting. On top it answered my dearest expectations. Fold after fold of mountains rising range beyond range into the cloudy sky. Of course, Washington was in clouds, but even what I saw of it, its huge base, was enough to convince me of its tremendous height and size. And the peaks of granite—the very peaks of granite I was standing on! It seemed impossible that I was now standing on that very peak which I had seen so far off at first! Then after a long talk with the fire warden up there, we went down to the cabins again and there we spent the cold bitter night, but thanks to a fire Daddy kept going all night we were reasonably comfortable.

The next morning, after taking a picture, we went down, crossing the seven brooks we had crossed coming up, stopping at the foot to pick a pail-full of blackberries from a huge patch, which were greatly relished at home.

Then we started for the cottage, but, of course, not without an unpleasant break-down. Thus ended our wonderful trip. Sometimes I surely want to do a trip like that with you alone, dear friend.

    Lovingly,
    Barbara.

William Sloane Kennedy (1850-1929) was a friend of Walt Whitman. (See, for example, Debating Manliness: Thomas Wentworth Higginson, William Sloane Kennedy, and the Question of Whitman, *by Robert K. Nelson and Kenneth M. Price, American Literature 73.3, 2001.)*

176 Armory Street
New Haven, Connecticut
October 8, 1924

Dear Mr. Showerman:

Goodness, you have written me many, many nice letters, and I believe I have only written you one, two at the most! I'm very sorry, but there have been many things that have had to be done first, letters to be written to people that I thought might get hurt if I didn't, whereas I thought you would understand.

Thank you ever and ever so much for sending me those precious, precious photographs. In my envelope I have another envelope, which contains only my most precious papers. They include some colored photographs—I mean paintings, of strange exotic butterflies and moths, sent to me by another friend, William Sloane Kennedy, a check for fifteen dollars—my first earned money, and those pictures. I shall keep these few things always, always, and they may, of course, increase.

As you see, by the above address, I am now back at Armory Street, in the oak forest. A few days ago I again climbed Mill Rock, where we went together, but did not dare to go as far as we went together. It made my heart sick to hear the sounds of hammering and an axe, for I knew they were building up those wonderful forests. Even if there is a city up there, I shall never, never forget the time there wasn't, that glorious day that you, my friend, were here!

Shall you be here again this winter? I certainly hope so.

>Lovingly,
>from

An undated draft to Mr. Oberg from about October 1924.

Dear Friend:

I am now at Armory Street again. Of course the confusion isn't over yet but we are getting help soon, and then I think it will be over in a short time.

I think you have written to me several times, with no letter from me in between, but you have no idea how many, many things there are for me—no, all of us, to do. Thank you ever and ever so much for your nice letters, the little French book, and especially the lovely, lovely butterflies and moths. Most decidedly they are Farksolian. The wonderful jewel-like colors! The thin fairy-like, gossamer wings! The odd shapes! Together these strange beauties form the loveliest design possible. I am simply wild to come and see the humming-birds you speak of, and perhaps real specimens, of those magnificent fairy butterflies.

Little Sabra is perfectly adorable. She is now walking when you hold on to her. She likes it here, but prefers, as I do, Sunapee. I feel sure she misses being turned loose in the sand. But maybe sometimes we can take her down to the beach on the sea sometimes and let her play there. There, I think she would like it better than in Sunapee, because while in Sunapee you only find two or three kinds of shells, at the sea you find hundreds. Sometime we shall certainly do it. I hope soon.

Well, goodbye, and thank you again for all that you have sent me.

> With love,
> from

An undated draft to Marion Hendrickson, later marked "Nov. 1924" by Helen. The S.S. Leviathan, *which crossed the Atlantic between New York and Southampton, was one of the largest and most luxurious ocean liners of the day. Helen and Barbara were seeing off Leo Anthony Meyette (1894-1974), their friend from New London (near Little Lake Sunapee), who was on his way to the Philippines.*

Dear Marion:

I am writing to tell you many exciting things, but mostly to thank you ever and ever so much for the dear little tea-set. Your father brought it up one evening. I love it, and love to look at it in the dining-room corner-cabinet. It doesn't show off the way it did in your father's living-room, but people that come into the dining-room usually notice it the first thing. I wonder who could read the Chinese figures on the little cups. They are fascinating, aren't they? I am crazy about the "semi-circle" tea-pot. It is a queer thing, the weirdest tea-pot I *ever* saw. Perhaps, when you come here sometime we can have tea in it together. Wouldn't that be fun? I shall keep it in my little house (when I have it) and when you come we can make tea in the little house!

Yesterday Mother and I went to New York. It was the first time I had ever been there. We went for two reasons. The first was to see a friend off on the *Leviathan*, and the second was to see the Aquarium. As I said before I had never been, and Mother hadn't been for several years, so we were expecting the worst things to happen. We expected to get lost at the very least and probably run-over or something like that. But we faced the prospect very happily. We found the first rather more difficult than we expected and the second rather more easier.

When we arrived at the Grand Central Station, we took a taxi-cab to the *Leviathan*, which was at Forty-sixth Street, Pier 86, I think it was. We got there safely and saw the monster. And it surely must be the biggest one afloat. I expected it to be big but not half—yes, just about half the length it is. We went all over it from top to bottom, and at last we found our friend. We talked a long time, watching the great flocks of gulls circling about and the smaller boats going around in and out of the wharf. At last the time came for it to sail, and we saw the four tugs push and pull and get it straightened, with the crew waving and shouting on board. We saw it off and then retraced our steps several blocks to Fifth Avenue, where we had something to eat.

After we had our lunch we rode in a bus to the elevated train, and in that we went to the Aquarium. There we stayed, watching the strange things for about an hour and a half. On the lower floor there were seven or eight big floor pools. In one there were a lot of gigantic turtles, in another a solitary penguin, in another a pelican, in another a group of alligators and snapping-turtles. Around the tanks were rows of little tanks, filled with strange, small fish. Around the walls was a row of big tanks, built into the wall. In about three of these were fancy goldfish, and in others were strange flat-fish of many different colors, sharks, muskellunges, bass, perch, angel-fish of gorgeous blues and yellows, with white ones and red ones; butterfly-fish, of creamy-yellow with fins of red-orange. Almost all of them were flat-fish, except a few which were *quite* the opposite. Some of them were striped, some were marbled, and others were spotted and mottled with all the colors of the rain-bow. There were some baby angel-fish, thin, transparent, and of a lovely sapphire blue. The angel-fish, pork-fish, and butterfly-fish, including many other varieties, were, as I said before, flat-fish. There were strange sea-robins with actual *claws*, sluggish rock-fish (almost all flat) whose heads stuck strangely out of the rocks here and there. There was one big tank which was devoted to three or four great sharks and shark-suckers (which were small blue fish which cling to the sharks all the time). The pork-fish are exquisite. They are a pale cream-colored species with very blunt heads and two shiny green stripes. Then there was a variety called the "queen-trigger-fish" which were big white flat-fish with transparent white fins and blue-green eyes which circled strangely in their orbs. Then there were rock hinds of red, green, blue, and white, which hung about the rocks all the time. In one tank was a number of small brownish sea-horses. Have you ever seen them? They have long tails, a little fin on their backs, and a head which looks exactly like that of a horse. They grow about seven inches long. When they go it is always (or, at least, almost always) along the bottom. They go along upright somehow, and that little fin just spins. They look exactly like tiny hobby-horses. They like to wind their tails about the grasses when they rest.

But almost the most marvelous part of this Aquarium was the way the tanks are arranged. Each tank is arranged to represent as nearly as possible the natural conditions under which the fish lived before it was captured. There is running water all the time. In some the bottom is rocky, in others sandy, and in others muddy, all overgrown with plants. And in some the sides and the bottom are solid rock. In one of the tanks in which are a group of trout there is an artificial water-fall tumbling in.

After we had been at the Aquarium all we wanted to we took the elevated train again back to have something to eat. Then we just got the five o'clock train, instead of the six, which we had planned for. In this way we had done everything about, and yet got back home one hour earlier than we expected, instead of waiting around for another hour. We had done a lot, and had a very good day, you see.

I certainly hope you will be here soon. We will certainly have tea in that delightful manner when you do. Thank you again for the little set, ever and ever so much.

   With much love,
   Barbara.

176 Armory Street
New Haven, Connecticut
December 12, 1924

Friend Leo:

Are you really there, safely? Did you see anything more exciting than angry waves and swooping gulls on the way over? Perhaps you caught sight of some strange fish (though I don't exactly see how you could from so high in the air), whales, or sea lions. You probably did see one or two whales spouting.

Perhaps you'd be interested to know that, listening to the radio one evening, I heard from a station in New York that the Leviathan, on its return trip, had encountered a terrible storm, that fifteen people were injured, and that waves over ninety feet high covered the decks. Those few who dared to try to get some sleep were thrown from their beds with dislocated ribs and whatnot. It made me hold my breath, when I first heard it, for I thought that possibly it was on your trip, but no, it must have been coming back.

Did you have fun living for five days on that big hotel? Did you like the pleasant rolling, tipping sensation of the waves (though it must take pretty big ones to rock 'the Monster')? I think, though I have never experienced the sensation of being on such a big one, that to lie and feel the vast bulk of it rolling and tipping must be one of the pleasantest sensations there is.

Is it not fun to lean over the railing of the high deck and watch the waves slosh and leap up on the side of 'The Monster'? When they really begin to get excited they must leap pretty high, on touching the steep sides. On Thanksgiving Day, when we went down to the shore, the waves were rising three or four feet, and the gray foam and spray that rode on them leaped up on the rocks so far that they touched me, standing twenty or twenty-five feet back as I was. Daddy and I sat on top of a small precipice, and watched these waves come bounding in, covering the rocks and the dark green sea-weed, and then rushing out again, and smoothing the sea-weed out in its direction. There was a place in the rock, where there was a narrow ravine, draped from the cliff with sea-weed. And the waves would come sloshing in and would wash the sea-weeds back and forth, and would cover quite the highest point where the sea-weeds hung from the rocks.

At New York Mother and I had the greatest fun! We went to the Battery, and saw the remarkable, remarkable, remarkable, remarkable fish that are kept there. There were butterfly-fish, angel-fish, pork-fish, rock-fish, porcupine-fish, sharks, queen-trigger-fish, and everything that can be imagined by man, and more too. Many of them, such as the angel-fish and the butterfly-fish, were flat-fish, but there were one or two like the rock-fish and porcupine-fish that were quite the opposite. There were some rock-fish whose heads stuck strangely, inconspicuously, and very suspiciously from the cracks between the rocks, and they had great bulging eyes. The queen-trigger-fish were great white flat-fish with oval eyes of blue-green, and the latter rolled strangely in their various orbits like planets around the sun. Oh, they are just too ridiculous to exist, anyhow, and I'm not sure that they do exist. Then they had, besides these remarkable, remarkable sea-fish, common lake-fish, perches, muskellunges, pickerel, and many others. Then there were five or six big floor tanks, in which were turtles, gigantic ones (one of the back of whose shell was about three feet long), alligators (of which you will meet in Africa, I think), and one tank had a penguin, another a pelican, and another a seal, sea lion, or manatee, I don't know which. Yes, it is a very remarkable place.

Do tell me what sort of experiences you had on the Leviathan. I am very much interested to know about it.

Goodbye—luck and joy be with you.

    Love from
    Barbara.

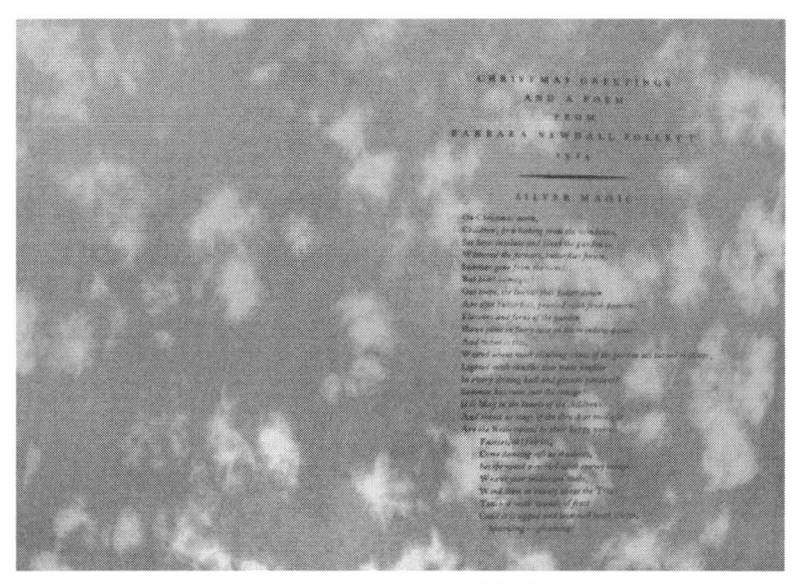

Silver Magic was set on mottled silver paper.

Christmas greetings and a poem from Barbara Newhall Follett, 1924

SILVER MAGIC
On Christmas morn,
Children, first looking from the windows,
See how desolate and bleak the garden is.
Withered the flowers, butterflies flown,
Summer gone from the woods.
But hist!—magic!
Out there, the leaves that flutter down
Are elfin butterflies, pearled with frost-patterns.
Flowers and ferns of the garden
Have come in fairy lace on the window-panes.
And what is this,
Wound about with climbing vines of the garden all
    turned to silver,
Lighted with candles that make fireflies
In every shining ball and glazen pendant?
Summer has come into the cottage!
It is May in the hearts of the children:
And sweet as songs of the thrush at twilight
Are the Noels raised by their happy voices.
    Fairies, oh! fairies,
    Come dancing soft as shadows,
    Set the wood a-whirl with snowy wings.

> Weave your iridescent webs,
> Wind them in beauty about the Tree:
> Touch it with wands of frost
> Until it is tipped and trimmed with icicles,
> Sparkling—gleaming!

176 Armory Street
New Haven, Connecticut
January 1, 1925

My dearest Mr. Oberg:

I have been very, very busy with Christmas books, baby sister, and—and eating peanuts! Otherwise I have had time to write a great many letters. But as it stands now, I have had time to do nothing.

Your box arrived in good condition—everything except the apples, which were a bit rotten. Sabra was crazy about Jimmy Jounce, and about the little blow-up doll and kitty. I was delighted with the little Butterfly box, and pleased to see that the chains had been mended. Sabra loved the peanuts, and was terribly funny with them. She would pick them up and put them in the box again. Before long, she had noticed how the stuffing was swept into the fire, and was trying to sweep the peanuts out of the box herself with her little broom.

We had a glorious Christmas, and much fun! This time we all had stockings; I bought one or two things to put in Daddy's, and Mother filled that. Late Christmas Eve, we went down together (Daddy and I) to buy the stuffing for Mother's. We bought first two pair of stockings, one of which was used for *the* stocking, then we went into a candy shop and bought some eats, especially a candy apple which just fitted the toe. We bought two bar pins, a gold and silver at a reckless price (for, as you know, Mother lost all her brooches) and felt greatly ashamed to have spent so much. Then we bought a beautiful cock of red and yellow, and had him filled with salted peanuts. When we got home with all these things, Daddy and Mother went off down town again, leaving Ding and myself to fill the stocking. That done, I went to bed, leaving a note for Daddy as to the whereabouts of it, and hanging my own. I was so excited I couldn't sleep; but after a while I went off, soon waking again. My brains were awhirl. I couldn't even think. All I could do was to lie there, biding myself from squirming, for I wanted to badly enough. I had no idea what o'clock it was, but finally I heard a sharp click-click, then a clock striking, but I was so excited that I couldn't even count it. It seemed to me as if I heard a small voice squeaking inside of me, "Now." The door opened. In he came and took my stocking off, returning it full and bulging over. All this while I was peering silently from under the bedclothes, but at last I tried to breathe hard and sham sleeping. Faint, oh, such faint light was streaming in the window, from the gas-lamp far away. My mind circled. "*Oh, if morning were only here*," I kept thinking and pinched myself angrily. But it did no good. I couldn't get to sleep, and, worse still, I kept seeing the faint, dark outline of it on the chair beside me. A clock struck. One. How exasperating. There I had been waiting to hear what time it was, and how could I know if it was one or half-past. Another long stretch. One, two, three, four, five. Only five. But then, it was later than I had thought. They must have stayed up very late to decorate the tree, I thought, because it must have been only four when he filled my stocking. Well, that was better than four anyhow, really I had expected it to be four, but there was an awfully long time to wait, and I knew I couldn't sleep. Five! I got to thinking again, but I couldn't for long, and soon I began to squirm. I wanted some water. I shuffled up and got it. Then I had a bright idea. If I pulled the screen on the piazza window up, it would be lighter, and they wouldn't say it was so dark when I could bear it no longer. But it was caught, and I couldn't pull it up. Moreover, when I started, the rapid snoring from the other end of the porch ceased, and I was scared to death. I tiptoed back to bed. The snoring began again, and I felt more comfortable. Ding. Half-past five. I got up, and tugged again at the screen. But it was of no use. Then I discovered that it was caught behind the baby's bed, which was too near the wall (of course, the baby was not in it; she was in her own room). Scarcely daring to breathe, I moved it, ever so slightly. Then I tried the screen again and, to my great joy, it yielded. More light came in, for now the light from another gas-lamp came through the window. Pleased at my success, I went back to bed. I could now see quite distinctly the outline of the stocking on my chair, and I could now see some packages piled out beside it. I stretched out my hand, and I got hold of something smooth and cold, with some sharp prongs on it. But I didn't dare take hold of it any more, for I was afraid it was breakable. Another long wait. One, two, three, four, five, six. Six o'clock. I got to thinking and for the next half-hour, the wait was not so unendurable. At last half-past six and then seven rang out. I had waited three hours, and, though I was afraid they would think it was rather early, I spoke. Daddy woke, and I unloaded my stocking. Then I clambered into Mother's bed, and Daddy came in too, and they unloaded theirs. Mother was, of course, delighted with the pins, and said "welcome," most heartily to every one of the caramels and pecan nuts.

After breakfast we went down, and I danced around the Christmas tree, and opened packages which were mostly books, lovely ones, too. Oh, but we had fun.

Thank you again ever and ever so much for all the things you sent us.

> Farewell, lovingly,
> B. N. F.

176 Armory Street
New Haven, Connecticut
January 2, 1925

Dear—dear:—

Oh, there are so many letters to write I don't know whom to say 'dear—' to next.

Dear, dear Mr. St. John:

I have been very, very busy writing Christmas letters, as you know, but not so busy that I cannot find a moment to write to you in. Thank you ever and ever so much for sending me that very interesting book (which I really got this time) and for the little picture. It is perfectly sweet. I have it now on my desk, and, as you suggested, I can really hear it singing, singing of you, bringing messages from you, telling me of times when—. When I was in that heavenly place, the home of fairies, gnomes, elves, nymphs, trees, dryads, butterflies, dragonflies. Where the poor innocent, ugly creatures come to find their own home, where they come flocking from where they have been abused and badly treated, to a home, a home which is restful, kind, and quiet. These creatures are tadpoles, lizards, snakes, frogs, little bugs and beetles, which people will insist on hating and abusing. That picture brings messages to me of the time when I was there, and I love it because of that.

We had a gloriously happy Christmas. In the early morning I woke at four to see Daddy come striding in to fill my stocking (you see, he had been up kind of late to fix the tree (I suppose)), (do you understand all the remarkable parentheses), and I stayed awake, squirming with impatience to know what was inside, until seven. Once or twice I got up to try to pull the screen on the piazza window up to admit a little more light from the gas-lamp, so that when I did wake them they wouldn't complain that it was still so dark, for I was afraid I couldn't wait until it was really light. I got the screen up after a lot of tugging (for it was caught behind the baby's bed (though the baby wasn't in it)), (another same case of parentheses), and a little more light came in, so that I could see the stocking quite clearly. You see, when the screen is down, faint light from the gas-lamp comes in, and when it is up light from another gas-lamp also comes in. Well, seven really came and I opened my stocking with delight. Then we went down and saw the Christmas tree and had *such* fun!

I would write you a longer letter, but I have so many to write, that if I make them any longer I shall never be through.

       Lovingly from
       B. N. F.

Barbara had sent Silver Magic *to Walter de la Mare.*

14, Thornsett Road
Anerley, S. E. 20. *[London]*
6th January, 1925.

Dear Barbara,

I had two Christmases this year—one immediately after I came home safe and sound on the "Orduna", and the other the day before yesterday, when your poem came. It is indeed a joy to have it, and I think it's a beautiful piece of work.

I wonder if you will think me very old-fashioned if I add that I can't get out of myself a sort of expectation of rhyme in verse, except, of course, in blank verse. I do hope you will try some rhymed poems as well, and in the old metres. This is just a selfish wish. Haven't you noticed at every Christmas one invariably, like Oliver Twist, keeps asking for more? And that's what I am after.

Please tell your father how intensely disappointed I was that that other meeting with him never arrived. Did he get a letter, I wonder, a week or two before it was decided that it would be impossible for me to go to Westover owing to my having to be back in New York at 11 o'clock the next morning? But this is an old unhappy far-off thing now. Please give him and your mother and yourself all my remembrances and my very best wishes for this New Year. I do hope you will all soon be coming to England—before I get a long grey beard. We hope to be in a house a little further from London than this is, by the Spring, and we'd love to see you all there.

       Yours ever,
       W. J. de la Mare

176 Armory Street
New Haven, Connecticut
January 27, 1925

My dearest Katherine:

I am sorry, but your wild endeavors to make me believe in God, have only been to the effect of making me say what I don't mean. For the time I was with you I certainly thought I did, but, now that my mind is clear and fresh, I see that I don't and can't. You don't realize—I can't do a thing so quickly that is so entirely contrary to my former ideas.

What is your "God" anyhow. Saying that He is a "beautiful spirit" doesn't mean anything.

Now I do believe in God, but in my own way, for mine and yours are the same thing with different titles. I move that I believe what I want, and you what you want, and not speak of it any more.

> I hope sincerely that I remain
> your true friend,
> [signed in Farksoo]

P. S. Your parents will know what I mean better than you, perhaps.

Robert H. Davis (1869-1942) was an American writer, photographer, editor, and author of the poem I Am the Printing Press, *which was reprinted widely (and on a poster).*

February 4, 1925
New Haven, Connecticut
176 Armory Street

Dear Mr. Davis:

I was very much pleased to receive your interesting poster. I think it is very interesting, and to me, it is rather unusual. Thank you very much for sending it to me.

I am glad that you were interested in my Christmas Greetings. I had great fun doing it, and, as you probably know from Daddy, I set it up in type myself. I had a much longer poem all ready, and we discovered that it would take too long to set up in the time we had. I also had ready a still shorter one which was made up from the refrains of the first and second parts of the long poem. But I thought that, as long as I couldn't very well have the long one, the one we devised from the second stanza of the long one was better than the refrains. I am sending the long poem in this letter, and, according to your desire, I am signing the card as it came.

Thank you again for sending me "I AM THE PRINTING-PRESS."

> With great love,
> from

SILVER MAGIC
Secret in the midst of enchanted woods
A little cottage is set among gardens.
Fir-trees, the wind singing through,
Are for ever swaying in their stately way.
There are flowers like strange butterflies at rest,
Butterflies fantastic as flowers on wing.
Bumble-bees of black and gold come tasting the pollen.
When tired children have come from romping in the woods,
Fireflies wink and glimmer in the trellised vines,
Light the garden with tiny tapers;
And the haunting silver voice of the wood-thrush
Thrills through the evening quiet.
> *Fairies, oh! fairies,*
> *Come dancing soft as shadows,*
> *Set the wood a-flock with feathery wings;*
> *Weave your webs of moonlight,*
> *Wind them in beauty about the trees,*
> *Touch the forest with wands of mist*
> *Until each tree is tipped and trimmed with filmy lace,*
> *   Shimmering—gleaming!*

On Christmas morn,
Children, first looking from the windows,
See how desolate and bleak the garden is.
Withered the flowers, butterflies flown, summer gone from
    the woods.
But hist!—magic!
Out there, the leaves that flutter down
Are elfin butterflies, pearled with frost-patterns.
Flowers and ferns of the garden
Have come in fairy lace on the window-panes.
And what is this,
Wound about with climbing vines of the garden all turned
    to silver,
Lighted with candles that make fireflies
In every shining ball and glazen pendant?
Summer has come into the cottage!
It is May in the hearts of the children;
And sweet as songs of the thrush at twilight
Are the Noels raised by their happy voices.
> *Fairies, oh! fairies,*
> *Come dancing soft as shadows,*

Set the wood a-whirl with snowy wings;
Weave your iridescent webs,
Wind them in beauty about the Tree;
Touch it with wands of frost
Until it is tipped and trimmed with icicles,
 Sparkling—gleaming!

The solar eclipse occurred on the morning of January 24th.

176 Armory Street
New Haven, Connecticut
February 7, 1925

My dear Mr. Oberg:

I want you to know that I have received the pictures—I have had them for a long time now, and I thank you for them very much indeed. I wish there *could* have been a little more light on some of them, but the little expressions are very nice, especially one, where she is laughing and laughing, and looks the little rogue she is. I am very anxious to see you, so that you can help me put them all in their places in my photograph-album. Also I want to see you for other reasons.

I will proceed to tell you why you have not been receiving letters from Mother. Please understand that she cut her finger rather badly on a tin can, and has not been able to use that hand much since, so of course she cannot write or typewrite. It happens to be on the most important finger of all—the middle finger of the right hand.

What did you think of the eclipse?????? Was it total in Rhode Island? It was here and we had the greatest fun. I am going to tell you about it for the pleasure of doing so, even if you have seen it. As the moon slowly covered the surface of the sun it grew darker and darker, and it got magical looking. Everything was difficult to see, and there was an opaline glow of blue-green over everything. Then when it was total, how marvelous it was. The corona was so lovely and silky and fairy-like, and oh!—there are not enough words in the English language to express how absolutely heavenly—exquisite it was—and the big solar prominences which flared out into that silky fringe of white light! Wasn't it all beautiful?

I am now going to tell you what makes me leap for joy within myself. You know well about the long story I have been writing, Eepersip. It is—it has been for a long time finished (that you also know) and now Daddy and I have been correcting it, to make it as perfect as we can—and, when it is all corrected and copied on nice clean paper—it *may* be published. In that way I may be able

to get royalties. Also even if they don't take it, it will do me good to see the story on nice fresh paper, instead of the dirty, pencil-marked paper that it is now on. Do you share in my delight?????
??

I will also tell you that I am very anxious to see you again. You will be down for my birthday, will you not?

Now I think I must take my leave, with much love from all of us.

    B. N. F.

176 Armory Street
New Haven, Connecticut
February 13, 1925

My very dearest Mr. St. John:

I am *so* sorry and so ashamed! Not to have written to you for *so* long! And you sent me a book and a perfectly lovely little picture, which I haven't even thanked you for! However, as you know, I am very busy, though that is but a poor excuse. I *do* thank you now, I thank you as much as is in my power. I love the book, I am reading it now, I have just begun it. It is very interesting, I think—so much about the wild folk that you and I both love so much.

And the picture is exactly what you said—it conveys to my mind exactly what you said—messages from you, messages from the wild woodlands. And, though I keep the brook, let its current turn back to you, bringing from me my thoughts of love, my thoughts of all the wild. Oh, it is all so lovely, isn't it?

I am having a birthday party the fourth of March—a children's party. That is one of the things I have never had—I have always just had my "grown-up" friends to a luncheon and a clock-cake. But this time I am really going to have the rough, noisy, school gang of children that go to the same play-class that I go to. I like them, with all their rough ways—they mean well. They are all about my age. One was born in March, on St. Patrick's Day, two in April, one in June, and the others are a bit older. So you see, we are quite well suited to play together, and we have pretty good times.

I wish *you*, however, could come down.

The most important thing that I have been doing lately is a correction of my long story, Eepersip. Daddy and I are doing it together. When it is finished, and copied neatly, we shall send it to the printer, and it may be—? Then I shall dance indeed. To have a book of mine—? Oh, wouldn't it be all so glorious.

    With love and thanks,
    B. N. F.

176 Armory Street
New Haven, Connecticut
March 5, 1925

Dear Mr. Oberg:

    I will write you a long letter as soon as I have time and my typewriter is working better. However, I *can* thank you for the little gold fountain pen that I am writing this little note with. I do not know how I am going to thank you, though, for I certainly can not find enough words to tell you how much I love it—to tell you how happy it made the happy day—happy as it was. It will improve my horrible hand-writing, too. (I hope you will forgive the latter.) Again let me thank you from my very heart.

               Much, much love from
               B. N. F.

As I mentioned earlier, Grace Parker Follett (1911-1995) was Barbara's half-sister from Wilson's first marriage—to Grace Huntington Parker, who died two days after her baby was born. In 1925 Grace was living with Grandmother Follett in North Attleboro. She became a nurse and worked in Mexico City and then at Massachusetts General Hospital in Boston.

About Grace's missing correspondence: Barbara wrote a note to her the month before this letter, which included the lines: "But don't put your letters inside of Daddy's any more; address them to me separately, because, when you enclose them in Daddy's letters, sometimes he forgets to give them to me. Do you suppose that accounts for their sudden disappearance?"

176 Armory Street
New Haven, Connecticut
March 12, 1925

My dearest Grace:

It pains me a great deal to acknowledge that I probably haven't written to you more than four letters, anyhow. But I will say that I haven't received all the letters that you say you write. I don't see any reason for their going astray if you address them to 176 Armory Street, New Haven, Conn. It seems very impossible to me. Anyhow, now that I have found a break in my work to write, I will make it as interesting as I can.

I was very glad to hear about your party. It makes me think a little of what I used to do on my birthdays. I would invite only two or three people to a little luncheon. I always had the same kind of cake: one with white frosting and a clock-face on it in yellow or brown. The hands of the clock would point to the hour which was my age. But this year I decided I would have a real children's party, and invite all the children of about my age with whom I play happy games on the Hillhouse meadows twice a week under the superintendence of a college student, a certain Mr. Collins. Now Mother doesn't care much about the fuss and the labor of having a party, and, to save her from this anxiety, my violin teacher, Hildegarde Donaldson, gave it for me at her house. She, herself, adores the work—the tiny details.

And another thing—it was all as much a surprise to me as to any of the children. The only things I knew about were the presents to go on the end of the cobwebs. Hildegarde and I went in town together to buy them. And they were certainly worth the hard struggles with the twisty strings that led to them. And the strings were certainly twisty! I cannot describe our emotions as we discovered with each new turn some new difficulty. But of course they came to an end at last, and we squealed with delight at our pretty presents.

After all the things were found we played games until supper-time. We played stage-coach, going to Jerusalem, musical bumps, etc. At last the long-waited-for supper announcement came. We formed a line and marched in while Daddy played the piano. And what a fairyland greeted our eyes! Hildegarde, knowing my love—my fiery passion for butterflies, had used this Idea as a foundation for the room. Strings were stretched across the room over the table, and from them were suspended butterflies. They were made of colored paper—and quite a job it must have been. Why, there was no end to them. I don't even now see how she could make them all. The room was lit with them. It even gave the effect that the walls themselves were covered with them. The paper tablecloth and napkins were designed with many colored butterflies—on each little candy basket was a pretty bow of soft Florists' ribbon—and a butterfly. The ice-cream was shaped like a big butterfly, resting on a mass of spun sugar—his cocoon. Indeed the pattern went even to the cake, instead of my name a—great big candied butterfly! Green ribbons, soft and delicate as fairies' wings, hung from the little lights on the wall, or were suspended from pictures, picture to picture. They were tied in soft and silky bows. You can guess that on them were more butterflies. Inside the snappers was a paper cap as usual, and, when we put them on, Hildegarde went around and pinned a specially beautiful butterfly on each one. So it was a butterfly party, you see. And now I begin to think I would like to see butterflies again, and Spring, and all the rest. They are coming pretty soon now.

But I haven't told you one thing about the presents that I got. My first was a small bracelet of green enamel and silver, a perfectly exquisite one—from my parents. Then, in the morning, when Hildegarde came over to plan for the party, we opened a four-foot package that had (unknown to me) lain two or three days in Mother's closet, or somewhere like that. It was my new violin, a perfect beauty. You see my Aunt Mildred Kennedy gave me my first little one; and now that I am ready for a full-sized one she got me that, too. Then came a present from a very dear friend of mine, a rather old man who lives in Providence, R. I. He is very fond of me, and always sends me something—it was a little gold fountain pen with my initials on it. A neighbor of ours came over with my present, a small silver pin that looked fairylike and like spider-webs. Then the things I got at the party—the present at the end of the cobweb (which was a small blue fluffy, soft feather fan), and the thing I got in the Jack Horner Pie (which was a small dog with diamond eyes, sparkling of green glass).

That was all, except those that the children brought me. But wasn't that a grand lot? And then the other day came a late present from Boston: a string of pink beads (they look like coral, but I don't believe they are real), a beautiful little necklace. I guess that is about all to say about my party, but I will tell you something about Sabra now.

She is *such* a delicious darling; such a rogue; so mischievous; so funny; so pretty; and so little. *That* and her mischievousness are about the best points about her I think. And she is so funny that she gets us into convulsions of laughter. She is funny in everything she does: even the way she walks with her little rear bobbing up and down is funny. And she knows it! Late in the afternoon before she goes to bed is her playtime (though she has playtime all day). But that is the time when Daddy, however busy he may be, comes down to see her, to play with her, and to show her her books. And the funniest thing about her is that, when she sees that people are amused by her being funny, she puts on more and more funniness, until, in the end, she is just a mass of squirms, of grins, of funny faces, of writhings, of delightful noises. But by far her *most* delightful noise is the way she says squirrel. (You see she has a book with some pictures of squirrels in it.) But there is no use in my trying to describe to you the way she does it: except that she curls her tongue around and sticks it out, and—explodes! That's all there is to it—she just explodes.

For "how do you do" Sabra makes a deliciously funny little bob, saying at the same time: "Do?" (How do you do?) She says "Cair-kee" almost every time you hand her anything. That means: "Thank you."

She loves to go out exploring in back. She pokes around in the woods, and discovers little things. Today she and I went out together for about an hour, and she had the time of her life. We found some pussy-willows, which she was very fond of; we went together and sat on the old wooden chair; when I poked away the leaves from the tiny laurel trees that grow everywhere in the woods, she followed my example; she made a new discovery: moss. She put her hands down on it and "loved" it in her screeching and *very* affectionate manner. Oh, we had a lovely time!

Well, goodbye, Grace. I shall write again, but I have to go to work now.

    With lots and lots of love, I am your friend,
    Barbara.

176 Armory Street
New Haven, Connecticut
March 14, 1925

My dear, dear Mr. St. John:

I was *so* glad to get your letter yesterday—and your lovely little poem. Nothing I have ever read sounds like it, and I know exactly what you mean. It is that feeling of being all alone in the woods at evening, when the stars are beginning to twinkle, when all is peaceful, and when, from the top of a tall pine, comes the soft tinkling notes of one of the inhabitants of the World of Joy. Little birds are so happy, aren't they? They are busy sometimes, when they have little birds to feed or nests to build, but, on the other hand, they are so free! They fly—they whirl through the air. They sing—no human voice is so lovely. They are afraid of nothing—until fear comes. Their motto is: "Don't be afraid of future trouble. Plenty of time to worry when it comes." It seems to me that, even if they don't plan for the future in quite the way we do, they are happier because they are not always thinking what dreadful things *may* happen.

Spring is here, I am sure. Crocuses are pushing their gay, cheery little faces through the earth, daffodils are budding, and—I am sure—did I—you know better than I do—was it a thought, or—this morning did I hear the familiar happy little trill from the quivering throat of a young sparrow? I am *sure* it was. I heard it all summer, and it was so planted in my mind that I have been hearing it behind my ears all winter—but—to really, really hear it again—seems to me too lovely to be true. There is not another song that is such a herald of spring—except, of course, the robin and bluebirds! Oh, it did me such good to hear it! It just thrilled me through and through with delight. (Please excuse all these ugly mistakes. You see, I cut my finger a few days ago, and have not been typewriting for some time.)

A few days ago my little playmate and I found some pussies almost hidden under a fallen tree, which spread its dead branches over them like a safe-guard. They were the first I had found, and so, though another time I should not have broken into that treasure-chest, my playmate and I each carried off a bunch of the same size. But a few days ago I found some more, as then tiny buds, and I left them there to grow, hoping that no one else would find them. Sabra likes them, too. She takes them and tickles her cheek, and laughs and laughs.

You know that I had a birthday party on March 4th. It was a children's party, given for me by my violin teacher, Hildegarde Donaldson, to save Mother the clutter and fuss that it would surely cost. It was just a party—though a very beautiful one. You would care nothing about anything except the room where we had our supper. Hildegarde knew how I adored those happy, flitting little insects—butterflies. She used this idea as a foundation for the decoration of the room. The paper tablecloth and napkins were designed with butterflies of many colors. Strings were stretched over the table with big butterflies of colored paper suspended from them. On the walls were green ribbons of a pale, fairylike shade, tied in soft, silky bows. It was that gauze-like Florists' ribbon. On these were hung butterflies, and there were so many that, on the first glimpse, we thought the walls were covered with them. On each little candy basket was pinned a butterfly, and on our paper caps Hildegarde pinned another. The ice-cream, too, was shaped like a butterfly, resting on his cocoon, represented by a mass of spun sugar. Even the delicious white cake with white frosting and eleven flickering candles was ornamented with a butterfly of candy. Yes, it was a beautiful, beautiful, happy little party.

There doesn't seem to be much more to tell, except again that spring is surely coming. It rained this morning, and the moss now shines out greener than ever. A few yarrow leaves are coming—those leaves that are like fairy lace or ferns. The grass is greening, too. But I never saw anything so lovely as the Whitings' crocuses. They make the whole lawn cheery looking, and welcoming. They make everybody who looks at them feel happy.

I love the picture you sent me with the letter. Have I ever written you a Christmas thank-you letter? It is shameful if I haven't, but I feel sure I have.

> With ever and ever so much love,
> Barbara.

176 Armory Street
New Haven, Connecticut
March 17, 1925

My dear Mrs. Eckstein:

First of all let me thank you for the outsides of the chocolates, as that came first. I have made some wonderful-looking beads from them—they have added greatly to the magical beauty of my little necklace. But now let me thank you for the *insides*, because, lovely though the others were, I am much more fond of the insides. The last layer of caramels is now fast disappearing. The box came with two other letters addressed to me, and, as I always like to do the most uninteresting thing first, I let the box sit in the middle of the table, with Mother's mouth hoping it was candy, and crazy to see *what* it was, while I read my letters. Then, as slowly as I could, just to torment her, I opened it. I put some heavy rules on that box of candy, about the amount they must eat a day—or, rather, must *not*. And Mother made me sell her extra pieces, and break all my rules. Then a friend came for supper one night, and we had some of it. Yes, it was the very same day that the box came. And, because Mother had had her share that day, I did not for a long time let her have any more. But she was so funny nosing into the box, and "wondering what was inside of that big fat thing" that at last I let her have one. Then, of course, all rules were broken, they dug in like moles, while I stood by, shaking with laughter, watching them excavate. So I turned away the rules, and let 'em dig right in. And that is what we have been doing. Yes, it is just the grandest present I could possibly expect, and a great pleasure to us all.

   With love,

176 Armory Street
New Haven, Connecticut
March 17, 1925

My dearest K.

 Listen, now, you must not go on criticizing my parents and my house. If you really care anything about me you must quit right off, or we simply cannot be together. I know your opinion—you don't have to repeat it every time I see you—once is enough. I see what you mean—but I don't think you exactly do. You don't dislike them really—you don't understand them, that's all. It's being horribly disloyal for me to let you say these things—I've been thinking it all over. You don't understand why I have my work to do—because, at this particular time, you have none at all. You don't understand why I can't come down oftener—but if you lived where I do, you would see the troublesome side of it. Even as it is, you are always expecting me to do all the coming and going down to your house—you hardly ever come up here, and when you do, you see how troublesome it is. Well, it is no different your coming up here from my going down there. The point is, you don't understand, and, as I have said, you are making our friendship very miserable. So we had just better quit and be friends, or, if you'd rather, keep on and not be friends. You will have to choose between them. Let the argument go, just as we did the first one.

   With love,
   Barbara.

176 Armory Street
New Haven, Connecticut
April 29, 1925

My dear Mr. St. John:

I was so sorry to hear that you are sick in the hospital. I think that the latter is one of the worst places there is, unless it's *not* being in one when you ought to be. The atmosphere is so dreadful, and everything is so disagreeable.

As you know, Spring is no longer coming, it is *here*. The only thing left is for it to unfold its green wings with a burst of sunlight to be fully developed. A little while ago I put in some cosmos and nasturtium seeds—the cosmos is now about two inches above the ground, and one little nasturtium is showing a little green leaf above the hard earth. There are butterflies dancing, white ones and brown ones and yellow ones and blue ones. Sabra loves them. When she sees one flitting about she laughs with glee, and says goodbye to it by waving her hand when it flies away. She loves to listen to the bird-songs, too. When I am wheeling her about and she hears one she listens with delight, and sometimes when Mother comes to take her up in the morning she is found sitting up in bed, motionless, and listening. The flickers are here, the noisy things. You see, when I was taking Sabra out for a ride, I suddenly heard a burst of sounds that sounded like birds quarreling. I looked and saw a flock of birds flying about in a most nervous way. I couldn't see—Sabra just came dashing into my arms all full of glee to show me her new dress—what they were, because the sun was in my eyes, but soon afterwards I discovered them in the opposite direction and as they flew I knew by their white tail and golden under-wings what they were. I like those birds very much.

I have a secret that no one knows except Mother, Daddy, and myself. But I am going to let you into it, trusting that you, too, will keep it a dear secret. Yesterday I was walking in the lovely woods across the street. I was going up to my outlook (a great precipice which looks out over the landscape, near the top of the hill) when suddenly I heard a squeak and a frightened scurry. Now on a former expedition up there I had heard the same squeak and scurry, but had been in time only to see some little brown animal go bounding down over the crags. This time I was in time to see more. It was a rabbit—the dearest little rabbit you ever saw. This time, however, he didn't try to get away. He just squeezed himself down into the leaves, in the vain hope of making me think he was part of them. I watched him a long time, perfectly motionless, within about five feet of him. But I was standing in a very uncomfortable position, and I didn't want to remain that way long. I cautiously edged a little nearer, thinking to sit down on a smooth rock which was just in front of me. I reached the rock all right, but when I went to sit down, I was just within the rabbit's limits, for the poor frightened little creature gave a little scramble and edged away another two feet. But just before he had done that I could almost have touched him—had I reached out my hand. I'm sure I was within three feet of him. Well, I sat down on the rock and watched. I watched a long time—both of us perfectly motionless. His nose was wobbling a little, his little black-brown eye was fixed steadily on me, he was trembling very little. But I decided I wouldn't frighten him any more, for I was afraid he would leave the place. So I went down. But I want to make friends with him. And perhaps you can give me a little advice as to how to go about it. Shall I leave food up there, or something like that?

The violets are at their best now, and the dandelions are beginning to go out, and Sabra loves the fuzzy little puffs. But, best of all, this morning I discovered a patch of those delicate wind-flowers or wood-anemones, snow-white and pink.

Sabra is now making serious attempts at talking. She uses the word "Mite" very frequently, indeed in the place of "little." The butterflies and flowers and birds and some dogs are all "Mite," while the other kinds of dogs and the cars are "big."

I must close now, hoping that you will be very well indeed, and also that we may see each other before long.

   Very lovingly,
   Barbara

176 Armory Street
New Haven, Connecticut
May 1, 1925

My dearest Mr. St. John:

I have made up my mind to write to you every time I find anything to say, for I know that it *does* cheer you up, greatly.

You know, not long ago when Mother and I were in Judds' bookstore we ran into a book by W. H. Prescott, with illustrations by Keith Henderson, in two volumes, called: *The Conquest of Mexico*. It is about the most fascinating book I've read in a long time. And the pictures! I've never, never seen such effective black and whites. They are just incredible. Of course, just as it always happens when I learn anything about history CORTES is my favorite hero. His courage surpasses everything I've ever known. He was cruel, and greedy, and terribly severe with his men. But—he had enough dangers without those of mutiny among his soldiers, and, too, if it was to be a war, there was no escaping cruelty—*and*—he was a sixteenth century SPANISH explorer which makes all the difference in the world from being a twentieth century soft-hearted reader. I entirely sympathize with him, and if he was cruel I look for his good parts. The Henderson pictures of him show features that could have been nothing by good-hearted. And he is—was—so handsome, with his long black beard and black hair, with the daintiest little curl you ever saw on his forehead. His armor is striking with its knee-caps, and leg-shields and mail. In one picture—my favorite—he has a rich mantle over one shoulder and under the other. He is bending slightly forward, almost touching faces with an Aztec prince whom he is arresting. The Aztec prince has drawn himself up to his full height (which is not so much as that of CORTES bending over) and is returning CORTES'S glance of pleasure with a haughty look that makes you feel quite surprised. His name is Cacama. I like him very much. CORTES wasn't so bad to him. I have just gotten to where he didn't do anything worse than to put him in fetters.

The main object of this letter is to find out whether *you* like this great man. I find that a great many don't, but in spite of all the massacre and the cruelty, I find that none of these bad things can keep me from loving and admiring him.

I am trying to think what else there is to say, but there doesn't seem to be much. So I will close, as before, wishing you good luck, and hoping that you will be well before long.

      Lovingly,

176 Armory Street
New Haven, Connecticut
May 21, 1925

My dearest Mr. St. John:
Everything now is here—including warm weather. For we have had some days hot enough to make the perspiration stream down my back in rivulets, also hot enough to do a great deal of good to all my young plants, my nasturtiums, cosmos, and morning glory. Hot enough to attract hundreds upon hundreds of butterflies, and make them lively and well-spirited. Hot enough to help the trees burst out in leaf, covering the woods with that soft green canopy, kissing gently the windows of houses, and shading and protecting us from the steady heat of the burning sun. And the heat has made Sabra well-spirited as well as the butterflies and birds and trees and

flowers, for I never saw anything so sprite-like, so full of life and so full of delicious fun and laughter.

And the birds!—you never heard anything like them. From every tree, from every bush you hear their cheery songs, gushing forth in sweet melody of springtime happiness. The other day I heard the soft, robin-like whistle of the rose-breasted grosbeak, and, peering high into the tree above me I saw him, with his gorgeous red and white breast. He was hopping about merrily from twig to twig. We hear, too, the cheery song of the song sparrow, the thrilling one of the brown thrasher, and, above all, when all is hushed and silent at dusk, when the sun is setting, from out behind the gently waving leaves come the silvery notes of the wood-thrush, that superb singer of the dusk. There are towhees here, too, for I have seen them a great deal, and am thinking that there should be a nest around here somewhere, so I keep my eye on them, as well as on the wood-thrushes. And I am hoping that the grosbeaks, too, will build here, and that I shall be able to see their nest. There is another bird around here that has always fascinated me. I haven't seen him, but I've heard him as he utters his spiraling song—the veery. I have also seen woodpeckers tat-tatting up the trees with their red crests, and Sabra has listened to their endless tapping. And, reminding me of woodpeckers because of the same tapping habit, are the little nuthatches, spiraling around the tree-trunks in search of insects on the bark.

Of course the buttercups are here, and the blue-grass, and the star-grass, and the pink azaleas, and the pink and white and yellow clover. Sabra loves them, every one, and, though she likes to pick them and take home great bunches, she never offers to pull them to pieces, and is always very ready to put them in water. She likes buttercups especially. The field on the corner of Armory Street and Edge Hill Road, the big field owned by the Water Company, is where she and I like to go. I wheel her down to the field, and then she walks to the buttercups, and we go about picking all kinds of flowers, and come back laden down with them. Ah, the little sweetheart, how I adore her!

And how funny she is! Last night she sat up on the bed with Daddy, going through all her delicious little squirmings, nosing down into his face and making all her delightful little noises, wiggling her pink feet until we went into convulsions of laughter, stroking Daddy's cheeks with her soft little dimpled hands, and kissing him. But her bath-time in the morning is perfectly uproarious. For she takes her face-cloth and soaks it with water and wrings it down her neck—or, over the floor. And she flings it about madly, making the bath-room a regular pool of water, until it is taken away from her.

But that never bothers her. Then she splashes with her legs and her hands, and has a perfectly glorious time. She has a great passion for little things—such as ants. She will watch an ant-hole, with the busy little bugs streaming in and out and carrying grains of sand for a long time. She loves to go for long walks with me.

I certainly hope that you are getting better, and that soon you will be out of the hospital, and also as always that we may see each other *some* time *soon*.

I am waiting impatiently to go to Sunapee, and my dear Secret Beach, and my chipmunks and rabbits and skunks and squirrels and minnows and baby horn-pout!

   With much love,
   Barbara.

176 Armory Street
New Haven, Connecticut
May 25, 1925

My dear Mr. Oberg:

How shameful—how shocking—for me not to have written to you. But I think you know as I do, that I am very, very busy—all the time. There is so much to be done, so little done—and never a beginning—that, of course they are never over with. In fact things to be done are like a big ball of twine with the beginning end inside, so that one has to unwind it all before one comes to the beginning, and in doing so, along hops another ball of twine to have the same thing done—before the other one is really begun.

But that is not the main object, which is—to be enthusiastic about the—?? dog. But how can I? How is such a thing possible, when I cannot be enthusiastic enough about one single bead on his blessed tail—or one single splotch of—(not paint———? I guess it grew there naturally) on him, one of his two delicious eyes, no matter which color, his majestically swaying tail, balancing his Lucky Bell—one of his white teeth—one single lump of "his last bark" on which his feet are set firmly, "to stay!" The truth is, he is (not almost unique) but unique—the last (or the first) of his race—one of his kind—a single specimen—alone—alone—alone—always alone—ever alone—in the midst of everything of the whole world—in other words, one of the wonders of the Earth—the eighth one. There is a story in which a great genie was to have set before him a task every day or he would kill his master—but if the master had asked him to make a ———? just like this one, it would have been impossible for him to do it—is it not so?? In fact, every time I look at him I am tempted not to believe my own eyes. In other words the English language will have twice ten thousand times as many word meanings as it has before I can say enough about him. In other words I never shall be able to say enough about him. ——— In other words, there is no use in my trying, and you will have to believe what I think, not what I write or say.

I have been with my friend Libby Crawford and her parents down at Madison on the sea, for Saturday and Sunday. We went in bathing twice and had a gorgeous time.

> With love,
> B. N. F. *[also signed with Farksoo initials.]*

Signe was Sabra's nanny.

176 Armory Street
New Haven, Connecticut
June 17, 1925

Dear Rosalind and Bruce:

I cannot tell you how glad I was to have the little bathing-suit for Sabra. It fits her exactly, and is as cute as can be. Sabra likes it, too, and is very anxious to have it on, and is anticipating the time when she is going "Fibbur" (swimming) in the "Gake" (lake) with her "Baiyee-poup," (bathing-suit), for I have told her all about Sunapee, the white boat, the ride in the car, and the little brown house, and the lake, and the sand, and the swimming and paddling. And Sabra, on her part, has listened with the greatest attention, and I think that she understands a good part of what I say, even though I cannot circle around a few words that she doesn't know. Anyhow, she goes around and tells everybody in the house all about it, and I'm the only one that understands her. For instance, I heard her say to Signe in the kitchen: "Mumma—Barboo, Faywee, Daddy—ri bote—Barboo Daddy payee——pick fowah—gowee awter." Which means that Mumma, Barboo, Sabra, and Daddy are going for a ride in the boat with Daddy and Barboo paddling, and that we are going to pick flowers that are growing in the water. You see, she is now getting up some fairly long sentences!

But of course, her anticipation is nothing compared with mine. I've been keeping count of the Sundays from the time Mother said that we should be going in about eight weeks. It has now dwindled down to about three. But—for Bruce especially:

But—it seems as if, however easily I can wait for eight weeks—yes, that seems bearable—but three weeks is different—it seems as if I can never stand three weeks or two weeks—less still, one week.

However, I am having a lot of things take up this week, and the next, but I'm sure that I shall entirely explode when the next comes. Do tell me about the trip, how the baby liked it, and what happened.

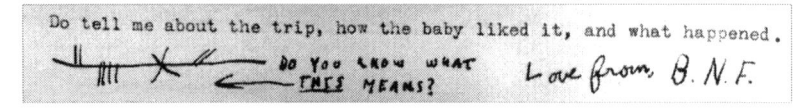

> Do tell me about the trip, how the baby liked it, and what happened.
> ⫽⫽⫽ ✗ ⟵ DO YOU KNOW WHAT THIS MEANS? Love from, B. N. F.

176 Armory Street
New Haven, Connecticut
June 21, 1925

My dear Mr. St. John:

Mother has written to you that I may come on Wednesday—but things have turned out so that I cannot come until Thursday, because Mother and Daddy are going on a trip in our new old Pierce Arrow, and are not coming back until Wednesday late in the afternoon. This is the latest of course, and they may be home Tuesday, but I cannot say, and had better not. So we will make it Thursday—and know that I have received your invitation with the greatest of pleasure, and am greatly anticipating the trip.

Sabra is watching me curiously, perched on my couch in my study, looking meanwhile at the little book of birds you gave me, and constantly telling me that she wants to go outdoors in the carriage with me, to mail the letter, and that she wants me to hold her up to the letter-box so that she can open it, and have me put the letter in. This she loves to do.

So I will close, thanking you again for your kind invitation, and expecting you with the greatest of pleasure.

>With a great deal of love from your true friend,
>Barbara.

176 Armory Street
New Haven, Connecticut
July 3, 1925

My dear Mr. St. John:

I'm writing to thank you for my most delightful and charming visit with you, and to tell you over and over what a lovely time I had (though you know it already). However, I can't thank you enough times, nor say by half what I felt like, in such sublime happiness.

But bread-and-butter letters are the most horrible things I know of—so stiff and formal, so I am going to change the subject at once. My little poppy plants are budding—I have four nasturtiums—except that I picked one—my pansies, cosmos, and morning glory are doing well. A few days ago I saw a tiny ruby-throated—bee! alight on my nasturtiums and then soar away again. I am expecting him again. I remember what you told me—the fact that the pollen is hidden in that long tube which only the hummingbirds with their long bills can reach.

It is now a matter of days before we go to Sunapee—and I am on tiptoe—of course.

I am anticipating my native element, the cool fresh lake, the pine grove where the nymphs and fairies dance, where the little elves hide among the needles. I am anticipating the riddance of the things that cling to my feet and legs like glue—shoes and stockings. I am anticipating the quiet and the peace of the woodlands—and above all I am anticipating so that I am thrilled through and through again and again those long quiet walks in the woods all alone at dawn. I shall see my native things, breathe my native air, dance and play with the fairies, and touch my feet to my native ground.

       With much love,
       Barbara.

176 Armory Street
New Haven, Connecticut
July 7, 1925

My dearest Mr. Oberg:

It is really shameful the way I have not written to you. Indeed I doubt that you have received a letter from me since you sent me the most beautiful mystery pup of Tut??? whatever it is.

We expect to be going to Sunapee Friday, and so we have already begun the exciting process of packing—already one trunk has been sent up there by means of express, so I feel that the time is really making progress, however slow it seems. Daddy is to return from New York Thursday evening, though he may not be able to make it. If he doesn't, however, the trip will have to be postponed till Saturday, and maybe Monday, because it is hard to travel Saturday or Sunday on account of the traffic.

Of course I am anticipating very very greatly our arrival there. They will not get to the cottage before I have stripped myself, put on my bathing costume, and swum and dived under water some distance. They may hear far away splashings when they get to the cottage, and they will see my little pile of clothes on the beach, but not even a shadow of myself. Oh, won't it be exciting?!

I have told little Sabra all about it in words that she understands, and so she is anticipating it all nearly as much as I am myself. The idea of putting on her tiny little bathing-suit and going swimming in the lake, has appealed to her ever since I have told her about it. And I know that she will be good in the car all day. She will probably sleep a good part of the way as she did last year and the year before last, and while she is awake I'm sure she will be happy and content. She has been for a ride in Daddy's new yet very old Pierce Arrow three times so far, and at such wide intervals that I know she will not be tired of it when the real time comes. She has loved it these three times, always hating to get out, and saying over and over "More ri car," (more ride car).

Well I will now close, only saying that if you are able to come up to New Hampshire for a few days we should be only too glad to see you.

  With love,
  B. N. F.

The Cottage in the Woods
New London, New Hampshire
July 18, 1925

My dearest Daddy:

The lake is still very high—it seems to me that it will never quite get ahead of the rains—for, you know, there have just been two big rains here, of the middle-size—just the size to keep back the progress of the lake, and for two days the lake has made no headway at all. These rains have brought lots of nice things, all the same. To begin with, there are lots and lots of mushroom and bright fungi around in the woods—also lots of Indian pipes. I do love those odd little things. If I look around on the leaves it does not take long to descry a clump of those waxen white flower-fungi—for that is what they are. I am beginning to learn where they are in the most abundance, so that when you come I can show them to you right off. There is quite a cluster of clumps near the path and very near the cottage, as yet unmarred by the blackness which they begin to show before long. And I am learning where they are for another reason—the fact that I hope with your help to make a fairy ring of them in my bower—bordered outside with lady ferns. It would be very pretty, I think.

There is a little chipmunk around here. I think he has a hole somewhere near, and so I have been feeding him and trying to make friends. I have put a lot of bread and crackers, etc., around, and I have watched him take a piece, sit up, and eat it in the most business-like manner.

THE COTTAGE IN THE WOODS (1923–1926)

I have begun collecting lizards again—the red ones. This wet weather has brought them out like everything. I have nine in the box now. They are great fun, and very pretty. I love the amusing way in which they walk, with the front leg—no, the hand, touching the leg of the same side. When you take one in your hand, they walk to the edge, and when you place your other hand in front of them, they hesitate a moment, as if puzzled that they have to begin all over again. Sabra likes them, too—and loves to have me hold her hand and let one crawl on it. I guess she likes the tickling feeling, for she laughs and says "Wuzheeds" (lizards).

The rain has made everything stand out so clearly. The moss and leaves are so green, the dead leaves are such a wet brown color. I really think it is more beautiful than when dry. Dainty dallabarda blossoms (I'm not sure about how to spell this) are peeping out from the brown leaves, pushing up their tiny white blossoms, and they look so fresh and dewy. And the white pines are so full of drops of silver water, all in between the needles—you know how lovely that is.

When you come, will you please bring the animal book—the Geographic animal book—that is, if you are stopping at the house on your way up. You will find it next or nearly next to the Holland Moth and Butterfly Books on the left hand side of the lowest shelf on the left hand side of the bookcase.

    With love from
    Barbara

P. S. I am longing to see you. Nothing ever happens unless you're here. I haven't been out to the raft since you've been here. I miss you dreadfully. B. N. F.

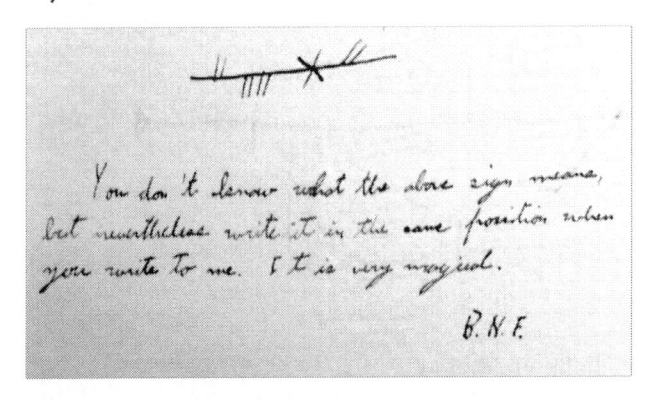

You don't know what the above sign means, but nevertheless write it in the same fashion when you write to me. It is very magical.

    B. N. F.

[On the reverse of the above]

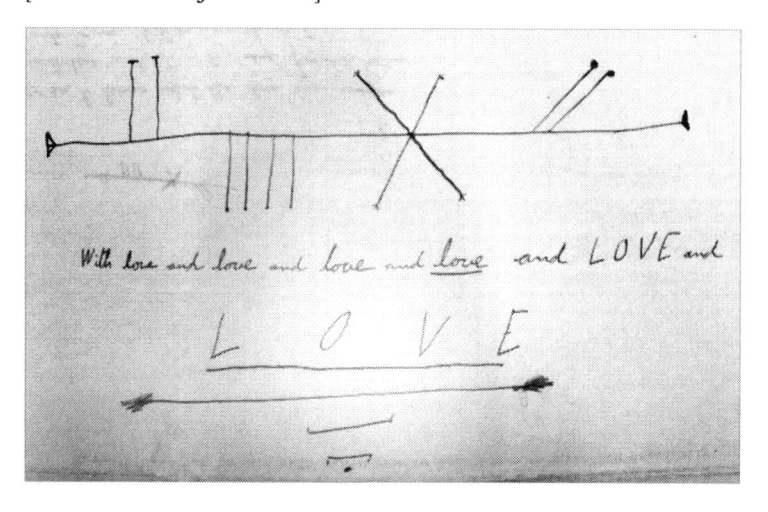

The American historian George Sands Bryan (1879-1943) and his wife, Alice, rented a cottage on the other side of Little Lake Sunapee. Mr. Bryan gladly played Captain Hook to Barbara's Peter Pan (while Alice became Hook's right-hand man, Smee). Later he chaperoned Barbara on her voyage to Nova Scotia on the Frederick H.

20 July, 1925
(Monday night)

Dearest Barbara:

I like your new sign very much—almost as much as the scent of balsam with which your letter is saturated. Not that I know what it means (the sign, that is: I know what the balsam means, all right). But I expect I shall know some day; and, anyway, it is very clear that it's pure magic.

Give my love to the lizards. I looked hard for them when I went up the lane and through the pasture, but without finding any. I knew *you'd* find them—and so you did!

I'm surprised at the rain, for there's been none here to amount to much—nothing but sudden, short showers. It was Wednesday that I left you. I drove down to Keene, and then over to Peterboro (that's near Monadnock, a glorious old hump of a mountain), and then down to Winchendon and Greenfield, where I slept Wednesday night at the Sprague farm. That was a beautiful day. Thursday I drove along home, the usual route; and it rained about fifteen minutes near the end of the run—hardly enough to start the windshield cleaner going. That night, Thursday, I slept at Armory Street; and just before I went to bed there was a terrific downpour—so hard that the copper gutters along the eaves couldn't carry it off, and it simply poured over the edges of them in a sheet, like a waterfall. But that lasted only five or ten minutes; and there's been no rain since—though this morning there was, for an hour, so thick a fog that one could see only a few yards on Fifth Avenue. The weather here is beastly hot and muggy, with about one comfortable day in four. To-night, as I sit here writing in the hotel room, I am damp and clammy all over.

Yes, I will bring you the book—that is, if I can find it, and I can if it is where you say. And I wish that may be soon; for of all the dismal and forsaken experiences in this world, staying alone in New York City in the summer time, with one's family in the woods, is about the worst. And when the family consists of members so completely nice and lovable as you and Mother and the Brat, why, it adds the finishing touch to one's desolation.... Tell Mother that I expected, on Sunday, to hunt up some old friends of mine on Long Island, the Burgins, but actually had to spend the day telephoning, waiting for the Public Library to open, reading some stories, and doing business with California by telegram.

I want a swim! I think I want any old kind of swim as fully as much as you want to get out to the raft—which I should think you might well enough do, with Raymond there and Mother to row the boat. But I shall have only the bathtub, for some days yet.

Don't forget to paddle your violin and your music and your stand over to the Bryans' once in a while, on days when there isn't too much wind.

This is all I have time for to-night, if this is to catch the last collection.

> Always with lakes and oceans of love,
> Daddy

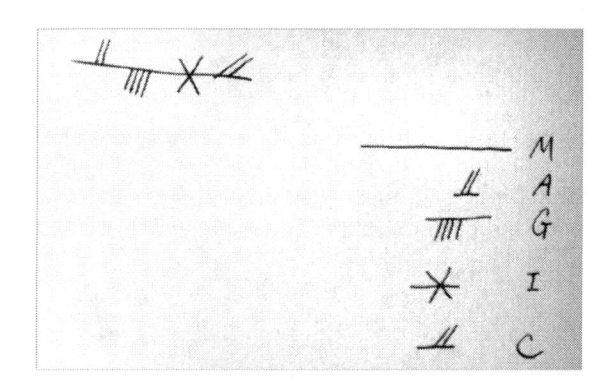

To One Styling Himself PETER PAN:

You must have One Thousand Dollars ($1,000) *in gold* deposited at the foot of the pine tree at the spot known as your Pine House, not later than 11:30 o'clock p.m., E. S. T., on Saturday, July 25th, 1925.

This is final!

        James Hook
        Captain of the Avenging Angels

The Cottage in the Woods
Lake Sunapee, New Hampshire
September 4, 1925

Dear Mr. Showerman:

Whenever I look at my beautiful little lake and I study the wooded shoreline, I know more and more that its image will never fade from my mind: the two high hills directly across, the dark pine grove at their feet, our pine peninsula of white pines with the birches and maple saplings around the edge; the long needle-point, with its high banks and ridge of glossy yellow pines, and the little Island-Peninsula, with the scarlet maple on the very tip. And I must not forget the picturesqueness of the Turtle Rocks, rock after rock, and the big Lone Rock on the outside, growing taller and taller every day, waiting patiently for his Brother Turtle Rock to rise by his side. One by one the rocks appear, and slowly they rise as if by magic.

And it is heavenly on a dark starry night to see the stars quietly trembling in the depths of the mermaid-haunted lake. The fairies dance on the surface of the lake when it is calm and quiet, ring after ring of them, one ring within another. The water-nymphs are on the outside, then the nymphs of the pine grove, next the water-fairies. Then comes a ring of small fairies of all descriptions, alternating with elves; next the tiny gnomes and pigmies, and, last of all a ring of night-butterfly-fairies, night-bee-fairies, gold dragonfly-backs and silver. And when no one is looking, a beautiful rainbow appears suddenly in the sky and the fairy angels in white robes with gold girdles, crowns of water-jewels, and golden-brown hair with drops of dew standing in it come tripping down. Soon follow the pine grove nymphs who have been to the rainbow treasury to replenish their rainbow garb. And after them come floating the winged fairies with green wings, one in silver and the other in gold, carrying between them a gigantic key, of quartz and brown stone, with bits of gold and beryl and mica. They are the rainbow treasurers, and they bear the key to the rainbow treasury. The fairies scatter and dance; gliding fairies shoot overhead like shooting stars, or water-gliding-fairies like water-shooting-stars. Night-air-fairies and night-air-queens dance overhead. The pine grove is lit with flashing lights. The same sort of thing is going on there, too.

This is a pretty complete tableau of the night-fairy scene. In the daytime they have to be more discreet, because human folk are about then. They have to disguise themselves. If you look carefully at the sunpath in the water, you will see numberless separate sparkles, which really are water-fairies dancing. The same with the moonpath sometimes. Butterfly-fairies and bee-fairies and gold and silver dragonfly-backs, and tiny winged fairies of the same sort are abroad then. Occasionally an impatient fairy glides across the air. Air fairies are everywhere you don't look, and common winged fairies dance everywhere. Breeze and wind and cloud and mist fairies, of course, are usually invisible, but they are there just the same. Nymphs, Dawn and Sunset, are queens of masses of innumerable fairies of blending dresses—tiny specks of color that, at dawn and sunset, gather together and help to constitute the magical colors seen at those times.

When you look closely into the heart of a flower, you will almost always find a fairy. The fairy of the gladiola is the most beautiful. Her dress is the shape of a petal and the color of her blossom. Her hair is in golden curls and crowned with green water-drops and dew, set alternately. A tiny, tiny creature, standing upright against the upper wall of the flower, or sitting on the edge of the lip, swinging her tiny bare legs. There is a dainty fairy for the lady-slipper, and a mischievous little elf for the Jack-in-the-Pulpit. So you see, wherever you look, you are sure to find fairies, and every kind thing you do will help and encourage them.

   With love,

Mt. Moosilauke's Summit House (a.k.a. Tip-Top House)—an old (1860) stone hotel that was given to Dartmouth College in 1920—burned down in 1942, but the mountain is still there and it's a lovely climb. Twenty-one years after Barbara's ascent, my grandfather introduced the mountain to my mother, who liked it so much that she organized a school trip for her classmates.

Summit House
Moosilauke
October 2, 1925

Dear Ding:

I am now sitting in the kitchen writing on the pine-covered table in the Summit House of Mt. Moosilauke. It is thick mist, and you can hardly see. The wind is howling and wailing, and I am still hoping that it will blow a hole in the mist, so that it will come off clear tomorrow. The day started beautifully with a clear blue sky, but one by one little white clouds came up, and they grew thicker and thicker, until now, as I said before, you can hardly see.

The Beaver Brook trail, which we came up, is a work of art. It comes up for a long way in a deep gorge with steep rocky walls, and tumbling down from rock to rock splashing and foaming, cascading from one rock and leaping down over another is Beaver Brook. The trail goes right alongside of it until you begin to climb out of the gorge. Every few yards you get magnificent views of it, up, up, up, at a waterfall which seems to come from the sky itself, or down, down, down, where it swirls and rushes on.

The trail is very difficult, and you have to climb on all fours for interminable stretches, but it's great, great fun.

The view must be something wonderful, only you can't see a vestige of it. But Daddy and I are going to stay up here several days, and we hope to have at least one clear day.

Mother and Daddy came up here and spent a night only a few days ago. Mother enjoyed it tremendously, and it seems to have done her a lot of good.

   With love,
   B. N. F.

Little Brown Cottage
Lake Sunapee, New Hampshire
October 7, 1925

Dear Mr. Showerman:

I can't tell you how I love your little gift. I love it for three reasons, besides the delightfulness of receiving it as I come back from a mountain trip with Daddy, which I will tell you later. Firstly, I love little trinkets of all kinds, especially to wear around my neck; secondly, because it came from you; and lastly, and the greatest reason of all, because Joan of Arc is my special heroine. I wonder if you knew this—if I told you during your visit last winter; or if you picked it up by guess-work when you went to Doremy? But this is nothing. I love it, and I can't express my feelings to you in written words.

But now for the mountain trip. We started sharp after an early luncheon on October 1. We drove along towards North Woodstock, and it was quite dark when we got there. I was terribly tired and half-asleep on the back seat. We spent the night at the Dartmouth Outing Club cabin on the Agassiz Basins, a series of pools formed by Moosilauke Brook, which flows just a few feet in back of the cabin. We were so tired that we almost fell asleep before supper.

The next morning we drove to Lost River, and gazed fascinated up the deep gorge up which we were about to climb. Up we went, first entering the woods of the Beaver Brook trail on fairly level ground, then rising steadily, until we were climbing up a steep, steep gorge with very hard rock climbing. We were in the same gorge with Beaver Brook, the mountain stream, which rushes down the gorge in tremendous forty-foot cascades, throwing jets of foam and dashing down in a pool, whirling round and round, and immediately down another terrific drop, and slithering down on the smooth rocks to another whirling basin.

Up and up and ever up we clambered with terrific views of the cascades with every few steps, and several times actually coming out on rocks where the brook dashes down, and crawling along in the passage of it a few feet. It was marvelous—simply marvelous. After a long time we gradually left the brook and climbed up the wall of the ravine and around the shoulder of Mount Jim, a rounded peak.

An interminable stretch of almost level ground followed, with the trees getting scrubbier and scrubbier and the temperature getting lower and lower. It seemed hours to me, because I was so tired. And when we got to the top, or near the top, we saw, to our great disappointment that we would soon be wrapped in mist. And it was true. When we were at the top, we could hardly see the Top House from the barn, which is just a little way below it.

I can't say much about the top, since we could only see a few feet, but, in spite of this, we had the feeling of solitude, of being above all the world, of being separated from everybody and everything.

We went into the Top House, stoked up a fire, went out and picked a few cranberries (I must not forget there is an extraordinary growth of luxuriant mountain cranberries on the summit of Moosilauke, and that these are wonderfully good when boiled up into sauce), brewed them up, and had a meal. We had no time with us, and so, when the sun was out of sight, we had no time at all. We ate when we felt hungry, got up when we felt like it, and went to bed on the same principle. It didn't clear all that day; we were in thick mist all the time.

It was still thick when we got up the next morning, and the morning was passed rather wearily. We wandered out to pick cranberries several times, and once we ventured down the saddleback between the north and south peaks a little way. We had glimpses once or twice late that afternoon, and a strong north-west wind came up, growing into a gale; and we thought it would blow a hole in the mist in no time. We were encouraged once or twice by glimpses of the moon, but it never really cleared.

The wind howled and whined all night. There was something awesome about the sound of it, something impossible to describe. All I can say is that if you whistle and hum at the same time, you will, on an insignificant scale, get something like the sound of it. It sounded from inside impossible to stand against (which was probably true).

The next morning we were disappointed. It was as thick as ever, yet the north-west wind was still raging outside. That afternoon we went along the saddleback as far as the Glencliff trail, which goes down the west side of the mountain; then we switched off on the trail up the south peak, and scrambled up. It was thick fog on top, of course, though occasionally we did get little glimpses of the Lower Benton Range to the west. Just as we were coming down the south peak we caught a fleeting glimpse of the north peak, a blue looming thing ahead. We couldn't see the whole outline, and we couldn't see it long enough to pick out the Top House, but we agreed that that one little view was worth the mile and a half walk in the wet mist.

But I must now tell you about the saddleback. It is covered with a fir forest, little stunted firs, two feet high and spreading out over a tremendous area, with thick gnarled trunks. Sometimes they are tall and thin like our trees of a normal climate—these are in sheltered places—but the majority for a long way is stunted and wide in area, sometimes being actually flattened down on the ground. It is a very interesting walk, even in thick weather, and we wandered down it several times, for the mere pleasure of being again among the little stunted trees.

That evening it cleared, so that we could see views of the mountains in several directions. It was so late then, however, that we could only see dark looming masses. The valleys were full of white clouds; we could see them gleaming, and in every direction there were strings of lights in the little town below. It made us feel so apart from everything, everything. It gave us the marvelous sensation of solitude—not until then had I known what solitude really means. The wind howled and moaned and whistled all night again with the same incredible, indescribable sound. And we were sure it would be clear next day.

And next day it was misty again, as thick as ever, and we would have to be going down the day after that anyhow, for our provisions were getting so low. I was grumpy for a good long time after that; it gave me such a shock to think of the likelihood of not one clear day out of all the time we were up there. But as we occasionally peeped out the door for any possible hope it seemed quite clear around the top, though the whole view, even the south peak, was clouded. And it began to snow, first thin wet miserable little flakes, and then bigger and nicer and drier ones, until all the rocks and the cranberries and the brown sedge-grass which covers the top were almost buried. It was so exciting that we ran out in the cold and frisked around happily. The wind went down a good deal. But toward the afternoon it was as thick as before.

There was only one remaining hope, a little time the next day before we started down; and I wasn't very hopeful. That afternoon two nice men came up to the house to spend the night and to go down the next morning. It was very pleasant to have them for companions, for on a mountain top a stranger is not a stranger, but becomes your friend immediately. It kept on snowing through the afternoon, turning to hard wet sleet. The wind rose until it was a gale again, and it howled and howled as before. Daddy and I walked down the saddleback a little way, to whet our appetites for a big supper, and what with the wind so strong that we could hardly make progress against it and the sharp cutting sleet on our faces, we had quite a struggle getting back.

I must not forget the animals we saw. Daddy saw about six cottontail rabbits, I saw none, but, as if to make up, I saw one little red lemming about four inches long. I thought he made up for the cottontails.

Sleet, sleet, sleet. Wind, wind, wind. Mist, mist, mist. And nothing else all night. Nice hot supper, and a tiny bit of hope for a sunrise early tomorrow morning. A little view. Shut in again.

The next morning Daddy poked his head out to see if there was going to be a sunrise, by any hook or crook. And actually the east was colored with a very faint purplish glow. We had breakfast. We went out. And there, surrounded by the radiance of their own fair beauty were the frost feathers. We were enchanted, as if in a dream. We pinched ourselves, opened our eyes wide, looked closer. No doubt about it. There they were, clinging to the great cairns outside the house, on the wire cables which support the house, on the house itself, even on the bare snow, on the grindstone, sawhouse and trail signs, everywhere, everywhere. On some of the stones on the west side of the house they were as much as ten inches long, and narrow. On stones on the east side of the house they were almost round and about an inch long. Some were less than an eighth of an inch long, and others over ten inches, and all shapes, though not varying from an unmistakable feather, and with delicate, delicate patterns traced all over them—oh! the mountain top was just paradise. There was one cairn with a hollow in one side of it, and this was all lined with frost feathers of different sizes, pointing different ways, like a little fairy palace. There is a D. O. C. trail sign sticking up from one of the big cairns on the north side of the house. This sign was symmetrically surrounded with middle-sized ones, and over the writing were little flat round scaly ones, just enough to cover the writing. And those at the corners of the sign were longer than those along the sides. There was one clump of stunted firs down a little way on the east of the house, which were covered with snow and icicles with the little feathers clinging all over it.

And I must not forget the sun and the weather. For all this time the sun had been pushing its way out of the mist and scattering it in all directions, and making it thinner and thinner. Now you could see faintly the outlines of the south peak, clearer and clearer, now thick again; then suddenly there came a great hole on the west, and the whole western view was before our eyes. First the low foothills of Moosilauke all red with the turning trees, and with the sun striking that maze of color a certain way which made it perfectly sublime, next the Lower Benton Range with the red colors not quite so red because the sun struck them differently, then range after range of high hills and mountains, the red fading away to russet and the russet blending with the deep blue of the Green Mountains on the horizon. It closed in again. We turned around. And lo and behold! the southeast and entire east was disclosed, with the bright foothills fading away to range after range of brilliant blue. It closed in for some time. And then each direction appeared to us, one at a time, the brilliant blue of the gorgeous mountains magnificently set off with [a] low bank of blue-white clouds lying just above the peaks. As gaps in the mist became more and more frequent, the sun became brighter and brighter, until the last of the mist went scudding—banished—away!

The frost feathers sparkled, the snow-laden trees sparkled, the mountains sparkled, the red trees sparkled, the fresh snow sparkled, the clouds sparkled, the whole air sparkled! And as we went around to the north side of the house, the whole of Franconia met our eyes. Osseo, Flume, Liberty, Haystack, Lincoln, and Lafayette, the last two capped with gleaming snow. Washington, as was to be imagined, was also capped; in fact, all of it that we could see was snowy white, and once, when the sun struck it full, it was too heavenly to be described in any words of mine.

We had to start down, to my great grief, but afterwards I reasoned out how nice it was to have our best day our last, and also that I should never have gotten over seeing the frost feathers melt. They were still at the top of their beauty when I left them.

With a feeling of regret we swung rapidly down through the first level stretches of Beaver Brook trail. Around the shoulder of Mount Jim, and thence down into the gorge with Beaver Brook. The little firs were all capped with snow and shining, some with not enough to cover the needles so that they were still sticking out all around the twigs, and others with the branches laden way down to the ground. We went through a forest of these heavenly snow-trees, with the frost feathers getting smaller and smaller, and more and more melted, until we were past Mount Jim and well along toward Beaver Brook. Then the snow and icicles left off, and we were entertained by a new thing—the ever-growing-nearer sound of the mighty cascades down the gorge.

And when we got down to the cascades we found them with almost twice as much water in them as when we went up, due to the melting snow on the mountain. The cascades were broader, there were new side trickles around rocks, the pools and basins were full to the brim, the waterfalls threw up fountains when they struck the rocks below (something which they did not do when we went up), and the whole thing roared much louder and was bigger in every way.

The thought of our beautiful, beautiful trip urged us on, as we climbed down the fifteen or twenty spruce ladders, walked cautiously over a slippery rock, or climbed down a particularly rough and steep bit of ground. There really isn't much more to say about the trip. The ride home was nothing unusual, except for the marvelous glimpses of the Franconia Range and other mountains, and also the hills near the road with the red, red trees on them.

So I will now say goodbye, thanking you again for the little gift, and hoping to see you again soon.

We intend to go down Tuesday this week. Shall you be in New Haven this winter, for I want to see you and tell you trifling details of my trip, which I cannot easily write on paper.

   With love,
   Barbara.

Tree-turning Time.
NEVERLAND.

Greetings, CAPTAIN HOOK:

Last night I woke suddenly to find it daylight, though I knew that it was TWELVE O'CLOCK at night. The sky was rather dark, and flecked with white spider-web clouds. Toward the NORTH, and directly over your PINE GROVE was a long cloud of a sunset rose.

On one end of it was a golden splotch, and it was all bordered with flecks of a robin's egg blue, but ever changing. Sometimes they were moonstone blue-grey, with a silver light which seemed to be moving about gently inside; sometimes of a liquid green with a gold light, sky blue, emerald green, ruby red, or like diamonds, or pearls; sometimes the pink of the cloud, and once snow-white with a constantly moving red fleck. Drops of liquid gold seemed to be falling from the sky, and each time the beads changed three green and white stones fell into the lake.

Suddenly the whole sky seemed to be on fire with sunset colours; the cloud was completely swallowed up, and the only thing that stood out were the now snow-white beads, which seemed to be stained with a sunset shade. The fire cleared away, the cloud was now dark blue, and the beads did not change again. Three golden arrows came flying and hit three of the beads, making a gap in the necklace, and through the gap came flying a butterfly.

Such a butterfly! I can give you only a very faint idea of how divine it was. It had six wings, the two upper pairs small, and the third pair like the lower wings of a luna moth. The upper pair was orange, and the delicate wings looked as though they had frost on them. The second pair was a liquid sea-green. And the last pair was snow-white and misty. The body was slim and black, and reached even below the last pair of wings. It was forked with silver and gold. The antennae were long and curved outward, and then way [went?] in gracefully, and they were tipped with tiny golden balls. Its eyes were two tiny red specks.

It flew majestically from bead to bead, alighting on each, and when it had gone clear round it went out the way it had come. Suddenly, by the gap, the necklace straightened out, and fell slowly, until it caught on the top of your pine grove, where, some time afterwards, I saw it hanging. This morning it was gone.

I think I can guess what it all means, but I want to see you and know your opinion on it.

    Salamus Cara.
    PETER PAN. *A S T H A V E C K I A*

Brookfield Center, Conn.,
xxiii October 1925

To Captain Peter Pan:
Right Worthy Captain and Sir:
 On Monday morning, xix October 1925, the stores previously mentioned and to us known were placed, with suitable protection,

at the base of the twin-spruce selected by you.

On the same xix October the certain secret lettering previously mentioned and to us known was visited and examined in accordance with your instructions.

I supply with this report a map-memorandum indicating the location of the treasure; also a sketch showing as accurate as possible the exact appearance of the lettering when examined.

You may also care to know that on the day preceding, xviii October, Smee, A. B., and myself made the circuit of our lake by canoe; the weather then being like that of mid-September.

    Respectfully,
    Jas. Hook
    Capt.

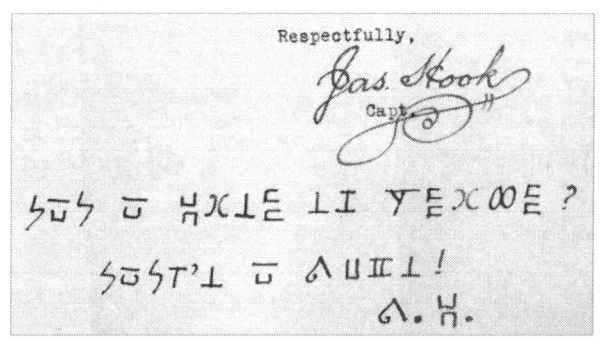

176 Armory Street
New Haven, Connecticut
25 October, 1925

Dear Mr. Oberg:

I am sorry I haven't written to you for such a long time. I have been planning to ever since we came home, but, you know, there is a great deal to do on getting settled again, and I have been very busy—so busy, in fact, that I have just barely had time to get in my practicing, see one or two of my friends, do my lessons, play a little and eat and sleep—all of which are very necessary as you will soon find if you try and omit one of them.

We have now been back since October 13, and it does seem rather nice to see all old my treasures again. One of my old treasures was as glad to see me as I was to see her.

I feel as if I couldn't—absolutely couldn't—wait until my birthday to see you, so I am going to propose your coming here for Thanksgiving week, coming Monday, and staying at least over the weekend. I am wild to see you for several reasons: the main one is to tell you about the many things that I have done this summer. The greatest thing I did was to take a gorgeous mountain trip with Daddy. We were gone about six days and we were in thick, monotonous, wet, disagreeable clouds for most of those days, but the story of it all takes several hours of patient narrating, nevertheless.

I know that you will be simply crazy about Sabra. She is too adorable for words. But if I should try to describe her to you, it would be wasted energy, for she is too beautiful to be described. I will say nothing about her at all, except that she is very fond of "Iting letters, ike Barboo," to various people that she has heard us talking about. I am enclosing one that she wrote some time ago to "Missha Oberg."

I do hope that you can come for Thanksgiving.

      With love,
      B. N. F.

176 Armory Street
New Haven, Connecticut
November 17, 1925

My very dear Mr. St. John:

I've got so much to tell you that I simply don't know where to begin. I took a gorgeous mountain trip this summer with Daddy, but, since that is the most important of these many things, I will save it till last.

Referring to your letter I find that you and Mrs. St. John have both been sick, and that you have been struggling hard with too much work and too little vacation. I am very sorry to hear these three things, partly because I was so very sorry not to see you this summer. In fact, I can't begin to tell you how much I missed you, and how anxiously I watched for you during August and early September. But I am very glad to hear of your new summer residence, and wish with you that I could be there with you to plan it.

Now follow answers to a few little questions asked in your last letter:

1. You *did* send me my pictures in the canoe (thank you very much for both those and the ones you sent in the letter).

2. I have recently been doing nothing very spectacular in the way of writing. I wrote a rather pleasant short story this summer, and the enclosed poem, written the day after seeing a uniquely splendid meteor. I am still keeping up my account of Sabra, and my account of the imaginary land.

3. I do not think that you ever sent the book on Story-Telling. I should like very much to see it.

4. We certainly did have a good time in Rivernook, in fact, I don't think I ever had such a good time with you anywhere.

You should really see my beloved little sister, Sabra. She is too beautiful, too adorable to describe. In fact I shall not attempt to describe her (trusting to luck that you will see her soon), except that she has lovely brown eyes, sixteen tiny pearl teeth, which shine delightfully when she smiles, straight brown hair, with faint, faint hints of reddish-gold, cut in bangs, and *very* bright red cheeks. She is running everywhere, taking long walks, and talking incessantly, to herself, to her four dilapidated dolls, and to everybody else in the world.

Sabra, of course, was crazy about Sunapee. She loved the beach with the nice warm sand, the woods where she went to pick leaves, and the sunny pine grove, where she went to play every morning. But above all these things she loved the water. She would go in bathing up to her neck, and splash and splash. She would hold her nose and dip her face under. She would vigorously work her legs and arms when you held her up under the stomach.

In my last letter to you I believe I asked you about the strange birds that I saw. I found out that they were Pileated Woodpeckers, but this knowledge was promptly replaced by another mystery. One of my friends at Lake Sunapee found in his garage a very strange lizard. It must have been about eight inches long, and about as big in proportion as are the little red ones. He had evil, beady eyes; he was black or very dark green, and was splotched all over with yellow spots of irregular shapes and sizes. If you know anything about lizards you could probably give me a little information.

And now for the mountain trip! Daddy and I climbed Moosilauke and spent several days on top in the Summit House. We started soon after dinner on October 1, and reached the Dartmouth Outing Club cabin near Lost River some time after dark. We spent the night there, right a few feet from some large, rushing brook, with that wonderful sound in our ears all night. I found a marvelous stone the next morning in the bed of this brook, which I will show you if you come here soon.

The next morning we were off for the Beaver Brook Trail. Oh, what a splendid trail, what a splendid brook and what cascades! They seem to come from the sky itself. Every few yards you have a view way, way up, where a big cataract comes pouring over a shelf, a drop of maybe fifty feet, hitting the rocks below and throwing up a fountain of spray, then whirling round and round in a basin, winding off around an outjutting rock, cautiously edging along a shelf as if afraid, and then down, down another drop, and another basin and another drop, way, way below! The trail is very difficult. It is steep and rocky and there are spruce ladders every little way. And sprawling over rocks and climbing up steep smooth places with nothing but roots to hold on to is very tiresome. But the thrill of the marvelous cascades made me forget everything but to hurry on to the next. In fact, I never realized how tired I was until I left the brook.

When we had started it had been perfectly clear, but when we reached the end of the gorge, and turned to say goodbye to Beaver Brook—lo and behold! little white clouds came sailing in, the Franconias looked far away and hazy, the peak of Lafayette was enveloped in mist. We pushed on around Mount Jim and by the time we had reached our first view of Jobildunk Ravine—well, there just wasn't any Jobildunk to be seen, nor any north peak looming up. In fact, there wasn't anything at all except a few feet of slippery wet trail ahead! And it grew steadily thicker and thicker, until, when we reached the barn, we could positively not so much as make out the dimmest outlines of the house, which is only a few yards above.

We were in thick mist for four days. After the first night a strong west gale came up, which we thought would blow away the mist in no time. But it didn't! There seemed to be an endless chain of mist, and we grew greatly discouraged at the thought of not seeing much of anything all the days we were up there.

Oh, the sound of the wind. There is nothing like it, nothing so magical in the world. And especially on a mountain top, where everything is so desolate and weird anyhow. The sound it awed my imagination, and silenced it. I can only say feebly that if you whistle and hum at the same time, you will, on an insignificant scale, get the sound of it ringing in your ears. We would sit in silence in the old Winter Room for long periods without saying a word, just listening.

Day after day of mist followed with only two small holes. One was when we took a hike over to the south peak and had a short glimpse to the north and south, and that evening after dark. We went out and saw the dark masses of looming mountains on all sides, and the little twinkling lights of the doll-towns below.

We had to go down Tuesday we decided (we had started Thursday), and that meant that if it didn't clear pretty soon we would have to miss the one clear day that we had hoped for. Monday it snowed, turning towards night into sleet. The wind was high. It was as thick as ever. We were pretty discouraged.

Here are the animals and birds we saw. Juncos, and plenty of them. Daddy saw about six cottontails, and I saw one little tiny red lemming, which ran out on the rocks and sat up, then scuttled away again.

Early Tuesday morning there was a faint purplish glow, oh! very faint, over the eastern horizon. The snow gleamed with a purity that it had not had the day before, and, smiling in the midst of their beauty, were—frost feathers!

Frost feathers! the magic name! They were all over everything, the rocks, woodpile, cairns, grindstone, trail signs, wire cables, house. They ranged from ten inches to so tiny as could hardly be seen. And these tiny ones were no less perfect than the larger ones. Have you ever seen them?

I can say no more about them for the reason that my vocabulary utterly fails me. You have probably seen them, so you can share my feelings. They are the very top notch, frankly, of beautiful things that I have ever seen, or ever expect to see, in this world.

>With much love,
>Barbara.

For Christmas 1925 Barbara composed Noël, *a song for her friends and family. Marjorie Potter, a librarian in Albany, New York, forwarded her card to the Knickerbocker Press, which published it around Christmastime.*

>Noël
>
>Il faut traverser le pays,
> En cette nuit sacrée,
>Pour se trouver—dans l'étable
> Où Jésus-Christ né.
>
>De l'est ils viennent, les mages,
> Vers l'étoile argentée.
>Ils offrent de tendres prières
> A l'Enfant adoré.
>
>Les bergers laissent leurs troupeaux,
> Ils suivent la clarté,
>Cherchant la crèche de Jésus,
> Pour faire des souhaits.
>
>"O Jésus, Dieu te bénisse!
> Accepte nos présents."
>Il sourit des bras de Marie—
> Oh! le divin Enfant!
>
>Words and melody by Barbara Newhall Follett
>who sends this Noël for Christmas Greeting
>MCMXXV

Noël traduit
We must traverse the land
　　On this holy night,
That we may find ourselves in the stable
　　Where Jesus Christ is born.

From the East they come, the magi,
　　Toward the silver star.
They offer tender prayers to Him,
　　To the Child adored.

The shepherds leave their flocks
　　They follow the light,
Seeking the manger of Jesus,
　　To make wishes.

"O Jesus, God blesseth thee!
　　Accept our gifts."
He smileth in the arms of Mary—
　　Oh! the divine Infant.

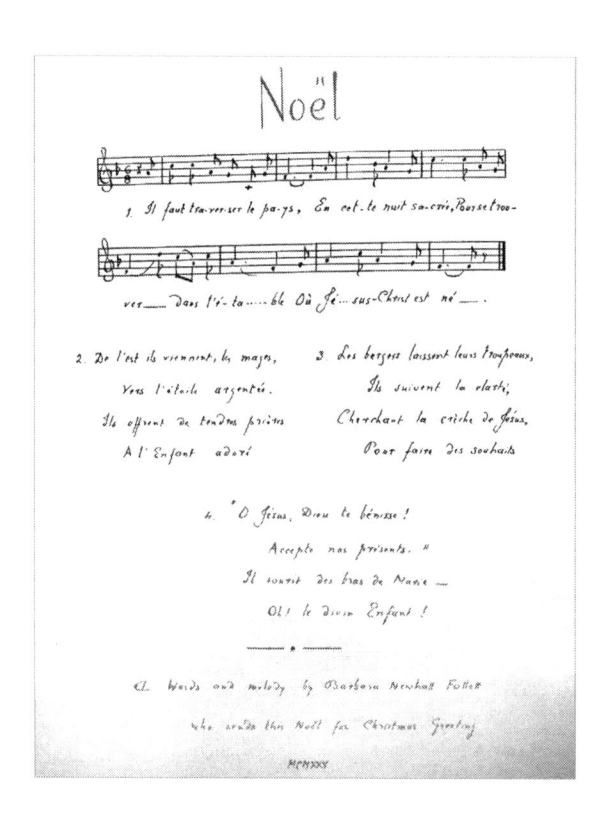

176 Armory Street
New Haven, Connecticut
December 30, 1925

Dear Lefty:

I can't begin to thank you enough for your gift of the gorgeous book with the fascinating illustrations. It is like a map of Fairyland which I have pinned on my wall, a map in which one is always discovering something new and exciting.

My family and my friends are as excited about it as I am, and are all eager to find out what the marvelous pictures are about. It has added immensely to the merriment and happiness of my Christmas.

I have begun translating already, and, though it is harder than anything I have had, the pictures are so wonderful that I am crazy, and everybody else is, too, to see what they mean.

And I mustn't forget to say that Sabra's kitty-muff is still a supreme success to her and to all of us.

        With love,
        Barbara.

Hill House
Taplow, Buckinghamshire
6th January 1926.

My dear Barbara,

This is only just to wish you and your Father and Mother a very, very happy New Year, even though it will not reach you until that New Year is well out of its cradle.

Is there any chance of your coming to England this year? That would be something to look forward to for us all.

I shall treasure your "Noel."

        Yours _____ *[indecipherable word]*
        Walter de la Mare

176 Armory Street
New Haven, Connecticut
January 7, 1926

Dear Mrs. Day:

I cannot thank you enough for your wonderful gift—more wonderful to me than anything one could possibly do to give me a thrill that will last my lifetime. To hear those beautiful mellow bells ringing out my own little tune made me feel as if I were in a dream—a beautiful, beautiful dream.

You would certainly have heard from me sooner, except that I thought I should see you soon, and be able to give you a better idea of what you have really done for me, than I possibly could by writing. Soon after Christmas we started out to see you, but out-of-town friends came just then, and we could not leave them. Even then, writing seemed inadequate; but, when we called yesterday and found you out, I decided I *must* write.

When may I see you and thank you again, and try to give you some faint conception of what you have done for me?

       Love,
       Barbara.

176 Armory Street
New Haven, Connecticut
January 10, 1926

My dear Mr. Oberg:

Your box was welcomed with joy, for it is always *the* event of the great day. And its contents were specially enjoyed by all of us. I suppose the odd and beautiful brush has been passed down in your family, or has a strange history of some kind. I would be greatly interested to know about it. At any rate, the box was enjoyed, for it is so customary now that Christmas really would not be itself without it. I was just wild about the little salt-and-pepper shakers, and I shall use them when I have my little house. (We love your way of packing things, because the stuffing is edible afterwards!). In short, the box was a great success.

Sabra knew some time before Christmas just what she was going to do. And when Christmas Eve really came, after days of busy preparations, but nevertheless tedious waiting, she was beside herself with delight when I really got a hammer and nail and hung up her stocking and mine under the mantlepiece! And Christmas morning, you can imagine the inexpressible delight with which each tiny package was carefully opened and its contents exposed and experimented with. And the Tree! That was the greatest event of all, for we skipped in, hand in hand, and danced up to it. And the first thing Sabra saw when she went in, was not the Tree at all, but: "Oh, *look at that little dolly* for me to have!" (But it wasn't little at all.) And she's had a beautiful time with that dolly ever since.

I don't think I ever had such beautiful, beautiful presents. And Sabra hopping around and asking to see everything and to have her new dresses and sweaters tried on made it all the merrier. For, you see, last Christmas she was really too young to enjoy it all, and the Christmas before that—well, there wasn't enough of her to call Sabra Wyman Follett.

The pictures were very good—at least, most of them, and one or two of the close-to ones were fine. Please tell me whether some of them were those that were taken with my camera, for, until you tell me, I still don't know whether it's working or not.

The monograms were very pleasing—I thought the best B.N.F. was the thick, heavy one. You know what I mean, don't you? I think I shall use it for my monogram, and I think it is very clever—graceful and handsome, too. Thank you *so* much for taking the time and patience to make them for me, for I daresay it is very nervous work.

And thank you again for the box and its content.

    Love,
    Barbara.

P. S. How are the butterflies getting on? I will send you some birds and animals when you let me know. B.N.F.

The new museum Barbara visited was Yale's Peabody Museum of Natural History. Its Great Hall was dedicated in December 1925.

176 Armory Street
New Haven, Connecticut
February 24, 1926

Dear Mr. St. John:

Don't think for a minute that, simply because you haven't heard from me, that I have forgotten you. No indeed, I have often wished that I might find time enough to write a letter of proper length. And even now, I am afraid that this one is not going to tell you one half of what I might say about yours.

To begin with, I took a snowshoe walk with Mother up to East Rock on February fifth, I think. We had a beautiful time. We crossed a small bridge over Mill River, and began to ascend the winding automobile road up Whitney Peak, next to East Rock. The river, as we drew farther from it, grew smaller and smaller, until it was a curving thread of water winding and twisting. The sun striking it near the bridge turned it into a mass of gold, paling toward the edges, with wider and wider gaps between each separate sparkle, until there was nothing but gleaming blue. It must have been such a day as yours. The woods were all clear snow, unmarred by footsteps, and the snow-laden pines and hemlocks were set off against a sky of the most heavenly blue, darker than I have ever seen it before. If I never see the sky as lovely as it was then again, I shall remember it—how wonderfully it made me feel, standing there in the snow and gazing into its distant depths. You could see miles into it—it looked as though it had suddenly come nearer than usual. Today it is far-away blue.

We saw rabbit tracks and bird tracks, also tracks of small animals that might have been squirrels—but what puzzled me were some small tracks almost exactly like those of a rabbit, but much smaller than any rabbit track I have ever seen. And I saw one snow-story, though I can give only a rough interpretation of it. Coming out from a small tuft of grass was a double set of those squirrelish footprints, as if some little creature of the grass had run out a little way and then back again. Nearby were five parallel marks, the end ones smaller than the next ones, and those smaller than the middle one. Might it have been this way: the little animal came out from his hole in the grass, and ran back just as some bird of prey swooped, leaving the mark of the tip of his wing?

Telling twigs from their "signatures" sounds very interesting, but I've never heard about it. All I can say is that the twig of an apple-tree is often more gnarled than most others. I can tell several trees by their leaves or needles, but I am not well acquainted with bark, so I don't know the trees in the winter time. This summer I learned a lot about needles, and can tell, without anything but the needles, all of the common needle-trees around Sunapee: yew-bushes, hemlocks, balsams, spruces, and white and yellow pines.

I think the pines are the loveliest of all. There is both a grove of white pines and one of yellow pines at Sunapee, and it is hard to tell which is the loveliest. The whites have a more delicate, fairy-like effect, but the yellows are dark green, massive, glossy, and more splendid from a distance. Have you ever been in just the right kind of light to catch a certain spider-web effect of the sun on the needles? I have lain for long periods beneath the shimmering green boughs, watching those little sparkles gleam and quiver in the wind.

I have heard of Christmas roses, and seen them when they are not in flower, but never the blossoms.

You have told me about the deer-mouse tracks, and I can imagine what they look like, their feet are so dainty, and their tails dragging. I love the deer-mice. They are beautiful with their tan coats, white stomachs, pointed ears, and black, beady eyes. The summer before last I had a pet one which I named Heather, and kept [him] in a large, comfortable cage. I grew very fond of him, and, when I scratched on the side of the cage, he would come out. I had one last summer, also, named Snap-dragon. Both of them were very young when I caught them, and I watched them grow up, their coats gradually changing from that infant grey to the lovely tan of the adult.

I've never seen a collection of birds' eggs, but we have now a new museum in which there are many animals and birds in their natural surroundings, with many nests and eggs. I saw a red-winged blackbird's nest once at Rivernook—don't you remember? and I think that they have the loveliest eggs of any I have ever seen. I would rather not see all the eggs in a collection without the birds and nests, too. I like better to poke through the forest and find birds' nests. In the museum the stuffed birds and animals are set up so naturally that one doesn't think of the robbing of the nests, or even the death of their owners.

I wish you could come and see me *soon*, not next month, but next week, and we'd go and wander about in the interesting place which I have spoken of. There are other things there, too, which I shall leave for a surprise to you.

If you could only see my two-and-a-half-year-old! These snowy days she has actually learned how to ski on my little old skis! She sticks her feet in them, and without any assistance at all, goes walking by herself. Sometimes she gets them crossed and then you have to help her, but not much. She is adorable.

If you do get to Rivernook around Easter, we'll see about a happy meeting there.

I *do* like your poem, and have read it several times. I'm glad that you like mine.

   Love from
   Barbara.

Born in 1878 in West Hartford, Connecticut, Ethel May Kelley was a writer living in New York City. I've included only the first third of the letter since the rest covers familiar Moosilauke territory.

176 Armory Street
New Haven, Connecticut
March 15, 1926

Dear Ethel Kelley:

I am ever so sorry I haven't answered your letter sooner—but there is no time in the day, none at all. It seems as though I never have nothing to do, that is true, for in spare moments I have: reading, story, account of Sabra, history of Farksolia, the book of fairies that I have been trying for weeks to start, and have succeeded in doing nothing but the table of Contents! besides many other things that I cannot think of now. So you see it is only once in a while, what with my lessons and music, that I write letters at all.

But perhaps you won't know what all these things are. The "story" is my *Eepersip*. I wrote it when I was about nine—but it was burnt up in the fire at Woodbridge. I rewrote it, and I'm now revising it with Daddy—but—I can't tell you what it's about because—well, never mind! I will say it is about a little girl named Eepersip, and that it is in three parts—The Meadow, The Sea, and The Mountains. You'll know more about it later—*perhaps*.

The history of Farksolia is the account of my imaginary country—in fact, my imaginary *planet*. It is the history of the people who live there, the queens who ruled there, the flora that grow there—as well as a written map of continents, lakes, rivers, mountains, deserts, and cities. Things that I see—only little things perhaps—but things that I like specially—are organized in Farksolia somewhere or other. As a matter of fact, there is a Farksoo language, too, which is carefully preserved on cards in drawers—both Farksoo-English and English-Farksoo; I am adding words all the time. There are Farksolian letters, too, and sometimes I write mystic things, secret things, with them.

Thank you very much for the little picture. I love to have pictures of my friends. I am sending one of me with—? *[Walter de la Mare]*. It happened this way: when "he" was here last spring, someone wished to take his picture. But he refused to have this done without my standing with him—to "help him out" he said! *[...]*

With love,

Barbara with Walter de la Mare, spring 1925

THE COTTAGE IN THE WOODS (1923–1926)

176 Armory Street
New Haven, Connecticut
March 31, 1926

Dear Mr. Barbeau:

I am terribly sorry not to have written about the pictures. They are beautiful, every one, and I am ever so glad to have them to add to the collection already put away in my album. I like them specially because I hope to see the places myself some day.

But I want to tell you what has kept me busy these last weeks. It is the revision of my longest story—the one written when I was nine, burnt up in that fatal fire at Woodbridge, and rewritten, tearfully, to be sure, but, of course, *much* better. Now that same story is—on who knows what desk in Knopf's building in New York? And I'm so excited that I don't know what to do!

It is gorgeous to really see pussy-willows and hear birds and feel warmish weather again, isn't it? It delights me to watch the lessening time between now and July—the blessedest month of the year—the month which brings Lake Sunapee the pines, and the granite-topped mountains; things the thought of which keeps my ideas for stories and poems flowing right through the winter.

Thanking you again for the pictures—good-bye!

    With love,
    Barbara.

A note to Dorothy Lathrop from about March 1926.

Dear Dorothy:

I expect that the "manuscript," the carbon of Eepersip, has reached you and I am anxious to know what you think of it after all this time and so many changes. Do you still feel as you did that day in my study, when you said: "I want to draw Eepersip's fern dress"? I have not forgotten, and, now that the story is so *enormously* improved (I must confess it was rather silly, parts of it, when I read it to you) I hope that you will still be interested.

It is now in the hands of Knopf, waiting the great decision. I'm faint and weak from excitement, growing more so every day, and I expect a letter any time.

    With love,

The Columbia archive has only a few of Barbara's letters to George Bryan, and I've searched his archives at the New York Public Library only to find no mention of her. However, one learns much from Bryan's wonderful letters. He wrote the following while researching at the Library of Congress.

Washington, D. C.
April 6th [1926]

Dear Peter:

Don't you care whether or no your faithful Hookie still breathes the vital air? Well, he indeed breathes the air; but, somehow—doubtless through his defect of mind—it seems less vital than that of Sunapee or of New Haven.

There is little of MAGIC to report. I enter this Library in the morning; walk across the Sun and the Signs of the Zodiac (all of which are of brass, set in the floor—a little like a fairy circle); enter Deck 7 (a trace of MAGIC here); step into my automatic elevator; press a button marked 4; step out at Deck 4 (having risen three in the scale—really risen, though reversely—a touch of MAGIC in this three); then walk to the North Curtain. My table is 162; and if we analyze this, it is possible to have: $1 + 6 + 2 = 9$; $9 = 3 \times 3$—a somewhat magical formula. Also, the great book-stack is nine (9) stories (decks) high; and there again we have $3 \times 3 = 9$. There is something reassuringly nautical in being on a deck, even when in a library; it is not displeasing to the soul of an ex-pirate.

Last evening, as Smee and I were working away in our cubby-hole, astonishingly a messenger from the reading-room said: "Mr. Taft wishes to see you." Immediately Smee looked very alarmed. "Oh, my!" quoth she. "What have you been doing, Gee Ess?" You see, she thought I had been breaking some law or other, and that the Chief-Justice had come to talk to me personally about it. But he turned out to be another Taft—a man from Huntington, L. I., to whom I had written for photographs and who, being on a trip to Washington, brought the photographs right to my very table.

Please remember me to Ding and Sabra and H. T. and Signe and all. Don't be bothered at all about your fiddle (Firefly has told me you are—a little). Think of how lucky it is to get started right again so soon, with the help of those who care so much that they would rather help than flatter and who know that you already are wise enough to *wish* the truth. Think, too, of the years you have ahead, you young, young Peter! (That is quite a preachment for Jas. Hook—who, shiver his timbers, is better with a cutlass at close quarters!)

    Yours for all old times & new times,
    Hook

The letter included a coded message to Barbara, which she solved. It read:

Hail, Peter

Hook will do faithfully what his friend requests. But not through fear of the curses of any god or goddess. Hook does not heed curses. And deities that made a business of cursing us poor mortals perished long ago.

       James Hook
       Captain

Transcribed from a draft dated April 14, 1926 to Chauncey Brewster Tinker (1876-1963), Professor of English Literature at Yale.

Dear Professor Tinker:

I was immensely glad to hear your lecture yesterday because I adore Shelley myself: I mean, of course, his poems, for I happen to be one of your listeners who has never read a biography of him, but who has been reading his poems for several years. I have never been able, never known how to express what I think and feel about Shelley; and now you have quite wonderfully done it for me! I have always felt that he seems to rise into the sky—"and stop of there—." Yes, there is that feeling of swiftness, of song pouring onward and breaking into flight—of "strange voyages."

When you read the poem from *Prometheus Unbound* (which I now want to read) I liked it better every time. At first it seemed a little vague; the second time I tried to follow the three changes of mood—and now I see that many of his poems are that way—and the last time it became clear to me—I grasped its magic, hidden meaning. As soon as I reached home I read it again.

The first poem of Shelley I ever read was *The Isle*. I don't remember how old I was but I know that it was some time ago. I don't remember why I happened to read it, but I know that it was of my own accord that I picked up this book, bound delightfully (to my childish point of view) in soft tan leather, and opened it to *The Isle*. The only thing I remember clearly was its magic effect on me—the effect of each line, of every word. From that time on I have read Shelley with adoration. When I read Fragment III of *Prince Athanase*, I came across these words:

> 'Twas at this season that Prince Athanase
> Past the white Alps—those eagle-baffling mountains
> Slept in their shrouds of snow—etc.

But "eagle-baffling mountains"! I have seen them—snowy mountains—and have long sought for words to describe them. In vain. Eagle-baffling mountains! What a gorgeous mountain-word! Never shall I forget how those words first thrilled me.

Please tell me what it was of Francis Thompson which you quoted yesterday—in which was something like this phrase: "Goldusty with stars." I should like to see it and read it again for myself—a habit of mine after I hear anything I like especially.

Again let me tell you how delighted I am—how grateful to you—because, as I said, you have told me what I have always felt vaguely about Shelley, but what I have never been able to express in words or even in clear, substantial thoughts.

On April 14, 1926, Blanche W. Knopf (1894-1966; president of Alfred A. Knopf and the publisher's wife) wrote to Barbara. Her letter included: "This is to let you know that I have just finished reading your manuscript and like it enormously. Of course we want to publish it and hope to if you will let us."

Elmer Adler (1884-1962) advised many publishers on book design and typography. He went on to launch The Colophon, *a book collectors' quarterly, in 1930.*

176 Armory Street
New Haven, Connecticut
April 19, 1926

Dear Mrs. Knopf:

This note is simply to tell you how delighted and overwhelmed I feel when I think of my little story out in the world between covers. And honored, too, for Daddy tells me that it will be designed by Mr. Adler. I have seen books done by him, and have always admired them.

But the feeling I have every time of it! I have never felt anything like it, and I feel sure that never will anything thrill me so much as that blue letter.

Again let me tell you how thankful I am—how delighted—how astonished, that you are going to *publish* it—my little story.

      With love,
      Barbara

Transcribed from a draft letter to Mildred Kennedy. The bottom of the first page is damaged, and the second appears to be missing, but I'm including what remains because Barbara mentions her first violin lesson with Hugo Kortschak (1884-1957), former assistant concertmaster of the Chicago Symphony, founding member of the Berkshire String Quartet, and Dean of Music at Yale.

176 Armory Street
New Haven, Connecticut
April 20, 1926

My dearest Aunt Mildred:

 I know well that I have owed you a letter for a long time, but somehow (what with news that makes me jump into the air every time I think of it—news that keeps my mind crazy for concentrated work) I have not managed it. The time does go fast, but it can't go fast enough for me! Now, for fear that the bubbling news would give my violin an anti-climax, I will leave your mind to be tortured with it, while I turn and say everything I have to say *first*.

 By a sudden blow I have almost broken the rope that bound me to my violin, just managing to cling on by a scanty hair. *I took a lesson from Kortschak.* And I found that I was all wrong, every way that I could turn. I was standing wrong; my bow-arm was wrong; my fingers of the left hand were good, but the left arm (wrist and elbow) were not. And so a single forty-five minutes undid all but a small fraction of what I had woven with such care—undid it all to take out some kinks in the beginning of it—and now I've got to weave it partly over again. It's an awful calamity. I can't practice long in my new position, I can't play things much with the piano for fear of slipping into my old habits again, I have to watch myself carefully—look myself over—every few lines. To be sure, I am coming out of it all right now, but I was certainly a mess at first. I'm taking lessons (now that Hildegarde Donaldson has gone to Italy) from Mabel Deegan, a younger and not so finished player; who is taking lessons from Kortschak. Now, part of the trouble of my left arm was due to not swinging my elbow in far enough, something which I have always been slack about, and naturally, too, because it hurts until you have a lot of endurance. Hildegarde was always very strict about that, but Mabel is not, so (for I had several lessons with Mabel before my lesson with Kortschak) you see, that may have been part of it, for that one little thing throws the whole left hand out; but *not all of it*.

 Sabra is too beautiful to talk about. She is over two-and-a-half. She adores to go walking with me, and I adore to have her—to have her thrust her little hand into mine, and talk to me—about things that she sees or that she is going to do when she is a big girl, or that she wants to do now. Her latest trick is picking up beads with her curly, pink toes, and *[two or three words missing here; "dropping them into" perhaps]* a little cup! *Won't* you come and see her? *[...]*

One of the surviving letters from Barbara to George Bryan. The dedication to "J. H." in The House Without Windows is James Hook; "S. W. F." is Sabra Wyman Follett.

Budding Time *[mid-April, 1926]*
Neverland

Captain Jas. Hook:

As Sabra says: "What do zhoo fink?" After waiting in suspense for days and days, with a despairing twenty minutes around ten o'clock every morning, the mail-man came and brought, atchally, brought—brought. . . . .

It is for a blue letter that I have been waiting—a blue letter with the famous white BORZOI seal on it. Once it came, but—it was in Daddy's hand, telling me not to be discouraged.

This morning, during the despairing twenty minutes, Signe came bouncing into the living-room, where we were waiting, announcing the mail-man. . . announcing that he had already come and been and gone, while we were not watching (though I don't quite see how he could have). Was there a blue letter, though? . . and I darted out the door. It seemed as if I heard Signe affirm, just as I closed the door, that there was a blue letter—that she had seen "him" place it in the box. I opened. . . white letters—on top. But near the surface of the stack *was* a blue letter! It was again *in Daddy's hand*. Discouragement for me. And I handed them all to Mother. But Signe said that she had seen *two* blue letters. . . and lo and behold! At the bottom of the pile was another blue letter, addressed to me, written on the typewriter. I simply threw myself down on the floor and screamed, either with fear for what it might contain, with joy for getting it at last, or with terrific excitement of the whole thing. There is a feeling, after you have been waiting a long time for anything, there is a feeling that, when it really comes, it must be impossible—a dream—an optical illusion—a cross between those three things.

Mother opened hers—but announced that she mustn't tell me what it was about (for the letter from Daddy was addressed to her). With trembling fingers and quivering hands I opened mine. And here it is:

[contents of Mrs. Knopf's letter]

Now: "What doo zhoo fink???" It is *Eepersip, The House Without Windows*, my *story*, my story in New York, with the Knopfs, to be *published*!! . . . PUBLISHED!!!!!!!

It is going to be designed by Adler in his best style—not a juvenile at all. No illustrations at first, but if children like it they will do it over, *with* illustrations—but not by D.P.L. . . . . for, I was shocked to hear, *she isn't good enough* in the Knopfs' opinion, according to Daddy's letter (for, you see, after I read my letter Mother read me the details in Daddy's).

When the book comes out (which it will next January) do note the dedication. No, I'll give it to you *now*:

For my two Playmates,
J. H.
and
S. W. F.

"What do zhoo fink?"

Library of Congress
Washington, D. C.
April 22nd, 1926

Dear Peter:

Now I know what all the secrecy was about—and I'm not dead certain sure that, after all that secrecy, I can quite so whole-heartedly confide in you. Here I've been so freely telling you of those old days of mine—spinning yarns of peg-legs, binnacles, yard-arms, lee-shores, marooning, cryptograms, boardings, and what-not; just holding nothing back but answering each question, even when the answer might tend to incriminate me. And what returns, pray, do I get? Why, this: you conceal from me, systematically and of malice, the most startling of news—and then, swelp me, you bring me up standing with it; sort of like a round-shot across my bows, matey, fired on a sudden out of nowhere. I puts it to you, would *you* like it?

I naturally had to lay up (no, not *lie*) for a pair o' days. Now that I'm more like James Hook, I send you this day a consignment of congratulations, assorted sizes, but all in prime conditions and valued at the top of the market. They are sent f. o. b. New Haven. Kindly advise me of arrival of same. If any should chance to be missing or damaged, please notify me, so that I may enter a claim at the Congratulations Office here. Smee tied them up in her best manner, with red ribbon and gilt paper and cunning little knots, such as she alone can contrive. (Smee, you must know, upon reforming, became a close student of Scripture; and she follows very literally and closely the injunction, "Rejoice with them that do rejoice and weep with them that weep." This, I know, is not at all modern; but there's something about it that suits old-fashioned and moss-grown critters of my kind.)

First, I ought to say that, whereas I have had books mailed to me, expressed to me, thrown at me, inscribed to me, taken away from me, and put under me to raise me to the height of the table, I believe I never before had a book dedicated to me; not even fifty per cent dedicated to me. And when that dedication is couched in mysterious initials, it makes one feel as if he were Bacon conspiring with Shaxpur—if you know what I mean. I went around saying to people: "I've just had a book dedicated to me." Such, you see, is poor old human nature that I couldn't bring myself to say gracefully: "I've just had a book dedicated to me." Besides, that would involve a lot of explaining; and that is something for which I lack gift.

Mrs. Knopf's letter was delightful; and I don't wonder that you had to do a *pas seul* all over the place.

Sometime, perhaps—I can't say when, I may tell you how and why there happened to be two marbles; and about the strange monument I saw, with *Scriptura mysterium symbolum ordo* on it; and the wonderful sun-dial that marks not only the hours but also the Holy Days—indicating the hours with the usual finger-shadow but noting the Holy Days with the shadow of a cross; and about the legislative days of the Senate, which don't coincide with the calendar days; and about the thirteen-ton statue of George Washington that strangely disappeared; and, oh, a heap of things. But now—now I am grieved to think of the trick that was played on me.

>Yours with mingled feelings,
>Jas. Hook

P. S.: This much I *shall* tell you: The wiggle under my signature used to be called my *rubrica*. On and around the Spanish Main, the *rubrica* was a most important part of every man's signature (i. e., every man that could write). A signature without its special *rubrica* was n. g. A *rubrica* without a signature was honored everywhere. J. H.

176 Armory Street
New Haven, Connecticut
May 9, 1926

Dear Hildegarde:

I was awfully glad to get your letter, for I am interested very much in the magical island of Capri. I should have written after receiving your post-card, but somehow I just couldn't find time. It seems marvelous that you should have gone in swimming—I envy the climate, and envy your living there, in spite of having no music. I adore lizards, of course, and also mysterious places like the Blue Grotto. I suppose you'll be going in the Green one, next.

It seems as if I am coming pretty well on the violin. I have had two lessons from Kortschak since you left, which corrected one or two little things that Mabel had been slack about, such as *vibrato*; it seems that I have been doing it too much with my whole arm—not enough with my wrist. I worked on the Country Dance, the Chopin Mazurka in A minor, and the Seitz Pupil's Concerto in D minor.

Sabra's latest trick is—she can turn a somersault herself! She puts her head down so that it touches the bed without her bending her knees!, walks forward a little with her head down, and in a moment—over she goes! It is an insoluble mystery how she gets way down like that. Of course she is crazy about the violets, bluets, and dandelions now in bloom, and we have made several little "gardens" of them, transplanted, in our back yard. What are the flowers like in Capri?

I hope you won't tell anyone about my book. It was intended for a surprise to almost everyone—and it would have been such fun to send it to Capri next spring. The point is, John Derby was one of the first people I saw after I received the news, and so I couldn't refrain from telling him. The few others I told I made promise to keep silent, but I guess I must have forgotten to warn him. However, no harm is done as long as it doesn't get any farther.

Thank you again for your letter—it gave me a great deal of pleasure.

    With love,

The Meserveys of Hanover, New Hampshire, were probably the Folletts' closest friends. Arthur Bond Meservey (1884-1952) taught physics at Dartmouth. He and his wife, Anne White (1885-1970), had three children—Ellen, who was a year younger than Barbara; Edward, who married Sabra about twenty years later; and Robert.

176 Armory Street
New Haven, Connecticut
May 9, 1926

Dear Mr. Meservey:

Your tail (or tale) of Roario King amused us all very much. I really laughed about it until I was quite hoarse—until the house rolled from its foundations with merriment. But I do hope that lions' tales (or tails) regrow and retassel after they have undergone such an awful accident. The thought of those splendid beasts going half-tailed through life makes me feel sorry all over.

Jolly Sabra is very happy to see ferns uncurling, dandelions dashing the lawn with gold, white violets sprinkling the swamps, purple ones flushing the greening grass with deep blue, bluets streaking the lawns and meadows, and butterflies darting here and there, black and gold bumble-bees buzz-buzzing about. I'm awfully glad she likes things of that kind.

The violin is coming well. I played on the piano in a recital of Bruce and Rosalind's best pupils—a Chopin Nocturne in G minor. It was glorious fun, after I got going. It was waiting with nothing to do that was nerve-racking.

I am writing quite a few things at the same time—make-up butterflies, make-up birds, and make-up animals, fishes, trees, flowers, etc. will be coming—I am writing young stories for Sabra and older stories for her [sic]—fairy tales. But when I sit down to write, I never know where to begin, for there is also my account of Sabra, and my history of the imaginary country. Also I have finished revising with Daddy my ninety-page story of Eepersip.

So you see I am quite busy, and, thanking you again for the tell-tale-tail of Roario King, I shall say goodbye for a while.

My love to the whole Meservey tribe,

176 Armory Street
New Haven, Connecticut
June 15, 1926

Dear Mr. St. John:

I am much afraid that I shall not be able to see Rivernook this spring. Everything is complicated now. A visit to Boston has been postponed three times for various reasons—and I never did get there. Next week I go to Cummington, Massachusetts—to study music until about July 4th, with Kortschak, violin; and Bruce Simonds, piano. I am looking forward to it—it will be the first time I have done music in summer.

Possibly you did not get a letter in which I asked if you have a record of my first trip—my canoe trip. If you have, please send it to me so I can copy it (for I find that I haven't a complete account of that trip) and then I will return it to you.

There is lots and lots to say. Mother, Daddy, and I drove up to Sunapee on Thursday, partly to try a car which Daddy has on trial; partly because the last postponing of the Boston trip was very disappointing. The woods were heavenly. In blossom there were pink trilliums; bunch-berries, heavenly little white flowers; a bush with blossoms a little like the wild honeysuckle of our woods; a small white flower something like an anemone, but with entirely different leaves, wild lily-of-the-valley; another flower something like it, but again with different leaves; blue-berries; that bush with leaves which turn such a heavenly color in autumn; and—beyond and above all— pink lady-slippers nodding there in their loveliness all amid the blossoming claytonias—pink lady-slippers, color of clouds at dawn!

I explored again the woods I know so well; I danced in the grove trodden by fairies' feet; I watched the waves I have so often watched; I talked to tiger butterflies, black-and-yellow; I visited each lady-slipper to music of the veeries and hermit thrushes—I was at home out-of-doors again.

We have started to have our place landscaped. According to my plan at present: the bank in front will be one huge rock garden, with evergreen shrubs, vines, ferns, close thick flowers (you know it as north bank. Would Pyrola grow there?); on the back of the house there will be a purple lilac on each side of the middle screen door; along beside the lilacs small flowers—daffodils, larkspur, etc.; from that middle door will be a stepping-stone path bordered with flowers; there will be a bird-bath with red and white flowering quince nearby, to attract humming-birds; the path will lead to the front of the little house (I've told you about it, have I not?); in front of the little house there will be rhododendrons perhaps; inside whatever hedge we have there will be iris of different kinds and colors; there will be a snowball bush on the south-east corner of the land—with quite a stretch of grass in the foreground. The ground has been seeded.

I'm sorry that it will be impossible for me to come to Rivernook. By the way, *how* is the fairy ring?

        With love,
        Barbara.

P. S. I wish you could see Sabra. Together we "act" in *Sleeping Beauty* now. She goes in, saying: "I fink I'm going to do my 'pinning now." She sits down at my big spinning-wheel and pumps the treadle with her little right foot—she dips her rose-bud fingers into the little wooden cup of water—she takes a strand of flax (placed carefully by me in a certain place to us previously known) and attaches it to the spindle with its rows of little sharp hooks. Then she "pricks her finger" on the hooks—and "falls asleep." I come in and kiss her hand (which she holds out to me stiffly)—that "wakes her up," and we go out together. A few days ago I dressed her up in bright laces and scarves, and we did it for Daddy. She is perfectly delightful! B. N. F.

Barbara stayed with the Simonds family at Cummington. I don't believe the poems she mentions have survived.

176 Armory Street
New Haven, Connecticut
July 7, 1926

Dear Rosalind:

I wish you could have seen the marvelous country that we went through on the return trip—for we came home a different way. We went through shady wood-roads, where the trees formed a green arch lovelier than any made by climbing roses on a trellis; winding lane-like places, and wonderful views out over the hills—fields of hawk-weed, daisies, asters, buttercups—which made the field north of Miss Roger's house (the strawberry field) seem pale by comparison.

We found the grass coming up nicely here—at least it looks so when you see it from low down—when you look down on it from the second floor it seems very patchy indeed. The flowers are doing pretty well—(perhaps Bruce will be happily disappointed to know that not one of the columbines has even dropped one leaf, though the blossoms were a little shattered when we got home)—and yesterday we drove out to the nursery and picked out two fine young Colorado spruces, one for each side of the front door.

Yesterday we found that I left my apricot dress there, in the closet of the little bedroom where I slept twice when Daddy came. Would it be too much trouble for you to send it down?

I think we have really discovered the cause of the famous "white movie." We thought it all out at supper one evening. Was it not from the thick paste formed in her stomach by the two junket tablets?

I am sending Bruce a poem according to his suggestion of my writing about mosquitoes—also I have copied exactly the hermit thrush poem. You can see how much I left out before.

I hate "bread-and-butter" letters anyway, so I thought I'd vary this one a bit by putting the bread-and-butter part of it last—because it is pretty hard to thank you for those happy and profitable two weeks you gave us (though I still regret the fact that you didn't allow us to pay the peanut butter bill)!

        Love from

Lake Sunapee
New Hampshire
August 23, 1926

Dear Mr. Oberg:

Certainly I was not aware of how long I had kept you waiting. This summer has gone faster than any summer I have ever known. As you say, there is even more to do here than at New Haven, if that can be imagined. I only wish I had the fairy camera to take the fairy pictures of fairy butterflies. It will have to be this way: my imagination will be the fairy camera; my typewriter, the snap-shots; and now, here are four films (each film a pair of butterflies for you to "develop").

LINDERO: a butterfly with wings of soft, pale green, trimmed with brilliant gold. The female is soft brown, mottled with light green. The spread of wings is three inches.

CREESOTHIMI: a white butterfly, whose wings are covered with black markings like hieroglyphics. The female is the same (do not paint her). The under side is marvelous mottlings of snow-white and radiant gold. A two-inch spread of wings.

WIRINEETA: the wings are snow-white, and a narrow green "ribbon" (about one sixteenth of an inch wide) comes down from near the body in the direction of the tip of the lower wing, doubles back, crosses itself, and ends just below the tip of the upper wing. The body is yellow, and bordered with black spots (very light yellow), and the black antennae are tipped with frosty puff-balls. The female is deep gray, mottled with rather dark yellow. About an inch and spread of wings.

VESPREENO: a butterfly whose wings are about of an inch across—deep brown with spirals of thread-like gold bands. The antennae are tipped with tiny golden globes of phosphorescence which shows at night. The female is brown and cream-color, delicately mottled.

There are my fairy films. You see I have left out details about the butterfly eggs, etc., which would not do any good for this particular purpose.

I wish you *would* send the title-page and the other completed butterflies. I am crazy to see them, and, since I have *[the rest of the letter is missing]*

"The Cottage in the Woods"
Lake Sunapee
September, 1926

Dear Mr. St. John:

Tomorrow I shall send two samples of berries, very common around the lake. One of them was growing in a wet place, more exposed to the sun than the other. It is a very tall shrub, and beautiful beyond description.

I also found a strange little flower in a swampy place, deeply embedded in some of that marvelous swamp moss. I shall look it up when I get home, but I would like to know about it now, and I am sending it to you—the little golden-berried one.

The other strange little plant is very common along a certain wood-path.

I hope they will all reach you in good condition.

>   Love from
>   Barbara.

A brief excerpt from a letter Dorothy Lathrop wrote to Barbara on September 2, 1926.

[...] I shall try to plan the drawing out while I am in New York, though I shall not be able to finish it down there [...] After that, I am under contract to Macmillan's for a book and to a magazine for three fairy drawings, so I begin to feel a little desperate! But don't lose hope! The drawing will be coming along sometime before many months.

My love to you all.

>   Affectionately yours,
>   Dorothy P. Lathrop

"The Cottage in the Woods"
Lake Sunapee, New Hampshire
September 9, 1926

Dearest Mr. Oberg:

I received the butterflies this afternoon, and they have been "the event of the day." The painting is beautiful, but now I am sorry I gave you such dull material to work with. Your butterflies on the title-page are lovelier butterflies than mine. Now that the mystery of the question-marks has been solved, I feel that the two -----s are more delightful than I could possibly have dreamt of. As you probably know, I am making up birds, trees, shrubs, flowers, fishes, and other various kinds of creatures. You said once that you would like to try some birds. I will send some, if your mind still holds, as soon as you like. And then the whole lot should be published in one huge volume with sub-divisions—one of which the butterfly title-page should be the beginning. I'll talk it over with Daddy.

Can you throw any light upon the big question-mark I gave you, after you had almost solved the other one? I will give you some hints: The idea of it is green. Arabrab is in it. Esuoh sselwodniw is one of its principal ideas. I shall be pop., etc.

Thank you very much for the pictures. Here is a little suggestion. Keep the flowers as different as you can from each other—they will go as *the* flowers—if you know what I mean.

> With love,
> Barbara.

Barbara described the view at dawn from Camp Penacook, near the summit of Mount Chocorua.

Dawn—September, 1926

The air is sparklingly clear nearby—farther off the hills are wrapped in soft blue haze, each little lake set amid the trees far below has a tiny spurt and fluff of white cloud above it, and there can be seen its reflection in the always unstill water.

Over there in the east is a massive bank of gray clouds, from the zenith almost down to the horizon—only one small strip of green sky above the hills. And now the clouds blush suddenly, colors dance about in the air—the sky there becomes a startling vivid green sea—the great cloud-banks are all rich maroon and russet and purple, the color reaching way up and blending into that soft gray. Higher up is a strange shade of yellow, and still higher delicate pink fringes, reaching into the pearliness and the snow above. The maroon grows brighter, richer, and suddenly it is tiered with dull deep blue.

To the right, what a contrast! There is a stern granite peak of Chocorua, looming up into the sky clear blue over there—and yet ruddy and golden light from the brightening dawn flings itself over there and breaks against the granite in a glory of echoes of color. Those stern walls are quivering, even trembling with reflected light—and now the sky way over there is tinted with russet.

Down below the lakes are full of color, and the hills seem to be almost hidden behind a curtain of golden and pearly mistiness—the blue tiers become more vivid—the maroon seems to fade—it changes into a sublime pink which reaches up almost to the zenith—the sun breaks out into the green but paling sea—the clouds break away—the light has gone from the great cliffs, the sky is serene blue—daylight has come!

Barbara's companion on Chocorua was Ralph Blanchard (1888-1960), head of the English department at the Berkshire School in Sheffield, Massachusetts.

Passaconaway was a hamlet along the banks of the Swift River just below Chocorua; its site is now a Kancamagus Highway rest area. The Champney Falls trail up the mountain is still there, however, and it's lovely.

"The Cottage in the Woods"
Lake Sunapee
September 9, 1926

My dear Mr. St. John:

What a gorgeous place your Passaconaway is! It's strange—this letter starts with a mystery—we all, Mother, Daddy, Barbara, Sabra, Ralph, went there. We wanted, most of all, to have Ralph see some mountains before he goes home—so he and I climbed Chocorua, up the Piper Trail—they dropped us off there, and then went on to your cabin. I carried three blankets in a tight roll, over one shoulder and under the other; Ralph carried Daddy's pack full of provisions hastily collected, together with two more blankets. Mine was certainly the hottest, lightest pack I ever carried. We were surprised (at least I was—Ralph had never climbed mountains in this country) to find all the millions of little brooks dry, which, the year before last, had merrily crossed the path. Before we reached Chocorua Brook, some fellows, inquiring whether we were going to spend the night at the Camp, informed us that the water supply was dry—stagnant. We were puzzled and worried; we thought of carrying water up from Chocorua Brook, which we could even then hear down in the ravine, with no canteen (which was decidedly foolish)—then we remembered that we could at least boil the stagnant water.

We reached Penacook, not exhausted at all, but willing to take a rest. The brook *was* trickling a little—drop by drop through the spongy moss—but we boiled it to make sure. The sunrise next morning was one of the most spectacular ones I've ever seen. A russet-purple cloud-bank with tiers of deep blue lay below bright sky-blue, and above a sea of mystic green, with islands and sharp, jutting peninsulas, seeming to rise above jagged black rocks in the strange sea. The mackerel sky was yellow, blending to smoky russet-gray, and fire, and delicate pink. And on our right the granite peak was such a contrast—gray, stern, quiet—while all the earth below was dew-fresh green, and all the sky was pulsating with fire or gently throbbing. And yet that great peak seemed to reflect the rosiness—the light leaped back from the granite walls, and burst into molten gold as the sun rose, fresh and sparkling as if it, too, had been dewed on like the trees. You know about Chocorua, about that shark's-tooth peak—how it changes shape from different directions, but always just as noble—you know about it—it must be one of the most glorious mountains in the world.

We climbed about the peaks—half exploring. I found mountain cranberries (not so good as those on Moosilauke), sandwort or mountain daisy, tiny tart blue-berries, bunch-berries, some kind of stunted yellow aster, and a little trailing vine which forms thick mats in the crevices and over the rocks (I am sending its leaf). It has delicious juicy berries—black, and about the size of the mountain cranberries. Do you know what it is? Looking through my friend's flower book from beginning to end, I could not find it.

We went down the Champney Falls trail, a steep zig-zag path through forested ground down to the Falls, which would be very spectacular if there was only a little more water in them. But it was marvelous to see a silver thread of water plunging down the weather-worn faces of the great cliff. The path was very rough and exciting for a way—in one place there was a huge boulder on our left and the brook on our right, so that we were startled by the echo of one of the cascades! Finally we crossed the brook, and an easy woodland path took us to the road, near which we met Daddy.

From there we went to your cabin, and, as I said before, I think it is a beautiful, beautiful place in its balsam-edged pasture beneath billowing mountains—like one of the many places where Eepersip must have lived.

We went home through Crawford Notch (if you have ever been through there you know it better than I can describe it). I will only say that I wanted, more than almost anything, to explore those fascinating granite-ledged hills, of strange mysterious shapes. Can't we do it sometime "next summer?"

The day before yesterday I was cantering through the woods on Barberry, when a great flapping arose over my head, and a bird somewhere between the size of a crow and heron flew off, crashing through the trees. I followed, softly, to where it alighted in a great hemlock. It perched on a dead limb, in full sight. It was sandy cream-color, with deep buff marks on its throat. But before I had time to observe it carefully, it flapped again. What do you think it might have been?

> My love to Mrs. St. John—
> your friend,
> Barbara.

P. S. I never saw any trees as noble—as majestical as your blue balsams with their Chocorua tops. With love, Barbara.

P. P. S. I will copy the trip-letter as soon as possible. B. N. F.

"The Cottage in the Woods"
Lake Sunapee
September 25, 1926

My dear Mr. Oberg:

Now it is my turn to say that I like your suggestions very much—I shall not attempt to convince you that it would mean too much time and labor, for you have already confirmed me that it would not be.

If you do change the pictures, please don't change the *blueetue*—I mean the butterfly itself—I liked the *blueetue* best of all.

Now to have the male and female together would seem to mean larger pictures, and I like the present size and shape very much indeed. But I can see that it would be a decided improvement, so why not make only two pictures on a page, one all across the top, the other all across the bottom. But you could probably arrange that much better than I.

I see now that I have been very careless about one little thing. In Farksolia, the planet where these imaginary butterflies flit, there are many different countries, as on our own Earth. Some of the butterflies I have sent you belong to one country, some to another, and it would be wise to have the flowers "match," would it not? Since you are going to change them anyway, I think it will make no more work for me to tell you what goes with what, instead of puzzling you with meaningless names. However, let us remember to hold to the idea of butterflies *with* flowers, birds *with* shrubs, fishes *with* sea-plants, and so on.

When the *blueetue* and the *pearleetus* come to you (of course they are in New Haven now), put the *blueetue* with the flower *pyranto* (already sent to you)—this is because the combination will show strikingly the protective coloration; put the *pearleetue* with the plant *moreetho* (described on next page). The four butterflies sent to me up here are supposed to go with the *heirando*, the *larandi*, the *arantho*, and the *moeetha* (all plants described on next page). Put the *creesothimi* with the *omaida* (on next page); the *lindero* with the *araimoss* (on next page); the *vespreeno* with the *coreena* (sent to you before); the *wirineeta* with the *florones* (already sent to you).

      With much love,
      Barbara

This backpacking trip on the Franconia Range of New Hampshire would be Barbara's last excursion with her father.

At Liberty Shelter: Franconia Range
October 7–12, 1926

OCTOBER 7

On the seventh we started out from Little Sunapee, cobalt blue and fringed with scarlet wind-tossed maples and dark pines and spruces—on a curving road over gold-prinked hills, among the draping boughs and fiery leaves. It was up beyond Plymouth when sunset overtook us, a marvellous and bewitching sunset, which we caught glimpses of from time to time. First we saw it over Newfound Lake with its two green islets—there we saw a long low bank of yellow-russet clouds, edged on top with a brilliant gold cloud of sharp mountain-peaks. The sky had a rosy glow above the clouds, and in the north and south were high narrow tiers of pink. We longed for it, but we could not wait—it vanished behind dark trees. Suddenly they broke for a moment—we saw another and an entirely different sunset. Now the west was a maze of fire, and nearer us, partly covering it, were dark purple clouds—drifting about and changing. Again we saw it—there were brilliant russet tiers in the north—but the west was almost concealed by those same violet clouds, much thicker now, and breaking open sometimes and showing through arching windows the fire and glow and rosiness. Now gone again—and for a long time we had no more glimpses, but at last, when we thought it must be over, the trees broke, and lo! all was changed—the deep violet clouds had vanished—now there were long narrow tiers of dark yellow in the west, blended with tiers of dusky blue shadow.

We passed the glorious green field from where the Franconia Ridge looms up, and we could feel dimly the presence of those sometimes terrible and awesome mountains—or smiling—sparkling—but always proud.

The Dartmouth Outing Club cabin is near the Moosilauke Brook—a rushing river which thunders over slippery boulders. In places it seems glassy black, ruffled with the white of eddies—sometimes they are strange foam-yellow—sometimes the whole great brook comes rushing through a deep crack a foot wide, with a mysterious crash and whirling foam. Sometimes a black glassy pool surges out from high crags and swings down a green cascade.

There are marvellous rocks to explore on, rocks full of mysterious pools with sheer walls. Often these pools carry several big stones—strange mottled mineral effects, sparkling with mica—all the stones smooth and oval or round. I discovered a tiny cave above a large rock pool, a cave set with stunted spruces and other shrubs. Just below there the stream ran silver and blue with sunlight, through a dark grove of solemn green hemlocks touching their foreheads to the cloud-fringed sky.

OCTOBER 8

If only I had waked Daddy up I should have prevented a disaster. Why didn't I? There is no adequate reason. I wasn't in the habit of waking people up—and I wanted to explore the brook. If I had only thought one minute longer than I did!

We broke camp as quickly as possible, and started for The Flume—from there we were to proceed up the Flume Trail, and up the slide, and on over the peak of Flume, down into the col between Flume and Liberty, then up and over Liberty's shark-tooth peak, and down to the little shelter on its flanks just below the summit.

The long stretch of green field was fresh and sparkling, and there above it were the mountains we were going to climb—here many hands have failed—here is an invincible challenge—for me mountain-fever is not an illness—but an indescribable longing.

First, way off to the right of the range, was Osseo, that low long mountain, and its sudden deep blue peak with sheer crags was seen behind the shoulder of a flaming hill; then Flume, gashed with its stupendous slide, the peak showing to the left of the same hill; then the green-flanked Liberty, with its summit wavering with sharpness, prinked with great brown crags; then dark-peaked Haystack, not showing far above its ridge; then far-off dreaming Lincoln; and Lafayette in its fringey mantle of white mist.

When I had been on my first northern mountains it was hard to believe where I was. I had heard Chocorua and Moosilauke spoken of, and I knew that I was going to climb them, but when I was really there I could hardly believe it. I have overcome that—all I feel now is an indescribable sublime isolation—I feel the character and spirit of each mountain upon me like a strange dark-eyed thought.

We pushed on through the crimson-draped roads—and often we saw Liberty before us, dull green, with bubbles of rock near the peak—Liberty with its arch of blue sky. Clouds were well down on Lafayette—now Lincoln was among them, too. We reached the

Flume House, parked our car, and struggled into our packs, then strode into the driveway that leads to the Flume gorge. All during that trip my pack seemed to grow lighter, not heavier, but at first I wondered whether, going up the great white slide, it wouldn't really pull me over backwards. I was worried about Daddy, too. His load seemed tremendous—I could barely lift it; it crumpled him up somewhat—and, well, could he carry it up the slide?

The first spectacular thing in the Flume was a long, undulating, but very smooth rock or rocks, over which the Flume brook runs in flood-time. Oh, it was slippery, even though dry! Our hob-nails slipped disgracefully on it, with no more hold than wet rubber soles could have given. If the slide was going to be as slippery as that—well, never mind what I was thinking!

The board walk began to grow steeper, foot-braces about a foot apart appeared—it was wet and the foot-braces were needed very much. Then I saw where I was. The echo of the brook beneath filled the air, leaped about and roared and thundered. My voice was feeble, and my thoughts could not hear themselves. The sky had narrowed to a small slit of blue, and on both sides of me were high dark walls of rock, covered in places with moss and little climbing ferns. It seemed to be raining slightly—the air was full of wetness from the lashing captive brook and dripping precipices.

"What is this famous Flume?" I had said before to Daddy.

"Oh, just a little gorge where the Flume brook comes through."

"Well, then, what are all these people crazy to see?"

"They get wild and excited about almost anything, because other people do, that's all."

I had to be content—naturally I didn't expect much. In fact, when we had come to the long smooth rock I had thought it was the climax.

"Are there any falls in this gorge?" said I.

"Oh, I think there's a nice little cascade there."

When we came to that long rock, I had said: "Is this it?" I was amazed even at that.

He was looking mischievous. "Part of it." I was excited.

At the head of those great walls were two dazzling, thundering silver cascades.

We left the grim rock walls a-whirl with their water echoes. We filled our canteens at a whirling pool of the same brook, where so many canteens have before been filled. Again a strange feeling—the anticipation of mountainous isolation was upon us, we felt it drawing tighter like a shadow as we strode up the beginning of the leafy trail towards purple-gleaming Flume and green Liberty. Sometimes we saw the slide ahead, steep—oh, steep! After quite a little walk, when we were near the foot of the slide, we sat down on a mossy rock and ate soft bread and butter and cheese—the bread left over from supper at the Agassiz Basins cabin. Then we had chocolate and small sips of icy cold water. A royal dinner could have tasted no better.

Soon afterwards we broke out of the woods and stood at the foot of the slide. There it was composed of small sharp rocks, loosely tumbled together, and steep bankings of soft sand. It began to rain slightly—the clouds were descending upon us, wisps and shadows of it crossed the summit of Flume as if enticing us along. In a sheltered place by the woods we repacked our packs with the blankets more protected and with the poncho on me. The grade became steeper and steeper, mist was all about us, and finally we climbed up through loose avalanching sand on bare wet rock. Sometimes the mist would break away a bit so that we could see the nearby foothills of Flume. Occasionally we caught glimpses of the westering sun—oh, much too near the horizon for us.

Hard scrambling began, over steep ledges where we had to take advantage of every little depression or projection for handholds and footholds. We must negotiate the slide without slipping and losing hold. If we had not negotiated it successfully where would we be now? A good long way below, down at the foot of the slide—if indeed there was anything left!

I had a strange wild feeling of desperateness—for Daddy was terribly tired under the weight of his dreadful pack—and also, here was serious and difficult climbing—not rock-skipping or aesthetic dancing—but here our lives depended on our ability to climb and to keep on climbing, tired or no.

The mist seemed to be separating oftener now—we saw often the gorgeous foothills near us. When we looked down, there to the left was a Flume foothill covered with the black of luxuriant spruces and the brilliant yellow of fall birches—to the right and farther off, we saw the flanks of Liberty, its summit in cloud, and there we saw the green of still unchanged trees and the bright scarlet of the fall maples. The sunlight was glinting far off on green fields and mist-hung hills, but every time I looked the shadow of it moved nearer, till we were in it—it warmed our numb hands as we sat on a rock near the top of the slide to eat a bar of chocolate.

Then, after a little more climbing we came into the woods, and except for our being tired we could go on with no obstacles such as sheer and terrifying ledges. I should say, for Daddy's being tired—to my huge surprise, I could not claim that I was—perhaps because it was such a relief to be on unobstructed ground again. Oh, that trail! It is one of the treasures of my memory. On the right was a steep bank of soft moss with little green leaves and vines running about over it, blended with the green of the trees, stunted spruce and balsam. On the right it was the same, but downwards—downwards into the space of the slide and brilliant hills.

Daddy needed a rest, and, forgetting that the trail went over the peak of Flume anyway, he said that I, being curious about that peak, could scramble up that and come right back. It was wasted daylight. I was partway back when I heard him calling me, and as fast as I could over the rough ledges I came down. Wasted daylight—and again I felt that it was my fault.

The peak of Flume is very bare, and just below it there is a few yards of knife-edge, with sheer dips on each side. Sunset—a marvellous sunset caught us on the peaks—but my worry about Daddy, who by this time was putting his utmost strength into every step, and the distance from the Liberty Shelter took the joy out of it for me—again I felt a strange wild desperate feeling, as if I was alone and more than alone among those awesome mountains.

I had some mind and heart to give to the glowing sunset, though— for perhaps even then I could not think of the dead earnestness of things. Even then I think that I alone could have reached the shelter before it was absolutely necessary to use artificial light, for I never knew the afterlight of any sunset to stay so long.

There was a long bank of dark blue clouds on the western horizon, rimmed with brilliant gold. Little wisps floated above it, and they were bright cloud-gold. The darkening peaks around us were draped with white mist, and many of the valleys were full of it. Still marvellous touches of fire could be seen on the flanks of Flume—fire of the fall trees. There was russet glowing in the north and brighter in the south, while the eastern sky formed great vaults and caves of violet-gray clouds and gleaming peaks. The peaks to the east seemed to be a different color from the western ones—the east weird olive green, the west purple and glossy blue.

Into the dark col we descended, between Flume and pointed Liberty. Still we could easily see without light—Daddy told me to go ahead of him if I wanted to—he had to rest. I went on into the black woods alone—here proud Liberty had been forest-fired, leaving gnarled gray distorted trunks and fresh green undergrowth. Suddenly black shadows leaped around me as I stepped into undestroyed ground where there were great spruce forests. There were little rustles all around me—I was startled for a moment. Then my eyes began to see ahead—where the shadowed trail went up out of the valley. I knew we were on the Liberty side then, and I was glad and relieved, for it seemed no darker than it had been just after sunset on Flume. Daddy came along behind me. Couldn't a miracle happen, I thought, just this once? A miracle, that would keep the light till we reached the shelter. Out of the darkness far ahead loomed the peak of Liberty—and the shelter was on the far side of it. We plodded on.

We actually reached the very peak before we had to use the flashlight. If the going had been smooth at all we could have kept on much farther. But we came to difficult climbing and were scared to break an ankle or something, so we fished it out. The mist hovered threateningly all around us, so the light only made a gloomy pathway upon it—and it began to snow—a fine hard dry snow like granulated sugar. But we had no time to think of being cold—except our hands—except our hands which we were always grasping the wet cold rocks with. My first memories of the peak of Liberty are bitter ones indeed. The wind howled and swept around us—at last we were in the black darkness. My sense of direction had vanished long ago. Daddy walked a few steps in several directions, but could not seem to find the trail down to the shelter. Once he thought he saw it, going down beneath great arching boulders, but it was only a dark clump of wet blowing mountain-grass. He seemed to find it, but I had no confidence. In the awful whirlwind of my brain I fancied he was leading us back towards terrible Flume. But no, it seemed new. We went along a little bit of smooth knife-edge, and on both sides of me were stunted flattened balsams, besprinkled with the sugar-like snow. We trod on many clumps of that same dark mountain-grass, down and down—and then we were in higher woods again—and any light that may have been cast down from the open sky was momentarily gone—and our flashlight was yellowing and yellowing; now one could look at it easily, now it was dark flickering yellow. There was only one thing to do. Both Daddy and the flashlight needed a rest. We turned it off, and were more helpless than we already had been—absolutely at the mercy of snow and wind and losing the trail and spirits and ghosts and cold and darkness. We rested—"anyway we've found the trail," we said.

When we turned the light on we were greatly relieved to find it bright again. We hastened to use it, but could not make much progress because the trail was quite rough. Daddy was leading, Daddy held the light. We had to move in relays, however much we wanted to use the light as fast as our legs could carry us. Daddy would move three or four steps down a difficult place, then he would turn back the light at me, and I would carefully crawl down—for it was more important to keep legs and ankles perfect than anything else at that time. It seemed eternities we were crawling down that trail. At last, looking down into the valley below us, we saw little flickering lights. We thought: "Maybe that's the cabin, and there are people there, and they've built a fire, and have wood stowed in." We would have been willing to go all that way, if that was true. Although usually I would have hoped to have the cabin to ourselves, tonight I hoped that we would have company and dry wood. Daddy said: "It's not the kind of shelter where dry wood is left—it's even a simpler place than that." Dry wood? That was now my chief anxiety. How could Daddy, as he was, in the dark, in the cold snow, wield a hatchet and haul in wood? How? All we could do was to hope that some kind-hearted fellow had left wood enough for the supper. But I had terrible doubts.

Suddenly we both realized that those lights were much too far down to be the cabin—we broke out in a little open place where there was a scrap of light, then the sharp angle of the shelter roof was outlined sharply against the dull blue sky—sharply, and right by us! We had reached it! It seems incredible to me now, but we had—reached it!

Up the three high steps on to the ledge we pulled ourselves—and had hardly strength to do it. We were there! Trembling from head to feet I peered into the cabin. Trembling Daddy lifted the light—the awful moment had come—the awful moment of doubt. In the corners of the cabin was a goodly stack for the evening—and smaller stuff for kindling, too. It was the greatest relief I ever experienced—together we sank down on the remains of old balsam beds left by many climbers.

But not for long! Daddy lit a candle, then he went out to get water from the little cold spring just behind the cabin, while I got the food-bags out of the pack, and hung the blankets up, ready for use. We soon had boiling cocoa in pint mugs—cocoa and hot fried biscuit. And then we spread out the blankets and were lost in slumber until morning.

OCTOBER 9th

Thick mist, and patches of crumbly snow. But, happily, the fireplace was sheltered by big old stumps which we left in it to burn out, and we soon had a hot breakfast cooking. That morning we swore to rest a little. But we walked up to the peak about a mile up, and explored about on the crags and among the little stunted balsams. We found some delicious mountain cranberries in sheltered places, and Daddy took off one of his socks to carry some in—for of course we were wearing two pair.

Each balsam had on every little green twig a row of little white crumbs of snow. Up there on the wind-swept peak I discovered the little plant mountain daisy, which I had found before on Chocorua. The blossoms are tiny and white, but very lovely. Up there we ate some chocolate and sipped water—then we frisked about in the snow some more, and went down.

Also that day we walked down the trail directly down Liberty for a little way, in the hopes of meeting Leo, our comrade whom we hoped to join that day.

That night a heavy wind came up, the mist thickened, the temperature lowered. I said that night to Daddy: "Maybe there will be frost feathers in the morning—no?"

"Not cold enough."

OCTOBER 10th

The next morning the nearer mountains were uncovered—the mist seemed to be lifting, but clouds still hung low over the crimson flanks of Kinsman, and the great cliffs and crags of Mount Cannon were draped with it. I went out behind the cabin to see, and there, on the north side of it, were frost feathers—little ones to be sure, about one quarter of an inch long, but unmistakably frost feathers. And that meant that there would probably be much bigger ones on the exposed rock of Liberty. After breakfast we went up, loaded only with the package of raisins, dates, cheese, and chocolate. But instead of taking the trail up on the peak of Liberty, we branched off to the left on the Ridge Trail which leads over Haystack, Lincoln, and Lafayette.

This was the beginning of one of the most beautiful walks of my whole life. Looking up a steep trail were banks of clean snow, unmarred by human feet, but often with the tracks of rabbits or small birds. The great tapering balsams in sheltered places were shaggy with snow, marvellous drooping white boughs, and banks and glades of balsams and snow. The little ones were often perfect in shape, and the little whorls of twigs below their tops were all white—like little silvery stars. And then you look down a trail into those glorious sweeping branches. Looking closely, we saw a small frost feather formation on the windward side of every twig, sometimes even smaller than the ones of the cabin, and these helped to make the twigs so completely white—only here and there the tips of fresh green needles burst through the snow.

We were on a broad saddle-back now, between Liberty and Haystack, and as we mounted higher and higher on the side of Haystack, we could see larger frost feathers on the exposed tips of taller trees, sometimes an inch long. The ridge became smaller and smaller—we were well up towards the peak when, over at the south, the clouds broke. Oh, there were the peaks of Flume and Liberty, small wisps of white mist drifting off them. Liberty was sharp as a tooth, Flume farther off, lower, more rounded, and showing the knife-edge passage along its peak. The sky was white behind them, the peaks themselves were dreamy quiet and green with half-snowed trees. Way down on their flanks the snow reached, then blended into Indian red and crimson. When we had seen Flume and Liberty from the long green field below, their colors, so sharp and clear, seemed to flaunt defiance to the sky—now they were its own pearly color, part of it, dropped down from it, and yet—clearly and dreamily outlined against the white.

To get to Haystack for lunch and back to the Liberty shelter in time to gather the evening wood supply would mean a steady plug, so we pushed on, just as we saw the clouds gather on the peaks again.

We plodded on, through the beautiful glades and paradises of the snow-balsams. Climbing up higher and higher towards the peak of Haystack, we scrambled now over difficult ledges, and the growth became scantier and scantier, also much more packed down with snow. We were near the top—now we looked down on a vast slope of stunted snowy balsams. We knew what a long steep slope it was, yet we could only see a little way down—then the balsams and the snow just blended with the mist.

Soon the trail was going nearly level again, and the balsams were much higher and shaggy. Here we could see frost feathers on their wind-tossed tops—some of them three inches long. We never knew what was coming to us, but we thought that these frost feathers were marvellously long, it was more then anything we had expected. Some of the tops of the trees were laden down with them and with snow—each little twig was blessed with them—and was moulded among its marvellous traceries and delicate patterns.

Thinking we were on the wooded top of Haystack, we spread out the old rubber blanket over a snowy log, sat down, and ate our candied luncheon, cheese, chocolate, raisins, and dates, and water so cold that it made our teeth burn in our mouths.

Again, on the way back, we went into ecstasies of delight over the snow-glades amid the balsams. Before I loved the white pine more than any other tree—now the balsam is my favorite—the balsam is the tree which Nature blesses with her mountain-ferns—frost feathers. Again we had a view of snowy Flume and Liberty even clearer than before. The sun struck Flume feebly and made it glisten, behind it the clouds lifted for a moment and showed, grape purple and russet, far-off mountains. There was a space of blue sky just over Flume, fringed with a curtain of almost gleaming mist—sky so blue it seemed to our white-blind eyes green, and then along on the horizon behind Flume were massive white cloud-banks. What a difference there was between the low russet and purple and the glistening white of the near peaks. We went on through the snow, and had a good margin of time to haul in wood.

OCTOBER 11th

And this was the day we were going to do the Knife-edge! There had been thick mist during the night, although once we had waked up to see a star, Jupiter, shining sometimes brilliantly, sometimes only half-heartedly through thin wisps. But the mountains were all clear below the four thousand foot level. Above that there was no break—but the mist was pearly and beautifully picturesque on the purple-shadowed hills and the scarlet.

We made an early breakfast—we were up in time to see a radiant lilac flush of dawn spread about the sky. And now we started, always admiring the little and big trees, now we turned down the junction, dipped steeply into the Liberty-Haystack col, now up gently, and then we came to two forests growing on top of each other—both laden with snow. The upper forest was long-legged snow-shaggy spruces, and down below was a starry undergrowth of perfect baby balsams. And there the sun flinted silveringly through. Up on the slopes of Haystack, on past the frost feathered trees at the top where we had eaten lunch—on on new untracked trail which we hated to touch with our snow-banishing boots. Up a little higher we went, above the trees on a summit covered with mountain grass. We were now on the true peak of Haystack and had broken out of the woods for good—out of the woods into the frost feathers. On the last trees they formed four or five inches long—they were rippled delicately all over the steep slopes on just the ground—each small scanty shrub was laden with them, and, above all, where the juice of frozen cranberries oozed out they were appleblossom pink, and every delicate and graceful pattern showed in that sublime pink. On the windward sides they struck out bravely into the wind, but on the lee sides they hugged the rocks scalily, and were small and round, like the lining feathers of a bird.

Here and there the blood of Nature had been spilled—long stretches of snow were pink with cranberries' juice. On over the peak, down into a shallow col. And here were vast slopes which had been forest fired, leaving the gnarled and twisted remains of skinny trees six and eight feet high. These had four-inch frost feathers all up and down their windward sides—sometimes the limbs formed strange shapes, such as witch-arms and witch-fingers, waving stiffly in the wind. We could not stop, but how we did long to examine every single one!

Now we are over the peak of Haystack, the mist is very thick, and, as we mount higher the wind grows stronger and colder. Now we have come to that strange succession of peaks each one of which may be the peak of Lincoln, there is no telling in the mist. Each one of these peaks had gorgeous drops and crags, off into ravines on each side like Jobildunk of Moosilauke, though we could only see a little way down. We could not keep the trail, but there was no danger of losing it seriously on a narrow knife-edge. We avoided going over the very tips of those sharp peaks. We would pass one of them, seeing marvellous caves and clusters of frost feathers everywhere. Sometimes we could even see them, in semi-circle shapes, hanging off those crags. They formed exquisite fairy palaces and caves among the boulders, caves fringed with some twenty inches or more in length and certainly four inches broad at the tip. Then there would be scale-like formations of smaller rounder ones inside, also pointed ones pointing every way, as the wind would go swirling about inside. We walked on them all the time, the ground was so steep that they formed on it. The longest ones were in clusters—small ones, four-inch ones, and the very longest, formed from the same root, formed and spread out their delicate tips, each one receiving support from the one beneath it.

The mist grew thicker and thicker steadily, it curled past us in strange bewitching shapes—it beckoned, it lured, it persuaded, it coiled up suddenly and flounced away. The knife-edge was at its narrowest, and for a few moments we thought of the terrific spaces beneath us—we looked through great hollows in the crag, looked through them as through a window-hole and saw white. We looked at the sky and saw beckoning dancing white, we looked at the ground and saw white, the rocks were white except the windward crags, where murky dull brown showed between the great feathers. And now we descended into a little col just beneath the peak of Lafayette. The ridge had broadened out into a saddle-back, and now we went down on a little path through knee-high and waist-high flattened balsams—if balsams they were. For every twig was covered with small frost feathers and snow. The only hint of green was on the bottom side of the very lowest branches, and often these were snow-buried. The little top twigs were so glossy with snow and small feathers that they made us think of the sleek tail of a white cat. The path was like a little rabbit-runway through those artificial trees, and sometimes, when a sharp gust sent a little puff of snow hurtling along, we thought it was a rabbit—there were tracks all through that little path. The ridge had not so broadened that we must follow the cairns, and the ground was not so beset with feathers. The grade rose suddenly, and almost without warning, we were on the peak of Lafayette.

And like a sudden squall across the sea, I felt again the strange mountain isolation, the joy of being alone with the mountains. We stood by the big cairn on top—there were perhaps the very longest feathers of all. We went into the old cellar-hole and ate our meal of frozen stiff cheese, raisins, dates, and chocolate, but we were glad to get through and stamp about to warm ourselves. Even in the cellar-hole were small scaly frost feathers.

There were two sharers of the clouds there with us in the cellar-hole—they told us that it was only twelve o'clock—and we felt relieved—we would be back in plenty of time.

After we had finished we did not wait on the peak. Except that it was the peak, in that mist all places were alike—we started down the knife-edge through heavenly paradises of frost feathers, always growing, always building up. The rock-caves were even more thickly lined with longer ones—they seemed to be three feet long hanging off the gorgeous crags of Lincoln, but there was no way of getting near to tell. It seemed to be a little clearer—we could see farther down in the great snow-lined ravines, we observed the great cliffs more clearly. And when we came to the forest of mountain ghosts of Haystack, the frost feathers on them had grown three or four inches longer—they were now six or eight inches long. Being clearer they were even more uncanny and beckoning and gnarled—all pointing one way, down the great slopes, seeming to entice us into evil by going down there. How different were the smaller but just as lovely feathers, swaying stiffly on the tops of the Haystack trees. Why must we go?

Down through that heavenly little stretch of trail just below the top, where the great shaggy balsams hurl down their feather-burdens in the wind. Down, down, towards Liberty, where there are no frost feathers except very tiny ones, but beautiful glades and paradises of snow. It must have been warmer down there, for almost every twig had a little silver icicle hanging off its tip. We caught glimpses of gorgeous billowing blueness, but we had come from the white mist into murky brown mist, and, except when it lifted or broke for a few moments, the air was heavy with it. We did not see then the dancings and curlings, we did not feel airy cold touches and pushes. And soon we were at the little shelter.

OCTOBER 12th

When I woke I saw, over in the south, a great patch of brilliant blue sky. Enormous white clouds were scudding across like the smallest of ships in the boundless sea. Sometimes shadows would fall over us, as a group of some of that weird brown murk flew over. The stern peak of Liberty loomed up before us, as we went out of the cabin, fringed with snow. There must be frost feathers up there! Dark blue Cannon with its stupendous cliffs loomed up out of the mist, its rounded peak clear, Kinsman, too, shook herself away from it. But still a long bank hung over the peak of Moosilauke over in the west. Its two smaller peaks, Mount Jim and Mount Blue, were clear, and when the sun struck them we could see their bright crest of snow. Slowly they crumbled away and lifted like a fringey curtain, and then we saw the peak, bright with snow, sharp and white. And then a sunlight shadow moved along the top of Kinsman, changing dull green to bewitching red, and now it glinted upon Moosilauke, moved up the peak until all that snow was rimmed with brilliant silver. For a moment it hovered there, then slowly glided along over the south peak and down, changing the blue and green to red—

magicking the snow-whiteness into silver. The farthest mountains were bathed in a flood of rich green light. There, on the horizon, the sky was green, and the mountains there were like part of the sky itself. Red trees gleamed scarlet even way off there, where the sun struck—sun, the magician of all. Dusky purple shadow lay between the weird little peaks off there, and the glow of golden sun shadow.

We tramped up to the peak of Liberty—we saw purple looming Flume with its cap of snow, magic-crested Moosilauke, shark-toothed Chocorua. But the chief glory of them all was frost-feathered Lincoln, with a sublime crest of snow where the sun broke and made it gleam. The peak of Lincoln looked like the peak of the Matterhorn—where in all the Alps could a mountain be more heavenly? Far off, at the end of the range, was Garfield, prinked with the whiteness of snow and then the Twin Range, the sun shining full upon the snow along that ridge. Spectacular cloud shadows drifted about in the valley between us and the Twin Range, drifted and cooled the fiery anguish of the trees, which slowly blended into the fresh green of balsams and spruces, which became also blended in among waving streamers of the snow-line, whiter and whiter way to the top of the knife-edge.

Then there was the great Presidential Range—still buried in crumbling mist—but we saw sometimes a lofty pointed peak, breaking, like a fairy dream, away. The snow reached far down on their flanks, the mist and clouds over there shadowed the white with the strange dusky blue of ice-bergs.

We could not get near enough to the crags of Liberty to see the frost feathers closely, but there were big ones there, certainly. Why must we go? The knife-edge was clear, why could we not stay one more day, and do it in the sunshine, and take some frost feather photographs to be sure of. No, we must go!

We dipped into the slope of snow-trees on the steep mossy trail to the shelter, shouldered our packs, and unwillingly plodded down. Through the Flume again—but what were those strange two-legged creatures mincing along with over-pink cheeks and over-white legs? It is a sad thing that we must go through the Flume again, not because I do not like the gorge. Daddy and I some day shall explore and explore until we find a gorge as spectacular that has not got five or six hotels in its bottom.

The sunset was glowing ahead when we pulled out of the Flume House Garage. The clouds were fluffy, soft gray on the dark side, bright gleaming pink on the sunset—there were heaps and billows of pink rolling in the sky. I happened to look behind us, and quickly I told Daddy to stop the car and look. Snow-crowned Lincoln was plunged in the glow of sunset, and all over its sharp peak the snow was a sublime pink, now fading, fading away to that cold moon-white which looms out of darkness. But shyly, Lafayette was shrouded with pearl-white mist, the edges of it catching the rose on Lincoln—veiled and hidden by itself thinking—wondering why on earth two such strange tiny beings had climbed her that day, but she had suffered them to come unharmed and see her treasures. And she gathered her long undulating shroud about her closer, and waited for the feathers to come. Some mountains love to stand free, but some like Lafayette and Washington and Moosilauke love more the white mist and the frost feathers.

Again we sped on, and reached the little cabin by the brook after dark.

OCTOBER 13th

Every day that we had been up there by Liberty Shelter we had been worried sick about Leo. Had he broken an ankle on the way up, alone? Had something gone wrong with the car in which he was driving to the foot of Liberty? Had something gone wrong with the trip in which he was taking Mother and Sabra back to New Haven? Had he stayed there to help them out of the mess of first arriving? That, and having our films developed, was the only consideration which made us wish to get down.

That morning we broke camp fairly late, and started out for Lake Sunapee again. The long green field was fresh and glittering with dew—there again were our mountains—glorious snow-crested Lincoln, and mist-wreathed Lafayette. We stopped, and watched to see if Lafayette was breaking from the clouds—once we saw her very peak free and gleaming white, but it shut in quickly again.

Onward, onward we sped, and between Bristol and Danbury, by the side of a rushing brook, the little Dodge died. We stopped some fellows headed for Danbury, and asked them to send us some help—then we sat down and waited. I explored in the woods and found two fungi. Suddenly a blue-painted car whizzed by like an arrow. All I saw was a flash of a red-and-black checked shirt, and a little blue cap. "Leo!" I screamed. The brakes went on—it was Leo. But not only Leo, for Captain Hook and Smee were there, too! Right behind them came aid from the garage at Danbury. So much help coming at once—we were overwhelmed.

It seems that Leo had had malaria chills every night, and thought it would not be safe to go into the mountains. But he had expected us sooner, and he was as worried as we were. He had set out to the rescue to find the Dodge, which he thought probably had broken down. And there it all was. We got the Dodge new parts, and started home.

Then it was that we saw the most gorgeous moonrise I have ever seen. The moon was behind long tiers of black cloud which her radiance fringed with silver—so the sky was covered with marvellous night caves set with fringey light.

Always dreaming, as I now dream, of mist-shrouded peaks, we spun along home.

Frost Feathers—seen October, 1925 and 1926

Frost feathers are not, as is commonly supposed, the delicate traceries and "paintings" of Jack Frost found on window-panes. Indeed, they are not a consequence of frost at all. They are found at high altitudes, after a cold windy night and very thick mist.

They are frozen mist—mist which freezes onto the rocks when it touches them—built up and chiseled away from the wind—chiseled until they have scalloped or crinkled edges, and until they are in the shape of a feather more perfect and lovely than any bird-feather—a feather, which, when taken apart, is found to consist of thin brittle layers. Each one has an individual tracery and pattern of its own—delicately shown in the snow-white.

Sometimes they are seen hanging almost in a semi-circle, off crags; sometimes striking out into the wind, sometimes, when on the lee side of things, rounder, like small inner bird-feathers, and lying close to the rocks, scalily; sometimes they form on the exposed tips of trees, and sometimes so thickly that the small limbs are glossy and rounded with them, like a white cat's tail; once we found them in exquisite little rosettes around the wire cables which anchor the Moosilauke Top House; we found them around the grindstone; often we saw exquisite caves of them, pointing every which way as the wind had swirled about; on Haystack we saw them on the tall, skinny, gnarled trunks of burnt trees, making them seem like pointing or beckoning mountain-ghosts; again they are seen, delicately rippled on the very ground—we found them formed over cranberry beds, where the juice of the frozen berries had pinkened all the snow—there the frost feathers had all their exquisite fairylike traceries all in a sublime pink.

The largest ones form in giant clusters—two-foot ones, down to one-inch ones, all joining together from the same root or clump, and peering out boldly into the cool pearliness of mist, and the wind-sculptor.

We seemed to be in fairyland when we wandered on the Knife-edge through paradises of them.

176 Armory Street
New Haven, Connecticut
November 13, 1926

Dear Mr. Oberg:

Have you received the butterflies yet? They were sent some time ago. I have decided that a good title for that special division of the whole book would be: *Butterflies of Farksolia*, rather than: *Farksolian Butterflies*. If you consult carefully the letter in which I described several butterflies and flowers, I think you will find everything you need at present.

Mother is in such a terrible mess now, with no outside help at all, that I am afraid she can't have anyone here at all just yet, but I am hoping that you can come down for March 4! We need to talk—about butterflies and such.

Please excuse the briefness of this note—I am terribly busy this afternoon, with practicing, and doing lessons for tomorrow.

>With love,
>Barbara.

Barbara probably read her Mint after the family's Thanksgiving on November 25, 1926.

FOR DADDY
An After-Dinner Mint

>*A man said to the universe:*
>*"Sir, I exist!"*
>*"However," replied the universe,*
>*"The fact has not created in me*
>*A sense of obligation."*
>Stephen Crane

Long legs were all right in the open country, perhaps, where there was plenty of room, but when it came to cramming them into cities and houses—why, it was impossible! The town was in danger of its life while my legs were free. They needed training, control, poise—and—aesthetic dancing-classes did not only train legs far too long and arms far too stiff, but they also developed a sense of rhythm, a love for beautiful music—they made one's soul like a butterfly for lightness and freeness, like a rainbow for colour, like golden flames for upspringing passion. My mother appealed for help to aesthetic dancing-classes, thinking that those legs of mine should become adapted to more ladylike postures.

It was a bad time for such experiments. I had just left the mountains—just left a mountain-trip so sublime that while it was fresh in my mind I could think of nothing else—life was a whirlwind of mist and snow and lofty dreaming peaks around me, and balsams laden down with snow, massive with snow, chiselled delicately from the heart and loveliness of snow.

But my mother did not know that—her only thought was to save the furniture before it was too late.

I was sent to a dancing-class—an aesthetic one—and I write this experience for the benefit of those other long-legged children, who, without advice, may be deceived and misguided by un-understanding mothers into the same cruel trap.

The advice is here—study it like a rule in first-year Latin, learn it by heart, forwards, backwards, sideways, say it over and over in your sleep: never, *never* trust your mother when she begins to talk of dancing-classes—especially aesthetic ones.

To begin with, I stood at the end of a long row—I cringed at the glance of the high-headed, eagle-eyed instructress—I wanted to hang my head. I felt as if that space of desert-like floor was huger and more desolate than all the Franconia Range, and I should much rather have been facing the dangers of bitter exposure to sleet and snow—the dangers of being night-bound miles from any shelter—the danger of the precarious Knife-Edge in high winds.

"Any beginners in this class?" asked the teacher, impatiently.

"I'm a beginner—" I ventured, very timidly.

"Oh, you're all right—you can do it," she said, hotly and convincingly.

Stiffly we stood in rows, confronting a double row of Mothers.

Lively, but absolutely expressionless music began—we revolved around the room—I tried to imitate their wavings, bendings, trippings—I could think of nothing but a long snowy trail amid shaggy balsams—of long icicles hanging from dark, wet ledges. What was that? The glimmer of icicles? What was that? The fresh green of matted balsams? But a terrible feeling of the cheapness of everything here overwhelmed me, as I realized that the glimmer was just from the strings of glittering glass beads dangling from hideous mis-shapen chandeliers—the green was only wilted branches trying desperately to add a touch of beauty to the place—and not succeeding. I could not understand why such unnatural imitations were being made—it seemed—

But again we stood stiffly in rows.

"Now, two three-step turns and then two coupées," remarked the teacher, agitatedly. "One, two, three—lively there!"

Three-step turns? Coupées? I never heard such names for mountains or trees. And then I suddenly realized where I was. I tried to imitate half-heartedly. What would happen if one was unexpectedly told to do such an absurd thing on the Knife-Edge? Why, on the Knife-Edge there is just barely room to walk, quietly and decently.

"Now, two slides—one, two—*begin!*"

This seemed more hopeful, for had *I* not climbed the famous Flume slide, scrambling over great precipices and sheer ledges, kneeling in running water, clinging desperately to any small projection?—I could do that with the best of them, I thought. But I couldn't—my legs would get terribly confused with each other, I stumbled, I became dizzy trying to whirl about as they did. She came over to me. I felt terribly ashamed—and yet I could do no better.

"What kind of slide is this you're doing?" she said, sounding very scornful.

I answered her miserably—"I thought you meant the Flume slide, and I can do that—but you didn't."

"I don't understand," she said, obviously much amazed.

Then she began to demonstrate. "See—make your legs twirl along over the floor—like this—" and she pirouetted. "Your arms! They are so stiff!" and her wild dark eagle glance almost pinned me to the floor.

"So were the mountain-ghosts," I caught myself saying—for a heavenly moment I had imagined myself one of those burnt trees—tall, skinny, gnarled—with their uncanny beckonings—mountain-ghosts laden with delicate rippling frost-work. Oh, if you could only see them—only be with them—uncanny or friendly, ghostlike or real.

We revolved some more, but I was none better, for a wave of dreams and meditations and heavenly memories rushed over me. Oh, the sun had been so beautiful, striking snow-crested Lincoln when the mist cleared away! And how dreamily ice-blue shadows had mingled with the white on the Presidential Range so far away, still hidden in great white clouds.

Again, as we stopped, the horrible situation dawned on me.

"This will never do," I thought. "I mustn't let my mind wander this way." I wanted to do something unique—stand stolidly still, or fall on the floor, but, in spite of ideas almost as strong as resolutions, I still tried to imitate, as we turned again and again. I tried in vain to use my marvellous mountain-plod, but that only made matters worse—such a glorious gait was not for aesthetic dancing—to my regret I saw that. Then I tried the steps which had carried me successfully up the Flume slide, but my strength had gone—I was constantly the last of the line, I fell behind with the weakest, I was more awkward and gawky than the poorest—and I felt it.

"Bourrée!"

But even this emphatic announcement could not bring me back from the mountains then—oh, those great slopes of snow-haunted balsams, and the tiny winding rabbit-trails! I was exploring among them with cold delicious mist in my face—exploring and finding fairy palaces and glades in the snow, and sometimes the trees were so white and laden with snow that they seemed to be carved out of it—exquisite fairy trees of the mountains————no I was not—I was standing foolishly in a stifling room—my tremendous imagination gave me a terrible jolt and a bitter disappointment.

As we brought up short, I became stingingily conscious of the rows of Mothers—I felt horribly conspicuous in my short butterfly-ish dancing-dress of flimsy gauze, the white silk socks which could hardly bear the pressure of my knotted calves—I felt *unendurably* conspicuous, so out of place, away from the wild free country and snow-crowned mountains.

My dreams ended for a moment—suddenly, and with a flash of joy, I saw the thing in a new light. The teacher was not so stout or so tall as I was—I could knock her over with a flip of my finger, trample down the others, and boost all the Mothers out of the immense windows—how easy it would be!

My impulse was so strong that I stood like a stone—my arms swelled suddenly with muscle, and solid waves and bunches of it stood out on my legs—slowly I felt my foolish silk socklets ripping—my foot was up, and then down with a savage stamp, as:—

"Alternate jetées with two-step turns—all around the room. One, two, three, *begin!*"

The door was huge, and beckoning, and standing grimly open. I thought of rushing for it, but I restrained myself, for I was at a far corner of the room. I kept up with the procession this time, though my legs and arms were again doing ridiculous things—my untrained mountain-legs, and mountain-arms, and mountain-shoulders built for bearing the strain of a pack—I thought of the cool pearliness of mountain-mist, of the dim and dreaming peaks around me when the mist broke, of the sunset colours playing on stately Lincoln's snow—pink—sublime—and of proud Lafayette, shrouded with mist, alone with the clouds and the sky. Suddenly the door, a vast and blessed sea-cave, loomed up in front of me as the north peak of Moosilauke had loomed through a fringey hole in the mist.

As I was about to dart through, the little teacher sprang to my side.

"Not so heavy!" she cried. "Be light as a feather, be lighter than a feather—think of feathers, think of feathers, *think of feathers!*"

The room came still with a sharp jerk, as I flung back my head and cried bitterly: "You don't know anything about feathers! You don't even know what feathers are! You've never seen them—as *I've* seen them—chiselled out of frozen mist!"

Quicker than a thought, I glided through the door—I knew the chase was beginning behind me, but I had a start—for a moment my words had frozen them stiff—desperately I hurdled chairs and tables, a standing lamp toppled after me with a crash, but I never saw the rushing and confusion, for, once out in the street in the open, my long mountain-plods had come back to me. Again I was on the Franconia Range—striding—striding my huge strides—now I was on Flume scarred with its stupendous slide; now on desolate Liberty, alone and content to be alone, even if it was holding hands with the other peaks of that chain; now Haystack, with dark and shaggy balsams fringing the cranberried summit; now frost-feathered, sky-bound Lincoln; and noble, snow-crowned Lafayette—that was where *my* legs belonged.

I could dream again of the mountains and the snow—alone—uninterrupted under the stars.

Barbara's present from Mrs. Howe was probably the 1921 American edition of the collection of Russian fairy tales edited by Alexander Afanasyev and illustrated by Ivan Bilibin—perhaps Russian Wonder Tales *by Post Wheeler (Century Company, New York, 1921).*

176 Armory Street
New Haven, Connecticut
Christmas Evening, 1926

My dear Mrs. Howe:

It is indeed rare to find a person of character who has "grown past" fairy stories—and those few must be immune to the laws of beauty. And even they *must* succumb to the Russian ones which you sent me. I think they are the most bewitching, fascinating, alluring, mystic stories of their kind that I have ever read—why, I simply could not leave the book until my eyes whirled in circles of red and gold, with concentration. Even on such a busy day as Christmas, I have managed to find time for the book, and I have studied the pictures carefully. Oh, what pictures! How they fit the stories! What inextricable tangles are formed by the writhing dragons and tongues of flame! And what superb, majestic, curiously foreign faces! What marvelous effects are made by the strangely tufted trees, and the inspiration of black and gold. Above and beyond all the stories I have read so far, is the story of *Ivan Tsarevich and the Gray Wolf*, with its whorls of iridescent magic, and the comet-like plumage of the Fire Bird dominating all the phrases, and the celestial dulcimer ringing through each word! And then the picture of the Fire Bird—dazzling fire trailing across a peacock sky, and the night-lit face of the amazed prince, and the billowing banks of dark forest trees.

But I must not be partial to *Ivan Tsarevich*—for my other favorite is the one called *Tsar Sultan*—the strange journeys over unknown wave-crests to the magic island and the fairylike city, where the squirrel under the fir-tree cracks golden nuts with emerald kernels! Often fairy stories are so much alike—but none on earth will ever have another squirrel cracking golden nuts—unless, of course, it copies this one. It seems to me that is the truest test of a fairy story—they are often much alike in plot, for they usually consist of princes and princesses, but they *should* have original ideas in places. And these certainly have a high percentage of originality—particularly that tremendous idea about the Fire Bird—that is probably the best idea in the book, so far.

Then the under-sea picture appeals to me very strongly. There is the strange sea-green face of the Tsar of the ocean, and the iridescent and brilliant fish of tropical shape, looking as if they were delicately feathering their fins, and gliding silently through the meshes of the ferny corals—what ideas those strange fish give me—I could almost write a story about them, and they certainly will add many inspirations of shape and color to my manuscript—several pages of imaginary creatures.

Oh, thank you a thousand times—that book has made me very happy—and I hope your Christmas was as happy as mine.

> With love,
> Barbara.

You'll recall that Mr. Oberg used unshelled peanuts as packing material.

176 Armory Street
New Haven, Connecticut
December 28, 1926

Dear Mr. Oberg:

Oh, what a Christmas we had! And oh, how your yearly box was welcomed. Your yearly box, you must understand by this time, is about the greatest event of all the Great Day. For one thing, space is not wasted with the packing, because that packing happens to be of such a very desirable quality! First of all, I should say that, though I've heard of metronomes, and thought of them, and had them described to me, I had never laid eyes upon one, or dreamed of the luxury of having one for my own. It is so nice to get a correct idea of the tempos of music, to be able to translate accurately and so easily expressions like ($\quarternote = 57$), etc. I find that I have been playing a great many things wrong, and still others about right.

It is by one of the greatest possible strokes of luck that you sent Sabra some dishes. She has been wanting them for a long time—for her doll tea-parties, etc. I wish you could witness her tea-parties—I can imagine how you would double up in a corner. She passes things around to her various dolls, and to Ding, the only living person present besides herself. Paper-clips, rubber-bands, and large wooden beads, constitute most of her diet—and these things represent cake, bread, marmalade, and shredded wheat, besides many imaginary things that I could not dare to name. Then she has what she calls her toaster, and her triscuits, which she toasts in it, and butters with rubber bands. All the little blue-and-white dishes are filled with food of various kinds. Also, she has found a lot of pleasure in the funny little cat that sits on the floor and squeals.

Oh, how delicious all the various varieties of candy were! How we went around and feasted all day long. Even for little Sabra all rules were off, and she sucked and sucked and sucked.

Thank you for your magical box!

        As always, your friend,
        Barbara.

3

TO THE SEA! (1927-1929)

The House Without Windows was published on January 21, 1927. Interest was such that all 2,500 copies had sold before it reached the shops, and a second printing was ordered.

January 8th, 1927

Dear Peter:

I am deeply grieved that you should suppose I had not written about the book. As a matter of fact, I *did* write just as soon as I received the package. For, although I did not open the package, I suspected what was in it. Smee can testify that I really wrote, and that to her knowledge (which surely you will not dispute) the letter was posted. Through what convolutions it now is wandering, who knows? Perhaps it isn't wandering through convolutions but is pursuing a fixed path and, like a comet, will return at a predictable time; predictable, that is, *if* we knew all the factors—which, of course, we don't. So that leaves it all *very* MYSTERIOUS, does it not?

It is well-nigh impossible, I fear, to recapture the first, fine, careless rapture of that letter bearing the familiar signature of JAS. HOOK. I believe I said that I was glad Peter Pan's Own Story had been told. Practically all that most folk know of Peter, they have had to learn through the medium of (Sir) James M. Barrie; and naturally Barrie may not be perfectly accurate about everything. Then I think I quoted from Phineas Taylor Barnum, a man who would have made a most uproarious pirate if it hadn't been for a number of things.

The book I discover, now that I *have* opened the package, to be as charming to the outward view as I had known it would be: binding, title-page, paper, types, and all. I haven't had the opportunity to dip into it; and I think Helen will explain why, if you ask her. It is (as you will admit) quite necessary that I have a free and untrammelled mind for the two readings of it. I say *two*; for you will understand that I shall read it once for the sheer story of it, and once for all the mystical allusions between the lines.

   Your faithful
   Gee-ess-bee

Alfred A. Knopf, Inc.
730 Fifth Avenue
New York
11 January, 1927

Dear Barbara:

I hope you will get a moment's pleasure out of learning that the second printing of *The House Without Windows* is ordered to-day, just ten days before publication. We shall try to make you a new and better jacket to-morrow. The correction "For what? Eepersip had not the slightest idea" will be made; and the sentence in the Colophon about the short descenders will be taken out.

>Yours hurriedly,
>Daddy.

January 19th, 1927

Dear Peter:

I think your book *looks* very charming, with its gay sprigged paper and all.

In fine—it's quite properly Peter-Pannish; and what more is to be said?

>Congratulatorily,
>Jas. Hook,
>Dedicatee

"Il pleut, il pleut, bergère" ("It's raining, it's raining, shepherdess") is a song from Fabre d'Églantine's 1780 operetta Laure et Pétrarque. *The narrative pirate poem is* Poppy Island. *I don't think Barbara got past imagining her "biography" of the gypsy girl.*

176 Armory Street
New Haven, Connecticut
January 20, 1927

My dear Mr. St. John:

Thank you for your two delightful letters in succession. You are the person whom I most look forward to hearing from, for you always have something interesting to say. You said in your last: "How strange it must have seemed to you that I have not written before now!" But I myself must now repeat that, and much more emphatically. I am very sorry about it—but how the time does fly!

I liked your last letter very much—for I feel that what you said about The House Without Windows really means something. I see now, perfectly well, my mistake about the vireo—but I was so over-eager in the revision of the story, that I never stopped to think whether the vireo nests in low clumps of grass, or not. Of course, chipmunks *do* sleep all winter—but, as you say, he was Eepersip's chipmunk. I'm very glad to hear you liked the book; it means a great deal to have it appreciated by people I care for.

Thank you, too, for the book of songs. I like them very much, and the pictures are delightful. Among the French songs there is one that I learned by heart some time ago: Il pleut, il pleut, bergère.

I was very glad to hear about the little rock garden that you are planning to make. I hope you are going to have columbine in it—the columbine is my favorite flower, I think. And then, would bleeding hearts grow in that kind of place?

Are you well now? It was very disappointing to me, to hear you were sick again.

By the way—Rivernook next spring?

By the way—why don't we climb Chocorua?

And, speaking of mountains, that reminds me: it is very possible that I shall be going up in the mountains late this month, for a few days, on snowshoes. I am going with two or three friends of mine, and it is very likely that we hover in the vicinity of Lake Sunapee, or climb Mount Kearsarge. And I was so delighted when I first heard about the possibility of it, that I wrote this little poem in anticipation (enclosed).

Here is a bit of news that made me very much excited: my book is in the second printing. The first printing is sold—twenty-five hundred copies—and it isn't published till tomorrow! Daddy tells me that it is very good selling for a book to go into a second printing before publication—that most books don't do it.

Speaking of books—*if* I recover from a bad cough, cold, and hoarseness before next Saturday, I am going to speak over the radio from New York. I shall probably read a narrative poem that I wrote a few days ago. I am both trembling and singing—at any rate, my blood is quite curdled. The trouble will be beginning. Then, I can't imagine how difficult it will be to talk and talk, and know that people are listening—yet just talking into a motionless, lifeless thing!

The narrative poem is like this (You may think I am very faithless to Eepersip and Nature, but, all the same, I am wild over PIRATES—their unknown islands, masses of blood-drenched gold, mystic maps, wild seas, wild fights, wild deeds!): it contains everything from Blackbeard to myself, from poppies to sea-shells, from butterflies to pieces of eight, from ghosts to living pirates, from maps to palm-trees. And, if you are interested in this (my first attempt at real rhyme and meter) I will send you a copy.

But already I have promised far too many copies that never seem to get far—but they certainly will come in time, for my motto is: Slow but Sure.

But besides this pirate song, I have managed to find time for a story. To be sure, it isn't written yet, but I have such a firm idea of what I mean to write that it will be very little trouble when I once get buckled down to it. It is about a little girl (nothing like Eepersip, however) who was always having strange, fantastic ideas about things, but most especially about pirates and gypsies. She writes little odd, quaint stories about everything she sees, and wants to be a gypsy herself. When her family moves from a tiny country village to a large city, she begins the business of fortune-telling, with the aid of a friend of hers—and for beautiful, written fortunes she is given various little odds and ends, mostly trinkets; and in this way she collects the necessities for a gypsy costume, until, finally, she is able to wander about dressed just like a gypsy—with golden bangles, and pearl bangles, and bracelets, and anklets, and a full flouncy skirt with bright embroideries. But it is her ideas and her writings that will make the main part of this *biography*; for I expect to put in many of them just as she might have written them. And in these stories, though she loved things of Nature, and was constantly making butterflies and birds and flowers play the main parts in her stories—she wrote mostly about pirates and gypsies: for her idea of pirates was much the same, mystic, blood-and-gold, unknown-isle as mine; and her idea of gypsies was simply a mysterious tribe who wore the golden bangles she was so fond of, and who told fortunes—just as she did. I am so overflowing with ideas for this new story that—well, if this letter should suddenly break off in the midst of a line or sentence, you would know why; I would be simply overwhelmed with a flood of irresistible ideas.

But all this time Farksolia is languishing. Not because I am tired of it, or because I have no more to say. Quite the contrary: I have had many admirable ideas about it, but simply haven't had time to write them down. I am looking forward to next summer to get a great pile of writing accomplished: I expect to work a great deal more next summer, rather than running about aimlessly so much. The Natural History of Farksolia has been elongating so that I have decided to make of it a separate volume entirely from the plain, everyday history. There is quite a variety of birds, butterflies, flowers, trees, reptiles, etc. etc. *almost* indefinitely.

I am enclosing: thanks for the book of songs, thanks for your letters, wishes for your good health, the mountain poem, a promise for the pirate poem (if you want it), a promise for the letter-account, the keys, and lots of love from us all.

>   Your friend,
>   Barbara.

Barbara's mountain poem, dated January 4, 1927.

SONG OF THE MOUNTAINS
>   I may never touch the snow-fringed Moon,
>>   White-robed, her sandals bound with stars—
>   Never walk on heaving waves,
>>   Or climb to radiant, fiery Mars.
>   I cannot dance the burning magic
>>   Of the Earth, with sunbeam rays,
>   Whirling, softly golden—yet
>>   On snowy sky-peaks I may gaze.
>   I have not trod those unknown isles
>>   Where raging winds like sea-ghosts blow,
>   But I know mountains, sky-kissing goddesses,
>>   And I have wandered amid their snow.
>   For my eyes there is no pirate treasure,
>>   Nor have I seen an albatross,
>   Color of snow, like the playful foam
>>   That laughing sea-winds gently toss.
>   But I have touched the feathers of the frost,
>>   Pale mountain-ghosts; and their rippled wings
>   Are lacy shells from the Sunbeam Isles,
>>   And whisperings from all magic things.
>   My heart is always with the mountains,
>>   Wind-swept; their peaks deep-fringed with sky—
>   Up there I still hear the waves,
>>   And the albatross—her lonesome cry.

I wish I had a recording of Barbara's appearance on the radio. As far as I know no recording of her voice has survived. Symposium *was an hour long, and the following listing is from the* New York Times.

Today's Radio Programs
WRNY, New York, January 22, 1927
 11:00 A.M. – Symposium. L. Carillo, James Connell, Barbara Follett, Hilda Gold.

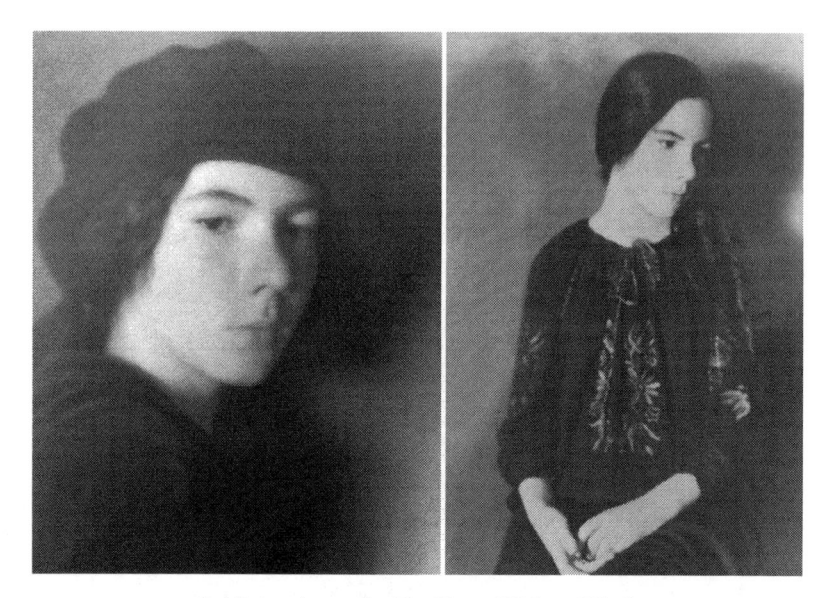

Publicity photos for *The House Without Windows*

Excerpts from A Mirror of the Child Mind, *Henry Longan Stuart's review of* The House Without Windows, *published in the* New York Times *on February 6, 1927.*

[...] From the moment of her escape on "the foothills of Mount Varcobis" to the last line of the book, Eepersip is the protagonist of her own adventure. No attempt is made to invest the birds and beasts that become her friends with any human attributes, far less human speech. An unbridled imagination is checked at every moment by a literalness of description that is apparently the amazing fruit of keen first-hand observation. [...] Barbara Follett may live and write to 90. But she will never give us the flight of sea birds more truly and vividly than in these dozen and a half words she wrote at the time: "Strong, narrow wings that beat down the air as the birds rose again, to hover and swoop and plunge." [...] There can be few who have not at one time or another coveted the secret, innocent and wild at the same time, or a child's heart. And here is little Miss Barbara Follett, holding the long-defended gate wide open and letting us enter and roam at our will over enchanted ground.

*Howard Mumford Jones (1892-1980) was a prolific writer. At the time of his review (*Barbara Follett: Child of Genius, *published in the* New York World *on February 13, 1927) he was teaching at the University of North Carolina. He would go on to have a long career at Harvard University,* served as President of the American Academy of Arts and Sciences, and in 1964 won a Pulitzer for O Strange New World: American Culture—The Formative Years.

The jacket of "The House Without Windows" says that the book "will be of special interest to teachers and parents who are interested in education; for it is the expression of a child who has never been to school." This is plain blah. "The House Without Windows" will interest anybody who cares a snap of his fingers for beauty and good writing. [...] The author has never been to school. There seems to be no sane reason why she should ever go to one unless she wants to. [...] She has the Mozartian calm. She writes as though she were living in that serene abode where the eternal are. It is as it should be. That is where she lives and where she takes us.

Excerpts from Lee Wilson Dodd's long review (In Arcady), *published in the* Saturday Review of Literature *on February 19, 1927.*

This strange, delightful, and lovely book was written by a little girl as a present for her mother [...] This is very beautiful writing. But there are moments when, for one reader, this book grows almost unbearably beautiful. It becomes an ache in his throat. Weary middle-age and the clear delicacy of a dawn-Utopia, beckoning... The contrast sharpens to pain. One closes the book and shuffles about doggedly till one finds the evening paper and smudges down to one's element—that smudged machine-record of what man has made of man. Of man—and therefore of childhood! [...]

176 Armory Street
New Haven, Connecticut
February 23, 1927

My dear Mr. St. John:
No words can describe how glad I was to hear that you will be in New Haven. I was quite beside myself with glee. Now you boil everything down to plain facts, it is a long, long time since we have seen each other and talked. Last summer has been gone a long time, and that was not a very thorough visit, anyhow. On Saturday I am free from all engagements, and I shall certainly keep it clear for you. When you arrive in the city, telephone Pioneer 5696, and we will make arrangements. My study is, you know, a temptingly quiet place for a good out-and-out talk.
I have my snowshoe trip to tell you about, my experience with the radio, my pirate tales, an interesting friend of mine (a little younger

than I am)—and loads of other things. *Please* don't change your plans! We shall be exceedingly glad to see you, and we all send love.

>Your friend,
>Barbara.

176 Armory Street
New Haven, Connecticut
February 27, 1927

Dear Mr. Jones:

I was glad to know that you liked my book; your review was delightful. That paragraph of *The Sea* that you quoted was the same one quoted from the New York Times. It is odd, but that place has always been one of my favorite bits, too. I always had a great deal of fun describing fishes.

I don't blame anyone for not being able to pronounce my names. It took a long time for me to settle into any definite spelling of them at all—they seemed to defy all attempts at writing down.

The mystic art of inventing and contriving such oddities is lost to me now.

>Your friend,
>Barbara.

P. S. I was especially glad to hear that Eleanor liked the book. I wonder if she likes pirates. I am very fond of them myself, and have been writing stories on pages of gold with letters of pure bright blood! B. N. F.

176 Armory Street
New Haven, Connecticut
February 27, 1927

My dear Mr. Oberg:

This is simply [a] hurried note in the midst of my business, to repeat the invitation which I gave on last October. Can you not plan to come away to N. H. on next Thursday, March 3rd—to stay over the week-end? We would all be very glad to see you—and I'm sure the butterflies need some talking over!

The reviews of my book are fast coming in, and perhaps we can find some time to file them up. All the reviews I have seen so far are very favorable, and it is interesting to keep them.

>There is much to tell.
>Your friend,
>Barbara.

TO THE SEA (1927–1929)

A letter from George Bryan from around February 1927.

Cartagene de las Indias
Nueva Granada

Dear Peter:
I know not whether you would much enjoy this place. The roadstead is indeed large and fine, and has at its entrance a goodly island—called, in the outlandish tongue common in these parts, Tierra Bomba. Seen from the water, the town is sufficiently handsome; for the beholder notes, first, gray walls of a prodigious thickness; then gray houses with roofs of red tiles; and back of these, hills of a considerable height, rising in a green ring.

But the spot when better known is less admired. The climate is by no means healthful. Great heat prevails, and neighboring swamps exhale vapors that are not at all salutary. Water for drinking is obtained chiefly from cisterns that have been built upon the town walls; in these cisterns the rain-water is caught. The streets are wretchedly paved and for the most part wonderfully crooked.

The Spaniards have managed this port as they have managed their other possessions in the region—that is, with the purpose of extracting all possible for their own enrichment and with no care whatsoever for the right administering of justice or for the welfare of the inhabitants. It would surprise you, my friend, to know how much treasure was hoarded here in the old days; and surprise you yet more to know how much was taken hence by some of the buccaneers in those fierce times of plunder of which I formerly told you.

These times are long past; and I am here not to land with a storming-party under cover of darkness but merely by way of a visit of the most peaceable nature. A brief season of leisure thus falling to me, I have been reading with the deepest pleasure the volume that I received from you and that was stowed in my sea-bag when I made ready for this journey. I now discover that the book is by none other than yourself. Upon the page dedicatory the initials *J. H.* are boldly printed. This is a high honor, forsooth, for one who once upon a time was in fair danger of swinging at Execution Dock!

On numerous pages do I find matters that you often have mentioned to me; only here they are given with a particularity and a smoothness belonging to the written word. Nor rarely do I fancy that I discover myself in surroundings and situations with which you and I in company were aforetime familiar. Unless I greatly err, there is much of yourself in this *Eepersip*—a name that I never encountered among the various peoples I have known on either side of the Atlantic. At times I follow you, I fear, but haltingly and laggardly, as I followed you in many a *pas de deux* under northern pines. But I nevertheless do seek to follow; and as I follow, do actually seem at times to float clear of earth and out into the sunset.

Our ship remains here until its captain has completed certain business. How long that may be is not yet determined.

>Yours,
>Jas. Hook

Bertha Mahoney's review was published in the February 1927 issue of the Horn Book Magazine.

176 Armory Street
New Haven, Connecticut
March 7, 1927

My dear Miss Mahoney:

This morning I received two copies of the Horn Magazine, sent from Daddy's office at Knopf's. It was a perfectly lovely little review of The House Without Windows, and I appreciate it very much. It was a beautiful idea to put Dorothy Lathrop's little Christmas card in. I have thought before of how appropriate some of her fairy pictures are.

I was also glad to see that you had printed my funny little door-slip.

At any rate, I was glad to see that you liked the book: my only suspicion is that it may start running away among young children, and consequently make me a lot of enemies. I already know of one little child who was tempted. Her father wrote to me about it!

>Your friend,
>Barbara Follett

176 Armory Street
New Haven, Connecticut
March 7, 1927

Dear Mr. Jones:

Until now I had not realized what my book is going to do for the world. But now it seems that it is going to make enemies for me instead of friends. But tell Eleanor to cheer up and finish the book. I have many plans up my sleeve for an Eepersipian escape, and I should be very glad to have a comrade—especially Eleanor.

Lake Sunapee in New Hampshire—where we go for the summers—is a place where one may very well play Eepersip. The small Twin Lakes are entirely surrounded with unexplored woodlands (or, at least, unexplored by everyone except myself) and hills, and very swimmable sand-beaches. It would be just the place for a rendezvous and head-quarters.

But tell Eleanor she must not go without me. I know all the tricks. You see, we shouldn't be entirely wild—we should be lightly connected with civilization, but I think our Lake Sunapee life would content Eleanor. I am out and across the hills from dawn till sunset.

My knowledge of pirates is rather limited too. Perhaps it is just as well—perhaps that is why I am so fond of them. My pirate learning comes from Peter and Wendy and Treasure Island. John Silver was a marvelous kind of pirate, because he could pretend to be so sublimely innocent. Billy Bones was different, but, somehow, I am exceedingly fond of him, too. The only real trouble with Treasure Island is that Long John should have been able to escape with his gang of rum-and-gold-lovers—with Flint's treasure in the ample hold of the *Hispaniola* (as he first intended). Of course, Jim Hawkins should have become a fascinated worshiper of John Silver's methods, and should have been converted, as Silver wanted. Then the doctor and the squire—also the captain—should have been slain or marooned. Somehow those three were not the kind of persons who should have become the possessors of that gold.

But I am not trying to teach anything to Robert Louis Stevenson.

Your friend,

A rare interview with Barbara, published in the March 13, 1927 Hartford Daily Courant. I've cut almost all of the long article—Peter Pan's Sister Writes a Book—*while keeping Barbara's and her mother's words.*

"What studies have you preferred?"
"I like Latin best."
"Do you read any other language?"
"A little French."
"And next to Latin?"
"Possibly history. In this I have read and read again the stories of the founding of America and the war of the Revolution. Just now I am all wrapped up in the life of Joan of Arc, especially with the historical setting in the fifteenth century."
"What other studies?"
"Natural sciences. These and their application fascinate me."
"Does your mother conduct your recitations?"
"Yes, in a general but not a formal way. She gives me problems in algebra, natural history or science and she hears me recite my

Latin declensions. She assigns me short stories to write and I have written several. My recitation hours depend somewhat on how busy Mother is."

"Did you ever try to drive an auto?"

Barbara's eyes flashed scorn at this suggestion of twelve-year-old activity.

"No," she answered. "I never even had a bicycle. But I love to walk. It was not many weeks ago that I walked twenty miles in one day and have walked over the Franconia range in the summer. I love swimming and I have swum half a mile at our summer home at Lake Sunapee."

"What authors do you read most, Barbara?"

"Shakespeare, Shelley and Walter de la Mare. I like to read the old authors again and again and I have read and re-read many of Shakespeare's plays. I have always been charmed with "The Treasure of the Isle of Mist" by W. W. Tarn. "The Three Mulla-Mulgars" by Walter de la Mare, I have read again and again."

"Are you interested in music?"

"I take piano lessons from Bruce Simonds and violin lessens from Hugo Gortshak [sic]. I have been going to concerts ever since I was six years old.

"Are you going to college?"

"No plans have been made for it. I have always enjoyed my home life and my studies at home." Which shows that Eepersip, Peter Pan's sister, has grown up, a thing Barrie never permitted Peter to do.

"Barbara's education," explained Mrs. Follett, "illustrates the advantage of not being put into groups. Much creative ability is killed by the modern school. Barbara has been given every chance for expression, and she is taking advantage of them all. Children have much more to say than opportunity is given them to express in the school room. We have tried to allow Barbara a full and free expression. This child has had leisure and tools to work with in her language and thought. She has used both in writing the book. She has never been bored by the things that bore other children."

Then Mrs. Follett took up the question of a college education where Barbara had left it.

"Selection of a college offers another set of problems," she said. "Some persons are not so fond of a college course for their daughters as they are. We, Barbara's parents, do not care much just now whether she goes to college or not. Whether she goes will depend upon conditions that develop later. If she wishes very much to go, she will go, but we shall not decide that for the present. If she shows signs of creative ability, I would not urge her to go for fear of affecting it unfavorably. If she turns out to be without initiative, we may have to send her. At present we feel there is not value enough in a college course for us to wish to force it upon her."

Brookfield Center, Conn.,
March 14th, 1927

Dear Peter:

Your picture in the paper was mighty pleasing, and I recognized not only you but the setting; but were you really reading proofs?—and do you actually aspire to be a pirate? As Togo, the Japanese Schoolboy, said: "I inquire to know."

I got a copy of the Wilson MacDonald book some little time ago, when the other Wilson spoke most highly of it to me. It seems to me quite worthy of the praise he gave it. I have read chiefly in the part called "The Book of the Rebel." "Exit" in "The Book of Man" is a fine variation on an old theme.

By the way, did you ever ask yourself whether that review by Elinor Wylie told you much about the edition she was supposed to be reviewing? Didn't it seem to you to be altogether too much about somewhat irrelevant things—especially about E. Wylie and various experiences of hers? She had been asked to tell us of a new and important (possibly *the* definitive) edition of the poet—an edition that most persons will be forced to see in libraries, if they see it at all (so costly it is); and I confess that she left me with no particular idea of the distinctive character and peculiar merits of it.

Thanks for the *alphabet* (you know *what* alphabet).

   Jas. Hook

176 Armory Street
New Haven, Connecticut
March 15, 1927

Dear Mr. Dodd:

I should have written to you long, long before this, if I had not been confident of seeing you and having the satisfaction of a private talk with you. Your review was perfectly lovely—it made me twice as happy as the others, though they were all favorable. It pleased me boundlessly to see you noticed my "daisied fawn." For, though I have never seen a young fawn, I think they must look like a daisy field in full bloom.

It seems very strange that I should have written so much about deer without ever having seen one alive. That is, up to a few weeks ago, when I went north to Lake Sunapee with a friend of mine. We stayed there several days, and, on one of our marvelous excursions over to a large game preserve, we encountered a herd of deer, soft-eyed, half-wild does, and feather-antlered bucks. I remember one small buck in particular, who leaped over a fence before our eyes (a fence much higher than he), first throwing up his delicate front legs, and then making his nimble heels "kick at heaven," as he landed almost silently on four feet of crusted snow. He was like a fairy, a real fairy, even if it is rather out of the ordinary to compare a quadruped to supernatural beings.

Never have I seen anything half so amusing as the antics of young kittens—I used to love to observe the various stray ignoramus cats we possessed at one time—that is why Snowflake is developed to such a great extent.

But I think we need a long afternoon to talk it all over.

> Your friend,
> Barbara.

From Lady Mary's Letter *in* The Star *(Wilmington, Delaware), dated March 27, 1927.*

Another Infant Prodigy Produces a Novel
There are so many infant prodigies in these days that people almost have ceased to remark them all.

The latest is Barbara Follett. [...] As a child lover I shall read the book, of course. But the work of prodigies often appalls when I examine it; usually these overbright youngsters amount to little later on!

Alice Carroll Moore (1871-1961) was head of children's library services for the New York Public Library system and was probably the most important children's book reviewer in the country at the time. Her essay, When Children Become Authors, *was published in the* New York Herald Tribune *on March 27, 1927:*

[...] I can conceive of no greater handicap for the writer between the ages of nineteen and thirty-nine, than to have published a successful book between the ages of nine and twelve. [...] What price will Barbara Follett have to pay for her "big days" at the typewriter, days when she rattled off, we are told, four to five thousand words of original copy at a speed of 1,200 words to the hour, producing at the end of three months a complete story of some 40,000 words. I have only words of praise for the story itself. [...]

Columbia's copy of Barbara's response is an edited draft.

176 Armory Street
New Haven, Connecticut
March 28, 1927

Dear Miss Moore:

It surely is very rash to slam down into the mud a childhood and a system of living that you know nothing about. There are things in your article of the 27th that are plain mistruths, which I feel the need of correcting. You write positively as if all children were alike, as if all children desired the same surroundings, as if they all liked the same things. Children are as different from each other as grown-up people; they are even more insistent in their variety of tastes; and a great deal more hurt when things do not go as they like. You say that you "can conceive of no greater handicap for the writer between the ages of nineteen and thirty-nine, than to have published a successful book between the ages of nine and twelve." And is that true about everyone? Why should it be true at all to an intelligent person? If you think it makes me feel vain and self-conscious to have published a book, let me say that that is untrue: I wrote the story in the first place because I wanted to run away, but, realizing the impossibility of it, I made someone else do it for me. The book was not written to be published—it was written for the sheer joy of writing. I am very much amused at the favorable reviews which are being written—I do not take them at all seriously—but I do take seriously an article which distorts into a miserable caricature my living, my education, my whole personality.

You also said: "Children need the companionship of other children"—but you seem to take it perfectly for granted that I do not. What made you think that? For I do play with other children, and up to a certain point I like it. It is undeniable that I do not go to parties and social events as much as other children do—I do not even play with them as much as other children do, but that, from my point of view, is *not* a forfeit. Neither am I forced to stay away from them. I do so because I wish to—it is by my own free will.

There are countless other objections to going to school, but with me the chief of them is this: if I went to school, where would I get the time for the violin and piano music that I enjoy so much; where would I get the time for comfortable reading of good books; where would I get the time for the writing which gives me joy more than almost everything I do? If I went to school I should have to spend the afternoon in weary "home-work." I should be able to write only during the summer months when I love to be outdoors and alone, and I should be doing hardly any music at all.

My life is very different from what you make it out to be: you write as if I was tyrannized over and coerced to be alone, coerced to write, kept away from children by main force. And that grieves me because it is so strictly untrue. It is also an insult to my parents.

Perhaps the most painful thing in the article is your absurd idea that I take a "professional attitude toward writing." That is so untrue that I am ashamed even to look at it—ashamed that a supposedly intelligent person should say so much about a thing she knows absolutely nothing about. You have no reason on earth to suppose that. As I said before, I wrote the story for the sheer joy of writing, without taking the smallest glimpse of the "professional" side of it.

If you had read the book from the right stand-point, nothing could have made you say such abasing things. The book is an expression of joy—no more—and to a careful person it *should* be an expression of my home-life as well.

Barbara Newhall Follett.

Eleanor Farjeon (1881-1965) wrote the words for Morning Has Broken—*a song covered many years later by Cat Stevens. Her review was printed in London's* Time and Tide *on April 25th, 1927, about when THWW was published by Knopf in London.*

This is an enchanting book. I will be brief with explanations, which are, however, quite incapable of explaining it. The tale is a child's dream of childhood, as it is and as it might be; and it is the work of a child of nine, rewritten, because it was destroyed, between the ages of ten and twelve. So the tongue of the dream is that of an age slightly advanced beyond the age in which the dream was created; but such nearness of speech and of conception can never have happened before in a work whose whole concern is childhood, and the radiant delight we lose as we grow older. Barbara Newhall Follett found her voice before she had lost anything; the book is bathed in a magical light which we older ones try to remember, or recapture, or assume. [...]

I do not think the perfection of this books is an accident; I have seen charming and amusing things written by children who in later life did other things; I have never seen a piece of writing by so young a child which made me certain that it was written under the influence of that movement which makes poets write they know not how. What will happen when her more conscious mind begins to direct what Barbara Follett writes, I do not know; but that she will always have to write I am almost sure; and if, in each age, she can produce something as true to her immediate experience as this, she will have a wonderful record. [...]

A letter to her father with an ominous opening line. The quote in the middle ("up to the pig-styes...") is from Rudyard Kipling's How the Leopard Got His Spots.

176 Armory Street
New Haven, Connecticut
April 29, 1927

Dear Daddy:

It seems to us that New York must be a sort of Louis XI's palace, full of snares, temptations, pit-falls, traps, and everything else for enticing and entangling its helpless victims. But now we have a stunning excuse for you to come home:

"The Brat" has a habit of calling at least forty-one times when Helen is in the house, but if she knows that Helen is out, she will hold her tongue. So *we* have the habit of going out for a walk every evening, as soon as the aforesaid "brat" is in. (She usually, however, has time enough to call three or four times before we are out.) Tonight, having nowhere in particular to go, we wandered over to see what the back-yards of our rich neighbors have developed into. (They are getting to be unusually nice back-yards.) Then a stunning idea occurred to me, and with much difficulty I persuaded Helen to scramble up Mill Rock a little way, and investigate the woods. Besides, I saw a patch of something green up high, which promised mystery. So up we went. The green proved to be a mass of plants which looked like overgrown mint, but among them, and up close to an overhanging rock, a columbine swung two or three red-and-yellow buds.

A long time ago, I had seen columbine up there, but I had never been able to find the place again. This time, however, I land-marked it carefully, and tomorrow I expect to take it up (since it is not a very large plant). But things developed tremendously in the course of a few minutes. There were multitudes of plants with leaves something like the leaves of bird's-foot violets, but with small yellow buds. I shall watch them. Up still higher we came on to a grassy path, which wound up the ledges. There were high, leafing bushes with graceful streamers up there, on one of which hung a few clusters of a kind of dangling barberry. Down on the right side of the path

(Not a whole garden is so lovely quite
As a prim path with flowers on the right!)

were clumps of leaves which looked as if they belonged to some kind of bulb (long, narrow, pointed), and, on investigating, I found patches of iris growing wild there, with some of them already budded. It looks from the buds like a blue variety. I expect to help myself to some of them. Still farther along on this mysterious path, we came upon masses of white and purple violets, possibly the largest violets I have ever seen. But still farther along was the great surprise of surprises. It was a wall—a high brick wall, with shrubbery showing over the top, and a red magnolia flowering at the foot. Near it were clumps of still another bulb—pale green shoots, not well matured yet. I shall certainly keep an eye (perhaps two eyes) on them. But I have some clue as to what they are, and I believe they are some kind of lily. For amid the shoots was a dried stalk, surmounted with a withered, stiffened, brown flower-cup, which was the shape of a lily.

I intend to make a great many visits, basket and shovel in hand, to this veritable Eden-of-cultivated-things-gone-wild, and I hope you will come along

". . . up to the pig-styes
and sit on the farmyard rails!
Let's say things to the bunnies,
And watch 'em skitter their tails!
Let's—oh, *anything*, daddy—
So long as it's you and me . . ."

And there really are bunnies skittering their tails. We saw an adorable small-sized one, as we came down, who flickered his white puff-ball, and he skittered from bush to bush, crouching quietly and melting "Into the landscape."

The wrens have again tenanted the green bird-house. Sabra was the first one to see them going in and out. Their songs are everywhere now.

The pansies are flourishing nobly . . . . lilacs are still budding . . . . seeds are coming up as well as could be expected . . . . daily I find new lily-of-the-valley shoots . . . . most exciting documents are pouring in from Brookfield Center way, including a delightful review of *T. H. W. W.*, also a great many important hints on the subject of *sunset-reading*, which I have not come to be very proficient at. The only thing I can think of at this moment that is not progressing, is my pirate story. That is because the time I would otherwise spend on it, I am now glad to spend digging out-of-doors.

I wish you superb luck on your writing (whatever it is), only I am sorry you couldn't do it here.

You will enjoy my new-found "Mrs. Derby's garden" up there in the wood. It is very like the woods in which we found so many wood anemones and violets and yellow adder's tongue, a long time ago. I always have remembered that walk: though I can't even remember how we got out into the woods, or where we were living. I still remember certain anemone-carpeted glades in those woods, and how we wanted to pick them all. Now, with my new craze, I should probably want to transplant them all.

Sabra is making such marvelous progress in her reading, that I am greatly delighted and proud of her. She picks out the words come, away, play, and run, anywhere in her books. I got her to copy "come away, come and play," from her first reader on the typewriter. This gives her a chance to learn the little letters. We try to do some every day. She still skips about singing: "It is, it is a glorious 'fing' to be a pirate king!" Tonight, as we went down the front steps, we heard: "Yo, ho-ho, and a bottle of 'er *rum!*" with a terrible accent on the "rum."

We do hope you will tell us where you are staying. If Sabra should dance out the window tonight, or should be wafted away like Persephone, we couldn't tell you of it until ————Monday morning!

(The Pirates————1940!)

    All good cheer to you,

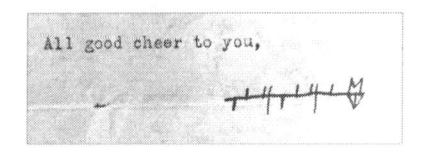

Regarding the treasure buried on Gardiner's Island in the town of East Hampton, New York, Wikipedia says: "The privateer William Kidd buried treasure on the island in June, 1699, having stopped there while sailing to Boston to answer charges of piracy. With the permission of the island's proprietor, he buried a chest and a box of gold and two boxes of silver (the box of gold Kidd told Gardiner was intended for Lord Bellomont) in a ravine between Bostwick's Point and the Manor House... A plaque on the island marks the spot where the treasure was buried, but it is on private property."

May 7, 1927

Dear Peter:

As you display such keen interest in the matter of *treasure*, I herewith communicate to you certain information that may prove of service.

The following valuables are supposed to have been found in a *swamp* on the *west* side of Gardiner's Island:

[A detailed list of treasure, including about fifty pounds in gold, included here.]

It is alleged that this treasure was found buried in iron chests, and that it was intrusted to Mr. John Gardiner by Kidd with the reminder that he (Gardiner) *must answer for it with his head*.

Now, it is possible that further treasure was buried at Gardiner's Island, either by Kidd or by others. As New Haven is on the coast, it would be possible for you to organize an expedition in the most approved fashion to sail to Gardiner's Island and search there.

It has also been said that Kidd had *caches* on the coast of Connecticut and the banks of its larger rivers.

      Yours for luck,
      Jas. Hook

Hilda Conkling (1910-1986), whose Poems by a Little Girl *(which included* Mary Cobweb) *was published in 1920, wrote to Barbara on May 31, 1927.*

[...] "Mary Cobweb" was my one and only friend of mine and I felt very lost and sad when she left me. When I come to think over the likeness between my "Mary Cobweb" and your "Eepersip" I realize that they aren't so very much alike after all. "Mary Cobweb" was more a "home girl" as they say while "Eepersip" was more for the out of doors. Though I love both equally well.

[...] I do like pirates! I used to tell myself wild stories of being caught by pirates. Of course there was always some handsome gallant that saved me in the end. But I'm sure that your pirate story will have it over mine entirely. What is its title? I wish I could read it sometime. Do you think I could?

      lovingly your friend,
      Hilda

In June 1927, Barbara sailed for ten days aboard the Frederick H., *a three-masted lumber schooner, from New Haven to Bridgewater, Nova Scotia. George Bryan was her chaperone.*

[undated, ca. late June 1927]
176 Armory Street,
New Haven, Connecticut

Dearest Shipmate:

As we figger it out, after great maneuvering, the 'hing weighs four lb. ten ounces; 74 ounces in all, divided by half, 37 cents, plus 10 for Special Delivery, 47—total 47; plus 2 for a letter which must be mailed: total 49. So here is 50 cents, and Gow Blass You.

This runs up a debt which could never be repayed, even though heaven should one day in the far future grant me the means, which it couldn't, with all its power, do, I feel such an inexpressible gratitude, and never, though you live to be a thousand, could any deed outweigh in either words or worth this very climax of all generosity—oh, I have an idea I'd better stop, before I fall asleep in my chair.

> The other shipmate,
> Barbara.

P. S. One cent tip, as you notice.

Lake Sunapee
New Hampshire
July 14, 1927

Dear Mr. Oberg:

I presume you must think I am dead by this time. Of course, there has been the usual rush getting off to Sunapee. Otherwise I haven't any excuse at all for not writing to you for such a long time. Oh yes! one excuse.

But that is a long story. Early in June a proud three-masted schooner sailed into New Haven, with a cargo of lumber from Nova Scotia. I went aboard her, climbed many times up to her lofty crosstrees, and out on her high jibboom. I became acquainted with the captain and the crew. A few days before she sailed, I had it all rigged up with a friend of mine to sail back in her with me to Nova Scotia.

Oh! that trip! It was marvelous—it will always be one of the treasures of my memory. We had unusually calm weather, mostly—the sails flapped and the reef points pattered. But when at last we had a wind, we had it hard. It was so hard, in fact, we took down the outer jib and the topsails. The waves were a vivid storm-green, crested with flying foam, and a furious white bone roared in the white teeth of the schooner. Over she canted, far to leeward. Imagine the thrill I had when we sat at table, using table-racks to keep the dishes from sliding off. There were times when even the sailors staggered a bit, walking from aft to forward. At night we almost rolled out of our bunks.

It seems to me, from what little I saw over one weekend, that Nova Scotia is a very beautiful country. And its inhabitants are very friendly and kind, even to strangers.

You should hear me repeat nautical words and phrases and sailor-slang; also, I like to show my knowledge of sailing ships.

I'll tell you more of this later, but this must be mailed now.

>Your friend,
>Barbara.

"The Cottage in the Woods"
Lake Sunapee, New Hampshire
July 22, 1927

Dear Mr. St. John:

I think I have never let so many nice long letters come from you without a word from me in the meantime. But, things in general have interrupted other things, and it took me a long time to get "settled" into the ways of civilization when I came back from my sea trip. Before that, I was so excited about the schooner, and going down to see her almost every day, that I could think of nothing else, let alone write letters. Then there was the usual confusion of packing and getting up here—and now, at last, here we be, and it is truly the first spell of real quiet I have had since goodness only knows when.

Do you love the sea and ships, yourself? I do not see any reason whatsoever why you shouldn't, but, somehow, I can't associate you in my mind with anything but the woods, and trees, and flowers, birds, mountains. Perhaps that's because I wasn't going on my sea-rage when I last saw you, though I remember I was fond of pirates at the time.

Well, I got on a sea-rage all right, and, long before I had seen the *Frederick H.*, I knew quite a bit about ships—ropes, spars, and whatnot. It was the most rash, suddenly unadvised thing I ever lurched forth upon. One day I simply decided I would go. And about three days afterwards I went. Oh! there is nothing in the world more thoroughly delightful than being under sails, the schooner leaning before a north-west gale, the green and foaming waves raging all about, the sails full and bellying out with wind, the howling and whistling of wind through the white canvas, the raging white bone the schooner would have in her white teeth, the far cant to leeward so that we had to use the table-racks, the calling out of "Hard-a-lee!" when we tacked, the bustle of men's feet to the blocks and sheets;

or in a calm for several days, nothing but the swell which rolled you out of your bunk at night, so that she almost rolled water onto her decks, and everything rolling and thumping, doors banging in the cabin, bottles and dishes jingling, the groaning of the booms as they would swing in and out, the billowing and flapping of the idle sails, the pattering of reef-points; and the sailor-life in general, the brief commands of mate and skipper, the nautical words and terms, steering by the light of the binnacle-lamp beneath the stars at night, when the moon would shine full on the sails, making them look like newfallen snow, the very reminiscence of the old sailor-life on clipper-ships, with watches, look-outs, two-hour tricks, the merry yarning of the crew when off duty in the fo'c'sle, the gayness of them all, the carefreeness—it was all just exactly as I had dreamed. Or being in thick fog; when you can't distinguish sea from sky, everything is a moving, ghostly space that one can see and feel. Or hauling and lending a hand anywhere—on ropes which needed tautening, taking a turn at the wheel, sweeping the decks by the hour for my special friend, the mate, helping the old cook over his meals and his dishes, talking with all the crew—it was my great delight. And I loved to go up in the rigging, too, especially on hot days, for there was invariably a breeze aloft, and you got shade from the vast expanse of the sails—up and up I would go, into the taut ratlines, feeling the life and joy of the ship as if she were a living, happy creature—happy leaning before the wind, happy in the foam she made, her white wings and the furious bone she held in her teeth; up where the taut ratlins quivered a little beneath the strain of the wind, and I would sit on the cross-trees and swing my legs into space.

But do not think that I have forgotten about the mountains. No indeed. I am very eager to get up on to granite peaks again. And so Mother suggested (and I strongly seconded the idea) that you should stop on your way up to Passaconaway, and take me along, and climb a mountain or two with me. For that would be two-in-one—we should have our wished-for visit, and a mountain at the same time—a pretty fine combination, in my mind. Do you suppose that could be arranged? It wouldn't matter to me *what* mountain! And it would be delightful if you could stop in this region two or three days, and become acquainted with Lake Sunapee once more.

As for flowers, Hooker's orchid seems to be pretty well attached to me. I have seen three this summer, and saw three last summer. They are the weirdest, most mysterious looking blossoms I have ever seen, that mystic green, with the two pollen masses of golden-brown, looking for all the world like two eyes in a little green face. The leaves are very curious, too, so shiny, round, and almost leathery. I suppose you are acquainted with the flower.

We have no plans at all for the late summer, and, having no automobile, it is impossible for us to do anything on our own account. But stop here on the way up, anyway, and we'll make plans then, and see about a capful of mountain-wind, or a shoeful of mountain snow.

>Your friend,
>Barbara (Sindbad, the Sailor)

The recipient of the next letter was almost certainly a descendant of Benjamin Stimson, who sailed with Richard Henry Dana, Jr., author of the 1840 book, Two Years Before the Mast. *The 1911 edition published by* Houghton Mifflin *had a painting of the* Alert *on its jacket.*

"The Cottage in the Woods"
Lake Sunapee, New Hampshire
July 26, 1927

Dear Mr. Stimson:

The book arrived late yesterday afternoon, forwarded from New Haven, and it carried with it a great mystery, and a great many questions. How in all this world did you know that I am what you might call mad, love-blind, over sailing ships of all descriptions, as well as over sailor-life in the square-rigged period? It has always been (or, not exactly *always*, but since about last fall), a great regret of mine that I was not alive during the clippers and square-riggers—before the age of steam. But it is too late now—to be sure, I can still go on schooner-trips, and I can still sail in the old row-boat of ours with a mast stuck into a whittled hole in the bow of it—but the old square-riggers have pretty well gone by, at least, in this country.

I can get them back, you see, only by means of books—and books do make things almost as real as actuality. From the very moment when I heard the title *Two Years Before the Mast* (which Daddy mentioned in a letter which he wrote to me when he forwarded the book up here), I thought to myself: "I think this is going to be a book I'm going to like." And when I first laid my eye on merely the *Alert* painted on the jacket, I said: "I'm *sure* this is a book I'm going to like!"

To be sure, I cannot yet say very much about the book itself, having already read only a few chapters—but what I have read are full of the spirit of square-riggers (somehow it is very different from the spirit of schooners), full of both the hardships and the merriment of sailor-life, full of many little nautical words and terms (and the more I see of those, the better, for I am trying to learn them, full of the very sound of the sea and the whistling of wind through the sails—

and it is the more vivid, of course, because it is the actual experience of the author. That is the best part of all.

Since you have been so mind-reading (or, perhaps, heart-reading) as to discover this close relationship between me and the sea, you may also know, through the same magical process, that I have just returned from a ten-day cruise on a three-masted schooner. To be sure you have—for it has appeared at least twice in News and Views of Borzoi Books! And so I thought you might be interested in a very condensed brief account of the voyage, which was a curious one, having both dead calm and a high gale, both sparkling clearness and a fog "thick as mud," as the crew said.

Well, I had been on a sea-rage all right, long before I had seen the *Frederick H*. I had been delving into a golden treasury of ship-words and diagrams in the dictionary, and I had really learned quite a little about ropes, sails, spars, etc. And so, when a friend of mine, who had been a sailor all his life, told me that a three-masted schooner had come into New Haven, I lost not a second in getting down to see her. She was lying close to the wharf, and it thrilled me as I have almost never been thrilled before, to look up at her long jibboom and flying jibboom, or up into the mazes of the rigging (which I had secret hopes of being allowed to climb). We hailed the skipper, who was sitting on deck, superintending the work or discharging the cargo of lumber, and asked permission to come aboard. This was speedily granted, and aboard we went, helter-skelter, over the lumber-carts. The first thing I did was to climb out on the spanker-boom, which slightly overhung the water, and walk along it to the very end. The next thing I did was to ask if I might go into the rigging. The captain said I might; only I was not to go off the rope ladder, and I was to "hold hard." I went, and never stopped until I reached the cross-trees. This was as much a surprise to me as to everybody else, for I had never dreamed of going more than a few steps. There I sat, just as Jim Hawkins had sat in his terrified flight from Israel Hands. I experienced great delight in knowing that I was sitting where he had sat on the *Hispaniola*! We became well acquainted with the skipper, Captain Read, and before very long it was arranged that he should take me and Mr. Bryan with him, back to Nova Scotia. I will not deny that the first thing I did was to dash upstairs to my dictionary, at full speed, and look up the points of the compass, which I learned by heart. Well, to cut a very long story very short (and at that this letter is getting long enough!) it was the most rash, sudden, unadvised, but most thoroughly delightful enterprise I ever lurched forth upon. Oh! but there is nothing more heavenly than being under wide-spreading sails, fore-and-aft, or square, or anything else, leaning before a north-east gale, the green and foaming waves raging all about, the sails full and bellying out with wind, the howling and whistling of wind through the white canvas, the raging white bone the schooner would have in her white teeth, the cant to leeward so that we had to use the table-racks, the calling of "Hard-a-lee!" when we tacked, the bustle of men's feet to the blocks and sheets; or in a calm for several days, nothing but the swell which rolled you out of your bunk at night, so that she almost rolled water on her deck, and everything rolling and thumping, doors banging in the cabin, bottles and dishes jingling, the groaning of the booms as they would swing in and out, the billowing and flapping of the idle sails, the pattering of the reef-points; the sailor-life in general, brief commands of mate and skipper, nautical words and terms, the reminiscence of old clipper-ship sailor-life, with watches, look-outs, two-hour tricks, the merry yarning of the crew when off duty in the fo'c'sle, the gayness of them all, the carefreeness—it was all just exactly as I had dreamed; or being in thick fog when you can't distinguish sea from sky, when everything is a moving, ghostly space that you can see and feel. Then I loved my part of it, too. I was often allowed a half-trick at the wheel, in daylight, or steering by the light of the binnacle-lamp beneath the stars, when the moon would shine on the sails, making them look like newfallen snow, or making the foam whiter and lovelier than ever. I used often to lend a strong hand on the hauling of too slack ropes, or sweep the deck by the house for my special friend, the mate, or help the old cook with his dishes, or just sitting and talking with all the crew. But the best of all was, of course, the rigging. Even on the hottest days there was breeze up aloft, and the vast white expanse of the sails shaded you. You think and feel that the ship is happy leaning before the wind, and happy between her furious white wings, and the raging white bone in her teeth. I used to go up there in good, fresh breezes, when the ratlines quivered a little beneath the strain of the wind, and the sails tugged furiously at the gaffs and booms.

Well, you can see what might happen to the paper supply if I keep on too long at this rate. I have been known to talk three hours at a time, steadily, fast, furiously, about this trip, and then do another three hours the next day, yet never repeat a word! I should be delighted to have a real talk with you sometime, on the subject of ships and sailors.

Daddy tells me, by the way, that you are the owner of a Block Island boat. A sort of small schooner without topsails, isn't it? *Do* tell me when you intend to take command of it, for I want to get enlisted in your crew. You will find me a pretty able seaman, all things considered!

Again, thank you for *Two Years Before the Mast*. I'm sure I shall be just crazy over it, as I already am of what I have read.

>Your friend,
>Barbara Follett.

Lake Sunapee, New Hampshire
July 28, 1927

Dear Mr. Oberg:

Thank you for your letter; also for Sabra's birthday cards. She liked them very much, and getting mail of her own seemed to her very important. Young children always do like that sense of independence—of importance—and Sabra does, especially. She had quite a little party yesterday—a two-layer cake, frosted, with four small yellow candles and a black-eyed Susan in the middle, stuck down into the frosting; and ice cream. She was quite excited over everything, and told the whole world that she was "four years old."

I don't think I ever had a more delightful experience than the schooner-trip. You now, I had always wanted to go on a large sailboat, and this was the most delightful opportunity. I was not long in arranging a passage, I can tell you! We had fair winds, and no wind, thick fog, and clear—just about all kinds of weather—mingled in with a good, stiff gale of wind, the waves raging green covered with white foam, and black squalls thundering up upon us ominously. The shrill voice of the captain could be heard through the howling of the wind, exclaiming: "Get down the outer jib and topsails, boys!" Fog is a very curious thing at sea. The air is wet, heavy, briny, and you can't distinguish sea from sky—everything is a ghostly, moving, uncanny space. It has no shape, no outline, no horizon—to hear the boom swing back and forth, groaning, by the hour—the flapping of idle sails, the ceaseless pattering of the reef-points. The mate would say: "I hate to do nothing but sit here, and listen to her flap her wings and shake her feathers!" And that was a true description, too. Well, I might write or talk all day about that trip, and yet never get anyone to *feel* it. They might *hear* it well enough, but to *feel* it would be impossible for one who has not been under sails. Have you ever been under sails? When you crossed the Atlantic—was that in a sailing vessel or a steamer?

In your letter you mentioned going to Boston on business. Couldn't you turn that business into pleasure, and take the train to Potter Place, and thence by stage up here. The driver of the stage is Mr. Crane, and he would undoubtedly stop at the head of the lane, between George's Mills and New London. We should love to see you, and I hope you will find the chance to get up here. Of course there are certain disadvantages—for instance, the trip is very long and tiring, as of course you know.

>Always your friend,
>Barbara.

This letter may have been abandoned: there's room on the first page for the start of a new paragraph.

The Cottage in the Woods
Lake Sunapee
July 29, 1927

Dear Daddy:

We have seen some most curious and marvellous cloud and sky effects today. In the afternoon, when Mother and I walked up to New London, a thunder-storm billowed up behind us ominously, and we received a spatter of rain, but it swung away to the southward, and, though it was obviously raining pretty hard on Mt. Sunapee and the southern hills, we got only a few rain-drops. The clouds were dark and grey, but very interesting, on the way back: there were ranges of sharp-peaked mountains along the horizon, there were billowy masses of greyish-white clouds in peaks, between which could be seen another and darker cloud which looked as though it might be the sea—that same dismal grey of dark weather. When we got down to the shore of the lake, a most curious range of sharp, steep hills was marching slowly, ever changing shape, over the actual hills, looking very mysterious and uncanny. At the same time the sky was full of long, fluffy tiers of white clouds, lighted up by the sun.

But at the sun's *eight bells*, when it was the sun's watch below, the sky and the clouds were the most marvellous. The tiers changed to pink, and pink mottlings dappled the zenith, while down low in the north-west the white clouds changed into a curious formation of wisps and bays and pools. The curious thing about sunset colours is that, while the changes are almost imperceptible while you watch, the clouds really go through such vast changes of shape and colour that one is amazed because it is so unnoticeable. The upper clouds were pink, and lower down were pools of dark gold, mingled with shadowy tiers of blue. Brighter and brighter it grew, and more and more colours kept showing, until the whole west, clear around to north-east, was brilliant with it. In the north-west was the bright pink, the gold, a burning, metallic gold mingled with the blue; towards the south-west was a long, narrow strip of blue-green sky, looking like a sea with islands, bays, coves, and peninsulas—the upper shore of which was a narrow rim of brilliant gold, above which was a dark blue cloud, and the lower shore of it was a purple-russet-maroon—all those colours intermingled. Higher in the south-west were brilliant golds, russets, pinks, and blue shadows mingled together into an indescribable brilliance, and across which stretched a dark blue wing of cloud, a sharp contrast with the pools of colour. A sea of fires glowed amid the lowest north-western clouds, growing steadily larger and brighter, and, higher in the north-west, there seemed to be a pool of blue water, with golden surf which flung itself high into the air along its shores, and almost concealed it. The blue clouds among the gold changed to a maroon, and the colours along the shore of the blue-green sea grew brighter. So it changed indescribably, until there was nothing left—nothing but wildly tossed about dark blue clouds, with a few quivers of scarlet among them.

An excerpt from the first of several letters from Mate Bill, a.k.a. William H. McClelland, first mate aboard the Frederick H. *Barbara had sent him a jackknife for a present.*

New York
July th 30 1927

Well Barbara
   I Reicived the jack-knife sent I came in hear I had left Bridge water before the knife reach there so they sent it to me here
   so now I am trying to think how I am gone to return the gif
   we was 16 days coming over hear we had light fog all the way over and lots of head wind I though we was never gone to get here Barbara I am sending your things to you I spoke to the old man about them and he made no offer to send them so I thought I would send them to you [...]

"The Cottage in the Woods"
Lake Sunapee, N. H.
August 30, 1927

Dear Jane:
   Thank you ever so much for your nice letter about my book. I like to think that some children of my own age like the book, because everyone seemed to think that there was too much pure description of Nature in it for children—not enough *story*.

A great many things, especially in the third part, "The Mountains," I have seen and known myself. I have been among "frost-feathers," and I have watched them form out of driving mist which freezes on to the mountain-crags and is cut and carved by the wind. And I have been on Mount Moosilauke when the clouds broke away and the sun burst out almost exactly as I wrote it.

But all of part two, "The Sea," is my imagination, for I have never lived by the sea, and I don't know very much about it—at least, I didn't at the time. I believe I saw sea-gulls once or twice down at the shore somewhere. Since then I know a lot more about it, and I know that if I wrote "The Sea" all over, I should write it much better. Early this June, I went off to sea in a three-masted schooner, carrying lumber down from Nova Scotia, and going back there without cargo. We encountered all kinds of weather—calm, thick fog, clear, and high winds. I lived "rough," like all the sailors, and I picked up quite a lot about sailing of a schooner, and I learned how to do things on board—and I saw how the sea looks when the fog is so thick that you can hardly distinguish the water from the sky, and how it looks in a gale, when the foaming waves are high. I wish I could have had that trip before I wrote "The Sea"!

Just now, I am having a great deal of pleasure writing a long pirate story. That, of course, has a lot of the sea and ships in it, all of which I picked up just from those two weeks off in the schooner! Do you like pirates and buried treasure?

Please excuse my not writing sooner. The truth is, I came back from the mountains this year with an infection in my hand, so that I couldn't use the typewriter.

I should be very glad to hear from you again. Perhaps we can keep up a real correspondence. Again thank you for your letter.

       Your friend,

On September 11 and 12, Barbara, Helen, and Bruce and Rosalind Simonds took two long hikes in the Presidential Range of New Hampshire's White Mountains. I've walked these same trails and it's a thrill to read Barbara's descriptions. On a clear day in late summer such as Barbara's party had, the Crawford Path above the trees is particularly spectacular.

September 11, 1927

I think no one could have had more splendid luck than H. and I, in the way of weather! Perhaps it was due to the favour of Firefly, perhaps it was due to the magic talisman I wear at my belt—anyway, I can't imagine a more gorgeous two days. Wednesday, when we drove up, the haze and clouds were low and thick—when we drove up through Franconia Notch Mount Cannon and the Old Man were clear—but Lafayette and the other peaks of the Franconia Range had vanished in haze. Even the nearer glimpses of the Presidentials, as we neared them, drawing further and further northward—were not glimpses at all! But in the evening, though the clouds were thick on Adams and Madison, at whose feet the house lies, there was a mighty north-west wind, and something sharp and cold in the night air promised good weather. In the morning, it proved to be the most gorgeous day of the whole summer—so they said—for climbing. Also, when we had looked out the window, long after dark, we saw the black clouds scudding along at a terrific rate, brightening with strange silver, and suddenly the moon, lacking three days, rose up, and rode proudly above the peak of Adams. We held a council of war—or, rather, a council of mountains—and decided to climb Adams by the Air Line, a trail branching off from the long Randolph Path.

Imagine the delight of not having to drive an inch before arriving at the trail. It begins practically in the backyard—and one is almost *under* the peak, which rises grimly above the world, like Olympus. First we ascended through low, open woodlands, crossing several small, mossy brooks and one large one; but the climbing begins almost immediately, and before long we could look back and see the mountains north of Randolph, rolling away and away to the sky. Then we came on to the summit of the first foothill of the mountain, and into forest-fired ground—which seemed like nothing but a path of destruction. Above us loomed gaunt, scraggly trees, which once had been mighty and green; about us were thick, new underbrush, and at our feet sprawled mats of snowberry, growing more thickly and luxuriantly than I have ever seen it, and spangled with pearly berries.

Then onward—up and up! We plunged into ever deeper forests of spruce and balsam, where there were high banks and rocks covered with moss on each side of the path—marvellously soft and vivid green moss. One bit of trail had a high bank on the left, overgrown with young spruces and balsams—growing in the midst of an even carpet of rich moss *glowing* with greenness, and sweeping, unbroken, down to the path. Then on, then on, and on—forever! For these mountains, rather than being more difficult to climb than some of the southern mountains, are just terrifically long—their spurs seem to reach out for miles and miles. But soon we began to notice a marked change in the luxuriance of vegetation. More and more stunted it grew, until, after passing through a few more banks of moss, we came out on the naked ridge—the bare knife-edge of Durand Ridge, which is the eastern wall of King Ravine. The wind was sweeping furiously across the crags—the bare crags with only little clumps of cranberry and other small mountain-plants growing in their crevices. There were to be sure, occasional clumps of spruce on the milder slopes, where they were growing flatter than juniper—but the great rocks seemed bare, treacherous, jagged. Then we began to have startling look-outs into the huge ravine, cut into the heart of the mountain. I was bolder than the rest, going so far as to venture out upon a crag overhanging space, the top of which was a narrow, pointed rock! Up and up the great Knife-edge we scrambled, and it seemed like a narrower and narrower ridge—between that vast bowl off to the west of us, and the Madison-Adams col east of us. Ahead of us were the two splendid peaks—the grey, rocky, but rounded cone of Madison to the left, to the right the sharp cone of Adams, looming far ahead, with wisps of cloud trailing delicately across it now and then; between them, and directly ahead of us, were the "sky-cleaving," "eagle-baffling" crags of John Quincy Adams—really part of the main peak. And yet not *eagle-baffling* quite, for, tacking majestically, with silent wings, against the wind, rode a great eagle!

What a terrifying position to be in! Ahead the impassive walls of the near peaks, on all sides of us sheer drops into ponderous ravines, beneath us nothing but bare crags, behind us space and the blue billows of endless, countless mountains! Oh! no one then could take away from me the feeling that I love to revel in—the feeling of awe, of sublime solitude.

The trail skirted the peak of John Quincy, and began to slowly ascend the peak itself. Still the wisps of mist were floating over it—but they were nothing but thin fair-weather clouds—and the blueness behind us was sparklingly clear. The cone of Madison seemed to grow more and more like a peak—it became steadily sharper and sharper—the ravine (of which we were now skirting the headwall) to grow even more terrifying—if that were possible—and our own peak to grow more mountainous and superb than ever. The rocks which we were now scrambling over seemed nothing but swordblades and rapier-points—they were jumbled together in a way that made you think they must have been hurled there by some great giant, landing at random anywhere. For they were all either on edge or on point—there was no smooth step anywhere! Madison began to rise surprisingly beautiful from a sea of surrounding blue summits—the Carter-Moriah range rose majestically to the right of it, making a gorgeous colour-background for the grey cone—now grown nearly as sharp as Chocorua. I have seen tawny peaks, dark grey peaks, blue peaks, green peaks, purple peaks, rose peaks—but never, until I had climbed Adams, had I seen that heavenly desolate light grey of the peaks of the Presidential Range (especially its northern summits), when you draw near to them.

Up and up! The wind grew staggeringly strong, *and cold*! Our hands were numb. The cone became more and more sinister, sharper and sharper as we went on, until, at last, we clung for shelter to the crags of the topmost boulder—before a mountain-wind, colder, fiercer than any I have ever known. The gorgeous thing about views from those high mountains of one range is that the most mountainous things you see are the peaks of the same range—they are so near that you see them in all their glory. Madison was now a sharp grey point below us, the Carters rose in their deep blue to the right, farther to the right was the huge bulk of Washington—a mass of blue-green crags and darksome, shadowy ravines and gulfs—with the carriage-road winding, a white ribbon, up its eastern spurs; further still to the right was Clay, from here nothing but a hump in the shoulder of Washington—farther still, and nearest to Adams except Madison, was the high, rounded hump of Jefferson, curious in that it did not seem grey like Madison—rather it was a brown velvet colour, because of the sedge-grass on it—though there were crags jutting out here and there. Its long spur, the western wall of the Ravine and the Castles, stood out prominently—so did the huge jutting crags—the Castles—along it. Then, to the right of Jefferson, and clear around the hemisphere back to Madison, were blue, far-off mountains.

The clouds had now ceased trailing over our peak—they hung high, and made the sky interesting. The Simondses said they had seldom seen a clearer day—we could easily see Mount Mansfield off in Vermont, and sharp Mount Blue far over in Maine. But the most spectacular were the nearest peaks of our own range.

I believe I forgot to say that, while we were ascending the cone, and while the clouds were still scudding across it, it often seemed as though the clouds were still, and as though the gaunt peak itself were slowly rolling and rolling over, like a great ship in a swell. You could feel the earth revolving—and it was most sinister and uncanny!

But it was impossible to stay long exposed to the full fierceness of the wind, so we floundered down again over those sharp boulders and ledges—down until we began to find little patches of warm grass, and then down farther until we were sheltered from the wind and could look things over. We were approaching the Adams-Jefferson col, and we hoped, if there was time enough, to go up over Jefferson itself. Now, looking back at the peak we had just come off from, it seemed nothing but a dark grey jumble of jags—the peak did not have a sharp form, as it did from still further down.

From the peak we had had two glimpses of delightful pools down below—one—Star Lake—just below the cone of Madison, and the other—Storm Lake—down in the hollow between Adams and Jefferson. Now, as we went down we passed tiny Storm Lake very close—I ran down the grassy bank and peered into it. It is a beautiful little pool down there, in that grassy hollow, looking up at the two ponderous peaks of Adams and Jefferson. From there our peak began to look more and more like itself—it became steadily sharper and greyer, and, by the time we reached the spring at the foot of the cone of Jefferson, it was looming up very much as Madison had loomed before—only higher—more impassible in appearance. First we saw the lower crags and slopes of it, rising gradually from the col, a weatherbeaten grey; then a more level stretch of barren ground, though still gradually rising; crowned with the unbelievably sharp grey peak, against the sky, and making a strange contrast with the deep, deep blue of the Carter-Moriah range, off to the right. It seemed incredible to have peak after peak rising off that way, without dipping below the scrub-line between—to have such a vast stretch of the peak of Adams especially, without a tree upon it. On other mountains I have climbed, when you are above the tree-line, you are practically at the top—here, the most exciting, and the most difficult part of the climb is above the trees.

We ate lunch there, in the shelter of a huge boulder, and gazing up at that glorious peak all the time—or off towards the Carters, or Washington. Afterwards we discovered that it was far too late to try to go up to the peak of Jefferson, but Bruce and I scrambled very hastily up to a large boulder jutting out from the shoulder of the mountain, to see what we could see. From there Adams was even more gorgeous than before—if that were possible—it seemed higher, and a little more distant, so that we could really see it better—it was gaunt and grey and weatherbeaten, as before, and the peak seemed even sharper—even more barren and desolate—and we could, of course, see much better, the flanks of the peak, as they rose up and up from the Adams-Jefferson col. It is needless to say that we could see much more of the Carter range—and they looked even deeper blue, and were even stranger as a background for that sharp grey.

Alas! We had to go down, whether we were willing to stay there all afternoon or not—so we presently started off down the true Randolph Path, beginning between the two peaks. For quite a way it was over bare ledges, then it dipped down into scrub spruce, so flattened down that often one confused it with that tiny evergreen vine, the crowberry! Then the trees grew more and more like trees, and, in surprisingly short time, we plunged into gnarled, stunted, rather mossy woods, steadily growing loftier and more luxuriant. The rest of the way down we went through very lovely evergreen woodlands, having blue glimpses of mountains ahead, through the trees every now and then. In the first part of the descent we had views of the round peak of Jefferson continually, and, after the peak had disappeared, we saw for quite a long way the ridge of the mysterious Castles, looming up opposite us. And there we were down before long, and, when we could look up again at the great peak towering above us—blue, wooded-looking—we could scarcely believe that we had stood on its highest boulder, and that it had looked so different—so much more sinister—that it had been so windy and cold there!

We came out of the woods just at sunset—the "glow" had begun to appear on the peaks—Madison, a rounded hump, was drenched in it, and the Carter-Moriahs had changed their deep, deep blue for that indescribable purple.

Another mountain-council was held, and another trip planned for the next day (for Bruce, being quite a good weather-prophet, thought the weather looked promising). We decided to drive over to the Crawford House—about an hour's driving away—from there we should hire transportation to the little station at the foot of Washington where the tiny trainlet starts up—then we should take the Ammonoosuc Ravine trail up to the headwaters of the Ammonoosuc in the Lakes-of-the-Clouds. We had it previously agreed that we shouldn't go up to the peak of Washington, for, by the time we got there, it would be about time for the train to arrive, so that the peak would surely be flooded with just the kind of people we most wished to avoid. Then we should go on down from the lakes, over the Southern Peaks (Monroe, Franklin, Pleasant, Clinton), by the beautiful Crawford Path (six miles above the tree-line), and down the Mount Clinton trail to the Crawford House again. I have always been eager to go over those Southern Peaks, and the idea of doing it the next day thrilled me so I could hardly sleep.

And—miracle of miracles—the next day was just as fair, clear, windy, and cold as the day before—in fact, the mountains loomed up even more sharply than before! I think it was about the first time during the whole summer that two such gorgeous days have followed on each other's heels!

We started off early, as we did the day before, and we had that heavenly drive over to Crawford House, with glimpses of Jefferson and Washington every now and then, and, later, of the Southern

Peaks in a long chain, with the great round dome of Pleasant seeming to dominate them. Then, after we had circled around Cherry Mountain, we had two or three looks at Lafayette and the rest of the Franconias, looming up, a gradual, very jagged peak, above the nearer hills. It seemed hardly five minutes before we had parked at Crawford's, and had hired a car to take us over to the station.

I think I never felt more disgust than I did at seeing those people, clustered about, waiting for the train. Something about them irritated me terribly. But, before long, we were out of sight of them, off on the Ammonoosuc Ravine trail. We went first through open woods, on a level, very rooty path. There were masses of ferns on each side, and banks of rich moss. We went along for long stretches by the Ammonoosuc River—now nothing but a gurgling mountain brook. Sometimes we crossed it, and, in some places, the crossing was very exciting and dangerous. Sometimes we went across on quivering log bridges—sometimes just stepping from rock to rock. A little bit of steeper climbing, and we came out at a lovely little pool of the river. It fell over cliffs in a series of delicate cascades, and finally landed in a deep emerald-green rock basin. The cascades fell through a deep cleft, and there were high banks of green moss and young evergreens on each side. We stayed there a few minutes—then on we went, until, as Bruce said, we "began to climb trees." It surely was as steep as climbing trees. In a very few steps we found ourselves high above the pool, which we saw, lying below us, like a gigantic pearl.

Now, behind us we began to have glimpses of blue mountains, rolling off, like billows, to the horizon. Ahead of us was ladder-like climbing over a very rooty trail, behind us the mountains, and on each side of us the high walls of the ravine which we were gradually climbing out of. We could see, on the northern wall, bits of the cog railway up the spur of Washington, and we could make out, now and then, little spurts of smoke, showing us how the train was inching along, up and up. Also, we saw the peak itself, through gaps in the trees—a great mess of grey rocks tumbled together—and that same mysterious grey that the peak of Madison and Adams had been, as we saw it from where we ate lunch the day before. And then we could see that the spruce and balsam forest was growing stunted.

Soon we came to a side-path from the main trail, leading down a few feet, to a view of two gorgeous water-slides. We clambered down it, until we stood on an overhanging ledge, and watched how the water slithered, in one long, smooth slide, from the top of the high cliff to a basin down below, rushing and roaring. Just above it the brook was split by a large boulder jutting out from it—the main water-slide on our side of that boulder, but there was another one on the far side of it—pouring down even more steeply than the other, over the cliff. We climbed down still farther, until we were almost at the basin in which they met, and we could look up and up at those great slides—they looked as though they were rushing down from out of the sky itself.

We climbed back on to the main trail again, and kept on going up—not so steeply now, but still enough to keep us going slowly. Soon we crossed the brook, where it was winding down a small rocky gorge, with almost sheer walls of vivid moss. We could look up at the brook—a long way up—and we could see the sparkle of the sun on cascades far, far ahead. Now we could see a decided change in the trees—they were beginning to be very mountainlike. We wound on, through forests of the stunted evergreens, always having gorgeous glimpses upwards at the vast peak of Washington, rising from terrifying ravines, which stretched their scraggly fingers of green trees up on the bare rocks, in zigzags and starlike shapes. Oh! the awe of it! It was like Adams, only huger, more powerful, more gaunt and terrible—yet the peak itself was not so pointed as Adams.

We came out on bare ledges, and began to scramble up over them, in sight of that glorious peak and its deep ravines all the time. We swerved off towards it slightly, and then, rising, bare and rocky, from a forest of stunted trees, we saw the cone of Monroe, the nearest to Washington of all the Southern Peaks. The climb became more and more striking—as we began to look back into the great ravine we had just scrambled out of, as well as off at jagged Monroe, or over at Washington. Great stretches of brown-yellow sedge-grass grew up there on the cone of the mountain, and they shone yellow in the sunlight, a strange and pleasant contrast to the grim grey of the rocks. Also, the long, gaunt fingers of scrub growth reaching up at the peak from the depths of the ravines, became more and more spectacular as we mounted higher and could see more of them.

The brook was now becoming very small—it was nothing more than a tiny trickle running down over the rocks. We crossed it many times—indeed, occasionally the path led over ledges of the brookbed itself. After mounting a few more ledges and pitches, we saw ahead of us the Hut of the Lakes-of-the-Clouds—right down in the col between the cone of Washington and the great jags of Monroe. For a moment I stopped there to get breath, then, seeing the little hollow in the naked rocks where one of the Lakes must be, I scampered up over the ledges, and stood above the tiny lake! It is so lovely to see it there, nestling, blue as sapphire, down in the weatherbeaten sternness of the crags. It seems to cower down before the awe of the grim cone of Washington—it is sheltered on all sides by the ledges, except in one narrow opening, where the beginning of the Ammonoosuc trickles out. The north-west wind—quite a strong gale, but not so furious as it had been on Adams—came tearing in through that small opening, and sent little squalls rushing over the tiny lake—the sun-fairies danced even more brilliantly here than on Lake Sunapee, or on the sea—perhaps it was because there the water is so much nearer the sun and sky! I climbed up the grassy ledges on the east side of the lake, and, when I reached the top, I looked down into another lake, north-east of the first one, even bluer, not so round, yet just as lovely, nestling in its own sheltering banks. Above them both towered that gigantic mass of rocks that was the peak of Washington, looking more awful every time I looked at it—looking more and more grey, with the golden-brown patches of sedge-grass looking like glints of sunlight in a dark forest. The fingers of green reaching out of the dark, shadowy ravines, seemed almost alive, as though clutching at the heart of the mountain.

We ate our lunch on the leeward side of a ledge overhanging the first lake. But soon we found that the wind was uncomfortably strong even there, so we crawled down deeper into shelter, and I found a little niche in the wall of a still higher ledge. Here I sat, in the midst of clumps of mountain cranberries, in the full sunshine, entirely out of the wind, and looking straight down into the little lake, feeling marvellously warm and comfortable for such a terrific altitude.

But never, as long as I live, shall I forget those lakes. The very name, *Lakes-of-the-Clouds*, thrills me whenever I think of it. Lakes-of-the-Clouds! What height—what smallness—among what barren ledges—that name suggests. Many things have been hideously named by mankind, but someone hit a lovely name then. Lakes-of-the-Clouds!

The long Crawford Path leads from Washington down to Clinton —about six miles from the Hut-of-the-Clouds. It leads just off the peaks of the southern part of the range, skirting almost below them. It doesn't actually lead over the top of any of them, except possibly Franklin—the exact peak of which is rather vague anyway. But Monroe looked so jagged and gorgeous, and I felt that the view from it back at Washington must be so staggering, that I longed to go up to the top of it. Accordingly, Bruce and I left the Lakes-of-the-Clouds before the others, and bounded from rock to rock down from the ledges by the lake, until we had gotten on to a spur descending from the peak of Washington, up which the old Crawford Path used to lead. Before we came to the top of this spur, however, a very mysterious thing happened. The bottom of the little col between the spur and the ledges on the south side of the lake was full of grey rocks tumbled and jumbled together in just the way—the edgy, pointed way—they were on the cone of Adams. And as we were walking cautiously over their sword-blade edges, we heard a distinct gurgling and chuckling down below us—the sound a brook makes running over and around sharp rocks. It was a miniature Lost River—there was a tiny inlet of one of the Lakes tinkling away down below us— entirely hidden by the helter-skelter formation of the rocks!

We walked along this barren ridge, exposed once more to the swoop and slash of the wind. Then we were down in the grassy hollow just below the craggy peak of Monroe, looming up in a sinister way. Down in this hollow are three or four more little pools which also rank with the Lakes-of-the-Clouds—though they are not so lovely—they are little boggy springs. We took the loop which leads from the Crawford Path up over the summit of Monroe. We went up so quickly that both of us were breathing very heavily before many steps, and we settled down to a slower plod. I couldn't go very fast up there—I couldn't if it had been level, instead of the steep, rocky climbing that it was. Behind me rose the peak of Washington, growing, as Madison once had, more and more sharply pointed. Off behind its northern shoulder reached the rounded peak of Jefferson— deeper grey than Washington—almost a purple grey, in contrast to the lighter, more weatherbeaten grey. A long spur of it reached down, just above that spur of Washington up which the cog railway ascends. The main peak grew more and more gorgeous as we went up, because the gap between Monroe and it grew deeper and deeper, and we saw more of the grey flanks and crags. The splotches of brown sedge-grass blended in with the grey, and the long fingers reaching out of the ravines seemed weirder all the time, until they, too, began to blend in with the colour of the rocks.

We came up to the top of a lower ridge of Monroe, then, at the end of a short stretch of level ridge, rose the peak, only a few feet higher—a mass of dark crags. We stood on top for several minutes and looked about us. I cannot say more about how Washington and Jefferson looked—I am sure that I have already repeated the same things over and over again. But nothing I could ever say would describe the impassive grandeur of it. Nothing! When we stood there on that sharp peak, east of us rose Washington and Jefferson, out of space itself, the great peaks rising aloft from their own ravines and gulfs; west of us we could trace the whole Crawford Path clear over to Clinton, going down over what seemed like peak after peak, mostly rounded in appearance. First, and right below us, was the grassy green hump of Franklin, the highest point of which swings off in a long ridge over the vast expanse of Oakes Gulf; then, farther down, yet seeming to loom higher than Franklin, rose the still perfectly rounded dome of Pleasant; and farther still, the long ridge of Clinton, with Lafayette and all its jags, and the whole Franconia Range towering bluely above it. South of us stretched a long spur (Bootts Spur) of Washington, the higher part of which was grey with bare rock-ledges, the lower part becoming greener, then blue; almost below us was another part of Oakes Gulf, a staggering dip off into space. South-west rose mountains, deep, blue, billowing like gigantic waves of the sea. North were mountains, too, but not such formidable ones as the southern ranges.

I have been on mountains, such as Carrigain, where the nearest thing is Mount Lowell, on which you can see the crags and slides beautifully—yet it is far enough away to look only jagged and blue. Other mountains, like Chocorua, rise up alone from a swirling sea of far-off peaks. Everything around you is blue and far-off (except, of course, the three smaller peaks of Chocorua itself). Passaconaway juts out all by itself—Whiteface having such a deep col separating it from Passaconaway, that you would hardly realize it as part of the same range. On these mountains there is hardly anything to break the blue monotony. Here, on a peak such as Monroe, and on others which I shall try to describe later, you have everything in one tremendous sweep around you! You can be made to feel small—the proudest spirit, if it has any imagination, can be made to feel small—by a sweep of blue; but to see some peaks towering a sinister grey above you, others down below you in an unbroken chain of tawny and grassy-green, and then, between the tremendous ravines to see the blue as a contrast to the nearest peaks—that makes you more insignificant than the smallest insect!

We scurried down again to the rest of the party, and joined them where the loop of the Crawford Path branches out from the main trail to go over Monroe. And then we started off on that walk along the top of the sky—the walk I shall forget not even if I live to be a thousand. First we dipped smoothly around on the southern side of the peak of Monroe, and then we could look up at the crags of it, overhanging the path—almost. Washington disappeared behind it. Then we looked off to the south-west at the blue mountains. Every step we took a new one rose up from behind the long Bootts Spur. We saw the Sandwich Range, looking more peaked and stupendous than I have ever seen it look, terminated by Chocorua, of which you could see the main peak and the Three Sisters—all of them sharp, but none so sharp as the main peak, which was nothing but a small jag on the horizon, yet keeping the shape of the mountain as I have always known and recognized it. We were getting into the shallow Monroe-Franklin col, and so the peaks ahead obscured some of the western peaks, such as Lafayette and the Franconias.

Now, right here I might as well say that it will be absolutely hopeless for me to describe what we passed over on the Crawford Path. It is too much—too glorious—too like—and yet too changing—for my poor English. A Farksolian might describe it, but that is only because in that language there are so many more words meaning little details for which you have to write a full English paragraph—and then imperfectly. But even a Farksolian could not make you *feel* it—he might make you see it dimly—but to get the wonderful feeling of loftiness and solitude you have to be there yourself.

Well, we skirted the peak of Monroe, along the headwall of the vast Oakes Gulf, over rather grassy ground, with clumps of cranberries and the delicate white starry flower, which I discovered is called sandwort. Monroe is famed, earlier in the season, for the beauty and rarity of its Alpine plants and gardens. Then we saw the nubbin-peak of Little Monroe, and we went on until we could look back between Monroe and Little Monroe, and see, as if framed by those two peaks, Washington, sharper and greyer than ever, rising majestically out of space! Then the peak of Monroe itself began to look more and more horn-shaped—we could see how much sheerer it is on the southern side than the northern—how it seems to be leaning out and looking down into the great hollow below.

Then we started the very gradual rise over Franklin. From where we were we could see more gorgeously than ever how Franklin seems, in all its greenness, to be swinging out over space. Up on its grassy dome we went, with the peaks still rising up in the south and the west—also in the east. For now we had the same view which we had had before from Monroe, only with another peak, Monroe itself, added. We saw the great horn-shaped mountain leaning out—outlined against the sheer grey of Washington, which seemed always to be towering higher and higher above us; then there was majestic Clay, on the northern shoulder of Washington, now becoming more and more a distinct peak, and whose long grey spur reaching down, showing just above the railway spur of Washington; then was great round Jefferson, showing from behind the long spur of Clay, whose own spur reached down still higher than that of Clay. All these peaks seemed strikingly near—all of them were grey, but in varied shades of greyness. The grey down on the flanks of Franklin, where they jutted above the tree-line, was the lightest; then came Monroe, a small shade darker; then Washington, yet darker, but still the same grey which I have seen only in those peaks of the Presidential

Range; then Clay, darker yet; and last Jefferson, almost purple-grey, and more mysteriously shadowed than any of the others.

It was the same way in the shades of green—for there was green reaching up from the hollows of them all. The lightest and the sunniest green was on Franklin, an almost golden-green; then Monroe, the green from whose ravines seemed touched only here and there by sunlight; then gaunt Washington, whose green fingers were dark and shadowed; and Clay, whose green seemed blending in with the dark, dark grey of its crags; and Jefferson, whose green was almost black—nothing but shadows stretching out from more shadows.

Again, it was the same with the various ravines between the spurs of each. The deep Ammonoosuc ravine, really on Monroe, not on Washington, was the brightest and sunniest; between the spurs of Washington and Clay we could see a ravine full of mysterious grey shadows; and on Jefferson, whose spur rose higher than any of them, and therefore of whose ravine we could see the most, there was nothing but a deep, deep sea, without depths, without soundings, full of shadows—a sea of black and purple and shadows.

Now we could see the glorious Franconia Range, surmounted with the sharp jags and *teeth* of Lafayette. Off south-west the Sandwich Range seemed clearer and sharper than ever—Carrigain loomed up like a great shadow, now that we were lower in altitude the peak of Chocorua was outlined more against the sky than it had been before, making it seem still higher. Of all the views of the White Mountains supposed to be gorgeous, I have seen nothing, even of far-off mountains, so lovely as from this Crawford Path. For each mountain, with its several spurs, interlaced gently with the others, so that the whole south-west country was made of these great mountains, deep blue, gently and regularly inter-woven together!

Then on, and on, along the sky-line, hoisted high above the trees, down into quite a deep col between Franklin and Pleasant *[since renamed Mt. Eisenhower]*. In this col, we dipped, for a few seconds, into very stunted, scrubby growth—because of the shelter of the two peaks—but I should hardly call it going below the tree-line. Every sign of a tree we had seen since leaving the Lakes-of-the-Clouds Hut had been tiny spruces, spread out as flat as crow-berry vines, on the grassy slopes. In going down into that col, we had, of course, to see Washington and Jefferson vanish behind Franklin—also Lafayette and the Franconias below the mound of Pleasant. But to the south we never, for a moment, lost sight of a deep and distant blue. That col was the most spectacular on all the Crawford Path—the dip being much more sudden, and seemingly deeper than any other. From tiny Red Pond—a little pool under the dome of Pleasant—we looked eastward at the huge expanse of green Franklin, looking like a very steep descent into the col; and westward we were overshadowed by Pleasant, rounder now that we were so near it than ever!

The path leads to the southward of the summit of Pleasant, but the Simondses thought that, in spite of the fact that we had none too much time left (having loitered and lagged all the way along), it would be very much worth while to go up to the top. The ascent is very steep for a little way—but grassy rather than rocky, as all Southern Peaks are. Up we went, through mats of cranberry and crowberry, until, after a steep but very even climb, we came on to the grassy summit of Mount Pleasant, with the green and brown sedge-grass rippling in the wind. The peaks of most of the mountains I have climbed have never seemed, when you are on them, as they look from down below. But Pleasant is unchanging—I have never seen it looking anything but round, and, even when you are on top, it is just as round and smooth as ever. On the very top is what looks like a very crude shelter—a small circle of stone-wall, not more than ten feet in diameter. On Pleasant you have the loftiest feeling of all the Southern Peaks, though it is not so high as Monroe, or even Franklin. But the view back at the Northern Peaks is just the same—except that it is more distant, and even more stupendous, and that you have another peak added, Franklin. First you look over at the great green slopes of Franklin, as it rises from terrific gulfs and ravines from all sides; then sharp Monroe, even more horn-like and craggy than before; and huge Washington, the grey of whose boulders seems softer and less stern; with Clay looming up from its shoulder; and then rounded, mysterious Jefferson. The shading of grey is just the same—growing steadily deeper all the way back to the spurs of Jefferson. But Pleasant and Franklin are a bright, sunny green, with tawny splotches of brown grass. The yellow-brown up on the cone of Washington looks more and more like glints of sunlight—but you can still see it plainly against the grey.

The Sandwich Range, the Franconias, and the other southern and western mountains, grow steadily more and more wonderful—they seem higher and more distinct the nearer we get. Again I was stunned by the sudden contrast in what we saw. To look from the grey boulders of Bootts Spur on sinister Washington, straight off into that sea of far-off blue ridges and spurs, interwoven, like a great woven pattern all over the world.

But we couldn't stay up there on Pleasant half as long as I should have liked to, for it was getting dark. No, not dark, but we could see that it would surely be nearly dark by the time we got down Clinton *[also known by its official name, Mt. Pierce]*. So we dipped down again into the Pleasant-Clinton col, again dipping below a little subway of scrub, but not seeming like such a deep or sudden col as the Pleasant-Franklin one. In an unbelievable short time we saw the dome of Pleasant behind us melt back into the range again, rounder and lovelier than ever. I think perhaps that the view from Pleasant is the most gorgeous all along the Crawford Path. But that signifies nothing: I thought the same about every peak we went up on to.

So we walked up on the long, long ridge which leads, eventually, to the summit of Clinton. But just below the summit the Crawford Path dips down into the woods, and down, and down, off those glorious sky-places, to our own world again. All those six miles seemed very short in time and distance to me! So short—far, far too short! And now we were going up the last of those peaks! I should love nothing more than to wander from the Lakes-of-the-Clouds Hut over the Crawford Path, starting early in the morning, and wandering up to every peak, by the branching loops, and spending as much time as I wished anywhere I wished, sitting for long hours on each peak, and stopping whenever anything unusually beautiful rose out of its surrounding peaks. But there we were, up on Clinton. There wasn't time to go even up to the top of the last peak—in fact, the Sandwich Range and the other Southern Mountains had vanished behind the long ridges of it before I realized that I had seen my last of them for the present. We paused for a moment before dipping down off the ridge—we looked back east again.

Oh! surely this was the most glorious of everything we had yet seen! Everything was just as it had been before—from mysterious Jefferson, up to the same "sky-cleaving" Washington, then over to Monroe, now grown small and uncannily hornlike, to the top of the high ridge of green Franklin, jutting out to the right of the glorious dome of Pleasant, green and tan! It was the same, only with yet another peak added! And Pleasant, so round and smooth and even, looked very strange down against the cone of Washington!

Well, goodbye to them! And we dipped below the scrub.

Goodbye—goodbye to them!

It seemed like dying by inches when, a few seconds afterwards, there was a gap in the trees—the stunted trees—and we looked back at them again—once—but it was the last look—really the last look. We never saw them again afterwards—except once or twice when, through thin places in the branches of the evergreens, we caught a fleeting glimpse of something massive, huge, and grey up there—which was probably the ghost of Mount Washington—or something shadowy, dark, unreal—the ghost of Mount Jefferson!

We plunged down at rather reckless speed through the beautiful mountain-forests of Clinton, arriving again at the Crawford House. Never have I felt such terrible sorrow at leaving the bare ridges—but I had been the whole afternoon on that heavenly trail, and I had let myself sink deeply into it—and when I left it struck upon me sharply. Nevertheless, the drive home was heavenly.

The sun took his watch below soon after we left the Crawford House. We saw that gorgeous "glow" all over the Southern Peaks, particularly Pleasant, when we came to that view of all the southern part of the range. Then, soon after we had come into sight of them for the second time, the colour had shifted from the southern peaks over to Washington, where it rested—only, instead of being gone, as we thought at first, it had increased in brilliance of purple—so that, when Bruce called to us to look back, it looked as though the whole great Mountain were wrapped in fire! Such burning purple I have never seen. Added to that, the sky was bright pink behind, and, in the midst of the colour, rode the moon, absolutely full, and a soft, rich gold! Imagine seeing it hanging over that flaming mountain—riding on high like a proud goddess!

We fled on before the night, but I watched the west, and what was happening among the clouds there. They changed into their usual gorgeous golds, purples, fire-colours, oranges, and all those other mysterious brilliances which you think of when you think of magic, and the Arabian Nights. (I don't know, though, why the Arabian Nights always make me think of strangely brilliant and magical colours.) But the shapes of the clouds were unusually weird. They seemed as though they had been flung about recklessly, and now they lay crossing each other in strange, wild patterns, one colour gleaming through another, and each tiny wisp a slightly different shade. Over in the south were long, horizontal bars of gold, which slowly faded to bright pink, and then to grey. But there is nothing more wretched than trying to see a sunset from a car, and the Simondses were in a hurry to get home before dark, so I had only to crane and twist around as well as I could. I wished we had been able to stay and watch Washington and the moon until it had faded!

When we came to the place where there is a view of the Franconia Range, we saw proud Lafayette, a deep, deep night-blue, outlined vividly against a still glowing sky. And when we came to where you see Jefferson and Washington again, they, too, were almost black—the last of their "glow" had faded, and the moon hung, more brilliant than ever, over Jefferson. A little farther along, and we saw her again, proudly riding over the highest summit; and still farther she lighted up the sky above sharp Adams; then she set again behind Madison. But soon she was up again—we saw her silvering the top of Madison as she rose from behind it—and then there she was again, hanging over the lower mountains and hills—we saw her gleaming through the trees all the way home.

My two mountain-days were over! All over! How I wished myself night-bound at the Lakes-of-the-Clouds! And what we did the next day—the drive we took—does not belong to Adams and the Crawford Path. Those mountains are complete in themselves, and I don't like to mix anything else up with them. The last thing I think of with that trip, was seeing Washington in the flames of the sunset, with the moon above that fiery peak.

Asthaveckia!

The Cottage in the Woods
Lake Sunapee, N. H.
September 13, 1927

Dear Bruce:

One of those impassible problems confronts me when I try to decide how I should thank you for those two mountain-days. I cannot use the conventional terms, such as—wonderful, beautiful, heavenly, gorgeous, etc. But I can say that those mountain-trips have meant more to me than any other mountains I have ever climbed or seen. When I think of the droning wind about the sinister peak of Adams, or of the Lakes-of-the-Clouds among their barren ledges, or of how the peak of Washington looked when we stood on Monroe, or on Pleasant—or all the Crawford Path—I can see that nothing I could ever say would tell you—or even give you any faint idea—of how I loved those two days.

One can't even attempt to describe Washington, as it looked when we were driving back from the Crawford House—the peak seemingly wrapped in burning purple fire, the sky bright pink above it—and then, in the midst of the colour, to see the soft gold moon riding [sic] proudly, over the peak. You can't describe it—you can't even believe it.

The other day Helen was saying to me: "Were we up there on the tops of those mountains? Were we really, really there?" And I replied: "No, we weren't—we couldn't have been. It is just one of those impossible things."

I have thought mountains of the second rank, such as Moosilauke and Carrigain, to be more glorious than anything else could ever be; I have considered the views and look-outs from them unrivaled— but, when I saw the mountains surging around me from Pleasant or Clinton—or Monroe, where those gaunt grey peaks of Washington and dark Jefferson loomed up behind into the sky; and where we saw that long chain of tawny-green humps of the Southern Peaks; and then, to see between them the glimpses of far-away blue—well, it was no wonder that Helen and I were pretty silent on the way home!

So I finally decided that it would be impossible, even to attempt to thank you. I have written an account of the trip—fourteen single-spaced typewritten pages—which perhaps you will see sometime when you have plenty of time! For plenty of time it will surely take to read it all! In that I strained my describing capacities to the utmost, and I found it very tiring work; but I did manage to make those mountains yield up a dim idea of some of their treasures, in written words.

> With love to you and Rosalind,
> Barbara.

New London,
New Hampshire,
September 13, 1927

Dear Mr. St. John:

I should have written to you much sooner, except that my hands became infected, and I had several yards of gauze bandage on them, for a long time, so that they were just about helpless.

But I want you to understand that I shall never, never forget the mountain-days I had with you at Passaconaway. I shall never forget the beautiful moss growing on the wet rocks up the slide; or the spectacular view from Signal Ridge on Carrigain. Thank you a thousand, thousand times for having me up with you for those few days.

Signe told us that you stopped here on your way back, Thursday. I was very sorry not to see you again—but at that same day, hour, and minute, I was ploughing slowly up Durand Ridge! Do you remember how, on Carrigain, we fell to talking about Adams? At that time, I considered Adams a far-away climb which I might take sometime in a year or two. And it was only a little while afterwards that I climbed to the summit of that great peak, in company with friends of ours who have been staying up at Randolph all summer! I must tell you more about that trip some day!

Thank you again for those few days I had with you.

> Your friend,
> Barbara.

[undated, ca. September 1927]
Dear Peter:

I have received from you such a sheaf of delightful letters that I hardly know how I should attempt to answer them. You must be acquiring an amazing speed on the typing-machine—otherwise you could hardly find the time to pour forth all those single-spaced pages. Me, I'm writing this in long-hand because Smee has fallen asleep quite near by and must not be awakened.

Down in this neck of the woods we have surely had the strangest season within recent memory. Almost all the fair days—and few enough they were—have been chilly; and for a good part of the time we have had cold, autumnal rains—easy and endless. The garden flowers have done badly for lack of sunshine, and even the wild flowers have lacked their usual abundance and brilliance. Piazza-sitting has been largely an impossible thing, and we have had hearth-fires and furnace-fires, both for comfort and to dry out the house. Sunspots may be to blame—I don't know; but the general impression is fairly uncanny. Smee digs in the flower-beds, trying to loosen the soil that the rains have tamped down. The hybrid tea-roses have hardly blossomed. If you have been having this kind of thing—only colder, because of your latitude—even you must now and again have been shivery.

I suppose the new camp—the one on your side of the lake—has been in operation. That wholesale kind of thing seems to be overrunning New England. The magazines carry infinite advertising of such places, and the supply is apparently none too great for the demand. However, if Hook were up there, I know that it would be possible to maintain something of the old mystery and charm. I know it because the letters of Peter Pan reveal so clearly the fact that mystery and charm still are there in full measure if one knows their secret.

What a gorgeous outing you must have had with St. J.! I followed your account from point to point, and I realized what a mighty busy time you must have had. Mr. St. John must be a pretty vigorous fellow to keep up that pace. I have got out my A. M. C. "Guide" and am trying to trace your trips. Somehow, as I do so, I keep picturing again and again that view of Chocorua from the highway, across the Chocorua Lakes—it must be the most beautiful view in New England. Certainly nothing we saw in the Presidential or Franconia country impressed us anywhere near so much. How I do wish Smee and I had a cabin in the Albany Wilderness—with a guest-room for Peter!

(A little later.)

With the aid of the excellent detailed descriptions and the careful maps, I have, as well as I could, followed each day's hike of yours. In one way, the White Mountains have a decided advantage. You can have some magnificent climbs without getting to such a distance into the wilderness that it is necessary to carry a lot of equipment and grub. None of your trips was such that you could not quite readily get back to your base on the same day—yet what a sense of remoteness and wildness you had! I wish I had had more out-of-doors life during the two seasons we were at Sunapee—there was always just a little too much work that *had* to be done!

> Yours, as ever,
> Jas. Hook

Judging by other reviews I could find, A.A. Milne's Now We Are Six *was published in October 1927. I can't tell from the faded clipping in the Columbia archive which publication carried Barbara's review of it.*

NOW WE ARE SIX. By A. A. Milne; with decorations by Ernest H. Shepard, New York (E. P. Dutton and company).

Here's our friend again, Christopher Robin! Three cheers for him! Has anyone ever had a heartier welcome? The more we know about him, the more we want to know about him, and the more we laugh at his childish caprices, the more we want to laugh!

And what comrades they are, Mr. Milne and Christopher Robin! One imagines them always together, playing, laughing, rhyming their small verses. With Christopher Robin's own eyes the author sees the world, as if through a magic crystal; and he writes, in enchanting rhyme, thoughts so young and so little that they are unmistakably Christopher Robin's. They are like the small, curly sea-shells which those two comrades are always collecting, as they walk, hand in hand, over the beach.

With the childish jingles, at which we laugh so much, there is much real and beautiful poetry. You have it in Us Two, in Blinker, and in even purer form, in The Charcoal Burner; so, too, in those exquisite little snatches, such as Sing Song, Wind On the Hill, Solitude, Buttercup Days.

Ernest Shepard, Mr. Milne and the immortal Christopher Robin seem to wander together very joyously—laughingly. We cannot think of the two without thinking of the tree *[sic]*, and we hope that they will always stick together, as playmates.

Mr. Milne has written a delightful little explanatory "Introduction," calling it an "Er-h'r'm!" to the book. But I hope, and I think you will hope with me that it shall be the "Er-h'r'm!" not only to Now We Are Six, but to a still greater acquaintance with Christopher Robin!

Barbara's review of Sails of Gold, *edited by Lady Cynthia Asquith (Charles Scribner's Sons, 1927), appeared in the* Saturday Review of Literature *on November 12, 1927.*

"SAILS OF GOLD!" One imagines a ship under full sail to her moonraker dashing proudly through the waves, leaving her wake of foam behind her, and cleaving the seas with her cutwater. One sees her sweeping into the path of the sun, where her sails look like golden wings; and one sees foam along her sides, swirling and racing away in two long mountain-ranges of snow-capped peaks. As a book, one thinks of sea-stories, full of the sound of the wind and waves, and the sparkling of pirate treasure.

But there is not one story in this collection, "Sails of Gold," that touches upon the sea; there is not even the echo of it that you hear within a great sea-shell. A strange and sudden shock! From the ideas with which the title fills your imagination, you turn to a totally different world. "Sails of Gold" sets you up for something wonderfully adventurous, full of the sea; but, on reading, you find almost every type of story that you can imagine—except stories of the sea.

Then why was it that the editor of this volume called her work "Sails of Gold"? Perhaps it was in honor of the authors, artists, and poets who built it up, sail above sail, into a majestic full-rigged ship. A beautiful idea—but it is not a *ship* which they built up.

But, after all, the title is not the most important thing. After you have let your ideas of wild adventure die down, you cannot help enjoying the book. For it is a perfect medley of everything under the sun, with prose and verse mingled together, and stories, totally different one from another, following upon one another's heels. There is John Buchan's tale of a magic-walking-stick which transported you from place to place—Merlin himself could not have contrived a better; there is A. A. Milne's curious story, "Tigger Comes to the Forest," which has in it Pooh, and Piglet, and Eeyore, and Christopher Robin, and all the others whom we have laughed at so heartily before; there is Algernon Blackwood's odd and beautiful tale which he calls "The Water Performance," and which has in it much of magic and mystery; Dale Mariford has written an extremely amusing bit of satire, called "The Dragon Who Didn't"—satire on that old conventional idea that any princess worth winning has a fire-breathing dragon who must be slain by the daring and heroic prince. And others, many others. Then there is the verse, which, let me call for my own pleasure, the rope-ladders between the top and top-mast-cross-trees. There are fairy poems, and mermaid poems, and flower poems, and a clever fish poem by Laurence Binyon, and even a giraffe poem—a very humorous bit of verse by Geoffrey Dearmer; though perhaps Ianthe Jerrold's poem, "A Lovely Lady," is the loveliest of all.

Verse or prose—the child or grown-up is hard to please who cannot find something to his liking in this book, something that will stir his imagination. I cannot help hoping that our friends, A. A. Milne, Rose Fyleman, Hugh Lofting, E. Phillpotts, and all the others who have found their places in "The Treasure Shop," "The Flying Carpet," and this new collection, "Sails of Gold," will keep on writing their delightful stories for children *ad infinitum*—that they may fill the holds of treasure ships brimming full of precious jewels and ornaments, and keep on weaving more and more of their wondrous golden sails.

The poet and literary critic William Ellery Leonard (1876-1944) was a professor of English at the University of Wisconsin.

176 Armory Street
New Haven, Connecticut
November 14, 1927

Dear Mr. Leonard:
It would be hard for me to say how much I loved receiving your delightful letter, and reading it. However, I take the liberty in contradicting you in one thing—that I may have "outgrown" Eepersip. (I have heard, you must know, altogether too much on that tack concerning another *thing*, and I don't want to hear it about her, too. So, *stand by to come about*, say I; or "Ha-a-a-rd-a-le-e-e-ee!" as our captain would whoop from the helm of the *Frederick H*.) I still love her, though I feel as though she might be written a great deal better; I love her because she is my way (or was) of writing down my own adventures—though, of course, in a slightly fantastic form. Much, more than anyone realizes, of that book is actual adventure—almost all of Part Three—the frost-feathers, the mist—is what befell Daddy and me on two or three trips across ranges of mountains. She is almost a diary, and so I could never "outgrow" her!

A little while ago, however, I faced about and tacked, as though in reply to some invisible helm, and set full sail close-hauled, starboard tack, one blast on the foghorn—close-hauled in an entirely nautical world (as you may have guessed). I was awed and conquered by a passion for sails, for square-rigged ships, for even schooners! The mountains sank momentarily in a cloud of spray. I yearned to know more, to see for myself, to live rough. It began with a wild craze for pirates; but, that failing, it took form in a simple longing for any vessel with sails—honest or piratical—and the common sailor began to appear to me nearly as thrilling as any pirate.

I thought a little while, and then I resorted to the Dictionary—like mad. I spent whole hours over a minutely detailed diagram of a ship, and other hours over the names of sails, and yet other hours over the points and quarter-points of the Mariner's Compass, and still more hours over looking up every ship-word that I could think of, whether I really knew their meanings or not. I learned some—but not enough—not nearly enough—I couldn't get from the Dictionary the real and deeply hidden meaning—the scent—the heart—the echo of the sea. I wanted real authority.

Then we discovered—Mother and I—a rich treasure: Mr. Rasmussen. He has been a sailor, mostly in square-rigged ships, for a great part of his life, but now he does 'longshore work as a carpenter. And he is full of tales and yarns of his seafaring days. Now, because he misses the sea so much, he owns a sloop, and takes her out every week-end that he is able.

But I didn't dare to ask about the condition of sailing nowadays, because I feared so much a bitter disappointment. At last I asked him: were there any schooners that came into New Haven now? And then fell the thunder-bolt! "Why, yes—there's a pretty little schooner in here now—a three-master. She come down with lumber from Nova Scotia, an' she's discharging now. Come in jist a couple o' days ago—jist before me. Yes, she's a pretty schooner enough—her name? I tink she's called the *Frederick H.*"

My heart leaped a mile! "Do you think," said I, and hesitated—"Do you think that they might let anyone come on board, mate?"

"Why, I think they'd be on'y too glad to let you aboard. The crew is all home boys and I reckon they's lonely down here where they don't know anyone."

I trembled all over. I quivered and shook so that I hardly heard the directions for finding her that Mr. Rasmussen gave me.

Need I describe the excitement of the following day, when, radiant with anticipation, I dragged the entire Follett tribe down the street? Need I say how thrilled I was when first I saw the topmasts of the *Frederick H.* fretting the sky, as we walked down towards the wharf? That was my first glimpse of her: I loved her from then till the last look I took of her.

You can imagine better than I can tell the meeting with the delightful old Captain Read, who could tell more in a minute than an ordinary man could in a day! But no one can imagine the glory of the moment when I received permission to go aloft. Up I went (I had always, always longed for a chance), hand over hand, clear up to the cross-trees! I felt—but it was indescribable!

I became fonder and fonder of the schooner, I felt that I could never bear the day when she had finished discharging, and would sail away, away, perhaps never to be seen again by me, leaving me here. The only solution I could invent was that of sailing with her! It was quickly arranged. I burst wildly and furiously through the ranks of defenses like rows and rows of sharp-pointed swords, which the family pointed full at me. I arranged with a friend: everything was settled—off I sailed!

Who could describe, the way they ought to be described, the adventures of that voyage? It answered gloriously to my romantic expectations. Even being bound by fog "thicker 'n mud" and delayed by dead calms, was exciting in its way. And when at last we broke away from the fetters of stillness, into a furious north-east gale— that was the supreme moment of the trip! We watched the waves mounting higher and higher; we saw great crests of foam, like champing white war-horses of Neptune; we watched the breaking mountain-ranges of snow-capped peaks made by the flashing cutwater of the schooner; we felt the wind so strong that we could barely turn our faces to it; we heard its singing through the sails; we watched the full moon rise from the heart of the sea on a breezy night three or four days before the gale, making the sails gleam like newfallen snow, and the sea look foamier than ever. That was the night we saw the mermaids playing beneath our swinging dolphin-striker, in glistening herds and hundreds. That was the same night when the sky was crazy—when the stars wheeled about uncannily, rising and falling and always circling. Oh, but I feel sure that I should be able to tell it better in words, and I think you would be one to share its mystery with me. So I will tell you more when I see you someday.

And there is much to tell of the mountains, too. I am torn between them and the heaving sea. Which is more magical, the howling and raging of wind when it drones about a mountain-peak at night; or the whistling song of it through the meshes of white sails? I can't say. The sea has its spray, the mountains their frost-feathers! The sea has its fog, the mountains their pearly mist. The sea has ships and sails, but on the mountains you are yourself, and nothing takes you, unless, like some, one chooses to ride up Washington in the cog railway train. As for me, I am not that sort. Again, I don't know. What do you think? Which do you love more?

   Your friend,

P. S. I shall write again sometime to tell you a little about this summer's mountain-trip. I wish I could put it into Eepersip. You must know that I recalled the galley proofs several times to put in new adventures in Nature!

Another welcome note from Mrs. Knopf. The Voyage of the Norman D. takes the form of a long letter to "Alan"—Barbara's nickname for Leo Meyette.

November 18, 1927

Dear Barbara:

I wanted to write you at once I had finished reading your manuscript but got tied up in so many things that I am only now able to tell you how much I like your letter and how you make me long to go on just such a trip. [...] I am delighted with it and happy that we are publishing it.

> With all kinds of affectionate regards,
> Yours sincerely,
> Blanche Knopf

George Bryan occasionally sought help for a psychological disorder. He spent much of the winter of 1927-28 at Craig House, a sanatorium in Beacon, New York. Future residents would include Zelda Fitzgerald, Marilyn Monroe, and Truman Capote.

Craig House,
Beacon, N.Y.
Nov. 26th, 1927

Comrade Peter!

It will forever be an impossibility for me to pay my epistolary debt; but the synchronous arrival of three letters from you in one morning's mail is so striking an event that it calls for acknowledgement and heartfelt thanks. So here, dear Peter, are both—and do not disdain them, proud youth.

Well, here I am, with the more or less lordly Hudson flowing a bow-shot from my bower-eaves and Mount Beacon, where Revolutionary watch-fires warned, hoisting itself in my back-yard. (It's an inconsiderable wart, from your sophisticated viewpoint, for it counts but 1,540 feet above the river's level.) I'm in Craig House, a one-time manorial mansion, with gables, turrets, wind-vanes, and a real terrace, inclosed with a balustrade and even now brilliant with pansy faces. My room is most spacious, with a practicable fireplace, colorful rugs, chintz hangings, and easy chairs. Here I hold forth with an attendant who (really!) boasts the name Earl de Courcey, who sleeps on a day-bed in one corner of the vast apartment, and who valets me no end, so that I am quite fussed by the unwonted attentions.

Every day I go to the gymnasium; every afternoon that it is possible I walk; once I have been to the cinema ("What Price Glory?"); once up the mountain (most improperly by the incline railway), once to Newburgh (which is just across the river, with frequent ferry-boats to take you there). You should come visit me and swim in the fine heated indoor pool and pass the medicine-ball with me. Then we should wander over the landscaped acres, admiring the rare trees, the secluded walks through the shrubbery, the conversations at Wodenethe (the main house of this numerous group of houses), the sixty pigs, the vineyard, the waterfalls, the haze on the far hills. What say?

In Craig House are a Steinway grand and a pipe-organ. You should hear me thundering out "Les Rameaux" on the organ, with the trumpet stop out! There's not much technique, but *O puer,* there's a deal of tone!

Yesterday I had two infected molars drawn. To-morrow? *Quien sabe?*

A friend sent me a review of the "House" from "The Nation," and pride swelled in the buzzum of

> Your shipmate,
> Jas. Hook

A pioneer in conservation and credited with saving the American bison from extinction, William Hornaday (1854-1937) was the first director of the New York Zoological Park (the Bronx Zoo).

Craig House,
Beacon, N.Y.
Dec. 7, 1927

Dear Peter:—

Here is the letter that was to have been written on Sunday but didn't quite get itself done. My schedule is, you see, though not terribly full, yet rather exacting—at all events it seems to one of my years and lazy temper. Egg-noggs are to be imbibed at specified seasons; exercise is to be punctiliously taken in the Gothic gymnasium; hydrotherapy is to be submitted to as gracefully as may be; walks are to be walked; errands are to be erranded in Beacon and Newburgh; the dentist (who presides in a white room filled with strange engines, the ultimate in such contraptions) is to be served; and soon, soon I shall have a pulley-weight affair installed in my own room and therewith shall do daily double-dozens for the benefit of that ole devil left leg of mine. Then shall my aged timbers shiver in right good earnest! In between, somehow, I have my social hours and my reading hours (just now I'm making a fist at doing Schiller's "Demetrius" in the original—an odd choice, perhaps, but I have only two-three of my own books here and must glean what I can from the extensive but queerly assorted library here at Tioronda).

(Tioronda, you must know, is the name of the house I'm in. Craig House, the institution, has sixteen houses and cottages. The headquarters are at Wodenethe. Then we have the Meadows, Fairway, The Lodge, Garden Cottage, South Gate, The Cedars, *et al.* It's a vast domain, with a special superintendent to look after the estate. The grounds around Tioronda were landscaped by the man that did Central Park, and they are filled with rare and exotic trees. I have pictures of this *habitat* of mine; and maybe you would one day care to see some of them.)

We had a bit of snowfall here on Saturday and Sunday and several of our group of serious thinkers have for two evenings been coasting down the hill in front of Tioronda. I could watch them from my window; the moonlight being uncommonly bright. The first evening, a nurse was injured when her sled collided with a tree. Later, if the winter holds, we shall have tobogganing.

I'm glad you met Hornaday. He's a marvellous person in his field; and all his life long he has fought against the so-called "civilized" majority to have fair play given to the wild life. He has been the greatest single influence in my time in getting decent game laws enacted and enforced.

You may be interested to hear that the de Courceys are famed in French history and that a de Courcey was with William the Conqueror. My Earl has the air of a Russian refugee nobleman. It is passing strange to think that a former Tsarist officer may be attending the former pirate captain

   Jas. Hook

Delicious nougats & caramels bearing Gilbert's imprint have arrived. Did you send them? If so, a 1,000 t'anks!!

Barbara (or her nears and dears) decided not to include Bryan in The Voyage of the Norman D.

Tioronda,
Dec. 16, 1927

Dear Peter:
  This is a mere fragment, sent in the hope that it may reach you on

Saturday. It is to say that, on thinking of the matter, I feel I should not even suggest what I am to be styled in your forthcoming *opus*. (a) Because I must not interfere with your auctorial preferences, of which at this writing I know o. (b) Because I must not get *myself* into conflict with others than *you*rself—those others who advise and criticize you. (c) Because I fancy I detect, even though you seek to conceal it, a feeling of impatience on the part of your nears and dears that you consider mentioning me at all. A similar, though less marked, impatience was in the air when you insisted on making me a co-dedicatee. Fly our paths, fly our greetings, wave us away!

   Yours,
   Jas. Hook

Tioronda,
12/18/1927

Dear Peter:

 You know, the ancient works were preserved to us through the labors of mediaeval scribes. Your old friend Caius Julius dictated to a secretary or amanuensis. The secretaries employed by eminent Romans were usually cultivated men; sometimes Greek slaves. Cicero had a secretary who employed a system of shorthand, and presumably other amanuenses had systems of their own. The shorthand notes of dictated material were ordinarily written with a stylus on wax tablets. Later, these notes were written out with a pen on strips of papyrus. A manuscript of this kind was multiplied by slaves, one slave reading aloud while a group copied. If a papyrus book were much used, it became soiled and worn; and fresh copies had to be made by manual labor. In the Middle Ages, it was usual for a monastery to have a *scriptorium*, where those brethren who were assigned to the task copied MSS., one of them reading while the others wrote. Now, in order to shorten the labor, conventional abbreviations were used, such abbreviations being readily understood by the readers of the completed book. Many of our books to-day contain a great quantity of abbreviations (examples are telephone books, "Who's Who," or the dictionary). Not only so; but errors constantly crept in: the reading brother was misunderstood; the copyists were cold or drowsy or in a hurry. Hence, the job of deciphering these MSS. demanded great skill on the part of the scholars who had to edit them when printing was introduced. The difficulty was increased by the absence of marks of punctuation. The earlier printed texts of the classics used a good many abbreviations, imitating the MSS. From the time of the Renaissance down through the eighteenth century, classical scholars were much busied with the study of evidently corrupt texts, and some of them were noted for their clever conjectures as to how certain passages ought to read.

Here endeth the treatise. I shall never again attempt to be so instructive! My next letter must be quite different.

    Yours,
    Jas. Hook

From a note H. L. Mencken (1880-1956) wrote to my grandfather sometime before Christmas 1927:

Let me see "The House Without Windows" by all means. You are bringing up the greatest critic ever heard of in America. Please give her my affectionate compliments.

176 Armory Street
New Haven, Connecticut
December 19, 1927

Dear Mr. Oberg:

This is a mere fragment, written hastily amid a perfect stack mountain-high of other work which must be done. It is to say that your large and Mysterious Box has arrived safely, and that we are longing to see what Mysteries it contains this time! We are indeed!

And now, my friend, I shall pay you back in your own coin. As you have mystified me, so shall I you. I have a Mystery about me, too—a Christmas Mystery, in reality—but it must be unseen for some months after the Day. If I should let it be known to you now, the charm would be broken. So, my friend, you shall know either in February, or in late January—my magic fore-sight cannot tell as yet such delicate matters. It is enough to say that it is coming, though late; and do not despair. Only get up in your mind a great deal of Excited Curiosity. That is the main point!

And here's the best of wishes for good cheer in *one-thousand-nine-hundred-and-twenty-eight!*

    Mystifyingly yours,
    xaaxaaa

Shortly before next year's Christmas, Helen will write the following to Anne Meservey. (Helen and some of my grandfather's older friends continued to refer to him by his first name, Roy, instead of Wilson—the middle name he preferred.)

Last Christmas there was something wrong, something not quite honest in the atmosphere, and I didn't have the slightest idea what it was all about, until that fateful telephone rang at two in the morning, and Roy's voice answering and saying: "I tried to, but I couldn't." Never can I get those words out of my mind.

Ding, who was living in Providence with her son Robert while healing a broken leg, had told Mr. Oberg that there was "an interesting picture of you [Barbara] in the December number of a publication called Silhouettes." *Mr. Oberg couldn't find a copy, and nor can I.*

176 Armory Street
New Haven, Connecticut
December 29, 1927

Dear Mr. Oberg:

I know it's a shockingly long time since I've written to you, and I am afraid that, even now, this will be only a pitifully short letter; but, anyhow, you know how it is just after Christmas!

It is to thank you for your wonderful box of mysterious packages, and their edible packing material: I thank you for everything—*everything* in it; the beautiful little hand-painted calendar, the pictures of Sabra and of the old house, and for the curious little rolling tow which comes back to you so lovingly as though it hated to be parted from you. Sabra was crazy with joy over that, and she has been rolling it around the house ever since. And, of course, the candy! You know how candy is around Christmas-time. One can't have too much!

As for "Silhouettes." It really isn't much of a magazine, being very dull and uninteresting, and it really isn't much of a picture, being only an extremely poor reproduction of a good photograph which was taken some time ago. But if you really would like a copy I will try to get one, though I don't know whether I can, it is so late in the month. I will try, anyway.

Well, keep on being mystified, and everything will go fine!

    Your friend,
    Barbara

On December 23rd, Barbara went to Craig House with Mrs. Bryan for a brief visit.

There's an unusually long gap in the archive for Barbara's letters at this time. I don't think there are any between the one above and March 7th. Fortunately, we have a few from George Bryan and one from Mate Bill.

Craig House,
January 4 [1928]

Dear Peter:

Imprimis: "Note by a Publisher" — Hay valla; I inclose it herewith. The talisman — Hay valla, in a private drawer. The letter from Mate Bill—loc; I have not seen it about, but I shall institute a thorough search. Are you quite positive you left it here? One item you do not mention—a large old-fashioned key. This and the talisman I can box and send to you.

Please do overlook my long silence. I have been living in many recollections of that happy December 23rd—those few brief, hurrying, hurried hours of afternoon! It seems, now, that you needn't have gone so early; but, as it was, you had a long, tiring day, and I don't wonder that you slept when you got back to 176. Don't worry as to Smee not understanding you. Smee, I am persuaded, understands a great deal more about some things than even you do. And if you were uncommunicative either in the station or on board the train, she took it all as a matter-of-course, in a spirit that both you and I (I believe I may include you) possess in a far less degree. Somehow, you and I are forever explaining, aren't we?

Did you, then, really so much enjoy your visit? What did you say about it when you got home? Did you truly find me very much the same? Would you care to come again? The outdoor tree was really very lovely. The indoor one has just been dismantled. It had become so dry as to create a fire hazard; but while it lasted it dispensed a magic of its own. There was a "make-and-break" arrangement that caused the lights to twinkle. Your casket of gifts was a marvel and delighted everybody that saw it. With all those protective charms, I should fare well in 1928. The necklace of cone-wings and that of bark-discs were especially symbolic. Perhaps the one of multicolored wax-beads is the loveliest. Has Smee seen all these remarkable things? They are proudly displayed on my bureau; and if she hasn't already examined them, she will certainly have pleasure in doing so when next she comes. I am not deserving of all that thoughtfulness and spell-working skill.

I don't know Babb's book—haven't, in fact, seen it advertised or noticed; but if you give it such an endorsement, it must be important to read and good to own. I wish you had had it to bring along with the other volumes that you showed me from your bag. As to Ludwig and Froude, I suspect that the truth lies somewhere between them. I know that Froude has some of what the Germans used to call *Tendenz*; and to judge by what you say, Ludwig must have a lot. But, somehow, I can make allowance for hero-worship (an ages-old human failing—if failing it be) far easier than for studied and systematic detraction. Lytton Strachey has made detraction a biographical fad, and I suppose the fad will have to run itself out.

This much for now from that most disappointing of pirates,

   Jas. Hook

Port Greville, N. S. *[Nova Scotia]*
Jan. 9. 1928

will shipmate

Got your letter and was glad to here form you I am home this winter. the Frederick-H is in Port Greville for winter. I may go in her in spring and would like very much to go to new haven again and see you all again there has been a lot of wind all right and fog to I wish that you could see the Frederick H now all snow I dont think you would cair to go up to hur cross-trees now it would be to cole. [...]

I will close hoping to here form you again

   your shipmate. Bill

The Benjamin F. Packard *was a square-rigger whose maiden voyage, from New York to Puget Sound around Cape Horn, was in 1883. She was retired in 1927 and became a tourist attraction off Port Washington, Long Island, New York, until suffering severe damage in the Hurricane of 1938. She was scuttled the following year. Barbara's account of her visit appears to be lost.*

Craig House,
January 21 *[1928]*

Dear Peter:

Your truly tremendous letter of January 8 (?) deserves an equal salvo of reply; but, alack! few are the romantic doings afoot here since Christmas came and went. I have, indeed, climbed Mt. Beacon (1,540 ft.) and seen the twilight from the summit. But we could not stay long; and as it was, we came stumbling down in the dark over a trail at once muddy and stony. The mountain-top was littered with débris of the fire that destroyed hotel and casino, and uglified by summer shacks of a ramshackle sort. New Hampshire's overnight cabins are no worse. We saw neither snow nor frost-feathers and had no stirring adventures. But at least no one else was there; the funicular was not running; the yawping excursionist was excursioning elsewhere if at all.

I went o'er and o'er your account of the trip to the "Benj. F. Packard." Of course, so prosaic am I, I should like to know how you happened to go; and what the "Packard" is doing off Port Washington; and what her destined fate may be. But until you tell me some or all of these things, I shall be more than content with the windswept, spray-wet narrative that reached me in such a surprisingly jolly bundle. I'm so 'tarnal glad that we still can correspond and that I may share with you your jaunts afield and afloat!

This brief word I shall try to slip into the four o'clock mail, so I'm abruptly ending it; but you may expect further tidings from

        Yours piratically,
        Hook

February 28th *[1928]*

Dear Peter:

Your yesterday's letter suddenly reminds me what a sluggish correspondent I've been. Perhaps you don't particularly mind, for you seem to have manifold adventures and manifold companions therein. Unfortunately, I am hog-tied to a major degree and don't go adventuring so that you could notice it. I've been to New York again, to see Smee and do some things that needed doing—that *was* an adventure, after all—the only one in long, rather monotonous weeks.

It is decidedly difficult for me to reconcile certain things. For example, you constantly imply that writing to me is an activity fraught with hazard for you. About every second letter of yours voices your subterfuges and evasions in connection with what would seem to be an interdicted proceeding. This very latest word from you depicts you as "trembling," running to the window, and "somewhat rattled," as you type the paragraphs. Yet you propose (and "H." proposes) that I appear in person—although you confess that "confronting" me is likely to be a queer and embarrassing affair, and so forth. Now, if I am so outlawed, why any such proposal (if it be serious), especially when queerness and embarrassment are the only features of the occasion that you find worth noting?

Besides, there are all kinds of (to me) more or less blind references to calamities and trouble and what-not—allusions that almost constitute a burden or refrain and that are anything but flattering or reassuring to the undersigned. Well, I've just written to "H." that it will not be feasible for me to be on hand on the 4th; and now I'm telling you the same, though in different terms. You ought to know that Smee and I used to come to Armory Street because we liked to but also because our coming seemed neither queer nor embarrassing—everything was simple and free and friendly. Perhaps you have not wholly forgotten. And when did Smee—*ego quoque*—not welcome you with good cheer to all we had? Yet, strange to say, you do not mention Smee or hint at all that she is included in your invitation. I am sure that neither she nor I would willingly make anything, let alone such an occasion, embarrassing or queer for you.

Please understand: I'm not meaning to dwell too much on this. And I don't see how it would be practicable for me to get to New Haven. All felicitations, Peter, and a right merry time! And many the junketings you plan be all you hope, is the wish of

    Yours,
    Jas. Hook

P. S.: I meant to write more but must get this into the mail. J. H.

Now Barbara's life takes a dramatic turn. The letter from her father, which she received two days after her fourteenth birthday, has not survived. I don't know when Margaret Whipple (my grandmother) began working as Wilson's secretary at Knopf, but I would guess in 1927, when she was twenty. (She didn't finish her degree at the University of Wisconsin but, like my grandfather, was a strong writer and editor.)

Sternway was the Folletts' rowing boat, which Wilson had outfitted with spruce branches for a mast and boom. The mountain "that we have always had vaguely in our minds" was Katahdin (or "Ktaadn," as Barbara preferred).

176 Armory Street,
New Haven, Connecticut
March 7, 1928

Dear Daddy:

I did receive your letter, yesterday afternoon, and I read it (as you may suppose) a good many times before I came to any conclusion or conclusions concerning it. And now that I think that I have, I feel that I must point out two ideas in that letter that seem like ill-concealed weaknesses, and that cannot help but make me suspicious. (1) Because you do not give any clue as to what your answer almost was, and especially *because you call attention to the fact that you have given no clue,* I am tempted to think that the answer you had in your mind was one that you are now ashamed to reveal. For, had the intended answer been the *right* one, why all the secrecy about it? (2) Because the question of the divorce was brought up, that seems to me to put all idea of choice out of the picture, and it also seems to betray what was in your mind. For, in the desiring of a divorce from

Helen (and I shouldn't have let her give it to you, anyhow), how is it possible that this answer which "rang clear as a bell" in your mind was the *right* one?

Then there are others—other points—though those are the chief ones that have anything to do with your letter. For instance, Helen clearly and decidedly eliminated the idea of divorce long before she and Miss Whipple left New Haven. I was in the room at the time, "neque temere incognitam rem pronuntio." *[Julius Caesar in his Commentarii de Bello Civili: "I do not speak at random on a subject to which I am a stranger."]* Besides this, Helen was actually not asking you to return to *her,* but to return to the family. Aren't we ever again going to cross the ranges of mountains in all weathers, or play about in *Sternway,* or steer a real windjammer through the seven seas, or take sailing-lessons from Mr. Rasmussen—as we once planned?

Such things do not reconcile themselves. For instance, if you now finally and determinedly drop all that, leave it behind, kick it out of the way, then how am I to believe that they actually and truly meant all to you that they seemed to at the time? And if they did, then how am I to believe that you don't feel any more the lure of *The Maine Woods*—the lure of that mountain that we have always had vaguely in our minds? This is the time of year when you are wont to have feverish spells of mountain-lure—why aren't you having them?

In short, and taking all this into consideration (as I hope you do), the whole wretched affair strikes upon me as being so absolutely nightmarish, insane, unthoughtof, that I can hardly convince myself that I ought to take it seriously. It seems to be like the last thing on earth that a person with any fragment of a brain or of a sense of responsibility would do. Doesn't it seem that way to you?

Then there's another very important thing. You say Helen needs me, and right you are; but I need you, too. Thus, when you think that out, how am *I* to manage? She needs me, and I need you; but there aren't two of me, are there? And I can't cut myself in two parts, and then set the parts fighting as you and Helen are fighting—can I? Besides, though you say a great deal, both in this letter of yours and at other times, about the destructive and "poisonous" relationship between Helen and yourself, you must remember (for even I can remember *that*) that it hasn't been true except during the last year or so; and that, even now, there is hardly anyone in the world who still doesn't believe that you and Helen are an ideal pair. Why, you are the only one who even entertains that wild thought! And, after all this, who is going to consider your thoughts the *right* ones? And besides, you cannot impress it upon me or anyone else that a relationship with a young girl of twenty is going (I mean, in the long run) to be anything but a worse nightmare than even *you* think your relationship with Helen is.

Now that I have said my say: there only remains one more thing. I feel that it is my duty to relate to you truthfully and accurately the details of my conversation with Miss Whipple. For I have an idea that she has gone to you, complaining that she has been maltreated in your house and by your daughter; and I have also a feeling that you are going to sympathize with her, and let her tell you what a beast I am, and all that. Well, you know that my memory is fairly sound on detailed conversations; and I here promise and swear that such fragments as I can't remember I won't set down at all.

To begin with, Miss Whipple asked Helen to telephone me where I was with Sabra, to tell me that she wanted to talk to me. And so I came. Naturally, we couldn't launch immediately into *that* conversation, and so at first there were only a few friendly remarks. And then—

W. You see, Barbara, I think he would be happy and contented with me; and you wouldn't object to his being happy and contented, would you?

B. You think you can make him happy?

W. I do.

B. Well, but is that a very honourable sort of happiness?

W. I don't know; you see, I suppose I'm in love with him.

B. Well, then I think you ought to try and get out of love just as quick as ever you can. Besides, can't you be on friendly, happy terms with him, without taking him away from his family?

W. People in love just don't do that—that's all.

B. Then what do you want; what do you expect?

W. I want to marry him.

B. Yes; but I might raise objections to that.

W. You see, your mother told me that if I married him I'd ruin your whole life, smash all your ideals, and all that. Well, I don't want to do that; you may not believe it, but I don't. Would it ruin your whole life?

B. I don't see how I can tell whether it would or not. It might not ruin the whole of it; but don't you see—it isn't that—it's simply the fact that it's dishonourable and unfair, that's all. Good heavens, Miss Whipple—don't you see what you're doing? Can even you, "in love," as you say, think that it is fair to take a man away from his family as you're doing? You can realize that you are not in the right of it, can't you.

W. Unfortunately, I'm not.

B. Indeed, and I think it's extremely fortunate that you're not.

Besides, do you want to know what I think? I suppose you don't, but here it is, anyhow: I think you've taken an unfair advantage of him when he was and is in a physically low condition—exhausted with work, powerless to resist your "love," as you call it. Because I can tell you I am absolutely sure that, if he were in his right mind, he would never think of such a thing—never even listen to it for a minute.

W. *(shrugs her shoulders; enter H.)* Well, Barbara's been trying to give me advice.

H. You can't blame her; she's only fourteen and she's having her father taken away from her.

(Here follow scraps of conversation; among them H.'s definite assertion that there will be no divorce.) (Enter Taxi, shortly.)

B. *(advancing menacingly upon W.)* Besides, I have another thing to say to you, and it's this: If I were in the painful position you're in; if I were doing what you are trying your best to do, I wouldn't stand up there, so extremely unashamed of myself.

W. *(mockingly)* Thank you; —that's all I can think of to say.

B. Goodbye, Miss Whipple; I'm going to swear at you behind your back when you've gone.

W. Mm-hm;—all right.

(Exeunt)

Now, there remain only a few general remarks. (a) You told me, over the telephone, Monday afternoon, to "hold my horses; and everything will be all right." Naturally I believed you (*must* I begin to train myself not to?) Did you want my horses held so that they (my horses) wouldn't get in your way—interfere with your plans? I cannot think of any other explanation; especially if this is the "all right" that you promised. (b) I never realized that my whole life has been simply a jumble of two persons "poisonous" to each other. I won't believe it, that's all; I won't. (c) I can also tell you that in the conversation between Helen and Miss Whipple, there were no dramatics at all, which was very fortunate; all *that* got out of Helen's system on Sunday. It was a cool, calm, deliberate conversation—and, as I said before, "non temere rem incognitam pronuntio." (d) Consider Sabra, among all the other things you have to consider. Can't you see that she is not possibly able to grow up decently in the midst of this whirlpool? Why, she will have to spend all her time struggling to keep herself from being sucked down into it—and, as you know, she can't quite swim yet. And besides, you can see—can you not?—that she can't in any way get along respectably with only two out of the three of us? It wouldn't matter which two you picked, she needs the third—she needs us *all*.

Well, I think that's all—every detail—every scrap. I depend very much on you; and I trust you to give another heave at the capstan bars, to get the family anchor started toward the surface again. After all, you have the strongest shoulders for heaving of us all! And, really and truly, you don't want the family anchor to remain forever at the bottom, do you?

  Barbara.

Alfred A. Knopf
730 Fifth Ave.,
New York
3/15/28 (Thursday)

Dear Helen:

  Thank you for your letter.

  You are evidently trying to work yourself into a forgive-and-forget mood and to smooth things over. Well, it's no good. Things can't be smoothed over, and there is a sharp and definite issue between you and me which you have got to settle before anything whatsoever happens from my side. If you leave the *status quo* as it is, it shall stay as it is forever as far as I am concerned. As to Barbara: I tell you again, as I have always told you, that I'm not going to be a party to any competition for her attention or affection. Her attitude of whole-hearted support of your position and hostility to mine is exactly what I most wish it to be, and I wouldn't for anything in the world curry any sort of favor with her. I am perfectly willing to be the one who is wrong, technically, legally, morally, or any other way you please. The fact remains that if you were four times as right as you think you are, and I four times as wrong as you think I am, you would be prolonging an indecent, dirty, and repulsive situation which is absolutely in your power to control. Apparently you had rather buoy yourself up with consciousness of your theoretical rights (which aren't going to get you anything) than face the facts of a situation which will in no wise change until you change it.

  I have been extremely ill and feeble and in that condition in which a man is likely to go pathetic; and, even so, I give you my word that I had rather flop in a gutter of this island which I loathe, die in a hospital ward, and be buried in the modern equivalent of a Potter's Field (if there is any), than compromise my position in this matter by one millimeter. Every one of us wants and needs his own kind of decency. You could achieve decency for us all, and at a stroke, if you happened to want that more than to sustain a fiction which does the most possible harm to all and good to none.

I suggest that we suspend all communication except on necessary mechanical errands until you have something to say that might do a little good. If it's a deadlock, let it at least be a silent one. If there's no move on your part in, say, six months, I shall arrange a legal separation which will assure you of your income as long as I am able to produce it; but action is the only thing I am going to be interested in. [...]

    WF

"Oxford" was Arthur Meservey's nickname (he'd been a Rhodes scholar).

176 Armory Street
New Haven, Connecticut
March 21, 1928

Dear Anne-White:

A thousand thanks for the scarf. It is lovely, in colour, shape, and in size; and I shall wear it according to mood, sometimes as a piratical bandanna (as which it is most becoming!) sometimes as a plain scarf, and sometimes in a curious, and rather piratical way, over one arm and under the other. It's all according to mood; and this one fits any mood.

I long to see Ellen again. The last time I saw her was at Sunapee, and we had such good times for a few days, tramping the merry greenwoods all day long.

And how is "Oxford"? My salutations (the nautical style, you know!) to him, as well as to yourself, and the whole family—and may you have fair winds and no beating against it to do, every day of the year, and every bell of the day.

    With love,
    Barbara

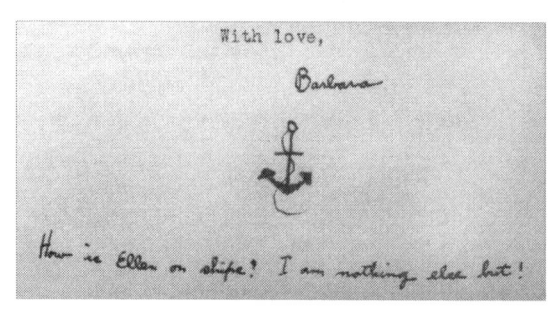

With the Folletts in turmoil, The Voyage of the Norman D. *was published. Or at least Barbara had received advance copies; press reviews don't appear until June.*

March 23, 1928

Dear Peter:

My many true thanks for the inscribed copy. The other I have sent to Smee. Were the whole background and *status quo* of things different, I dare say we should be celebrating the volume's appearance in some Pan-ish manner, as would be fitting—but *dis aliter visum*.

But you have many others to celebrate with you! Your letters bring tidings of hearty activities and gay doings by sun and moon. The postscript to yours of March 6 (if you remember it—and I am going to expect you to remember it, just as you expect me to remember everything) carried, however, something poignant beyond what you were likely to guess. Sunapee—wind—wave—cloud; the pines; all that setting looked for me as we used to see it in so-happy summers. Northern woods and waters always held for me more than sea or schooners can, I guess.

The whole air of your March 20th letter is so spontaneously jolly that I take it for granted that all the ills you tried to conjure up out of vasty nothingness for poor, harassed Smee and myself have fled like vapors. It strikes me that if the Macedonian cry, straight and sincere, is to be raised, Smee and I are the persons to raise it. Result? A flock of echoes?

If the "Annie C. Ross" goes, some other sailing-ship will doubtless come along. The sailing-ship has been disappearing for thirty years, and has no more disappeared than the hand-loom has. That's partly a false alarm to make a headline in a Sunday supplement.

        Yours,
        Jas. Hook

In the next letter Ralph Blanchard is I think suggesting that Margaret Whipple had told Helen she was pregnant by Wilson. To the best of my knowledge she didn't become pregnant until 1934, with my mother.

176 Armory Street
New Haven, Connecticut
March 24, 1928

Dear Mr. Meservey,

[...] About ten days ago Helen called me up, in a terrible state, and wanted me to come down to see her. [...] She thinks that perhaps it is all her fault, and that if she would take herself out of the world Roy would take up his responsibilities with the children and things would be better for him and for them. It is a desperately bad mess.

[...] I don't believe that Roy is in any such mess with the girl as the girl said. I think she simply lied about that. The rest is made up of familiar enough psychological phenomena. The difficulty is in Roy's case that he has overworked gravely, allowed himself to get run down physically, been under a good deal of worry, and lived for several years a very unwholesome life with little to take him out of himself. Add to that—we must face the facts squarely if we are to help—that Helen, with the best intentions in the world, had ways that got on his nerves and nearly drove him frantic. Mind you, I am the friend of Helen as well as of Roy, and am as anxious to help her as to help him. I wonder if you know how much she rasped him. Don't—if you value her life—ever let her know that I wrote this. But I have seen so much of it in these last two years. [...]

>Yours sincerely,
>Ralph L. Blanchard.

176 Armory Street
New Haven, Connecticut
Tuesday, 27 March, 1928

Dear Oxford:

Thank you so much for your letter. I feel that you are quite right about things, but I am too mentally worn out to see things clearly and sanely. You see, I am so horribly tied because Follett will neither let me write to him, nor will he see me; yet he demands that I break the deadlock by giving him his freedom to choose what he shall do in a case where, it seems to me, there never has been any choice, and where, according to various letters and remarks, the choice would necessarily be one of great harm to him as well as to us.

The horrible part of the delay scheme is that Barbara is becoming so totally alienated as the days go by; she has on now a steely indifference. Her words: "I envy Ellen in having a father she can worship," are significant.

Barbara is about to form definite plans for sailing on a four-master from Bridgeport, Conn. to Georgetown, S. C.! A rare chance for the girl to get away for several weeks, and I have already given my consent, though it hurts a bit to lose her. I have more or less promised my friends the Blanchards (you remember Ralph) that I won't stay here alone with Sabra. So I hope the Meservey family won't fall dead with surprise if Sabra and I should bumble in some day of, perhaps, next week. If I can find an appropriate person to stay with me, then I shall probably stay here for a week after Bar goes, for there are many things to be done here, and there seems to be a lot of people who are looking at the house.

I'm glad you like the Sunapee scheme. The cottage rent is mine, and mine only; it will be heaven to have you, and perhaps some of you can stay all the time. Living there is very cheap, and there are no clothes, and there is quite a lot of everything that matters.

But I shall be up to see you very soon now if you think you can stand it.

    Yours devotedly, and with all my love to you all,
    Helen

I don't know who Miss Sieve was, but you'll recall Barbara writing to William Leonard last November.

The University of Wisconsin, Madison
Department of English
March 27, 1928

Dear Miss Sieve,

Barbara's *The Voyage of the Norman D.* is as amazing a creation in realism for a twelve years' child as *The House Without Windows* was amazing in fantasy for a nine years'. I see the same gifts, however, in each: the child's zest for living, changing normally from fantasy to realism in just those years, the wholly extraordinary thing being the degree and the coherence of that zest, the completeness of the child's absorption in the experience and the completeness of the absorption of the experience by the child. But the call of life is so healthy; there is none of the hectic and exotic of the "prodigy" in her *living*, apparently. And her *writing* has nothing of the child's imitation: it is complete, zestful transmutation of her child's experience into amazingly effective language—and, as such, is as much art as any grown up's transmutation. [...] For the first time in history it would seem the abounding healthy child has become the authentic child-artist.

    W. E. Leonard

176 Armory Street
New Haven, Connecticut
Thursday, 28 March 1928 *[although Thursday was the 29th]*

Dear Anne:

Thanks so much for your nice letter, and everything you said in it is very precious to me. But don't raise up any hope about my "mind." I am so very, very tired, Anne, and I can't stop my mind wheeling round on the same subject and keeping me awake nights.

If something would only lift the weight my head seems to be carrying! My bad nights are giving me horrible days.

What Follett is living on and where I don't know. His salary cheque comes to me with– [*without*] deduction, and I am sending (at his request) him nothing.

I feel, all the time more persistently, that I have brought a great man to a humiliating condition. He, I am sure, feels that the responsibility is mine, and I take it. He is a greater person than I am, and he is greater, apparently, without me, whereas I am worth little or nothing without him. That, I suppose, is the tragedy. How gladly would I give myself up if he would be a father again to the children, make a home for them! Please believe this. Have I a right to hold him to a principle which he doesn't believe in? The principle, I suppose, of a man's having his *choice* to continue living with his family.

Little Sabra this morning: "When *is* Daddy coming home, he's been gone so long?"

You know I crack under things like that, Anne, and I feel that I must give up everything to give back Bar and Sabra their father.

Bar's schooner trip is not going to pull off this time, unless, by chance (and there is a chance) of its going to the West Indies. We'll know a few days later on. So I shan't be a-packing up quite yet to run up to you. Really, I have no business to betake myself to you and your family, for I'm in quite rotten shape, and go to pieces in no time at all. And I think I'd better stay right here.

Will Oxford or you write down the name of a good elementary Physics book for Bar to get started on?

      Love, you know,
      Helen

Norman Vaux Donaldson (1899-1964) was an editor at Yale University Press and Barbara's fourth important correspondent. His wife, Hildegarde (1893-1957), a graduate of the Royal Conservatory of Music in Brussels, gave Barbara violin lessons. Barbara wrote a song for Norman after a recent excursion in his car, Hermione.

> The stars were off their course one night,
> The trusty compass-points went wrong,
> The Bear hung upside-down—sad plight!
> And told your mate to sing a song——
>   A song, a song for the waves and gulls,
>   And haul, my hearties, haul!

Hermione struck a reef one night,
Her skipper standing by her helm.
A coral reef she struck—sad sight!
Said Davey: "Come to the shadow realm——
    The realm, the realm of the bones and shells,"
        And haul, my hearties, haul!

She struck—her jibboom pointed square
At glassy windows of the World;
Said Davey: "*She* will never dare
To cruise again—her life is furled——
    Is furled, is furled like seagulls' wings,"
        And haul, my hearties, haul!

Her skipper waited for the tide.
He found it high! The east wind blew,
And angry, curious seagulls flied,
Or, better yet, the seagulls flew——
    They flew, they flew like ghosts of foam,
        And haul, my hearties, haul!

The skipper tried to find some barge
To rescue him, but all he saw
Was one lone creature (very large),
A REPRESENTATIVE OF THE LAW!——
    Of kind intent to please and serve,
        And haul, my hearties, haul!

Hermione slipped off the rocks
To hoist her wind-swept sails once more.
The winds and waves she gaily mocks,
More pert she seems than e'er before——
    Than e'er before she seems more pert,
        And haul, bold matey, haul!

    Norman D (the skipper of *Hermione*)
    From his shipmate
    B. N. F.
    April 4, 1928

Helen occasionally gave lectures about home schooling and in particular the potential role of the typewriter.

176 Armory Street
New Haven, Connecticut
12 April 1928

Dear Oxford:

I had to call up Roy on the telephone this morning for mechanical reason in re mortgage notes, etc. And he asked me if I had seen "Oxford," and said that he had a letter from you that you were going to Boston and then were perhaps going to New York and would see him. He wonders why you haven't showed up.

Please see if you can, Oxford. That is a very good sign, and very significant.

Barbara is in a very bad condition spiritually, and though, perhaps, at bottom she has faith in her father, her words against him are very, very bitter. A friend, Donaldson, who has taken care of us this winter, and has been especially nice to Barbara, in loco parentis, says she has changed terribly even now, and he is quite worried about her.

I said to Roy over the telephone this morning that I had to go to New York next week, and that I'd like to see him. "That is up to you," he said. But, of course, according to his new code of living, that means I must say he can have a choice before we discuss ways and means. And I can't yet say that.

Tell Anne I am speaking on the 23rd at the Bookshop before 30 EDUCATORS, dinner at 6.30 and then me. They are paying my expenses, and putting me up for the night. A mighty discussion will follow. I'd give a lot to have Anne come down and go with me; can't you persuade her to? Tell her I have found the cheque she sent me, and that it is hers, and now she should use it, not me!

But do keep on with Follett, Oxford, Please.

       Yours,
       Helen

Le Marquis
12 E. 31st St.,
N. Y. C.
April 14, 1928

Dear Peter:

Your letters were forwarded to me—three of them. It isn't very clear to me whether you are or are not going on that schooner trip. I suppose I shall find out in due time. The ship must be much more interesting than the "Frederick H." The ideal thing to do would be to charter the "Benjamin F. Packard," refit it, and go sailing away for the Spanish Main. Did I say "it"? Forgive me, great Julius!

Or I have another suggestion: See whether you can acquire the replica of the "Half-Moon," built for the Hudson-Fulton celebration some years ago. "It" must still be lying around somewhere and perhaps could be purchased. Nothing more romantic was ever described by de la Mare or drawn by Rackham. You could have Cap'n Hendrik's own cabin in the high sterncastle, under the lantern. Wouldn't that be fun? And you could have gorgeous ornamental sails, with all kinds of symbols on them, and do your cooking at a fireplace below deck. I'm not sure that any marine insurance company would take a risk on you; but if you could get Mate Bill as skipper, there wouldn't be any risk. You would learn about more sorts of rigging than even you ever heard of before. And you could carry a small piece of ordnance and throw solid shot.

How would you like a voyage in a canal-barge? The stormy winds and fogs would disturb you not a whit, the coast would always be in sight; but there would be compensations. You could tip up and go ashore whenever the mood struck you; and you would be spared the nuisance of handling sail. I commend it to you as not without its merits. Some of the barges are painted gaily indeed. A few of the old-time canals still function, but I guess most of them have substituted electric traction for horses or mules. This you might not like at first, but I think you'd soon get used to it.

But by this time you may, for all I know, be afloat in the "Albert F. Paul," bound for somewhere-or-other. If it's a three-week's trip, as you wrote a while back, I shall miss your letters. Smee is glad to know the flowers are doing so well; and so, too, is

       Yours,
       Jas. Hook

From Mr. Oberg, on receiving The Voyage of the Norman D.

April 29, 1928

Dear Barbara:

Thank you for the beautiful solution of the Great Mystery which you prepared for me some time ago. You may be sure, I wondered into what it would finally develop. I must tell you, however, I received a little advance information as to its import, before my dear little friend, the "Cabin Boy," arrived, through the fact that your

"Grandma" told me in a letter from the New Haven Hospital, that she was reading it at the time. She did not, of course, know that you were planning a great surprise for me. I have read the greater part of it and expect to finish it when I get home to-night. [...]

I have not heard from you since December 29, 1927, or exactly four months to-day—but of course, I know you are always busy with your studies, cabin-boys, etc., but I hope you will be able to steal a little paper, ink, and time, from the old gentleman who to-day is starting his yearly season of untruthfulness, with no intention of reforming, until the end of next October. [...]

By May 1928, Barbara had convinced her mother that sailing to the West Indies—following the course of the Carnegie, *which they had recently visited in Virginia—was their best next step. Helen elicited Wilson's help in finding a publisher who might finance their travel in exchange for Barbara's writing about it. Wilson was not at all keen on the idea.*

"McFee" is William McFee, a writer of sea stories and frequent contributor to Harper's. *"Sedgwick" is Ellery Sedgwick, publisher of the* Atlantic Monthly.

Alfred A. Knopf
730 Fifth Ave.,
New York
May 17, 1928

Dear Helen:

(1) You have cost yourself exactly $14.75 by overlooking my feeble petition for my $10.25 in royalties, because I have had to hold out a $25.00 Mercury cheque on you, and this is your notification that you're that amount under your expectations at the bank. I will return the $14.75 if I can manage to collect what is coming to me.

(2) Thanks for telling me, at last, what the scheme is. I'm sorry, but the last thing on earth you ought to try for is getting such a thing arranged except when all hands are in a good clear sound condition of mind to cope with it. It is just faintly possible that something of the sort can be contrived. But it can't be done all in a minute; and it oughtn't to be done at all unless you can pull yourself together. Trying to sell editors and the public an author who, by your own account, is going to pieces and needs to be saved is pretty weak tactics. And you can't sell anybody anything by acting the way you did here Monday: making a deliberate appointment with one person, then another with another person for nearly the same time, and not really keeping either of them. The whole business of fancying that

the experience itself will pull you together—either of you—is not sense. If you aren't capable of engineering it sanely and collectedly, it's nothing you ought to have. I don't seem to hear anything about what you are going to leave behind you—what you are doing with your mother, what is to become of Sabra, what arrangements are made for the house, and so on; all things that I naturally have to be somewhat concerned about.

McFee is a nice person, but the idea that his name is worth thirty cents in such a connection just won't hold water. Sedgwick could, if he took a notion, sell the idea to, say, Harper's Bazaar and get an advance out of them—but what likelihood is there that he will take a notion, or that you will present the affair to him in a way to create a good chance of interesting him? I can see a dim chance that the Hearst publications might bite: and another that McCall's would take a chance. But the whole matter, for any sane editor, would take a lot of chewing over and study. The more you succumb to your present hysterical state of mind, the more possible openings you are going to plug up by alienating persons who could and might help (there aren't too many) and the less progress you are going to make. In fine, you have a job on your hands if you stick to this project, and it's the first principle of the job to approach it in a condition to do it. I am perfectly willing to do my share of the investigating and interviewing if anything happens to get me convinced that the affair has a gleam of sense to it. As long as it is presented in terms of lost souls and with more than a suggestion of lost wits, I am bound to feel that I do you the better service by keeping out of it. [...]

You are telling me something I delight in hearing about Sabra. Sabra, bless her, was always much more to me than you thought or than I had any way of expressing. If there were any one thing or person for whom I would undergo what you seem to think you can reimpose on me, it would be she. The problem doesn't exist, because, not being completely daft, I realize that to vacillate for her sake, or for anyone's, would ultimately be the worse for her and me and everyone.

   WF

On June 6th, Barbara took the train to New York to visit her father unannounced. Shunned, she quickly returned to New Haven. Early the next morning, without telling her mother, she took a train to the Bryans' home in Pelham, New York, where she stayed at least through June 12th.

Alfred A. Knopf
730 Fifth Ave.,
New York
June 6, 1928
(Wednesday)

Dear Helen:

Won't you *please* try to understand that I refuse to have any dealings with Barbara and Sabra apart from you, or to do anything that could possibly create a needless cross-pull? Their attitude, or at least Barbara's, is exactly what I want it to be. They must go with you, be yours, and be on your side in any issue that exists. That is right; and I should think you might try to detect in my part of it an attempt at my kind of decency, and not indifference to them. When Barbara asked Norman whether I had asked for her, there was no reason in fact or in sense why he should not have answered quite simply, "Of course." If you don't comprehend my permanent and helpless devotion to those two, you don't comprehend much about me, that's sure. But I will not, now or ever, engage in any sort of contest for their favor or for possession of them. I think you owe it to them, to yourself, to me, and to ordinary expediency to offer me my freedom of action on decent terms. But that is your problem. I can only define and declare my own attitude during whatever interval you elect to practise this fearful retaliation of a sort which no human beings on earth ever merited, regardless of what they had done.

I will answer the details of your letter when I have a chance and a typewriter. This is merely a note to forbid you to charge to airy indifference my failure to make overtures to Barbara today. As for your offer to absent yourself, I know it is meant obligingly, but it doesn't oblige.

WF

Excerpts from a review of The Voyage of the Norman D. *by Margery Williams Bianco (author of* The Velveteen Rabbit), *printed in the June 9, 1928 issue of the* Saturday Review of Literature.

[...] "The Voyage of the Norman D." seems at first glance as unlike the story of Eepersip as could well be imagined, but in reading it one recognizes more and more strongly the logical development. In Eepersip the experience took place largely in the mind; here it is in every day life, but the spirit that made the imaginary adventure real lifts the actual one, in turn, into the region of vision and mystery. [...] "The Voyage of the Norman D." is a fine, sustained, and vivid piece of writing that would do credit to a writer of my age, and I very much doubt whether an older mind would have got so much out of the experience or brought nearly so much to the writing of it. [...] Through the whole story of the voyage, as exciting in the telling as any buccaneer yarn, one finds the same fervor of description, the same untiring joy in living and keen reaction to natural beauty as in the earlier book. [...] I regret only once exception, and that is the individual referred to as the author's shipmate. He was there; he seems indispensable, since we gather that without his company Barbara herself could not have made the trip. But over his personality, almost over his existence, has been drawn a rigid veil. He remains to the last a creature of mystery. [...]

176 Armory Street
New Haven, Connecticut
Tuesday night *[likely June 12, 1928]*

Thanks, Anne dear, for the telephone, the letter and for everything else that you do and are. I thought at first I'd enclose some recent letters to show you how the land lay, and then I decided to wait until after Oxford had seen Roy. Roy wrote to my Mother a terrible letter calling our whole marriage a dreadful mistake, and causing my poor mother inexpressible anguish. You see she knows all about it because she has lived with us, and she knows the greatness of the whole relation from the beginning, and she knows too that if he had never gone to New York, that greatness would have held. In cleaning up I have come across hundreds and hundreds of letters from Roy to me, and from me to him; and Oh Anne, they are just too wonderfully permanent for me to ever believe they were nothing but literary flourishes. You see we were never away from each other without a daily letter; I thought at first of burning them, and then I decided that I couldn't because someday I want Bar and Sabra to know something of the greatness that was so fine and is so rare. More than that, no one in the world could be convinced of the mistake he refers to in this letter to my mother. As recent as last December, he wrote to Ethel Kelley, a copy of which he sent to me: "Helen understands me pretty well, or will; these things are in her hands—good and safe hands, I feel; ....."

And now he threatens me that he will disappear and there will be no money if I don't take steps to release him. But Anne, I'd rather he would disappear, cut off all the money or even commit suicide than allow him to marry a girl who said the things to me that girl said, who is the girl she is, for as Alfred said, "if you let him marry that girl, it is the end of Wilson Follett." I cannot do it no matter what he does to me. And I feel sure that if I can hold out my friends will stand by me much more closely than if I give in.

I do want Oxford to know that I would make any arrangement in the world for him other than that. I can never have a home again without him, for he has been a part of it too long. Barbara will never stay without him; already I am having difficulties with him about this thing. She worshiped her father in a terrifying way, and now she cannot settle down. The morning after she came back from New York completely overcome by his indifference, she left this house at three in the morning, walked to the station and was on a four o'clock train to Pelham, where the Bryans live. I knew not a thing about it, and went mad with fear when I got up and found she had not slept in her bed. She is still down there. It is a very difficult and dangerous thing to deal with; if Bryan were well, I could make him show Barbara that she should not do a thing like that, but he is vague himself. That action is nothing more nor less than her challenge to her father. But it is awful for me.

Roy writes to Ding something to the effect that while we are all good enough as individuals we have a warping and deadly effect on each other. That is bunk. He seems especially mad that I am breaking up the house here and sending Ding away, Sabra too, and that Bar and I are trying to get off. I wish I had never mentioned anything until I actually got away, but there were difficulties about Bar's next book which had come up, and Norman spoke to him about the thing. What Roy doesn't see is that none of us can think of a home without him, and if our mutual effect had been evil, we shouldn't be anything but glad to break up. He said to Barbara and to me: "I will never be a member again of any household in which your mother is a part." And Barbara said, "Why?" but could say no more. But it still does seem as if we should do things [for] beings for whom we are both responsible and who need us both and who need a home without a thought for ourselves. I have never asked him to come back except as a father of the children. He says he is getting to be a real human being after all these years of misery but he writes my mother the cruelest letter imaginable and has completely shattered her.

And the horror of it all is that I am in love with him, that Barbara adores him, that Sabra talks of him every day, and that Ding loves him. He writes to me of his "permanent and helpless devotion to those two" (the children), but he won't, apparently, sacrifice one bit of what he wants most in order to make a life for them, take his happiness from them, and thereby give some happiness to them. And yet at the same time he repeats to me that he will never see them or have any relations with them without me. What does it all mean, Anne? If I divorce him (which I shan't) he would never see any of us again. And Barbara refuses to give him totally up. And I feel, too, that I must hang on to that shred for them, for Bar says she couldn't stand the horror of knowing that such a thing had happened to such a private family!

I do want to see Oxford.

I am renting this house the first of July at a low rent but I must get away or go mad. And Oxford doesn't know anything about this letter but he does know that you found me thoroughly smashed and anything else that he likes. And I do think it wise to see Knopf at his home, if possible.

        Love from
        Helen

Between 1909 and 1921, the Carnegie undertook six long scientific expeditions—"traversing all waters between the parallels of latitude 80° north and 61° south" (Carnegie Institution Newsletter, October 1972). On May 1, 1928, she embarked on a trial cruise before beginning what turned out to be her final voyage in June. Captain James P. Ault planned to cover 110,000 miles over the next three years.

176 Armory Street
New Haven, Connecticut
June 17, 1928

Dear Mr. Oberg:

I suppose you think that I have entirely forgotten your existence, do you not? I confess that it seems that way. But no one could be sorrier or more apologetic than I. No one.

To tell you the truth, I haven't been so busy as I have been wandering. Yes, wandering! We have been down to Washington, D. C., there to see a little brigantine, the *Carnegie*, which has just sailed for a three-year cruise for scientific purposes, around and around and yet around the world. We saw much of that little sailing ship, I climbed clear to her royal yard. Then we came home; and then, lo and behold! we were off again, this time for Newport News, Virginia, and to see the same little vessel again. This time we saw her off for England, under all her sail, and I say she was a beautiful thing to see, with that column of square canvas, one above the other, swaying and lifting and rolling against a bright sky—swaying over the huge swells.

High up in *Carnegie* rigging

Down at Newport News I became acquainted with five large coal-schooners—the same sort of vessel as the *Norman D.*, but larger, and with four masts instead of three. There are, as a matter of fact, two four-masters in New Haven now—the *A. Ernest Mills* and the *Charles M. Struven*. The last is far superior to the first, I think.

Then, too, Helen and I have a wild project in hand. We are going down to the West Indies (Barbados) this fall, in a sailing vessel if possible, to be gone no one knows how long, to do no one knows what—but mainly to meet the *Carnegie* when she stops there. Aren't we mad? Oh, it is going to be glorious fun. I have just now been writing to certain schooner-captains I know, to see if they are going down that way this fall.

But first of all comes Sunapee. I am more excited about going up north this summer than ever before. It is so hot and dusty and crowded and tiresome in a city. I want to get out into the open lake, and get my small green row-boat down again, and step the little crude mast in her, and unfurl her little crude sail, and go sailing in the waves across that little bit of a lake. And I have not heard "lake water lapping with low sounds by the shore" for a long, long time, so it seems to me; though indeed, last night I heard a few sea-waves. It is years since I have heard a hermit-thrush, centuries since I have seen a blueberry worthy to be called a blueberry; and eras since I have heard pine trees sighing; and aeons since I have sailed in my crude little sail-boat, whom I call *Sternway*, from her habit of sailing backwards.

Enough of this. I hope in the future to carry on a correspondence with you that is a little more *like* a correspondence. Anyhow, I am going to try to.

    Your friend,
    Barbara

Seeing off the *Carnegie* at Newport News, Virginia.
Barbara is in the foreground.

Standards were quite different in 1928. It doesn't surprise me that Alfred Knopf would choose to fire my grandfather to avoid a scandal.

46 Perry Street
New York City
June 26, 1928
(Tuesday evening)

Dear Helen:

You will not, I imagine, be unduly surprised to learn that my job with Alfred ends on August 15, and as much before that as I can contrive. My best efforts to keep the job indefinitely and to make myself progressively more useful in it have proved insufficient to overcome the handicap of the difficulties against which I have had to work, and Alfred is now as determined to have me out at the earliest practicable moment as he once was to keep me permanently.

I imagine that this unexpected *contretemps* will impress you as conclusive enough evidence that, so long as my social position remains what it is now, my career as Wilson Follett is done. To put it crudely and bluntly: no divorce, no job—and no income. I would never think, so far as my own sentiments are concerned, of stating three facts as an argument for a divorce: with or without a divorce, and with or without position or income, I am going to live with Margaret Whipple as long as she wishes me and wishes that. But the fact that you have destroyed your income is a fact which you must face, and which I have to face in its bearing on all of us. What I wish to make clear is this: There is no reasonable likelihood of a job and an income that will keep you in comfort, or keep you at all, so long as I am frankly living with a woman to whom I am not married, which is what I am going to do until or unless I can marry her; and if I am left in my present situation I shall simply be forced out of my name and connections and into disappearance from the scene. This does not represent my choice at all: I am morally committed to working for you and for Barbara and Sabra and your mother, and am honestly ready to do it for my natural life. But there is no point in readiness to do it if in the circumstances people don't want me or my work—which is the fact.

It strikes me that, in the circumstances, it would be a sound and useful idea for you to come down here before you go to Sunapee and thrash some of these things out in a triangular conference conducted in the best spirit we can muster. It's a pretty serious situation; most serious of all for you, though serious enough for any one of us. I am anxious not to let you down in any way that is humanly avoidable; and—well, I wish you could bring yourself to a corresponding point of view. It seems as if our community of interest is, for once, obvious enough; and I find myself clinging to a hope that it will be enough to bring you to a reasonably calm consideration of the inescapable facts which we are up against.

Don't imagine that my allusion to a possible disappearance is in any way intended as a threat, or as a lever. I resist the possibility with all my faculties: it is, none the less, the probable alternative.

WF

Thursday, 28 June, 1928

Dear Oxford:

The enclosed speaks for itself, but I do need some advice. I have written to Alfred to find out the truth. I wish he could be persuaded not to let W. go, because he will not find another job right away, and, as you know, I can't support my entire family in a minute and a half. More than that, Follett's only hope lies in keeping that job.

The letter is entirely illogical because it is not true that he can't get a job unless I let him go. As a matter of fact, it would be laughable to go after legally a man who has no job! He must have his job first.

My family are in a bad state—Bar, especially. She begs me to take her to Sunapee Saturday, and I shall try to go and hope to see some of you soon after. If I am to have no more money I am in a serious hole, I assure you. But I shan't now give up the idea of the trip which I still want to pull through if possible.

    Helen

From Gordon Campbell, a sailor on the Carnegie *whom Barbara befriended on her recent visits.*

Hamburg
July 2 - 1928.

Dear Shipmate

I hope you will forgive me for this long delayed letter but in England after I received your very nice letter I kept posponing the reply as there was a lot of talk about some of the boys paying off in Hamburg. [...]

We made good time all the way to the Irish Coast I think the most we made was 286 miles in 24 hrs. and that was sailing by the wind and I don't think there are many square riggers that could do that. [...]

Well Barbara the Skipper is a real Gentleman he never fails to say good morning to each of the boys when he sees them on deck and he has been very pleasand to work for all the trip I never saw him growl at any body yet. [...]

Mr Unanda has John Daryso, Person, Charlie Ness and Myself. So the third mate Henry has Whity Agge, Charlie Hendrickson, Harry Olsen, and Sampson a new man from Newport News he was on the "Maud M. Morey" some time ago. [...]

All the Boys send their best regard to you barbara and they would answer those post cards but we are a poor lot when it comes to writing letters I wish I could write such a lovely letter as you wrote me I will always keep it Barbara [...]

    Till Barbadoes
    Gordon

James Norman Hall (1887-1951) and Charles Nordhoff (1887-1947) met while they were pilots in the Lafayette Flying Corps during the Great War. Both writers, they collaborated on a history of the Corps before going to Tahiti in 1920 to write articles for Harper's. *These were collected in the book Barbara mentions—*The Faery Islands of the South Seas. *They would co-author many adventure books, including 1931's* Mutiny on the Bounty. *Nordhoff returned to the United States in 1940 while Hall spent the rest of his life in Tahiti.*

Box 65
New London
New Hampshire
July 6, 1928

Dear Mr. Hall:

From reading *The Faery Lands of The South Seas* I have grave doubts as to whether you will ever receive this letter; however, we'll hope for luck and start it along! Mother and I may get to Tahiti long before it does! We intend, you see, to start in the fall and peg along slowly, first down to the West Indies—probably Barbados. Then we want a complete shift to the South Pacific; we have such a small geographical knowledge of the world that we have a sort of feeling that once in the West Indies, we can simply *step* to the South Sea Islands! Which is probably not the case.

Our first idea in starting out for the West Indies was that of following the *Carnegie*. Have you ever heard of her, in your remote corner of the world? Briefly, she is a brigantine, carrying eight sailors and seven scientists, bound for about everywhere in the seven seas, for scientific research. They "want to make the north pole behave better," as the crew puts it. She sailed from Washington the first of May *[actually June 1st]*, bound for England; she ought, about now, to be in Germany. She was going up to Iceland, and from there clear down to Barbados. We saw her at Washington, having a great curiosity about sailing ships, from lumber schooners to full-rigged ships; we liked her very much; I was up at her royal yard in a short time, and the same day I ate dinner in the fo'c'sle with the crew, listening to their yarns, for I have a way of making friends with sailors.

So we decided that we would try following her about the world a little; and since we couldn't leave before fall, we thought we would try for Barbados in September—she is supposed to arrive there about the middle of September. So we made a little arrangement with Mr. Wells at Harper's to write our adventures as we went along; and Mr. Wells promptly referred us to you and Mr. Nordhoff. The

Carnegie is going to Papeete, and she is supposed to get there early in March, 1929; but, because she is a sailing ship, with only a small auxiliary engine, she is already behind her time, and may be even more by that time.

Well, we read *Faery Lands of The South Seas*; and we decided that the West Indies couldn't compare with the south Pacific, and now we are more determined than ever to get to Papeete, when the *Carnegie* is there. Oh, she is a beautiful little brigantine. She has a great, lofty foremast, and carries a royal; her bow and stern are like a yacht, and she has a long, graceful jibboom. They told us that she would sail fifteen knots without her engine; a speed which nearly equals the old clippers.

As I said, I am very much in love with sailing ships of almost all descriptions. I had a little experience myself—ten days on a three-masted lumber-schooner, with about all kinds of weather—calm clear days, a little breeze; calm, foggy day; another breeze—and so on, until we arrived at Nova Scotia. I wrote a letter about it which amounted to a hundred and ten pages, and turned into a book, somehow or other. Ever since that voyage I have kept my eyes peeling for mastheads over city buildings; and I have acquired a long list of three- and four-masted schooners; and an even longer list of young sailors, old salts, experienced, wise old mates, and long-winded, loquacious old skippers. And I must have felt several *[that's where the first page of the letter ends, and the next appears to be missing.]*

A letter to Norman Donaldson shortly after Barbara's father visited Sunapee ("There have been Family Scenes"). George Bryan is the "Third Factor"; recurring abbreviations in Barbara's letters to Donaldson include "phil" (philosophy) and "S.-C. F." (usually So-Called Friend, I think, although in this letter it's Self-Conceited Fool).

July 7, 1928

Dear Shipmate:

I would have written sooner, except that I spend a good deal of my time Constructing Something. Exactly what it is I don't quite know yet; but it looks like a cross between a prairie schooner and a gravy boat, *built* from memory. It isn't intended to be either; but it looks rather like that. And I work on it rather ferociously, from four till eight in the morning; for I must get it finished before next week, for next week Mr. and Mrs. Third Factor are supposed to arrive—which is fortunate, since the Financial Transactions are growing extremely limited.

This is a wunnerful place for pondering on the problem of the universe. When I want to ponder, I take *Sternway* out to the swimming raft, tie her (a bowline in the end of her painter), hop out, lie down on the raft, and go to it. I was there a whole hour one day, wondering about the universe, but I found that it was a rather Large Subject. It made my little, little brain crack-crack. But the phil. . . holds firm. SHE is more true and alive than ever; myself is much more worth-while, in spite of occasional external difficulties (family scenes, etc.); and as for the Third Factor—well, the Third Factor is about the same, so far as I can see.

Anyhow, it's grand up here. Oh, Norman, I wish you could see *Sternway* sail! I had her out in a raging westerly gale o' wind, day before yesterday; and by jings!, Norman, I nearly sailed her under water! I shipped over the leeboards, and there was no tacking her—I had to wear her, and she changed like lightning, the little boom whizzed over like mad, and nearly carried us all under the salt sea. If there had been anyone with me, I should have been more careful; as it was I was very reckless, for I held the sheet until the leeward side was far too low in the water, and until the slender spruce mast bent nearly double, and I felt sure she would snap clean in two. Or perhaps three.

And yesterday I had her out in a raging westerly wind. I couldn't resist letting her run before it, just for the speed, but I found getting home was *Quite* a Different Matter. I might have gotten there, sooner or later, but Sabra was with me then, and she got impatient, so there was nothing to do (no Crustimoney Proceedcake) but furl up and row home—which I did.

Did you go down to the *Mina* to deliver my message? If you didn't, I *shall* be angry. It was so mean of me to run off like that without saying goodbye.

There have been Family Scenes. But only when WF was up, and they Had It, if ever there was a case. But I retired to the raft, and thought how external all those things were, and how unimportant, and how beautiful the lake was, and how huge the universe was, and what a fly-speck the Earth is (God must have to use a microscope), and what They were missing, squabbling away in the cottage, and how fortunate I was to be able to keep myself from being drawn into it—and numerous helpful thoughts of this kind.

Say, I thought you were going to write to me! Go down to the *Mina Nadeau*, and then tell me about it, you . . . . . . ! And, by the way, why don't you and Hildegarde come up some week-end? Jings, but wouldn't we have a sail? Say, my hearty, you don't know nothin' 'bout ships, without you've seed *Sternway*. She'll lay it over on any ship you've ever seed before. Jings, *I* never seed a ship like her; I never seed a ship carry on like she done 'n that gale 'o wind t'other day. Say, shipmatey, she was sailin' some twenty knots, I'll wager; she was goin' too fast t'heave out the log, 'twould 'a hauled me out o' the ship!

But really, seriously, it's beautiful up here, shipmate. There are two hills; the western one fairly low, and fringed with spruces on the top, and the rest of it pastured; the eastern one is a little higher, and is bald on top—it thrusts its crown of gold-brown into the full sunlight; over behind them, a little to the east, but showing on the west shoulder of the eastern hill, is Royal Arch, a high hill covered with a thick spruce forest, always looming darkly over the nearer, lighter hills. Then there is a valley between them—a valley of maples which turn most gloriously in the fall—a green valley which spreads up both the hills like a soft fringe. And square between the two hills, down on the lake, is the Pine Grove, dark against the background of maples. It is the most beautiful bit of woods in the whole world— you could sail the Seven Seas forever without seeing its like; it is mostly of yellow pines, with their long, dark, massive needles; here and there are white pines, more delicate and pale, but less glorious to look at; there are so many spruces away in the heart of it, and hemlocks along the water's edge, with here and there a white birch; and on this side, at the very tip, there is one curious little maple. This maple has been distorted by the thickness of the pines, until it is nothing but a tall, curving trunk, with a patch (square in shape) of leaves at its top. And in the fall, the lower half of that patch turns to bright scarlet, while the upper half is still bright green, giving a most weird effect.

And the hermit-thrushes! Norman, there is no sound of bird or man or wind or sail or wave, in all the universe, so beautiful as the hermit-thrush singing at dawn or at dusk, his throat lifted. He perches on the very highest twig of some grand old tree, and after every trill he looks about him alertly, on a perpetual lookout, like the lookout on the fo'c'sle deck who whistles to himself through his melancholy two hours. But the thrush's song may not be compared to the sailor's whistling! That is, the whistling may not be compared to the song.

Jings, but life is worth living—————ain't it? You ought to see Treasure Island—it's a real little green island at the corner of the lake—a glorious little uninhabited place. The Third Factor has a place 'way down at t'other end of the Twin Lake—I should guess 'twas about fifteen minutes brisk, hearty rowing—not so good as when T. F. was just across the lake. But the fifteen minutes hearty rowing will be good for my arms. They are already *much* tougher 'n afore, by carrying cargo to the place where the Something is being constructed. I will tell you, by the way, what this Something is, when I know!

Till then, Adieu! And write to me, you "Self-Conceited Fool!"

    Your shipmate,
    Peter. Barbara.

P. S. I just noticed that I signed your letter "Peter." I was the most surprised person in this universe, I tell you! You know why, don't you? That is T. F.'s appellation for me; and I clean forgot that this letter was to you! Isn't that the most absurd thing?
    B. N. F.

July 7, 1928

Dear Daddy:

I have lately had two glorious sails in *Sternway*. One was the day before yesterday. There was a gale of wind from due west—well, such a gale that it was extremely difficult to row the boat. The whitecaps went tearing at a mad speed past Cape Horn; and there was an ominous darkness out there. In fact, savage little cat's-paws came shivering into even this cove, every once in a while.

Well, I hadn't had *Sternway* out in it very long before the rope which ran through the sail from masthead to the end of the boom busted; the sail bellied away hopelessly, and the boom fell down. That was discouraging. So I took her in, and ran a new rope through the sail, and made the boom tighter than ever. Then I took her out. We sailed with annoying slowness through the cove, but suddenly one of those little blue squalls swept around the corner, caught the sail, heeled her over, and the next second we were out in it. By "We" I mean *Sternway* and I.

Well, I never seed a ship carry on like what she done. She tore along through those white-caps, tossing her bow around, like mad. When the squalls tore along, she dipped her leeward side; and I was as reckless as any sail-carrier, for in the worst squalls I would *not* let that sail out—I just held her to it for the sheer fun of it, and watched the water pour in over the side. At one time I felt sure she was going over, but I held the sail, and I wouldn't let it slack up an inch. And the mast took a terrifying sweep, and I felt sure that it was going to snap clean in two. Or perhaps in three. But it didn't.

You know, ever since I put that new rope in, I think it is no longer true that the tackle would bust before the ship went under water. Nothing gave way—not even the old sheet. The mast held marvellously—that's a good little stick, that mast, and the boom is another. But it was startling to tack. You would put the tiller down—and whizz-zz-zz-zz! Before you could get the water out of your eyes, you would be about, the sail having jibed with a terrific slap, the water would be pouring over the other rail, and *Sternway* tearing along like a mad creature on the other tack, piling up mountains of foam.

The other grand sail was yesterday. It was a most astonishing day, yesterday was. For it blew a gale dead east—a gale nearly as strong as the westerly one the day before; yet the day was clear till night, and today the wind is west again. I never saw it blow east all day without rain or fog—never. But it blew all right. The white-caps went sweeping and swirling in struggling knots. It was very appropriate, too, for at that same time I was reading about Aeolus and the struggling winds—in Latin.

Then I went out sailing. I couldn't resist running before the wind a way, just for fun. Sabra was with me, so I couldn't take the risks about the wetness of the leeward rail, but we had a jolly good speed some of the time, nevertheless. I was beating home, but she got tired of the beating, and so I had to furl up and row, which annoyed me. There haven't been two days of strong wind—two successive days—for a long time.

Well, *Sternway* is a great little ship. Last night I went out in her, with the oars, to observe the sunset, for it was still much too windy for the canoe. And I sat at the helm of her, with the oar held as a tiller, and let her run before that raging easterly wind, straight to the west; and she ran as though she had a sail in her, I swear. It was so glorious, and such a good way of seeing the sunset, that I let her run half-way to the west end of the lake, and then, there being nothing left of the sunset but a bunch of huddled, wild, black mountains, I turned around and rowed. And it was some row, out around Cape Horn there. That point in Cape Horn, you know. The way the wind goes tearing around there, as if it wanted to blow a hole in the lake, and bear away the hills! The squalls are fiercest there, the white-caps whitest and swiftest, the waves most ferocious. And the bow went up a smooth mountain, and *slap* into a rough valley, and sent a cloud of spray flying. It blew so hard during the squalls that I could hardly get my oars back for a fresh stroke. And it made me laugh so hard that I was not pulling dreadfully strongly, anyhow.

It certainly was a queer day, yesterday. In spite of that easterly wind, the sky was a glorious blue, and was full of great big white clouds, that went flying over to westward, under full sail. There was not even a wisp of haze, anywhere. And when I was out sailing, I was in sight of the peak of Kearsarge all the time, and it was clear purple—bright and sharply outlined against a rich sky. And the sunset was a sea of gold and crimson, full of islands and bays and Cape Horns and little silver waves, and trees with golden leaves, and it was framed in great mad mountains of darkness. One would have thought that the wind was west. It was a perfect west-wind day.

Well, so long for a while.

>With love,

You'll recall that The Voyage of the Norman D. *was a long letter to "Alan"—Barbara's nickname for Leo Meyette, her friend from New London, near Little Lake Sunapee. Despite Barbara's advice, Leo went ahead and married Maybelle Wells.*

Lake Sunapee.
Box 65
New London, New Hampshire
July 10, 1928

Hail, mate Alan!

And yet, on second thoughts, not "hail" neither, but "get to the devil." That was what I meant to say. Alan, Alan, shame on you! Alan, if you knew how I felt, walking home from New London yesterday afternoon, as I read those cursed words of your letter—Alan, if you knew how I felt then, you would turn into salt water. Why, Alan, you've gone to work and taken malicious joy in busting three perfectly good hearts already—your own sister's, mine, and Helen's. If not even the cat's. For I am sure she feels it, too.

Alan, you must not marry. You must not. I am going to talk to you and damn you up and down to the devil like a Dutch uncle, so be prepared. Alan, Alan, you must not marry. Do you hear me? Oh, hell—would you could hear my voice, with the true quiver of rage and sorrow in it, instead of reading these dull written words. If I had a red ribbon I would write with that—it would be more the colour of hell.

Alan, you must not marry. Do you understand me? Can you hear me, across these mad seas? Shipmate, shipmate, I am not trying to be unkind; don't you see I am only trying to save you? Alan, you would be the sickest and saddest and sorriest pirate on all the seven seas, if you allowed that moment of weakness to conquer you. Alan, if you marry, I'm done with you—you've lost one of the best friends you ever had. You didn't know I was one of your best friends, did you? But I am.

Alan, I can't have this. I am hurt to the very heart already; and if you go and *do* it, I don't see how I can bear it. Don't you remember anything at all? Didn't you practically swear to stay free and wild and happy? Oh, when I think of it all! It is too terrible. Do you remember when you were shingling the roof of the farm, and the urge for climbing a mountain came suddenly over you, and you threw your hammer into the air and climbed a mountain? You mean to tell me you don't remember when you were making a door, and felt that same mad impulse, and left the house chock-full of chips, sawdust, and shavings? Oh, Alan, Alan, Alan! How can I support this? Tell me, shipmate, how am I to support it? Have you thought at all? Have you thought how sorry you yourself will be?

Alan, I should have been far less surprised to see the sun collide with the moon and throw off a tremendous shower of brilliant sparks, which fell to the earth and turned into opals bigger than grape-fruits—far less surprised to see this than to see Alan Gold-belt getting *married*. It is, with absolutely *no* exception, the very last of the possible or impossible that I expected. Absotively and posolutely, the very last. And also the very last that I should have *liked* to see.

Do you remember the time we were out walking, Alan, and you suddenly said: "Bar, can you imagine me in any other way than ragged, penniless, and out of a job? Could you imagine *me* married?" And I said I certainly could not. And I can not. I mercifully can hardly believe my senses. For if I could believe them, I think I should sink into the earth.

You must not, *you must not*, YOU MUST NOT! Don't you understand, mad shipmate? Where's your freedom now, where will it be later? Where the mad adventures, where the rivers of gore and mountains of rotting flesh? Leo, we won't look at you with a wife. If you have her, keep away from us, that's all, or we'll blow you up and send you to your lover, the devil who resides in the land known as Hell. You keep away from us, and we'll keep away from you, for, by thunder, we'll not be shipmates any more, you and I, Alan. You're no true pirate. You're a disgrace to the ship, and must walk the plank, or swing from the yard-arm.

I boil with rage. Alan, Alan, Alan, who used to be my shipmate, my pirate friend, my treasure-hunting companion—how can you go and bust up my heart into little hard splinters like that. Need I remind you of the grocery days, when you sent high-hatters astray so maliciously and gloriously? Those persons whom you misdirected to Soonipi Park are undoubtedly driving away yet to the eastward. Need I remind you of the day we followed the gorgeous little brook in the winter, walking on mysterious snowy soap-bubbles which let us down into caves and chasms; of the time we hiked over the hills and valleys to Little Sunapee, and over some more hills and valleys home? Need I remind you of all that? Alan, do you hear me? Do you hear me?

Well, I am hurt; and when I am hurt I am hard as nails, and bitter as the salt sea. I would save you, my shipmate, if I could, but the ultimate decision lies with you. You know my mind now. You must write to me, and tell me what you have done, and whether you have given her up or not. And if you have done what you should do, we will welcome you in true piratical fashion—if not, go to the devil! I say again, Alan, for I'll no more of ye.

    Your enraged shipmate,
    Blackheart

P. S. I would have told you about our sailing craft *Sternway*, my schooners and sailors, treasures and mysteries, and the heaps of queer things that have taken place since you left, on land and sea and air. But I will tell you nothing more until you have told me what you mean to do. Then we will see. B.

Barbara's "three" was another recurring theme at this time. I believe they were the goddess Virodine, a brooch in the shape of an anchor that Norman had given her, and her philosophy.

July 10, 1928

Hail, shipmate!

And yet it isn't a very cheerful hail, either. I am in sad need for consolation. I am not so wrought up as I might be if it weren't for my three—without them, I should be completely at sea, and tossed about by the wild waves, without rudder or compass; but as it is, I have a little piece of kelp to entangle my hands in and hold to. Now is the trial of the three, if ever there was a trial. And, just as I expected, the goddess comes out by far the highest of the three; she very kindly puts a white mist in my mind, so that I am sleepy and not fully comprehensive of it all.

I will be brief. Yesterday I had a letter from LAM, the "distant friend." And Leo is getting married. *Married.* This month, sometime. Helen and I and his fine sister Grace, are all three nearly in tears. We are sending a cable this afternoon, telling him to stop in the name of the devil. Oh, it is too distressing! that happy, carefree soul! Norman, Norman, if you knew him you would see how horrible it is. He is the sort of person who would throw his hammer into the air with a scornful jerk, in the middle of shingling the roof, if the urge to climb a mountain came upon him. He is the sort of person who would leave a door half cut through a partition, and leave the house full of sawdust and shavings—when the mountain-urge came upon him. A glorious, carefree soul, with a sense of humour that would appeal to the devil's own dam.

Oh, it is a terrible, terrible tragedy. He will, I fear, go off the list, if we cannot stop this—and if he goes off the list, who is there that may stay? Oh, my poor Virodine—now is her testing! It is some task to veil me to this, yet she succeeds, partly; for I feel as though it could not happen, as though it were a nightmare, as though it were not true, as though he were only joking. And, though it comes over me in horrible nightmarish waves of fright at times, yet I have hopes . . . . . . And if it can't be stopped, I shall resign completely. I thought I had resigned, but I hadn't resigned from Leo. I gloried in Leo—otherwise the *Norman D.* wouldn't have existed. I gloried in Leo as he was, all alone, wild, and laughing, and piratical; and I wanted him to be exactly as he was. Well, tell me what you think of it, shipmate.

> Your shipmate,
> Barbara

P. S. I wrote a letter to Mate Bill yesterday, hoping to draw a fourth marvel out of him. BNF

New London
New Hampshire
July 11, 1928

Dear Bruce:

Well, we're here, thank goodness, at last. The weather has been perfectly glorious for a whole week; but yesterday was the beginning of showers and haziness, and today looks dubious. But that week was perfect. I was up between four and six every morning, hiking through the Wet Wild Woods, all by my Wild lone. The woods, by the way, have never been so beautiful as they are this year—I suppose that is due to all the rain. Anyway, I have never seen the ferns so green, the moss so luxuriant, the hemlocks so feathery, the balsams so sweet-scented. The bunch-berries are still in flower, which shows how late the season is. And there are still ladyslippers! The first morning I found fifteen or twenty pink ones all growing near together, in their prime. But they are fast withering, now.

And of course the hermit-thrushes, wood-thrushes, olive-backed thrushes, song sparrows, white-throated sparrows! This morning, at six, there was a most delicate chorus of hermit-thrushes from across the lake—several of them, singing their little moonlight arpeggios together. But there is something buoyant and joyous about a song sparrow; and something shrilly beautiful about a white-throated sparrow; and something furiously happy about an olive-backed thrush; and something cool and dusky about a wood-thrush. In spite of all these, however, the hermit-thrush is lovelier than them all combined—I think.

We have A Cat. A Kitten. Not nearly so interesting, so far, as the little grey-and-yellow one we had last summer, with that tail like a grey squirrel's. This one is very small. It is a plain Kitten, that's all, just plain Kitten. It is about eight inches long, not counting the tail; it is delicately formed, like all Cats; it is grey on Its back, with white showing here and there, and It has a neck of pure snow, and a small pink nose and white paws. Quite an Ornery Kitten. But It has a charming way of kinking up Its ratty little tail, and side-stepping when you play with It. It also bites your finger very playfully, apparently with great enjoyment. But It supplies a good deal of entertainment.

You should see *Sternway*, our row-boat with a spruce mast and boom, and a crude sail! She sails backwards most dexterously, hence her name; but I have seen her sail like chain lightning *forwards*—for example, a few days ago, when it blew from the west blamed hard. I nearly sailed her under water, and I was quite positive that the mast would bust in two. But it still exists, and not even a rope gave way—not a shred. A pretty good little tackle she seems to have, though I hadn't realized it!

Well, life is great, ain't it? Sometimes. Not Usually. So long, and good luck, and love to Rosalind.

   With love,
   Barbara.

Port Greville NS
July 16 1928

Will Shipmate

reiced you letter was glad to here form you again will I have home all summer the Frederick H. must be in Boston now the cook is hur the capen is home you sed you wish I could see your Ship I spose you are capen now. [...] how is your Father and Mother give them my best wishes will ship mate I will close hoping to here form you soon

   your shipmate
   Bill

Barbara's new mate aboard Sternway *was Edward Bliss Meservey (1916-2009).*

TO THE SEA (1927–1929)

"The Four" refers to Barbara's closest and most loyal friends: I believe they were Leo Meyette, Norman Donaldson, George Bryan, and I'm not sure about the fourth. Sabra? Virodine?

Box 65
New London
New Hampshire
July 17, 1928

Dear Norman:

It's the oddest thing! You know, there have been repeated cubes of H 2O under low temperature in the hollowed, cubical container for H 2O under low temperature, and—Jings, this sentence is mixed up, ain't it? I guess I had better start anew. What I *meant* to say was that there have been cubes of H 2O under low temperature in the container, ever since last *Saturday*, and today is *Tuesday*. The P. V. becomes dubious! Apparently the V. is not so P. as was thought, which is unfortunate because of the Extremely Limited Condition of the F. T.s—also, I begin to sense a vague wish for the Ph. to *coniungere, convenire, misceri,* as P. as possible. (You can look up those Latin Verbs, if you don't Understand them).

Last night I rowed down toward t'other end of t'other lake (Jings, but my little ship goes down there a thousand times more readily than she comes back, and partly because the Prevailing Winds are Fair), and the windows were *ouvertes*! Yes, the windows of the living-room were all ouvertes just a crack. Thinks I, Jings, this is pretty good, ain't it? So I *clam* (look that up) went around and looked in all the windows, but I didn't see no signs of life, so I went up and looked in the garage, and the Templar wasn't there and hadn't been there—so I just concluded the conclusion that Mr. Messer had opened the windows to Air Out the place. Well, *that* seemed to denote an *Extremely* P. V.—*especially* as I found a fresh cubical figure of H 2O under L. T. in the C. for H 2O under L. T. Is *that* clear?

So this mornin' I rowed down there *agin*; and the winders were still open, and the new piece of you-know-what was still there, and I was Sure I Heard Sounds from Above. Thinks I, Jings! And then I didn't think no more, 'coz I was too Excited to think anything but Jings. It was as you were meeting Hildegarde (you see I *haven't* forgotten to whom I am writing), when you said that by the time it could be reckoned in Minutes, you would be too Excited to Reckon it at *all*. So, after I had thought Jings several times, I hit the Brilliant Conclusion that it would be a good idea to sit down and wait, and say good morning (Jings) and then clear out adroitly and tactfully until they were Somewhat Settled. Meanwhile *Sternway* was banging around on the rocks in front, in the waves of the west wind.

Well, I sat there; and I inscribed the "Latin poem" on a piece of wood, and put it—oddly enough, in the container, thinking that was a Safe Place of Concealment, and one where it would be sure to be found. And then I was *SURE* I heard Sounds—running water! Jings! thinks I, several times. But then I suddenly thought: "Unjings!" For there were no signs of life in the kitchen—I mean luggage—and there was nothing in the Container except the H 2O under L. T., and the Templar wasn't there and hadn't been there—and so I hit another conclusion—and this time it was that the Sounds were proceeding from the next house. Then I thought "Un-jings," so many times that it *quite* made up for the time I had thought "Jings" before; and I reproached Her for that deception, and then I apologized, and she said she Quite understood my frame of mind—so that was all right. Do you see?

Such is life, ain't it?

Well, there was a beautiful Gale o' Wind yesterday—Oh, Normy, you would have gone mad with joy over that gale of wind. We took *Sternway* out, but she was Cranky, and was always turning toward Wildwood, and wouldn't stay in the wind at all. I think that was because the wind hadn't come to its climax yet—it was just a series of violent squalls with dead clams* [* in margin: "isn't that a marvellous accident?"] between. Finally—disgrace of disgraces! we brought up on the leeward shore—and I furled the flapping sail as Fast as Possible, while Edward shipped the oar-locks and the oars. He lost an oar, and Jings! I never seed anyone get down in the stern of a wessel quicker than wat he done. It was meerackuluss. 'Deed it was. And he got the oar, and reshipped it, and then we rowed home.

Well, the wind continued to come up, and when we went in swimming it was quite terrific—I have never seen it blow any harder. I ought to say that I and Edward rowed over to the beach just for the fun of it—all went well until the last stroke, as the waves hurled us up on the sand—and with that last stroke I went over backwards into the bottom of the boat, while both the oars went floating serenely out of the oar-locks. We agreed that that couldn't be beat for Gracefulness.

We went in swimming, and it was simply grand—it was really hard work to swim. I went out over my head, and treaded water for a long time, rising adroitly for every wave, but sometimes letting them break over me for fun. One hugeous one turned into a white-cap right over me, and torrents of hissing foam poured over my face. So yesterday I really fell in love and gotted engaged—to the West Wind. And when I went out in *Sternway* afterwards, and let him blow me (sitting at the stern, steering) clear across the lake, and then turned and rowed back again, and did it again, and then rowed across the lake, broadside, and then rowed straight against it with the bow riding up a mile or two and slapping the foam left and right, and drenching me and herself, and the bow getting buried all the time in monstrous sock-dolagers of waves—when I did all this, I ree-ee-eely came to the conclusion that the West Wind would make a purty good husband. So we will have a public wedding, and foam for the bridal cake, the next windy day. Will you be present?

Well, Jings, you can laugh all you like, Norman D, sir; but it was a pretty gorgeous day yesterday, with the old white clouds under full sail serenely clipping (fifteen knots, I'll be bound) over to eastward, leaving their wakes of foam, and with foam along their bows. And I never saw the West Wind more domineering, or the mermaids more playful. When I was out in *Sternway*, the way he danced us round was esstrordinery. And when you looked to the westward (no fooling, now) the whole lake was just mad dark tearing blue—one continuous squall—but it was also covered with roaring, hissing white-caps, of a whiteness unrivalled by snow. And to feel the little boat cavorting around, *burying her bow* like any ship—and to feel the wind furiously on my back or in my face, and the clouds of spray and waves mingled flying against me—well, I don't know how to finish this sentence except by repeating the statement that I fell in love and gotted engaged. Let me give you a tip—those infinitive constructions are Dangerous. I always get into trouble when I use them—for you never can finish. It's very odd.

Well, Norman D, my fine friend (S.-C. F.), I invented a wunnerful game this morning, which we must play. It is played with three pebbles, two of them more or less alike, one strikingly different in colour. I played with two dark grey ones and one pure white one. You throw them into the air and catch the white one and one of the grey ones, two points; if you catch all three, five points; but if you lose the white one (even if you catch the two grey ones), five points down; if you don't catch any, ten points down. It's greater fun than you would think—that is, if you're fair and throw them decently high. I was thirty-eight down once, playing by myself. There are two ways of playing—either by picking a number and seeing who makes it in the fewest throws; or by fixing a number of throws, and seeing who comes out highest after that number of throws has been thrown. Is *that* all clear? And don't you think it is a foolish, amusing little game? I do.

Well, farewell, Norman D. I wish I could have written you a funny letter; but, you know, our discussion of that other letter rather spoiled my ability to be repeatedly funny—if you know what I mean. However, here's hoping you'll excuse it. And, blame it, why don't you write? And, blame it, I guess you'll be at the Danger Point about now, won't you? Well, S.-C. F. beware! It is foolish of you to risk your life by Swelling; because, I will tell you frankly and bluntly, *there is nothing to Swell about*. Of course, you *are* one of The Four, and not by a long shot the least of The Four, either; at the same time, Swelling is Dangerous.

>Your shipmate,
>Barbara.

P. S. It is unlikely that I shall ever make the mistake in signature again!
B. N. F.

From Astrogle.com: "If a star is present on Mount Venus then it does not allow a person to succeed in sexual matters. Wastage only of time and money comes his way."

From: Wofs.com: "... It suggests misfortune caused by the opposite sex. You tend to be unlucky in love not because you are unattractive, but because you are never satisfied. When you feel betrayed or double crossed in love, you have the ability to enact revenge to soothe your jealousy. This can cause misfortune. You should work at keeping your temper under control, or you could end up the biggest loser."

Box 65
New London
New Hampshire
July 18, 1928

Dear Norman:

May I rely upon your stainless honor in-so-much as to ask you to hand the enclosed to Hildegarde, *Unopened*?

It's the oddest thing! I was down at W. again this morning, and the winders are *still* opened, and everything is spick and span as can be, but there are *no* signs of life. Jings; or Unjings, rather—ain't life queer? What now? What next? What heretoforeagain howsoverasmuchas?

Anyhow, I got a wonderful letter from Gordon Campbell yestiddy afternoon. I reckon you've kinder forgot who Gordon Campbell is, h'ain't yuh? I can imagine you scratching your head in perplexities. Well, I'll explain. He's my favourite in the crew of the *Carnegie*. He is not my favourite as a sailor, if you see what I mean, but he's my favourite because there is more *to* him, if you see what I mean. And I think he is rather more of a *person*, if you see what I mean. He drinks with the crew, but very, very little; because certainly he was the stiddiest on his feet the next morning, if you know what I mean.

Well, anyhow, it was a wonderful letter, and here is an accurate copy of it. I don't prize it so much as Bill's letters, to be sure; but just the same———well, here it be.

[Campbell's letter of July 2nd transcribed here.]

There; isn't that priceless? You see I wrote him a long letter, asking for a thousand details of the trip, the arrangement of the watches, the skipper, the mates, and the kittens—and see what I got for my pains? That is by *far* the longest letter—and the most like a letter—I ever got from a sailor. He is much more literate than many, too—notice the apostrophes in "don't"; the correct spelling of "received"; the way he struggles with his "two"s and "to"s and "too"s. And read it carefully and tenderly, Norm, and don't miss a word. Catch the subtle undertone when he says "Some of the Scientists were not feeling too good"; and of the skipper: "All the trip I never saw him growl at anybody yet"; and of the mate: "Of course he has had a few argument with some of the boy but that can always be expected on a ship." And I love the place where he says: "The last we saw of the missing one was the both of them climbing up in the forrad running Gear." The last we saw of the missing *one* was the *both* of them.... Do you catch that odd little grammatical twist. And when he says "*Mister* Campbell has wrote at *last*," he was referring to our joke about *Mister*—and also he was referring to my saying in my letter: "Well, you just tell that Mister Gordon Campbell to write to me—" or something like that.

Well, Norm, it is Obvious that now that the ph. is gradually (though not so P. as I should like!) coniunxing, you will receive the Cream of the Correspondence. But don't—oh, look out! I shouldn't have said that! Don't Swell! But there is no doubt that you are the SECOND of The Four. Ain't that what you might call a Compliment? You better look out, or you'll lose your reputation—you'll have some job to keep it ahead of LAM—that is, unless LAM marries.

I guess you are beginning to learn, a little, what my long documents to the Third Factor were like. But you mustn't be misled;

because they weren't at all like this—they were much more serious, somehow. There were Jocose Moments, to be sure, but they were mostly Serious and Descriptive, if you know what I Mean.

Well, the Coniunxing of the ph. looks Dubious don't it? What do you make of it? Anything?

        Your shipmate,
        Barbara

P. S. I am not generly "supersticush"—isn't Campbell's spelling of that divine?—but I have a spidery, horrible star on my "mount of Venus." You ask anyone what a star on the mount of Venus means, and they will tell you—that is, anyone that palm-reads at all. So I am in the greatest of worryment, although I am not exactly supersticush. But it was a *hint*, if you see what I mean, and kinduv oped my eyne to the Possibilities. Also I am to beware a man with a Vandyke beard!!!!!!!!!! Isn't that Barba ?????????? BNF

P. P. S. Virodine and I got together and swore to overthrow the predictions of my palm. And we will! B.

Box 65
New London
New Hampshire
July 18, 1928

Dear Hildegarde:

This is going to be, as Pooh would say, an Extremely Short letter. It is just to tell you that things have been going all right, or pretty nearly so, since a few days after WF left. There were some storms and rain-falls then, to be sure; but the sun came out shortly, and ever since there have been nothing worse than slight gratings and irritations, such as appear in the best-ordered families—if you know what I mean.

You must come up again *soon*—SOON—and stay *longer*—LONGER. You have no idea how grand it is here when it's really windy and the white-caps go flying past the old Cape Horn, as we call the point. Day before yesterday I got engaged to a West Wind, it was blowing so hard and foamingly. We are going to have a talk about the wedding-day pretty soon, but we haven't quite decided when it will be.

        With love,
        Barbara.

July 19, 1928

Hail—I mean Hi-Hi!, shipmate!

Helen walked to N. L. *[New London]* this afternoon, and brought back two *such* letters! Two is not One of the Larger Numerals, to be sure, but they were two such tremendjously grand and gloreeuss letters—Oh, Norm! One was from the T. F.—a page and half another, and ne'er a word about when they are coming up!—and t'other was from—well, guess! Form your idea before you read the next paragraph, and then write me what your guess was.

It was Mate Bill! The fourth letter from him! And here it is:———

[July 16th letter transcribed here]

There: isn't that doubly priceless? To be sure Campbell's letter was longer and all that—but isn't this just———? If you see what I mean? Here is a new spelling of received———"reiced." By "your Ship" he means *Sternway*. This is my favourite remark: "I spoze you are capen now." Isn't that Bill all over? That remark introduces you to him, if an introduction you need! "Our trit" means "our *trip*," evidently.

Well, Helen is pestering me about the racket of this thing, so I will Close hoping to here form you soom.

        Your shipmate,
        Barbara

P. S. The envelope was addressed to Miss Barbara Florrie. B.

"Fts" might mean final thoughts, and I think "VSD" is Very Secret Delivery. WW and ph. remain the West Wind and philosophy. There will be more of these mysteries that I'll leave for you to decipher.

July 22, 1928

Dear Shipmate:

Reiced you letter was glad to here form you. The very first thing I sawed (even without looking) were the Fts. And, as you may well believe, I was Very Much Puzzled about them until I arrived at your explanation. To speak as between shipmates, I will confess that I thought they were all intended for return VSDs, and I thought that my shipmate must be getting very Swelled Up, and that I had better take him down a peg or two. Well, your explanation was an explanation, all right, but so illogical! And so delightful! Now anyone else would have sent as many FTs as there had been unanswered letters from *himself*. See what I mean? But you———Jiminy, what an odd idea!

Isn't this a Great and Historic Correspondence, though? Jings, but it's going to be lots of fun. I accept all your rules perfectly, and I have one rule, also——that I shall only write when I want—that is, when the divine mood comes upon me. I shan't either try to answer your letters—I never did approve of answering letters, if you know what I mean. I may run them over systematically, discussing certain points, because if neither of us ever answered the other's letters as such, it would no longer be a correspondence at all—it would simply be a series of entirely isolated VSDs. Do you see what I mean?

Of course your letters (and mine, too, you yunnerstan') are VSDs. In fact, they will be as S as anyone could desire—they will be as S as any D could be. I am an S. person, as you know, fond of Ss and SDs.

Well, I had a discussion with the WW the other day; and I said that if he wanted to marry me he would have to get along without either of my thirds. Oh, I haven't told you, but my ph. is progressing *famously*. I have even writ it down in detail (three pages, and an Ser D than that (if you see what I mean) could not well be imagined). I have found out that I—I don't know whether you are or not—that *I* am divided into three parts—three Main parts, although there are fringes. These parts are heart, imagination, and head; and they are evenly and completely distributed among the Three Factors. See if you can find out which Factor has which Part? Then write and let me know, and we'll see if you hit it right.

Well, I told WW that he would have to get along without any of these three, and he gave me a slap (kiss?) which sent me under the water, choking! But it was apparently a playful slap, because he accepted my conditions, so we're still engaged. The next west-windy day is the wedding day.

I writed a pome yestiddy, about some poor soul who had not been to sea for years and years, and was Moping about it, as Eeyore was when he lost his tail. It was in blank verse, and so Sad that it almost made me weep myself, and then it seemed so funny to weep over some bum pome of my own that I laughed till I wept again. It was all about sailing beneath the stars, the wind a-singing and sails a-sighing——or was it wind a-sighing and sails a-singing? I dinna ken.

Well, such is Life. I have lately had opportunity to use that expression—for yestiddy some persons turned up that I didn't want to see, and the cat did something she shouldn't in the dining-room (if you know what I mean), and Sabra talked herself and everyone else luny, and it rained today, and the house was, is still, hell; and it is still raining; and if I had no ph. I might be in the awful midst of that wild whirlpool—while, as it is, I stand above it, I and my inward peace, serenely smiling and unworried. Inward Peace is an Enormous Improvement.

Well, Norm, you are too damned old-fashioned, and I am too goldarned wild-reckless, and the two of us make a good pair. Anyhow, you're all right.

> Your shipmate,
> Babou (Barboo?)

P. S. TF has not encore vented—if you see what I mean, Pooh. BNF

Thanks for the info. about the seven (7) schooners. I should have preferred to be on the *slowest*. Do you know why? B.

A short letter from Einar, another friend from the Carnegie.

Raykjavik Island
July 24/1928

Dear Barbara!
Few lines to thank you for your wonderfull present and to let you know that Carnegie is still floting around with the old crew, all in good spirit even if we are away upp north in Island. We have had so far a lot of head wind plenty of rain and squalls but I think it will be better when we starting working our way to the southern a bit. We are leaving here for Barbados coming friday it will be about a sixty day trip. [...]
They verry best of regards and wishes from Einar

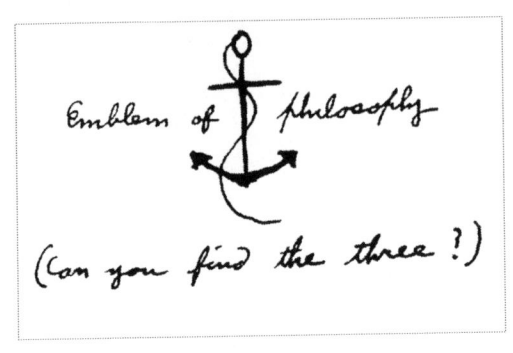

Emblem of philosophy

(Can you find the three?)

Another puzzle for Norman, drawn at the end of the July 22nd letter.

Shipmate:
Pst! Pst! Send this to your brother. Eh? And tell me what he says ... The WW is a great old fellow, and I am hugely in love with him. I get jealous and suspicious sometimes, but he slaps other people so hard in the face, that I am soon reassured ... Sent another

devil of a letter to Leo... How are you?... Have you found out about the anchor yet?... So long!

      Your mate,
      Barbara

Barbara enclosed a coded message with her note to Norman.

July 26.
[written in the shape of a large X]:
The north wind has blown all night, But I am hoping WW will arise soon.

New London
New Hampshire
July 26, 1928

Dear Norm:

    Thanks for the info. about the spelling of my name. I just got your letter, and—but we weren't going to discuss that. I will only say that the closing sentence (you naughty young man) sounded rather like a love-letter! Hem! To be sure, we weren't going to ANSWER letters as such, at the same time, questions should be answered, and I will answer yours, but you must answer mine. You answered (or tried to) one of mine, but there were two others in that same VSD—why the anchor is the emblem of philosophy; and why I should have preferred to be on the SLOWEST of the seven (7) schooners.

    Well, Mr. S-C f (notice the F is small, and the S-C large, which, I hope you realize, is meant for an insult) your answer to the Division of the Three Parts Among the Three Factors was WRONG!!!!!! Try again, please—don't be discouraged, but try again. This is great fun—a thing like this going on over the mail——ain't it?

Now for the answer of your question, which, by the way, is a MOST DIFFICULT one, for the Reason that I don't know the Answer of it. But here is what I THINK is the Answer of it: being by nature a Very Secretive Person, and having by nature Very Few *Real* Friends, and accumulating by nature Plenty of Ideas (such as they are), and yet, by nature, not Revealing them to Many Persons——I find that when I find a Person, to whom I may Reveal my Plentiful Ideas (such as they are), and with whom I have Many Humorous and Serious Understandings, and whom I Consider Quite a Delightful S-C F, although Without Doubt an S-C F——well, that's the Answer, if you see what I Mean, Pooh.

Your FTs are being employed——but I guess I had better not tell you. You will notice that your *own* VSDs are in Stamped Envelopes—but then, I don't want to discourage the arrival of the FTs. They are HANDY.

I have written everything down, Norm, and it took a prodigious load off my mind. I wrote down the Principal Ideas and the Principal Sub-Ideas, and all the Sub-Sub-Ideas, if you see what I mean, arranged extremely Systematically, if not Mathematically.

Well, answer me those two other questions, and then I will try not to ask questions for a while, for I know that they are a Nuisance in a Correspondence of This Kind. However, I *should* like to know about the anchor and the slowest schooner—and, oh, yes, tell me your second guess about the Parts of the Factors.

        Your matey,
        Babou.

P. S. Thirty-five. BNF

July 28, 1928, New Hampshire

Dear Mr. Oberg:

I can't tell you how sorry I am that our correspondence has slowed down so much, but I have only one excuse for everything: "Such is life!" That is what the cook aboard the Norman D. used to say whenever he became unbearably irritated against the captain. And what with the confusion, the hurrying, the tearing, the work of getting up here and settled, renting the house in NH, and what-not, I think we have done fairly well to keep on our feet at all.

But now we are here, by the beautiful little Lake Sunapee with its two gold-brown hills and the valley of maples between. Those hills are so beautiful against the sky! But I hasten to add that the sky is not very beautiful today, for it is full of wet, low clouds, and the tops of the hills are buried in fog, and it has been raining. Such days are not welcome up here, because you can't go out very advantageously, and what is the meaning of this place if you can't go out?

The other day we all went up Mount Kearsarge, that big blue mountain with one big round dome with a smaller one beside it. Sabra went, too, and she climbed all the way to the top without being carried at all—indeed, she went so fast that we were all glad she didn't go any faster! And then she went, without difficulty, all the way down another trail, a much harder and rockier one than the one she went up.

And the day before yesterday I climbed the eastern of the two hills across the lake. It was a beautiful, clear day, and when I saw those hills so sharply outlined, I couldn't resist. So I had a beautiful time climbing it, and looking at the mountains and lakes spread out around it. It couldn't be clearer—that is, not in July. I ate blueberries, raspberries, and strawberries (quarts of them) all the way up and back. And there are going to be blackberries galore, too.

We have a little grey and white kitten. We got her to keep the mice away, but she is much too young to do any good with them. She does nothing but frolic around, playing with pine-cones and flying leaves; she sleeps hour after hour, until you would think she would never wake up but she always does. She wakes up, stretching herself out long and lean, and then arches her back stiffly, rubs her eyes, laps her paws, and starts to play. After a little of that, she turns to and sleeps again. Her life seems to be one continuous "Watch below!"

Well, goodbye for the present, but I hope to write again soon.

    Your friend,

An undated request to Norman from about this time. Hildur Alida Anderson (1909-1971) was born and raised in New Haven, but I don't know her connection to Barbara.

Hey, Norm!

Normy, will you mail the enclosed for me? And will you do it without *ever* telling *anyone, ever,* no matter *what* happens? This is MOST IMPORTANT; and by this the devotion which you avowed in your VSD will be put to the test. And you will never ask me any questions about it, either, *will* you? I may tell you a little something—but until then, *silent!*

The enclosed may amuse you—I mean the *other*—*not* the letter.

> Your shipmate,
> Babou

P. S. Norm, I can't find the right kind of envelope. So I shall have to ask still more of you, and this tests your devotion, your philosophy, your honesty, and your morals *hugely*. The thing to amuse you is marked OTHER: the thing to mail is not marked. Now you must take the unmarked thing, and write an envelope for Miss Hildur Anderson, 116 Lilac Street, New Haven; stamp it, and mail it. It must be a BLANK envelope, and the "Hildur" must be spelled just that way. Don't dictate the envelope—write it YOURSELF, and show it to no one—mail it YOURSELF. And don't—oh, please be careful to open the thing marked OTHER. If you do all this all right, my devotion will increase ENORMOUSLY. Let that be your bribe—if a bribe you need—which I doubt, my darling S-C F.

P. P. S. Don't forget to put the unmarked thing in the envelope! When I said BLANK envelope, I meant that there must be no return address—Yale University Press, or anything of that kind.

Oxford had invited my grandfather to go hiking with him in the White Mountains.

106 Perry Street
New York City
August 1, 1928

Dear Oxford:

I'm sorry, but it just can't be done. I could elaborate endlessly with details, but the whole thing boils down to two facts, which I give you in the order of their importance to me:

I. It doesn't in the least tally with my notion of decency to leave Margaret Whipple (who has nowhere to go and no consolation for staying) in this inferno while I enjoy anything so desirable. She has tried in every known way to send me, but I can't make the grade, owing to the way I am constructed, and it would be idle to pretend that I could get the good of the expedition with that awareness in my mind all the time. I'd gladly renounce this form of selfishness in the interest of *your* enjoyment, purely and simply, if I could argue myself into thinking that your enjoyment ought to get precedence over her need (this sounds like conceit, but isn't). But I can't argue myself into that, either. It's no go.

II. You had little more than got away north when Alfred A. Knopf,

Inc., discovered how much better off they would be without me than with me. Hence, I am on the town; and it would be tough on the family's income and their accursed South Sea trip to omit any possible effort to hook on to a satisfactory job and salary that will see them through. This also would be a very hard fence to shin over, even if I weren't confronted with the other impassable fence.

To these considerations I might add that Helen is pounding me to know if the car is sold. She wants it disposed of and the value of it made available. I shouldn't bother about that if the coast were otherwise clear, but it's an additional discomfort.

There's a possibility—how tangible I can make it I shan't know for a week or two yet—that I can get my income out of some syndicated writing that I've projected. If so, I—we—shall live up north in the wild, within a few hours' easy drive of you. Then we can devise ways and times to do things—or, at least, so I should hope. But we daren't count on such good fortune until it comes to pass. Until it does, I'm afraid my way (which is plain and inescapable) lies right here, in a place which has long been to me so ghastly that it seems fantastic to have to construe it as the scene of any human being's obligation.

Love to Anne. I'd give my ears to be with her, and you, and the youngsters who will have grown so far away from me. You must get your trip—and how sorry I am that it isn't to be with me!

        Yours always affectionately,
        Follett.

I think the article Helen refers to is Education à la Carte, *which wasn't published by* Harper's *but by the* Pictorial Review, *and not until July 1929. Or it could be an entirely different article that wasn't published anywhere.*

New London, New Hampshire
4 August, 1928

Dear Anne:

After I talked with you yesterday I came back to the cottage and found Mrs. Meyette there. And that resulted in her taking Bar and me to Newport today (she herself having to go there, anyway), to get our passport pictures. I thought that would be a good thing out of the way. Came about that after the Bank and a Law Firm had told me there was no way of making out an application blank this side of Concord, I walked into the Clerk's office in the Court Building just to be told once more. And, lo and behold! he said he could do it; that he had never issued an application to a person not living in his county, but that there was no reason why he shouldn't. So there we went through the proceedings, and he, after getting the pictures to stick on, will mail them to me, who writes money orders and mails them to Washington. And then, if all goes well, we get the passports sent to New London.

So after you have gone to a lot of trouble I can now, when it is too late, relieve you from further trouble about that!

I expected that Follett would not leave New York. I think the situation there is very bad about his getting a job, and I am almost down and out, but not quite. I am hoping Harper will take the article which is, in my opinion, a hundred percent better than when I read it to Oxford.

It was grand to have him here, and Bar envies you all in just having him. She seems very indifferent about her own tragedy, but it comes out in one or two phrases that mean volumes. The thing strikes deeper into me all the time; and of course I am frightfully jealous of the person who has usurped my place, the particular place which I have always longed for—of living with him and writing with him alone. We could have had such a time! I think, perhaps, it all accounts for my indifference to the children: they have kept me from him, and they have been the cause of my losing him. And without him, they seem to touch me so vaguely. Perhaps I can get over this, I don't know. Only, I do know that I myself am needed and wanted so little, that I don't promise to go on. I do promise, however, not to dump them on the world without taking adequate justification.

I wish someone would drive us over to see Ellen. Bar wants to see her so much. And I do, too. And Anne, the days that Edward was here were just too lovely; of course we fell in love with him. We want him! And he is so beautiful to look at! Robert is a darling, too, as you know; but we didn't have enough of him!

Do thank Oxford for coming over; Bar and Sabra fell all over him, and he was lovely to me. Yes, we all envy you—and him.

      Love,
      Helen

An undated letter to Norman, written as a solid block of text diagonally on square paper. I think it falls somewhere between the July 26 and August 15 letters.

I venture to dare to suppose that there is No Use in Trying to Conceal the Reason for this Breach—this Sad Breach—in our G and H C. I suppose you are now Congratulating yourself on thinking that you know all about the Breach—that is, you with swelling [three or *four words missing: perhaps something like "chest and thinking"]* yourself very subtle in being able to make the erroneous guess that I am Spending a Good Deal of Time—with the TF. And it *is* erroneous. I only wish it were not, but I tell you it IS. And I can prove it to you very—extremely—easily. All you have to do is drop a line to P. NY, and you will discover that the TF is *still* there. 16 Young Ave., in case you are Suspicious. But the Real Reason for this Sad Breach is only our plain and simple Rule no. 1—that is the rule which enables us to write *what* we feel like, *as often* as we feel like, *as much as* we feel like, *in what manner* we feel like, *when* we feel like. QED. That is, to be briefer—the rule which Enables us to write Only During Propitious Moments (or Hours, as the Case May Be), if you see what I mean, my devoted (and devoted-*to*) S-C F. Well, well, well. Hereinafter, I shall say WWW, and you will know what that means. We must get as many abbreviations of that helpful sort as possible. I am now going to State the three things which I want your VSD to contain. Which reminds me—I forgot to write your VSD on your birthday; and I'm sorry: which also reminds me—how near was my guess? Now I will State the three things, if I don't get interrupted by some stray Thought which pokes his head in the way like a comet. I want you to hazard a second guess on the division of Parts and Factors— and we must have an abbreviation for that, by the way, let it be GDPF (G/rand D/ivision P/arts F/actors). That is one. Then I want you to work out why the anchor is the emblem of my ph. And I want you to try to find the three factors and the objective, on that anchor. That is two. Then I want you to try to work out why I should have preferred to have been on the *slowest* of those seven (7) schooners. That is three. And Three should be, to you my nautical devotee, *much* the easiest of the Grand Trio. That is a Grand Trio——ain't it? We will call it GT. WWW, ph. is a Great Help—ain't it? Jings, mine is working in Great Shape. I was out last night with Signey under the stars, watching the flashes of weird lightning, and the meteors, and the high, luminous bank of Northern Lights. And then there was a lightness in the east, and soon the red moon arizz through the fog, and came into a crystal clear pool of light, and shone goldenly. And, though any ph. is very small and insignificant when brought face to face with the stupendousness of the universe, yet it is amazing how well an airy anchor constructed of nothing more substantial or tangible than ideas will hold on *any* bottom—be it rock, clay, gravel, sand, or mud. Ain't it great? And say, Sir Devotee, I have to laugh when I think of that last sentence in that second VSD of GDPF. And I want to know; because that is now one of the most important cylinders of flukes of my ph. And you are *such* an *authority* on such things. Yes, I want to know whether you Approve. And if you don't, I shall Argue, and we'll have a reg'lar old sock-dolager of a Hargyment over the mail—which will be fun, if I know anything about anything. Or Anyfing about anyfing, as Sabra would indubitablyously say. Well, shipmate—or, as I should say, "will shipmat"—I am going to begin to "close hoping to here form you soom." You must answer me in the very next VSD about the G/rand T/rio; and in the VSD after that you must tell me whether you Approve of the GDPF. And if you don't—Jings, you will have such argymentative VSDs that you will be very much surprised, and whether you will be flattened or swelled I don't know. That, by the way, will be interesting to observe; whether you will be flatter or sweller after such an assault! Very interesting for a specialist in flattening and swelling. I think I shall have to hire one to observe you and communicate with some Bureau of Scientifics. So I will close my shipmat hoping to here form you soom agin. Farewell!!

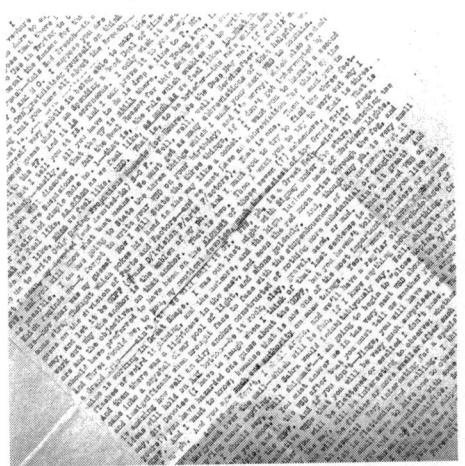

The next letter suggests that Barbara had a contract with Knopf for a third book. I suppose it might have been for her pirate story, which doesn't appear to have survived, or perhaps the book about Farksolia, which she didn't finish. It's a very long letter and I've cut out some material about the Folletts' dire finances.

106 Perry Street
New York City
August 5, 1928
(Sunday)

Dear Helen:

[...] First, it would be an awfully good thing for you—and, in a lesser way, for me—if you could get the idea of hurry out of your mind. Very few, if any, of the things you feel pressed about make any real difference as between one week and another, or even one month. This Harper article, for instance. And all your projects of rushing to see people in New York and elsewhere. There is every inducement to go slow about all such things, do them at leisure when you are good and ready, and get things right by taking the necessary time. You made me spend forty-seven cents for a telegram to say that I would read the Harper paper, not to speak of going a long distance on foot to hunt a telegraph office in a temperature of 88 Fahrenheit, knowing already that I was to do everything possible about the article—and, anyway, it would have been perfectly easy to send it by mail with a note asking me to work on it if I could and return it if I couldn't. It came late last night. You want me to "have" it copied—which means my spending five hours to copy it myself, in addition to the many hours of work I shall have to do on it if I do any—and then to deliver it to Harper's. I am going to work on it and copy it, but not deliver it to Harper's; it isn't going to help you any with them to have your stuff apparently connected with me, and you should deliver it yourself.

The plain fact of the present situation is that there is nothing that any of us can do that should take precedence over my trying to arrange a regular job and a reliable income. The basic facts are that you're all right if that comes to pass and all wrong if it doesn't. It would be philosophical and helpful if you were to perceive this and let your perception take the form of not spending an unnecessary cent until you knew that the treasury is going to be all right. After a winter and spring of pretty lavish expenditures of an avoidable sort (besides the unavoidable ones), you are talking with a freedom which alarms me about trips to New York and New Haven, hiring a motor car for a week, and so on. It is a pretty poor time to be going in for such things. And you are, on the financial question, raising the ante altogether too blithely. In one letter you asked for $6000 a year. Very reasonable: you shall have it if it can be got, and I am willing to live like a wharf-rat to supply it. In the next letter, you asked for $6000 *plus* enough to take care of your mother and Sabra in your absence. That is something else again: frankly, you won't get it, and I doubt that you would get it—in that spirit or for that purpose—if I had $25,000 a year. That I should live the kind of life I shall have to, and in the place I shall have to, to put five hundred dollars a month into the bank for you to spend *solely* on a trip that you ought to supply for yourself if you get it, is altogether too much of a roast. If you can't do better than that, with the house rented for enough to take care of itself, your whole idea needs some pretty drastic revising. Does it ever occur to you that you are proposing to exact and enjoy without a qualm the profits of my carrying a load pretty certain to include the following components: (1) living in New York, the most loathsome of all the works of man; (2) working long hours at work mentally degrading and morally worthless; (3) living on a scale which involves physical privation; (4) accepting the impossibility of doing any work that I want to; (5) accepting the impossibility of a respectable social status, the sacrifice of common, ordinary human rights such as practically all decent persons enjoy—I say, has any of this occurred to you? I am willing, and fully expect, to put up with all of this that is necessary to your comfort (assuming that I can get the chance to put up with it); but there really is a limit. If I detected any sign at all of your being concerned about me—I mean, not words, but actions—it would make it somewhat easier to believe that I'm not just trying to make money to pour into a hole. —Well, what I have to say boils down to this: you will have your $500 a month if I can possibly raise it by any amount of scrambling whatever; and you won't have a cent more than that (regardless of whether I have a surplus or not) unless you can show a clear mathematical necessity in terms of a way of living that makes sense to me. If you were planning to make a tenable and continuous home for Barbara, Sabra, and your mother, and to live without needless expense but with every comfort in some place like Hanover or Burlington, I could gladly slave as I never did before to provide you with everything possible. When you go to putting a trip that nobody in his senses would grab at *until* the prior claims, the automatic necessities, had been taken care of, I have to call a halt. While your plans are on the present basis, $6000 a year is the mortal limit as far as I am concerned. If I can get any margin above that, I shall, with a good conscience, either tuck it away against future troubles or use it in the interest of decencies and comforts of my own.

Well, I recommend that you sit tight and hang on to your slender cash until you learn what your income is to be. Then you can cut according to your cloth. Every railroad trip you take for the present is simply holding my head under water until the bubbles rise.

It is in the nature of things that Harper won't run your article until some acceptable stuff has come through from Barbara on the trip, so that they can see where they're at. Then they will use your piece as an introduction and ballyhoo for the other. It doesn't make a darn bit of difference whether you give it to them this month or next, or next after that. Nor is there anything whatever in connection with it that can't be done exactly as well or better by mail. Whatever you require of them by way of letters, documents, etc., should be stated in a clear typed list on which they can check off items as they get round to supplying them, and with a carbon copy on which you can do the same.

I am going to give you some general and specific advice about your affairs with editors and publishers. I imagine you will think it dictated by irritation and allowed yourself to be forced by excitement out of the posture which I recommend: well, the advice is good advice anyhow, and I am going to force it on you. In the long run, you are going to have the publishers hating the sight of you if you don't keep the indebtedness from them to you instead of the other way about. If they know every time they see you coming that you're going to ask for help—no matter how excellent the claim may admittedly be—you're going to incur a relationship that will soon make you even more uncomfortable than it makes them. Don't levy any sudden demand for payments: supply your work, give them a good comfortable interval to find out without hectoring what they think of it, and take your pay when it comes. The only exception to this should be if a month or two were to go by, when you might reasonably write mildly to ask if a letter had gone astray. You shouldn't broach the subject of an advance—as I remember, one was agreed upon—until you actually know that you are going to board a designated boat at a definite time. And, if you do accept that advance, it should be the only favor asked; and after it your concerted effort should be to get the balance in your favor as fast and as emphatically as possible. Otherwise, believe it or not, you are simply going to jockey yourself into a position where you will have to beg for favors that will sooner or later be refused, instead of having people falling over themselves to confer favors.

You mention going to see Alfred. (I take it for granted that that has nothing to do with me, and I explicitly rely upon you not to talk over my situation with him in any way—either the present or the past parts of it.) If you are going to do that, you should be provided in advance with an exact appointment and an explicit list of what you want from him; you should keep the appointment exactly; and any demands you make should be of extreme reasonableness. You can't suggest money (except for drawing any royalties that may have accrued), because you have gone elsewhere to enlist interest and help without broaching the affair to him or going through the motions of finding out if he were interested. You can't fairly or honorably ask him to release his rights in the third book (if he has any: I haven't the contract to refer to) unless you are prepared with a fair offer to take over the copyrights, plates, and stock of the other two; to ask this would be unmitigated gall. And to confess that you have promised the third book elsewhere (if you have, and if the contract gives Alfred a claim to it) would be to admit at once a lack of responsibility and a lack of sense. —Most of this may be firing in the air, because I don't know what you want of him, and am merely slamming down notes on what occurs to me as possible. In any event, I should seriously think over whether an orderly and careful letter stating the facts and the requests wouldn't accomplish more and accomplish it more quickly. The advantage of a letter is that it gets both action and attention *at once*, as incidents of the day's correspondence. You *see* a man and tell him your story, and then you wait for him to act until he feels just like it; and it's ten to one you have to write and prod him after all. Even in the office, nine-tenths of all business is done in writing, and rightly so. [...]

No, I don't think you can get anything regular out of the Pictorial Review that you could keep up while travelling. I hope you can sell them at least one thing before you take off; but if you could persuade them into a monthly department—which you could by showing them plenty of sample goods, and in no other way—you would have to stick by it and be in touch all the time. That is obvious.

That cleans up pretty much everything as far as the Harper article, I think. Or everything that there's any sense in descating on. [...]

I think it quite possible that you may get by with the article about as it is. The point for Wells will be that it raises, in an interesting and discussable way, an issue which affects enough of his readers to kick up some dust. That is all he is obliged to be concerned about; and on that basis he may, as I say, be content. He is not obliged, as I am, to concern himself with the light in which it may leave the author with the readers. From that point of view, I think I had better say certain things; and here goes.

First, the article is too personal not to be more personal. Either there should be more circumstantial information about Barbara in it, or there should be practically none. I understand the difficulty arising from her attitude, but I think you will have to cut through that regardless. (As a fact, I believe that there'll have to be a lot more iron in your control of her in the next two or three years, or else she'll go completely to pot.) If you are going to write technical articles, you have to write them about your work, your data. Barbara is the chief of your data, and has no more personal rights in the matter (granted the rudiments of taste) than an internal combustion engine would have if you were an engineer. She might as well understand this, and learn that she is simply obstructing your possible career out of an empty kind of pettishness. The natural thing would be an article reporting the developments of the last nine years—a factual sequel to "Schooling without the School"—with a trifle of theorizing somewhere in it, as before. Naturally, I can't do anything about this aspect of the paper.

Secondly—and I can perhaps do a little about this—the tone taken is in many places a little too young and a little shrill; shrill with the wrong kind of truculence. "Imperturbable" is the kind of epithet no human being should use about himself unless he is really trying hard to infuriate readers; and that is an example of the tone I mean. The article ought to contain more of the force of understatement, I think. You are humble and inquiring about things you know perfectly well, and peppery and cock-sure about things that perhaps nobody will ever know. (I am exaggerating, but you see the idea.) I shall try to urbanize the tone a little without loss of matter or real emphasis. [...]

I was going to write Barbara at this same time—I owe her a letter in answer to a very delightful one of hers—but this has exhausted me pro tem. Tell her that I got a dinghy and spent two hours on a three-masted schooner of Boston, the Albert H. Willis, in from Georgia with a cargo of Southern pine and anchored in the middle of the East River, and was hospitably received by the mate, Mr. Green, who joined the Annie C. Ross when she left New Haven and made the next several voyages in her; and I spent two hours on the fore deck of the cargo steam El Capitan, Southern Pacific Lines, and watched her loading from the dock on one side and from lighters on the other, for New Orleans. The Astors have a full-rigged three-master, a barque, which they use on short trips about Long Island (unfortunately, under her auxiliary power chiefly), and which, I was told, will go to Santander, Spain, in the race for the largest class later this summer. (I suppose you have read about the wreck of the Rofa in the race for schooners.) Do not infer that I am planning an escape to sea: I promise you that I shan't let go the bear's tail until there's far too little of me left for any manner of getaway.

   WF

August 6, 1928

Hi hi!

H. says she is going down with Signey next Saturday, and she also informs me that I must inform you that she intends to steer her course direct to no. 14 B. L., there to stay at anchor a few days. And she will steer direct without any further arrangements, unless, of course, the weather report at your end is unfavourable.

Which manoeuvre strikes me is bold and unprecedented—nevertheless, 'tis none 'o *my* affair, thank V———

> Hi hi, from
> Bahbuh (a spelling I think you did *not* suggest, in your list!)

P. P. My next VSD will probably be devoted to a nautical adventure which took place a short time ago. But you never can tell about my VSDs! Nor yours, either, I find!

Helen wrote the following letter to Wilson and sent a copy to the Meserveys (hence its survival).

New London, New Hampshire,
8 August, 1928

Dear Roy:

Will you go to the West Indies and beyond with Barbara? It would be the greatest thing in the world for both of you. And all you will need is your passport, your typewriter, your passage; with Barbara's job, and the kind of stuff you can write, there isn't a chance in the world of your not working your way along indefinitely. At Barbados you can pick up schooners; and the two of you can earn your way so much more easily than Bar and I can, for, as you know, I can never hope to earn money with my pen or typewriter. So far as Sabra and I are concerned, I have a standing invitation to teach in a school in Boston, and have Sabra with me. You wouldn't have to think of us at all, this I can promise you.

Won't you try it? You still have time to get a passport. And you would be free of New York, and you would get some health back, would have a gorgeous time with Bar, would be able to do many things with her that I cannot possibly do, would make the trip a far richer affair,—and you would make me exceedingly happy.

Thanks so much for your kind and detailed letter, the advice of which I shall try to follow. I shall, however, have to go down, anyway, inasmuch as I can't have my wisdom tooth out by correspondence.

> (signed)

106 Perry Street
New York City
August 11, 1928

Dear Helen:

If I were you, I think I should try to raise some cash by sending something like the letter of which the following is a rough draft:

Corona Typewriter Company
Rochester, New York
Attention of the Sales Manager

Dear Sir:

A daughter of mine, Barbara Newhall Follett, now fourteen years old, has been from her third year entirely home-educated, and by instruments of which the chief was a Corona Portable of the vintage of 1913. An article about her education to the age of five, written by her father, who is a fairly well-known writer, was published in Harper's Magazine for October 1919 under the title "Schooling without the School." In 1927, at the age of twelve, Barbara published her first book, *The House Without Windows* (Alfred A. Knopf), written entirely on her Corona at the age of nine and rewritten later. In the summer of 1927, having made a voyage to Nova Scotia in a lumber schooner, she wrote—also on a Corona—a book about this experience, published early this year by Alfred A. Knopf under the title *The Voyage of the Norman D.* Both books have been enthusiastically reviewed, with not a dissenting voice, by many of the principal critics and nearly all of the critical journals of the United States and England. (See, as a typical example, what Mr. William McFee writes of *The Voyage of the Norman D.* in the book section of the New York Herald Tribune of Sunday, May 20, 1928.)

Beginning in September, Barbara and I expect to continue her education by a trip which may last upward of a year, to be taken in cargo schooners and slow freighters in the West Indies and the South Seas. She is commissioned to write for one of the oldest and most eminent of American monthly magazines a series of records of her trip. A Corona typewriter will be the chief item of her small outfit of luggage, and whatever she writes will be written on it.

Barbara's young sister Sabra is also being Corona-educated in spare minutes, and now, at the age of five, is able to rattle off on the keyboard all the common words that she knows.

I find myself wondering what it would be worth to you if I were to write you (a) a letter incorporating the above facts, with permission to use it at your discretion, or if I were to work out for you (b) a booklet based on my own experience, giving parents rather detailed and valuable suggestions about the systematic use of the small typewriter in the education of children of from three to twelve, or if I were to do both of these things. I notice that the Royal people, in connection with their portable model, are consistently exploiting ideas which I feel got their first working-out in my own household and which I have always therefore felt should be of uncommon interest to the manufacturer of the machine actually involved—as they may well be in connection with an educational experiment which has turned out to be really of some public significance.

If any of this interests you, I shall be glad to hear from you at the address given above. Needless to say, I do not now wish to sanction the use of any facts here mentioned, pending my subsequent permission.

> Sincerely yours,
> Helen Thomas Follett.

That, or some modification of it covering what you can make yourself want to say, ought to fetch them to the tune of a comfortable sum, especially if they should happen to want the booklet, as I think they would. (I could rattle off a pretty fetching one in short order if you were to get stuck.) But for the Lord's sake don't just jump at anything they offer. In fact, it might be a good idea to show me their come-back, if it's serious at all.

If you can snag some easy money out of them, you might be able to hold off from drawing the Harper advance until you have actually shot them some eligible stuff. That would go big with the Harper outfit, who will really make a difference to your whole future if you handle them right. These typewriter people don't make a darn bit of difference to anything beyond this instant minute (thought I haven't much doubt that you could get them to set you up in an equipped school at a good salary, with their machines among those present—especially if it could be called the Corona school).

If you *do* do anything about it, for God's sake keep a file of carbon copies of everything you write and the original documents from the other side.

As to going to the West Indies, I have no ideas except these: (1) My whole instinct and wish, the instant I can shed New York, will be to head north, not south; (2) I don't feel like heading anywhere leaving debts behind me—anywhere, that is, that would make a difference to my contact with the debts or to my rate of payment; and (3) I've responsibilities other than financial which wouldn't be at all well served by my running away with Barbara, and which I should still need to serve even if I didn't heartily want to, as I do. To thus much

I might add that if by spectacular luck I should get abreast of the financial difficulties with any margin of ease to spare, I should want to use the margin to make something of myself after all these years, and to get out a few of the things that I've had seething where they make me uncomfortable. Barbados may be the way to accomplishment for you, but it isn't for me. I don't put myself first, but I don't see any good reason for not putting myself next after the discharge of my material obligations.

By the end of the week that begins tomorrow, I shall hope to be giving you some idea about your future income. I am sorry to be so slow, but these things are more complicated to arrange than a thirty-a-week clerical job, and they are likely to take time—besides which, it hasn't been every day that I could make my battered head stand up against the ninety-in-the-shade weather and do its best.

      Yours,
      WF

Isn't there a dentist up there who has a shot of novocaine in his locker?

August 11. *[1928]*

My dear shipmate:

Norman, I want you to help me. I am in serious mental difficulties, and I want you to write me *soon* a long, philosophical letter. I want it to be philosophical, and I want it to deal with the subject which I shall soon tell you directly. I don't want any roundabouts, or any other subjects. I want you to give it to me hard. It must even have advice, if you have any handy. But above all it must be Philosophical. Don't fail me.

Norman, the situation of my mind becomes more and more horrible. The GS (eographical eparation) becomes *ghastly*. And that is what I want the philosophical letter to be about. I want you to hand over some philosophy that will *last*—not that will look pleasant for a minute, and then fade. It must last; it must be really substantial. It must be of the sort that I can read it over in extremities.

The Anchor has held marvelously. No one could have asked more. It payed a good deal of service just tonight, and even more of a one yesterday. I have not lost my temper for a long time. And I have always been inwardly happy. But the Anchor can't very well deal with something inside itself—can it? I must have an anchor within the Anchor, if you see what I mean. By the way, you haven't answered yet my question about the anchor. Never mind: the other is infinitely more important. It is enough to tell you that the anchor represents both the holding quality of the philosophy; *and* all the factors and the objective (which you still don't know about).

I got a letter from the second mate of the *Carnegie* today.

Now, Norm, don't forget, will you? I need your prim, old-fashioned, devoted PH. Really—*really* I do.

>Your shipmate,
>Babou

A most generous letter to a young admirer of The Voyage of the Norman D.

Box 65
New London
New Hampshire
13 August, 1928

Dear Bob Hatfield:

Well, to begin with: I *could* read your letter without any difficulty; I *did* accept it, and, as you see, I *am* answering it, though not very promptly. However, I *never* answer letters promptly. I am not made that way. And so, if we have any sort of correspondence (which I hope we shall), you will have to be extremely patient about it. All my friends become dreadfully exasperated with me; and I don't blame them!

It was quite needless to explain that you are a respectable sort of person. Any person, from the old salts to sea-mad children, who are interested in ships (sailing ships) is plenty respectable enough; that is, for me. Sailors are the most delightful beings on earth. Somehow, I don't feel that enough persons realize it, but they probably do. Anyhow, I repeat—I think sailors are the most delightful beings on earth; and I have spent some of my most amusing and even thrilling hours yarning with an old salt who is cook on a four-masted schooner of my acquaintance. This old cook, Bill Barrett, was left in charge of the schooner while her captain was in New York hunting for a charter (the poor sailing ships are neglected in these modern times); and the skipper had instructed the cook to drop him a line now and then to tell him how things were going aboard. So, once in a while, old Bill would fetch out a pencil and a scrap of paper, and dictate a note to me to the captain. He used to say, shaking his grey head sagely: "Ye know, I ain't much of a *scholar*. Oh yes, I kin read all right; but I ain't much on *spellin'*." Another time he dictated a note to a friend of mine, and I found myself absolutely obliged to step into the next room and visit the cat, because of the laughter within me!

They are all like that. No, of course, they all aren't, but in general they are—you know what I mean. I just mentioned old Bill because I know him better than most; for the schooner was in port in New Haven for a long time before she found work, and I saw Bill as often as I could. And some of his yarns—about drunken mates and tyrannical captains and gales and shipwrecks and square-riggers—were simply marvellous. And he knew how to tell 'em, too. Those old fellows, you know, have grown up in the old square-riggers, and they are filled with the utmost scorn and contempt for the young sailor-lads in the "fore-and-aft rigged wind-jammers." They think they're greener than grass.

Well, I want to try to give you a little information about getting a job on a schooner. I admire tremendously your wanting to do it, and I wish I could help you more. I think you should write to some of the various ship-brokers. There is J. F. Whiney Co., 10 Bridge Street, New York City; he takes care of most of the Nova Scotia vessels—in fact, he was Captain Avery's broker for the *Norman D*. Then there is Allen Hoffman Co., Newport News, Virginia; to him there belonged a number of delightful four-masted schooners, among them my favourite *Maud M. Morey*, commanded by one of the most charming little old grey-headed skippers anywhere on the seven seas, old Captain Colbeth. Then there is Gilmartin and Co., 116 Broad Street, New York City; I know one fine four-masted schooner of theirs, commanded by a man by the name of Tyler. Then there is the Crowell and Thurlow Co., 131 State Street, Boston; and I know several schooners of theirs. I have one other suggestion about getting hold of a schooner: that is, to write to some Lumber Company, asking about their vessels. I don't know any of the Lumber Companys of New York; but I know one in Bridgeport, Connecticut—the A. W. Burritt Lumber Company; and I know another in New Haven—DeForest and Hotchkiss, Water Street.

Whether all this will be of any service to you I don't know; but I should think you might find out about vessels belonging to these various companies. If you want to find vessels, New York is the place to go, for there are always schooners there. There is a very useful man, by the name of Walter Goldfrank, Stein Hall, Madison Avenue, New York; and if you went to him, or wrote to him, he could give you lots of information. Whitney's vessels are off Bridge Street way; but that, I am told, is a difficult place to find.

But of course I don't know what sort of vessel you would like to ship on. My opinion is that lumber-schooners are by far the pleasantest. They are incomparably cleaner than coal schooners. When loaded, their deck-load rises high above the bulwarks, and must be good fun to scramble over, though I have done it only in port. And there is something clean about lumber, too, which coal can't be compared to. Then I imagine that there are still plenty of Gloucester fishermen still in working order and sailing, but I suppose most of the vessels are auxilliary by this modern date. I know very little about them.

As for the schooners themselves; the finest vessels I know are the *Annie C. Ross*, a fourmaster, Captain Joseph Zuljevic; the *Albert F. Paul*, fourmaster, Captain Jones; the *Maud M. Morey*, Captain Colbeth; the *Lucia P. Dow*, Captain Loesch; the *Josiah B. Chase*, Captain Chaney. Then, of course, there is always my little *Norman D.* (her real name is *Frederick H.*), whom I believe to be now commanded by a Captain Nolten.

Well, I wish you all the luck in the world on your enterprise. Of course, it is needless to say that if you know the names of a few ropes and sails and blocks, and the points and quarter-points of the compass, and how to blow a foghorn, and a few odds and ends of things like that, you will make a good impression with the mate, and the mate, of course, is the man whom you will have the most contact with—that is, as an officer. But, if you are interested in ships, I suppose you know all that I could tell you. Besides, on a schooner it is easy enough to catch on. It is the fast-vanishing square-riggers that take the real seamanship; and the old cooks and skippers cannot be blamed for their amusing contempt for the schooners.

Mentioning the square-riggers makes me think of my two most sublime nautical achievements; and I can't resist mentioning them, because I am really quite proud of them, and, I think, not without reason. I was down in Washington, visiting a little brigantine who is now on her way from Iceland clear to the West Indies—she is on a scientific cruise of three years in all oceans. I had a most gay time fooling around with her Danish and Norwegian sailors. I climbed her rigging, sat on her yards, looked at the Potomac from her top. And then, one fine day, I decided I would climb to her royal yard. Now, as you know, the royal is the highest yard of all ordinary square-riggers, except those few glorious ships who carry skysails, too. And this brigantine's royal yard was about a hundred and fifty feet up. And as I went, ratline after ratline, it struck me that it was quite a long way. I got out on the foreyard, up on the stay, from there on to the top (a cowardly way of getting there—avoiding the futtock shrouds!); and then I started gaily up the topmast rigging, which (I thought), was considerably wobblier than the lower mast rigging—in fact, I thought, to be frank, that it was a little *too* wobbly. And then I came to the topmast cross-trees. Well, I thought I should never get over them (they are not like the comfortable cross-trees of a schooner, that you can slide between—but you have to go out and around them). I tugged and pulled, and finally I was over, breathless but triumphant. But the most difficult part of it was yet to come. I looked down at Washington, but looking down never troubles me; then I looked up, and there was the royal yard, tantalizingly near. Well, I started on the last lap of the rigging. But, gosh darn it!, if the topmast rigging had been too wobbly, what was this? Dii immortales! It seemed as though the strongest of the rigging should be up there, not the feeblest! Every ratline quivered and shook. Well, I was up; I climbed on to a little trembling cross-step suspended over space, I embraced *most* affectionately the royal mast, and I gently lifted myself on to the little shaking yard—and sat down.

But if getting up had been hard, what was getting down? By jings! I felt like a cat, "stuck" in a tree. Perhaps I should say, "marooned" in a tree. But I found the cross-step at last, and then a little block, which was helpful, and then a broken ratline, and a cobweb-like shroud. And there I was; and that "wobbly" topmast rigging seemed firmer than boulders, after the ethereal nothingness of that royal rigging.

The other thing I was proud of was a genuine meal in the fo'c'sle. In the *Norman D.*, of course, I ate in the cabin, with the skipper and the mate; I had looked into the fo'c'sle as the three sailors were eating, once or twice. But there was a crew of eight in the brigantine, and they all ate round a large table in the middle of the fo'c'sle (which, by the way, was below-decks), and one day, to my great delight, I was invited to "come down and have a bite." And I sat at that table with the rest of them, and watched them guzzle their boiling stew, and reach out their long arms to spear potatoes with their forks. Poor Aage, the tow-headed Norwegian, was too far gone in something worse than wine (he had been out on a "spree" the night before) to do anything but lie around on deck in the sun, with a sick expression; but the rest were all there, hale and hearty, and how they ate! . . . The reason I am proud of eating there with them is because sailors are very reluctant to admit any outsider at all into the fo'c'sle; so it was as much an honour as if the king of England had asked me to dine with him. And it was much more delightful! though you needn't tell the king of England that.

You know my mate Bill of the *Norman D.*? And you know his letters? Well, since the book was published, I have heard from him thrice more. And in the fourth and last (so far) letter, the spelling (or, rather, the *mis*-spelling) is, if possible, worse than ever. Also most delightful. I have three letters from a mate named Jack, of a four-master I saw in Bridgeport. I heard, a little while ago, from one of the sailors of the brigantine—a long, detailed, amusing letter; and yesterday I heard from the second mate of her—he who taught me a good deal of my knowledge of ropes—that is, the ropes of a square-rigger, about which I knew very little. I have also a charming letter from an old captain, which he wrote to my father after he had been sent a copy of the *Norman D.* So I have a marvellous nautical correspondence, and I encourage it as much as I can.

As a matter of fact, I am a sea-captain myself. You didn't suspect that, did you? Well, I have a row-boat, with a mast in her, and a boom, and a sail, and some leeboards, and an oarlock on the stern to hold an oar which serves as tiller. She is great fun. You must know that I am on the shore of a little hill-surrounded lake; and it can kick up a good swash at times. I have magnificent fun bouncing around in the sailing rowboat. The other day, in a fresh westerly "breeze-o'-wind," I nearly bust the mast clean out of her, and I shipped a lot of water, and the sail tugged like a kite. But I was a daring sail-carrier, and held it just as close-hauled as I could, and let the water come in over the leeward side. It was grand fun.

But here I am, running on, and running on, and on, and on; and I guess you have begun to wonder whether I intend to go on forever; perhaps you regret having written to me! However, I get excited about these things—ships, and sailors, and rigging—and there is no stopping. But I will stop now, and I hope to hear from you again.

    Your friend,

There was another Follett on the Frederick H.

Parrsboro, N. S.
August the 15ist 1928

Dear Friend
  Received your Verry Welcome letter to day Was glad to Hear from You It was quite a suprise I though you Had Forgoten Us Before this
  Well the first question was about the Capt. the last account of Him He Was out of His Mind and they sent Him to the Bug House [...]
  Well Barbara My advice Is If You and Your Mother goes to the West Indies Is to go By steamer There Isent Maney Vessls Has Accomidations for Wimen and going Out to sea In the fall and Winter Is not like It is on the
  On the Cost In summer There is Verry Heavy Gails and Ruf sea and the sailing Vessels Is Not fited for that [...]

    Yours Respectfully
    Oscar Follett

August 15, 1928

Will shipmat—as Bill says:

Well, Norm, I hope that letter of mine didn't scare you black and white—perhaps I didn't mean to Put It Quite So Strongly, if you are sure you know what I mean, Pooh. So I will write a Cheerful Letter, instead—now; though I want the philosophy from you, just the same.

Well, I nearly died of busted sides laughing when I read "that was too easy (for *me*) to feel it worth answering." And later when I read: "but you must admit I did that one hundred percent perfect and rather easily." Of course, I don't know how easily you Came to Your Conclusion—at any rate, the Conclusion was NOT Correct!!!!!!!!!!!!!!!!! You are apparently, more of an S-C F than ever.

As for the Fs in the Ph, I will discuss that a little. You said that my head went to TF, my imagination to V., my heart to myself. I know what you said, for here is the letter before me. Perhaps you wrote it wrong, but that's what you wrote, anyway. And that is not how it goes, at all. So you will have to hazard another guess about that, and another about the slowest schooner, and you must work on the A, for that is very Interesting, if you know what I mean.

WWW, you're a darling of an S-C F to mail the MI for me, and I am so trembling with real gratitude (good rhyme for your favourite word, *platitude*!). I can't tell you how grateful I am—I can't tell you how I admire your honesty and devotion (I can see you swelling from here)—and believe me, my devotion is much more on the increase this way than it would be if I had told you what the MI was. For to know that you were consumed with C (quite naturally), and yet to know that you heroically abstained from gratifying that C (if you know what I mean)—well, it just made me admire you so, my S-C F—really it made me admire your qualities of heart, head, imagination, and soul to a perfectly Terrific and even ALARMING Extent. So there you are.

As to your brother—if he shows any symptoms of going mad, let me know, and I will send him the key to all the vowels. But not until he is at the Last Extremity, if you know what I mean.

As for my ph: it is really wonderful, I am mad with joy over it. The A is the sturdiest little piece of iron that ever felt a sea-bottom— it will hold on clay, mud, sand, or rocks, equally well. Really, life is overwhelmingly adventurous and beautiful when you look at it through the eyes of a ph—not through your own eyes. Of course, there is a flaw at present, and you know too damn well what that flaw is—but that is not Permanent, if you see what I mean.

I am enclosing a pome of Shelley which expresses my outlook quite admirably, and is, besides, a beautiful little fragment of verse. As a matter of fact, thanks for your enthusiastic comments on *my* pome—whether it deserves it or not, I don't know; but the point is, you seem to think it does, and that's all there is to it.

You know, I am extremely interested in this inflation business of yours. I am always wondering what will happen next. Even supposing I *never* prick the bubble, that same bubble can't swell quite for*ever*, can it? Won't it BUST sometime with terrific and alarming explosion, its fragments strewn all over the world? Much those things interest me, if you know what mean. Gosh darn it, though we are both devoted and devotees (you know what I mean, don't ye?), I cannot help *experimenting*. I feel it out cautiously, and try to form calculations about it. And the amazing thing is, I am learning to govern it at will—make it, within short notice, any size I like!!!! (*Do you see what I mean, Pooh?*)

So now I will again enumerate the things you must do, so you won't forget them. (1.) Philosophical letter concerning the you know. (2.) Work and report on the A. (3.) Work and report on the Fs of the PH. (4.) Guess again about the S/lowest S/schooner.————————
We are apparently, therefore, no farther advanced than EVER, if you see what I mean.

Of course I now know *exactly*. You were exactly 630 days on the minus side of my guess, n'est-ce pas? But if you are Delicately Inclined, you need not mention the subject.

       Your shipmatey,
       Babu.

This is the reason for your failure concerning the slowest schooner. You tried to be too simple—you weren't *subtle* enough! B.

The larger is the poem—the smaller is an Experiment in Practical Physics—*if* you Understand me *Completely*.

August 22, 1928

Dearest Norman: (There being no other N. I can safely conclude, following your excellent example, that you are the both Dest *and* LEAST D, if you quite understand me!!)

I am going to begin at the end of your letter. I am not going to worry or guess again about it, if you know what I mean, because I don't care a damn how old you are: so there.

Your answer about the S/ S/ was so nearly correct that I think I will help you about it, so that we can cut that one off the list. It was not only because of the Cursing and Swearing, but also it was to hear the delightful alopogies which the old skipper would make for his vessel, and all that. By the way, do you know what an alopogy is? It is my own invention, or perhaps I had better say it is my typewriter's own invention!

You were wrong about the G/rand D/ivision P/arts F/actors.

Now for the most important part—the ph and the two As. I am, to begin with, sorry to have made you break the rules of the G and H C, but it won't happen again, if I can conveniently help it. So there. I know I was asking you an *awful* lot—you needn't have stated that. Of *course* you can accept a PH, even when you ain't wise and strong—but I don't think you can very often accept whole-heartedly all of some one else's, if you understand me. I think your PH is grand for you, anyway—I never said I didn't, did I? Damn it all, your PH is all right; but you forget that neither A, G, nor F has *anything* to do with my particular difficulty. You didn't think of that, I fear. Now, here is something that will swell you a little. I think you marvellously GENEROUS with your PH, to offer it to me like that, for a SECOND A. I *admire* your generosity of spirit, exceedingly. So there. I shall hold NA, NG, NF for a reserve A, and I shall put it over the bow, ready to drop in case the other starts to drag—which, damn it, I don't think it will. (I mean, bless it!) I never did think it would, really. In fact, I have entirely strengthened the A for this immurjensee, if you understand me. In fact, I had it already strengthened by the time your letter came, so there. But just the same, thanks for your letter; that TWO A business was the most helpful suggestion, and it really did help. So that's a compliment to you, ain't it? So there.

Thanks. I didn't want your Advice, anyhow, so there.

This all sounds awfully sullen and cross, I know. So I am going to change my tactics a little. N., I am prodigiously grateful to you for something you won't remember or think of at all. It was perfectly *adorable* of you to do it for me, and I feel my eyes moist now with pure gratitude, and admiration. I confess that it didn't do any good, but you TRIED, anyhow. And I think it was perfectly *wonderful*—it showed the pure gold of your heart and your spirit. If I were That Sort of Person I wouldn't need an A or a PH or *anything*. You are almost—perhaps more completely than I even realize—*divine*. May the trouble it must have cost you be repaid to you a billion times. If you know what it is, so much the better. I don't think I will tell you, but you may guess, if you like. Anyhow, I can never forget it; and I fear I can never repay it as it deserves. It made me feel how low and ornery and foolish I am, in contrast to such undiluted beauty of spirit. You shouldn't even associate with the likes of me, Norman.

You are a saint; you belong with the immortals; and yet, out of the greed of my mind, I still wish to have you for my shipmate. So there.

Now for the GDPF. This guess of yours is pretty bad, Norman. It is absolutely the ONLY thing which makes me think you still belong to the world of mortals. I am quite surprised you couldn't do better. I thought you would probably fail in the first, but I had NO IDEA you would fail so *completely* on the second. For this is even worse than the first. And if you work that out, that ought to give you some clue. For that must mean that *something* was right in the first; but—well, I was going to say that NOTHING was right in this guess; but there *is* something right. All of which should, if you study both combinations of yours carefully, give you the correct answer next time. Please hazard again, as soon as the time is auspicious, and as soon as you may do so without violating the rules of the G and H C. So there.

Well, I think I have finished. You would have heard from me as soon as I got your letter, but I went off to the mountains. But believe me, my mind was simply bursting with gratitude and wishes to write to you; and I don't think there is going to be anything to prick the ego-bubble this time; unless a slight prick might be accomplished by my telling you that I am now going to write to the TF, in reply to a LONG DOCUMENT which I received IN COMPANY WITH YOURS, a few days ago.

> Your grateful shipmate,
> Barrboo

P. S. I hope you will get Prodigious Amusement out of the Enclosed. I did. Babbu.
Don't worry: it's nothing that will dis-inflate you. I am too grateful to do that.

"Sec. Kellog" was Frank B. Kellogg (1856-1937), Secretary of State in President Coolidge's administration.

The explorer Hiram Bingham (1875-1956) made public the existence of Machu Picchu in 1911. At the time of Helen's letter he represented Connecticut in the U.S. Senate.

James Rowland Angell (1869-1949) was the president of Yale University from 1921-1937.

New London, New Hampshire,
22 August, 1928

Dear Norman:
I am making a collection of letters of introduction from various

important people who can, perhaps, help me along my uncertain way, such as Sec. Kellog who asks all Consuls to be nice to me. And I shall have one from Sec. Wilbur of the Navy. I have written to Hiram Bingham asking him to suggest ways by which Barbara can get into his Inca excavations, in case we go to Peru.

Now it occurs to me if someone would write something about ME as A EDUCATOR, I might get a job, if money should give out. Don't you know someone in Yale, even Mr. Angell, himself would do, who would write a letter to the British Board of Education, or whatever they have at Barbados? Couldn't your friend Hutchins pull me something like that. I could, then, get a chance at some people who might hand me some interesting material, and who, in a pinch, might help me out by giving me a job. I don't think the Department of Education would mean much, coming from Yale. Ask Mr. Day if he thinks I am crazy.

Also, who at Yale might know an archaeologist down that way, or an entomologist, or any other kind of a "Scientific" perhaps at the B. W. I. or at Balboa, or Callao, or beyond? I want Bar to get as much science of one kind or another as is possible, and a letter from one bug-man to another might do a lot of good. Nice bugs, including cock-roaches, down that way. W. T. Hornaday has given Bar a commission, that of finding out about the golden plovers who fly directly down there from Nova Scotia. He has a sad story as to what happens to them down there (which is too long to tell now) and he wants Bar to find out the truth about it.

There is in Barbados, a college by name Codrington, and through a letter from Yale, I might get on to somebody or something that would lead to someone or something.

Bar is up in the mountains with Tyler, Ralph Blanchard is here with me, and we shall be going down soon. Ralph is coming over here from Boothbay again to take us all down. Some friend, what! I may be down about the fourth if I can get down with the Tilsons; if not about the eighth with Bar and Sabra, shall you be there then, and if not, can we go there? Don't say you won't be around to see us off on the fifteenth—second class, Lamport and Holt.

    Love, always, hot stuff from the *South Sease*,
    Helen

I've had the impudence to say that I can be reached in this country through the Yale University Press, care of you. Is that all right?

Sch Edwin. G. Farrar
℅ John G Hall
114 State Street
Boston Mass
august 26 1928

well shipmate

I am Back at the sea again I am with a captain from brigwater the schonner is a little bigger then the Frederick H:

The Frederick H is in here now on loading lumber: we have ben in Boston about four weeks now on loading lumber well shipmate I cant tell you where we are gone from here yet we may go to brigwater and load I dont no for sure well shipmate [...] good time this sumer with your Boat I would like to sea you and your Boat and take a sail with you. [...]

    From your shipmate
    William McClelland

R.M.S. "MAUNGANUI"
At sea, en route for San Francisco,
August 27th, 1928.

Dear Miss Follet:-

Your letter came just before I started north. I haven't been at home for a long while and I am homesick to see the autumn foliage. That's what I miss more than anything in the tropics — the change of seasons. [...]

If you mean to follow the Carnegie about, you'll be so dizzy by that time that you won't know where you are, very likely. I saw a chart of her proposed cruise, and there are so many loops and turns in it that it looked like one of those fancy designs on embroidery.

I showed your letter to my friend Nordhoff. We'll be on the lookout for you. I must warn you though that Nordhoff is a very retiring man, so I'd better say *I'll* be on the lookout for you. [...]

    Sincerely Yours,
    Norman Hall

August 27, 1928

My deah Norman:

Hi hi! I have a friend. Don't worry, he ain't to go on the list! He is not the kitten but one of the numerous small sworn foes of the kitten, if you know what I mean. It is, at this very moment, squabbling over some choice scraps of cheese-rind which I laid out for it on the bookcase—that is, unless it has been scared away by the sudden and vigorous commencement of this machine—I say "sudden and vigorous" because that's just what it was: I have written just now to the TF and I thought I would bathe my spirit in another gasp and gurgle of New Biddeford—and that, my deahrr shipmatey, you supply better than *anyone*.

Well—WWW—what we cannot kick we must needs embrace. That's what I am doing to the expo. Since it can't be lumped, it must be accepted, and the separ which it involves—though that is such a very heavy dose that the strain on my old anchor is rather large—BUT, I haven't yet needed to lower the SECOND—although, there it is, hanging over the bow, all ready for service in case of trouble.

Hay? Ain't yuh ever goin' to guess again about the GDPF? Oh, forgive me! I almost forgotted the hallowed laws of the G and H C. The only thing is: we sail the 15th, so there is a TERMINATION to the G and H C. Do not think I flatter (a thing I NEVER do—"What, never?" "No, never!" "What, NEVER?" "Well, hardly ever!") when I tell you that I shall miss that, too—though of course I shan't miss it (I NEVER deceive my four—"What, never?" etc., etc.,) so much as I shall miss the you-know-what. Jings, Jings, Jings, but that was a complicated sentence, but you can work it out *if* you disregard the parenthetical remarks and READ *THEM* AFTERWARDS, as a sort of finish.

WWW, as I was saying, there is a termination to our G and H C, and also the S/ublime C between me and TF—I don't know which C I shall miss the more—but I guess *you* know. However, I tell you frankly, I don't know! Well, I shall try, old shipmatey of mine, to drop you a l or two once in a w, but you must be patient, for you must realize everything. I shall also try to continue the C with TF to a certain extent; and some m for fts has suddenly appeared out of the very s—if you understand me. Of course that m won't do any good—that's the only trouble—for it is American. But, I shall probably use it to advantage. I may use it for an excursion down to P to say farewell to the TF.

THERE is a thing on which I want to ask your opinion (I won't name it ADVICE): *should* I say farewell to TF? I don't know. I could do it by C, but that wouldn't suit—it would leave us both unsatisfied. AND YET, we might BOTH be STILL MORE unsatisfied, should I go down there. I ought to explain that my poor TF hasn't come to Sunapee yet—old M'Giddy rallied and then relapsed and is still in the hospital—they may get up for a week or two in September—it's not at all certain.

Page 2:
The next day—I went to bed last ni.!

WWW, my deearrest shipmate, I have made a Momentous Discovery. You know, I have always been suspicious of these Accidental Personages—if you know what I mean. They are Different in Some Way, I think. Well, a Discovery—! I, I, I, yes, *I*—your own shipmatey—is an Accident!!! Imagine it!! I AM AN *ACCIDENT* !!!!!!!!!!!!!!!!!!!!!!!!!!!! !!!!!!!!!!!!!!

WWW, guess whom I heard from yesterday. Mate Bill again—another master-piece. So now I have five letters from him, and one from his wife. By the way, was it You or the TF I told about the letter from his wife? I seem to forget.

WWW, now I think I shall avaunt myself from your world until the next VSD. I don't want to Violate the Laws of the G and H C, but I SHOULD like to hear your next guess about the GDPF—I want to get that all straightened out with you before the 15th. When you get it all straight and clear, I will send you a long rhyme I wrote about the Presentation (if you know what I mean). It's a beautiful and CLEVER Rhyme—more Beautiful than Clever—and the ONLY mention of the Presentation is in the last two lines. You see, each stanza has four lines, of which the second and fourth rhyme—NOT the first and third. The first two lines of that last stanza are "You must think it strange that I,/ Who followed where clouds flew. . ." See if you can gather any hint for your guess about the GDPF, from that. Oh, the whole pome is a MASTERPIECE—really and truly. It expounds the whole A, in Disguised Terms.

Well, old Normy, fare thee well—or ill, as the case may be!

        VERY D————ly,
        Babooooooooooou.

P. S. Hi Hi! If I should prick, you'd better put Mercurochrome on it At Once—because the pin is RUSTY! B.

From a transcription typed sometime later. As is the case with many of Mr. Oberg's letters at Columbia, the brittle paper has crumbled away.

Sept. 10, 1928

Dear Barbara:
Please forgive me for not answering your letter of July 28 until now. I am just reading yours of June 17th in which you tell me that you are planning a trip to the West Indies this fall. I hope I have not delayed writing until you have left Sunapee and started your travels. I would certainly like to do some more travelling especially in our

home country.... So you are now a mountain climber. I have never yet attempted anything in that line. I have once climbed some rather steep foothills of a granite range that forms the backbone of Scandinavia. This happened in 1872 so you see I began my mountain climbing a while before you began yours! [...]

    Your old friend

Helen's Education à la Carte *was published in the July 1929 issue of* Pictorial Review.

New Haven, 12 September, 1928

Dear Anne and Oxford:

    This it the last word I can get off to you for a while, but I will have something to write about, possibly, from Barbados. At least, I can tell you better at that time about our plans than I can now.

    Things stand now something like this: Barbara's job with Harper is still on, and we start with her five hundred dollar royalties plus some more money of hers accruing from her books, making in all something over a thousand dollars. This will be in the form of a letter of credit, and traveller's cheques. How long this will last I don't know, of course, now.

    I shall not go away from the West Indies until I hear by cable from the Bank that money is being deposited monthly by Follett. Or, unless, something I can write will bring an immediate cheque. And I will save out enough money to get home.

    I am sorry Follett is against this trip, as he seemed to be when he wrote to Norman. He can't seem to imagine my position at all, and the impossibility of our remaining in his vicinity while he lives the kind of life that he is living now. Everyone else, including all Yale, just about is so enthusiastic and so helpful about it, that I wish he might be. The trip began, as you know, as an escape from the kind of torture which I can't seem to get used to. To the world it is an extremely interesting educational procedure, and will be watched as such.

    I have agreed with the Pictorial Review to write the story of our education up to the present. Eventually this will be the first part of a book: the second will be what is going to happen now. In order to make me feel that the Pictorial Review is in earnest, Mr. Waxman handed me fifty dollars as a sort of bonus, or whatever.

    I shall have all my mail here sent to the Yale University Press where Norman will take care of it, or deposit any possible cheques.

    Sabra will be here with Margaret Tyler, who will let you know if anything in regard to her comes up about which she needs help or advice. Follett is more than welcome to come here to see her, if he comes alone. I will not allow him to take her away to live with him and M. Whipple, nor will I allow him to take her away to New York to visit them. If he should give up his present mode of life, and lives alone, he can of course have Sabra, if he can make suitable arrangements for her. If he should come here and deliberately take Sabra away, Margaret Tyler will communicate with you.

If I die on this trip, or go insane, or anything else that keeps me out of the class of responsible parents, then whatever you and Ralph, the Donaldsons, or Tyler decides is the best thing for Sabra—so be it. If you and Anne will decide alone, that will suit me perfectly. The others are my best friends outside of you both. But, in all matters pertaining to me and my family, your decision stands with me.

If I die on this trip, and Barbara survives, I would like Oxford to be her guardian. If the time comes that Follett wishes to resume his moral responsibility toward these children, it goes without saying that he may. But until that time, I do want Oxford to act in that capacity. And, in the event that we both do come back, I wish that Oxford would be this sort of guardian advisor to Barbara. She needs a man very much to take the place of her father in matters of advice. I do not think I am the one to take all the responsibility of guiding her, because I don't think my influence on her is valuable at this time. If Follett ever takes up his responsibilities as a father, she will, of course, have to accept his guidance and discipline.

The house still remains in Follett's name. I couldn't bring myself to have papers made out for him to sign: it seems like the last straw. If Oxford suggested it to Follett, all well and good, but I couldn't make myself do it. And I think he will be perfectly fair about the property. If he wishes to make it over at any time that is all right. But it hurts me to break our last and only bond.

I am awfully tired. The last details are overwhelming. And it all seems terribly unnatural. This breaking away is a very terrible thing for me. But I shall hope for some results that may make it possible for me to stand things as I have to stand them.

I will come back whenever I am needed. And will always be in touch with the Consul at Barbados, leaving my address there. And anytime Follett is ready to help co-operate with me in any way that seems reasonable to you both, I will do all in my power to help save something for Barbara and Sabra. You both know that.

That is really all I have to say, except to bless you both for what you are, and what you are doing for us all. If I pull off anything on this trip that is significant in the smallest way, it will be because I don't want you to be completely disappointed in me.

        Yours — with love — Helen

William Beebe (1877-1962) was a biologist from New York who spent many years exploring marine life in the tropics. In 1927 he married a woman half his age with the understanding that theirs would be an open marriage. Thus Wilson's warning, I suppose.

106 Perry Street
New York City
September 12, 1928
(Wednesday night)

Dear Helen:

    Thanks for the various informations.

    You misapprehend me as completely as could be on nearly every possible point, though on none have I changed my tune; so I will confine myself to the briefest condensation of the things I have already said.

    1. My attitude toward the trip is (a) that I hope it will do you both good, (b) that I am willing to do anything in reason to help it along, and (c) that I regard it as pretty poor sportsmanship to expect me to break my neck supplying money to be spent that way when there are so many prior claims.

    2. The reason why I have shown no interest in your remarkable collection of letters is simply that you have kept me consistently in the dark as to the entire business, making it very clear that the one thing with which *I* could supply the trip (if I had it) was money.

    3. I shall be glad, as I have said all along, to edit and try to market whatever stuff comes in. I can say no more than that, and nothing different. I mean what I say. It's up to you entirely.

    4. I have put myself completely at the disposal of Hook for anything he wants, or thinks he wants; force myself on him further I can't. As to your gibe about "the man who can do no wrong," Hook may just recover enough to understand that a man who has done the wrong thing for fifteen or so years does better to stop than to continue. But that's as may be.

    To the foregoing, let me add the following new jottings:

    1. I will write immediately to the Lincoln station to take the car out. Why didn't you say so before? As for the Smiths, I never heard of them and don't know who they are.

    2. Don't get the idea that the house is at your disposal for anything except renting.

3. If you're going into Beebe's vicinity, be damn careful to keep Barbara under your eye.

I still think that you would have started this trip in better shape and got more out of it if you had gone about the thing with some patience and made more of a job of cleaning things up behind you. But that's only an opinion, and I suppose you are acting in what light you have to go by (as I should suppose you might also give others credit for doing). In any case, I wish and hope for the best possible results for you both. I am sorry not to have been able to contribute more to your preparations, and I shall expect to contribute later to the full limit that I specified.

If you leave the country without settling for the cottage, please let me know the fact and the amount.

I shall write a good-bye to Barbara tomorrow, whether or not it reaches her.

>Yours with all good wishes,
>WF

77 Mansfield Street
14 September, 1928

Dear Anne:

This is my last letter from these parts. I am sending the enclosed to you *[Wilson's letter of September 12]*, for no reason dear, except that I can't have it around me. It seems so cruel to send a thing like that to me for the last word, and I have had my awful day as a result. I will not answer it. You know I can't write Roy a personal letter there, for there will be nothing private or personal about anything that enters the place, I am sure.

It is torture to me to have him speak of our fifteen years as he does, and this letter simply upset me all over again with the enormity of it all. Can't he understand that I can't stand the proximity of living near him and the girl, that my nights are nights of sleeplessness and horror, and that my going away is only an attempt to escape that horror. I haven't been a cheap sport about anything. It will be Barbara and I who will go without, for I have taken care of my Mother first, and I shall take care of Sabra second; and that all the money that is being taken on the trip is Barbara's savings account plus the advance royalties from Harper. Nothing has come from him; and I can't see how I can do anything different. I have paid one-half of the taxes, and have ordered the other half to be paid from next month's rent, and I shall pay the cottage from Bar's money. Why does it make any difference where I am if I assume all the responsibilities? Do you notice what he says about the house now? But *I* couldn't suggest it be made over to me; and he would have been made very angry, I am sure.

Will the thing go on forever, Anne? Is there no hope in the world, nothing to look forward to, nothing to come home for, and no home to come home to, and no reason for having a home? I can't bear it, Anne. But I love you so much for your faith in me, for your encouragement, for your love. I can't say more. I feel old, and tired, and very, very lonesome tonight, and hardly able to go on.

    Helen

106 Perry Street
New York City
September 14, 1928

Dear Anne-White:

Thank you for your letter. No: I didn't know anything about the sailing except the date, and, since they make it pretty clear that they prefer not to be bothered, I'll just stay out of it.

Your assumption that I chucked my marriage because I fell in love with somebody else (which you state very explicitly indeed) is an idea which, an hour ago, I would have sworn to anyone on earth you are incapable of. Nordic males of reasonable intelligence and decent intentions simply don't act that way, as far as I have had any chances to observe. I expected you to understand, without my engaging in any propaganda or joining the contest of insinuations and lies, that I abandoned my marriage because it was going irretrievably wronger and wronger; that, for reasons of innate maladjustment, it was providing a more and more impossible atmosphere for a home and for children; that, of pure human cowardice and feebleness of will in the face of a clean issue, I sidestepped the operation for years; and that my belated present knowledge of what, after all, a marriage can be is an experience that I should never have had if it had still been possible for me to make any contribution to my home that was not an injury to everybody concerned. Helen, who will not let herself remember such things now, had offered me unconditional release from the farce for years, at intervals; and always the chivalrous fool said "Oh no—no thank you. I wouldn't dream of it." (Of course, I don't think for a minute that the offers would ever have been made except in the expectation of such answers.) That is my really disastrous sin—keeping up the travesty for those years. Nobody has any right to ruin himself as I was doing except in the interest of almost overwhelming benefits to others—and I was ruining the others too.

Generally speaking, a man can't be any good to others under a cumulative load of shame and disgust that makes him no good to himself. Also, he has to be the judge of how much it is morally possible for him to carry. Suffice it to say that I was at the end of my strength, and lived for several years with the conviction that I had missed everything and was to spend the rest of my days a cripple incurably. Now, I'm not so sure. I have—compared with anything I had dared hope for a decade or so—a good conscience. Which means that I think I've acted in a way to make the best eventual outcome of a bad matter. No irresponsible hysteric is going to take *that* away from me by throwing fits about unrealities. It is, of course, a sharp pain to sit tight and find old friends lied into the position of strangers to all one's realities. But I can bear it, since I have to; and I rather think I can do some work that'll show what life has come into me.

The thing that does genuinely amaze me is your failure to read how disastrous I have been to Helen in the fact of her cheap and sensational behavior about the whole business. If I had ever meant to her anything like what you now so easily assume, she would have faced this in a way to command everybody's respect—including ours—and to get some good out of it. A woman who, when her marriage busts up, spends several months creating the most dismal mess of debts and complications that she can contrive, as a prelude to running away and leaving others to face the music, is giving a pretty darned sick demonstration of how much she got out of her marriage. The simple fact is that the sooner you face such things the sooner you get over them. Helen will find that out—in the British West Indies, Jolo, New Haven, or anywhere else. The greatest shame I shall ever know anything about is helping a woman get the way Helen is—and will stay if she doesn't take hold of herself. [...]

        Yours,
        Follett.

On September 15th, Helen and Barbara boarded Lampert and Holt's steamship Voltaire *in New York and, with a suitcase and a typewriter each, steamed third class to Barbados. Sabra, Margaret Tyler, and the Donaldsons saw them off, but not Wilson.*

S. S. Voltaire
September 19, 1928
High Seas

Hi Hi HI, old Matey!
    I sit here, Norm, with my lips compressed in one grim determi-

nation, but my mind is one grim blank! Oh, how uncannily the old sea affects me! I sit here hour after hour, sunning and sunning, and humming; and walking around the decks, and exploring the steamer's gizzards; and I have picked up two or three really grand acquaintances—but I have not had any really worth-while thoughts for some time, and H. is the same way.

WWW, now I have started, I will tell you somethings. Weather: the first, second, and third days out, around wicked old Hatteras, ye know, we had a rather large swell, but not much breeze. It made even this old thing do some rocking stem and stern, and oh! how sick all the lady passengers were, and how unsick your old mate was! I strode around with my well-balanced sealegs, smiling upon the melancholy ladies with an air of condescension; I ate first cautiously, then more and more heartylike—and now I am eating like four and sunburned like twenty.

WWW, matey mine, the separ went kind o' hardlike—more so than I hexpecxted. It is a disconsolate experience to feel that you are going to be seriously missed—and by someone you care more or less for, too. I felt like a guilty creature, especially since I was going off to have just such a wild good time, you see? Once in a while, even now, I feel that my inward peace and contentment is not due to me. But enow of that.

Oh, the sea! Norm, Norm, how I adore the old sea! And it is just the same as ever, except that I think I never saw it so divinely blue—oh, so blue, blue, blue, under the hot sun. The ship rocks lazily, like a great cradle. . . I see stars out my porthole at night. . . and our waves clash with the sea's own, and fountains of spray fly up with that grace which spray alone has. Oh, what is there that is more beautiful than flying spray? And what snow-mountains boil around the windy bow of her!

The bo's'n is a real sailor, Norm. He's English. And he's just grand. He's been at sea thirty-eight (no, I guess it was twenty-eight) years, and knows more than any sailor I ever met—about the stars, and the fish, and the birds, and the way an engine is put together, and the weather, and nigger sailors, and the way a lady passenger's stomach operates, and why she's seasick. Moreover, he has a deep, cutting sense of humour. I talk with him by the hour. And the carpenter is an old, old sailor who was brought up in the squ-ri's, if you know what I mean; he is white-haired, and blue-eyed, and thoroughly a sweet old sailor.

You know, Norm, although I am a passenger, I see and do things that no other passenger sees and does. I explore the internals and vitals of this old concern with the second engineer (and to see those enormous pistons walloping over that propeller shaft is a terrifical thing to see); I go in the forrad storerooms with my bo's'n; I go astern where no one save the crew is supposed to go; I visit the skipper (whose name, by a coincidence, is Captain NORMAN); I walk with the chief officer over the bridge; and I harangue with the fourth engineer in the first class apartments, where I really should not be. In short, I have run of the ship. You would love to see my dear old carpenter standing at work in his mouse-small workroom—it is a great sight.

Sometimes I go away up forrad in the very bow, and watch the boiling foam with the flyingfish flying out of it as the ship scares them; and I yarn (mostly by excited gestures) with the Spanish third class rowdies who are always around dancing and singing incomprehensible Spanish songs. Ah, it's a good life; and how I love the old ocean! And how I wish there would come a little breeze-o! It was as calm as a millpond yistiddy; and today, in spite of a little spirit which the sou'-east trades seem to possess, it is very hot.

Well, Normo, I have given the old sea a hextra salute from you. I didn't ask your permission, but I didn't think that was necessary. Whether V——— is here or not, I hardly know; but I have had inward peace in the Fullest Degree of late, and there is only one rasp, and that a small one. And the sea is so blue that you would think a glassful of it would be blue—only (beggin' your pardon) it seems to be more or less purple at present—there are clouds in the sky, and the bo's'n predicts showers, and I believe him. I should be surprised if he failed in *anything*. He's that Sort of Person, see?

There *is* mystery tied up in some inexpressible way with the sea, ain't there? I don't quite know what it is. I feel the mystery in a schooner, while in this iron concern I just feel comfortable and hot and happy; but there is a mystery. H. expressed it fairly well when she called to attention the hundreds of different ships out at sea this minute, a good many of which are out of sight of everything, just as we are. She thinks that expresses the boundlessness of it—how so many ships can be out, all out of sight of each other. But there is something beside that: the heaving and throbbing of it, the deepness of it, and its terrible fickleness. Oho, such is life.

Do you ever pause to consider your old matey? I wonder. Wouldn't it be queer if, even across this terrific span of waves which separate us, we were considering each other at the Same Time? I imagine it happens occasionally. There is a mystery there, too, which I have allus meant to hask your hopinion hon—that invisible wireless, as it were.

How big the sea is! And how etc., etc. You'll hear from your matey again, maybe.

> Sleepily,
> B.

September 20. *[1928]*

Dear Eeldigarda:

Well, sometimes I am a mis*e*rable an*i*mal, and sometimes a fastideeous one, but on the whole my momen*tum* seems to be functioning, and my appe*tt*ite is *amm*azing.

The sea has been *ee*nermuss, you know—just big and blue and a-glitter with diamonds of sunlight. We sighted land this afternoon—a corner of Guadaloupe, which rose sheer and purple and surf-fringed out of the sunlit sea; tomorrow we shall be in B., disembarking. It's very exciting.

Well, my eel, I shan't forget in a hurry the famous afternoon when Hildegarde got on a hunt with her face set in one grim determination. There were dismal moments, but the outcome more than made up; and I ain't a-going to thank you, cause that ain't in my line; I don't want to mention it, but I just mention it. See?

And I have been just as treemendoss and jigun*t*i*ck* as ever, and I yawn all the time. I am yawning so hard this minute that—(heigh-ho!) I don't see why (ho-hum!) my head doesn't (ha-ho!) come (ho-ho!) off—if you see what I mean, Pooh.

Norm will give you parti*cul*ars, if you are interested; but I am (dearie me!) altogether too sleepy to relate them again, as you would realize if you might observe me. I wish to turn in, I'm going to turn in—(heigh-heigh-oh!) a thousand times goodnight; and maybe I shall be more coherent in the morning.

> YAWNINGLY,
> B.

In the next letter Barbara spelled Meservey without the third "e"— a most uncharacteristic mistake.

September 20. *[1928]*

Dear Meservys in general:

Now, since I can't answer a whole bunch of you individually, I will answer you all collectively, if you see what I mean. I am in a good humour, for the reason that I am still laughing about what the bo's'n said this morning, when we were discussing the nigger sailors: "They're all right by daylight," said he—"but at night you ought to put luminous paint on 'em so as to see 'em."

I can at last fathom the fascination of a steamer. Yes, I've been down in the engine-room, with the second engineer; and although it is Fah. 112, I stood at it for at least an hour. Oh, it is grand to see those enormous silver pistons galloping and plunging, and walloping that propeller shaft over and over; and to stare into the roaring oil furnaces; and to ask questions AT THE TIPTOP OF YOUR LUNGS of the second engineer, so that your voice is a barely perceptible squeak above the thundering and booming and hissing. But I learned something; and the next morning I went down again, and watched the second at work on the indicator cards.

It's been calm, lazy, sleepy weather. There was a little spray in the engineers' messroom once which I didn't see; apart from that, none of the waves have been obstrep... if you know what I mean. They're afraid of the bo's'n, I guess. Certain it is the bo's'n can be more vehement, even without the aid of honest-to-goodness oaths, than any bo's'n of my acquaintance. He is a fine old sailor.

And as for the old man, why there isn't a wave in the sea who would dare to throw a grain of salt in *his* whiskers————for the obvious reason that he hasn't any. He comes down to supper in the first class saloon all dressed up with a white cement shirt-front and four gold bands. As a mate of my acquaintance once put it: "The cap'n of a steamer ain't a cap'n at all—he's a chauffeur." Which just about states the case.

And there's the chief officer, and the first officer, and three other officers, and the bo's'n, and a whole lot of stewards, and two carpenters, and sixteen engineers, and twelve firemen, and thirty-five sailors, plus thousands of extraneous beings who don't seem to know what they are. It's too complicated for me. They all have their uniforms, and one has three stripes, and one has two, and one has two with a whirligig, and one has three on purple, and another two on white, and another two zigzags—and so on and so on. We *always* take the bandmen for the stewards, the chefs for the officers, etc., etc. What a mess of red tape! Jings!

Well, I request that each Meservy tender my especial compliment to every other Meservy—first from left to right, and then, in case any are left out, from right to left. And by the time that is done, I hope to be sound asleep and snoring, for we disembark at Barbados and bugs, tomorrow.

    Very sleepily and (heigh-ho!) yawningly,
    Barboo.

Thursday Morning
21 September, 1928

Dear Anne:

Tomorrow morning we land at Barbados! And another chapter begins! I wonder what will happen next, and, even so early in the game, I look forward with amusement and excitement to what is next. So that is all to the good.

But to go back. We went down to New York on Friday, and saw Alfred Knopf, and I came away from him feeling much better, although what he told me was not too encouraging. He applauds what I am doing, thinks it the only possible thing to do for the time being; thought the Harper scheme first rate and didn't see how anyone could do more for us than they had done; had a letter of introduction written out for us a good deal like the letter from Harper with the added information that he published Bar's books. Then he, of his own accord, talked about Follett, for he wanted me to understand his position. He thinks Follett is unbalanced; last fall when I asked Alfred about Follett's work, he could say nothing but it was all right, but, since that time, it had been falling off, and Follett himself had become so irascible in the office that no one could work with him or under him, that he had kept him even longer than he wanted to on my account; that he did think he was a good editor and a good stylist, and that, therefore, he should be able to get some kind of job. But what is more serious is this: Alfred is convinced that if Follett doesn't chuck what he is doing that pretty soon he will be no good to me, the children, and what is much worse, to himself. He is really worried about him, and he thinks he is on the way to real deterioration. So that is the pleasant truth. He himself can do nothing, because Follett didn't even come in to say good-bye to him.

Bar had a steamer letter from him, but it didn't please her much for a last letter being entirely devoted to putting me in my place. It is all too horrible, Anne. Alfred said that all this stuff about his life with me, and the mistake of these years was all stuff that made people think his judgment completely gone to pot because the case is so entirely against him, as everybody knows.

Well, our letters from all our notables have got us the run of the ship from the bridge to the engine room. And Bar has asked all the questions that came in Oxford's delightful letter to her. She has made friends all over the place, especially with the Bos'un a man of the late fifties, Britisher, by name of Heap who lets Bar travel around after him all over the place down below where the heaps of cable lie coiled up and where the supplies are kept, and down to his cabin in the stern of the ship where we both go and spin yarns with him and the ship's carpenter. The Captain has allowed us on the bridge, let us use the sextant, chinned sailing yarns with us. In this class there are many colored people, lots of and lots of 'em, small black babies who, says the Bosun, should have luminous paint on at night (!). Neither of us has been actively sick! We took the sodium nitrite, four grains when we got on the ship; it was seven hours late leaving New York, and so we can't tell whether we felt queer from the excitement or the nitrite. And we felt none too good for a day or so, lazy, didn't want food, but we were not sick, not sick in the delightful sea-sick way. You could hear the big black ladies whooping around, praying in their cabins: "Dear Lord, take us safe (whoop) to Barbados (whoop, whoop)."

The weather has been superb. Bar and I go way down to the bow and watch the ship cut through the unlimited stretch of the bluest water, kicking up the small transparent flying fish. No land in sight yet, but tomorrow morning we sight it. Today is choppy as you can see if you notice this typewriting. It was an absurd performance—our going in the swimming pool this morning at six o'clock—great waves sloshing over us choking us with salt. All we could do was flounder around, and exclaim in the words of the niggers: "Dear Lord, take us safe to Barbados."

It has been so far, absurd to try to write. My mind has been completely blank, just plain blank. I can't remember when I cared less about anything. I just sat, and sat, and didn't care when or where I did another thing. A glorious vacuity. And Bar said, after a day: "I haven't been so happy and contented for a long time."

Your letter was just what I wanted! What you are to me is something just beyond any words of mine to express. That you understand me and have faith in me are the important things in my life just now, and I hang on to them as to nothing else. Bar, you know, adores you and Oxford, and I feel that, you and he, together, can save her from complete disillusionment.

This attempt to write with the ship a-heaving up and down is too much, and I give up. I'll send this from Barbados when I land tomorrow that you may know I love you all, and that I am dependent on you—spiritually and morally to help me make something of myself in spite of such a knock-out as seems to have taken my life with it.

Tell Mother White we loved her little card. Bar will write when she settles down a bit, for she loved all the letters from all of you.

I shall move away from the Marine Hotel just as soon as I can find a cheaper place, but, I am planning to make Barbados my base of adventure coming back there for my mail, etc.

Take care of Follett for us whom you love, — Helen

The line in Walter de la Mare's The Three Mulla Mulgars *that Barbara tried to remember in this terrific letter to George Bryan: "And a thin, twangling, immeasurable murmur like the strings of N manossi's harp rose from the tiny millions that made their nests and mounds and burrows in the forest."*

Marine Hotel
Barbados (Bridgetown)
September 22, 1928

Captain Hook:

Hail! Don't you think I am extremely diligent and faithful? I do, considering that we only landed yesterday, and that we've been trying pretty hard to "get our bearings" ever since. You have no idee of the disconcertment (if that's a word) of landing in a Foreign Country—if that's what you call it.

Well, it was pretty beautiful from beginning to end. Yesterday morning we were up at about five, watching for the landing. It was just beginning to be light—it was, in fact, that mysterious hour when it is neither dark nor light—just twilight. Orion shone bright overhead, and old Jupiter was very brilliant, considering the light. Ahead there was a line of darkness along the edge of the sleeping sea, and at the end of that line a light winked, and winked—and—winked. Fifteen minutes later another light showed, but this was a steady one. Half an hour later it was fairly light, and the line of darkness was obviously land, even without the two lights. There was a terrific pile of huddled clouds away on the southern horizon. They were dark grey-blue, and the sun was somewhere away beyond them. They formed terrifying spires, turrets, ancient castles, dragon's head, alligator's jaws. What would we have thought they were, I wonder, had we not known they were clouds?

The stars gave a last feeble wink, and went out, one by one. Gold shone through the grim duskiness—the dark mystery—of those awful cloud-shapes. Fire. . . splashes of red seas . . . pathways of gold. And the sun was up. And Barbados lay long and slender across the horizon, and grew steadily until we could see where the shore sloped up to a hill, and where Carlisle Bay was. One flyingfish leaped suddenly out of the foam beneath the bow, and flew, with tremulous wings, ahead of the ships for nearly a hundred feet, then dropped down with a little splash just ahead. A minute later the bow scared him up ahead, and this time he flew safe away to windward. A seabird darted, with slender brown wings, across the bow—like a small, swift thought.

Then I saw something standing up against the coastline—tall, slender, dark—the masts of a ship, with her bow or her stern straight toward us. Could it be the *Carnegie*? Could it really? I dashed away aft, snatched the bo's'n's glasses, and rushed amidships—then looked. No, it was not the *Carnegie*, but it was nearly as good—a four-masted schooner, lying at anchor, bow toward us. Then I fell to scanning the shore lazily with the glasses. I saw houses packed in closely together, palms, surf, beaches, and myriads of masts, everywhere. A little later I looked at every mast, to see if I could find the *Carnegie*. No, they were all little two-masted trading-schooners, and there were lots and lots of them. I looked everywhere, except right against the sun, where I could see nothing.

A little later, when we were all anxiously watching, and picking out more and more trading-schooners, palms, and houses, I gave a start. What was that little two-master with just a pretty sheer, such a long jibboom, and with those curious nubbles on her foremast? She was side on to us, and it looked as though those nubbles might be the ends of her yards, in line with the mast itself. "Give me the glasses—quick!" I said to H., and I looked. It was—it was—it was—the *Carnegie*! "There she is! There she is! There she is!" I shouted. Well, we watched her steadily, and saw her grow larger and clearer, and we saw someone walking about in her, and she was just as beautiful as ever—quite unchanged, so far as I could make out, by her two-month trip from Iceland.

But now things were becoming exciting, aboard. We were steaming very, very slowly into the little bay, and I could see the steamer's forefoot down in the clear blue water. Boats—oh, thousands of little brown boats, with two or three duskies in each one, were gliding out toward us. Now, the telephone rang in the peak, and chief officer answered. It was from the bridge. "All right, sir!" Then he turned around and shouted "Let go!"——and then there was a sudden rattling and rumbling and splashing, and down went the anchors.

I was quite dizzy with excitement—the water was so deep that we couldn't see the bottom, even in that clearness. Oh, it was so clear! And it was so blue, and full of sunlight, and hot! The duskies were out of the boats now, swimming around the steamer, begging for money. Once in a while someone would throw a shilling in, and it would go twinkling silvery down down, until picked up by one of them, and then it would promptly disappear in the mouth of whoever was quick enough to catch it. There were all colours in the little boats. Some of them were sleek and rich brown, like Malays; others were swarthy and as black as possible, with barbaric looking earrings. And they were all shouting for money, and asking to take the passengers ashore, and rowing around us, and bumping against each other; and all under that hot sun, and in that blue, blue, sapphire-blue sea. And there was the four-master on one side, the *Carnegie* on the other, and straight ahead the town, with palms spiring up here and there.

At last out came the launch belonging to a friend of a friend of ours, and we walked down the steps toward the bouncing skiffs and the excited negroes. It was all very exciting. And we motored off toward the four-master, and went behind her stern. She hadn't such a pretty bow as she might have had, but her sheer was fine, her masts were unusually straight and even, and her counter was beautiful. Badly she needed painting—but I can forgive a schooner anything, when she is as really good-looking as that one. Her name was *Kathleen* Something-or-Other—we couldn't quite make it out.

We landed, we stepped ashore, in the bustling gang of blacks; we got into the friend of the friend of the friend's car, and drove off through the centre of Bridgetown.

It is the quaintest little place I ever saw in my life. The masts of the curious little trading-schooners grow all through the town, as though they were palms; there are absurd little rickety-wheeled donkey-carts everywhere, and baby Eeyores drawing them, with their sage ears nodding; everywhere are women with huge baskets of fruit and meat on their heads, walking the streets, and selling their wares; added to that, the streets are narrow and crooked and lined with absurd, dirty little shops; the traffic cops are black as jet and dressed in ridiculous uniforms; and added to that, everyone keeps to the *left* side of the little streets.

We drove through a good deal of this, and then came out in fairly open country on a little bumpy road. The houses here were smaller and farther apart, and quaint in build; and there were gardens, and they were full of bright, unheardof flowers. Vines grew gorgeously over the little fences. And always were the donkey-carts, with those absurd little animals plodding contentedly along, with a decidedly philosophical angle to the ears. Some of the wheels are amazingly rickety, and some of the donkeys themselves are extremely dilapidated. I saw in the midst of the town the most really good-looking negro woman I have ever seen. She was standing on the sidewalk, holding ten or fifteen strings of red and white beads over her arm; she wore earrings, of course, and had a white cap on. And she looked very wistfully into my eyes, as if to say: "Now then, mistress, won't you have a little something?" But they all look a good deal alike.

Then we arrived here. This is a fairly large hotel, with a noble old palm-tree just outside our balcony, and numerous other unknown trees and shrubs, fruits and flowers, butterflies and birds. This is the beginning of the rainy season, which means that showers may arise suddenly without any warning; which they did all yesterday afternoon. There were clouds above us at times black as the ace of spades—it might be raining pell-mell; but a little farther off the sun is always shining brilliantly, and the sky is blue. There is a curious tree outside our windows—a variety of palm, I think, which grows just beneath the first one I spoke of. It has long, long branches, and they grow from the bottom up, rather than from the top out, like a true palm. And those long branches are waving all the time, like great fans, with a slow, uncanny, Egyptian movement. The real palm, however, is a noble old tree. And how marvellous it is by dark, black against the sky, with stars caught in its silent branches!

We swam yesterday noon, in that blue sea. Near the shore it was thickly clouded, because of the showers, but we swam out way beyond the cloudy water, and could look down through that blueness to the white coral sand thirty or forty feet down below us. I walked upon the beach, too, picking up things. What a collection I shall have! The sand, too, is the most beautiful I ever saw—clean, ground from white coral, and full of pink and red grains. There are beautiful little pieces of white coral everywhere—delicate as frost-feathers.

There were tiny little fishing boats putting out to sea—no more than skiffs with little leg-o'-mutton sails, brown and tan. A trading-schooner, all her sails set, was standing out to sea. Oh, how strange and different and quaint everything is!

This morning I took a walk all by myself, away toward the country. Everywhere were the black women, with their baskets of fruit and meat upon their heads, dressed in white cotton, walking erectly and sturdily down toward the town, calling out their wares now and then in strong, not unbeautiful voices. Farther up I found several little dirty fruit-shops, and there the women were loading up their baskets. Once in a while a donkey ambled comfortably along the road, drawing its little cart hardly bigger than a baby's go-cart. They are invariably little dingy one-seated wagons, with two big wobbly wheels, but there is a great range in size and liveliness of the donkeys. Some are old, patched, dilapidated looking beasts; some are quite lively and spirited. But how those little carts must bump-bump-bump.

There were palms everywhere, some of them bearing coconuts. They are strange, beautiful trees. I shall never forget looking out of this window last night, and seeing our tall, shapely tree, silhouetted in its soft black against the clear sky. There was not a breath of fresh air, and those leaves (now green and sparkling with sunlight against the burning sky) were motionless. And oh! the sounds here at night—crickets, swamp frogs, cicadas, and myriads of other insect voices—they all blend together in one long, shrill, chirping note, with only a little fall in the cadence of it now and then. It reminds me of parts of the *Mulla-Mulgars*—what is that marvellous line about the "thin, immeasurable twangling of the tiny millions who made their burrows in the forest. . ." It is something like that, I think. I wish I had that book here. But, as it is, I find Shakespeare fuller of richness than ever.

Farewell for the present. In the midst of all this quaint and different sort of loveliness, I think of you a great deal—indeed I do, Hook. I wish you had come along down with us. How we would explore those curious little trading-schooners! How we would pick up corals and shells and coloured pebbles!

Oh, the sea away before us is blue and burning! Oh, how green the palm-leaves are, and the leaves of other rich, strange trees. The flowers here are big and bright and lily-shaped—all the scarlets and oranges and bright pinks of the earth, I should say. None of them are familiar to me.

Yours,

After two days in Barbados, Barbara wrote a poem.

> Darkness and mystery.
> The moon shining
> Upon the white, deserted streets.
> A heavy, rich fragrance
> From thousands of tropic blossoms.
> Leaf patterns from the guava-tree
> Upon the white coral pavement.
> A palm against the sky—stately—solemn.
>
> Look! Is that snow
> Upon the little stone church-step?
> No, only the moon.
> Far off, a cluster of staring lights
> Like an enormous crocodile of gold—
> The *Dominica*, asleep in the harbour.
>
> One last sage-eared donkey brushes past.
> Little grey philosopher,
> Are you really contented,
> Or are you only wise?
> Who knows his quiet secrets?
> Who knows what he is thinking?
> Who understands those nodding ears?

Silence.
Only the countless, innumerable voices
Of cricket, beetle, cicada,
All blended into one shill, chirping note.
They sing without pause or fall.
The island's heart is singing.

The white flowers are white as moonlight.
The orange ones are fleeting phantoms.
The pink ones are the colour of the wind.
Mystery—singing silence—moonlit darkness.
Why?

Those two are whispering
Over the little white gate.
Why?
What are they saying?
Their voices lift and fall, in whispers;
And their cheeks are ebony.

Away in the wet fields
A lone hut, dark against the sky.
Who is there?
No light—no voices—nothing.
Only—joyous music—
Joyous but melancholy
Music for dancing, music for gayness.
Where is the laughter?
Where is the dancing?
Music—and, in the darkness,
Shuffling feet....

Barbara Newhall Follett
Barbados, September 23, 1928

"HP" is Dr. John Harland "Harley" Paul (1900-1971), surgeon and observer aboard the Carnegie.

Marine Hotel,
Bridgetown,
Barbados, BWI
September 24, 1928

Captain Hook:
    Well, H. has gone down town, leaving me here all alone. I'm glad of it. I haven't had a chance for some time to think at all. I don't

know myself any more. I've forgotten what I'm like. But here I am, and I can think whatever I want until she gets back.

This is a marvellous place, and I realize it more and more. To be sure, it is thickly populated, and there is no doubt about it; but the quaintness of the little coral-paven streets, the tinted walls, the little trading-schooners, the coconut palms, the fantastic little donkey carts—these all atone for that. And then there are the beautiful beaches—sometime I am going to send you a sprinkling of the sand we swim over all the time—and the busy little harbour—Carlisle Bay. Imagine a small, white-beach-fringed bay—a bay of green and blue water distinctly separated, with the sun throwing gold over it in the afternoon; imagine the stately old palms and the quaint, crowded city on the shore; imagine such a place always full of shipping—and shipping of the right kind, too—trading-schooners, an occasional steamer, and the *Carnegie*. Imagine it, and then do you blame me that I am entranced by it?

There is a small white schooner in now, a three-master, with extraordinarily tall and straight masts. She is loaded high with lumber, and her bow is a little bit too high for the best of looks. I saw her all day yesterday and the day before, and she looked extraordinarily familiar. Finally I asked about her: "She's a Nova Scotiaman," I was told. My heart gave one enormous thump, and then—stopped. "What's her name?" I whispered hoarsely. But she was only the *Charles* Something, and my heart finally started going again.

There is also a three-master now getting ready to go, if she has not already gone. In dock is another three-master, and countless dingy, quaint little top-masters; and then there is the four-master I spoke of before. Then there is the *Carngeie* (Why *do* I always spell it that way?), and two steamers. There are always sails on the sharp blue of the horizon—more trading-schooners coming in or standing out to sea (one went out yesterday); and often the edge of the sea is pricked with a line of tiny little sailing boats with their brown or tan sails, going out to fish on the reef.

The fish are amazingly beautiful. HP and I met a gang of negroes yesterday, walking across a field, one of them carrying a big catch of fish of all sizes, shapes, and colours; big blue iridescent ones with white pearly teeth and blue-lined throats; pink ones, lengthwise striped with red; little shimmering purple ones. There are always little bright white and silver fishes playing about the beaches, and sometimes they all leap out of water at once—a little silver cascade of fishes.

Some of the natives here live in a most primitive way—it is a great relief. They live in odd little dingy cabins back off the roads; they keep goats (oh, the goats are too charming for words; little snow-white ones, brown-and-white ones, black ones, mottled ones), chickens, and pigs (we met a man with a family of pigs, who said he sold the littlest one for sixpence!); they raise corn and sugar-cane and yams and aloes; and they have a little bright bank of yellow and orange and pink flowers about the door of their huts. HP and I, walking on a small grassy hill over the sea, saw a child singing an incomprehensible, flowery little song, the only words of which that we could catch were: "I love the dover; I love the dover—" whatever the Dover is! HP suggested that the child had heard it in church, and substituted "dover" for "Saviour."

Yesterday we drove in the ricketiest of rickety hacks, out into the country for five miles or so. I wish I could describe those roads to you. The whole atmosphere is so new, and different, and quaint, and beautiful. The little road, baked and white under the midday sun, wound on ahead of us, bordered on each side by the walls of the house—walls tinted in shades of salmon, pink, lavender and cream. The houses, with their little flower-gardens, were farther and farther apart the more we drew out of the town; and the palms grew thicker and thicker, until finally we stopped in a thick grove of coconut palms along the shore.

Here there were five or six lizards on the rough trunk of every tree—bright blue-and-green ones, with long, pointed heads, malicious little eyes, and ridiculously long tails. They run around those trees like chain lightning, and then, when they know they are out of reach, they lie against the trunks and watch you warily. We found some baby ones, too; so little that they seemed no more than wisps of some brown, dried leaf.

We went down on the white, gleaming beach, and looked out to sea. First there was a strip of light green water, where the waves broke into emeralds on the sand; this green deepened until it was a mermaid colour—then suddenly changed to the most dazzling of blues—a colour which grew steadily brighter and brighter toward the horizon. And on the very edge was the reef, where the waves broke ceaselessly—and that was a sharp line of white. And far out was a bank of black clouds, which were pouring rain down madly five or six miles away.

Down this beach a way was a huge gang of negroes in swimming. Horses, donkeys, men, women, children—all in one shouting, happy bunch; why, those people swim most of the time! It is amazing. It is likewise amazing how everyone has something to sell and no one ever buys anything! There are no buyers—because they are all selling.

No one ever worries about anything here, so far as I can see. The butterflies, flowers, birds, leaves, sun, and sea are all amazingly dazzling and brilliant; the natives all amazingly black and cheerful; the lizards amazingly bright and lively; the frogs and crickets alarmingly and loudly musical; the mosquitoes dreadfully plentiful; the donkeys charmingly philosophical about the cars; —the rain wet, the sea warm, the harbour full of sails and masts, the Guava jelly delicious—in short, everything is just as it ought to be. You ought to come down here—you really ought. It's the best sort of medicine.

I have a whole lot of odds and ends of shells and scraps of white coral and coloured stones; and I am going to send you a collection of 'em if I can, in the near future, dig up a box and some paper and a piece of string.

Farewell for the present, and here's hoping we don't get too seriously cheated over the English currency—which *is* confusing.

   Always yours,

The Okeechobee Hurricane of 1928 ransacked the West Indies between September 12th and 16th before reaching Florida. It left almost 2000 dead and hundreds of thousands homeless. Guadeloupe, Martinique, Montserrat, Nevis, and Puerto Rico were particularly hard hit.

[October 2, 1928]
Marine Hotel, Barbados, B.W.I.

Dear Anne and Oxford:

I should have got off a word to you before had I really been able to snatch the time from the stuff I had to write. Now, for the first time, I think I can see daylight. Which means, that I have been trying to work up something to send to the Pictorial Review; when I left New York, Percy Waxman gave me fifty dollars as a sort of clincher that I'd do something for him. It made me feel that I had to do it. I couldn't write on the boat as I had hoped to; and I couldn't get going here for some few days, what with the heat, and the newness and all. And now, I am about to jump off again. So I am trying to finish the first part of the article and send it north next week before we take off for the other islands.

It's a lovely place here! Hot and lovely in the daytime; cool and lovely at night. We met our friend H. Paul, and he has devoted all his spare time to taking us around this island. We love the place: the wharves are full enough of schooners to give Bar all the thrills she wants, two-masted affairs, and three,—we discovered a fine three-masted one with a white captain (many of them are colored) and found she was from Nova Scotia. We should be going on her if she were going anywhere but to Turks' Island, and we should willingly go there except we have no way of getting away from there back again, and there is nothing there but salt!

You have read about the hurricane in these parts! Pretty terrible! We want to see some of the islands that have been hit, and so next Wed. we are sailing by steamer to Dominica, making that island, which has been only partially hit, as our base and then taking schooners to the various smaller islands up north, St. Kitts, Nevis, Saba, and then Martinique. We shall probably come back here, leaving some of our luggage at this hotel, and making it our definite base for cables, etc., and go south to Trinidad.

Bar has been writing up this island in attractive prose. But I don't think that, as yet, she has got the makings of a letter for Harpers. It strikes me that these devastated islands may do that. Anyway, she is going to have her chance to see them, and write about them, and the schooners we have to take to get around. We can live over there on Dominica cheaper than here, although here it is half price now during the off season, paying $2.50 a day each including all meals. So the islands should be half of that again, which I can afford.

I must make a go of the Pictorial Review stuff and send some from here next week. The trip is beginning auspiciously, but we don't want to have to stop before we finish. In other words, if you can find out for me that Follett has started to contribute something to my account, could you cable me here at Barbados? I am not quite sure that I can get through the canal and to Tahiti without more money, for it is going to take so long for me to hear anything form the Pictorial Review, and for Bar to hear from her stuff. I have a feeling that we shall be able to manage in time, but boats are so scheduled that it is better if I can possibly know at the earliest moment whether I can plan on sailings to Panama. I feel that if Follett doesn't come across soon, he just won't at all; and I want him to feel that you both expect him too. There are bills in New Haven for Sabra which must be attended to, and so on. I haven't heard from the Harper article, and probably shan't hear for a long time; it seems to take forever to get anything away from the place. We have had no mail whatever since we have been here.

I planned not to leave Barbados until I had heard about Follett's money, but I think there is money in this hurricane business, and I think I may very likely get something out of it to write myself as a news article, and, of course, in a few months the devastation will be gone. We haven't any idea what a hurricane will do here, although we had an earthquake here the other night, and the pictures gyrated around, and queer things happened to the buildings.

Barbara is off today and tonight with Dr. Paul visiting some pirate caves he has heard about in some distant part of the island. The moon is full, and it is one of those perpetually tropic nights that one hears about, and that sometimes one sees and experiences for himself. Here is a bit of verse Bar wrote about it *[the poem of September 23rd]*.

This is not a letter describing anything; it is simply to tell you that we are glad we came—so far. The real adventure begins next week. This island is so safely British that you can't make a mistake, and everyone is kindness itself to us in helping us make plans to get around. The smaller islands will prove overwhelming scenically, anyway.

I must confess, however, that Follett's money would help relieve this awful pressure, a sort of hysterical pressure that Bar and I both have about our writing. And it will be months and months before we can get the stuff ready to send, and more months before we can get an answer. This is not completely true about mine; I shall send a sample to Waxman before I leave this island and ask him if he likes it enough for me to go on to cable me here. A deferred cable to the U.S.A. costs only 12 cents per word. A letter from you will answer the purpose if I can get it in the next couple of months. I can't help hoping that something will come for I am convinced that this trip will work out beautifully if I don't have to work under such a strain as I feel now, and, naturally, I hate to have Bar feel that strain too. I find it impossible for her to write her experiences up every night; they have to soak in with her before they become transmogrified into something beautiful.

It is to you both that we owe our being here. And I think it will mean life to me; certainly Bar seems very happy and contented.

Remember the Marine Hotel. I shall leave all extra luggage here and keep in touch with them in case of any need at home.

   Devotedly,
   Helen

Thursday, 4 October *[1928]*

Dearest Anne:

A short note before the ship leaves. We left Barbados yesterday and are on our way for Dominica where we stay for a while, hoping to get schooners from there up north to see what a hurricane can do to the islands. Dominica is about as far north as is safe to go to stay.

We shall come back to St. Lucia, a heavenly island where we can live with a nice colored woman for one dollar a day. That includes meals.

Bar is fascinated with everything. The Chief Engineer on this boat is a delightful Scotchman who is telling Bar all sorts of things about his engines. Tonight when we pull out, we are both going down again to see him start. Bar is almost being won over to steam! Which will make interesting material for her letters to McFee.

I'm counting on this northern trip for her first letter. Then we go down to Trinidad, by schooner, we hope. From there we shall try for Balboa, and the South Seas. We are going to be dreadfully disappointed if we can't make it.

I have almost finished the education stuff for Waxman, and shall hope to send it off soon now. But it will take so long for me to hear.

If Follett doesn't come through with any money in the next couple of months, I shall think he has given us up. We need some money quite badly. The pressure of having to write every minute is bad for both of us. But I shall keep going as long as I can. It is just too good for both of us to give up.

I long for a cable from someone telling me that deposits have begun to come through. It would make such a difference!

I shall return to the Marine Hotel some time, and shall keep in touch with it.

This is really written to give you my love and send you some stamps. Isn't Edward collecting them? Or is it someone else?

    All our love,
    H.......

Also to Anne Meservey. Chief "Bert" is Andrew Burt.

St. Kitts
8 October, 1928

Dear:

This island is not so intriguing as St. Lucia and Dominica; or that may only be because Bar and I are extremely tired. We're in a funny little house managed by a nice colored lady who takes us for three dollars per day—both. And we shall stay here until Saturday when we shall take the Skirmisher down to St. Lucia, and stay there a while. We may, however, sail over to Nevis, and there take a boat.

Bar is all engines now, thinks, talks, and eats engines. The Chief is an extraordinary person, Bert by name, a Scotchman, not too young. Bar spent all her time trailing him around, and I spent most of mine in his cabin or tying to find them and, invariably, they'd be down with the engines. I spent several sweaty hours down below myself, but I got the Chief to really explain things to Bar, and I think what she writes now may be fairly correct. This will please Oxford, I know. She began writing today, and the stuff is pretty fairly interesting.

I decided that it was foolish to leave the West Indies before we knew anything about them. So this trip. It may mean that we don't get into the South Seas at all, in which case I shall try to go to work either in Barbados or Trinidad. I still have hopes from Follett that he won't let us go completely. He, himself, and Her must be living somehow.

We have both been working today, and I send off my stuff this week. If Waxman likes it I can do more; and I shall ask him to cable me to go ahead. I shall have to have more money before I start the South Seas business—I am sure of that. And yet think how cheaply we can live on the islands in comparison with anywhere else. In St. Lucia we can live—board and room—for a dollar each a day. You can't live at home any cheaper, can you? So it seems to me I should stay here, and not try to get back for a while anyway.

I'm awfully homesick tonight. I want to see you, Anne dear. And I want Sabra! This is the first time I have dared to think of her!

I haven't the energy to write to you about the islands in a purely descriptive sense, for what energy I have I put into the article which I need so badly to get off. And there is heat here, and you can't work so hard! But we already love the islands, some more than others, and we could spend much time on any one of them with the simple people. The Government people are a sporty crowd who drink squizzles all the time, dance, and get nicely drunk, and then rather, rather silly. A little of that kills me and sends me to bed early for nights after.

The hurricane has been merciless. In Montserrat, the barometer readings went like this: 12 September, 8.30 A.M. 29.80; 6:15 P.M. 28.33; 6:30 28.10 then up again to normal about 30 in the morning. A wrecked place, houses all over in the street; whole families sitting on top of their ruins; stone church knocked all over the place; steel piers carried miles down the beaches. The natives still smile and wonder what to do next. But Nature is good down here, and things are green again so soon. The lime orchards were ruined, so much poverty will follow.

More later. Who collects stamps at your house?

Something happened aboard the Canadian Pathfinder *to cause Barbara's anchor to drag—something to do with Andrew Burt, I think.*

Hotel St. Antoine
Castries
St. Lucia
Windward Islands
October 24, 1928

Hi hi, S-C F!

This morning a divine little green schooner beat her way into the exquisite bright blue harbour, and anchored. How white her sails looked in the tropic sunlight, and how they gleamed against the blue of the tropic sea! She brought us mail from Barbados; among it was your letter to H. Well, it suddenly struck upon my mind what a sluggish correspondent I have been—and how the G and HC has deteriorated, as it were.

And even this is not going to be a very long letter. You see, this is an island—quite naturally. And being an island, it is only natural that mail must go to the mainland by boats. And, going as it does by boats, you must sort of take advantage of the boats that come in; because, take my tip, matey, they don't come in any too often. So, being as that is the case, and seeing as the s. s. *Dominica* is expected for a short visit tomorrow, and seeing as we want to get our mail ready tonight, and seeing as there's lots more mail I want to write—well, you see what I mean, Pooh—don't you?

WWW! An accurate account of what has taken place to me—even externally—would occupy pages and pages—and—pages. But an account of what has taken place to me *in*ternally; well, it would occupy thousands of pages. So, supposing I put them together—well, it would swamp the Harbour of Castries in a shower of manuscript—and the trusty old s. s. would sink under the weight of it.

So, as it were, I can give you only a very brief account. (a) We've done a lot of touring around through these entrancing islands: Dominica, Montserrat, Antigua, Nevis, St. Kitts. (b) We've seen a lot of the hurricane wreckage, which is simply incredible. (c) We got none of the hurricane ourselves, except, on the way down, an unusually heavy swell off Hatteras, which turned up the toes of the lady passengers—all except *me*. (d) We stay here til tomorrow, then we sail by launch to another town of this island; then we return to Castries; shortly after that we sail for Martinique; then we return again and pick up a s. s. for Trinidad—that's the temporary schedule, as it were. (e) I now understand steamers—I'm wild about engines—I've been in a real triple reciprocating engine-room, and I've started and stopped a little s. s., the *Canadian Pathfinder*, and I've been called her "sixth engineer," and I've become acquainted with her chief—a rare find.

There's five things already. But the momentous is yet to come. (f) The A dragged!!!!! But not through what you would think would be the cause—no, it dragged through a different cause entirely. That is, my wind failed me when I was dangerously near a lee shore!!! So I made use of the trusty second anchor which you suggested, and which was hanging from its cathead, in readiness. Now everything is all right again—or nearly so.

As to the cause for the dragging of the A; that, my dear and trusty matey, you shall NEVER know; neither shall ANYONE else!

Well, in case I don't have a chance to write to Hildegarde, give her my love just the same; and the same to Helen Deane—and to Midget and Sonny, too—tell Midget I *hope* she isn't dead yet.

Farewell: it's sort of distracting to write with ten thousand thousand thousand mosquitoes and all sorts of etceteras buzzing around your ankles at the same time.

>   Your shipmate,
>   Babu.

Hotel St. Antoine
Castries
St. Lucia
Windward Islands
October 24, 1928

Dear Oxford:

This is the most magical time of day in the tropics. It is dark, but not yet completely dark; the Insects, etc., have begun their loud, shrill singing (in the forest the noise is deafening), the fireflies are flashing brilliantly all about through the branches of such dreamlike trees as guava trees, mango trees, breadfruit trees, coconut trees, tamarind trees; the lights are winking down in the little town so far below us; and everything is very mysterious and peaceful.

Peaceful, did I say? Immortal gods and goddesses! It is indeed difficult to Write Coherently with an army of Peculiarly Distracting Mosquitoes buzzing around one's ankles—Mosquitoes Guaranteed to Bite.

Well, what I mostly wanted to say was that the exploration of the *Voltaire*'s innards on the way down to Barbados was nothing compared to the exploration of the innards of a little steamer which we sailed in on our trip up through the islands devastated by the hurricane. You see, in that steamer coming down, the chief engineer was not much of a person; and it is the chief that matters if you want to get into the engine-room. But in this other small steamer I was mentioning, our chief was a real character—a fine sort of person—and we really *lived* in the engine-room. They called me "sixth engineer," and a first-class engineer I was, too. I really learned a good deal in the three days and nights I was in that boat. The chief often used to let me start or stop the engines as we came in and out of island ports; and that was a great experience, to see those gigantic, galloping piston rods yield to my inexperienced hand!

Now it is darkening rapidly—the sea and land have become merged together into one mysterious Shape; the insects are increasing their songs; multitudes of soft-winged bats are swooping about, darting on the balcony and out again; a "whistling frog" is going "Snap-snap-snap—snap-snap-snap—snap-snap-snap" in a thick vine outside, like an insane typist. He makes an awful racket, and he's always there every night.

You would think you were dreaming, if you could see the brilliant, incredible flowers, the blazing butterflies, the madly coloured hummingbirds racing among the hibiscus blossoms; you would likewise think you were dreaming if you could draw one breath of the fragrance which spreads through the air at night, arising from thousands of tropic blooms—why, it is an even intoxicating fragrance. Also you would pinch yourself to wake up, just to look down into the incredible blue of the little harbour, watching the motions of toy steamers and snow-sailed schooners, far, far, below, between emerald hills.

Much love to Anne, and Ellen, and Edward, and Bob, and "Other Ding," and yourself—in other words—MESERVEYS IN GENERAL.

   So long for the present,
   Barbara.

Mrs. De Brettes' Boarding House
Castries, St. Lucia
Windward Islands
October 31st, 1928

Shipmate—Hi-Hi!
  WWW, as the saying goes. You would laff a most tremenjous laff if you could hear all our experiences since we left St. Kitts. I wrote you once from here, I believe? Well, of course in that VSD I didn't have a chance to tell you very much—and of course the details are the most exciting. I want to tell you such things as the sign-boards which you see all over this town: "Licensed to sell intoxicating liquor." The brutal frankness of that appeals to me immensely, if you know what I mean. But at Nevis, near St. Kitts, there was a sign: "Licensed to sell spirituous liquor—" which, in my opinion, is priceless.

But by far the most amusing event during the whole expo so far has been our pursuit of the *Camelita*. That sounds mysterious, does it not? Well, it's quite a long story. When we were at Barbados, we used to walk down among the fascinating shipping a good deal—I sent you a picture of what that shipping was like, I believe. Well, among those dirty little two-masted trading-schooners was one by the name *Camelita*. We came near to going to Dominica in her instead of in the steamer; in which case my A would not have dragged, and a lot of trouble for me would have been saved. But, unfortunately, the *Camelita* was going too early; with the result that we waited for the steamer, as you know.

Well, a week ago we went by motor launch to Soufrière, a little town of this same island of St. Lucia. When we arrived at Soufrière, by thunder! there was the *Camelita*. We hailed her like an old friend, and determined to find out where she was going, so that perhaps we could sail back in her to this town of Castries—which is the capital of the island. Well, we hung around Soufrière for nearly a week; we spent a night at Vieux Fort, a little town at the tip of the island (I never saw so many mosquitoes in my life as we had that night!). When we were ready to come back here to Castries, the *Camelita* was still rolling off the jetty, and we heard she was to sail at noon on Sunday (this is Wednesday—and it was last Sunday she was to go).

So far so good. We met the black, good-natured skipper of her, and arranged to sail with her Sunday at noon. Then he, considerately, agreed to have her sail at four or five instead of twelve; as it would be so devilishly hot at noon. Well, we went to see the skipper's agent—to find out if he were a decent guy, you see. We were informed that "he's not a sober man—oh, no—not a sober man!" But we were also informed that there was a "revenue officer" sailing in her, too; so that we decided to go in spite of this reputed insobriety, and place ourselves under the protection of the revenue officer, whoever he might be. Well, the agent thought that would be all right; and he also agreed to go down to see what condition the skipper was on Sunday morning, and he would report to us. Sunday morning we were informed that the skipper was in fairly good condition, and that it was all right for us to go. Which sounded promising.

We were to sail at two. First it was to be noon, then it was to be four; but when I asked the skipper that morning, he said it was to be two. Well, this was queer. For one thing, the skipper came walking down the jetty (he'd just been ashore) with a decidedly unsealeggish sort of gait. For another, he didn't seem to know "what is which and which is what." This was our conversation:

"Good morning, Captain Desrochier."

"Mornin'."

"When do we sail, Captain?"

"Four."

"Well, but Mr. Eudoxy (the agent) said that it would be a good thing to sail earlier, because he said we wouldn't get to Castries till late."

"Hm?"

"Mr. Eudoxy said that four was too late."

"Wind too light?"

"No, he said that four o'clock would be too late."

"Vessel too light?"

"No—four o'clock too *late*. Couldn't you sail at two?"

"No, four."

"Yes, but four is so late. Couldn't you make it two?"

"All right."

Then he got aboard in a decidedly unsailorly way. Meanwhile I was being heartily chuckled at by the crowd which is always on the jetty. No wonder—my struggle with the rather unsettled skipper was anything but solemn.

Well, I decided (somewhat cannily, I thought) that I wouldn't tell Helen about this, as it would upset her so; and I knew that this so far unseen revenue officer was to go, so it would be all right, and I didn't want to miss the chance to sail in this mysterious little *Camelita*. So I didn't say a word about the somewhat unsettled condition—I merely remarked that we'd be sailing at two.

At about one a messenger came in from Mr. Eudoxy. "Mr. Eudoxy," he began, "says that the cap'n and whole crew's drunk; and he advises you not to go in that schooner." Well, you can imagine the effect this announcement had upon us! We were thunder-struck. Our only chance, we decided, lay in the revenue officer—we'd go see him and observe what condition he was in. Which we did. We found him in a mysterious little shanty back on the hillside; and he vehemently vowed he'd look out for us; and he also vowed that this captain was not the man who was to sail the ship—rather the mate was to sail her, the best sailor anywhere around. So that was all right.

At two o'clock we were aboard the *Camelita*, standing beneath the fore boom. The cap'n was ready to go, and hoisted the foresail, and was about to get the anchor up. He was very much out of sorts and feeble-looking, and wandered disconsolately about like a lost soul. Suddenly it was observed that this mate, who was to sail the boat back to Castries, was not present. And suddenly he appeared on the jetty. But the captain evidently had some row with him, and the mate (a gigantic, jet-black, finely built negro) was greeted by: "Don't you touch her rail!" accompanied by vehement gesticulations of a bamboo cane.

But the mate was equal to the occasion. "I will touch her rail!" he exclaimed haughtily—"See! I touch her rail," and he banged upon the bulwarks with his bamboo cane. Then everything was very exciting. There was a lot of rowing going on in Patois, and the result was that the mate vowed by all that wasn't holy that he wasn't going to sail the blankety-blank hooker back to the Castries. He threw a bundle of his clothes ashore to a negro who was standing on the jetty, he started to jump ashore himself, and was vigorously retained by the same revenue officer, who had begun to come into action. Then they quarreled. The mate wouldn't go—the revenue officer insisted and threatened.

Then there was a good deal of playing ball with the mate's clothes. The mate threw them ashore, the officer had them thrown back, and the mate tore them away and threw them ashore again. Then the officer threw them down the hatch. Meanwhile the mate tore loose and went ashore, with the officer after him. Then there were alarming preparations for departure going forth. The captain ordered the stern rope to be cast loose, and the mainsail was hoisted.

"Are you going to leave the revenue officer?" I asked.

"Yes."

"But we can't go without him," says Helen, white with terror.

"Why not?"

"Mr. Doorly wouldn't like it at all—" you see she introduced the name of the Administrator of St. Lucia. So the anchor was dropped again, and the captain blew furiously a whistle that had the colic. After a long, long wait the mate turned up in company with the revenue officer. He was somewhat humbled, and agreed to go. Later we discovered that the officer had taken him to the police station, where matters had been satisfactorily arranged. So it seemed to be all right.

But while all this had been going on the breeze had been slinking away, and now the foresail was flapping feebly. So we had to sit and wait for a draught. There was an awful lot of quarreling all the time. Those niggers were just like so many chillen. We went ashore. We went back to where we were staying. We had tea. The *Camelita*, with her sails hoisted, and her stern-rope cast off, was floundering about the jetty of Soufrière. We had supper. Still no breeze. We went to the jetty, and got our bags, and took them back to where we were staying. We cancelled everything. We went to bed.

In the morning the first thing that met my eye was the foremast of the *Camelita* and a patch of her foresail. All day long, while we explored the hills of Soufrière, she rolled around there with her bow-rope taut and her anchor down and her sails hoisted. At night, in spite of a favouring breeze, she was still there. They were having too good a time to depart. The mainsail came down—either accidentally or intentionally. It looked as though those halliards wouldn't hold a patch of gossamer, anyhow!

Tuesday morning the *Camelita* was still there. At eight o'clock she went out, limpingly and drunk, heading for the open sea. We went aboard the motor launch back to Castries. By the time we were aboard the launch our schooner was sailing nobly with the wind on her port bow, heading for Castries. I wished I were on her, out in the sun on the blue, blue sea; then I thought of the reeking gang aboard her, and I was glad I wasn't.

But she seemed to be going all right. Suddenly, just as the launch pulled out, a most astonishing thing happened to the little schooner. She had too much rum stowed away in her hold, and she was drunk, too. She swung gently into the wind's eye, and started around in a circle. Was she tacking? Yes—it was a head wind. But was she tacking, when she turned completely around, and started sailing for the mountains known as Pitons which dip down sheerly into the sea leeward of Soufrière? Was she tacking when running before the wind dead away from Castries? Ye Gods, no!

The poor drunken schooner had been left to herself. The helmsman must have left the wheel for a row, and the schooner had swung into the wind and was now running away from Castries, and going rapidly ashore at the foot of the enormous Pitons. We passed the point in the little launch. We left her out of sight, and she was still running for the Pitons. A moment later the point interposed, and we saw her no more. This is Wednesday morning. She has not arrived in Castries yet. Undoubtedly she is being bandied back and forth with the powerful current about the Pitons.

That is the pathetic end of the tale of the *Camelita*. Charming yarn, n'est-ce pas?

>Your matey,
>Barbara.

To George Bryan.

Castries
St. Lucia
November 6, 1928

Hail, shipmate!

I am mad with sea-worship again today. It ensnares me with a mysterious, uncanny spell. I have just been thinking of my schooners again. And yesterday a silver-grey steamer turned up here, the old *Haiti*, southward bound. I didn't care anything at all about her, but I watched her go out, after dark, and nearly expired with the longing.

I heard her whistle hoarsely and strangely three times. I rushed out of the house and into the dark, deserted streets, and down to the wharf. I pushed away from the crowd and stood alone on the very edge. A step more, and I should have been too near the sea. A shark played about at my feet. The steamer had swung her stern outwards from the wharf, and her engines were going "Slow astern." The propeller blades sheared through the water one after the other, slowly and sternly: "Thump-thump-thump-thump! Thump-thump-thump-thump!" with a rushing of water and a great white fountain at the stern.

But it was the shape of the steamer, and her darkness, and the lights upon her masts. She hung there like an awful phantom; her starboard sidelight burned a brilliant green, and above it was the masthead light, bright gold. And the two reflections, the green and the gold, mingled in the sea below in a shifting, brilliant pool—bright green, bright gold entwined together in the velvet blackness.

"All right! Let go!" called a voice out of the darkness. And there was a swish as the bow rope was dropped into the sea. Farther and farther outward she swung—awful, vast, dark, glittering with a few lights, and with that terrible fountain at her stern, and the propeller's thumping. Suddenly I heard a faint "ting-a-ling-a-ling!" far away inside her heart; and my heart gave an enormous leap, because I knew so well what that signal was. It was "Stop!" in the engine-room, and I knew that now someone was turning the wheel to shut off the steam. And I saw the fountain subside, and the propeller ceased. And now the *Haiti* floated, silent, gaunt, and awful upon the black water.

Fireflies flickered through the air. Always the reflections of the green and gold lights played together in the blackness below. How silent! How lofty—how terrible she was! There was a long minute of suspense; and then again I heard that faint bell, ringing away from out a fathomless depth, it seemed. And almost at once the propeller started wheeling, throbbing, swishing, and the white fountain burst upwards again. Now the black, dreaming hulk swung backwards away, and away, and yet further into the black circle of the harbour. She turned her bow—the green light vanished, the red one appeared. Another pause. Then I heard the mate, far forward, call out: "All right, sir!" And then the bell again rang, faintly, tinkling: "Slow ahead!"

Like an awful ghost the steamer wheeled about, headed for the open sea. Smaller and smaller she became, yet she seemed to crouch away on top of the water as a duck or a seagull crouches. As she drew farther, more and more mysterious and gorgeous she became. But suddenly, as if to keep me from seeing more, a tremendous shower of rain blew out of the blackened skies; and, brave though I am, I unfurled my heels and ran for shelter.

I have been thinking of my schooners—my northern schooners. I remember (and you do, too) our *Frederick H.* as she sailed that night in the brilliant moonlight; I remember her again stepping briskly down the seas with the wind in her face and the sky angry and the sea green; I remember her as I saw her from the crosstrees as we sailed into Lahave. Her sails, gently puffed with the breeze, were—well, you know how they were. Besides, it wasn't the look of her—it was the *feeling*, somehow, that always grows and grows upon me when I think of the rigging, and tall masts, and white sails, and the sea. I could no more describe that feeling than I could fly.

Then I remember the rigging of that big four-master, the *Albert F. Paul*. It seemed an interminable climb, I remember; and the wild west wind was tearing, and whistling through the taut shrouds that day; and I climbed, and climbed, up the purple, mysterious spars; and slowly I rose out and away from the dirty, crowded town of Bridgeport, and knew only the wind, the rushing, the quivering, vibrating shrouds, and the purple masts.

And then there was that heavenly, unbelievable climb on the little *Mina Nadeau*, that three-master from N. S. It was on a brightly moonlight night, and I remember looking upwards among the rigging, and feeling powerless to resist. I scurried behind the fo'c'sle, and in a moment I had climbed over the port sidelight case, and was up, and up, and up, into the moonlight, into the wind. There was a wind blowing in from the sea that night—quite strong, quite cold, and it was some sort of hail—a signal—from the old sea to me. I reached at last the crosstrees, brightly frosted with moonlight; and there I stayed until that breeze pierced even my sturdy being like a spear of ice.

And I remember some of the jovial afternoons NVD and I used to spend, walking down the old, rickety wharf in the teeth of a biting breeze from the sea, watching the seagulls swerve and swoop, and seeing the sun make silver trails upon the sea far, far away. We used to walk down by the side of the green, stately four-master, *Annie C. Ross*, and spend the afternoon with the hoary old cook, spinning yarns, and writing letters from his dictation.

Then there was the wild, windy, rainy, bitter day I steered the noble old four-master *Charles M. Struven* out into the sea behind the tug. I remember the steering, and I remember, when we left the schooner at anchor to wait for a fair breeze instead of this foul one, how she looked standing gaunt and grey through the mist and the rain. Oh, how alone the noble old ship was then! She stood, stern and weathered, looming dimmer and dimmer, more and more ghostly, through the fog.

How strangely I feel when I remember these things. Oh, how I wish and wish I could explain the feeling that surges through me. It was never a feeling of *fun* that I had; it was not exactly the beauty of it, either. It could hardly be called mystery. But I did—O Virodine—I did feel so absurdly and strangely happy aboard those schooners. It was not that I felt like laughing and playing—no—it was just contentment. No, it was not contentment, either, because I never feel more restlessness than when I long for the sea. There *was* mystery, I guess, and remorseless glamour, and some bitterness, and some sheer loveliness, and the allure of the horizon, and the beauty of a ship—it was all those, I guess, mingled together into one great feeling that surged through me like an enormous, crashing wave of green and blue.

And each of those happenings had a different feeling. I remember the glorious sense that NVD and I used to have, walking down that old wharf, in the teeth of the bitter breeze from the sea. There was a sense of freedom and wildness we had; and seagulls and wind and grey sky—I wish I could tell it. And there were those peaceful moonlight nights, too, when the spars gleamed as though they were frosted; and there were, besides, those dark, rainy nights, when NVD and I and *Hermione* (our schooner) would tear down the rain-drenched streets, just to catch a glimpse of the black, deserted harbour—just to strain our eyes to make out the outlines of a mast, black and sinister through the rain.

Here, I have seen extraordinary and lovely happenings concerning schooners, too. One was what I wrote to you about before, when the little *Camelita* lay by the black jetty, her spars silhouetted against the orange flame in the west, and against the shifting, mysterious silver-blue sea. There was a cluster of black heads grouped upon the jetty; there were the silent black masts of the little schooner; and there was the one silver star over the sunset. . . .

But by far the loveliest and weirdest that I have seen was from the balcony of the hotel, when we were living up there. I don't know how I escaped telling you of it. It was on a brilliant tropic day, when the sky was bright blue and the little harbour burning blue fire— when the sun blazed down upon the town and the sea, and the blueness and the brilliance was dazzling. But there was rain somewhere behind the hills, and a great rainbow swept across the town, one foot imbedded in the heart of the harbour, and the arch stretching away across the green hills, casting strange tints upon them. Suddenly, around the bend, a little schooner hove in sight—a little two-master with all her sails set. She was beating against the breeze into the blue harbour; and the sun made her sails whiter than snow against the incredible blue. And how tiny she was! She tacked again and again, gaining ground with every tack, and finally she sailed into the very spot where the rainbow sprung out of the harbour. For a moment she was a fairy ship—her sails were filled with iridescence, her grey hull was lighted with colour. Then the wind caught her, and hurried her out of the enchantment, and she became her own sweet self again, drenched with sunlight. And soon the rainbow vanished.

Which reminds me, this is a land of rainbows. I can remember so well the first rainbow I ever saw—a faint, dull, fraction of one. A half-bow is quite a happening up north; and a complete one is quite rare. I remember craning my neck out of a window to catch a glimpse of a fragment of one through the trees. Here, there are rainbows all the time, nearly. Before showers, after showers, during showers, you may always find one away off at sea somewhere. I have seen them lying across the green hills, so that you could see the hills themselves through the iridescence, as it were; I have seen them immeasurably distant, rising out of the sea; I have seen incredible brilliant fragments of them across the clouds; I have seen the one I spoke of whose foot was imbedded just below, in the harbour itself. But out of all the bows I have seen here, and many of them complete, I have seen nothing as perfect and glorious as the one H. and I saw on the way home from an early morning walk. It was raining slightly then, and the sun was shining brilliantly; and over the sea hung a complete and unusually brilliant bow against the black rainclouds which had just passed. Both its feet descended into the blueness, and cast iridescence about them. And outside this bow, behold! rose another—fainter, and seemingly more distant, but complete and perfect like the first. It was like a tremendous dream—the iridescent sweeps of colour, the lowering black clouds, and the blue sea drenched with sunlight.

Well, I guess I have ranted long enough. It may seem very strange to you that I should go to work and talk about northern schooners! I suppose it is strange. But I'm sea-mad again today, that's all. And I'm not going to be daunted, as they'll see. Oh, I'll give 'em all the very devil, as I said before. Life is too short to be wasted. I shall do what pleases me. If I find that a tame, sensible, proper, civilized existence won't suit me (which it won't) why, I shan't try to make it suit me. I'll get away and be happy. Yo-ho for the old sea!

Yours,

In October 1928, my grandparents rented an old farmhouse overlooking Penobscot Bay in Maine.

Tenant's Harbor, Maine
November 8, 1928

Dear Oxford:

Well, I must thank you—wrily, but sincerely—for all this trouble. I thought Helen understood clearly (a) that I should have the New Haven bank inform her by cable (they have her address: I haven't) of any financial arrangement as soon as made, and (b) that she was putting her head into a possible noose by starting off on this crack-brained expedition when I hadn't a job and when the accumulation of anything like an income might turn out to be a very slow and uncertain business, as it has. Yet she is keeping the cable hot with these inquiries, or rather with the same inquiry over and over—first through Donaldson in New Haven, then through the bank, and now through you. I can only iterate to weariness that when there is any money the bank will instantly cable her about it, and that her non-receipt of a cable means the non-existence—as yet—of the money that she, in the face of all explicit warnings, expects.

As for "failed to locate," I don't comprehend that. I left New York on September 30, leaving explicit forwarding arrangements. I have received mail forwarded, from others, and have replied to this same missive before, via Donaldson. I know of no effort to "locate" me. I have even been in direct communication with the bank.

I left New York (a) because I could no longer cope with it witout going wrong in the head, (b) because there was no likelihood of a paying job there anyhow, and (c) because it costs too much money to live there prospecting. Inasmuch as I seem to be on the defendant's side of the rail, I will remark that I am paying $12 a month rent and living on a scale which gives two persons all that is desirable in existence for a total of about $750 a year, a good deal less than half of which, so far, I am supplying myself. In time, when my syndicate stuff gets going and I can build up, I shall pretty surely accumulate a good enough income. I may be able at any minute to wire the bank, for Helen, a goodish sum. If she counts on it for any particular time, she is—well, to put it mildly, a person to whom words don't signify the usual things. There is nothing under heaven that I can do, or shall consider doing, except sitting tight here, doing my work, getting back some health and well-being into my body and my mind, and in short leading a sane life, in an effort to produce an income sufficient to cover the needs. This is the answer that I should make—for the nth time—to Helen if I were hearing from her direct, and it is the only answer I can make to the succession of agents whom she (to my chagrin) saddles with the queer task of doing this fruitless soliciting. Nobody is more worried about her predicament than I am. If she doesn't know without further telling that the material objective of my existence is to enable her to pay her way, I don't believe it will do much good to reiterate that fact—any more than it did any good to point out the mess she was very probably letting herself in for.

We didn't go to the mountains, out of reluctance on my part to take the two days and to do the trip without paying for it myself. I couldn't have seen you in any event, since I don't leave my companion dangling for anything, however important to me. (It was made wholly clear to me that in no event do we go there together—which is all right, on the understanding that neither of us goes there at all.) I hope you will find the pack useful a few times this winter: it's better than any American contraption I know. If there's an Engineer Corps compass stowed in the thing somewhere, I should appreciate your mailing it to me before the winter's over.

>Hurriedly (to catch the mail),
>and always, affectionately yours,
>Follett.

St. Lucia
9 November, 1928

Dearest Anne:

It has been almost impossible for me to find time to write letters. And I don't for the life of me see how I can write the kind of letters that would make good reading! All day I mutter and putter over these articles for Waxman; then I walk for an hour or two, and then go to bed very early. And I haven't any ambition left to put on paper all the excitement, the descriptions, and the life of these islands. Whether I shall ever do it, I don't know; but I rather think I shall. And the heat is pretty bad to work against, so that I find my energy has all gone by the time I can get through what I have made an attempt to put through for the day.

Strange to think that today is the ninth of November! The old schoolmaster was out this morning budding his roses! And last night was so hot I couldn't sleep! And there are roses on the table, and I am in a powerful sweat this minute, though it is six o'clock at night, and quite dark. Things are so inconsistent here; early evenings like yours, roses, hot nights and mosquitoes.

We have been on this island for nearly a month, and have been living excellently well for ten shillings a day including meals. When we first landed we went to the hotel and paid twelve shillings a day; a lovely inn way up in the hills, and sloops that came in. That is where I got off my first article to Waxman. I sweat blood over it, and hope you will never see it. And I hope more that you will never see the next one—that is, if there is a next one.

I have lived here long enough to know that sickness is not an unheard-of thing, and that I should be very silly to squander away the letter of credit which I took away with me. So I cabled Follett sending a loving message from us both and asking him about the deposits. I have heard nothing from him since the last cheque last summer from Knopf. You know I saw K. the last day I was in New York and he cautioned me severely and emphatically not to let Wilson think we could get along without his financial help; K. swears that making our support a necessary part of his life is the only thing that may possibly save him. Knopf, you know, said he thought W. was unbalanced, and cited instances in the office. He was exceedingly kind to me, and said the trip was the only possible thing for me to do for a while, anyway.

Dean Lyman at my Bank in New Haven wrote me saying that no deposits had been made to my account, asking about Mr. Follett, who had given him to understand that deposits were going to be sent monthly, that bills had come in that couldn't be paid, etc. The cable which I sent to Follett on Perry Street was returned, so that is why I cabled Oxford hoping that he would look him up and convey to him that we needed his help.

We can't get to Tahiti without Follett's help. I think we can't now, although I am still waiting to get word from the steamship company about passage, etc. Of course we do want to get there. But we have the alternative of staying on one of these islands at a cheaper rate than we could stay at home, and I have also the chance of getting my stuff out which I shouldn't have at home—wherever that is. The stuff may get me a job. I am waiting to hear from Waxman about more articles; I shall have another one finished in a week or so. I am not telling this to Follett because I think he should know that he must, if he can, work for us, and help us along, a little, anyway. If we can make Tahiti, it means that we shall be off the map for thirty days; it means that we shall try for a cheap cargo boat, or the third class in a passenger boat, and I have got to have some money to stay there on, and get home with. I have had to ask for an advance on the house rent, asking the bank to borrow this for me; I didn't like to do this, but I don't dare to stay around here without it. Follett doesn't know this, I think; I do hope he will let us know what I can count on each month, and then I can have a draft sent here when I am in need, and I shall have enough for Sabra, too. Knopf also said that an intimate friend like you should make Follett feel that you expect him to look out for us, that of course he will, etc. Knopf feels very strongly about this, and I feel that he knows Follett really better than the rest of us; thinks he will go to the dogs unless you can make him feel this responsibility toward the family. So I feel, too.

Barbara is difficult, Anne. I wish she could live with you and Oxford for a while until you can discover what she needs most. She does exactly what she wants to do here, and I allow her to do so for any peace whatever. She needs a man to be her guardian; and if she can't have her father (I wish she could!) she must have someone else. I am naturally worried as to what her independence will land her in; but I can do nothing but wait and see. I think she needs a year away from me; she needs mental work, and hard work; and she needs someone to tell her what she must do. This is an easy place to go soft in, I know that; and I force myself into working with no clothes on, sweating unbelievably during the hottest parts of the day just so as not to fall into the tropical laziness. This trip is admirable for her, but she can't keep it up without harm, I think. You and Oxford must help me decide about her; whether her father will take her on; whether you and Oxford will (you have enough!), whether you think Ralph would do it. I should have a guardian made legally for her; and with a man, I think she will come out all right. She is a great person, but the last two years have made a different person out of her, and I fear for her future. I should like her to forget me for a while, for she has been so close to me that she can see me only very critically; and she bitterly complains about me to my friends. This is a wrong attitude, for one thing; she doesn't see me clearly or with perspective, and she makes it difficult for my friends. Moreover, it is the kind of thing that is not honorable or decently becoming.

13 November, Tuesday Morning

This is a sort of a continuation. Yesterday I worked all day getting my second article written, and I am very tired today.

Came Oxford's cable, for which thank him. I cannot yet believe that Follett will let us down unless he is really ill, and down and out himself. And I shall still expect to hear from him. Knopf said there was no reason why he shouldn't get some kind of job, that he was a good editor, and a good stylist. I should like to hear from you about him and what is happening.

Shall I return or not? Can I do anything by returning now? Should

I get back, take on Sabra, and face the music, by which I mean try to get a teaching job in a school in Boston where I can have Sabra? am I dodging things this way?

We are both in good health. I went flop for a while after landing, and thought the "trops" had certainly got me. But since then I have put on six pounds, and should have more were it not that we walk up hills for miles. Bar and I walked sixteen miles over the mountains last Sunday, and I suppose the thermometer was anywhere from 85 to 90! Sweat!

I am quite serious about Bar, Anne. She must have a man to look out for her. Please help me about this, for it must be arranged as soon as I get back. She maintains that she has perfect freedom, and we can't argue in hotels and boarding houses. But her freedom she takes for license. The life on the islands fascinates her, and she will bring back much; but she has the habit of using her brain, of using it hard, of being with intellectual people (there are none here), and she needs those same hard contacts again.

I am getting myself into pretty good shape. The writing is coming easier, and I am sure I should never be doing it at home: I should have to be teaching. And the writing may get me a better job. Knopf thinks it bad for Follett to think I can earn the money, and I think it probably is. And I really can't. I am writing under extreme difficulty—the worry and the heat. But I don't for a moment regret coming.

I must go to work now. Please write me at Barbados on receipt of this. I think then I may get it, for I shall probably be there until the end of the month. And then I think Martinique. A dollar a day at the French Is. and from there I can get a cheap steamer straight to Tahiti if I can get to Tahiti at all. But write me at Barbados. Or send any word there. And give me some advice as to my returning.

You have all my love and devotion.

Helen

This appears to be the second page of a letter to Anne from about mid-November 1928. "Prescott" is William H. Prescott's 1847 book, A History of the Conquest of Peru.

[...] There is almost no hope of our going to Peru unless something breaks during the next month, unless Follett comes through with something. Or unless by hook or crook we can earn a passage on a cargo boat, as I think I mentioned before. That is doubtful but not totally out of the horizon. Bar has been reading Prescott and has the Peru fever; I have always had it, and thought it would be a great change for her letters. It goes without saying that the truth of the matter is we are homesick for the mountains!

And, unless Follett helps out a bit I really think the Tahiti thing is off the map. I don't mind landing there broke because I think I could earn something by that time, and living on all the French islands is cheap now, about four shillings a day. But I shall do nothing about it all except to get sailing schedules unless I feel that I am safe in trying it. And if Follett really gets no job by that time, a month, say, from now, it seems to me as if I should come back and try to support him. What is he doing that he can live at all? He felt so badly you know about Sabra and my mother—well, it is all inconceivable to me. And do let him know that we are still counting on him, and still waiting to hear that he is going to help us some, anyway.

You know we haven't had a cent from him since the last cheque from Knopf in the middle of the summer.

I really expected encouraging news by this time; and I should now be planning for Callao and Tahiti for the December sailing. You see boats go only once a month, and it is necessary to plan right away for the next one, which, of course, I can't make.

Oxford was an angel to cable, but I must say it made me pretty low. Still, I had to know! Let Follett himself cable us if he has anything important to tell us. I wonder what he thinks we are living on!

Have been working all day; it's terribly hot, and I'm feeling low. Write me at Barbados; I'm trying to get Bar down to Trinidad and Demerara sending her in care of the Chief Engineer. And I'm trying to send her for the price of deck passage; she will write something for the boat. This is one reason I wanted to hear from Follett, for I shouldn't be sending her this way; nor should I be giving up Trinidad myself if I could help it. It will be cheaper for me to stay in Barbados and then go to Martinique, leaving the southern islands alone. So your cable came just in time; I felt there was no very good news. We have to go deck passage tonight to Barbados, which means—well I don't yet know what it means. But it means two dollars per day instead of eight. H.

[added in pen] Bar has written several times to Follett and has sent him stuff to sell, so far she has heard nothing.

Castries
St. Lucia,
November 13, 1928

Dear Norm:

Yo-ho-ho! and a bottle of rum! I don't know whether I am on my head or my tail. It's most awfullishly hot, and there's a breeze, so the green palms are tossing against a burning sky. Gosh! Were it not for my old A, I'd be in a pretty hard way. It dragged once, sure enough, but I think it is reinforced sufficiently now, and ought to hold. However, I am coolly and deliberately and consciously and wilfully putting my head in the lion's mouth—at six o'clock tonight. May V———— be good to me!

V———— has, by the way, been most marvellously good to me of late. Well, I needed her. I have been trailed by an old fool named Tucker, who wants to convert me, as it were (he doesn't know anything about V————, of course, but just got on to the fact that I wasn't quite respectful enough as regards his vile little church.) And H. is quite attached to this old fool; and the old fool is quite attached to H. !!!!!!! What next?

There have been exciting doings as regards Harley Paul. Very exciting. And H. is at present in the depths. Oh, well; I don't know whether I'm on my head or my tail. It's four bells in the morning (fourth engineer on watch aboard me old steamer, and third mate on deck). Me old steamer is, at this hour and minute, discharging cargo at the neighboring isle of Dominica. She'll be here later, and I'll see the old gang.

I wish I could write you something coherent. But my mind is, alas! pretty seriously tied up at present. I can't think of anything but my own affairs—the dragging of the A, the means of redragging it, V————, certain extraneous fringes, the advisability of bewaring of three persons, and so forth.

By the way, old dear: you know the advice you gave me in private about not trusting other white persons met in these wild latitudes? Well, thanks for that advice. I've stuck by it faithfully and firmly, which H. has not. That advice has come in damned handy more than once *already*.

By the by: the bo's'n of the S. S. ———————— is a loon. Don't let me forget to look out for him. Though I guess I'll look out without advice from you, hearty. I've certain rudiments of horse-sense.

Hi hi! But I'm happy, happy, happy. V———— and I have set out on a conquest of the universe. We've succeeded. I am firm in the face of appalling odds. You may not believe it, but the odds are terrifying. The universe does not yield to me—but it cannot daunt me.

    Your matey,
    B.

20 November, 1928

Dearest Anne:

If you think the other letter may do any good, send it to R. if you know where he is. I think it despicable of him to leave me in a hole like this with three other people on my hands. It is awfully embarrassing to have to leave all to Tyler, you know. Her school and clothes.

I've finished my second article for Waxman. You needn't mention them to Roy. It will be time enough when they come out, and this one may not go. And Oh Boy! I'm tired. It's nice to have Bar away, though. I can work better, and don't have to talk to a soul. The stuff must go tomorrow so I can get word by the first week in December. It means a lot to me whether he takes the second thing. He will probably take more, in that case.

I loved your letter which was here. But I don't like what you say about Edward, and hope you will send better news the next time you write.

You are the only one who can help get money out of Follett. It isn't so much for myself, Anne, but I can't support the gang. And what is more, I shouldn't have to. He must have some money to run the car and live in Maine. Must. Can't you wire him to send me some money right away. He should help us some out of whatever he has, I think.

There are no jobs here. Absolutely none. I'll try to write you a letter about darling St. Lucia after Wednesday, tomorrow. Even my back is broken tonight. Day after day of work from six to nine at night. But I must get this off to you so you can pass it on to Roy. I really want him to get on to his job and help us, and then I can help Sabra and my mother. Between you and me, I've borrowed on the house rent for three months. But you mustn't tell this. And so, of course, I can't pay the interest on the mortgage due in Feb. The house will have to be sold unless Roy comes across pretty soon.

Please try once more to get something definite out of him as soon as possible.

I loved your scheme of travel. Well, I guess it's up to me and Waxman. More later on in the week. Love, and devotion. H

A second letter written on the 20th, replying to a letter collected while mailing the first.

20 November, 1928
Barbados, B. W. I.

Dearest Anne:

I cannot believe that Roy would let us down so unless he is ill and can't work. He just isn't that kind of person. I cabled him you know, and the cable was returned. So that's that. Barbara has written him letters, and sent him little sketches, and has heard nothing.

We really need some help from him, and we have had none since the middle of the summer. Hildegarde got Barbara's clothes for her, and we lived on our friends in New Haven for several weeks. Bills are coming in for Sabra's school and clothes, too.

I can't keep going without help, Anne. That is, I can't support four people, and it doesn't seem the square thing to me that it all should come on me. After all, what have I done? Except fail as a wife? That is everything to Roy, apparently, but I don't believe he should extend his punishment so far as leaving us stranded now. I didn't mean to fail, and what's worse, I didn't know I had!

It would be even harder were Bar and I in New Haven. The nervous strain of living there would knock us both out, and the expense, too. We two are living here cheaper than I could get an apartment of three rooms in N.H. I don't want to come back because it means I shall have to go back to teaching, and how I dread that. I suppose I could have Sabra with me, but what should I do with Barbara. I feel as if I couldn't go on even down here.

There are no jobs on the islands. They are poor as poor. The teachers in St. Lucia get sixteen shillings a month. Colored teachers who live in thatched huts under a coconut palm.

I'm trying to write stuff for Waxman. I hate to do it, hate to expose myself, my life, and Barbara. And if I were getting any help from Roy I shouldn't have to. I should like to write up about the trip as an educational adventure, and I think I might have some fun doing that. But this tears my heart out. And I am dog tired.

I want to get to Tahiti. I want Bar to know Hall and Nordhoff, and I feel they are our friends. I'd rather use every penny to get there and then go stranded with friends. I can go from Martinique to Tahiti for something like a hundred dollars, each—that's second class, on a rotten little French boat. Some friends are trying to get us passage on a Canadian cargo boat. But if we don't hear soon, I'll try to go the middle of Dec. as there is nothing else to Tahiti for several months, and I should use up my money (someone, I don't know who, sent me a little money) by that time.

Barbara wants to get into the South Seas, though I think it is her excuse to go on the sea for a long time. She has gone down to

Demerara now under the care of the Chief Engineer of the Pathfinder. I couldn't afford the time or the money, and I think her getting away with the grand old Scotchman will help her. You've no idea how she has changed, Anne. She declares she has as much right to her freedom as her father has to his. Perhaps she has—but where do I get off? What about my freedom?

Whatever either you or Oxford advises me to do, you know I'll do it. Remember that. And remember, too, that a cable will get me. I am more than well known in St. Lucia, and at Barbados.

If you can get hold of Roy do tell him that I am counting on him for some help, anyway. He must be earning something, Anne. I can't believe it otherwise; and I can't believe he can know we are up against it unless we hear from him. Do I miss him Anne? You answer me that.

Have him cable me a foreign draft, Royal Bank of Canada Barbados, the minute you can reach him by wire or by anything else. Or he could cable money, I suppose direct through Western Union.

Don't lose a moment about this, will you? I shall have to leave this place for a cheaper place, and may be on my way to Martinique by the second of December. It is so hot down here that I lose all track of time, and can't get the hang of our being so near to December.

This is a dull letter. I'm dog tired, and can't eat. Hope I'm not getting malaria—it's down here. That would be a mess, if that happened. But I am sure things will be all right when you get hold of Roy and he understands the hole we are in.

I've expected, you know, news from Dean Lyman that deposits were coming in monthly, as Roy said. Lyman must think things are queer. Well, they are.

> Love to the whole tribe of blessed Meserveys, from
> Helen

The main part of a letter—to Mr. Oberg, according to Barbara: The Unconscious Autobiography of a Child Genius by Harold Grier McCurdy and Helen Follett (U. North Carolina Press, 1966). I don't agree—the letter of December 2nd suggests that it was Barbara's first to Mr. Oberg from Castries. Helen transcribed this one "from a frayed carbon copy, too faint to be read with pleasure" when sending material to McCurdy in the early 1960s.

ca. November 1928, from Castries, St. Lucia.

[...] The few who have not adopted modern costumes and customs seem to be the elderly women of high class—judging from their extreme nobleness of countenance and their cleanliness of dress as compared with the others. I have visited the Catholic church here several times and I have a queer fancy that the only persons who really and truly belong are those fine, middle-aged women. I sometimes step into the church during the afternoon before the evening service, just to watch. One of those gorgeous creatures sweeps along the aisle toward the altar, with a steady, slow, queenly gait. She kneels and prays upon the red velvet carpet. And she *belongs*. She wears a long, quaintly cut, flowing garment of rich purple cloth adorned with a marvellous pattern. This dress has a high neck and long sleeves, and a skirt which sweeps to the ground, and which is caught up on the side. Beneath it she wears a white petticoat trimmed with stiff lace, and around her neck she wears a bandana handkerchief of a plain colour. There are gold earrings in her ears, and she wears a red or blue bandana tied fancifully about her head. Really, she is quite noble and glorious to look at, as she sweeps up the aisle holding her rosary, and as she prays upon the red velvet carpet.

There are many of these people, and they all dress much alike. Some of the colour schemes are extraordinary, but always seem to show a certain kind of good taste. Purple seems to be the favourite colour, but there is also old rose, lavender, cream, dark red. Always it is a richly patterned material. It seems incredible that they should wear such thick clothing in this climate, but they must be used to it.

I have shed bitter tears, standing at the back of the church. There seems to be services all day long, and the whole town seems to be there. Between services there are still many natives sitting there with their rosaries. I stood at the door one evening during vespers. A poor woman, with nothing but a few rags about her, passed along the sidewalk with a big basket on her head. She took off the basket, and knelt upon the hard stone church-step, knelt there all through the service. A dog came along the sidewalk, sniffed the door, walked in. I held my breath. He walked up the aisle as if on tiptoe, and then lay down halfway up, and rested there through the whole service! Why?

Why do these people attend church all day long? Is it merely "something to do" in these peaceful islands? Is it fear of Hell? Is it actual piety? What is it that wrings their hard-won pennies from them into the collection dish? I have wept and wept about those pennies. I know just how hard-won they are, and what a penny means here to a native. For a penny one may purchase four big breadfruit. For a penny one may purchase a dozen oranges. I have watched these people dip their hands in the stoup of holy water, and cross themselves with it. And I know what vile, feverish water it must be by the time hundreds of people have dabbled in it. Ralph Blanchard has had actual experience of holy water visibly squirming with mosquitoes. Oh, how ghastly it all is!

And you should see the wayside shrines in these Catholic islands! There is one not far from here, along by a very muddy river. It is a sad little place of stone, in the midst of the cemetery; and within it—O God!—within it is a ghastly crucifix and pictures of Mary, with several other dreadful little images. Before these things are placed faded artificial flowers in dirty glasses. And the native women walk up those steps, take off their baskets, kneel for fifteen or twenty minutes before that shrine, and put their haypennies in the slot. Now, I don't condemn the images and flowers and crucifix. They are no doubt atrocious and even scandalous, but I don't condemn them. After all, these people have done the very, very best with them, and they mean something to them, it seems. I think the faded flowers very touching. I could weep bucketsful about the whole thing, anyhow. I saw one poor woman approach with her newly born baby in her arms, and, after kneeling, she rose and held up the baby, as if to show the holy Mary the very best she had to show. How touching—how ghastly touching—how uncannily touching it all is, anyhow.

The Catholic church in the town is a grandiose structure and very respectable, but there is another church near this shrine—a little hovel with a cross upon it. We went inside one day, H. and I. More little images, more faded flowers. H. approached the altar, but I could not bear to intrude. There was a sick candle burning in a dirty saucepan in a corner—there was the altar overhung with unbearable pictures of holy personages. Perhaps I am to blame but I feel dreadfully about such things. It is because I envy it so. As I said before, I should like to be one of those gorgeous Negresses, with their long dresses and their rosaries, who approach the altar in the town church, and kneel upon the red carpet. Happy, happy, happy that they are!

Yes, I envy anyone who can kneel for a half-hour upon a hard stone church step, and rise feeling happier than before. I envy anyone who can contribute a haypenny, feeling that it moderates their chances for Hell. I envy the trust, the faith in the presence of these mysterious beings in the presence of a mysterious country where they wander about in white robes and play upon harps . . .

I will continue this account of St. Lucia some other time.

        Sincerely your friend,

Written after her unchaperoned trip with Andrew Burt to Demerara (now part of Guyana on South America's northern coast), where Barbara "picked up a new and glorious acquaintance—the devil."

Castries
St. Lucia
December 2, 1928

Hi hi!

I ain't going to say "Such is life!" for the reason that it isn't. It just plain isn't, that's all. So I hereby change the password to "Such ain't life!" which is much truer. Because, as I said before, it just plain ain't. For one thing, it seems too good to be true that we are actually sailing from Martinique for Tahiti on the 15th of this month. It just can't be. "Such ain't life." For another thing, the trip I had a while ago—alone to Demerara and back—that was also too grand and glorious to be true. "Such ain't life." For a third thing—well, that concerns me and V——— alone. "Such ain't life." Now do you see?

I have picked up a new and glorious acquaintance—the devil. He and I are on very friendly terms. He stands by my helm and pilots my gallant bark in an east-south-west-by-northerly direction—which is an extremely jolly direction to go in. My A has been retrieved, and is holding famously. It didn't really drag so far as I thought; stress of weather just strained it a wee bit. Happy? I don't think I've ever, in my life before, had such inward peace as I have had of late. This minute and second, there are seventeen particularly malicious mosquitoes around my ankles, and they are a bit distracting—but that's just external, if you know what I mean, Pooh.

Well, how's things? Have there been any skewners in since the *Mina*? I have seen several three-masters out of N. S. down this way, but I am interested in the engines at present. Not that I've deserted the old sails, ye knaow—but when there's a steamer about that I have been aboard of before, I usually go for her. As one of my engineers put it: "Schooners may be pretty to look at 'n' all that; but they've got no *innards*." Which is the truth. But oh, you S-C F—between Trinidad and Demerara we passed a full-rigged ship!!!!! She's a German training ship, and she was holding her own with us until a squall came up, when she drew ahead very slightly. I nearly went off my head. But the breeze dropped down, and very slowly we left her behind, and the last we saw of her was her sails head-on to us, leaning whitely out of the fog.

"Such ain't life," Norman, such it ain't. Good luck! Farewell!

      The devil's mate,
      Barboo.

Castries
St. Lucia
December 2, 1928

Dear Mr. Oberg:

It seems incredible, does it not?, that I should actually be writing to you from this quaint little West Indian town. It likewise amazes me when I realize that this is the 2nd of December, and there are roses and green leaves out the window. It is hard to know just what to write. I can hardly dare to venture forth upon a description of these islands, because I could not describe them did my life depend on it. Or, were I to describe where we have been and what we have done—that would look rather like a steamer schedule. Enough to say that we have been having a glorious time, travelling up and down and back and forth among these beautiful islands; and that we sail tomorrow or within the next few days for the neighboring island of Martinique; that we stay there till the 15th, and then sail by steamer for Tahiti, away in the South Seas! Doesn't that all seem incredible?

The trip to Tahiti will involve about a month at sea, in the wide Pacific. I am looking forward immensely to that. I have never been at sea half long enough. And this will be the real sea, too—out of sight of land for days and days and days, instead of sailing among hundreds of little green islands all the time. Yes, it will be grand. Perhaps we'll get into a typhoon or something.

Well, it seems funny to wish anyone a "Merry Christmas" when there are roses on the bushes instead of icicles; but all the same I do wish you a merry one, and the best of luck besides. You may write to us Care of James Norman Hall, Papeete, Tahiti, Society Islands. Any letter addressed thus will reach me sometime in the far future.

    So long for the present,
    Barbara.

Tenant's Harbor
Maine
December 14, 1928

Dear Oxford:

Thanks no end for sending over the rucksack and contents (it arrived, oddly, a day or two ahead of your note). I don't believe I shall have a chance to use the pack before spring, and it would have been a pleasure to think of you—and perhaps Edward—using it a few times this winter. What I really did want was the compass. However, probably it was simpler for you to send the whole mess; and thanks. Everything came in good shape. I'm enclosing the amount of postage that was on the ticket.

Since I last wrote you, I have received from Barbara a carbon copy of one—evidently not the first—of her Harper letters, from an address which I understand from the Pictorial Review people to be superseded. I mention this to correct my earlier remark about knowing no address for the travelers.

I would send my love to Anne if I thought she would have it, but since she won't I suppose I had better keep it to myself. I shall be thinking of you a lot in the holidays: I always feel specially near to you then, somehow, and I feel it coming on again.

    Yours,
    Follett.

The correct spelling of the French cargo ship is Louqsor.

Fort-de-France, Martinique
18 December, 1928

Dear Anne:

We are waiting to be allowed on board the Luoqsor; we have given up our bed worth eighty cents a night, and are bumming around till we can take up our home for three or four weeks on board ship. It is a cargo boat, and the second class is not very inviting. However, the agent here is nice to us, and has spoken to the Purser, and is going to speak to the Captain this afternoon. This will probably mean that we can have a cabin to ourselves (six-berth cabins), anyway. The agent has also sent on to Marseilles, the home office of the Messageries Maritime, a letter I wrote yesterday asking to be allowed to write a folder for the line and to be refunded our passage money if said folder proved acceptable. We'll see what will happen: the second class fair went up from eighty-three dollars to one hundred dollars. Which leaves me pretty short. But it is the best investment I can make of the little money I have, so I think. As I wrote you I am counting on something to break my luck at Tahiti, something that will serve to give a definite direction to my course. There is nothing here in the islands that can do that: humanly speaking, they are pretty low, educationally speaking, they don't exist, physically speaking, they are gorgeous, and natively speaking, they are fascinating.

We are down to the real tropical tramp condition, the real American bumming state. Here at Martinique, we could afford only a bed for eighty cents a night, and we have eaten all our meals on the benches of the park—fruit for breakfast, amounting to four or five cents; cheese, biscuits, chocolate, and perhaps a stick of nougat for lunch, and the same for supper. We have had three meals aboard vessels here. At St. Pierre, there was a superb Danish bark, three masts, two square rigged; beautiful and alluring. Here, at Fort-de-France, there are three northern four-mast schooners from the north; and we have dined on the Kohler of Baltimore, in a truly sumptuous fashion. There is also a four-masted bark, three masts square rigged, which is a Belgian training ship. We came here at the right time for the sailing vessels, for they are bringing coal down from the States. And even now we could go to Haiti on the Kohler; but we have decided against changing our plans now, especially in view of the possibility of writing a folder that may give us back our two hundred and the chance of getting on further on that line. She goes to France, you know! And maybe I'm playing for that—I know that such an idea has entered my mind more than once.

We have climbed Pelée. We have spent several days in her town where no English is spoken. We have bought all our food there at the market, in French, we stayed at an Inn, indescribable as to "local atmosphere" for forty cents a night; we have had two dresses made for sixty cents each including material; and we have done it all in French. We have learned more French here than in any number of French lessons—I am sure of that. The night before we climbed Pelée we stayed at a boulanger, and saw all the bread baking done at night—a marvellous sight—all done by the light of two or three bougies—naked colored bodies leaping into troughs of dough, kneading dough with their elbows—baking it on long shovels. More French vocabulary. We climbed the mountain with two native boys, superb country; too much rain and fog for entire visibility; and we were not allowed to climb the cone which was too slippery. I am enclosing *une violette de la montagne* which we picked way up on the side. I think I have an article in my head on the teaching of French which may prove interesting. Then back to Fort-de-France.

I am now in the office of the American Consul. Bar has taken herself off to the schooner, Kohler; and we are both waiting to be allowed to go on board the Luoqsor this afternoon.

I want to get this off to you, so you can begin a letter to me at Papeete. It will take so long for mail to get there. And I feel that you must help me decide some things. I may have sold two articles; I have not heard from them. And I have asked the bank to try to get hold of Mr. Follett and cable me some money here. Nothing has happened. I haven't enough to get home, and I don't know that I should come home, anyway. That is where you must help me. This is incoherent, but here are few of the things I'd like help and advice about.

Mother and daughter somewhere on their travels

Is there a chance that Follett is going to support us? Is this chance any more sure if I should return than if I should stay in the Pacific islands, somewhere?

If Follett is refusing to help us—is there any reason for it? Is he trying that as a way for my letting him go?

Has he any right to support someone else and refuse to help us?

Should I get a lawyer to see him and convince him that he is obliged to help us?

And what about Sabra? Shouldn't I come back for her sake? Or would it be, in your opinion, all right to have Tyler bring her to the Philippine islands, and then stay on myself.

Well, I could go on forever, but what's the use? Anyway, I haven't money enough at the moment to go back to the States if I wanted to, but I can live on the French islands for an incredibly small amount. Do you realize we haven't had a cent from Follett since the middle of the summer? And that I do think he should look out for Barbara and Sabra. And do know, Anne, that I cannot support four people in the States; and that I am convinced that he should be made to contribute something. Please try to get something out of him, and have it sent to Dean Lyman at the Union and New Haven Trust Company, for I am writing him now to cable my money at Tahiti.

I shall try to get a MMS. for a book written at Tahiti. Bar and I are going to try one together, about this trip, how it was done, the help we have had, the people we have lived with. Our need of economy has really sent us to live with the people, and become part of their life.

This island is the filthiest place I have ever struck—a human sewer runs down the gutter of every street, and the stench is horrible. The French islands are so different from the British in this respect. This is a rich island, but filthy with fruit and human refuse floating down the streams; the food is horrible, and the mosquitoes offensive. Yet I am delighted to be here, though I long for the sea and some fresh air now.

Our love to you all. And write me at Papeete, Tahiti, pretty soon, so I'll get some idea what you think I should do. I wish you were with me; I can think of almost no one else to whom this real bumming trip would appeal; and, let me tell you, this *is* a real bumming trip, a little more so than I really like! H.

But my funny-bone is intact; and my health O.K. So———

On board the *Luoqsor*
23 December, 1928

Dear Anne:

Tomorrow some time we stop at Colon, and shall be there long enough to get off the boat for a while, mail some letters, and get generally straightened out before the three more weeks of the sea and then, Tahiti. Things are all so beautifully vague from now on, and Tahiti is ahead of us like some queer dream that may turn out happy and that may turn out evil. As Bar said last night: "the less our money becomes, the farther away we go." Which is true: I am scarcely aware that we shall be so very far away, so much farther than the West Indies! And, as yet, we have no way at all of getting away from the place! A woman on board who lives there tells me that ten or twelve dollars a month will give us a cottage, and that a dollar a day will feed us both. Well, I'm not taking anyone's word for such things; three months in the West Indies have done some things to me.

I am writing again, and Bar will send something off at Colon. I have two articles not heard from; this will make the third. And when we get to Tahiti, Bar and I are going to write a book together—at least, she hasn't quite promised to do so, but I think she will. I thought a mother-daughter book might catch on, having her write great lots of description, and I do a lot of the education stuff. I don't know how it will come out but I think the idea is good.

You know that mail takes forever to get to Tahiti, so I hope you will write to me as soon as you can. Many things will have to be decided during the next few months—what I shall do with Sabra, whether I shall return or not, whether Follett has abandoned us for good and doesn't expect to support us at all. This last, if you can find out, will help me a good deal in making my plans. You see, Tyler is coming to Europe, I think in the spring, and that means something must be worked for Sabra, either Tyler must bring her to me, or I must go back to her. Don't you want to bring Sabra to me at Tahiti?

It is hot today, and they say that Tahiti is having its hottest weather. And I don't like the weather! We've struck the hottest weather at every island. Christmas at sea! The first Christmas away! And it has always been such a lovely day with us, such an important day. Last Christmas there was something wrong, something not quite honest in the atmosphere, and I didn't have the slightest idea what it was all about, until that fateful telephone rang at two in the morning, and Roy's voice answering and saying: "I tried to, but I couldn't." Never can I get those words out of my mind.

Well, I suppose you think it is easy for me to forget all that, to get going fresh and new, to pretend that life is grand and great and exciting, not too easy, Anne. There is something always lacking, something I always miss. Something has happened to crack the universe for me, and it is hard going with so little to go on. Really! I work all the time. And, at Martinique, it was very different, because I had to save every sou for our passage. Did I tell you of our forty-cent bed, and our fruit and biscuits which we bought and ate out-doors. A bit romantic and all that, but it is not so easy to work and have so little to work on! Really!

But, Anne, I'd rather anything than back at New Haven teaching brats in school, or the old cooking, teaching, house-keeping combination. I could do that for love, perhaps, but not from necessity. So you see why I need your advice.

The blue Caribbean, so blue, so hot, the prow of the old boat kicking up schools of flying fish, iridescent in the sun; the passengers who speak French, or Dutch, or Swedish—so many going to Tahiti, some sick of the fogs of London, seeking fortune in copra, wanting to live simply without "worries" as one man said. All seeking something in the coral islands of the Pacific; a Swedish honeymoon couple, beautiful to look at, eager, enthusiastic, full of faith and belief in the coral islands. Out for life, life that is simple that makes living worth-while. Some believe that they can pick up a copra trade immediately, and they have very little money; and some have not enough to go home on, should there be an explosion of their dreams and hopes. Rather sad, and somewhat depressing, but they are buoyant, so why should I worry?

I planned to cable you for Christmas that you might know that I am more with you than with anyone else. But I find I can't afford it, and that you should get this small note by New Years, anyway.

Ellen would love this. I wish she were with us. All our dinners for weeks to come are on the forward deck—chickens, beef steer, goslings for Christmas. Pens of lambs, too. I like them all better where they are than in hash on the table. But the French love to eat, and how they do it! Bar despises the French, everything about them, including their language. Martinique was a filthy island, and the French are a dirty lot—that's true. But I like the language. I have finished reading *Sapho* which the American consul made me a present of when I departed!!

I hope to find a thatched cottage at Tahiti, where Bar and I can work. Harley Paul will be there for a few days in March on Bar's birthday, he hopes. He's been an angel to me, and I am quite happy when he is round to play with me. I wish I could go to Yokohama with him, for he was born there, and I can't imagine any more fun than parading around there with him. But I can't even think so far ahead as that. And it may be just as well.

Some day Anne, I want you to go away with me, will you?

Helen

There are no letters from January 1929 in the Columbia archive, and relatively few until the summer, so we must rely on Helen's books for news: Magic Portholes *for an account of the month-long voyage from Martinique through the Panama Canal to Tahiti; and* Stars to Steer By *for their first month in the South Seas.*

Mr. Oberg will have looked in vain for Barbara's essays in Harper's. *She sent in one piece that wasn't good enough, apparently, and we will soon learn that Helen stopped her from sending in a second. And to continue traveling they were forced to spend Barbara's $500 advance, which weighed on their minds for some time.*

February 3, 1929.

Dear Barbara:

[...] Speaking of travel, you are surely doing some great things in that line. I have done a little travelling myself, although none of it has taken me to any but the universally rather well known parts of the world. I am looking forward with pleasure to the chance of following you in your interesting travels, by the kind aid of "Harper's Magazine," where your Grandma tells me your account of them is to be published. It may be that the first papers have already appeared, but I have not yet had a chance to go to the Library, to look. Even if the beginning is not in the current number, I can find the back ones in certain drawers where they are filed for reference, later to be bound in book-form.

[...] I have lately had a letter from your Grandma who as you no doubt know is now back at 20 Wyoming Street, Boston, from her recent visit in Providence, where I called on her. She is getting along surprisingly well for so old a lady, after what she has gone through. I have sent her your Tahiti address, which she did not yet have, when here. If any mail for you arrives there after you have left, it will no doubt be forwarded to your new address.

[...] Please let me hear from you, when you can spare the time.

Yours sincerely,

On sending things to Waxman at the Pictorial Review, Helen writes: "now he has, already one about which I haven't heard," which I think means that he now had four articles, and Helen was still waiting for his reaction to the third.

3 February, 1929

Dearest Anne:

I don't think I could go on without these letters from you. The news wasn't too encouraging, but your whole belief in me is the one thing that matters. For, I can tell you, my darling, I have horrid fits of not seeing how in the name of heaven or hell I can go on! I am sending Waxman another thing by boat next Tuesday; now he has, already one about which I haven't heard. If this new one about our learning to speak in French in Martinique doesn't go, I guess I am through. I can't leave this island, anyway, for Dean Lyman at the bank tells me that no money has come through from Follett. He wrote him a registered letter in order to get his signature, which he did get. So I guess the Bank is disgusted with him, too.

Here are a few things that have occurred to me: (1) If I were not away, he would not be having the chance to live exactly as he wants to in Maine and doing what he wants to do, which is writing; for he would have to be hustling somewhere to support us in New Haven or thereabouts. (2) I am glad he is getting back his health, and I will give him about two months more in which to finish the job and make his hundredth attempt to make a living by writing. (3) And if at the end of two months he is still in Maine, making no more attempt than he is now to help take care of us, then I shall get someone to call his legal attention to the fact that he will have to get a job somewhere and have a certain income for us. (4) If he is well physically and mentally, he cannot have any legal excuse to dodge his responsibilities. (5) I do not propose, unless he is mentally or physically incapable himself—in either case I will do anything in the world—to take a job in New York and so absolutely go to pieces myself, and, at the same time, lose all contacts with my children. (6) I wish you would help me to get the house made over to me; there are bills all the time on the place which are sent to me, and the confusion causes everyone to complain. Roy has said over and over again that he would make over the house to me, and now I think he should do so. All that has to be done is this: a note to Mr. MacDonald, William Hotchkiss, Real Estate Agent, New Haven, and ask him to make out the papers to be sent to Mr. Follett for his signature. (Moreover, Anne, rumor has come to me that Whipple is going to play for the house, next—this came from New York.) And Follett is the kind of fool that may fall for it. (7) The tenants like the house but want some things done to it; which I can't do until I get some help. (8) Andrew Jackson, an old Dartmouth man, an old friend of mine, located at Rockaway, New Jersey, Eastern Iron Ore Company, is a lawyer who would do anything for me without a noise, without money; he would give me advice if I asked him. (9) I don't like the lawyer business but, Anne, I can not think it right for me to be shoved into New York to kill myself trying to make a living for four people, while he, in perfect health, tries again to write under just the conditions he has always wanted—he shall have his chance again, but sooner or later he should face his responsibilities like a man, and get a job, even if he doesn't want one. (10) I don't for a moment believe he couldn't get some job if he tried, even if it wasn't what he wanted.

I have come to the conclusions above because of various reasons. I don't think that physically I can get a job that I can hang on to. And more than that, I don't think it is good for Follett to be allowed to get off so easily. I will work of course and help all I can, but he will have to get a job, too, and give up this idea that he can write and support—how many now?—on his writing. Barbara's stuff is not coming through well. I have refused to let her send her second installment. This means that I may have to pay Harper back his five hundred dollars. She can't seem to get going, as I wish she would. You've no idea what an effect this whole business of her father has had upon her. And the only thing that I think will save her is to have a guardian legally appointed—Oxford, or Ralph, if either one will accept—and get her back to do some studying. Norman Hall is in town now and I think he will help me plan some things for her to do here. But I am so handicapped because I can't afford to get around. We can't take trips into the back country, to the place where the pearl divers work, etc. Not now, at any rate. I shan't leave here until Barbara gets some material, anyway. She thinks she can write better when she gets back, and perhaps she can. She has certainly seen

Polynesian Life enough, but there are many things you can't write about, if your aim is artistic writing.

So, darling Anne, my plans are still indefinite. I'm not going to leave here for a while, anyway. It may be that I can crawl along to Samoa, or later, the Philippines, but I can't do anything unless my stuff has sold. Traveling is expensive, if it is only by schooner; living here is cheap. Which is what makes me believe that Follett is lucky. It might be advisable for me to go back, and live in the house again, so that Follett would see his responsibilities in front of him, which he couldn't dodge so easily as he is dodging them now.

I'm willing, Anne, to do my share, for everybody's sake, but if Follett is well and sane, I am not willing to do his share, too, if he can be made to do it himself. This is all very demoralizing to Barbara; she thinks it very picturesque and striking of him to be allowed to evade his job toward us, and get away with it, throwing, thus, the whole thing on me!!

This island is heavenly in physical beauty. Humanly, it is a queer mix-up of Chinese, Tahitians, French. Loving is nothing but picking out the brown girl you want. I can tell you yarns. Follett et al. should be here, where it is done—with the exception that living is so cheap, that no one evades the job of contributing to his children, no matter where they are located, and they are very apt to be scattered widely. We've been out to Vairao in the country, climb[ed] the mountains (in my union suit) beat[ing] our way through the tropical bush of bananas, plantains, and oranges, and coconuts. I took, at the request of the family, a picture of a dead baby, half Chinese and half Tahitian, in a native hut; I smoked with the Chief of the District, and drank his wine. He made me a present of the dancing dress—the Hula-hula—and quantities of beads. He is a half-caste, and not too pleasant to look at because he has elephantiasis!

Do write me again. I must have letters from you. Must, Anne, because, although my sense of humor is on the up-grade, I still have moments of horror.

        Love to you all, from Papeete,— Helen

TO THE SEA (1927–1929)

The following was to Ellen Meservey. Barbara got up to something that Helen thought scandalous in Tahiti, but exactly what it was is not clear.

Papeete, Tahiti
Society Islands
February 28, 1929

Dear Ellen:

"Other Ding" wrote me a letter, describing eloquently the snow and frozen pipes and plumbing difficulties, and whatnot. How unreal that sounds down here: Flowers are growing luxuriantly here, the sun is shining, and jiminy! ain't it hot? Oh no, I guess not. We swim in the luke-warm waters of the Pacific Ocean!

Your little telephone adventure had all the atmosphere of a mystery yarn in embryo. But I myself have mysteries to recount, not by mail, but by spoken words—someday in the future. You must know all sorts of things happen in Tahiti that wouldn't *dare* to be true up north. Why, you even believe in the Devil down here!

I spend my time thus: sitting here writing like a fiend while the sweat runs down my neck in streams; strolling along the quiet little streets of the town, watching languid-eyed Chinese babies lolling on doorsteps; wandering from the neighbouring atolls—little, two-masted trading schooners, fragrant (if you can call it fragrance!) with copra; taking brisk walks for miles and miles up the valleys into the mountains; or getting happily down into the ponderous gizzards and other anatomy of the two mail steamers that come in here once a month, one from Australia and one from 'Frisco. You know, the anatomy of those steamers is most wonderful—beautiful to look at besides merely mechanically interesting—I never get tired of 'em. They are quite alive somehow, you know.

You feel sure that they are alive when you are at sea with 'em. It is beautiful to explore among all the various gadgets, oojars, oojar-gepivvys, and ookum-snivvys. They are all going about their work very nicely and independently; though, to be sure, not always so nicely. You see the enormous cranks walloping around about the shaft, whirling it by their own mad violence; the piston rods that drive them flashing and leaping; the eccentrics busy with their quiet, graceful dance. 'Tis a marvellous contraption or contraptions—there's no doubt about that. To be sure, you always want to see the things that you can't—the insides of cylinders, of boilers, of condensers. But that's the way of human nature, isn't it?

By the by, your honourable mother was reading my palm (or trying to) last summer on one of the hills over Sunapee lake; and she predicted that I was to have some sort of very startling and really adventurous adventure. Of course, that got me beautifully excited, because I love adventure, and never could have enough of it. Well, you tell her that I have already had a pretty wild and glorious adventure; and tell her likewise that before three weeks are up I'm likely to have by far the wildest one I ever had in my life before!! Perhaps there *is* something in palm-reading, after all, though I never used to think so. Likewise, tell her that I haven't seen as yet any sign of various persons which she mentioned in this palm business. But the adventure is unquestionable.

My love to everybody in the Merservey tribe. Unfortunately I can't write to them all—they are too numerous. "Various other jobs too numerous to mention," as an old engineer said. Well, that's like you people!

      With love,
      Barbara

P. S. Don't let school tame you down, Ellen! It's dangerous, you know. I shall be disgusted if I find that you are as tame as most that cleave to school. Be wild! Have adventures! If you knew how extraordinarily wild I was, you would get a good laugh out of it. Why, I make friends with the devil all the time. B.

Cyril Crossland (1878-1943), the son of painter James Henry Crossland, was born in Sheffield, England. He devoted his life to collecting and studying marine flora and fauna, spending much of the 1920s in the South Pacific.

Apia, Samoa, 13 April

Dearest Anne:

Here is my last address, but by the time this gets to you, we shall be gone, off to Honolulu. Write me there in care of the Bank of Bishop and Co., Ltd. There is such a complication of reasons for our being here, and for our going there that the story will have to wait a while.

I adore the islands, and for some reason, Samoa is the loveliest of all. Only for some reasons, however. I am going to spend a week living in a thatched Samoan house, sleeping on a mat on the floor, eating native food, and trying to understand the people, somewhat. They are pure Polynesians here which you can't find in Tahiti. But I love Tahiti, and would go back there in a minute if it weren't up to me to make a last stab for a job. In all the ten or eleven islands there are no jobs! Not literally, of course. I could work in a store, but

I couldn't get enough for two people to live on. And there are interesting things to do in Tahiti if I didn't need money to keep going on.

Sudden was our departure for this island. Between us and Dr. Tyler, Bar has had a smash—emotional and nervous. It was bound to come sometime when the condition was right for it. And it came to a climax in Tahiti. Follett's attempt to smash his family for his own individual freedom has worked one hundred percent. Bar is now the victim. I can't tell details.

On the French boat to Suva, Fiji, I was robbed of all my money; had taken cash because I was landing on Good Friday, and wanted a passage to Apia. Great difficulties, because the last small cheque was not enough to get me to Samoa. So I had to yell for help.

We are going to leave here May 10 for Honolulu. I have hopes there of a job. Yale colony, Bishop Museum, and I have letters to friends there. And the climate is fine. Which means that by the first of June I should know whether or not I can spend the summer and winter there. Only four days from San Francisco, and sailing from Honolulu everywhere in the world. I hope things work out there so I can get a job, and have Sabra with me. I must have her, if possible.

I don't want to go back to New Haven. If Follett can do nothing for me down here, how in Heaven can he do anything for me up there. Will act, however, on your advice. Would he get a job with a regular salary were I to give him his divorce? I must have his help if I can get it. Bar needs help, badly. And I cannot get money enough for all of us; doubt if I can for any of us. Haven't heard from but one thing which sold. I am, however, saving the stuff for a book which I hope Knopf will be interested in. Bar has gone to pieces temporarily, and can't write.

Ask Oxford about the following: Crossland is a coral expert working on a lagoon in Tahiti. He is collecting for U. of Cal. and for Cambridge. Now I can go to Papeete, live in a cottage (ten dollars a month, lots of room for you) on the loveliest coral beach and work with him in his bamboo and coconut palm laboratory. Would Dartmouth be interested in a collection of coral? This is what Crossland writes to me; what he says about Yale would apply to Dartmouth equally well:—

"If you feel like taking on a real heavy job, but one certain to be of value, and make a *serious* collection for Yale Museum, I had better warn you it means a lot of hard work (and lots of pleasure, too). My 1925-6 collection came to about a cubic ton and cost £20 to get to Cambridge. So you might write and ask them if they would value them enough to pay freight—say £15 and the small expenses of packing. I'd mention there are other things than corals of scientific value, e.g. you might take on the wims or slugs, lovely things I do assure you. Those of my 1925-6 collections are being named at the British Museum and Edinburgh respectively, so there would be no trouble in their getting the names, unless they found new species, not at all impossible. Other groups, Zoophytes, etc., being also named at Brit. Mus. Hydroids at Copenhagen, Seaweeds by Setchell, Berkeley, Cal. and so on. You'd have to come to live hereabouts to do the thing in this style. The house next door will be vacant in a month or two....... Perhaps you do not want to take things quite so strenuously; I think Yale would like *specimens*, though these have not the scientific value of a whole collection. I wish I knew who is the Chief Biologist there. One could send a series illustrating reef formation, reef rock, coral modifications and so on ....."

I think that would be lots of fun, and would, somehow, justify my trip, if nothing else does. I can and will do it for Dartmouth or Yale, if I have enough money to live on there. It doesn't take much, to be sure; but, as things are now, it is pretty uncomfortable going. I shouldn't get paid, probably, for the work. See if D. would care (possibly they would care enough to give me a few hundred dollars for the year's work). I couldn't go wrong working under Crossland's direction. He is an Englishman, and really knows corals. Oxford perhaps, and you too, know him by name.

Don't you think it is time that Follett got a man's job, and stopped fooling around with his pen? Can't anyone jerk him out of that kind of thing before a lawyer does it? A year is enough for him to fiddle around in Maine trying to write. I don't want to come back until he has been given his chance. But I haven't the slightest idea of calmly going into a N. Y. office to work while he is playing around in Maine. This trip, so far as he goes, is the easiest thing that could have happened to him. He would have had to support us if we had stayed at home. And he could not have just gone off with his pen and his girl.

I can get to Honolulu third class. But I shall have to get work immediately, and so will Bar. If she can.

I could collect any number of things on this island if there were any way of getting them home. But every shilling counts for me, and I am afraid of the duties. The tapas here are gorgeous; I shall try to get some of those. Write me at Honolulu. Are you going to England?

Helen

TO THE SEA (1927–1929)

10 May, Pago Pago
American Samoa

Dear Anne:

I wonder if you and Oxford have gone, are going? What fun for you both, and I do hope you pull it off.

We arrive in Honolulu on the seventeenth—I think I wrote you. We must, Anne, find out where we stand. We cannot go on like this. Barbara has gone to some kind of pieces, emotional, and physical.

I do not believe any of us is doing right to let Follett go on like this and I mean, now, unless I hear from you that he is going to help us (or from him, which I doubt) to throw the entire family on him. And if necessary get hold of a lawyer who may make some impression on him about the obligations he owes to the family.

I'm sorry if you think I have fallen down on the job. I've sweat blood over my writing. I know well enough that I have an interesting book in the making, and I am doing some of the best writing I have ever done. Bar, even, says she is flabbergasted. But I can't go on, unless I have some help from Follett. If I return it will be all the harder for him, for I shall certainly make him, somehow, take care of the children.

Barbara has gone to pieces. Her writing job is not anywhere near finished. She has lost interest in things, in living, in writing. She says, herself, she is "homesick." But there's a reason. She has missed her father terribly; and has discovered that she needs someone else to take his place. A Scotchman, a fine man, her father's age, the chief engineer on a Canadian boat we were on. A problem which she needs other advice upon, than what I can give her.

I cannot write and get a job too. If I can get any help from Follett, I think I can persuade Barbara to stay away a while longer, perhaps get her to re-trace the trip, a thing which I want to do very much, thus making a unit out of the thing, piling up backward impressions. Then she would finish her job, and I should have a book to offer someone, and I should feel as if the trip had not been a complete failure. As it is now......

It has been the greatest event of my life even with the struggles, and they have been, and still are, awful. But I can't keep on with Barbara going to pieces this way. A tragic thing, Anne. Homesick and nowhere to go. So she wants to see again this one man who is in Montreal, I think, this person who has "fathered" her. You see what I am up against! I can't send her to him; and he can't possibly take care of her, so I should say. He is not married, and is on the Canadian Aviator cargo ship. I liked him so well that I allowed Bar to go down to S. America with him while I stayed in Barbados last

Fall. And she has learned "engines" because of him. Bar, of course, thinks I am her enemy in all this.

I beg you, Anne, to give me some advice as soon as possible. Unless I find work in Honolulu, and Bar, too, I cannot stay there very long, for it is expensive. Shall I come back, see Follett, and find out what he intends to do for us? Shall I try to stay away longer with Bar, and borrow money on my house to do it in order that she may finish her job, and that I may have some something to show for the trip?

I detest the very hope of coming back. I love the natives in these islands, especially in Apia, Samoa. I have lived in their houses, slept on their floors with them, eaten with them. And I have made an attempt at their language. I'd never go back, if I had my way! And it still seems incredible to me that it is Barbara who is dragging me back, and who is such a drag here. It doesn't seem true, even now as I write it. She will regret it so much, especially in the light that she has no home to go to, and that the chances that this man will take care of her are so very slight—in my opinion.

Barbara must have, you can see, a guardian. She is in a critical condition, and likely to do anything from running away to suicide. And my advice is not what she wants. She must have a man to help her.

Shall I try to get the cottage again, and try to re-organize myself and my family up there where there is some real climate?

Please write to me at once. Honolulu is an easy place for mail, and we must know where we stand before we can go on. I have written two more things but have not heard from them.

I have a horror about going back. Even this step toward America—this Naval station, white uniforms and all, this lovely family—the Doctor here—all these things make me so homesick, Anne. Whereas, the farther away I am from homes, families, houses that resemble my own—the happier I am. An Apian *fale*, a coconut-thatched house, a bamboo house in Papeete—the idea of collecting corals as I wrote to you—these things make me almost happy. But Barbara makes me unhappy beyond words.

Shall I let her go back to the States, have Norman Donaldson meet her in New York, have her see Follett, let him take a hand? And shall I stay away a while longer to finish my own job of writing. Would that be the square thing to do?

Write me. All my love.

Helen

TO THE SEA (1927–1929)

Barbara wrote the following for Harper's *while sailing from Honolulu to Samoa. It wasn't accepted for publication.*

S. S. Sonoma
May 14, 1929

Dear Mr. McFee:

Oh, 'twas to be a grand feast! One of the numerous sons of the Keane family would be departing in three days for 'Merriky. Yes, 'Merriky! He was going there to work, to seek his fortune; visions of gold mines flitted across the brains of the grey-haired parents. He was going in a steamer, too; yes, an actual steamer. This was unheard of to all of them, except to one daughter who had been to Honolulu. And the son himself appeared to treat it all quite casually—oh, 'twas nothing at all, nothing—nothing for *him*! And someday he'd come back in fine clothes, with lots of money, and swank around before his old simple native friends, and be high up and above them—a veritable *popaa*.

But there must be a farewell feast—of *course*! Oh, they would have a wild time, and drink, and dance, and eat, and sing, and all this till four or five in the morning. And we were lucky enough to be staying out with the Keane tribe at that time; so we were in on the whole thing. There was plenty of excitement, and "plenty too much work." Boys went out and gathered huge armfuls of leaves—big, shiny ones; girls sat cross-legged on the floor and shredded them with their finger-nails until they were green ribbons; these, joined in pairs with another sort of leaf, were hung all over the wide porch, until you would have hardly known the place. Friends were called in to help. They called for more leaves, and the boys brought them in from the river, cool and fresh and shining green; and you could hear the many fingernails hissing through them. Chickens were killed, and pigs were killed, and fruits and vegetables were gathered, and roasted outdoors in a huge fire—roasted on hot stones, and covered deep with breadfruit leaves to hold the hot air. The table was laid out on the porch—oh, no one was idle, they were all working at full speed—laid with a splendid centrepiece and wreaths and bouquets and drooping chains of leaves.

An hour or so after dark the banquet was ready. Wreaths had been sewn together—long, patient labour with flowers and berries—the table from head to foot was glittering and steaming with *kaikai*—food. Plates piled high with evil-looking oysters, and then chicken, and pig, and breadfruit, and yams, and potatoes,, and taro, and cooked fish, and raw fish in coconut sauce—oh, there was not room for another single dish upon the table. The girls came in, with their gayest frocks; and the boys, sleeked and combed; and certain wandering *popaas* (white persons)—we all came and sat down at the long, steaming, decorated table. No grace, or anything of *that* sort; no speech, not a syllable. We dug in, without waste of time.

Most of the *popaas* sat at another table at the end of the porch, and enjoyed themselves in the feeble, foolish ways of *popaas*; the wreaths on their heads made them look ridiculously out of place. One man might have passed for a very dissolute Bacchus; and another was a solemn caricature of Julius Caesar. But the natives! Ah, they were made of different stuff. Of course, they couldn't content themselves for long with eating in silence like that; oh, no, they up and fetched their guitars, and strummed, and sang in chorus, stamping their feet and clapping their hands.

And wine was brought, white wine and red—oh, this was a regular party, and no mistake! Glasses twinkled with jewel lights all around the long table, sparkling from among the dark green leaves. And it was marvellous how they sang and talked, and yet how the chicken and pig and taro and breadfruit vanished. As they drank the wine, glass after glass, the singing became louder—oh, they were warmed up now with food and drink, this was *their* party, they would have their fun in their way—and never mind those dull, stupid *popaas* there at the other end! They stamped more and more boldly, till the room shook; they clapped their hands till their palms were sore; and they sang, they sang, they sang—wild, hilarious, reckless Tahitian songs. Their faces, a row down each side of the table, were full of the sheer joy of existence—their eyes flashed and their teeth shone; linking arms all down the table, they swayed back and forth against each other to the rhythm of the excited guitars.

And then the time came, of course, when they were too happy to stay in their seats any longer. One by one the girls and boys were up, and, after a few preliminary wriggles, started dancing in earnest. Old Keane, with large hibiscus over each ear, getting tipsier and tipsier with the good wine, encouraged them from the head of the table. Oh, and this was *their* dancing—none of your European jazz! Lizard-like, they wriggled—oh, they wriggled splendidly!—they made sinuous, snake-like movements with arms and fingers and bodies; they quivered from head to foot, while the muscles rolled under the sleek brown skins; they hissed and whooped and laughed long, wild laughs.

As I watched them, clapping my hands to the music of four or five guitars, I suddenly remembered my friend Mere, sitting comfortably upon the porch of her house in Papeete. "I don't want go heaven," Mere said, a mischievous twinkle in her black eye, as she unfurled the ebony waterfall of her hair. "I want to go hell. In hell—plenty sweethearts. In hell—have good time, sing, dance around the fire, play on guitar." There was truth in what she said. The Tahitian dances would have astonished St. Peter; but the Devil and his imps would have howled with glee.

Corie wore a dress of green with a full skirt. Her hair was looped back and adorned with a wreath of red and white flowers. She was the most wrigglesome dancer of them all, and fiendishly excited. Her eyes flashed fire—those usually placid black eyes. She displayed two rows of gleaming ivory teeth. Every once in a while she would utter a long, hilarious whoop of joy. As she danced, there was a *feeling* growing strangely upon me—an ability to see into the heart of it, to understand. I suddenly *liked* her dancing, envied it, felt the spirit of it surging like fire through my bones. The native passion was aroused in Corie to the utmost; she seemed tireless, eternal. The crystal beads twinkled about her strong neck, flopped upon her green dress, flashed forth sparks of blue and red fire like diamonds. Her teeth shone—and her savage, beautiful, barbaric eyes. . . By Jove, she *was* beautiful! She had awoken out of her usual everyday lethargy and sleepiness; she was awake, and having her fun now, and in her glory; and she danced, she danced the very soul of life, beating the drum of life, with nature, with nature, living and dancing and dying, close to nature, in the heart of things.

One of her sisters carried into the room a baby—a wee thing, blinking tearfully from the sudden glare of light. I cast loose from my safe moorings at the table, and went to see the little creature. It was a blessed, fatal move. The guitars struck up in a burst of hilarity, Corie uttered an excited cry, seized my arm, and exclaimed, "Dance! Dance!" It was a perilous situation, that: Dance, and make a fool of myself; or not dance, and make a fool of myself? In the bright course of a second I had thought the thing out; and instinctively I made up my mind. And beside Corie, in the centre of a flashing ring of native boys and streamers of leaves and flowers, I stamped and leaped, and clapped my hands with native ardour. And so delighted and surprised were they all that they forgave me for not participating in lizardian and snakesolian wrigglings. Oh, she knew life, did Corie; she lived close to it, and dealt with it primitively, just as she was was intended to long and long ago. What a heavy brown arm it was that she flung across my shoulders, when we had finished! Oh, I was her life-and-death friend now, I had shared her emotions and secrets; all barriers had been mystically broken down.

The amount of wine consumed had been tremendous, and beer, and whisky, likewise. It astonished me how those lads stayed upon their feet. But they stayed mighty well on their feet, and danced as though they had not tasted a drop—only they were a bit excited, that was all. But then, I reflected, there hadn't been really enough time allowed. . . . About half an hour later, when the phonograph was wound, and the "European" dance started—then it was that things became different. Rudders were off centre, and steadily more and more so; individual craft when tacking about over the verandah with a strong head wind, under jury rig. Ah! They might have called it "European," that dance, but it was more of a devil-dance. Boys, with wreaths set at rakish angles and falling piratically over one black eye, violently seized upon their sisters, cousins, relations, friends, or even each other (for there weren't nearly enough young ladies); and, arms thrown around each other, they kicked up their legs and knocked their knees together and floundered about the piazza, bumping into other people very hard, staggering, stumbling, clawing hysterically at each other. European? Well, maybe . . . . Even the hilarious, steady rhythm they started off with was rapidly melting away—they could not bother about rhythm—no time to worry about rhythm—what was rhythm, anyway? Dance, dance, dance—and every once in a while back to the table for another glass.

But they were happy, that was the main thing. Two of the lads, dancing with each other, were surprisingly clever at avoiding shipwreck, in spite of the fact that they were rolling their decks full of water. I expected every moment to see them go under, but, grasping each other desperately, they kept at it. Their only chance was to hold on, and they knew it, and held! A third lad came and asked me to dance; but I had one look first. When he explained that there weren't enough girls, I had one sniff—and then told him to go and put on a girl's dress. . . . Ah, this was his last effort. He disappeared around the corner and subsided on a bench, lost in the most complete and perfect form of happiness—oblivion.

The Dance of the Whisky Devils went on and on. It was becoming more and more uncivilized. Several of the boys were lost now; old Keane had vanished somewhere; but the girls were still in good trim. More drinks, more music, more dancing, but 'specially more drinks. The more they had, the more they wanted, of course. The piazza was as though a hurricane had just passed over. All the leaves were strewn desperately about the floor, and the decorations were in rags now. And I wondered quietly—I thought of the hours of patient work that morning and afternoon to prepare those trimmings and wreaths and leaf-chains—and now?

At one o'clock we turned in. There was nothing left of the dance but a few badly aimed stumbling about the porch. At two o'clock the lights were out, everybody had vanished somehow or other. There was a decidedly alcoholic atmosphere—rottenly fragrant, stifling, depressing, sickly. Dead silence outside—pitch blackness. Nature quite unchanged, but very still. There was a dull thud somewhere on the porch—a groan—and sounds of broken glass. . . .

A very few days later, on twelve-hour notice, we sailed out of the harbour at Tahiti in the French cargo-steamer, *Andromède*! That's the way we do things, you see. Settled down comfortably in New York, one, two, three, hey presto! and we're off to Abyssinia. Settled down comfortably and indefinitely, hey presto! and we're bound for Samoa, via Fiji and the Tongas. Pleasantly crazy? That's what we thought to ourselves, as the *Andromède*, a black silhouette against the sunset-lighted peaks of Moorea, passed the reef and began to lift and fall in the mysteriously toppling domes of a moonstone sea. Indeed, it was so strange and queer and wild, now to be at sea again, after those two peaceful months among the tiare wreaths of Tahiti, that we could do nothing except grasp the rail of the old cargo-steamer, look into the sea, and wonder.

Quaint ways our old *Andromède* had! The whole week's dinners mooed, grunted, and squawked astern; a Chinese lady with blackened teeth and a baby roamed about the hatches; a mischievous old man in a decidedly shabby costume sat outside a door marked "Chef Mecanicien"; and a wild, terrible gang of pirates went and came incessantly—oilers, firemen, sailors, a butcher, a blacksmith, a bo's'n or two, some Oriental waiters, a gigantic hulk of a cook, some lean dish-washers—oh, a dark, wild horde!

We were at sea again, on our way, on, on. . . .

Barbara began asking her friends for money, which I think she planned to use to run away to Andrew Burt in Montreal.

At sea, S. S. *Sonoma*
May 16, 1929

My dear Norm:

Poor Barboo is sadly and definitely up a stump—a rather unusual sort of stump, too, especially for poor Barboo. Do you think you could extend a helping hand—that is, fetch the step-ladder by which I might descend? Do you think you could, without telling *anyone*, cable to me a Sum of Money? It wouldn't necessarily be a *Very* Large Sum (say twenty-five dollars), and it would be Soon Repaid—on that you may count.

If you should, by the Grace of The Lord, find it in your Most Noble Heart to do this Deed of Love—if you *should*, I say, please cable it personally to *me* at Bank of Bishop and co., ltd., Honolulu, Hawaii. Oh, but this would be Very Much Appreciated!

I will tell you the remainder of this Very Thrilling Story, when we have our next tête-à-tête (which we *shall* have someday, for a' that an' a' that), contentedly drinking until Canada be Dry.

    Barboo. (with Belated Affection)

Honolulu, Hawaii
May 24, 1929

Dearest Anne:

Sometimes we all feel, I suppose, that all the powers of fate are rising in a conspiracy against us alone. I know *I* do. That's how I feel now. I feel that things are ingeniously and maliciously schemed to be inconvenient and difficult for me—as though the high powers had a personal grudge against me. And, although I blush deeply behind my trusty old Corona, I am writing to ask you a favour. I hate to ask favours of people, but this is one of those cases where there's no alternative.

Well, it's like this: Seeing that you are dead certain sure to lose that five-hundred-dollar wager of ours, do you suppose you could find it in your heart to advance me twenty-five dollars of it now? I realize that it's a bit early, of course—but still. You see, to stop beating about the bush, I'm up sort of a stump, that's all, and I need that little bit of money like the very devil, and I can't ask Helen for it, for several reasons. You know very well why I can't ask her—you know as well as I do.

Well, I ain't no orator, as Brutus is, but as you know me all, a plain blunt man. Therefore I can't write or speak how infinitely much just twenty-five dollars would mean to me. It would make *all* the difference! ALL! I can expect to repay it within two months, I *can* repay it within three months, I can promise and swear to pay it within four months. And I know you're my friend—one of my very few *real* friends. If you feel that you can't or won't do it, I'll ask you only not to tell *anyone* that I asked. If you *will* do it, I will ask you to cable it down to me personally, care of the Bank of Bishop and Co., Ltd., Honolulu, Hawaii. And don't say anything about it just yet, not to Oxford or anyone. You see, there's a rather long and complicated and exciting story connected with it, and I kind of feel that that story is meant for you alone. And someday you shall hear it.

My love to every one of the Grand Gang.

    With love,
    Barbara.

Honolulu, 4 June, 1929

Dearest Anne:

I've been ill! Funny kind, a bad heart, so the Dr. wouldn't let me swim. Otherwise we have both been perfectly well, physically, since we left N.Y. Barbara not so well in Apia; climate pretty bad, there. But what a place! And how I want to go back.

Have only a few minutes to get this off. The latest is this: Bar and I are sailing around the thirteenth on a *five*-masted schooner, the Vigilant, Captain Peasley for somewhere round Puget Sound! We pay, of course, about steerage fare, but we may be gone fourteen days or thirty. After that, still uncertain. I won the heart of the old Chinaman who owns the ship; he quoted Confucius at me, and consented to let us go if the Captain would consent. That, easy.

Barbara has been in bad shape for some months. Dreadfully homesick, and the thought of no home, and no father! She said once to me: "You know I used to pretend I didn't care, but I did care more than anyone will ever know."

She wants to get a job, and earn her own living. And she may stay in the States somewhere with a friend. I don't know really.

I wish you or Oxford would write her, or both. She is discouraged about her writing, no word from McFee having come through; and she has given up writing at all. If she had had someone to hang on to hard and tight, she never would have been in this emotional state she is in now.

I have great hopes of this schooner trip for her. I didn't care where the ship was going, east or south so long as we could get aboard her.

I want to go back to the islands and gather up the material Bar dragged me away from; and also take some pictures. I think I have a book coming; and I am writing better, I think, and so does Barbara, than ever. It has been an awful fight, however, awful, Anne.

If Follett doesn't break through soon, if he can't see that he has got to come out of his Arcadia, get a job in a city, and face the music, I think a lawyer ought to point it out to him. Now, after a year of trying to get back his health, and write (and how many times has he tried that?) I think he should be made to help us.

Margaret [Tyler] has been an angel with Sabra; and she thinks I should stay away longer. I can't think of a job in New Haven. I can think of lectures in Boston, perhaps. There are no jobs in New Haven except at the Press. I am fast getting lots of material for lectures or for the book. Bar has been in very bad shape, Anne. I can't seem to make up my mind about her.

There is a chance of my seeing M. Kennedy in Los Angeles, or in her coming to Honolulu if I return here via the schooner, and it is possible she may help out with Bar until she can get a job. Please don't mention M. K. to Follett under any conditions.

So try for the next address: care of Security-First National Bank of Los Angeles. I'll write any more plans when I know them. And know I love you and am always ready for advice. How about the corals?

    Helen

You'll recall Mildred Kennedy from Barbara's childhood.

Berkshire School,
Sheffield, Mass.,
June 17, 1929.

My dear Meservey,

[...] Do you hear any news from Helen? I had one letter yesterday, in reply to one of mine answering an inquiry whether I could take charge of Bar this summer. By this time they are on a schooner from Honolulu to Vancouver. From there they go to Los Angeles, where Helen hopes to leave Bar with Mildred Kennedy. She intends going back herself to the South Seas, to do some writing and perhaps to make a business of collecting curios.

I couldn't offer to help with Bar, because I have cut loose from school-teaching and plan to keep free to go wherever fortune leads me. I am sorry, for I believe that Bar is at a very critical time in her life, when she needs to be associated with sane and well-balanced people. I am afraid that Helen has not been just that. [...]

    Yours sincerely,
    Ralph L. Blanchard

Five thousand miles apart, father and daughter were both suffering. I don't think my grandmother would have written this letter unless she feared for Wilson's life.

Box 75
Prospect Harbor, Maine
July 2, 1929

Dear Mr. Meservey:

Would it be possible for you to come here, see Wilson Follett, and take him away with you for a trip to the mountains, or a trip on a schooner, or anything that your two heads could hatch up? I scarcely ask this because I want him somewhere where I am not: I ask it because I believe that he is a very sick man and that his only salvation is to be away from me and with someone to whom he can talk freely or be silent, someone before whom he need not be afraid to show what he is feeling.

I thought that when we got away from New York and into the sort of country that he seemed to like, he would be able to do the work that he has always wanted to do, and by means of it be able to make a decent living for himself and his family. None of these things occurred, and from the burden of his worry over his inability to work and thus to meet his responsibilities, he has gone rather badly to pieces. He tells me now (at more frequent intervals than he has all winter) that he never expects to be able to work again, that he has no mind left, that he is rapidly getting into the condition that George Bryan is in (I've never been able to find out what condition that is except that it involves a sanatorium), and finally that no one has any respect for him any more or expects him to amount to anything—and mentions you as one of the persons cherishing this idea.

That last is not my idea at all, either of what you think or what I believe. But it is my idea that he isn't going to get over it until someone beside myself tells him it isn't so, and it is also my idea that he's not going to get any better until he gets away from me long enough to find out what he wants to do, how he wants to do, whether he wants me with him or whether he wants a chance to go it alone for a while or forever.

I do believe that if he could see you, talk with you, and do something with you (leaving me quite out) that he would be able to get some sort of grip on himself again. I don't know anyone else who could do it for him, and I don't know anyone else to whom I could appeal.

I ask you to believe that this letter is not written in a fit of hysteria on my part. I am not much given to that disease, and if I were it would have exhibited itself some months ago. As a matter of fact, I did consider writing to you before, but I felt that in all fairness both to you and to Wilson I should say nothing to anyone until I was sure that his despondency was not just a mood. I am sure now.

Mrs. Meservey (if you speak to her about this letter—and I do not ask you not to) will say, quite correctly, that she predicted this a year ago. I do not know what you will say. I know, certainly, that I feel miserably guilty without being able to determine in what way I am culpable.

       Yours always faithfully,
       Margaret Whipple

Barbara on the *Vigilant*

On June 15th, the Folletts set sail from Honolulu to Hoquiam, Washington, on the Vigilant, captained by Ralph E. "Matt" Peasley (the inspiration for Peter B. Kyne's 1916 book, Cappy Ricks, Or, the Subjugation of Matt Peasley). Second mate was Ed Anderson, who plays an important role in Barbara's story.

The voyage took a month. After spending another week with Anderson in port, they made their way to Pasadena, California, where they were met by Mildred Kennedy and her friend, Mrs. A. Brown from Concord, Massachusetts. It will have been unanimous that Barbara and Helen live apart for a while. Helen rented a room in Los Angeles before returning to Honolulu in early September to begin work on Magic Portholes, while Barbara stayed with Miss Kennedy and Mrs. Brown in Altadena, a little north of Pasadena.

Bridgewater
July 4, 1929

Well shipmat

I reicived your letter was glad to hear that you rive home saft again well Barbara your things you was speaking about they are here the old man sed he would send them to you from new york. [...]

I no you like to go to sea what king of a trip did you have gone home

   So long from your shipmat.
   Bill

Anderson was right about Joan Lowell's book, The Cradle of the Deep: *despite garnering praise in the press for its authenticity, it was a fraud. It supposedly described the author's first seventeen years living on board her father's windjammer in the South Seas, and earned her $50,000 in royalties. In 1957 Lowell was imprisoned for writing bad checks.*

1788 Meadow Brook Road
Altadena, California
August 5, 1929

Well, old girl:

The above is where I live—no, not where I live now, but where I shall live after Thursday (this is Monday). I wouldn't descend upon us until Friday or Saturday!

Everything's all right. When I say that I mean it the way a corpse does—you ask a corpse lying in his coffin how he is feeling, and he lifts his head to say: "Fine, an' how's yourself?" So I'll tak' that back and say that everything's wrong. Don't ask no questions, and I won't tell no lies.

I was readin' i' the shippin' news today that the S. S. *Tahiti* (C. E. MacPherson, 2nd E. Thompson) lost a fifteen-ton propeller in the act of docking here the other day, and that divers worked four hours to retrieve it, and that it *was* retrieved and replaced in dry-dock. A wee sma' thing, perhaps, but it was quite exciting to me. I live i' the wairrld o' ships. And the Can. Gov. Mer. Mar. came across most nobly, and presented me with schedules and scedules and skedools. I have 'em from Montreal, and I have 'em from Halifax. Too late, alas!

I have letters for you—a stack. It looks as though one was from the Messageries Maritimes, and another from Leo—but, of course, I haven't opened them. I got a stack of mail myself, including (a) a letter from Effie, (b) a letter from Anderson, and (3) an iron belaying-pin. Anderson's letter was a scream. You'll laugh your head off. The *Vigilant* sails today or tomorrow for Honolulu, Charlie Ness had a wild adventure, Anderson thinks Joan Lowell's book is a fraud, he hasn't purchased either ice-cream or cherries, and he's having a "frightful time with the Farksoo," and he sent best regards to "The Mater."

The belaying-pin I won't discuss now.

Mildred hears! Music, the human voice, over the radio with the Vibra-Tone attachment. Really quite marvellous, ye ken.

I feel subdued. There is nothing that subdues better a rampant person than a crack over the coconut with an iron belaying-pin, is there.

>Barbara Follett
>(That's how my belaying-pin was signed, if you please, sir!)
>*Insult added to injury, I ca't!*

Barbara had met Togasü Riggs during her brief stop at Tonga en route to Samoa. "Lopua" is the Lokoa, *on which the Folletts had been traveling since Fiji. The scene of Riggs cutting a lock of Barbara's hair appears in* Stars to Steer By.

N. Fugamisi *[Tonga]*
20th Aug. 1929.

Dear Loving friend

Just a few line to let you know that I am still alright.

But I want to know a good news from you & your mother. And how are you getting on. [...]

Then I want to make this few words to let you know that I am still Remember you my dear girl. But I thought you forget me long time ago.

By my heart was on your hairs that you cut for me last time. And I always think about you and Mother I never get anythings for you this trip. [...]

Please send some other Hairs for me next boat, Because I never know that you are in Apia. Also let me know which place that you stayed. And let me know how the place.

I thought you never think & Remember me because you got a boy there. If you do that My dear that not fair to me.

Like my way my dear girl. I stopped friends with Tongan girls now because I always Remember you my dear girl. I never forget you till the end of the world. [...]

> I remain
> Your Loving friend
> K. Togasü Riggs
> A HEAP OF Kisses to you
> XXXXXXXXXX, XXXXXXXX.

[postmarked August 21, 1929, 4:30 p.m.]
3880 West First Street
Los Angeles, CA

Dearest Anne:

I have at last got your letter of June the last day, I think! I wish I could tell you about our thirty-day trip in the wind-jammer, but I shall have to save it, for I have only a little time here, and I must get down to the essentials so that I can hear from you again before I move on.

But I must say at first that I am awfully disturbed about Edward. You must tell me more accurately what is the matter with him. Please. And is he a stamp collector by chance, for I can send him some interesting ones of the islands in the South Pacific.

I cannot even take time to write to you about Bar and her condition. She has given up her job of writing as I told you. The emotional climax hit her when she was away, with very bad results. She worshipped her father, as you know, and she has constantly picked out people here and there to talk to them about her father, her trips with him, etc., etc. The second mate on the Vigilant whom she selected out of the bunch for a special friend told me that she talked about her father all the time to him: "How she must worship him," he said to me.

Well, the point is: I am going to try to write the book of this trip. This is a financial obligation to Harper, and a moral obligation as well. I don't say they will take it as a substitute for Bar, but I have hopes even now that Bar will contribute portions of writing here and there. There are excepts from letters which she has written and of which she has copies which I hope she will give me to use throughout the book. Her contribution, so that the book will be by us both.

In order to do that, I feel obliged to get back to Honolulu and the Bishop Museum for a while. There are jobs there and I feel pretty sure that I can do some kind of clerical job at the Museum for half a day earning board and room, and giving me the other half to write that book. The Bishop Museum has all the scientific material from the islands which I shall have to use. And they have in their show cases all the things which I have seen but which I should have to see over again to be sure of details.

No word, and no money has come from Follett. This is the purport of this letter. Can you get in touch with him immediately, and find out if he has sent money, or if he *will* send some to me. The need for both me and Bar is imperative. Bar is in no condition to go to work in an office, as any doctor can vouch. Follett should be made to realize that he has got to get a job and take some care of us. Knopf said that if Follett is allowed to think we can get along without his financial help, he will go to the dogs; that a job with a responsibility of us is the only thing that will save him. I am not ashamed to take his money for either Bar or Sabra. I want to hear right off about him, because it will make all the difference for Bar and for me too.

I am ready to turn the whole thing over to a lawyer. If you see Follett you can tell him that I am ready to let him go on condition that he gets a job and supports us and also makes the house over to me. This last he has always said he would do anyway, because it was my friend's money that started it anyway.

Now, about a lawyer. I don't know anyone. But it occurs to me that Oxford's friend in New York is the man to take it on; Follett then can have no kick at all. Will you find out about that? And what I should do next? I have not enough money to get East, and can't leave here immediately anyway. And if there is no personal need of my being along, I'd rather not go at all. The job of writing my stuff for the sake of Bar is the one thing ahead of me if I can pull it off.

So, can you write me soon. Please, Anne dear, find out if Follett has sent any money, or intends to do so. This is imperative for Bar and me. Then let him know that he may have his separation on the condition that he will get a job and support us. It seems absurd to me to divorce a man who has no job, and who is very likely never to try to get one, unless pressure is brought to bear on him. I know him well enough for that.

Oxford's lawyer friend, it seems to me, is the man. Of course, if Follett has a job now and can make some definite settlement on me, I am told I can get a divorce easy enough out here in Reno!

I can't keep going on like this. Barbara's illness has made me determined to appeal to Follett for his help once more, for as can be verified here her whole condition is traceable to the terrific shock to her at a critical age. I can not get a job, look out for her, write her book, without some help. And I cannot believe he should be allowed to go along longer dillying around. It is silly to pretend that he can't get a job.

There is no need of his knowing where I am. The money sent to Honolulu will get to me wherever I am. I shall go back to H. alone.

Things are very serious with us, Anne. And I can't make this letter sound anything but gloomy!

I hate to urge all this on you and Oxford again. But what can I do? Please write to me as soon as you can. And take all my love.

    Helen

A telegraph exchange between Helen and Oxford Meservey, August 29 and 30, 1929.

Please wire collect care Postal Telegraph Pasadena Calif Wilson's address where he can be located stop Is he well stop Has he a job or is he trying for one any hope of money for answer all questions immediately stop Here with friend short stay love to all

    Helen Follett

Wilson at Prospect Harbor Maine. Saw him recently. Shows little change physically. No prospect of money. Not seeking city job. Little work for Bookman. Doubt if he could do steady work.

    Meservey

Margaret Tyler had been caring for Sabra during Helen's absence. At the time of her writing the following letter to Anne, Barbara had been put under the care of a Swedish psychiatrist, Dr. Ture Schoultz, and had registered for classes at Pasadena Junior College—her introduction to formal education. Neither experiment would last long.

195 Church Street
New Haven, Conn.
Sept. 12, 1929

Dear Mrs. Meservey,

Did you have another letter from Helen just after we left you? I found one here waiting for me, and have had another since then. In the first one she said she was sailing back to Honolulu that Saturday, Sept. 7th, that Bar was to stay in California for the winter and go to school there, being under the care of some doctor. The fact that Mildred Kennedy is helping Bar she is very anxious to keep a secret, at least from Wilson, also that she has been with them this summer. Helen wants to get a job with the Bishop Museum out there and also write up her trip. Helen said that M. K. sent her off with a lot of new and lovely clothes, so she felt quite gay. One of the amusing things in her letter was that she had seen a doctor herself, who had forbidden her "to think about Sabra"; sort of in the class with "I do not choose to run."

[...] Poor Bar also wrote to Norman Donaldson for some money, and he sent it, much to his wife's distress, as she wondered what Bar would do with it. [...]

Thank you for taking us both in, with your big family. I loved being there, it was a great pleasure, as well as a great help as regards Sabra. We may worry and laugh over the troubles of the Folletts, but I always do admire their choice of friends; that is one reason I was so happy to see you and visit you, and I hope we may come again.

    With kindest regards
    Margaret Tyler

A handwritten note, undated, but probably about September 16th. I don't know who Florence was—perhaps a housekeeper or neighbor. Probably not Mrs. A. Brown, who I think might have been Mrs. Alice M. Brown from a prominent Concord family and who was about the same age as Helen and Mildred Kennedy.

Dear Helen:

Promise you won't be flabbergasted? Brace yourself!

This is my last hour in the town of Pasadena. I'm leaving for the far east, via Vancouver, where I'll be met. Then I plunge whole-heartedly into a very large job which consists of being private secretary for a whole class of marine engineers who have gathered together for the purpose of working out miracles and life-old dreams in a prospering engineering shop. And I'll live, by myself, very quietly and respectably, in a tiny apartment, and work like the very old Nick.

I'm not going to tell you, for the time being, where I'll be; and names, jobs, and headquarters have all been completely changed, you see. So we're unfindable. Besides, I want to be alone with my Disillusion or my Fairytale—as the case may be.

And I expect I'll be seeing you again in this incarnation.

    Love,
    B. F.

Florence and Mildred are acquainted with the situation; or will be tomorrow.

After writing to her mother, Barbara ran away to San Francisco. Whether she was planning to travel to Montreal to see Andrew Burt, or to meet up with Anderson, or to strike out on her own, I'm not positive—but

I'm fairly sure it was Andrew Burt. Whatever her plan, she didn't get far. She registered as "K. Andrews" at a boarding house on O'Farrell Street in the Tenderloin district, only to be arrested on September 19th after trying to escape from the police through a window. (MIldred Kennedy had contacted authorities in San Francisco, thinking it a likely destination for the runaway.) She was detained in the Juvenile Detention Home while the local probation officer, Warren Prescott, awaited word from Los Angeles about what to do.

Over the following week Barbara's escape was covered by the California press. The wire services picked up the story and soon newspapers all over the country joined in the hoopla. For such a private family as the Folletts, this will have been a particularly grueling time.

Nancy Barr Mavity of the Oakland Tribune *interviewed Barbara; her story appeared on the front page on September 20th.*

[...] Today she is held at the detention home in San Francisco on the request of the probation authorities of Los Angeles, after her arrest at an O'Farrell street hotel in San Francisco where she had registered under an assumed name.

"I hate the idea of school. Even more than that, I hate the idea that if I had gone to the Pasadena junior college, according to the plans others made for me, I might grow to like it," she declares. "I was not given the conventional upbringing and it is too late to try to standardize me now." [...]

"Causes do not matter—the result is that I am here," she remarks with adult fatalism.

"I do not know where my father, Wilson Follett, is. Both of my parents are literary—perhaps that is the trouble with them, and with me. My mother and I had some serious difficulties, into which I will not go. Two friends in Los Angeles gave her the money to go to Honolulu to pursue her writing and I was placed with Dr. Schultz to go to school.

"I am told that I am wanted in the south for forging a check. Well, I might do anything else, even murder, for there is a streak of crime in my nature, but I didn't do that. The money I had with me was given to me in cash."

There is a touch of very youthful bravado in the beautiful face with its deep brown eyes and crown of copper hair as she calmly announces her streak of crime.

"What I hate about it all is the sordidness and vulgarity of being arrested," she burst out.

"It has none of the beauty of grief or tragedy in it. If it were beautiful, I wouldn't mind so much." [...]

"I can't be treated as if I were a normal girl of 15," she says gravely.

"At 10 or 11 I went through all the storm and stress usually associated with my present age. I have been suppressed until I can't bear it any longer. I have plans for myself—the only logical plans that have ever emanated from my family, I think."

"I wouldn't be here today if I had a normal upbringing. But then, I might have been in a worse place. Who can tell?"

"At any rate, I hated Los Angeles, with its blatant sunshine, never a wisp of fog or a cloud, and I love San Francisco. I am so glad that I went to Golden Gate Park yesterday morning. It is one of the most beautiful places in world, I think, and I need that beauty to remember."

"When my money was gone, I planned to go to work. I thought I could get some small office job, for I typewrite well and have a good knowledge of English. If I failed in that I could begin as a waitress or a clerk. I know that I couldn't support myself by my writing yet, but I could be perfecting it, seeking real criticism and development.

"That is the life I planned for myself, and all I ask is to be let alone to do what seems best to me. I am proud enough and sensitive enough to hate this sordid end of things horribly." [...]

Her father, Wilson Follett, author and at one time connected with the publishing house of Alfred Knopf, wrote of her as "an example of the norm of childhood, undevastated by the average perversions."

But Barbara's lips curl in a bitter smile at her father's description of her unfettered childhood and the success of the experiment of home training without formal education.

"It sounds very lovely—but I know what the literary temperament is, when confronted with a typewriter," she comments briefly.

"I don't know how I will handle the situation when I am forced to go back to Los Angeles," she says, "but one thing is certain. The minute I can do it decently, without fear of arrest, I am coming back to San Francisco."

Floyd J. Healy of the Los Angeles Times *also quoted Barbara in his story of September 21st.*

[...] "I came away because I felt I had to have my freedom," she said. "I felt utterly suppressed, almost frantic, under the plans that had been made for me. I did not want to enter college nor live the standardized existence. I have never been to school in my life. Perhaps I might like it—I do not know. But this I know: "I do not want to like it. And so I came away, and I suppose I will have to go back."

[...] "All the plans were made. I had picked out my course of study—botany, Spanish, English and algebra. I was to play my fiddle in the school orchestra. But I couldn't stand it," she said with a gesture of repulsion. "The whole atmosphere of Southern California seemed poisonous to me. I had some money my mother gave me before she went away. It was enough to last me quite a while. So I came to San Francisco by stage. I left a note behind and I took an assumed name.

"I had been to San Francisco before and it has been the dream of my life to come back.

"This has been a sordid, humiliating experience, but perhaps some day it will be literary material. Four little girls in their blue uniforms in their cages next to mine. Looking through the bars. One of them even tried to wink at me. Why are older people crushing us in this way? It seems to me I cannot wait six whole years until I am twenty-one in order just to be free."

Excerpts from the following days' papers follow.

Los Angeles Times, September 22, 1929
Child Writer in Revolt
Three days in the juvenile detention home have not lowered Barbara Newhall Follett's passionate resistance against returning to college and the care of her mother's friends in Pasadena. The young literary genius protested to such effect today that Probation Officer Astredo refused to release her to Mrs. A. Brown of Concord, Mass., and Miss Mildred Kennedy of Boston, who, armed with the authority of the Los Angeles Juvenile Court, appeared at the home to claim her.

"She showed such serious disinclination to go with Mrs. Brown and Miss Kennedy," Astredo explained, "that it seemed wise to keep her here until we can communicate further with the Los Angeles Juvenile Court."

Barbara said she found the arrangement "unbearable." The situation was "poisonous," she said, and she felt "suppressed, crushed, and almost insane" at the curtailment of her freedom. So she ran away to San Francisco.

"I am an expert typist," she said. "I have used a typewriter since I was 4 years of age. I corrected the galley proofs of my own books. I have lived all my life with scholarly, well-informed, cultured people. Though I am only 15 and inexperienced in the business world, I am better equipped than most who enter it and succeed."

I'm surprised that Dr. Schoultz (that's the correct spelling) traveled all the way to Maine to see my grandparents, but that appears to be what he did.

The thought of my grandmother raising Barbara is intriguing. She was certainly smart enough to keep her engaged intellectually, but she could be very mean and was a master at passive aggressiveness. She always treated me well but was cruel to my mother and other members of my family for long periods of time.

Box 75
Prospect Harbor, Maine
September 24, 1929

Dear Anne-White Meservey:

I owe you an apology, first, because I seem to have misconstrued what you said to me when you were here about Wilson's past history, and second because I was so foolish as to repeat all the nonsense to him. The latter, I feel, was particularly asinine. I hope you will forgive me on the rather feeble grounds that all women must be fools with the men they love.

I believe Wilson is going to write to you about what we have learned about Barbara and her mother. Helen herself never wrote to him, but a Dr. Schoultz from Pasadena came to see us yesterday, and told us all about them. It is possible that we are going out there to try to make a home for Barbara. I hope so. I think that I could help to make her happy again. I shall be grateful for even the chance to try. And I believe that at last we are going to have a divorce and the chance to marry.

Wilson tells me that Edward is still in the hospital. I am sorry. Do you still plan to take him out West? If you do, and if we go, it will be rather a nice feeling to know that we aren't separated from all the Meserveys by the width of a continent.

        Yours always sincerely,
        Margaret Whipple

Further excerpts from the Los Angeles Times. *Confusingly, Mrs. Brown has been given the initials "J. L."*

Los Angeles Times, *September 24, 1929*
Girl Novelist Returning with Guard Escort

Barbara Follett, 15-year-old novelist, is expected to arrive in Los Angeles from San Francisco today in the custody of Harry W. White, deputy Juvenile Court officer. The girl was detained by the police in San Francisco after she had departed from the home of Mrs. J. L. Brown and Miss Mildred Kennedy in Pasadena a week ago.

Los Angeles Times, September 25, 1929
Girl Novelist to be Kept at Juvenile Hall

In the technical custody of Harry W. White, deputy probation officer of Juvenile Court, Barbara Follett, 15-year-old authoress, who was detained by San Francisco police while in flight from Pasadena friends in whose care she had been left by her mother, will arrive in Los Angeles this morning.

There is no charge pending against the girl other than that she is a juvenile "without parental control"; and it is understood she will be taken immediately to Juvenile Hall until the receipt of instructions of her mother, who has been notified of her detention.

Los Angeles Times, September 26, 1929
Runaway Authoress Returned

Miss Follett, who was detained by the San Francisco police last week at the request of the Los Angeles authorities, was taken immediately to Juvenile Hall, where she will be held pending a hearing next Monday afternoon before Referee Van Waters on a petition stating she is without "proper parental control."

Los Angeles Times, September 28, 1929
The Lancer column, by Harry Carr
The Child Novelist

Now that they have locked up Miss Barbara Follett, the child novelist, what else are they going to do with her?

In spite of the fact that Los Angeles is a "poison atmosphere" for higher intellects, I am constrained to rush to her rescue. After all, we novelists have to stick together. Some folks write them at 15, as she has done; and allow themselves years to live them down. Others wait and die with novels still in their consciences. Everyone writes one sooner or later.

I haven't stated mine yet, but who can tell? Inspiration is liable to overtake a fellow anywhere and at any time.

By now Wilson and Margaret had arrived in Los Angeles and insisted that Barbara's court hearing be private. Helen did not get back to Los Angeles in time for it.

The family in Pasadena was Alice Dyar Russell (1881-1964), her husband Bert (1874-1933), although I think he was living in Detroit at the time, and their daughters—twenty-one-year-old Elizabeth and Phoebe, who was fifteen. Alice became a great friend to Barbara.

Los Angeles Times, October 1, 1929
Barbara Follett Made Juvenile Court's Ward

Miss Barbara Follett, 15-year-old authoress, who "ran away" from her guardians in Pasadena and was taken into custody in San Francisco a week ago, yesterday was made a ward of Juvenile Court and placed in a private home in Pasadena.

Juvenile authorities declined to reveal the name of the family with which Miss Follett has been placed and also refused to disclose details of the hearing on the petition stating the girl was "without proper parental control."

It also was learned yesterday that a special secret session was conducted last Thursday in the girls' court at Juvenile Hall, at which time Miss Follett's case was passed on and it was decided to place her in a private home until her mother returns from Honolulu or until other provision is made to appoint a permanent guardian for her.

The hearing was conducted with the greatest secrecy, it is reported, and special efforts are said to have been made to prevent newspaper reporters from learning that the hearing had been conducted, in spite of the fact that a widespread public interest in the girl's case was indicated.

Dr. Miriam Van Waters is referee of the girls' section of juvenile cases, but her report and recommendation on the hearing last Thursday still were held secret yesterday and had not been filed in the juvenile department of the County Clerk's office.

Helen returned to Los Angeles sometime in mid to late October, while Wall Street was in free fall at the beginning of the Great Depression.

October 30, 1929 (31, I mean)

Dear Oxford and Anne:

Things are very complicated here—to say the least! Follett brought Whipple with him, and that, as perhaps you can imagine, has made a dirty mess. He was asked to come alone. And he has taken Whipple everywhere with him.

That is all I am going to say. One reason is that Follett told me that Anne-White, Tyler, and Hildegarde—all of whom had seen him and Whipple—held me in lesser love and faith than before. This is under-stating it. The effect, however, that I felt turned into ice.

It has been difficult here, and still is. They twist the knife. I spend three hours with Follett in a lawyer's office, and then come back and find Whipple in the living-room of the house I am staying. Not so very easy to endure.

Some day, when I have some money, I'll give it to Oxford if he will come here and see the two lawyers—Follett's and mine—and hear the story. Both are fine men besides fine lawyers—recommended by Lee Higginson, in Boston.

Follett himself will tell you the story which you may believe as you will, or not. He does not know the circumstances or any of the details of the mess except as Barbara has seen fit to tell him, and Barbara is not an entirely reliable source of information now. He will not allow anyone to tell him the story nor will he read any of the evidence.

I have no way of telling you, and no way of convincing you of the truth, and yet, I'd rather you two people know the truth—as bitter as it is—than anyone on earth. The only thing I can do is to ask you to have faith in me. To believe that I am being guided by a man of unquestionable reputation as a lawyer, and unquestionable as a man and human being.

I do not know what is ahead for any of us—whether I shall have to stay here all winter, or not. Things are complicated, I assure you! And Follett, for once in his life, cannot blame me, for he has been warned again and again that he did the most senseless, brainless thing he could have done, and the most insulting to Barbara and to me. The reaction on Barbara is a complicated psychological one, which I refrain from unravelling until some day hence. And which, I can assure you, Follett himself only knows the surface.

My lawyer here is James Shepherd *[actually Sheppard]* of the firm of Haight, Mathes, and Shepherd, Rowan Bldg, Spring and Fifth Streets, L. A. This I give you for no special reason, but just for any reason.

My love to you all. I want to hear about Edward especially. Please write me a note here at the Security First National Bank, L. A. Did the shells arrive, and what else can I do. If anything, please let me know.

Here are a few nice fish for Robert.

    Helen

Once again the details of Barbara's "moral break-down" in Tahiti "must wait."

The article Helen sold to Good Housekeeping *was* Questions! Questions! Questions! A Child Asks, a Mother Answers—*and* Both Learn a Lot. *It discusses the first ten years of Barbara's education at home, and her fascination first with punctuation (and other "tiny things"), followed by the typewriter, clocks, colors, flowers, butterflies, mountains, and the sea. It was published in December 1932.*

Thursday, November 14 [1929]

Dearest Anne:

I want to write to you the whole story just as soon as I am able to—I mean, physically able to. It is a long one, and one that only a few people know anything about—certainly not Follett who will listen to nothing that doesn't fit in with his own moral code of living. But I want to write it to you alone—you and Oxford—and I want to do it carefully enough so that every detail can stand the test of investigation, leaving out all the emotional upsets along the way.

I never knew about Barbara's attempt to borrow money from you. I know now there were several other of my friends whom she wrote to at the same time. She turned against me in Tahiti because I could not allow her to commit the one action which she was obsessed to commit. I couldn't do it, no matter whether I sacrificed myself, her friendship, my friends. You could not. That is the story. But it must wait. It was the beginning of Barbara's moral break-down. Her formula which she quoted to everybody was that her father could live as he wanted to live, that he could do as he wanted to do and that no one had ever stopped him—therefore, she could do with her life what she wanted to do with it. Fortunately my decision was intensified by the fact that I didn't have the money to let her go where she was obsessed to go. Therefore, her plans for money; therefore, her turning against me, as a power of restraint, law, or whatever.

What her own suffering has been due to this obsession is something about two people know anything about—a cruel, cruel experience. I can tell you that. But the experience would have been a thousand times worse if I had given my sanction, my permission to her. She was not quite fifteen at the time, remember. The details in which this obsession worked itself along are not pleasant, are quite awful, in fact. They must wait.

In order to justify her own thinking processes which had become inverted she pointed to her father as an example. This is absolutely so, as those in Tahiti know, as those who took care of her here know. Follett does not know, nor would he believe.

Her running away from a delightfully healthy experiment which she had entered into freely, gladly, and of her own will was a piece of the same moral break-down, of a piece with the same kind of perverted thinking. It was pitiful, and as dangerous an attempt as any child ever made. She will know sometime what Mildred Kennedy saved her from. All she knows now is that she was thwarted in her attempt to get away to the person she wanted to get to. It had to be so. Then she turned around for some one to excuse her conduct, and she found her father and Whipple out here, ready to make fun of the Juvenile Court, the officers who had been kindness itself to her and to me, and of Mildred Kennedy who has done for Barbara this summer what no human being can ever believe—in the way of kindness, sympathy, generosity. And they found me to blame with the whole affair. Follett contending that it was all my fault! That I had failed with her, and it was time she came to him.

I have never kept Barbara from her father. I do not now, but I affirm, and I know—and here I have every kind of authority backing me up—that Barbara is in no moral condition fit to make a rational statement of what she wants to do.

It has been a disgraceful thing for Follett to bring Whipple here. Mildred offered to pay all his expenses if he would come out here alone. Instead of that, he borrowed six hundred dollars to come here and bring Whipple, which amount he has to pay back to *[here Helen has redacted the name]* before I can have a cent from him! *[written in margin: "So he says!"]* The Juvenile Court of which Dr. Van Waters is the head, now doing something at Harvard has been up against it in regard to him whom they cannot regard as a proper parent. He has taken Whipple up to the Court with him, to his lawyer, and everywhere else. It has been unpleasant and not a little insulting to me. And then some.

The Court issued an order that Barbara be placed in the home of Alice Dyer *[actually Dyar]* Russell, a nice person who writes and who became acquainted with Barbara years ago in Cheshire *[Connecticut]* through being interested in the article about the Typewriter which came out in Harper's. She was placed under my custody and Miss Whipple was not allowed to go there. The reason was perfectly plain and not unreasonable, although it had nothing whatever to do with me. I had not complained to any authority whatever. The Mann Act might have put Follett into jail, as you know.

The Juvenile Court has no right to decide between parents in the custody of a child—that belongs to the court of domestic relations. But they said very plainly that they thought Barbara belonged with her mother, because the father had deserted the child and had failed to support either the mother or the child. However, Barbara is under the parents' guardianship—both—at present. "To save Barbara" is a happy but ironical phrase coming from Follett and Whipple.

My lawyer wants me to clean up the mess. He has talked hours with Follett, and is sure that his whole line of reasoning is entirely false. Follett has complained out here—in my presence—before two lawyers—that I had spoiled his chances of getting a job, that I had ruined I have forgotten how many lives. It sounded hollow, and not a little puerile. Especially to me who has gone through with Barbara one of the most terrific emotional experiences that I can imagine. All I said was that I had been faithful to my family; I had not deserted them; I had been faithful to my children; and I had been faithful to my own moral code of right and wrong and the truth.

That is all, Anne, that I can say. Barbara will see some time—and not too far off—that I had to risk her friendship, her love, all, because there was no other choice. She has condemned me to my friends, has told untruths about me in her obsession to get away and live her own life.

We are trying to make an arrangement for Follett to sign about the house, and the children. A divorce court will not give him the children—either one. I will not give up my guardianship of Barbara to anyone while she is in this abnormal ill condition. Follett thinks she is morally upset because of *me*. *[In margin: "my influence! Bah!"]* But I have learned quite a lot about anyone who blames everything on someone else. I've been a fine goat for Follett; but soon the goat may grow horns, you know.

I was in Honolulu trying to get a job when this broke through here. And working at the Museum too, where I was checking up details relative to the islands. You see I am responsible for the Harper stuff somehow. And I had to come back here. Now, I don't know what next.

What I really was hoping was that you were coming to Tucson! It's not too far from L. A. and I was thinking of a winter with you! I'm glad of course about Edward, but I'd love you here.

I want to get a little stronger nervously before I tackle New Haven, Sabra, and the house—settling that up. Follett wants the four-poster bed—the one we had so much fun in discovering in his grandfather's attic, restoring, etc., and a lot of other things. One must have "guts" to go through that kind of sorting out, you know. Everything had been so completely *ours*. So I don't want to get back to N. H. until Spring.

I sold a thing—not very good—written down at Fiji when I was stranded—to Good Housekeeping. And I've sent off another. I do hope I can pull the writing through. That will be the thing to hope for.

Your letters have been the comfort of my life all along the way. I've waited for you and Oxford to say the thing is hopeless and that I had better clean up things. Just know this; it is difficult. I have to stay here a year in order to give him a divorce in this state, but I don't think I can do it here unless he is here, too. So that remains still in the air. I offered Follett in the presence of my lawyer to choose any divorce from the list he wanted—cafeteria style—with one exception (infidelity) and I would blindfold myself and sign it without contesting if he wanted to go to Reno and pay the bills over there. You can't do more than that. The lawyer wanted to know if he would do it, if he had the moral courage to commit that kind of perjury. Follett would. Moreover he professed himself—in the presence of the lawyer—willing to take Barbara into his home as it is now. And the lawyer said he could never advise anyone (meaning me) to allow a child in adolescence to live in a house of adultery. It might sound foolish, but he didn't believe that that kind of living should be encouraged.

Hasn't Follett smashed, Anne? Isn't he going round in circles? Or have all the rest of us smashed, and is he only right? It's either one or the other.

Whipple has done more harm than anyone because she has gossiped and said untrue things. Friends of mine have heard her say such things against me that even Follett himself winced. I remember so well when she first came to the house that she used to amuse us by her gossip about the Knopf office—it was funny, much of it—some a bit off; but clever and laughable. But it disturbed me and I said to Follett I wondered a bit at anyone who would gossip so about the people she worked for. Barbara has handed me some pretty touch remarks which I am sure she never originated. And the Court has a distinct reason for stopping her seeing Barbara. Remember that, also remember that I have complained to no one in authority about her presence here. If you will be sure not to misunderstand me, I'll say that I kept off because of the fear of drawing Barbara still deeper into the depths of unpleasantness.

Follett and Whipple have been to see Tyler and Sabra and Hildegarde. I don't like Whipple's going to see Sabra in my place. But I don't like to say anything about it for fear that it will sound jealous or mean or priggish. But I don't like it. Follett, yes, of course.

This must do for a starter. I have written this to no one. I don't want anyone but you and Oxford to see this letter. I don't like to write it.

I think I am pulling through. My mind seems pretty clear about the thing. Now—but Anne, what a Hell it has been, and still is—I've reasoned myself out of the worst of it. And I don't think I could do it had I not seen the whole thing pretty clearly from the beginning on, and that I have exposed my thinking to some pretty severe and exacting tests. I don't think I am going to worry much more for with all the bungles and messes I have made during the last indescribably terrible months, I could not, would not have changed the direction of my course. I feel so sure of this that I can say you would not, either. No sane person could have.

Barbara will see this some day, unless something very precious has snapped permanently during this adolescent growth of hers. Either one thing, or she is and will remain a psychopathic case. There are signs that her thinking is getting clearer. But I shall leave her alone for some months to come.

And of course I am dying for Sabra. By the time I get to her the worst in my life will be over, I think, and I hope I shall have something in myself great enough to give to her.

Write me. PLEASE.

Helen

The article in the August 1929 issue of the Atlantic *was* Fear *by "One Who Knows It" (my grandfather occasionally wrote anonymously or used a pseudonym).*

On November 29th the Carnegie, *after 291,000 miles at sea since 1909, exploded while refueling in the harbor of Apia, West Samoa—the same harbor Barbara and Helen had visited six months earlier. The ship burned completely, and Captain James P. Ault and Tony Kelar, the cabin boy, perished.*

[envelope postmarked December 10, 1929]
2001 Marengo Avenue
South Pasadena, Calif.

Dearest Anne:

Things have been so complicated in this part of the world that not a day has passed without its own private and personal cataclysm. The result is the only thing now that I have the time to pass on to you. The details which determined the result are soul-tearing, and heart-breaking.

I left this house because it was too much to watch Follett and Whipple around here, and to see them play the game for Barbara. I moved in town and stayed alone at the hotel, not seeing Barbara for a month. She was to stay with Mrs. Russell. During that month she saw her father et constantly, day after day. It had been determined that when the time came for Barbara to leave Mrs. Russell then she should have perfect freedom of choice as to her course.

Mrs. Russell's affairs changed very suddenly, owing to her daughter's illness, and her husband's losing a job at the time of the stock slump. Mrs. R. had to go and live with her daughter and take care of her. Barbara had to make a decision sooner than was expected.

She stayed here alone for a few days at Thanksgiving time. She made her own choice definitely and finally, and it was not for her father. He turned upon everyone, anyone who did not agree with him all the way. You know how he has now only use for the person who agrees with him. He hurt Mrs. Russell awfully, and it was Mrs. Russell who saved Barbara's life in many ways.

Now Follett is stating that I am "periodically insane." Can you beat it?

My friends here are working to get me established. It may be in Honolulu. I shall be in New Haven in March when the coldest weather is over and get Sabra, and shall take her away where Barbara and I will make a little home for her. Follett does not know this. Margaret Tyler wants to go to Germany, you know. She declares she will take Sabra with her [in margin: *"if I can't take her"*], but I think she should be relieved of her.

I can get not a cent out of Follett. He is not broke. Did you read Fear in the August Atlantic? That's his. And not yet has he made over the house to me. We wonder where the snag is there.

I have kept many of your letters, Anne. Not once did you let me down. Not once did you fail to keep me going, to have faith in me, to believe that I could sometimes get myself expressed in a creative way. That is even now my hope. It is the only thing I can do, perhaps. The regular school here is off me; a private school, possibly. A friend is trying for that in Honolulu.

I write hard here, and look out of the window and see Follett and Whipple go by. The Gods now are trying me out. And Anne, I am equal to them. I believe firmly that I have got inside myself and that I cannot be hurt any more. And I have now the faith in myself that you have held on to in me. I marvel at you; I marvel that you could and would believe in me in spite of every persuasive word used against me. I noticed that Follett fell a little low in his enthusiasm for his oldest and best friends. He cannot stand criticism. And it is pouring down on him. A doctor in Pasadena reported to me that Follett et had left no stone unturned in New Haven to hurt me. I can't bear to think of Follett engaged in that stuff.

Barbara is coming through gorgeously, finely. She has been put through things unmentionable. She has grown up, but every day I can see the old Barbara shining through—bitterness, suspicion, hatreds leaving her. She is relieved, I really think. I wish *they* would leave town.

I wish I could tell you how I feel about you, and about the fight you have put up for Follett's sake. I can't. You can do no more with him. No one can. He will have to do it for himself. And one wonders when and how.

I shall probably leave Barbara here to make a home somewhere while I go east by water for Sabra. The climate in Honolulu is superb; swimming all the year. And not anywhere near so expensive as New Haven. It looks good for me. Barbara wants San Francisco. That may turn out if I can make any connections there.

I do envy you and the family the lovely Christmas that is ahead of you. I had intended sending you some Samoan tapas, but I was called away from H. so suddenly, that I didn't get them. If I don't go back I can send for them. You may like them for the porch walls, perhaps. Some people like them extremely well.

Isn't it awful about the Carnegie? The survivors will land with the body of Captain Ault on the S. S. Ontario, the 19th of this month. Some day I may hear the story.

Of course I shall see you somehow when I hit the east. What do you want or need of my things for your house? I shall try to hang on to the choice antiques, but may get rid of rugs and other things. To get passage back to the islands.

We shall stay here till Jan. 1. After that we don't know. If Mrs. R. can take Bar I shall start for New York by way of a slow cargo boat. If not, I shall leave Bar somewhere to await my return. You see I have almost got to the point of planning. It's Helen Follett I'm going to concentrate on for a while!

I want to know about Edward. And what next for you? And my love for you all is very very deep. You hung on to a person struggling in torments that persisted in choking out life itself. Can I say more? I can, perhaps, say it in better language, but the truth is there.

Helen

After a long gap between letters from Barbara, finally one to Alice Russell. Helen wrote "Pasadena 1930" on it when gathering material for Harold McCurdy, but I think it's from a little before Christmas, 1929.

Tuesday Morning

My dear "Shipmate":

This morning came a package from down town; and, because there is no Christmas with us, and because one day is like another, we opened it, and found your *David Copperfield*. Oh, thank you ever and ever so much—it was grand of you to think of it, and to remember that I had wanted to read it. I shall start in with it as soon as I have finished *Kim*, which I am reading now. I have started *Kim* at least twice before, but never could get far with it. But now that I know a bit about foreign people, and have become interested in different tribes and castes, I find it magnificent, especially if you read it slowly.

I've finished *The Mill on The Floss*, of course; and it left me with mingled feelings. I suppose one would expect to have a sense of great victory and triumph; instead, it made me quite depressed. I haven't worked it out yet to any satisfaction. I hold to this: that if that was how Maggie felt, why then of course that was how Maggie should have done. I feel the same about Jane Eyre. The two climaxes in the two books remind me a great deal of each other. Both of them are depressing to me, because I can't decide whether it is *worth* it, or what it means, anyway. Only in *Jane Eyre* at least there is an ending which soothed your vitals somewhat. In books with such climaxes there *should* be soothing endings. A sensitive soul can't stand the strain imposed by a book like *The Mill*. I don't feel happy about that book; nothing has been done, everything has been sacrificed and lost, and sacrificed for nothing except vague and shadowy ideals. I don't deny that all *should* be sacrificed for ideals; what tears me to pieces is that anyone should be so made as to be forced by inner feelings to follow those ideals, at the cost of everything. I'm afraid I have a rather devil-may-care philosophy of life, dealing principally with the Self, and with happiness as the only ideal and the only aim. My soul and Maggie's are simply a terrific clash. I understand her, and admire her, and love her; and I know that she did only what she *had* to do; but it is depressing to me, as I said before, to feel that anyone should have to go to such an unreasonable extreme merely to satisfy an inner craving. That inner craving must be satisfied, of course, and it is right to satisfy it; but what irritates me is that such an illogical inner craving should exist at all. Apparently a soul like Maggie's never could be happy unless it starved itself, and no soul should be like that. What was G. E. like? Anything like that at all?

But enough of this. To return to the world again, the mails are most desperately tied up. There are "substitutes" all over the streets, and the P. O. is jammed. Nothing comes through at all, except for two or three occasional Christmas cards, which I shall diligently save for you. I am writing a little, for a bribe! And I am extremely happy. I've found out lots of things. It is a great old game, keeping on trying to adjust two natures like mine and Helen's so that they will fit. The couplings are mighty delicate, and fly first one way and then another, but I keep them nicely under control now.

I've discovered that one of the great points is to have plenty to eat, and plenty to sleep, and no worries. Whenever anything happens, I start planning what I shall have for dinner, or else I play a Symphony. I'm making good my boasts about winning. I have as good as won!

We both wish you such a Christmas as never was—inwardly, at least, which is the main point. And thanks ever so much. And if you're as happy as I, I shan't be worrying about you!

      Your shipmate,
      Barbara

4

NEW YORK CITY (1930-1931)

Compared to the previous two years, 1930 was calm and Barbara's emotional state continued to improve. For the first two months of the year she and her mother lived in Los Angeles working on Magic Portholes. She also corresponded with her two new friends, Alice Russell and Ed Anderson (who lived in Seattle between sailing gigs), and continued to receive love letters from her "dark suitor," Togasü Riggs.

Fugamisi *[Tonga]*
7th Jan 1930

Dear Loving friend.

[...] When I read your letter its makes my heart beating like an earthquake shocking. Because its on the letter. You going to try to come back to the Island again some time. *[...]* I want you to married with me. But I want you to let me know about this things that I point to, and I want you to be sure to me my dear girl. *[...]* And I let you know that time to be married with you. Let your families knows it. Let them know that I am goin to Marrie you. *[...]*

About your Hairs. I always kept your hairs in my P. Book. But I dont what Am I sent to you for treasure like your hairs that you gave to me. I wont for get that till the end of the World. *[...]*

> With best wishes to you & relations.
> B. T. Riggs

The next letter was to Alice. Barbara's grand pirate ballad was 1927's Poppy Island: A Ballad of Pirates, Treasure, Poppies, and Ghosts, *which didn't appear in print until 1966, in* Barbara: The Unconscious Autobiography of a Child Genius.

J. B. Priestley said of George Meredith's 1859 novel: "So far as English fiction is concerned... there can be no doubt that the modern novel began with the publication of The Ordeal of Richard Feverel.*"*

Saturday Morning [ca. mid January 1930]

Hail, Matey:

I feel that I owe you twenty-one thousand and seventy-nine apologies and alopogies and agopolies and other things. I am humiliated, and disgusted with myself, and I'm darnation sorry. But you forgive me, I trust, and hope. Don't you?

Things really are all right—momentary disturbances and subterranean mutterings, that's all. Being on a pinnacle of happiness and exaltation—I mean, of course—ex*u*ltation—I find that I am likewise on a pinnacle of sensitiveness, and a tiny spark fired off a whole train of things that started cavorting round inside till I lost my course and my compasses and got momentarily reversed. But they got back all right, in short time.

Your account of the earthquakes was most exciting. We had a few little quivers down here, but nothing like *that*. I don't like the darn things, I have to say. After all, the earth is all we've got, and when it begins to play tricks one feels terribly insecure and feeble and useless, somehow—not at all pleasant.

If you've got an idea for a yarn—stick to it. Don't let these other cooks join in the making of the broth. Wave them away as though they were flies. Be polite but uninfluenced! I wish you luck, and more luck; and I've a good deal of faith in you, what's more.

Helen had a ghastly day yesterday—went to the Progressive Educational meeting and came back like an over-used dishrag—and you know what *they* are! She got slam-banged and squelched and hurt and depressed, and it was very frightful. Unfortunately, it happened to be the day when I wasn't feeling up to standard either; so we were quite comically blue for half a day or so—she tearful; I grim, glum, and silent.

But we've been writing! I've been writing a lot. Nothing extraordinary, but enough to make one feel glimmerings of self-respect. I've done lots of steamer-stuff, and island-stuff, with light and breezy conversations in it—just what our MS has been needing, you know!

There's been six inches of snow in Seattle, and bitter cold; and this has prevented Anderson's job from going through—yet. And, because he also is a sensitive individual, such a little spark fired off a long train just as it did with me. He's all balled up, about *himself*, which is the worst kind of balling-up anyone can have, as you know. However, I think that also is decidedly on the improve, and I'm trusting so.

Helen has been considering jobs in China and Alabama. Both sound intriguing, except that China is such a darned mess right now.

I shall be sixteen in a little more than a month. I've had thoughts, at times, that instead of going back east I'll settle down grimly and take the first job I can get, no matter what it is. But Helen is insistent on finishing the book first, and perhaps she's right, now that she's got so far with it. If we could only serialize it! If only I could pay off Harper's! If only I could write!

Do any of your young folk's juvenile healthy-minded periodicals ever take long poems, or ballads? I wrote a grand pirate ballad a couple of years ago, which I was in love with then, and am in love with still. Vanity Fair once offered to take it, if I would cut it down in length, which my father wouldn't let me do. It amounted originally to forty-two four-line stanzas. This made about three and a half pages. I can cut it down to twenty-seven stanzas, making a little less than two and a half pages. And it's a grand story, and quite a breezy piece of verse, I think. I like it, perhaps because I never did anything else of its sort, and perhaps because it has got so much adventure and mystery and colour in it. Well, enough—I'll send it to you. I'll send you the poem as it is cut down. The stanzas which I took out were purely descriptive—of the island, of the treasure, and so on.

Meanwhile, my dear, one last word of advice from a sage and experienced character: don't let those children of yours up there interfere with your writing. Let *them* do the dishes for a change!

        Yours ever,
        Barbara

P. S. I'm at present being intellectually tumbled and lifted and slam-banged by reading one of the greatest books ever written: *The Ordeal of Richard Feverel*. I'm insane over it; I think it is magnificent, but crashing and smashing. It has the same effect on my mind that the sea has on my heart—if you know what I mean.

I think "That Person" was Andrew Burt, but I don't know about "the ban upon a Certain Region of the World." Did he forbid her to come to Montreal?

The Awakening of Helena Ritchie was a 1906 novel by Margaret Deland. "Max" is Max Lewis, Elizabeth's new husband—they married on New Year's Eve, 1929. As for Barbara's Idea—I have none. I guess it didn't work out.

[undated, but I think late January 1930]
Sunday Morning

My dear Watchmate:
    What is the Postal Department of the U. S. A. coming to? Lord

have mercy on us all!

I reicived (Mate Bill's spelling) your letter day before yesterday—was glad to her form you agen. Your letter from England was most amusing; but then, after all, what can one expect? I suppose it's entirely reasonable; though, as Anderson would put it, "It is to smile."

In regard to China—I'll quote from Anderson. "The news of the unsettled conditions prevailing in China comes as something of a relief, in so far as it affects any immediate emigration of the Folletts. Frightful place, China. I've been out there a couple of times, and always felt a bit silly riding in a rickshaw. Takes an Englishman in a top hat to carry the white man's burden, so called, with any degree of dignity. I suppose I am as observant as the average, but at that I failed to notice much in the European part of Shanghai that differed greatly from any city of equal size anywhere else. What novelty or glamour exists within the native quarter is more than discounted by strange sounds and bewildering smells. The American concession is more American than New York or San Francisco, and so it is with the British concession."

Anderson is distinctly a satirist. He says that he "can't understand why it should be continually necessary for lawyers to write 'final letters' to Follett." When I reminded A. of Helen's belief that A. considered her exceptionally sane, he replied that "the memory of it eludes me." A. is really about the only entertainment I have, you see: you have no idea how one must suppress and curb one's Self when living with Helen!

By the way, I have news of That Person who had put a ban upon a Certain Region of the World. The ban is now lifted—hurray! This is not direct news, but indirect—through Helen. Will wonders never cease? Things always happen in the most unexpected manner, don't they? Well, it does not worry me. But I'm glad that we've finished that part of our writing which was saturated with ghostly atmosphere—I have a feeling the ghost may sleep in peace now.

I've read "Helena Richie" and am struck with Helena's resemblance, in more than one respect, to our own Helen here. I think it's a fine book—not a tremendous book; but then, one doesn't want all books to be tremendous, for it would make a dishrag out of one very soon.

Max's praise is overpowering—I can't think what evoked it. Maybe it's a touch of Max's typical sarcasm and cynicism.... By the way, I've come, incidentally, to some conclusions....

What really and truly pleased me, was your praise of my little pome. I think your suggestion of the St. Nicholas was a good one—we'll try it. I've hidden it from thee because, my dear, I haven't had a copy of it till recently, and had nearly forgotten it—just had a smouldering recollection in the anterior of my cere—whatever-it-is. Shipmate, do you think I could find any market for an exciting and colorful and mysterious pirate yarn which I may write shortly? I adore pirates, and can "do" them up to the limit. I propose treasure buried in caves on floating islands, and whatnot.

Friday we drove down to Wilmington with —— —— the Palmerstons, who have been very, very good to us. We saw a disgusting vessel which was a cross between a schooner and a motorship, boasting four masts and eight Diesel engines. She brought in eight hundred tons of raw copra, and we watched the copra mill for some time, and were escorted through it by an elderly gentleman whose name is McDevitt, and who writes a letter without using a single punctuation mark, and who spells *does* "dose." But he showed us the whole works, and was very kind. And I yarned to a Danish skipper, and a lone lorn engineer who hadn't talked to anyone for ages and ages, and was so glad to unloosen his tongue that he bored us all to extinction.

I've had an idea—I'd better say An Idea—and I wish I had a red ribbon to write it in—large red capitals. If it works, and I haven't yet found any nigger in the woodpile, it should improve the Folletts' finances considerably and pleasantly. I shall find out all about it next week; and it may be a definite reason for our coming back to California in the future.

No yob has turned up—I don't think we particularly desire one, too much. By "we" I mean not particularly Me, but Others. Dinna be askin' me, mon; I'm tellin' ye plain, I dinna ken.

More power to the Story!

Tell me, shipmate mine, am I being pickled in brine and preserved?

Yours for better days,
B. F.

Oh, G-D this —— —— —— writing! xx! x! It's doubtless "good" for me—but it's fiendish, devilish, hellish Hell; it tends to give me yellow fever to the nth degree; and I'd as soon drink ten qts. of cod liver oil. And I cannot even express my feelings on the subject—except to thee, my dear. And the pressure gauge reads "Danger."

However, don't be worried! At that, I'm happier than any mere human has any right to be: and I don't need no bluebirds, neither!

S.M.S.
Fugamisi
1st February 1930.

Dear Loving friend

[...] Soon as your letter reach to my little office and I am very supprise to read it. The first thing I am looking for to have look at the end of the letter to know where the letter came from. And when I saw the name and I stopped read, and I looked down to your name, and I leened down my head and cry because I am very pleased to hear of some good news from you my dear loving friend.

But one thing I want let you know my dear. Please can you send me one of your real Photo and you write your name on. I also write my Poor name after. [...] I never finish with you till the end of this poor world.

I wished you had a good Luck then. But myself I am always think about you dear. I won't forget that on the steamer. Also I am still kept your Golden hair I alway put in my pocket when I travel about. I never go to any other country because I want to meet you here again, can you try to come back here some other time [...]

      I remain your trully friend
      I, B. Togasu Riggs
      Heap of kisses {xxxxxx} xxxxxx }
      xxxxxx xxxxxx

I don't believe Alice's White Doom *was published. Mark Twain's* The Mysterious Stranger *came out in 1916, posthumously.*

[undated, but I think early February 1930]
Saturday Morning

Dear A. D. R.:

Yesterday afternoon came your long, imposing-looking manuscript-envelope, forward out from South Pasadena. And now I'll tell you exactly how *White Doom* affected me. When I read it the first time, I realized that you had put your finger right on the secret of my feelings about the desert. I feel *just* like that about the desert! Whether or not that's an indication that it "comes off" I leave you to decide. *I* think it does. It's so brutally inevitable and terrible—it simply freezes the marrow in one's bones. That's what it should do. That's what the desert does. Yes, I'm sure it comes off. I've read it three times, and like it better every time. It grows on you. But I *don't* hate it, except that I hate the desert in the same way that your story does; and I do see why you wrote it, though that's lots harder to explain.

What's more, I don't think there's another thing to be done to it, and Helen doesn't either. It seems to me to be in grand shape; all the details seem just right to us. I'd leave it as it is. I don't know anything about how or where it could best be sold. It doesn't seem Pictorial Reviewish, somehow. In fact, one doesn't often read a magazine with a grim and terrible story in it. Or if they are grim and terrible, they always turn out well in the end—the wrecked sailors rescued, or the suffering fireman rewarded with an admiralty badge, or something. In fact, you don't see marrow-freezing stories! So it seems a problem to me; but that's a minor problem, anyhow, and doesn't matter nearly so much—except as regards finances, of course!

I do want to see you, very frightfully much, if you know what I mean, Pooh. We'd rather like to push our feeble and abortive attempts beneath your nose—though since reading your story I rather quake in the knees about doing so. What we are doing is so unspeakably *puny*. I've just read *The Mysterious Stranger*, by the way; and I've brought the book down here to read it to Helen—whenever I think of anything trivial and puny I always think of that book—what a glorious work of unfettered imagination it is!

A. D. R., if our feeble and abortive attempts aforementioned ever come to anything, may we dedicate them to you? We'd like to so much!

I didn't mean that *you* were pickling me in brine—I just meant, *was* I being pickled? And I can't remember any of the other mysterious allusions I may have mentioned in that letter. That's how correspondence is! I swear they've gone clean out of my mind. But I don't mind your hunting them to their lairs, if you've a mind to do that.

I can't give any tid-bits from Anderson this time, because I've not been supplied with any since I last wrote to you. BUT! I received a four-page document from my Tongan friend in Vavau, in which the amiable lad proposed marriage to me in the true native fashion, and winded up saying that his heart was "beating like an earthquake." Isn't that exciting? Rather a problem, though, to know just what to do about it. Shall I go and keep house in a grass hut in the Tonga Islands? I can't imagine myself doing it, somehow, even though Fugamisi may be the son of a very high-ranking native chieftain! (I wouldn't mention this to anyone—it may be humorous, but it should be a secret, for all that.)

Did I tell you that the ban is lifted in Jamaica? Let's go down there and hide and remain in obscurity together forever! I think you and I'd get on first-rate. Our many and various families can get on without us, for a change. The ban seems to have settled, however, upon the Tonga Islands. I wouldn't dare to go down there! Not that I want to see the Tongas again, anyway. They haven't the lure for me that they have for Helen. I think the West Indies are much more beautiful.

Oh, I do want to see you! As soon as you come down, mind! Telephone us, or something. Our number is WAshington 2819. There's so much to talk about, and explain, and understand, and so on.

Well, as a closing word, I repeat: Don't do anything more to that story of yours, because it's perfect as it is, and needs no more work at all.

    Your shipmate ever,
    Barbara.

3518 West 3rd Street is in Los Angeles's present-day Koreatown, not far from MacArthur Park.

["Feb 1930" according to Helen's note]
Tuesday Night

Dear A.D.R.

Forgive! I make no excuse—I am obviously indulging in a selfish and *bad* spell of utter laziness—too lazy even for Farksoo!!!

We were put out of our apartment on account of a newly-wed pair of permanent tenants: now we're in a confused and tiny place belonging to the same establishment—3518 W. 3rd—just roun' de co'ner.

Honestly, A.D., I'm *no good!* Haven't the gumption of a weevil in a biscuit—and don't particularly want to have, either.

I can't say right now anything *definite* about the *Marsodak*. Even the S.S. Co. don't know any too much *consairning* her. But there'll be tons of time to write to Panama.

Anderson is still at sea in the yacht. Bless his heart—he sent me a telegram when they sailed so suddenly that he didn't have time to write. Weather reports say "gentle southerly wind"—this of course is all wrong for him—sails, ye ken.

Ye'd better be disillusioned about me *right away*, A.D. Really, I'm not worth the respect of a *mosquito*. But I'm happy as I can be!

    Bar.

[undated, but I think late February 1930]
3518 W. 3rd St.
Tuesday Night

Dear A. D. R.:

Helen received your letter yesterday; and she said that she thought at the time it was too late to answer it, as you were coming down this week, and as mail is so absolutely, hideously———well "What is the Postal Department coming to?" says Anderson. A sentiment with which we all agree.

Anyhow, she telephoned Gladys, who also agreed; and then tonight we both changed our minds, and so I'm tapping this off in a hurry. Oh, my dear, forgive me that last nasty little note of mine, won't you? I want to talk to you face to face, instead of writing.

Cause: the cargo-boat is late. Effect: We shall probably not sail until Saturday, possibly Sunday. Remarks: If we sail Sunday Gladys can't take us! Query: What then? Item: Such is life.

Helen is very much interested in a Pathé Studio dramatist, which may—I repeat, MAY—mean a reason for our coming back here sometime in two incarnations from now. (I hope you don't believe in reincarnation?) We've had lots of excitement and confusion, and don't quite know where we are. Right now we're in that stage between twilight and night—or, rather, twilight and dawn—where we don't know whether we're in California or Arabia, and where we both desire above all things to go to bed—and can't see any farther ahead than to that particular consummation-devoutly-to-be-wished.

This Tuesday has been not a day but A DAY. One of the grandest, and one of the most awful imaginable things took place this afternoon right on each others' heels, leaving us feeling in somewhat of a "Mid-air status quo," as Anderson puts it very effectively. (He, by the way, has been having Adventures, too; and now has got two jobs instead of none at all!) He won't be down here, though.

I did such an awful thing this afternoon that "poor sap" would be far too mild a term for me. "Damn fool" would be better, but it is too common. So I'll call myself a "jobildunked blastoderm"— which, if violently pronounced, is at least interesting-sounding. I—I repeat—*I*—left open the door of the apartment of our friend the-lady-who-believes-in-reincarnation, and her priceless yellow Persian cat escaped and can't be found, and the lwbir (see above) is absolutely heart-broken, and I feel like a worm—you know that feeling, I guess.

As for your story being sent back, I think that's too awful for words; and my heart goes out to you with a feeling of real impulsiveness—you know what I mean. It's too damn awful, that's what. And why, why, WHY? Well, as I've said before, such is life.

How's this for a headline: LITTLE CUT-UP MAN CARVES WIFE. !!?!!??!

> Yours while the earth doth turn,
> Bar.

Gordon Campbell included a few photographs with his letter, including two of the Carnegie *in the Arctic and one of Captain Ault holding a sextant.*

At Sea.
March 2nd 1930.

Dear Miss Barbara.

[...] Well I suppose you heard the bad news about the "Carnegie" being burnt up and the Captain getting killed. I was wondering if you could give me any information about it as I was at Sea at the time just happened to pick up an old newspaper and saw where Captain Ault was brought back to Washington.

I did not hear if any of the others were hurt or not, and I thought may-be you would be able to tell me as I suppose Doctor Paul hase given you all the news by the way give my best regards to the doctor next time you see him and also my best regards to your Mother.

[...] I am at present about 200 miles NE of Cape Hatterass bound from New Orleans to London so I will post this as soon as I arrive in port so I will be dissappointed if I have no mail on arrival in New Orleans.

[...] Don't forget Barbara give me all the news of Tahiti and write soon as you know you never answered my last letter. But I forgive a shipmate a little thing like that. *[...]*

> Your Shipmate
> Mr. Gordon Campbell

Barbara's sixteenth birthday was momentous. With the Russells' help she cut her long hair into a bob, and she and her mother began their voyage back east on the Marsodak.

S. S. Marsodak
March 4 *[1930]*

Dear A. D. R., *et al*:

Just before I opened that package of yours, I felt it all over, and I studied its weight with great care; and it seemed vaguely to me that I had seen something like it, somewhere else, sometime before. And the longer I felt it and looked at it, the more this conviction grew, until at last I gave a sudden whoop, and said: "Aha! I know now what it is." And when I opened it I was right. Well, it's a grand thing to possess—especially seeing that it is such a very historic copy. I like books with histories—or anything with histories, for that matter.

Now to the story which was so ardently requested; for lack of an ability to draw, I shall perform my bestest endeavor to portray with accuracy the—well, the Results. I stood on the corner of Sixth and Main, as agreed, and about ten minutes later the roadster pulled up, loaded down to the plimsoll mark and a little over. Helen glanced at me as I stepped bravely out, and suddenly said excitedly: "What have you done with your hair?" She told me that she had thought I had "put it up differently, or something." And then, when she saw the true state of things, she emitted a sound of combined emotions; and for a few minutes there you'd have thought it was the most tremendous thing that had ever happened in the history of the earth, and infinitely vaster and more important and vital in effect upon the whole of humanity than anything that ever took place in the annals of the universe.

Barbara with hair long and bobbed

The rest of the day, at intervals, she kept saying how different I looked, and how queer; and I don't think she really liked it very much, though of course she couldn't help seeing the practical usefulness of the thing—oh, how practical and useful it is!—and then it faded gradually into oblivion, where I hope it may remain. But it was one of the best afternoon's works I have ever accomplished—or perhaps ever shall; and I thank the Russells for the inspiration to my failing courage, and their spiritual splicing of my main brace!

The S. S. *Marsodak* is all my heart could have desired, and more. She's the most informal, happy-go-lucky, undisciplined ship afloat. There isn't a white uniform aboard; everyone mixes with everyone else—the captain works like the rest—one of the junior engineers is likely to come in to the captain's room and slap him staggeringly on the back—they're all intimate, informal, and unrestrained. It's simply *glorious*! There are six passengers; four of them men, so that Helen and I are the only feminine things around except the ship herself and, of course, the wives of the seagulls and flying-fish. That's lucky, too—the usual first-class type would not enjoy the *Marsodak* to the full—I feel convinced of that.

Alice Russell and Barbara on her sixteenth birthday

The captain's a fine soul, just about the most human skipper we've met, I think. The deck department is an amusing assortment; for the first and third mates are gigantic men, enormously stout and pompous; and the second mate, who sits between them at the table, is a man smaller than I, though sturdy and well-built; so that it's quite ludicrous, and everyone laughs over it, and nobody minds in the least. The engine department is a bunch of grand, taciturn characters; and there never existed a more likely-looking set of A. B.s than the sailors—men of Anderson's stamp inwardly. The gulf which yawns between him and them is nothing but the gulf of the education he has given himself; which most of them haven't. But you can see the terrific close affinity—as, indeed, you can among all seafarers.

We're carrying a deckload of lumber for Norfolk, and a hold-full of copper for Baltimore. So she's well loaded, and steady as a ferry. The sea has been millpondish since the very beginning, and getting hot now as we go southward. I sit out in the bow, or on the upper deck, and read *The Rescue [Joseph Conrad, 1920]*, which is one of Those Books that simply *go through* a person, if you know what I mean.

Well, that's about all, I guess—pleasant, lazy life for me! I shudder to think that it must ever end. Farewell for the nonce; I can't give you any address now except the New Haven one; but I will write to you at Baltimore. We may stay there some time. . . . I had some vague idea when I started this that I might be able to say something appropriate to you. But I find I can't, you know; so I'll have to pass on the unspoken thought instead. Believe me, it's just as much in existence for not being put down on paper!

    Yours for happy days,
    Barbara.

The apartment in Washington was between the White House and the Lincoln Memorial—an easy walk to the cherry blossoms circling the Tidal Basin.

"The Source" was Barbara's father. He and my grandmother reviewed scripts for MGM while living in the Pickwick building on South Grand Avenue—or at least that's where they were in April 1930, when the census was taken.

Potomac Park Apts.
21st and C Streets, N. W.
Washington, D. C.
April 7 [1930]

Brave Matey:

I received your letter just where I should have—at that quaint, friendly, slow-moving town of Savannah, where we stayed six or seven hours. When one goes to sea, one thanks the lord almighty that one is out of the range of telephone calls, jazz orchestras, agents, and gas bills, "and the benefits of civilization generally"—but let me tell you, it is an extremely pleasant sensation to see the customs official or the ship's agent come up the gangway with a hearty smile and a packet of mail, and on the very top of that packet a letter addressed to oneself in a well-known and well-beloved handwriting.

The *Marsodak*, to me, made up for just about everything. I am sure she made up for the extreme discomfort of landing on the east coast. When we arrived in Baltimore, where there was no one, and no mail, and no money, and no telegram, Helen and I had a mild attack of hysterics, and were quite light-headed together for awhile. And Helen said: "Shall we wear these stockings, or had we better not?" And I replied: "That is the question." You have no idea how heart-rendingly pathetic and funny and ridiculous it all was.

Washington is a very beautiful city. I remember it as such, and I am not disappointed. The cherry-blossoms are out around the Tidal Basin. But there is always a "but" to these things. And in this case the "but" is a financial one—and that is a very important variety, as you will admit. You see, we have not received as yet any of those phonetically aesthetic phenomena known as "large checks"—and the absence of those seraphic esculents does *not* add to the scene. When one considers, too, that everything is eggsackly twice as expensive in this diminished West Longitude from Greenwich, why then—well, one yearns, for more reasons than one, to be again in the increased West Longitude from Greenwich, and to be there At Once.

Do you know anything about what has gone wrong with the alleged and assumed source from which the large checks *au mirage* were alleged and assumed sometime in the future to flow? If so, I confess to a mild sort of human curiosity on the subject. Also: do *not* reveal to the alleged Source the exact whereabouts of Us. Helen wishes this to be a secret for awhile. If the Source wishes to communicate, he (or It) may do so *via* thee, my shipmate.

The news of E.'s being in the hospital for appendicitis was a terrific shock. Give her my love, and a hunk of salt horse to munch, which is the sailor's remedy for all ills of mind or body, and a good one! I hope business is improving in the desert, and that there will soon be some Vast Sums (oh, mellifluent sound!) rolling in the general direction of the Russells. And of us, I may add!

The General Course of Action of the Follett Clan (perhaps "Clan-Follett" would be better) is to remain here for more or less a month, and work like the devil—like two of 'em, rather. Helen is doing some corking writing, and I edit, copy, re-copy, and suggest; and together we are making very palatable corned beef hash. Your wish for "excitement and happiness" has not been listened to by the celestials—but that's all right. I had a grand taste of it in the *Marsodak*. I learned how to navigate—picked it up like lightning amid the praises and good wishes of the entire deck crew. And I watched dolphins leap after flying-fish, and porpoises playing under the forefeet, and tropical sunrises and sunsets, and the spray flying clear over the bridge on that day when we had a stiff breeze and lost the bottles on the table. And I made one or two friends of the sort that the sea gives you at its best—those that share your sense of humor, and your general tastes, and your sensitiveness, and your introspectiveness, and would give you the shirts off their backs gladly, and know the same of you, and will be your friends forever and ever.

I want some more news of the Russells—how Pheobe is, and how E. is, and how The Great Exception is getting on, financially and otherwise; also if there is anything to say about the Source and Co., I should be much interested. I may write to It when I have time. Now I am going down town on some Urgent Errands, and so I must say farewell for the nonce.

>   Yours ever,
>   Barbara.

P. S. I *do* like the type—it's quaint and different and artistic, I think.
P. P. S. Have you heard anything about who won the contest? B.
P. P. P. S. What *does* your last headline-contribution mean? I can't make head nor tail o't: "Suds slap stars silly." Can an explanation be offered? B.

"Dr. P." is John Harland "Harley" Paul. His book, The Last Cruise of the Carnegie, *was published by Williams and Wilkins Co. in 1932. Barbara edited the manuscript at 15 cents per page.*

Washington, D. C.
April 28 *[1930]*

Dear A. D. R.:

Still here, and working like fiends. The writing becomes more magnificent every second; it really is *grand*, and it really must "go," I think. There is no longer the faintest trace of a "narrative style" about it; the whole thing has split itself into little episodes, each one a complete little entity, with a definite climax and a definite "point." Some of them are screamingly funny, others quite sad and wistful. These episodes are split from each other by little section-marks consisting of a triangle of dots. There isn't even any attempt at strict chronological truth any more. The imagination has come into its own.

These episodes are not even uniform in length—they are just as long or as short as they want to be. Some are eight or nine pages, others half a page. The whole book, every line in it, is entertaining and thoroughly charming, I think. There's not the repetition of an idea; and even the sea-stuff is varied to an extreme. The characters are uproarious, picturesque, consistent. Negro characters, nautical characters, scientific characters, and ourselves—anyone who knows us would find our self-portraits just true enough to be very humorous.

But it is heart's blood, believe me! I wish I could draw an accurate graph of Helen writing an episode. On one side of such a graph would be the progress of the episode; on the side at right angles to it would be Helen's corresponding state of temper, in which high would mean very bad. Thus, the beginning of the episode would be very high, where she realizes that it's got to be written. The temper remains about the same while she flounders around—then she gets an idea, and the temper drops abruptly to a very happy frame of mind, near the bottom of the scale; there it remains a short time—then difficulties galore are encountered, and the temper line shoots to the very peak of the scale, and the apartment is an accurate representation of the nether regions, for a while, varying in length from half an hour to two days; then the difficulties are worked out; and with another abrupt drop the temper-line returns to a frame of mind in which the universe seems to be her special oyster, and a very nice one.

To be entirely fair, I own that my own temper-line would have to be marked in such a graph, along with hers; and I think the curves would be more or less similar, though not quite so exaggerated... Well, maybe I'll work this out sometime. If I do I'll send you a copy!

The other job seems a bit indefinite; though I've already hauled in a good deal of pocket-money from Dr. P. Helen now tells me that I'm absolutely indispensable to her, and must go north with her, and help clear out the house, and so on. But if I see the prospects of landing a job here, nothing shall daunt me!

The job performed by the Russells in Pasadena, on Saturday afternoon, was a noble job. The hair started curling up tight as soon as it was set free; it doesn't bear the faintest resemblance to what it was then. It has a wave in it that hardly anyone will believe is natural! And it is really the best thing that ever happened. While I'm on that subject, I believe I will quote from Anderson's latest. I wrote to him from Baltimore, sitting at the saloon table of my beloved *Marsodak*, asking what would happen to me if I should cut my hair off (tactfully not saying that it had been done, you see!) And here is what I got back:

"It seems that I am called upon to remark upon two matters of some importance, if one can consider the matter of a haircut of any importance. As you are probably bobbed, and even possibly shingled by this time, there's nothing to do but yield with good grace, and submit a word of commendation upon good sense, and convenience, in place of an approving glance. Bobbed hair is really charming, you know, when it doesn't hang straight down like rope-yarn from an Irish pennant. As you assure me that yours is wavy and inclined to curl, we may count the tresses well lost."

In the next breath he springs the Arctic adventure, the absolute out-of-touchness with the world for four months, and the element of risk and danger—all quite unconcernedly, and in the same somewhat humorous and heavy literary style. He then professed great concern for my personal welfare. At that time there had been quite a tempest, financially and otherwise, and I sort of expected I should have to walk the streets any minute for any kind of labor I could find. During this crisis, I wrote to Anderson. And he came back with putting his worldly fortune at my disposal, at any time, and with expressing great grief and concern over it.

"I only pray," he says, "it doesn't cast you into the day-laboring class. I've been in it long enough to know what it amounts to, and what its probable end is. The sort of existence that leaves a woman a slattern at forty, and a man a dolt. Or if they have some perception, leaves them with a sort of misanthropic cynicism, bereft of ideals and appreciation of life.... This must all seem very serious and dull, coming from me."

Maybe I'm prejudiced somehow, but I think knowing a person like that is a great adventure.

I could also quote ad infinitum from the letter which arrived just before the last one, in which he remarks that there is one thing I have in common with my father—"the tendency, or ability, to dream." Then he said that my dreams were "beautiful and sane," instead of being "distorted, perhaps through long suppression, who knows?" Then he became somewhat grandfatherly, saying that dreams would have to be put on the shelf for the present, under these entirely practical conditions. Then he charitably said: "Sure! Don't I know? Haven't I sat on deck in the moonlight, and let fancy put on its seven league boots, and go roaming?"

Well, enough of this! This takes me too far away from the immediate present, which I've got to set my mind on pretty hard. I keep busy now from getting-up to going-to-bed, and time whizzes. I am happy, on the whole. Not ecstatically so, one couldn't be; but sort-of at zero, if you know what I mean. Not definitely one thing or another. I am hardly a person right now—I am more like a machine. Typewriting, typewriting, editing, editing, cooking, sweeping, mopping.... That sort of thing. And busy as the devil, every minute, though not about the same things! (I hope.) I want to remain that busy until about next January, when I think I'll take a vacation of some sort—if not materially, at least mentally and spiritually—come down to Baltimore and look at a ship again, or lock my door (wherever my door will be then!) for a week or so and work on Farksoo and think; or take a train up to New Hampshire and look at the winter woods; or climb Monadnock and sing a song.

Dr. Tyler, who is taking care of Sabra, came down a few days ago, on her way south with some friends; and she dropped in to spend the night. It was very nice to see her, but made us all feel a little queer, if you can imagine it. She talked a lot about Sabra, and made us all very homesick—made me want to send a telegram to Follett and say: "Drop it, you poor fool—and come HOME!" Helen hopes to have money enough this summer to take the cottage in the New Hampshire woods. Then I could have the woods again, and Sabra. I think that is a gorgeous scheme; and I only hope there *will* be money—though God knows where it is to come from. If we went up there I should still keep busy. More physically than mentally. I should climb hills and swim lakes, and sail my boat, and play around with my little sister (that will be some job, for Tyler says she is a positive "whirlwind.") I'll entertain her, and keep her busy, by building her a little shack in the woods, and making a wild-flower garden, and that sort of thing. And I should hope to do some writing, too.

In fact, wherever I am, and whoever I am with, I am going to keep very busy until about next January. And by that time, if I've controlled my temper at all the crucial moments, and my tears at all the appalling ones, and my patience at all the nervous ones, and my sense of beauty at all the hideous ones, and a degree of common-sense at all the flurried ones, and prevent myself from becoming hard and bitter during those damn-fiendish ones that tear your vitals—why, then, I think I shall have earned a vacation, by about next January.

The cherry-blossoms are over now. We have seen Mrs. Pratt just once—tomorrow she is coming to take us out to Capitol View, and to drive us about a little. She seems like an extremely nice person; and we all sat and talked about the Russells, and old times, and it was very jolly. She described the Russells' flurried and hasty departure for California, and the two tea-kettles left over; and it sounded so much like the Folletts that we laughed until the tears ran down our cheeks.

Even if I don't get a regular and permanent sort of job here, I think we shall stay here about a month longer. We are not needed in New Haven till August, and Helen yearns to get as much as humanly possible of the book finished. She works altogether too hard, of course; but by Jove what writing! We hope to get the book completed, and the final copy made, up to Tahiti, before going home. That should be half of it at least. That will be enough to exhibit the King of England himself. There is a good deal of work about the beginning to do—you see, she improved so vastly that she found the beginning positively *rotten* by contrast, and worthy of the garbage can; so she has rewritten the whole beginning. And it's *infinitely* better than anything you've seen of hers. I had no idea she could pull off anything of the kind. It's full of light-hearted, humorous conversation, beautiful little patches of description, not too much; and—oh, well, there's just no use talking about it, that's all! It makes my own stuff sound dull, and heavy, and thick, and formidable, and sluggish, and thoroughly awkward and ridiculous.

Speaking of writing: I hope the pot-boiler and the whole-hearted young man (God! how I yearn to spit at these whole-hearted young men!) sells with a bang; and I don't doubt it will—*that sort* always does. But I always think of *your* writing as being the other kind—the soul-mauling kind.

Well, I can see that I shall have to stop. This won't go into an ordinary envelope, if I don't stop soon—I can see that. Anderson wrote me a ten-page letter once, quite a long time ago, and wound up with: "If I write any more, I'll have to send it by parcel post!"

> Your shipmate eternally,
> Barbara

Washington, D. C.
May 26, 1930

Dear old Barnacle *[Norman Donaldson]*:

Isn't it satisfactory to have the old mail packet under sail again? Believe it or not, here's *one* old sea-dog who is thrilled to the marrow about it!

You are Dead Right, matey—N.H., Conn., is NOT the place for anyone with the name of Follett and the temperament of a navigator instead of an anchorer (always spiritually speaking, you unnerstan'). You are Deader Righter about New York as The Place, and about the Absence of Jobs. They are surely conspicuous by their non-existence.

Howbeitsoeverinasmuchaswhichly, I have Formed a Determination. I am going either to Have a Job or a Definite Prospect for A

Job, by June 15th, if it's in a coal-heap in the W. I.'s. And incidentally, *may* I use your name as a person who could assure another person that I am neither a vamp nor a pick-pocket, but a reliable and middlingly intelligent coral polyp? Because that might perchance be Useful, if you Perceive my Meaning, Pooh.

Just above my solaplexus and somewhat a-starboard of my 'art, there is a certain silver pin with a certain full-rigged ship on it, presented to me by a certain lady whom you know very well indeed. That pin has been continually in the same Lat. and Long. on its earth, while its earth has wandered the Lats. and Longs. of the Earth, while the Earth has wandered the Lats. and Longs. of the Universe in General. That ship, anyway, chronometers or no chronometers, has been christened *Undaunted*, and has come safely through many a perilous adventure unscathed. It has been used as a shirt-button, a slip-strap, a Pricking Weapon of Defense (we won't go into details), a Symbol, a Friend, a Bribe, and a general Shipmate. So you can readily understand that I am attached to it immensely, and you may tell the certain young lady so. By to Hell with this—what I meant to say was that the ship, the *Undaunted*, represents ME!!!!!

Did you ever hear that grand old negro spiritual: "I got a home in-a dat rock, Don't you see?" It's my very most favoritest song, and I'm going to sing it to you someday over our NBR (Canada Dry?).

I told you, did I not?, that I am now working in the employment of one of the observers who was in the *Carnegie*. This particular observer is a certain medical gentleman, whom you *may* just *possibly* have heard of. I am editing, in my most expertest manner, his official narrative of the cruise, and receiving from time to time one of the Succulent Tid-bits known as CHEQUES. Fact is, I receive an almost super-salary. (The word "super" is so much the vogue, don't you know?) No, there is no more to tell. That's all. I just told you because I wanted to prove to you what a marvellous person I really am.

Furthermore, I am negotiating two businesses simultaneously, in addition to my Secretarial Labors for both the M.D. and for Helen. These two businesses are both glittering gold, succulent, splendid, unlimited. Neither of them has worked out yet, though.

I have been to Monsieur le Commissioner of Civil Service. However, that's definitely Out of the Question. I couldn't make it now if I wanted to, and by God the thundering king and his whole armada of angels, I don't want to. When I am forty-nine years old, I'll consider it—if I'm still an old maid, that is. Until then, heaven defend me from the damn thing.

This all sounds like a great deal of busy-ness, doesn't it?—until one stops to analyze it. Then one finds several things that haven't worked, and one thing that did. That one thing, ceasing as it does very shortly, because of the departure for unknown regions of the M. D. above-mentioned, may also be considered as non-existent. So what this all boils down to, as one of your marvellous business abilities may easily perceive, is exactly o—in other words, a great deal of Hot Wind.

Well, well, well! That's life for you.

Helen's writing is stunning, glorious, superb. I am a partic'lar person, too, and a good critic. It's magnificent stuff, and ought to go like a half a gale. To tell the truth, I am a trifle uneasy about Harpers. You see, I had a contract with 'em which I did not keep. In fact, I disgraced myself, probably, in their eyes. There will be no hope for my reputation until Helen's book lies at their feet. Then there is still no hope for me until they read it, like it, and accept it—and all of those desirable consummations may not consummate, if you know what I'm talking about, at all. In which case, my reputation as a person of any stability is non-existent. I couldn't even hint about a job with them, unless they get really enthusiastic over this writing. *This is all strictly personal.*

So really, when one comes right down to the barest of bare facts—and I *love* bare facts, and I hate these silken individuals who insist on delicately draping them with scarves and banners—to come right down to salt as salt, and north-west as north-west—it all boils down to absolutely o.

Isn't that crashingly cheerful?

And I'm absolutely happy, and sing to myself, sometimes aloud, sometimes deep down internally: "I got a home in-a dat rock, Don't you see?"

I believe I'm getting long-winded. I've suspected it for several paragraphs past, but then, what the Hell, etc., can one expect from an old skipper? Especially one who has had an interesting voyage? Would he keep quiet about the winds, and the sails, and the cargo? Not he!

We should leave here the end of this week. I have invented a table, called Discardination of Local Apparent Time, being a table which my excellent friend Mr. Bowditch absolutely forgot to remember—this is a table for keeping track of D-vo, D-vai, MN, MB, and sundry other details. It also is a calendar, condensed, and complicated by many other things, and it's very Useful. Anyway, as I was saying, we should leave here the end of this week, about Friday, or maybe Saturday, or possibly Sunday. We go to New York, and there we stay to Transact Things. What sort of things—Quien Sabe? God himself hasn't decided yet. We may come to New Haven after that, we may not, we may drop dead, we may go cuckoo. Quien Sabe again? I suppose we'll come down. There are Other Things to Transact there, as you can readily imagine. So I suppose that, unless we either die or go cuckoo, I'll be seeing you again fairly soon—that is, always assuming that *you* don't in the interim die or go cuckoo.

With which touch of cynicism, I wish you not Good-day or Good-night, but Good-sextant.

        Poop-ishly,
        Barbara.

P. S. In case I forget it, I have a shipmate who is going to write to me next October, care of you, on returning from a voyage to the Arctic in a trading-schooner—a very nautical and square-rigged shipmate, even square-riggeder than you. So next October, in case I forget it, as I said, you are to take care of my mail!

Washington, D. C.
May 29. *[1930]*

Dear A. D. R.:

The MS is nearly FINISHED!!!!! The heart's blood has all been shed, and nothing is left now to do but to add a few finishing touches. We've been here two months now, and our rent expires, so we are going out into one of those delightful little one-horse villages in the Virginia backwoods, to spend a week of sheer rest, walks, and finishing touches, before we sail for New York. We've earned it, don't you think? At least, Helen has.

My job goes out to the back-woods with me. You see, I am now a full-fledged Editor. I edit, and suggest, and copy for that certain medical and scientific gentleman whom you have heard of. This, incidentally, is the typewriter I use for him—I use it myself to keep in practice with it! And that certain gentleman rewards my distinguished efforts at frequent intervals with one of those succulent tidbits known as Wages. In fact, I get paid fifteen whole cents for every single page; and since this type is large, the pages count up mighty fast.

Well, what I mainly wanted to say is already said—about going off into the back-woods. They are going to hold mail here until we get back to Washington, in about a week from now, or perhaps a little more. Then—New York! Helen has a friend there with whom she can stay for nothing, and I am going to stay with my Strange-Marriage Family, which I told you about, in Pelham, twenty minutes from New York. Thus we shall be SEPARATED—which will be good for us both. Furthermore, she can transact her business in N. Y. alone—just as she wants.

Then I'm going after a job. I made a definite determination that by June 15th I was either going to have one or a definite prospect for one. I have a vague feeling that Harper may land me in his Bookshop—especially if he likes the MS. Then there is Percy Waxman, Helen's friend at Pictorial, and there is always A. A. Knopf. I am one of his authors, and he is almost bound to do something for me if necessary, though that is the last resource—as I despise the place, the chilly, rapid-fire efficient business money-atmosphere of the place. There is also a Jew by name Goldsilver or something of the sort, a friend of a friend of ours, a wealthy and influential person, who might help.

I've been into the Civil Service Commission here, but that's definitely out. If I live to be forty-nine, and am still an old maid, I'll consider it—not until then! Anyway, I have a fancy that New York will do something, it being so tremendous and—oh, well, there's no adjective for it. In New York, the first few days, it takes the whole set of a human being's faculties just to keep his head through the uproar. But one improves with a little time.

Anderson sailed on the 16th, as per schedule, sailed right out into space. Look up Point Barrow on a map of the Arctic regions—that's the end of the route—then they turn around again and circle Alaska toward home—if they don't encounter a nor'-easter, or an iceberg, or the pack-ice. Before they sailed he sent off one dashing letter, of quite a different tone from what you'd expect of a person embarking on such a mean voyage. He described his own particular position aboard, half-way between sailor and engineer (there are four gasoline engines for sails and cargo, you see); and then he wrote several pages in mocking echo of the "tourist literature" on Seattle, concerning statistics and what-not. And then he seemed to run out of material, and said "Well, goodbye!" or words to that effect. A person like that sort of takes one's breath away, seems to me. Very startling and over-powering.

Farksoo progresseth, even with everything else that is on hand. I improve it every time I take out the MS and breathe gently on it. Sometimes I arise at six in the morning and gloat triumphantly over it. I've combined the two vocabularys (ies, I mean!) into one, Farksoo and English all mixed. It's much better that way; and the Grammar develops *magnifiquement*.

How is The Exception? And the Devil's Limb? And the Other One? And Thyself? It seems a very long time—almost a kickworthy long time—since I heard from you! Maybe there'll be a Royal-typed letter awaiting me when I come back from our retreat in the woods.

We have seen the Pratts, and spent a most glorious day at Capitol

View with them. I think those woods are too beautiful to be true—oh, how well they satisfy the hunger of one who has spent a year and a half away from New England! Pinkish bronze oaks, gold-green maples in the sunlight, dogwood and red-bud flowering.... And I saw the quarry pool, and the daffodils growing wild on your lawn, Shipmate. And the apples and lilacs were flowering, then, and there were violets and spring beauties everywhere. And Phoebe's bench is still up there in the branches of the enormous old cherry-tree.

But this *won't* do, in this curious old world of ours! Anyway, here's a whole steamer's cargo of love to you.

>   Your matey,
>   Barbara.

Barbara was now living with the Bryans in Pelham, about fifteen miles northeast of midtown Manhattan. Near the end of this letter she mentions that she's planning a new book, which would become Lost Island.

16 Young Avenue
Pelham, New York
June 16, 1930

Dear Shipmatey;

You know, I really am a wonderful person. Three different makes of typewriter in three days. This is Mr. Bryan's Remington Portable—my own is in dry-dock at present, as one might say, if one were nautically inclined.

It is glorious, in more ways than one, to have this *really* private address. I wish Anderson were here—correspondence would be very enjoyable—no restrictions, as one might say. Well, we'll make the most of this opportunity, won't we.

There's so much to say, my dear, that, to put it very tritely and very truly, "I don't know where to begin." About the Farents. I know nothing about them, and I really don't care a damn now. I only care in so much as I sympathize deeply with the situation confronting you and E. when they came trooping up to the desert. It was—well, it was one of those Grand Accidents that Occur Occasionally. I don't particularly want to think about them. I tried sincerely to get myself to write, but failed of course. They don't seem quite of my world at present. I am truly very happy now, and I want to keep to this particular circle, for the time being at least. You see what I mean? And don't you think I'm right?

The only thing that makes me unhappy now is that my dreams are going through their death-flurries. I thought they were all safely buried, but sometimes they stir in their grave, making my heartstrings twinge. I mean no *particular* dream, you understand, but the whole radiant flock of them together—with their rainbow wings, iridescent, bright, soaring, glorious, sublime. They are dying before the steel javelins and arrows of a world of Time and Money. I am happy the whole live-long day—happy as a bird—but when night comes and I settle down in bed for a night's sleep, then my tortures begin. I don't know when I've had a night's sleep without a prelude consisting of an hour or so of writhing! By day I think it's a grand old adventure; by night I think it's Hell, and double Hell.

I am seeking a Yob. Yobs are (as the Naturalist said, speaking of the "big game" in the West Indies) few and far between. I have several lines out, and something may bite someday. It *must*. I can stay here as long as I like, and I have forty-five dollars, earned from Dr. Paul, and he owes me about ten dollars more—that will pay carfare to N. Y. for some time to come. (G. D! how I hate this machine.)

The MS *may* sell. Harper has rejected it. Helen is in the hands of two female agents, who seem to be very influential people around here. They make lavish promises, and Helen believes; Barbara, the skeptic, says: "A bird in the hand, etc." Anyway, Collier's, American, the Companion, and Good Housekeeping, are all interested, and will all have a shot at it—and, as I said, these two ladies seem to be influential. Someone telephoned their office about it while I was there talking, and one of them said: "Oh, but you'll have to stand in line, you know." Which delighted Helen beyond measure, naturally.

Oh, I wish, and WISH Mr. R. and Phoebe could go to Russia alone. I think it would be the best thing that could possibly happen, for both of 'em. Meanwhile, you and I will hold down the continent of North America until they come back, in the very distant future—or, perhaps, until you follow them over. In all events, they should go alone for a while, and you and I should be together somewhere, with our cocoa cups.

You and I could have the most excellent laugh about these people right here, for instance. I told you a little about them when I was out there. They have become even worse. They never go out of the house at all. If Mrs. Bryan has to go down to the village on some little errand, Mr. Bryan stands by the window and peers anxiously forth until she returns. At night every bolt and lock and key in the whole house is drawn or turned; the chain bolt on the front door, both locks, the knob on the screen-door, the key on the inner door, and all the windows fastidiously bolted. I never saw such terribly, appallingly fastidious people in all my days. They're worse than Mrs. Hayball. There are two "objects" in the kitchen, and neither is ever used at all.

The "swamp angels" are fastidiously removed and put outdoors at once. They say that those two objects are merely for use in the winter, when it is too snowy or dripping to go outside. It seems strange, when one considers all this, that Mr. B. doesn't keep the type of his Remington in better shape.

Mrs. B. never does any house-work at all, except for very superficial "picking-up" and dusting around. Every Saturday she has a man come to clean house. The Two themselves do nothing but sit, first in one chair and then in another. They don't know what to do or think about—and the result is o. They listen to the same things every night on the radio, and go to bed in the same way. But it amuses me infinitely. I enjoy it, I have to say. I am more private than I've had the privilege of being for a long time. I josh them good-naturedly, and they seem to like it—but they don't know what to make of me. You can readily imagine what vague, scandalous, unaccountable, phenomenal sort of Thing I am to them!

What are you going to do about the pot-boiler? Take out the fox-meat? It's somewhat ironical that the market you scorned should have dumped you, isn't it? That's what comes of being snotty, even if it's only mental. Well, good luck to it (damn this ribbon!) I think, as always, that the whole great Thing we call Life is one huge practical joke, anyhow. If we *take* it as such, it is instantly powerless, and we may with impunity exult. THEN—the old Joke treats us Well for a change, and we begin to forget that it *is* a Joke—with the result that we are unprepared for the next battering. Then is heard the rumbling, ironical Laughter of the Gods. I think a good, sound, healthy pessimism is a Wise and Noble Thing.

Don't be so humble and modest. You're a wonderful safety-valve; and I damn well hate to think that you were nothing but that (Oh, the language which is going on inside me about this ribbon!)—a safety-valve? No, no—you're about the best friend anyone ever had, or ever imagined. To be a safety-valve is just a small item which is an automatic and natural part of a Friend, don't you think so? As for Anderson, he has served my needs a whole year now, and a rest will do both of us good, I suppose—though it is a little strange not to be able to anticipate those pencilled, air-mail envelopes! I shall hear from him—barring accidents—about the first week in October. I expect he will show up on this coast shortly afterwards. It would be like him to do so. Besides, I flatter myself a little that perhaps my friendship did something for him, too. I think we were mutually very good for each other—let the Farents say what they may!

Do you realize that a year ago yesterday I set sail from Honolulu harbor in my beloved *Vigilant*? I was rather glum all yesterday thinking of it. It hurt. I suppose it will be years before I go to sea again, and I may never even see that schooner. I suppose that I spent about the happiest month of my life during that sea-trip in her. And it lasted even during that week in port, when I took over the cabin-boy's job, and when Helen, Anderson, and I had cherry- and ice-cream-parties in the cabin after everyone had gone ashore, and when we used to walk up into that virgin forest two miles up the road, and eat salmon-berries. Life was beautiful then. This doesn't seem like the same era. Here the beauty consists of great stone towers against the sunset—sublime, symbolic, but away above the plane of us poor ants that hustle along the swarming streets at their feet, so engrossed in ourselves that we never even *see* a fellow-mortal, but bump into him with a bang, and then hurry and hurry on.

Oh, my God, my God!

It makes one's heart and soul suffer—it stabs them to the quick. Oh, for wings, for *wings*!

Wings!

That is, in general, the theme not only of my own heart, but of the book I'm going to write. I *ought* to be able to write it—I live it constantly. My heart is the field of a thousand battles every day.

But I'm happy, really—you understand that, don't you? And I'm coming up, and up. Not a day passes but that I myself climb a little—somewhere. I am getting gradually to a point where I can trust myself, put faith in myself. Gradually, and cautiously. Once I tried it before I was ready, and the cargo spilled. But I'm Building, always. If I can put unbounded faith in myself, I don't care what happens. And I can, as time goes on.

>   Your shore-bound mate,
>   Barbara.

P. S. Dr. Paul spends time and postage writing me love-letters! He also sends me now and then a batch of stuff to edit and typewrite. This is Well—it means Cheques! B.

New York's YWCA was at 610 Lexington Avenue, three blocks east of St. Patrick's Cathedral. (As of this writing it's a construction site for a 709-foot luxury hotel/condominium complex.)

Founded in 1917 with Rockefeller money, the Lincoln School was an experimental "laboratory school" under the aegis of the Teachers College at Columbia University.

16 Young Avenue
Pelham, New York
June 26, 1930

Dear First Officer:

How do you do? How are your dreams today?

Mine somewhat materialized last Monday—that is, the puny, coined, earthly little dream somewhat materialized—when I got a sort of a job. I was in Pelham until Sunday noon, then I suddenly became very tired of sitting like a fisherman at his lines, with nothing biting at any one of them. And I decided I'd have to change and be like a Tahitian fisherman who takes spear in hand and dives after his prey, instead of waiting for it.

No sooner thought than accomplished. The tears of horror stood silvery in my een as I left the house, and increased with nearness to the City, but I turned not back, Skipper, I turned not back. That was Sunday night. I stayed at the Y. W. C. A. (Ugh!) and Monday morning I———went to work! Who can boast of such a thing as that?

It happened when I was on the roof garden Sunday night, gazing o'er the colossal brow of the etc., etc., etc., and there was also on the roof garden an old lady. It transpired, after friendly conversation, that she ran an employment agency for domestic service, and that she needed some typewriting done, and could use me for "an hour or two in the morning." I went, stayed all day, all Tuesday, all Wednesday, and half of today, receiving fourteen dollars and much praise.

The Great Trouble, though, is that I am now "laid off"—oh, the horror of those two words!—for the regular girl, who had been out, comes back next week. So that's that. Now I'm going back to Pelham to spend the week-end; and that's always my mail address, for they will forward anything anywhere.

I've read *all* of Barrie's plays, now, and wish there were hundreds more. But "Dear Brutus" is more gorgeous than the island one, "Mary Rose."

I haven't seen a picture of Masefield for a long time, and I don't know whether you're right or not. I'll look it up someday.

Follett did *something* about the house, I don't know just what. It belongs to Helen now, debts and all. She's been in N. H., seen Sabra, slept in the house, had a Hell of a time, and pulled through very well, in spite of a horrible row with Dr. Tyler which was humiliating and irritating to all of us. I shall see Sabra next Monday. Helen is going to bring her to New York to have her see someone at the Lincoln School. We want to get an unfurnished apartment near the school, move down some of our stuff, and Get Settled. Sounds simple, doesn't it? Yes, I know it does.

The Farents can g- t- H—, if you know what I mean; I won't think about them yet awhile. You have my devoted sympathy, however, as you know; and you have it every time you see them—so when you *do* see them, remember that my sympathy is floating around somewhere in the atmosphere. I'll lay up a "special fund" of it for that very purpose.

I wish one of you were Here, so that I'd have a real kindred spirit close by. I need one! Correspondence is as inadequate as clouds are to a parched country longing for rain—I mean, when the clouds just drift away overhead and perform nothing! I wish Anderson were around, failing yourself. However, it is doubtless magnificent training for me not to have the people I want and care for, but to be forced to stand on my own pins, mentally and emotionally speaking.

Helen's MS is in the hands of agents who talk a great deal. Via them it is in the hands of Collier's. I'd like to report a two-thousand-dollar check—but, alas, am unable to do so at this sitting! Helen's address is many and various. The best guess, I reckon, is ℅ Dr. Margaret Tyler, 75 Mansfield St., New Haven, Conn. I don't guarantee it, though. By the way, Helen says she wants you more than she ever has, and she sends you her greatest love. That woman is—well, what she is going through isn't even printable, and only a deep-sea sailor could even begin to hint at it.

You ask slyly and subtly and cautiously about Dr. Paul. You've asked so *very* cautiously, in fact, that I don't exactly understand what it is you're asking about him. You needn't be so Extremely Reserved with me, you know! I don't give a puff of wind for Dr. Paul, one way or another, if that's what you want to know. Helen got banged up, some, but she's getting over it. Her knowledge of his attentions to me (which are probably lighter than thistle-down, I'm not sure) has waked her up with a whang to what sort of a juggler he really is. So I guess that's all right, especially as he's going to Spitsbergen or Lapadaeczvia or somewhere, and can't be even written to for a year.

The more I see of everybody in general, the more I know that there are a few simple, quiet souls (like Anderson) who unconsciously and entirely unmaliciously knock everyone else into so many bedraggled cocked hats.

        Yours for aye,
        Barbara.

A postcard to Anne Meservey from Helen.

3 July [1930]
Y. U. L. A.
38th & Lexington Ave.
New York

I've torn up 3 letters to you. Just tore up another. So much to ask and tell you about. How is Edward? I do want to know that! And what are your summer plans. I must see you if possible. Write me at 176 Armory St. New Haven. I'll be living there alone in an empty house from tomorrow on for a week. Then here again job-hunting.

H.

Fox Film Corporation became Twentieth Century Fox.

16 Young Avenue
Pelham, New York
July 18, 1930

Dear Mate:

CUBS HAMMER MOSS, SCORING ON ROBINS. How's that, my dear?

Well, 'ere I ham, as one might say. Your letter arrived a rather shocking long time ago (it's make my heart beating like a earth shocking), and I would be 'shamed if I weren't so almighty damn-fired hell-bent busy. You see, I am no longer begging for work, I am *in* work up to my ears, and over them at times. Yes, I have bearded New York in its lair. I find it not so appalling, in fact I rather like it, as one likes some colossal piece of machinery; and struggling into the sardine-packed express "L" at quarter to nine in the morning is almost exhilarating. It thrills me to see all those millions of faces, all going to their respective puny jobs, and all so tense and rushed. I don't know, but New York has so far done me much more good than harm. I feel more of a sympathy and understanding for People In General than ever in my life before, because I am One Of Them, which I never was in my life before. I find myself buying my chewing-gum from a cripple in the street, rather than in a drug-store.

Yes, I long and long and *long* for the sea, and woods, and quiet, and more sunshine, and the wind, and a little more room, please, and not so many people on my feet, if you don't mind. And there are times when I feel my heart beginning to curl up just a little at the edges—the first step, the warning symptom, to its sickening and dwindling. I keep holding out my arms—I mean my spiritual arms—like an amoeba or sumthin. A ceaseless need. Sometimes I think it's the sea, and sometimes I think it's Anderson's correspondence, and sometimes I think it's just space I need, and the wild. And I can't have 'em!

You see, I am now taking a course at the Packard Commercial School, and studying shorthand with might and main. Already I have caught up to the class which started two weeks ahead of me, and I've only been there five days! You see, a really good and intelligent stenographer and typist can always get some sort of a job, while there's damn little chance for an inexperienced nothing-in-particular, as I am. I really am having a fine time at the school. The teachers are good souls, both of them, and it is as fine a bunch of young womanhood as I ever set eyes on—those girls.

I am also writing synopses for Fox, at six dollars apiece, which is fun. Then, too, occasionally someone drops a bulky MS into my lap and says: "Here! I'll give you five dollars for your opinion on this, expressed in two pages." That's a tribute to one's critical sense, ain't it? Furthermore, it's pin-money—lunches and stockings and toothpaste and what-not.

About Sabra. Please don't let your imagination go running away with you, or I'll die. You know, after all, she is only a little, little girl. It was almost a terrible experience, if you want the real truth. I rushed to her with my heart wide open, and my soul ready for the balm I felt she'd give—and the beautiful dream melted, and I found a little child—a darling little child, to be sure—who took all I could give, and gave almost nothing in return, because she *could* not, of course, and I was ridiculous to expect it of her, but expect it I did. She could not fill any need of mine—not the need I thought she could fill, that is, but something entirely different that hasn't got oriented yet; and the other need, the greater one, is still hungry. And it's dying now. You can't keep anything hungry forever, without eventually just starving it to its death. There is a limit.

Well, just what will happen I don't know. I have been in New Haven a good deal, slaving away in the attic of No. 176. It's fascinating! Sorting out books, and junk—amazing junk! I've pretty well worked things out. You know, we've rented an apartment in the city, and we're moving into it the first of August, and we stay there until June, 1931, at least. At that date the building is going to be torn down, so I suppose we may just conceivably have to clear out. And I think it's lucky. Otherwise we might become appallingly rooted there.

So far my life seems to be nothing better than a mess, so far as the future is concerned. I have to work, that's certain, and if I get a regular job I'll have to stay with it, and that means—well, it means just what I'm having now, more or less. I have to heave a sigh at times. Sometimes I even get very morbid and decide that I'll marry the first person who offers a chance to get out of it. And then sometimes I change my mind. I don't know. Anderson informs me that dreams have to be put away on the shelf occasionally—usually, he should have said! New York, New York. Two weeks vacation. Slaving for your salt and matches and tooth-paste, and your cup of soup and crumb of hard-tack. I always swore I would never get into the "mood" about it all, but I seem to at times in spite of myself.

But don't mistake me. When I'm busy—and I *am* busy—I am really happy, you know. I don't have much time to sit down and think, and I guess that's lucky. I haven't any time but for the ten-of-eight train in the morning, the 3rd Avenue express, the Packard School, lunch, afternoon business, the trains again, supper, Amos 'n' Andy, work, bed, and the ten-of-eight in the morning again. I meant to go down to New Haven over this week-end, but the prospect of two quiet days in the "timid little house" was too tempting to resist. I meant to go down to Baltimore when the *Marsodak* came in last trip, but didn't. I mean to go to N. H. next week, but probably shan't. I also mean to go to Baltimore next trip, but really I can't possibly. I also meant to write and do Farksoo, but somehow I keep missing the mark. My nose is shackled to the grindstone! I never can lift my head to get a peek at the blue sky!

And you—you are a grand, gorgeous soul, and I am with you more than you know. And I'm glad you agree with me about the cocked hats.

    Yours ever,
    Barbara.

P. S. The house is getting ready to be sold now. Helen and Sabra are living there. I was to stay there too until August 1, but joined the school instead. You can imagine how that flabbergasted Helen, who had counted on my staying down there and helping out. But I figgered that I would be a coward either way, and so I took what I guess was the severest course after all!

Russian looks to me worse than Gregg shorthand, and not nearly so convenient! B.

Helen and her daughters lived in the apartment building on West 122nd Street for less than a year. It was on a quiet corner of Manhattan—steps away from the Hudson near Grant's Tomb and overlooking Sakura Park (so named after a gift of 2,500 cherry trees from the Committee of Japanese Residents of New York in 1912).

620 West 122nd Street
New York City
August 1, 1930

My Deah:

Well! Here we am, as you might say. It really has become a rather usual occurrence, all this moving around, yet still, it has not lost a certain spice. This is really a grand little apartment of three rooms, and we have our own old furniture, and a whole bookcase full of books (the pick of the flock) and a little kitchen which is concealed behind two vast doors; and I can't imagine a better place for us to live in————————that is, all things considered, and seeing things as they *are*, my boy, as Chester used to say to Marlow.

You mustn't feel sorry for me at all, though. I really am quite happy, because I am so busy from morning till night that I haven't time for anything else. I'm good in school—in fact, one of the best in the shorthand class, now—and Fox Film likes my work for them, and they hand me out a bit of praise almost every time I come into the office, which is about three times a week, and they pay me in cash in sealed pay-envelopes (can you imagine anything more pleasant?) and so I can pay the school and my car-fare and all my odds and ends, and feel quite independent. There's nothing better than that. Of course I simply detest the work I do for them—it's enough to give a rhinoceros the ear-ache, let alone me—but the getting paid more than compensates for that.

So I'm in good shape, and find time passing swiftly. Our old, old, old friend Leo Meyette (who used to be the grocery boy in the little one-horse New Hampshire town where we spent the summers, and who is one of the grandest persons in the world) is here, with his wife and his younger brother; and his antics in the great City keep Helen and me laughing. Then, too, it won't be so very long before Anderson is home, and I believe I could go through *anything* with an occasional letter from him to keep me going. I never realized before how he and I had gotten to depend on each other's support. We each have had such ghastly times! It's quite beautiful, I think—two hungry souls beating their wings desperately and finding such joy and strength in one another.

I really think it is grand for Phoebe to be off—though be sure that I can sympathize with *you*. It must be like being wrapped in an unlighted cloud, to be alone after having such an iridescent creature with one for so long. I want to see all the Russells *together*. I'm damned sick of seeing people who are starved for each other separated by circumstances—especially such petty materialistic circumstances—finances, for instance! Bah!

Sabra is a great little thing. She is not with us now. I think that is a mercy for all of us. School begins late in September, and she would be miserable here unless she were busy. She is now at a camp in Lyme, Connecticut, which is run by a grand woman who is an old friend of hers. All the children are about Sabra's age, and she is a gregarious little thing, so it suits her to a t. Furthermore, this is a rather unusual sort of camp. It is excessively informal and care-free and happy-go-lucky. For one thing, most of the children wear—not a single blessed shred of any kind! Nothing could be better, in that glorious sunshine and fresh country air. They are brown as Polynesians, and just as happy, and so deliciously unconscious of themselves that it is a rare pleasure to watch them playing.

I'll never forget Sabra's eyes when she first saw them. We drove up in the camp truck, and they stood around us in a semi-circle, motionless, staring, and naked, just as the South Sea babies run out from a native house to stare at strangers. She was quite taken aback, and amazed. So were we; it was somewhat unexpected! About half of them are little boys—S.'s first experience, you see. But she was entirely acclimated in half an hour or so, and now she is having the time of her life. I think it's the best thing that could possibly happen, both for her and for us. It will put her, for one thing, in corking physical shape for a winter in New York. She needs all the reserve strength and health that sunshine and the country can give her.

God knows my own health is standing me in good stead. I don't know where I'd be without it. Those subways at eight-fifteen A. M., when the masses and millions are tearing in to work . . . .!!!!!!!!!!!!! Does that give you any idea?

Well, news seems to be consistently lacking here. I give the best of myself to everything I do—no man can do more than that. I work like a dog, sleep like a pig, tear around like a deer, eat like a wolf, laugh like a hyena (sometimes), spit like a cat (other times), shut up like an oyster (for a change), and pull long juicy worms out of the ground, like an early bird. There. Doesn't that give you a picture? Someone who can draw caricatures (Phoebe, for instance) ought to take the matter up.

   Your mate, in foul or fair,
   Bar.

NEW YORK CITY (1930–1931)

620 West 122nd Street
New York City
August 15, 1930

Dear Oxford:

You would be surprised at my reason for writing to you, on this thoroughly disgusting dreary rainy afternoon—surprised and probably amused. So first I'll tell you that. Ever since I can remember—which is a fairly long time—there has been a framed photograph among my very various possessions—the photograph which you once took of a rabbit reaching up to sniff at the blossoms of a strawberry plant which towers above him! That picture has always delighted me, yet I don't believe I ever spoke about it to you. Now that I'm back from my roamings, and have it on the wall of the dining-room of our very small new home, it delights me ten times more than ever—so much so, in fact, that I simply couldn't resist the impulse to sit down and write to you about it.

It appeals to everything there is in me—love of animals, sense of humor, sense of wistfulness, love of beauty. It is without doubt one of the most perfect and rare photographs in existence. I should like to hear the history of it. Leo Meyette, who is here now, but leaving for New Hampshire tonight, asked: "Where did he get a rabbit so small?" I told him that I was sure it was a chance meeting-up in the woods. That's true, is it not? And that strawberry plant—was it an exceptionally large one? For the rabbit is really incredibly small! If it is an ordinary strawberry plant, the photograph must have been enlarged to approximately life-size, I should say. That leaves the rabbit about two and half inches from the soles of his hind feet to the tips of his ears—and he has lifted his forefeet from the ground to stretch himself up, too!

Apart from this I believe there isn't a great deal to talk about—not via the U. S. Mail at least. That is a most unsatisfactory institution. It is not the fault of itself at all: indeed, one must admire nowadays the celerity and certainty of it, and all that. The difficulty is more fundamental than that. It lies in the expression on paper. That's a real obstacle. Letters are confounded nuisances, except when they deal with things so remote and impersonal as—well, the weather, or the rabbit-photograph, or what price butter-beans.

I think Leo expressed it rather accurately in one of his letters to Helen. He closed it: "In a devil of a rush and mess and damn this city I hate it." My sentiments to a t.

                With love,
                Barbara.

Many Red Devils Ran from My Heart is from Stephen Crane's first collection of poems, The Black Riders and Other Lines *(1895).*

"To mark, wi' envy in my gaze, the couples kittlin' in the dark between the funnel-stays" is from M'Andrew's Hymn *by Rudyard Kipling (1893).*

Joseph Conrad's blessing does not appear to have survived, nor Barbara's photograph of one of her favorite writers.

620 West 122nd Street
August 18 [1930]

Splice the main-brace, ahoy!

All congratulations on your latest entries in the unofficial log. It arrived this morning, and so you see I am SETTING YOU AN EXAMPLE. In fact, I wrote you a letter before this one, but tore it up. It contains too much really Tough Language, and all That Sort of Thing! I suppose I picked it up from the Unmentionable Movie Trash which I Read For a Living—anyhow, where-ever I picked it up, it certainly is NOT the proper thing to send in a letter to one who is writing Healthy Young Men for a Living.

My dear, don't you ever yearn to spit in their faces, and to create for a change some perfectly Horrible and Gritty young men who would hammer and mash and batter and whang up all the healthy-minded maidens? I suppose, were a list of detailed rules for healthy stories written out, they would look something like this: "No kisses of more than two seconds' duration," and that sort of thing. Wouldn't they?

Well, anyhow! Dang it all, I'd like to see all you Russells together. It's not right for people to have half-continents and such trash shoved whang into their faces, between them and those they love, is it? We are just Victims, that's all. There are half a dozen or so great Wheels grinding around toward each other all the time, interlocking on the rims, and if we happen to get caught between them——we just get mashed.

> Many red devils ran from my heart
> And out upon the page,
> They were so tiny
> The pen could mash them,
> And many struggled in the ink.
> It was strange
> To write in this red muck
> Of things from my heart.
> *Stephen Crane*

Tough going at times, my beloved mate!

I wish I had some GOOD news for you! Alas! I am fairly busy over my eighteen-a-week (more-or-less). I have a fairly regular round of housework, synopsisses, tipe-riting, an' a' that. My sole pastime, so far, consists of walking along the river-bank park in the evenings after dark—"to mark, wi' envy in my gaze, the couples kittlin' in the dark between the funnel-stays." (If only there *were* some funnel-stays! Alas!) Helen's Manuscript is less and less sold all the time. Sabra is still at camp. Finances become lower and lower. You can't live—here—on *my* salary—though I daresay I could alone. And to think that I'm the only one of the family who has a "yob!" *That* tickles my sense of humor fine!

My sense of humor has had more and more heavy responsibilities of late. I really need fuel for it—fresh fuel from the outside. However, I can say very truthfully that it has never yet failed me, and it isn't going to either. . . . Leo Meyette (have I told you anything of him?) and his wife, and his brother, and his sister, have all been here for a while, but now they have departed for New Hampshire and the old home-farm again. It was a delight to have them here. Leo, in particular, is really one of the greatest persons in the world, as well as one of the very simplest and humblest.

Have you Seen or Heard anything of the Farents? I confess to a mild sort of curiosity. I suppose I should write to them, but—oh my, oh my! You see, I feel that if I can stick out this particular present-minute, present-place situation, and get on top of it, and yammer at it, and smash it, and domineer over it, and be Snooty and Disagreeable to it, and Awe it, and just make it Cringe—why, then, I guess I'm doing all I have room for. And I *am* doing just that. So picture yourself an Amazon, mounted upon a Bucking Elephant, and hammering that elephant over the head with a Fijian war-club.

Anyway, there's a picture of Joseph Conrad over this table ....

And NOTHING can daunt me!

"I got a home in-a dat rock."

Wings! I have 'em!

And Joseph Conrad sent me his blessing and his love. Not so very long ago.

And Anderson comes home in October.

Well!

Lots of things have Occurred to Me, anyhow. I think I'm ready to live a much happier sort of life from now on—I mean, to make the best of circumstances and of myself, and get a lot of pleasure and fun out of anything and everything. I wish poor Helen could do that as effectively as I have learned to do it. She hasn't. She's under water. God! And I can't rescue her. I do forty-nine fiftieths of everything that is done at No. 122, as it is; and I sing as I do it: "I got a home in-a dat rock, Don't you see?"

And in October, Anderson comes home. And I'll have that fresh fuel for my S. of H. Besides, I may earn a whang on the back from him, and that's worth anything.

But I want all the Russells to be together. And why must Phoebe go to school, with her scientific father to superintend her? I think school is really and primarily a place for children whose parents are banging each other over the head with rolling-pins, or whose parents are absolute morons, and whose parents are both slaving at outside work for a living, or for children reared in utter poverty and misery. (This is not supposed to cast any reflections of any kind upon the Russells, I *hope* you understand!) But rainbows shouldn't be stuffed into sofa-cushions, should they?

I love you, A.D.R.
Yours ever,
Barbara.

620 Etc
August 29 *[1930]*

Dear Mate:

Having allowed the dentist to put a gold inlay into a tooth, having written, delivered, and been paid for three synopses, having seen Helen off for New Haven again (thereby making three trips back and forth from here to town in the course of the day, via that devastating subway), and having, alone and in peace at last, partaken of my bowl of soup and crust of bread—having done all this, and being still quite alive, I will now proceed (oh, luxury!) to sit down and quietly, and in leisurely fashion, write a letter to you.

How I have chuckled over your contributions from Pasadena headline English! I would answer in kind, but I scan the papers in vain. New York headlinists don't seem to have that ingenious knack of balling things up; in fact, for the most part they are altogether too lucid to be interesting. DRIVE CAR DEATH LEAP TIES UP TRAFFIC, is the best I can do, for the time being.

Dash it all, now that I've really sat down—after three days of trying to—there doesn't seem to be anything more to say than there was last time or the time before, and one shouldn't repeat oneself. School begins again next Tuesday. Thank God I can pay for it—the whole thing. I can also pay my own dentist bills, and buy my own clothes, and my own amusements and necessities. That's more than I was ever able to do before; and I can tell you, it makes me feel quite uppity when I go sailing into that Fox office on Broadway and receive my weekly pay envelope!

Helen is rather desperate. I don't know what to do about her, at all, at all. It makes her feel rather badly to think that I have a job and she hasn't; it struck her hard that her MS didn't sell with a bang; and as for finances—well, I don't know where the rent comes from. She is always so secretive about those things, and she's such a fool, really, when it comes to money and Practical Things. When I say "Fool," I don't mean it harshly, you understand. I guess you know what I mean as well as I do, anyway.

She has gone down to New Haven now, to mull over the house, and get it ready for renting. She is kind of wild here, because there's a steam-derrick half a block away going all day, and making a fearsome racket. My typewriter goes too much for her nerves, too; but I don't see how that can be helped. I'm hoping she'll find some quiet in New Haven for a few days now, just as I'm finding peace here alone. When she comes again, Sabra will be with her.

Well, what next? I'm fairly contented, and have a rather pleasant sort of curiosity about the future. It can't fail to be interesting! I think the masculine farent should be whanged on the head and wake up to find himself shanghaied to sea; and I think the feminine farent should tackle the first job she can light on. He isn't what you'd call a Man. He isn't half the man that some of the Dago workmen are down the street. He isn't halfway the man that Mate Bill is, or Cap'n Colbeth, or Anderson. He should go to work and do some hard physical labor, under someone who can't be talked back to, and who doesn't care a damn for all the long words. Nothing could be better for him than to take a trip in the *Vigilant*, under old Captain Peasley, and first mate Jacobsen. Jove! He'd "yump" around then, all right!

Yes! I *have* some news for you. I went and saw *The Green Pastures*. It is the loveliest, and most real, and simple, touching, glorious play I ever knew. Marc Connelly's negro play, you know. It interprets the negro's simple belief and religion. Lord God Jehovah is exactly like some kindly old white-haired preacher: he has a little office up in Heaven, and every morning two angels, with dust-covers over their wings, come in and dust it. The whole story is there from the beginning—Adam and Eve, Noah and the Ark, Moses, the pilgrims on their way to Canaan; and all through it the choir sings negro spirituals, most of them familiar—and you get to the point before long when you just want to lie down and weep.

Speaking of weeping: the steam-derrick which makes such a racket down the street here is doing a job for a company which calls itself

The House-Wrecking Company. If that ain't the limit!...
     Yours,
     B.

I just received a letter from Detroit, enclosing E.'s masterpiece. Oh, I *do* so hope you'll all manage to get away together on some gorgeous Exposition before long! B.

620 West 122nd Street
New York City
August 30, 1930

Dear Mr. Russell:

 Some time ago, when I used to take annual mountain trips with W. Follett, I also wrote long and happy letters about it to friends. E.'s gorgeous epistle made me feel definitely wistful. The White Mountains—I mean the eastern ones—are all old friends of mine; and while they are undoubtedly mere foothills when you compare them with the Sierras, still—"there's no friend like an old friend." Besides, the White Mountains are at times not only an adventure, but really dangerous; and not only very rugged and glorious, but so lofty and so far-seeing that to you upon their summits they seem the very ultimate, the crest of the infinite itself.

 It's a long time since I've had a mountain trip to amount to anything. But the sea has taken the place of the peaks, and I have not been hungry. You might be surprised to hear that a mere steamboat ride to Coney Island and back, is brim-full of possibilities. For one thing, the C. I. boats have beam-engines, which are old-fashioned and truly beautiful, although the passengers will insist on calling them "see-saws." Such things rub the wrong way the fur of anyone who admires and feels machinery. Then the trip itself is out among all the shipping in the world—down the Hudson between docks on Manhattan and New Jersey; out into the harbor, past tugs and ferries and freighters and liners and tankers and barges and scows and a wreck here and there. And a glimpse of the open sea itself, too, and the faint ghost of the open sea's lift and fall.

 The reason I gave you no address when I wrote from the Zone is that I hadn't at the time the remotest idea of what it would be. From there we went to Washington, where we stayed two months, I think, during the loveliest time of year. We took trips once in a while down into Maryland and Virginia, sometimes to the Blue Ridges. I like that Virginia farm-land in April and May—rolling and fragrant and welcoming, somehow.

After that we came straight up here, and for a while we were like two goldfishes when the bowl has been upset. We dashed back and forth between New Haven, Pelham, and New York, like mad things. And then we finally settled here—after having "wrassled with dragons," as Phoebe says. When we took this tiny little apartment, we had no idea that we were landing in such a first-class part of the city—it was all an accident—and we haven't gotten over being surprised, yet! We contemplate Grant's Tomb from our front windows (cheerful, isn't it?). But the Hudson is beautiful at night, with the little lighted ferries slipping back and forth.

Well, we *have* made port, for the time being, at least. Now the thing is—*to pay our harbor dues.*

    With love,
    Barbara.

A note to Helen while she was in New Haven, written, I think, on September 4th. I'm not sure who "M. C." was—probably the Champernois in the next letter—one of Helen's literary agents.

Thursday

Hello, how's everything?

  Here is some stuff from that paragon of activity, M. C.

  I have jumped up into another class—the second "yump" since I joined. The whole Packard school asks my opinion now!

  Fox is out of material over the week-end, which means that I *may* have to cash the tenner. You see, we've got to have an ironing-board. I have exactly one dress which I can wear to school, until I wash and iron a little, and even then I may have nothing but the one. And you can't wear one forever—at least, not *quite* forever.

  Weather's improving.

  No need for you to come home; everything is O. K., Gabe!

  What are you doing, anyhow, and why so uncommunicative? Anyway, don't drop on me out of the sky without letting me know, will you? That would be inconvenient, as I haven't even bought towel-racks, yet, and God knows we'll need towel-racks, about ten of them.

  I am having a delightful and restful time, and have no desire for a change (no offense intended). I guess I'm supposed to live alone, anyhow. I don't believe I'll ever get married; or if I do, I'll insist on a house-boat all to myself, on the *other* side of the lake, or bay, or whatever it is.

  Haven't had any mail from anyone, except Norm, who wrote me

a delectable letter from Maine, in which he stated that he was sitting as nearly naked as possible outdoors, and that some fat old dowager (were there any such about) would have quite an experience were she to come down the road at that moment. Such a condition must be a pleasant relief from the chains of Elm Street and Briar Lane, even though he seems to relish his chains. He'll be down on the 8th—I mean, down from Maine.

  B.

A hurricane struck Dominica on September 3rd, leaving 8,000 dead.

[ca. September, 1930—I think the 12th]
Friday

Dear Helen:

  I saw Champernois this afternoon, and Champernois (that's not how you spell it, is it? Doesn't look right) says that you shouldn't be discouraged about the MS. There is still a chance to sell it to a magazine—they have a perfect right to do so until it has been published definitely as a book. It is now in the hands of Brewer etc. What did Blanche say?

  She also has an idea about some reading for you to do—for The Dial. But this is vague, also. The job for me is to come in sometime next week, I take it. Altogether, I've had no stint of odd jobs, for both the Miss Carneys have been using my expert services quite frequently, and paying me, of course, though I resist heartily on every occasion.

  I had a grand dinner with Norm Wednesday night. We didn't talk so much, but we laughed our heads off—just giggled, idiotically and foolishly, you know.

  I've heard from Frisco, and Frisco says that the *Marsodak*'s skipper and first mate are changed still again, so that any chance of coming up to New York is all off. Which is something of a relief to me.

  Took a test today which I'm almost sure I got a hundred on. The marks haven't been told us yet, and won't be till Monday, but I know there was one paper which got a hundred there, and the teacher gave me a curious pleased glance, and furthermore I feel rather sure about all the material in it. If that really goes through, I'll probably come out with an A and get a Packard Pin or something! Ridiculous, isn't it?

  They are also giving me a course in business correspondence, which is useful and full of pointers.

  Norm's got a yob for me. He wants me to take the forty issues of "Genius Burning" and pick out the best therefrom, to be compiled into a small but delicious volume of poetry. You know, the Hermione gang in Capri. That gang I'm still jealous of, deep down!

By the way—Dominica's devastation was reported over the wireless by the skipper of "The Canadian National Steamship *Lady Hawkins*"—thus says the New York Times. The skipper of the *Hawkins* is Armitt, I think. Sister to the *Nelson*, anyway. Which is rather amusing.

I've heard from Detroit, and Detroit delivers loud and resounding whacks on the back. But Phoebe has gone back home. She was "a very small animal surrounded by apartment houses," and it evidently didn't work. But the Russells are planning a gorgeous trip next year in the Sierras.

I've heard from Hanover, too. Bless their 'arts.

[a postscript] I'm reading "Far *[shorthand mark]* Madding Crowd."

The "tragic discoveries in the Arctic" refers to the last camp of Salomon Andrée and his two companions. Andrée was a Swedish adventurer who tried to reach the North Pole by hydrogen balloon in 1897. His team left Svalbard on July 11th, but after ten hours fell to earth. The balloon bumped its way north for two days before its final crash, forcing the men to travel by foot on pack ice, which was drifting in the wrong direction. They survived about three months. On August 5, 1930, their remains were found by chance by a Norwegian expedition. There are haunting photographs of the crashed balloon online.

According to the Internet Broadway Database, Marc Connelly's The Green Pastures *ran for 640 performances at the Mansfield Theatre (256 West 47th Street), from February 1930 through August 1931. It won the 1930 Pulitzer Prize for Drama.*

620 West 122nd Street
New York City
October 4, 1930

My dear Mate:

Your letter arrived here on Wednesday, the 24th of September. I remember that, because it was sent on the 22nd, and I remember my delight and amazement, and my admiration, too, for this world of wonders. A letter across the continent in two days? What next?!

I sat down at once and wrote an answer to it—yes, the very day I received it, mind you. Then, on reading my letter, it seemed too puny and putrid to exist, and hopelessly inadequate, so I tucked both your letter and my embryonic one away in a drawer. Then came the week-end—a week ago, and I firmly intended to answer you then. You see, Saturdays and Sundays are my only real days, and so I save up everything all week to do then, with the result that I get about half of the things done.

Well, I thought so very much about your letter, and my answer to it, that I thought myself into a state of believing that I *had* answered it, and it didn't really occur to me until this morning that I hadn't, and that my embryo was still lying in a drawer. You don't know (yes, I guess you do, though) what a day—a week—is like in New York C I T Y (as our friend Leo Meyette always writes it on envelopes!).

Now whatever I was going to say has entirely slipped me, so I'll begin over, having all day to do it in—that is, if I neglect my washing, and the meals, and my week-end home-work, etc., etc., etc., which I intend to do if I desire.

Your headlines are very juicy. Of the four I deciphered one—the one about the icy doom stilling the heart, don't you know, and the record thrust within clothing. I suppose that was eventually intelligible to me only because I have been following, off and on, the tragic discoveries in the Arctic. Speaking of the Arctic: the other day my red hair was made to rise stiffly on end (like quills, etc.) by seeing a little piece in the Tribune about an air-plane which effected a rescue of the crew of a trading-ship somewhere north of Alaska—a ship owned by the Seattle Fur Trading Company. My high pitch of excitement (to put it mildly) did not abate even when I learned that the ship was a motorship, with a name which not even a newspaper reporter could have confused with my *C. S. Holmes.*

Imagine Phoebe studying punctuation and grammar! The funny part of that is that I, also, am studying punctuation and grammar. At the commercial school whose walls enfold me half of every weekday, they require one to take a little subject known as "business correspondence"—more briefly, "correspondence." This embraces spelling (such words as "separate" and "February" and others that Anderson would laugh at), also grammar (such things as the "can" and "may" hitch, etc.). Apart from this it is quite interesting, and I think I am getting something out of it—although some of my friends would doubtless say that what I mostly need is not a correspondence course, but a hush-up course.

But this is a mere digression. What I started to say in the paragraph above this one is that Phoebe is a brick of the best no. A1 material. Isn't it disgusting—how Things Are? Degrees and credits———bah! To sweat for one's shelter, clothing, and bread! Ye Gods, let's go to Tahiti. I like, and I don't like, to think of Phoebe in school. It isn't right, and yet it's marvellous of her to be attacking her dragon by the hind legs and pinning him down.

There is school, and there is school. Sabra seems to be enjoying hers terrifically. She is happy as can be—comes out at one o'clock hopping and prancing and singing. She learns cooking, and handicraft, including carpentry, painting, etc.—really they show a great deal of imagination and skill down there. The children mess around with smocks on, make as much noise as they like (within reasonable bounds, of course), do more or less what they like. As you perhaps know, this Lincoln School is a so-called "progressive school." That means that children are not "sat on" or "squshed" [sic], or boomeranged with "mustn'ts" and "don'ts" and "be quiets." Which is an extremely good plan—for that tender age, at least.

"Green Pastures" is easily the most tremendous thing, in a dramatic line, that I've ever seen or heard of. I think it beats—for effect and appeal to one's innermost vitals—Hamlet, or R. and J., or any of the old stand-bys. Is this a literary sacrilege? Well, I can't help it if it is. When Jehovah (a kindly, fatherly old preacher in a frock-coat) produced the firmament in a terrific thunder-clap, I wept and wept. I don't know why. They have staged it to perfection. The thunder shakes the theatre. They have a real sea for the Ark, and a long sandy stretch of road along which God walks for miles, it seems, while bushes and trees and houses float past. It is a rolling platform, of course, but one gets the effect of walking forever and ever, and before the end of it comes everyone aches from head to foot, so real it is. I suppose someday the play will leave New York, don't you? If it ever gets within reach of you ———well, I guess you don't need any advice on the subject.

Such things are——what's the plural of *oasis*?——oases, I suppose, though it doesn't look right. They are——that——in a desert of grindstones, inhabited only by dragons with scalesome, flailsome tails. Isn't that a picture? I bet Phoebe could draw it admirably. Get her to try her hand at it, if it appeals to her. The dragons would be something like Kipling's Bi-Colored-Python-Rock-Snake, I imagine.

I have set aside a few days around the middle of this month—marked them off mentally with red ink—for the days during which I may hear from my wandering sailor. Of course one can't tell—I might hear tomorrow, or I might never at all. Rather uncomfortable suspense. I don't know quite what would happen to me in that case, and I don't care to speculate. If I don't hear before November, I shall be worried. I haven't many bulwarks. My family isn't a bulwark at all. You are, and he is. He is so simple at heart that he would be laughed at by some of this world, and distrusted by most of the rest—my farents, for example—my fermenting farents. He is the soul and essence of the sea. He can sit on a schooner's taffrail at night and become so utterly a part of the ship and the sea and the night that it makes you cease your breathing for awe. He is rugged and uncut, and, though so far above the standard of most sea-farers, he still falls far short, in some ways, of the shore-world's standards. He is ignorant—of the little things that don't matter. But he is so real that he puts to shame thousands of people who probably would consider themselves far "above" him.

And he answered a need of mine that nothing and no one else could answer, by knowing how to laugh, and by being serene and tranquil and deep as the trade-wind Pacific. Bulwark, oasis, anchor—what-you-will. Mysterious, too, in his comings and goings, as the sea with its tide. A romantic soul. "Sure. Don't I know? Haven't I sat on deck in the moonlight and let fancy put on its seven-league boots and go roaming among the stars?"

He and Conrad would have hit it off grandly.

Forgive my "uplift" trend (as old M'Andrew would have said), but one *does* get a bit romantic and poetic over the week-ends. At last I know what the week-end really means to the hordes and hundreds! Helen and I stand by the front windows and watch the pantomimes across the street and in the park opposite—you have no idea how interesting it all is, to see these hundreds of human figures, young and old and medium, gesticulating and running and arguing and laughing—like a puppet-show, don't you know. It is excruciatingly funny, and excruciatingly sad—sometimes we laugh at it, sometimes we weep. Always we feel about three centuries old—in comparison to Sabra, for instance, who is so full of energy that she quite appalls both of us.

Well, what's one to do? Here we are, all of us, kicking and straining and growing black in the face to keep up to some invisible, tyrannical Mark. I don't know, but I'm in the fight. The shorthand? I don't know how much longer, but I know that I can't afford it forever. I think about a month more, and then I shall get a little job out here in Columbia. I have made some important friends, got them interested in me, and built for myself a reputation which I probably can't live up to. More struggling—to keep up with *that*. There is nothing very Iridescent in sight. Helen has no job, and neither the MS nor the house is sold. Cheerful! Ja gewis. Fox Film Corp. has given up all outside readers. So farewell to the putrid novels—farewell, also, to that handy little twelve or eighteen dollars a week!

What more shall I say? I don't wish to end this in a minor key. You are NOT to think I'm discouraged, or despondent, or anything, because that would be disobeying orders, and at sea we respect orders from mates. And anything can be shattered with a laugh. Remember what dear old Satan said about that, in *The Mysterious Stranger*?

"Power, money, persuasion, supplication, persecution—these can lift at a colossal humbug—push it a little—weaken it a little, century by century; but only laughter can blow it to rags and atoms at a blast. Against the assault of laughter nothing can stand."

Besides, it's Good to be alive and healthy and young, wherever you are, or whatever you're doing; and there are wonderful things even in the newspapers. In the last Herald Tribune Magazine there were a couple of pictures which an astronomer-artist-engineer had painted of the planet Mars, viewed from one of its own moons. Could anything be more glamorous than that?

>Yours for fair winds,
>Barbara.

Old No. 620
October 13 [1930]

M'dear Mate:

I am taking advantage of this unfathomable holiday (Columbus Day, I think) to write to you. The last few days (extending from last Monday to last Saturday) have been as momentous as any days have been for a long time—in fact, so momentous that I haven't recovered from their effects yet—not by a long shot. However, lest you die of suspense, let me proceed.

Monday, when I came home from school (this was a week ago exactly) I was informed by Helen that I had been solicited for a job, that she had accepted with alacrity for me (wise woman!) and that I was to go to work Tuesday afternoon, for half-time work indefinitely, along with school, you see. The office is the Personnel Research Federation, and the boss is an old friend (more or less) of the family.

So Tuesday afternoon (that's enough excitement for one paragraph, don't you think? that's why I'm changing!) I wandered into this office with my school-bag in my hand and my only hat in (on, rather) my head. That hat was dug up in the New Haven panic, and is at least eight years old, but it was a twelve-dollar felt hat, and one advantage of them is that they LAST. (I don't know why I put that in.) As soon as I entered the office I was asked whether I took dictation—and how glad I was to be able to say "yes."

My job is that of any ordinary stenographer (and I am almost equal to it!), and I am enjoying it hugely, and getting twelve dollars a week for half-time, and promise of a full-time position as soon as I finish school; and I have a desk of my own and a large old Remington Noiseless, and it's a great life and New York's a pretty good place. There!

But, my dear, that's a mere fraction!—a puny, putrid, infinitesimal fraction. Don't faint away. I know one shouldn't put so much vital material into one short letter, but that's the way things happen—they drag on forever and ever and ever, and then pile all on top of each other in a rush. I guess you know what has happened.

By the time last Saturday came (that was day before yesterday) I was very tired indeed, and when I left the office Saturday noon I had a curious pain in the region of the solar plexus, which increased, until I was fairly hobbling down Sixth Avenue. I got home all right, but it was a hard job, and I couldn't think what was wrong with me. When I came stumbling into the corridor at 620, I felt a little better—the worst of it seemed to be over. Then I came into the dining-room, and on the table was your last letter with the delectable headlines, and the explanation of "hunger's bloated ghost." (But what about the hopi bean and the baby lima???)

I read your letter, sitting in the brown rocker beside the front window, and I laughed so hard that it was real torture, for laughing hurt where the pain still lingered, and that seemed to me so comical that I laughed still harder and it hurt still worse.... Then your letter was finished.... I leaned forward to lay it down upon the windowsill.

... And upon the windowsill....

I saw.....

NEXT PAGE

I can't say this dramatically, so I won't....

I saw there that very familiar pencilled air-mail envelope, Seattle-post-marked, and flavored with Camels and oakum.

Helen had played that windowsill stunt on me, and damn foolish of her it was. The truth must be told. It was more of a shock than anything else. Of course I had expected it for weeks, but my expectations were always naturally ended as soon as I came into the house from school and saw whatever mail there was. This time it had been your letter—a glorious treat. I wasn't ready for this that followed. It was like a terrific earthquake.

The result was that—having answered the little note—I relapsed on the dining-room day-bed, and didn't move the rest of the day nor Sunday morning, wondering what the hell was wrong, and what I should do about it, and what I managed to do to myself. I lay there grinning but in very real physical pain.

The pain is all gone now, and I know what was wrong, and it was nothing serious—I'm not going to die or anything exciting at all, so that's all right. And I've recovered, more or less, and I feel merely buoyant and ready to tackle New York with fresh vigor for another new week, beginning this afternoon, in the office of the P. R. F.

You can imagine, of course, how disorganized the poor man is. It was only a tiny note, just saying he had arrived. It was dated *September 7*—instead of October 7. That's a good enough illustration of what a long voyage of that sort does to one. He hinted, in a way that made my blood run cold—"the breeze of wind you suggested turned out to be a man-sized affair, and it threatened *not* to be all right for a while."

O God, these wild people of the sea!

Of course I can't believe it yet. It's been a terrible gulf. It will be a long time before things can be as they were. I had half expected that the threads would just pick up again where they broke, but threads don't do that. There have been too many vital changes. But maybe I'm wrong. Maybe I'm still stunned. And I still hear that "man-sized affair" howling about split spars and streaming rags of sail. I know!

When he gets more or less organized again—not before—I shall gently hint that we would both like to see him this winter. I have a good idea that he'll take the hint. It's very easy to ship coastwise, especially in the winter, and it's rather hard to ship anywhere else except offshore. I feel somehow as though we should have to talk and laugh before balance can be recaptured. I am all up in the air now. I have concentrated all my faculties on trying to believe that that little letter is genuine, and not some ghostly aberration come to haunt me. I felt as though I were writing to a ghost, Saturday afternoon.

Stunned but happy, happy but stunned....

Well, was I right? Will you admit that last week was a momentous one? If you don't, I'll make you eat your words!

We're all coming out to California next summer, so beware!

Then here's to the day you and I can do dishes once more, in our incomparable and sublime manner!

       Your mate,
       Barbara.

Twenty-five dollars a week was an excellent wage, particularly for a sixteen-year-old during the second year of the Great Depression.

620 West 122nd Street
New York City
November 2, 1930

My Dear:

I heard from your own particular Mate just before your letter arrived, in which he remarked that he had been handing you a "raw deal"—that was how he expressed it. But if, as you say, he is to be happier and healthier because of the change, I don't call it a "raw deal" at all. That's just what you would want, isn't it? I mean, let me quickly say, Under the Circumstances. Of course it is not, NOT as it should be to have a part of oneself drifting about on the other side of the continent from one, is it? But I should think that Washington would be immeasurably more pleasant to live in then Detroitmich, as we write it in shorthand. And Air Mail across is remarkably rapid, though, of course, not rapid enough.

   Don't allow your feelings to be too much mixed about my job. You see, I really am having quite a good time. Don't imagine that it's a desperate struggle, or anything of that sort. Taking letters in shorthand is still quite a glamorous proceeding to me; though the last few days I have been addressing fifteen hundred envelopes—invitations to the very formal banquet of the Annual Fall Conference! That is rather monotonous, but it is just part of it, you see; and I like the people I work with—we all get along admirably well—and none of them works very hard; so I couldn't have landed in a better place for a first job. After November 7th, I think it will be full-time, at twenty-five a week, or thereabouts. That is a remarkably good wage for a person so inexperienced as I.

   Helen has just triumphed over a very crooked deal that was going on in New Haven concerning the house. She found that she had gotten into a "nest of crooks," so to speak, and by supreme courage and daring she managed to call their bluff, and we don't think any radical harm has been done. She is going to give a little talk soon, about the trip. She seems to be quite cheerful, and is riding the waves in great style. I like to see a ship riding the waves.

   The way you are, my dear Matey, and Phoebe, and the other member of the family in Detroit, and also the Deserters—of whom what news, by the way? I hope there will not only be cocoa when next I sail into port, but also Graham Crackers. I laugh still when I remember that colossal carton which Phoebe so thoughtfully purchased for my luncheon one day! Is it empty yet?... Last night Helen and I, with California resounding in eyes, nose, and mouth, bought and ate two large red-gold persimmons.... Not long, now, Matey—not long! I'll be there!

   I really think you are a thorough-going Traitor not to have been dumb enough to have been surprised; though, certainly, you *would* have been dumb, come to think of it. Don't think that that "dramatic arrangement" was at all pre-thought-out. It just occurred to me that the announcement needed a page to itself. It occurred to me just as I got to it—not before; and so I just naturally took that page out of the typewriter. It wasn't until afterwards that I slipped it back in to indicate that the letter didn't jump off in mid-air right at that point.

The dropped stitches have been carefully retrieved; or, I'd better say, the torn sails have been carefully patched, with marline warranted to hold "till the cows come home." (Funny, that that should be a nautical expression, but it is used by every sailor on earth when he's speaking about tying knots!)

It would be hard to tell what a relief it is to me. I don't any longer get to wondering whether the schooner is hemmed in by icebergs or getting battered by Arctic gales, or any such horridiferous thoughts. He, being a cautious soul, has decided to stay aboard a while longer, because there aren't any jobs for sailors any more than there are for anyone else at present. The vessel is laid up in Seattle, and he and the mate are alone aboard. They take turns cooking and feeding the cat, and they work whenever the weather lets them. So I guess he's lucky, and he is certainly quite right to stay where he is. It was, as he termed it, a "professional compliment" to be asked to stay on, alone of all the other men, anyway.

Seems to me this was a specially juicy lot of headlines. The New York Times and the Herald Tribune never indulge in such things, and I chuckle over these long and heartily. I can't make any of them out, which certainly proves that the headliner is a "bright fella." More power to him!

More power likewise to the "pot-boilers!"

God bless us, every one.

   Yours,
   BF.

Wesley Hill, who played the Angel Gabriel, was killed on December 10th.

620 West 122nd Street
New York City

December 13, 1930

Heave 'n' paul! How is you?

I think you are just too kickworthy for anything: how I'd like to get you across my knee. Bother my astral presence!

However, your letter with its little cascade of headlines, did finally arrive; and here I am sitting down to answer it, although if I had the gumption of a weevil in a biscuit (or even *half* a weevil!) I should be romantically doing the dishes and mopping the floor. Dishes and floor I absolutely refuse to acknowledge on Saturday afternoon. And those dishes can stay there till 1932 for all I care, and the swamp angels besides.

Saturday is a great day. Out of the office at one o'clock. This day I walked all the way home, about five miles, I should say. It's the first time I've done it, but I was feeling so utterly happy today, and it is such a beautiful day, that I kept postponing taking the subway, and saying I'd walk to the next station, and then the next, and so I got home.

To answer some of your questions. What has been happening? Yes, I work full time and on full pay, and I get a *great* kick out of it, really I do. The saddest thing I know of that has happened is that the Angel Gabriel of "The Green Pastures" was killed the other day by a taxi-cab. The play won't be itself without "Gabe." I don't go to the docks. New York docks aren't goable to (should I have said go toable) by unaccompanied femininity. It has been mostly Conrad. Yes, Sabra is rather "separate." There aren't many excitements to share, and I guess she finds me a rather dull lump most of the time! Christmas? Don't ask!

I haven't the least sympathy for anyone who will work four hours on Algebra! It's positively criminal — insane — unheard-of!

Your descriptions of the California weather made me gasp. Heavens! It can be beautiful, I know! I'm coming, Matey, I'm a-coming! I think the ideal thing would be to live in Southern California during the winter and spring, and get North for summer and fall. You can't deny, Matey, that L. A. in the summer is — ! & ^ $$] ::: ! ç — — ^^^^ .... (I hope you grasp the full significance of that!)

I admire Elizabeth, and I envy her her studio, and I send her my love. That's very few words, but there's a lot in back of them.

Yes, I s'pose the U. S. Government notices an increased return of about $0.30 per week since mid-October, and maybe that's one of the reasons they have been ballyhooing of late about the return of prosperity. Anderson and I commune continually; we nibble delicately at the earth as though it were a piece of cheese, and we fool with stars as though they were a handful of beads. He (wise man!—) is hanging on to his job for dear life, while I stand by and approve. On the other hand, I hang desperately to my job, while *he* stands by and approves. Thus we get along, though it's very unsatisfactory not to be together. I think he writes better and better all the time. His comments are really immortal.

I've just read your story again, and oh, I like it ever so much! I do hope Helen manages to get it into the proper hands. Of course it's not the thing at all for these women's magazines, which demand pleasant, sweet, impossible stories, brimming over with love interest and the triumph of right. Well, I don't know: when I glimpse at such magazines, which is not often, I, too, demand sweet, pleasant, impossible stories. I should read them, if I read them, just *for* that sort of story. Yours is banished from there! But there's a place for it somewhere—not in the pastures, but up on the high barren cliffs.

Helen is riding the waves valiantly.

I saw a headline today in one of the New York dailies: FAY CALLED CZAR OF MILK PRICES BY PROSECUTOR. No' sae bad?

May your stars shine!

>Yo' frien',
>Barbara

620 West 122nd Street
New York
December 28, 1930

Dear Meserveys (or should I say "Meservies?"):

A thousand thanks for your grand Christmas bundle, which did much to make our little Christmas a *real* Christmas. Having been in wild out-of-the-way spots in the South Seas and such places for the last two Christmases, I found myself very much out of practice this year, when it came to even cards; and this may account for the fact that I appeared to be so very Caledonian, and that no one received anything-at-all from me!

Your choice of gifts was most happy. Sabra was not the only person who was tickled to death over the kitchen set: we all sat around and admired every piece of furniture for a long time. She thinks it was the nicest thing anyone sent her. Fortunate, too, because she has a doll's house, and the doll's house happened to be weak on just exactly those items: furniture for its kitchen!

As for Helen's and my stockings: that shows real insight, and how you happened to hit on our exact sizes is more than I can fathom. Usually people forget that I have large, hiking feet! Anyway, silk stockings were just exactly what both of us needed, being here in New York, and having jobs, etc. The fact is, Helen put on hers to go out to dinner on Christmas day, and I put mine on the next day to go to work! As I said before, real insight!

I suppose you all had a tree twelve feet tall, and about twelve feet of snow besides. We had a tree three feet high! And the snow we had was weak and watery. We thought of you, and wished we might have been with you. It was awfully good of you to have asked us. But oh, this business of working is so very serious and solemn! And there's nothing to do about it, and I'm lucky to have a job anyway; and after all, offices go on, mail comes in and mail goes out, Christmas or no Christmas; to get Friday and Saturday morning off was an impossibility.

Well, this is all I'll write for now. It's just a "thank-you" letter, I suppose; but let me assure you, it *means* a lot more than most of 'em do!

    Love to all,
    Barbara

Did Barbara's well-intentioned "Uncle" have anything to do with her "moral break-down" (Helen's term) in Tahiti? This is the only letter from Uâ in the archive.

Papeete, Tahiti, January 4th, 1931.

My dear Barbara,

No,—I haven't forgotten you. You were only a chrysalis in those days, but you held the promise of a wondrous butterfly; otherwise I should hardly have bothered to tell you the difference between the sham of life and the reality.

[He goes on at length about his love for a girl twenty years earlier, and his grail of finding such a divine and ideal love again.]

So, perhaps, now you will understand *why* I talked to you as I did; I saw (or I *thought* I saw) a gleam of pure silver in the physical matrix that was You, and I wanted to break away the impeding rock and soil so that, perhaps, some day, in the crucible of love, a pure metal might be born.

It was just possible (one chance in a hundred million and two) that some boy might love you as I had loved *her*, and I wanted you to be free—yes, utterly and gloriously Free—from all those age-old and encrusted lies and inhibitions of our limiting inheritance and environment, that you might go to him with wide arms [...]

If you think back you will remember that I did not again talk to you in the same way after you told me of your engineer, for somehow I could not bring myself to believe that he fitted into the conception of the boy I visioned for you.

[Here he writes about his disdain for the world's "false standards and inhibitions," preferring to live with the "unspoiled children of Polynesia."]

So, Barbara, *au revoir*, my dear. If you think it is worth while then try to keep burning that inner flame which I *thought* I saw in a gleam of silver. If you never find the living counterpart of the ideal I have tried to show you, it will not matter in the least.

Think of me occasionally as a sort of well-intentioned 'Uncle' who, if he talked at all, would *not* utter the standardized lies of our degenerate civilization.

    Your friend,
    Uâ

620 West 122nd St.
New York
January 5, 1931

Dear Mate! *[Alice]*

Happy New Year! Five days gone a'ready!

A thousand thanks for your Christmas gift, which was a very happy thought indeed, and which I shall read with the greatest of pleasure—and wistfulness, too, I guess. I can't forget the torment of *Wuthering Heights.* It's a haunting thing to me.

I don't think it was so *very* terrible of you to open It before Christmas. It was quite my fault. Then, too, as you know, I am somewhat of an atheist; and to tell the truth quite despise the mercenary thing Christmas has become! The real thing goes far deeper than that.

We enjoyed all your gifts ever so much, including every scrap of gilt ribbon, even! The "edibles" were quite ambrosian (speaking of ambrosia!) The soap-Santa-Claus made such a hit that it hasn't been used yet! It's one of those sad problems: "You cannot eat your cake and have it too."

We had a three-foot Christmas tree and a lot of fun buying things for Sabra, mostly from Mr. Woolworth. That's about all.

Well, to tell the truth, the graham crackers which you so subtly allude to, Matey Mine, *are* somewhat more chocolate-covered than before—not to say "gilt-edged," which doesn't seem to fit the metaphor so well! I'd hate to think you really were so blind as you suggest that you are.

Anyway, Christmas is gone, and here is another year, brand new, just out of its chrysalis!

Thanks again; and to all of you I wish the best luck in the world.

   Your pard,
   Barbara

Pardon the puny dimensions of this, won't you?

Helen was successful in getting Magic Portholes *published by the Junior Literary Guild (now called the Junior Library Guild). Helen Ferris, the editor-in-chief of the Guild and a close associate of Eleanor Roosevelt (who was on the editorial board), chose it for publication in June 1932.*

As for Helen's "radioistic ambitions," there are a few scripts in the Columbia archive but I don't know if they were ever performed on the radio. However, Helen was interviewed several times on air about her adventures with Barbara. There are transcripts at Columbia, and there's a photo showing Helen and other guests on the Herald Headliners *(Boston Sunday Herald) program from March 5, 1933.*

N by E was Rockwell Kent's report of his voyage to Greenland in 1929, where his boat was shipwrecked.

Alice's daughter Elisabeth Lewis was a talented painter. Her work was featured on several covers of House Beautiful *around this time (see, for example, July 1933).*

Helen is between the microphones.

620 West 122nd St.
New York City
February 24, 1931

Dear A.D.R.:

I hardly dare to write to you at all now! Oh, I admit it, I admit it, my dear, it is simply horridiferous of me to have neglected no. 2001 so very long. I know—I don't have to be told so, or mercilessly scolded, or kicked, or shaken!

Human nature, I've decided, is a very ornery sort of thing, when all's said and done. In spite of my inward resolution to make no excuses for my long, dastardly silence, I am going to proceed at once to make some! To begin with, Helen has been down and out with the "flu." She's been up for some time now, but for several days the place was pandemonium, and there was no doing anything save just dragging along from one hour to the next. Everything seemed as wrong as possible. Even Anderson, the unfailing standby, was summoned up-sound with the owner of the ship, with the result that I didn't have any word from him for over two weeks, which was uncomfortable. I learned afterwards that the two of them had been cutting down a tree for a new mast for the schooner. Still romance in the world, eh, what? I like the idea of cutting down trees for masts—in 1931! Seems too good to be true.

Even at the office, things were deadly, as the Director had to go out West to a big meeting, to deliver a couple of addresses, etc., and when he's away there's hardly anything to do down there; and if there's anything I hate, it's keeping up a semblance of having something to do when in reality I'm *not*. The time hangs awfully heavy at such times. Now, however, Helen is well, A. is back, the Director came back today; also a deluge of proof for the technical Journal came in in the morning's mail, and my down-town desk is loaded!

I have other exciting news. The other week, in pursuing through the Shipping News, I came upon an item about my old schooner, the *Frederick H.*—that is, of course, the *Norman D.* It seems she had gone ashore off Mount Desert (Maine) in a gale o' wind, and damaged her rudder. (Follett would know about Mount Desert.) Well, that set me thinking. I got to thinking about that "worthy mariner" (as Anderson calls him), Mate Bill, and how he was, and how Mrs. Mate Bill was, who wrote me once; and whether the schooner was badly knocked up, and whether Bill still remembered at all the little red-headed girl who kicked about the decks of the *Frederick H.* so long ago, when she was only about up to her own shoulder, or less!

So I typed off a letter to Mate Bill.

And in reply:

Port Greville
Feb. 12. 1931

Dear Barbara

we got your letter O K and was glad to here form you again. Bill is not home so he got me to drope you a line Bill was in Frederick last summer and this summer to he left hur about 3 weeks befour she went ashore she is in river now not hurt much. we was tacking about you about a week befour Bill got your letter he was useing knife you give him and sed I like to no ware Barbara is now he though he would never here form you again Bill sed he would make you a boat like Frederick and take it up to you in summer.

if you think you could fine him he would let you no Bill ofen speek about that man that came down in Frederick and would love to see him I am send you some snaps of Frederick H. now Barbara I will Close for this time Please write soon again form Mrs McClelland

Bill working in woods about 16 mile form home he diden have aney chance to write he in a camp with about 28 men so you see he would have no place to write please excuse him

Real honest-to-God sterling people? Yes! And what difference does it make whether they can spell or not? Not a sand-small bit—though of course it's preferable, I think, to have, as a steady correspondent, someone who *can* spell and punctuate and form good Anglo-Saxon sentences and paragraphs!

Well, I was overjoyed. So it seems I may be seeing Mate Bill this summer, "if I can fine him" that is, which I think I can do, even among the dingy, complicated, disgusting wharves of New York. If I do, there will be a story. And yet—I confess I have a vague fear when it comes to seeing Bill again. Bill remembers me as a little kid. I've put on so much stature, etc., I'm afraid he may be rather flabbergasted. However, I don't see that I could have done anything about it; though I do think it would be nice to have some magic gift by which one could become twelve or thirteen years old at will. Don't you?

Other news I have none, I guess. Helen's manuscript is battling for dear life. There are three very powerful ropes out now, and any number of smaller fish-lines. Some of it is in the hands of St. Nicholas, which has so far reacted favorably. Helen, with the help of a new-found actress friend, is dramatizing it with radioistic ambitions, as perhaps I've told you. And then the Junior Literary Guild. One of the three ought to *happen*. I should think, anyway! If all of them happen—but that isn't to be expected. But if any one of them happens, it will help the other two!

She herself is working like an Injun most of the time. I, on the other hand, ain't working no more than I have ter!

Sometimes, still, I spend week-ends at that quiet, timid little house in Pelham, with the elderly poet and his elderly wife. I spent this last week-end on holiday with them, reading Sherlock Holmes and Sat. Eve. Post stories, and in general having a good relaxation. I also did some writing. I find it rather difficult to get all the writing done here that I might like to do. It's rather thick at times!

Have you heard anything, or seen anything, or felt anything, of Follett? Or of The Other? I wonder, I wonder, what they can be doing, and how they are, etc. How's that "menial job" which Follett said he had?

Your story, I regret to say, hasn't sold yet. I'm going to take it down to Ethel Kelley next week-end, and read it aloud to her. She is a very precious friend of both Helen and me, you know; and is well up in literary things, and knows a lot about possible markets, etc., even if she has been flat on her back for three or four years.

The only other bit of news is that my German friend, the young and fair-haired second mate of my last steamer, the *Marsodak*, came for a "wisit" with me the other week or so. I came home from work and found him sitting at the table with Helen, laughing, and looking quite like himself. We had a very jolly time. He went out and bought two immense porterhouse steaks about three inches thick, and a dozen pastries with whipped cream in them. Lord-a-mercy! when these sailors get ashore! That's one thing I like about A: he doesn't force fanciful boxes of candy upon one at every corner. But the German mate was very entertaining, as usual: he spun yarns till nearly midnight. It seems his ship, the *Marsodak*, is laid up in Baltimore: he got transferred to another of the company's ships, which just came into New York. He was shivering, however, and talked a great deal about California, and his favorite town, San Francisco.

The weather *has* been rather beastly, though not half so bad as I expected. It's been alternately cold and warm, cold and warm, all winter long. There's been real northerly spice in the air, and quite a lot of snow; and there have been some of those clear, cold, north N. E. (that stands for New England!) days that make one feel very virile and full of life and energy. These last three days, on the other hand, have been gloriously like spring itself.

In your last letter you commented with great, great enthusiasm, on N by E. Funny that our tastes in literature should clash, even a little, isn't it? I can't praise the book with the whole-hearted eagerness that you do. You say that Rockwell Kent is a Man and a Seaman. I don't think he is quite either. There are some gorgeous bits in the book, and I love some of the pictures; but damn it! there's too much Rockwell Kent at every turn! I have a feeling, also, that there's affectation in the book—it doesn't quite ring, to me, with the genuine wholesome sound that it ought to have. It can't be said that I am prejudiced, either, because I started out with the feeling that I should certainly admire and love the book straight through. But it doesn't seem to me the book that his earlier one, *Wilderness*, is. (Pardon this *atrocious* sentence!)

Another thing that doesn't ring with me is the breaking up of the little party.

Another thing that's out of place is the episode of the Greenland girl.

I'll tell you, though, of one really gigantic piece of writing that has come to light. It's in the February issue of Harper's Magazine; and it's William McFee's article, "Engine Room Stuff." Now on the whole I have had occasion to be hugely disappointed with McFee's writing. But this one piece is epic, cosmic. It's without doubt one of the best short pieces of writing I've read for a long time. It has, in fact, only one bad line in it—which one can skip when reading it aloud to friends, as I do. I suggest that you dig it up. It's far more than worth the trouble.

My love to the fambly. I suppose B. R. is in Washington, now. Alas! These continental separations! Atrocious, aren't they? If you will give me his address, I think I'll write to him again shortly. How's Phoebe? The House Beautiful covers are GRAND!

There are lots of things I should have said that I haven't, I'm sure. Yet this is, at least, a starter, isn't it? I hope you don't feel too thoroughly exasperated with

> Yours ever,
> Barbara

It's not surprising that Barbara wished she and Phoebe were better friends. They were almost exactly the same age—Phoebe being three days younger (and Elisabeth six years older).

620 West 122nd Street
New York City
March 12, 1931

My dear mate:

How glad I am that our last letters crossed in the mail! I had a genuine feeling of shame when I received that little admonishing letter of yours—but think what that feeling would have been had I not been secure in the knowledge that my letter *was* on its way to you as fast as the faithful little plane could take it. Just think! Only three days from me to you, clear across this old continent—two days if you happen to hit the mail just right! How many months did it take in olden times?

Well, anyway.... Everything is going well here. Helen's book is, I believe, on the very threshold.... Oh, I know, it's been on that threshold a very long time! The job holds. Anderson is marvellous. Honestly, I don't see how I could possibly get along without his twice- and sometimes thrice-weekly communications: all done in the best Andersonian manner, and never less than two pages in length. He is—a rock.

I have had two other bits of mail lately that have been interesting, besides the letter from Mrs. McClelland. One came from my dark suitor in the Tonga Islands. In his quaint English he expressed the opinion that it was a "poor world." The other was from a half-caste girl whom I knew in Samoa, and came to like very much. I thought she had by far the most personality—as we measure personality—of anyone I met down in those outlandish parts. At that time there was something in the air about her marrying a white man—a wireless operator aboard one of the Navy ships, I believe. That was two years ago. I was interested to hear this time that it was still in the air—in fact, she is to be married in April. I am a little distressed of course, because I don't like inter-racial marriages, and can't help having doubts about the man. She has great dreams of coming to live in the States. Poor child! A Polynesian is a "nigger" here, you know. If only one could *say* those things. But no—you have to be silent.

It *does* seem too bad to let Phoebe grow up. I know you won't *try* to prevent it, though, for of course you realize that that is misery-making. Oh, Mate, I can give you all sorts of sage advice on those points! I remember certain things so very well, you see—things that have grown a little less real and vivid, perhaps, to an older person. I think growing up *could* be a most glorious experience. But, oh, it can be so *ghastly*.

Incidentally, I wish Phoebe would write to me someday when she feels like it. I wrote to her two or three times, and hoped for a brief word sometime. I got the impression that perhaps she was very much disappointed with me—and I honestly don't blame her. She started out with the idea that I was such a romantic character, you know, and of course I wasn't. I felt at the time that perhaps she had built up something around me that was too iridescent and fragile and beautiful for any mere mortal to live up to. Oh, I know.... Butterfly wings .... Touch them, and the powder comes off on your hand....

I have been meditating a good deal the last few weeks on the rather abstract problem of whether or not I should go to college—that is, of course, assuming I could get in, which I doubt. I don't feel the faintest ray of desire or enthusiasm—in fact, I feel a decided antipathy. But I *do* believe it to be an asset, if you can display your A.B. or B.A. or whatever it is, when applying for a job. I have decided to get the opinions of several of my friends, on the subject. That doesn't mean that I will promise to *follow* their opinions, of course, even should they all turn out to be "for" it—it just means that I am interested to see what they think.

I am not only vague in the extreme on that point, but I am also vague about the immediate future—this summer, I mean. The building we are living in is to come down in June, at least our lease ends in June. Helen wants to go away somewhere. I do, too, but if the job holds I intend to cling to it with might and main. I don't believe it will hold all summer, as the Federation goes very slowly from June to about September. If Anderson were going to be here I should certainly make some sort of effort to see him, but he is going up North again, as perhaps I told you. Not such a long trip, he says, but I feel rather bleak about it. He is going because he wants the money and is saving it—For A Purpose. Also, times are so damned hard, he thinks quite rightly that he had better stick while the sticking's good! So with him away, I don't care much where I go, but I certainly want to go somewhere. Anywhere Helen decides on will be agreeable to me, I guess. We'll probably hunt up a schooner and sail to the coast of Maine, or maybe to Nova Scotia—or maybe in another direction entirely, toward the West Indies. All things hang on two "ifs"—*if* my job doesn't hold, and *if* the book goes. Otherwise I guess we stay here—(Heaven help us!)

I'm writing a preface (trying to, I mean) for the book. They think it will give it the punch of authority and genuineness, if you know what I mean. I'm hoping to be able to pull off six or seven good pages, but have produced so far only a bit of garbage. *You* know. When it's done I'll send you a copy for criticism. I'm also sending out two or three other copies to my friends—when it's done. That's the way Dr. Bingham, Director of the Federation, always writes an article, and I think it's a good scheme.

Well, I guess that's about enough dribble for this time, isn't it, Mate? Anyway, you can see that I'm at least making quite an effort to take my life and put it up on a peak where—alas!—it isn't. I'm happy in the effort. And I love you. You and Anderson are the two best friends in the world.

    Yours,
    Barbara

Fugamisi
30th April 19/4/31 [sic]

Dear Miss B Follett.

I received your most welcome letter with best.

I got your letter last night, and I am very happy to hear some good news from you and also from your mother,

I am very pleased to hear that you are ready to come back to the Is.

[...] Please dear I want you to come back again to see me.

I am back from trip to NZ last month. But I want you to come here and I can take you to NZ with great love.

[...] I am very please to get a Photo from you my dear. Well give my love to your mother also your friends.

Now I am closed with best wishes to you. I can send my photo next trip. I haven't ready yet, because I am very busy.

> I remain
> Your best recard.
> K. B. Riggs

Anne Meservey had found a summer cabin for the Folletts in Norwich, Vermont—just across the river from Hanover, New Hampshire, where Barbara was born. (Barbara's half-sister—my mother, Jane Follett, who also was born in Hanover—lived with my father in Norwich when my sister was born in 1961—again in Hanover. Alas, my sister died within twenty-four hours.)

620 West 122nd Street
New York
May 2, 1931

Dear Anne:

It is wonderful about the cottage in the woods. It isn't too far in the woods, is it, for three females without man, dog, gun, or car? But I trust you for that.

When we can come is still a little up in the air. As I wrote you, Barbara can't come anyway until July. It is possible that I may be detained here for some weeks in June myself. That depends a good deal on what I hear from a publisher who has my manuscript now. I expect word this coming week.

Would you and Oxford like my old canoe? So far as I know it is still in excellent health—an Old Town. I don't like to give it to Mrs. Stanley, but I shall probably do so unless you want it, because I don't know what else to do with it. It is in the Sunapee cottage, with a rowboat that belongs to me also. If you have a car, it wouldn't be such a difficult job to hitch it on to a trailer and take it up to Hanover. I shall probably never go to the cottage again at Sunapee.

You mustn't consider being financial host to us at all. Barbara and I can do that. That you want us to come, and anticipate our coming—those are the things that matter to us.

I'll write you next week. Perhaps I can tell then when I will get up, but at this moment I can only say that I will come sometime.

> Love from
> Helen

"SOME of those things ought to come through!" None of them came through apart from offers from Macmillan and the Junior Literary Guild. The novel Barbara had begun in her new, curt style was Lost Island.

150 Claremont Avenue
New York
June 1, 1931

Dearest A.D.R.:

I am really almost afraid to write to you at all. I feel quite dastardly, and all that. But I've been endeavoring to do sixteen different major things at once, and you know what that is like. Furthermore, the scheme of the universe was just about as full as I could manage, and I had to keep going pretty tight to keep up with it at that. Now there is one extra corner. You can have it!

Your last letter was really a very grand one. Maybe it will help a little for you to know that I answered it twice, or started to, but the answers never got finished! Also I never received the headlines which you enclosed in it. They had a tragedy. You see, I opened the letter as I was on my way from the house to the subway station, and so they blew away! I chased them a little, but there was quite a wind, and they eluded me. Of course, knowing your habits, I should have been prepared.

The best thing that letter contained was your news about B. R., and yet YOU merely appended it in ink, as an after-thought! It is too grand to be true that someone is going to see somebody they want to see. I envy you and rejoice with you all at once.

We have some rather good developments of late. Helen's book is TAKEN!!!!!!!!!! By Louise Seaman, of Macmillan. Furthermore, it seems that now it's been accepted, and a generous advance offer made, certain other publishers in N. Y. are on its trail—which is flattering, you know. Well, the joke's on them.

Now, I don't want this to be mentioned. It's a great secret, for the time being. You must share it only with Phoebe. Helen is very anxious to have it a surprise to W. F., and for that reason I think it would be better not to tell even the Deserters. Furthermore, the Contract isn't actually signed, nor the Check received; but it's as good as done, and I don't think it can really go wrong now.

There is still more editorial work to be done on it. It was accepted on faith, so to speak. Helen has gorgeously revised the first four chapters, and the faith is that the rest of the book will be pulled up to the high standard of those four. That will be done this summer. The book will doubtless be out next spring.

Helen says she's going to get that book serialized before it's published, then accepted by the Junior Guild, then published, then radioized, and perhaps a few odd chapters accepted by Harper's Magazine in payment of the Debt! Well, SOME of those things ought to come through!

Other things have happened. One sad one. A. has gone, of course—which leaves the corner in my time which I was speaking about before. I'm glad to have the corner, of course, and yet — It was more of a jolt than I had anticipated. I feel quite nebulous, not quite sure of whether I'm here.

Other things have happened. We're moving, as you can see by the heading. Just an apartment round the corner, because this building is to be torn down, beginning tomorrow, supposedly. The new place is bigger and airier and sunnier and expensiver, with a grand view of the New Jersey hills, Grant's Tomb, and the rear of the statue of Butterfield.

Other things have happened. I'm to have a two months' vacation, and we're moving up to Hanover to spend them in a little cabin in the woods, just across the river from our old and dear friends the Meserveys. Really in the woods. Wood-thrushes and crickets and pine trees. Oh, my God! And stars, and smells, and green grass. A little log cabin, all furnished, facing Mt. Ascutney, for $20.00 a month. Not too extravagant, eh what? I shall climb mountains and tear around. Just the worst two months here in the city. What luck! July and August.

Other things have happened. I'm writing a book. A good book. The one about wings. The first chapter is done, and the second is well under way. The plot is mapped out rather clearly—in my head. It begins rather dismally, but soon acquires some sun. There will be sea (naturally), and a romance (?), and a satisfactory amount of misery. The plot is exceedingly old and trite, but it's going to be handled in a new way. It's about a shipwreck, an island, and so on. But it doesn't turn out very well. It leaves you a little poised in mid-air.

Well, I think that's all that has happened, summed up in brief. I think you'd better move east next winter. It's going to be a good winter. I'm to have the same job, "with added responsibilities and an increased stipend." The last clause is particularly inducive, I think. "Increased stipend" has a pleasant ring, has it not? Someday I'll buy an island yet! Or a boat. Or both.

As I said, it's going to be a really good winter. Helen's book will be on its exciting trip through the press, I shall be working up mine, plus a few articles for Harper (say I lightly!). We'll have a little more breathing-space, too. Why, I shall even have a room all to myself, which I haven't had for ever and ever so long. And how I shall work!

I was going to say a lot about your comments on college. But that is so long past that I'm quite out of the mood at present. I saw your points at the time, I believe; in fact, they were obvious points. But somehow I don't believe it will happen. Everything can't happen, you know. I'd rather cut it out than some of the other things. One has to choose. The point is, weed your garden, don't you know?

What are you doing, and planning to do? Damn, damn, it's a long time since I've seen you. Come east next winter. It looks as if I shouldn't go west for some time yet. Got to stick at the wheel and weed my garden. But it's really awful how all my best friends are thousands of miles away. It's as if I had a cursed circle around me that my friends can't get into. A geographical circle, I mean. The only real friend I have in New York is Ethel Kelley, and she's too sick to see me at all most of the time. When I want her most, she's invariably too sick. Also, she's trying to write a book too, and giving all her spare energy to that. The only other person who is at all in reach is Norman D. of New Haven, who comes down to N. Y. once in a while on business. Otherwise, I'm damned alone, if you want to know.

But that doesn't matter, and isn't interesting anyway.

This style of writing of mine sounds rather curt in a letter, doesn't it? It's a new development. I think I rather like it. The novel is more or less written in that style. Some sentences which aren't really sentences, you know; and no long, involved ones. W. F. wouldn't approve of that, I suppose, he being the champeen sentence-twister and wordsmith of the generation! Incidentally, any news of him? And don't forget! He's not to know about Helen's book.

Do you remember that beautifully involved sentence in the introductory sketch to *The Scarlet Letter*? It begins "In my native town of Salem...." and ends, halfway down the page, "there stands a spacious edifice of brick." Words to that effect. In between those two clauses, which are the complete structure of the sentence, he describes the whole town of Salem, I should say, with dashes and comma-dashes and semicolons galore. Incidentally, it was my first reading of the book, just yesterday. I never could plough through Hawthorne before. I used to get snowed under before I could find out what it was all about. But I got such a tremendous kick out of that book that I had an attack of hysteria or sumthin very like it. The suspense is crushing, and the whole structure is built up magnificently. I didn't know he wrote like that!

That's all I've read for months. Except galley proof, of course. There's always lots of galley proof to read, when a good eye is available. I read just about all the proof that comes into the office, and am getting quite famous for not passing up errors. Very uninteresting material, though, for the most part. Scientific and technical and deadly dull! Scientists can't write a good English sentence, somehow.

Anyway, I still think *Lord Jim* is the greatest book in English, and a point above *Nostromo*. Tell W. F. that when you see him. Then he'll know I still disagree with him!

I suppose California is getting hot. We've been fried and frizzled the last three days. Helen and I have been carting basketloads of books across the street to the other apartment, and we're about done up. I think S. F. would be grand about now. But not so good as little old Hanover!

I hope you'll condescend so far as to forgive the long silence and write me. I'll try to make up for it; but my tryings never seem to amount to very much. Letter-writing is a delicate matter. It has all sorts of strange bumps and valleys. It's a quicksand affair. But even quicksand serves to pave a river with.

>Yours with love,
>Barbara

150 Claremont Avenue
New York
June 28, 1931

My dear A.D.R.:

I wonder, wonder, wonder. IS anything wrong with the R's? I'm rather worried. I'd hate to think so. Or HAVE I done anything wrong—other than not writing for a long, long time?

Sometime I'll tell you why that long break occurred. It was horrid of me, I know, but I was in a snowdrift and could not get out, and didn't care much.

Or maybe that last letter of mine went wrong—in which I told you about Helen's book and Macmillan's acceptance of it; and also of my projected book, of which three chapters are now in existence. Maybe that letter smashed in an airplane or sumthin.

Anyway, I do want to hear from you — ever so. About how you all are. I suppose B. R. has been west by this time, hasn't he? Or did something slip up there? I am rather worried. I do hope that everything's well with you and yours.

My love and Helen's to Phoebe, et al., and plenty left over for yourself.

>Yours
>B.F.

P. S. If it is true that that letter didn't reach you, please don't say a word about this to anyone. W. F. mustn't know — yet!

July 4, 1931

Dearest A.D.R.:

Your letter came just in time—I leave tomorrow morning early for the month, and Helen follows in a few days. The address will be: ℅ A. B. Meservey, 24 Occam Ridge, Hanover, New Hampshire.

Oh, I am so sorry that things are going so rottenly for you. There is no justice in Heaven or Earth, it seems. Really, I cried over your letter—as if that would help any! How I wish I could *do* something! My heart would tell you to pack up and go to B. R. *at once*. But there's poor E. So I would compromise. I would go to him as soon as ever her need of you is abated a little. I don't believe it's a case of Money, A. D. R. ... But then, of course I am probably all wrong. Only you *mustn't* say that about not seeing him again. You mustn't even contemplate such a thing. There *is* a limit to what the gods can do, you know.

There are three chapters of my book in existence now—pretty fairly good I think. Its title so far has been "Lost Island." Does that sound intriguing? The few persons whom I have so far confided in have liked it—also have been enthusiastic over the outline of the story. I am having a good deal of fun wrestling with it.

I think it's *swell* that The American Girl has been chasing you for material. That is about the highest compliment a writer can have, isn't it? And you *must* find time to do the work. If I think of a rip-snorting Idea I'll let you know. But maybe you already have plenty of Ideas. Apparently that is the easiest part! It seems to be with me.

There are no further developments on Helen's book. I imagine it will be out next spring sometime. They are casting about right now for an illustration—a "tropical bird" preferably, as H. says. Whether it will work out I don't know. Also, we are still revising the MS. One can revise till Doomsday, it seems. We probably will!

Alaska *is* a Hell of a long way off! No mail until October. But that's something to anticipate. He is such a faithful soul. Two letters a week, and sometimes three, from the time he landed last fall till the schooner sailed this spring. He'll come back. I have an idea that he's unbreakable and eternal.

Oh, A. D. R., I don't know what to say, but I'm *sure* you should come east. The bus costs only $55. Could you stand the bus? If it's lack of ready cash, I could remedy that—yes, even I, incredible as it may seem. And oh, how I'd love to see you myself! Of course, there will not be that old California glamor—that subtle, fleeting thing that surrounded us before. It might be a little unreal. I haven't carried over much of that atmosphere. But we could have cocoa and graham crackers even here, and I could whirl you around. How about next fall?

Next fall looks just a little dreary to me anyway. To be sure, I'll have that same job again, and probably it will be a bigger one. My employer has industrial ideals—that your job is your own property, so to speak. But oh, oh, in N. Y. the moths feed on the wings of your soul. This is probably an unhealthy attitude, I know. But I *do* think the world is rather horrid. Most of my dearest friends seem to be in deep trouble, and I can't do anything about it.

Perhaps that's why I cling for dear life to A. He, with no tools and no material, has nevertheless made something most beautiful and real out of life. I don't know just how. But he is a rock and a shelter. I'll never forget or forgive WF's attitude toward him. That was mainly what caused the sharp and sudden break between him and me. It was unwarranted and ridiculous and *mean*. My respect for WF did its loudest blowing-up over that.... A. is a treasure.

Anyway, you come East this fall—or sooner. One can get to the point where one doesn't know what to do and consequently does nothing, whereas an outsider, acquainted suddenly with the true situation, at once forms rather definite opinions. Of course, this outsider isn't pretending to be God! But I know how easily one can let Money rule one—especially if Money is thought of at every step. Soon one ceases to take steps. I know!

If you will come, you know that you could stay here with us—we have plenty of space now, and anything we have is yours. Helen longs to see you, too. You would be quite close to B. R. and could run down to Washington often by bus. I feel sure that everyone concerned would be happier for it. You could rent the house; and if Phoebe couldn't come too I know she would understand, and would be glad to carry on for a while. And oh, we would welcome you so! So *do* think of it seriously.

This is a nice, cool, comfortable apartment, with lots of light and plenty of good tables to work on. You could get a lot of writing done. We would all be writing together. Wouldn't it be fun? Also, we live right near the Hudson River, which is really beautiful at night—dreamy, promising. There is a nice park—a public spoonery, to be sure, but still very nice. I think we could have a grand time.

This is the great 4th of July. It seems strange and incongruous somehow, to hear the snapping of toy pistols and firecrackers. Silly. It makes H. and me a little depressed. Seems so utterly futile.

One very nice thing *did* happen this week. The Chief wrote to me — at last. H. had been to Boston, and his boat was in. She went down to pay a friendly visit. The letter is more or less the result of that, but that fact doesn't make it any less pleasing. It's just the kind of letter that was needed to square that account. It has relieved me more that I imagined, and given me a freedom from that vague and horrid sense of guilt and discomfort. Until now there was still something pending—waiting to be settled. Not it's all definitely fixed, somehow—the account has been cleared, and well cleared. Until now I had vague feelings of sadness on the subject, which have completely vanished now.

Now for the woods! I *am* looking forward to sunlight and trees — the Earth. Except for a curious and indefinable loneliness, which I have experienced a good deal of late without exactly knowing why—except for that, I think the next two months will be glorious. One *does* get lonely in the springtime somehow, when the wind is warm on your face and the grass is green.

I need you a great deal. I *know* we each have a lot to discuss and propound which we wouldn't by mail. At any rate, mere quiet companionship would be very soul-satisfying.

Do give our love to the "fambly." I am holding my thumbs for you, my dear, and I *do* want and hope and long for things to be better. I won't say "pray," because whatever small part of God I may once have believed in, I don't believe in any more. But I believe in love.

    Yours,
    B.

As we will see in August, Barbara's article for Harper's *didn't get far.*
    Coniston *was a 1906 novel by Winston Churchill (not that Winston Churchill!) about New Hampshire politics. The small town of Coniston was based on the hamlet of Croydon, New Hampshire, five or six miles west of New London.*

Norwich, Vermont
July 14, 1931

Dear Mate:

The Meserveys brought over your letter yesterday, and I was very glad to have it, even if it was a rather sad sort of letter. Although I still doubt whether the gods are "equal to *anything*," I know they are equal to a hell of a lot, and I've been worrying about "you-all" a great deal. I'm awfully glad that E. is getting better. Doctors, I think, are generally pessimistic. They are rather interested in their infernal fees, and they are quite pleased when somebody springs a strange new disease or combination of diseases that nobody has ever heard of before.

I do hope Phoebe won't crash up next. Or you. I don't see how you manage to avoid it, with all the mental and physical stress you must be under. Of course, if one can keep from losing one's head, that's the main thing.

I suppose you are right about B. R., if he really is that way. I hadn't thought of it in just that light before. Still, I think he's wrong; but if that's how he *is* he can't help it of course. I wish, for the sake of all the R.'s, that he weren't quite so much of a Stoic, or had quite so much of a hankering for self-dependency. Of course I know he wouldn't want to be "hovered over and looked out for and taken care of and protected"—and he isn't exceptional in that, because I don't think any man who *is* a man wants that. It isn't exactly a question of "hovering over," in my mind. Of course a great many women can't do anything but "hover" (that's a wonderful word!), but you aren't like that. I can't rid myself of the feeling that you could do him more good than harm; but probably you know better. That's just my feeling.

Anyway, I hope that the "psychological moment" comes soon, when he will be a little bit swayed by his feelings. I do want to see him swayed by his feelings. Everyone ought to be, once in a while. A. and I were discussing that in our sage transcontinental manner just before he left, and we came in perfect accord to the conclusion that you can't build an intelligent life solely on a foundation of either Reason or Passion. It's a question of blending them and getting the most out of each, and shedding the husks and putting them in the garbage can. And when A. and I come to a decision—well, it's a Decision, that's all!

Please don't think I'm trying to tell you anything, because I'm not. But I've worried a great deal about you, and wanted to say some of the things I've felt. And one of the things I feel most strongly about is that separation is Dire. It seems that most of my life I've been parted from the people I've most wanted to be with. It's a kind of doom that hangs over me. But it's a dire kind of thing, that I oughtn't to yield to. I think togetherness is the best way of fighting sadness and despair, just as cleanishness and good Ivory soap is one of the best ways of fighting drab poverty. I think even you once said that if people were together that was half the fight. I think that holds good. I mean, of course, if the people are congenial, and happy to be together. I merely assume that that holds true of the R.'s.

As you say, it is rather a "weary, futile world." There isn't very much to be said for it most of the time, A.D.R. It's a disappointing

Jinx. And the only way of beating it is just not to let it weigh you down. What I should like to do is to pack B. R. up in a crate, labelled conspicuously "FRAGILE. PERISHABLE. HANDLE WITH CARE.", and address him to No. 2001 via Airmail. This might be utterly the wrong technique, I can't pretend I'm right, but somehow I'd refuse to let the old Jinx cheat you out of everything. It's bad enough as is, without all these damned infernal separations.

It's strange that I should be given a physical endurance, at least, that is nigh unending, and yet that I can't come out and scrub pots and pans and do the cooking, or tend the store in the desert and help Phoebe out. I'd be very good at that sort of thing. I'm getting quite Practical. But I have my own little circus, and have to run it. It's only a one-ring one, but it's all I can handle, as sometimes the elephants are rather unruly, and come near squashing me against the wall.

This summer won't grant much of a respite, but it is a grand change. I do ninety-five per cent of all the work that is to be done, which is considerable of a job in a camp. But I don't mind that. What I do mind is an article I'm still trying to write for Harper's. I've decided that that is going to be done this summer, whether or not I get much ahead of "Lost Island" (which I probably shan't). But "Lost Island" is pretty well started, and I don't think it will miscarry now. Three long chapters, and the story well under way. The next thing really is this Harper article, and it's going to be done.

This little cabin really is very enchanting. It's up in a pasture, on a hill, with sumac in front, and hemlock and woods stretching indefinitely behind. The hermit-thrushes sing nearly all the time, and are quite tame. The field is white with daisies, and alive with big orange butterflies. The steeplebush is soon coming out. There is a huge patch of rhubarb down below the cabin a little way, so we have a continual supply of super-excellent rhubarb sauce. The hemlocks make a grand harp to the wind. And it's good to be wearing old black pants again. They have shiny streaks on them which is varnish remover from the *Marsodak*; they have spots of engine-room oil on them; they have a streak or two of whitewash from A.'s large brush aboard the *Vigilant*—in fact, quite an atmosphere.

There's nothing like these northern woods and hills and wild flowers, anyway. We have the cabin full of wild flowers, just ordinary ones, like daisies and buttercups and meadowsweet and Queen Anne's lace; but they have a delicate and subtle Something about them which isn't to be equalled in a Fifth Avenue florist's window. And I am also peacefully reading "Coniston" for the first time.

So you saw W.F.—well, well. If he gets much sourer, A.D.R., he'll turn into curds, and have to be combined with a good deal of baking soda and made into gingerbread.... I made a perfect one last night, with some milk that was terribly sour, so sour I had no faith in it whatsoever, since it was *solid*—but the gingerbread was superb, which just goes to show that you can't daunt a gingerbread.

I believe that W.F. has become the prince and king of all Fools. I think that probably the reason he and M. turned against A. and were so utterly mean to me about him was that they were somewhat afraid of him because he was upright and honest and aloof and didn't approve of them. He's ten times the man W.F. is, and maybe W.F. sensed that—you sometimes do—and naturally would resent it.

Anyway, A.D.R., don't you lose your sense of humor, whatever happens. If you have that, you can keep your head above water—*just*. Sometimes it's by a hair's-breadth, but still it's above water. Without it one may as well lay down and die. That you still have plenty of yours is evidenced by the last headline you sent me. I can't make anything out of it at all. It does sound somewhat vacationy, though I can't define the reason for it. What masterpieces that headline fella does pull off!

I certainly don't think there is much to be said for this so-called civilization. It's barbarous, that's what it is. The primitivest of the primitive were never capable of such outrages as this Jinx civilization. That's one of the things "Lost Island" is about—sort of a fling, a kick, a dig at the world. Not a nasty one, just a grieved one. I wish we were back to the cave days. Even nowadays there are some tribes that are happy. Look at the Polynesians, for instance. Naturally we can't be happy in their surroundings, but that's not the fault of the surroundings. It's our fault—and civilization's. Damn, damn!

But lest you think I'm becoming very despondent myself of late, let me assure you that this is my normal state of mind, when I allow it to come to the surface. That is, I *always* am grieved at the world. But I usually don't allow it to come to the surface. I sink it. And I do love listening to those hermit-thrushes. They are divine. And there are a few beings whom I love a great deal, and who make most of what there is of Good in life. But I don't believe in God. God got discouraged and gave up long ago, and I don't blame him, I'm sure!

A.D.R., I do with all my heart hope things will come somewhere near right for you soon. If you would come east this winter, even if you still felt that you should keep away from B.R., we'd adore to have you. Why don't you come anyway? And then if the "psychological moment" arrived, you'd be that much closer. I think that's a good idea. I think we could find a certain amount of peace, and might really get a lot of masterpieces done. I feel all energy at the very thought. And cocoa is an inspiring drink. You see, friends have to stick together in the face of the Jinx.

>   Yours with love,
>   B.

Norwich, Vermont
August 20, 1931

Dear A.D.R.:

I was glad to have heard from you at last. Of course, I realized that you couldn't be writing letters; the only trouble being that I worry about you.

After reading your letter three or four times, I felt pretty sure that you were feeling better about B.R. You didn't dare to say so in so many words, and I don't blame you—but still, there it is, isn't it? I was also awfully glad to realize, by your quotations from his letters, that he still has plenty of his own sense of humor, and that nothing can alter that.

As for you, you don't have to worry about old ladies' almshouses, or anything of that sort!

When I turned the page of your letter and read the "further happenings of this horrible summer," I said to myself: "This is more than the limit. It can't be true." And I laughed a little, it seemed so utterly far-fetched, if you know what I mean. Well, what can I say? Ye Gods!

Thanks for the clippings. Yes, I sympathize very much with that poor chap who wanted to be let alone and to have a row-boat.

You want to know Things. I should say it was you who had the Things to relate. Helen says that she would write to you, only she can't think of anything to say, because there is too much to say. She feels for you quite tremendously, I am sure of that. Her revision is all finished now, except for a few details. She is now working on a new prospect, a rather vague one as yet, in connection with radio broadcasting.

We haven't gone back to New York yet. I may not for nearly two weeks yet. I haven't gotten very brown, and I've worked pretty nearly all the time, but I've enjoyed myself a good deal. Somehow I can't make this summer a parallel with the one of yours that you told me about. I am a bit depressed, and anyway the hermit-thrushes have stopped singing now. But the goldenrod is glorious. I console myself at times by indulging in long conversations with an ancient farmer who has friendly blue eyes and an immense white moustache behind which he smiles secretly.

The Harper article fizzled, because I couldn't, if you know what I mean. The book may just possibly escape fizzling. I have nearly finished the sixth chapter now. That is about half of it, I should say, because they are long chapters—fifteen pages each. I still hold to my opinion that it's a pretty good book.

I think it was grand that you got that Thanksgiving story off. I don't know how you managed it, with all your sixteen worries, each one being plenty for one person at a time. I get thrown all off the track myself by reading in the newspaper some little item about the ice being bad up Point Barrow way.

The thing I have been gladdest of this summer, I think, is that I have been working on Farksoo again, after a long spell during which it rested in a drawer untouched.

I am lonesome as hell, and wish I could see you. It was partly for selfish reasons that I suggested that you come east this winter. The invitation still holds good, in fact, it always holds good. If I ever come to live out west, you'll come to see me sometimes, won't you? We can have cocoa and discuss the events of the world. I believe I shall come, someday.

I guess that's about all. I feel miserable because I can't do anything, for you or myself or the ice or anything. I think impotence is about the worst sort of curse. If ever there is anything I can do, you'll let me know, won't you? And if anything does happen that makes you change your mind about coming east, remember that we want you.

Anderson—God willing—will be back toward the end of September.

      As ever,
      B.

Sept. 28 *[1931]*
Mon. night

Dearest ADR:

Do let me tell you how sad I was to hear about your mother. It must have been *terrible* for you, when everything else in the world is wrong at the same time. Did she keep on writing that pleasant poetry of hers right through? A life-saver it was, for her, I should think.

Oh, I do crave so to hear some *good* news from you! Of course, it *is* good that you have been able to stand up so well under these catapultations, and keep on composing wholesome young men and healthy-minded virgins. It seems nothing short of miraculous. I think you're a grand scout, and I'm behind you somewhere in the east, with all my strength.

Your husband's words about Gabriel and the empty belt were glorious, even in their sadness. I love people like him and you. "Like," I say. Well, there *aren't* any, that's about the size of it. But I love him and you.

Do give Phoebe and E. my love, too. I feel much for the trapped nymph. Being trapped by life, in her case school, is *not* good for one's wings. I admire her. As for E., may what gods there be lend aid.

I should treasure a few lines from you sometime when you feel me-ish. But don't hurry. I *do* understand.

       Yours ever,
       Barbara

Oct. 5 [1931]

Dear Alice:

Your letter comes at the end of a day so atrociously busy and hustled that I simply cannot tap a key on the dratted machine; but I want to answer it right away, because I liked it so much; furthermore, since I don't ever have air-mail envelopes on hand, it behooves me at least to be more or less prompt with my ordinary ones! Forgive the _____ effects *[here Barbara drew a shallow bell curve]*: I am unspeakably tired, and my handwriting, as you know, doesn't amount to much at the best of times.

First I want to mention Phoebe's poem. I adored it. It is inexpressibly passionate and wistful, with a depth and a wildness to it—*also*, a preciseness of technique and structure (to be prosaic)—that convinces me that P.A.R. is rapidly growing up. What do you think?

I haven't written a poem for __ years. I guess the fountain has gone rusty, and gotten choked up with stale moss. Pleasant thought, isn't it? But at the best, I could never produce a poem like that of Phoebe's. If I have any ability at all, it lies in prose, I think.

Your mother was a dear, brave soul. I like the little stanza you gave me. It was sad, because true. Almost everything that is true seems to be sad. There's almost no *magic* in the world—in fact, even that "almost" is superfluous!

You might, sometime when you feel like it, give me a bit more out of B.R.'s letters. I do hope so much for him! His soul so gets the better of the world at every turn, that it seems as if his body *must* soar alongside, impelled upward, as it were.

About my job: it's all right. We're working now hellishly hard, because the Fall Conference is impending, and also because of a series of radio addresses on "Psychology Today" (drat psychology!) which we are getting under way.

The book progresseth slowly. You'll see it, not too long from now.

I hadn't thought about the farents for some time—bless their little wee souls!

I'm terribly, terribly glad that you feel me-ish at times. That helps more than you know, perhaps. How I would adore to see you! Well, one of these days....

    Yours,
    Barbara

P. S. No, he is not back.

The "magnificent illustrator" of Magic Portholes *(and three other books by Helen, including* Stars to Steer By*) was New Haven-born Armstrong Sperry (1897-1976). Ten years later Helen would write about him for* Publisher's Weekly *(June 21, 1941) after he won the Newbery Medal.*

The Kirbys *was indeed by my grandmother. It was published by G. P. Putnam's Sons in 1931 and includes a stove catching fire and burning down the Kirbys' house, à la Orange Street in New Haven, 1923. (The Maine coast story was* No More Sea *by my grandfather, published by Henry Holt and Company in 1933. It's not really about the Maine coast but about a mother who moves inland with her son, far away from the perils of the sea. One of the characters, Charlotte Robinson, bears a striking resemblance to Barbara.)*

150 Claremont Ave.
October 19 [1931]

Dear ADR:

Just a vibration from yours in New York, to let you know that I'm still quite alive, strange as it may seem.

I've been doing some thinking about Phoebe's poem. Would you like me to try peddling it around a bit? Have you, for instance, sent it to Harper's? I think it's gorgeous, and she might make a small handful of pebbles out of it. It's worth trying, I think; though I've never had any luck in that way myself.

The only development here in New York of any great interest is pertaining to Helen's manuscript, which is trying hard to put itself across on the radio. I think it may. If it does———! Oh, but I'll talk about that when it happens—and IF.

Another development there is that she's put salt on the tail of a perfectly magnificent illustrator—a shy little man who has been down to the tropics himself, and *knows*, who has an adorable sense of humor, and who can play the ukulele and sing Tahitian songs in a simple sweet way which makes me weep—*me*! He's caught, I think, better than anyone else could have done, the spirit of our trip—its gaiety, its colors. You wait till you see!

"Lost Island" cometh along. I've nine whole chapters now—considerably more than half, for they're long chapters.

I'd love to hear from you—about you, and P. and E. and M., and B.R. Are they all still in trouble? Is everything still just as wrong as it has been, which is, I should say, as wrong as possible? I've thought of you much and deeply, ADR, though I've been dour and uncommunicative. I've a great deal of personal faith in you. I'd feel that the world was even wronger than it is, if it kept on banging you over the head.

It seems that someone by the name of M.W. has gotten out a book—the story of a midwestern family, "The Kirbys." Is it *the* M.W.? I thought her projected novel was a Maine coast story.

Best of luck and love to all of you.

   Your Barbara.

P. S. Does this envelope suggest anything?

A letter from around November 1931—between the October 19 and December 22 letters, anyway.

Thursday night

Dear Adr;

Really, you are too unsubtle for words! As if I could *write out* such an event! As if there were any words that could convey the tiniest fraction of it! Oh, well, we dense human beings must have words, I suppose.

In words, then, know that he has returned, and all's well. He has been writing to me in his usual clear, faithful way, and between us we've just had the Airmail-envelope presses going to their full capacity. He is one of the world's best, I think—and if other people don't think so, they needn't, and you can tell that to the farents, and be damned to them!

I'm very happy over it all, of course, but not so much so that I didn't read with something akin to rapture the letter which seemed to say that things are brighter for you in several ways. I am so glad, and may it keep on! All your little items of information were absorbed and treasured. Of course, I was sorry that the editor (damn the black hearts of editors!) couldn't leave your story in peace. I *really* can sympathize, too, because Helen's editor has been something of a nuisance, too.

I can't write more tonight, though I'd like to. I should have written to you *first*—but I didn't. And *that* always takes me much longer than I plan on. However, some Sunday I shall write to you and do nothing much else all day!

> My love to all.
> B.

150 Claremont Avenue
New York
December 22, 1931

Dear A.D.R.:

I'm not sending any cards, either, so that's all right. Christmas doesn't really exist this year, anyhow. Six to ten million human beings unemployed and suffering, and the weather messy and warm and rainy, and nobody with you whom you love—well, it just *isn't*, that's all. I'm damned if I'll send any cards!

You ask for a pleasant chatty intimate sort of letter. You have me stumped, A.D.R. I don't know where to begin. We don't go for walks, much of any. One soon exhausts the possibilities of the neighborhood, you know. There isn't any pleasant little hill.... Ouch! Idiot! Fool! Sabra is well enough, only I don't see very much of her, and when I do see her usually neither she nor I are at our best. My best goes into the job, which isn't where it should go; and her best goes into school, which she really loves. Besides, she's rather outside my pale, you know (or is it pail? I hardly know).

I'm glad to hear the hopeful sound in your words when you mention B.R. Also it's good to know that E. is writing. Painting? And how is the business-in-the-desert? Phoebe, I suppose, finds it difficult to see rhyme or reason. Well... don't we all?

The book crawls along—crawls is just the word to describe its progress the last month or so. It's about two people who found out the rhyme and reason for a little while, but had it snatched away again. It's *supposed* to tear one's heart, you know. If it doesn't, a little, here and there, then it's no good. Promise you'll be torn, A.D.R? I may send you a copy of it before I show it to Messrs. Harper etc. I want to try to get a copy to E.A., you see, and perhaps I'll ask him to send it to you, or you to him, or something like that.

He remains the best thing that I can see in life. (See???) It's his steadiness and strength and complete trustworthiness that makes him stand out so, in a complicated and discouraged world. I won't do any quotationing now, because I haven't time, but sometime I will. In the meantime, oh, thank God I've got him!

I hear that H. is going to do something about your little serial in John Martin's. I've glanced at it, and it really is adorable. Something ought to be doable about it, of course. I hope she'll succeed. What are you writing now? Healthy things, always? Oh, well, I suppose we can't afford to do the others until we make our fortunes first!

I want to see you, very much. Who knows? The world is fairly small, when all's said and done, and I've an odd presentiment that I shan't be sitting at this desk for more than a certain amount of time—another year, say. I don't know what's going to happen after that, but I just have a small, dim suspicion, that's all. If the world has *any* justice (I never believed it had much), or a shred of happiness in it, or even the most erratic tendency to keep its promises—well, I shan't, that's all. And if that sounds vague and mysterious and so forth, it's just because I don't *dare* to do more than vaguely, dimly hint that things could take a sudden turn. (Sudden???) And if the world so much as suspected that I was in danger of telling you anything about its secret mechanisms, it would swoop down on me at once and cut off my head.

My love to all the fambly, and—no, I *won't* say "Merry Christmas." I don't feel the faintest ray of that sort of sentiment, and there's no use in cluttering up the air with it. But my greetings, anyway.

As for the poor Hoovers being crammed into art. Well, I don't feel qualified to give many comments about that. However, perhaps this will give a clue. My new shorthand abbreviation for "article" is "art," and oh, you, more than anyone in the world, will appreciate and see the irony of that! Especially with the dry, scientific, technical "arts" which are submitted to our little publication, the *Personnel Journal*!

Oh, yes, I do laugh now and then. In fact, I'm not honestly so gloomy as I sound. I've gotten into the habit, I think, of writing rather cynical letters lately. You will make due allowances. I probably say either more than I mean, or not as much.

        Yours,
        Barbara

150 Claremont Avenue
New York
December 27, 1931

Dear, Noble Meserveys:

What a box! Oh, Lordy, what a box! Oh, Lordy, Lordy, what a box!

Sing, oh, Mighty Chief Oxford, an anthem in praise of that box, in praise of jams, jellys, marmalades, syrups; in praise of sticky ears and fingers and mouths! praise the honey in its comb, and the jars so adhesively snug and dripless! Sing praise to the colorful box, and the tiny box within for a little girl; for pictures of frost and maidens fair; for noble verses nobly sung!

Sing, oh, Mighty Chief, an anthem in praise of all the love that packed the box, of the sprigs of ground pine that smelled so woodsy and good to city noses!

Praise the Noble Tribe of Meserveys for all their love, their hilarity, their goodness, their fidelity! And praise the Maker of Jams, Jellys, Marmalades, who in her infinite wisdom believed in the enchantment and the magic of such gifts for the bringing of happiness, and gaiety, for the sweetening of dispositions, and for the soothing of appetites, to a lesser Breed, a lesser Tribe, a Tribe unswerving in its devotion to the Great Northern Meserveys!

A noble anthem, I ask you to sing, oh, Chief!

We praise you all!

Hallelujah! We, lesser tribe of Folletts, bow low with love, with thanks, with adoration. Hallelujah!

Barbara Newhall Follett: *A Life in Letters*

5

LIFE WITH NICK (1932-1939)

The following letter from Ed Anderson is perhaps the only one that survives of the probably dozens he wrote to Barbara while she was living in New York. (And, as far as I know, none of her letters to him remains, though I'd love to be proved wrong.) It's undated, but "Soon, it will be spring" suggests February or March 1932.

Finding much of anything about Anderson has proved tricky. Crew lists suggest that he was born in the U.S.A. in about 1904, his middle initial was probably "S.", and he was about six feet tall. I don't even know what "Ed" was short for—Edward? Edmund? Edgar? Edwin?

Foss Pier. 660 W. Ewing St. *[Seattle]*

Dearest:

When I suggested that visit, I should have added that it be entirely on your own terms. It did not occur to me that it was necessary to say so. Evidently I am something of a stranger to you after all. The reason I asked a definite answer was because I knew it would be either extremely hard or else quite easy and simple to answer it. Under the circumstances I think one can be forgiven a little curiosity. How else could I learn if this reacquaintance of ours is prompted by sincerity or just a whimsical moodiness; a sort of nostalgic doldrum that sends the mind foraging amongst the old curios up in the attic. Those outmoded articles that are set aside when new interests, and new friends cause them to appear old and boresome by contrast.

Your reply to my direct request has strengthened a vague uneasy feeling that your letters are perhaps urged by some exigency of the moment. I have a feeling that all is not quite as it should be. What it is, I haven't an idea, but this is the impression your words give me. When you say that "the inconvenience and little pain" that would be caused by your leaving now, is also to be considered. I have uneasy forebodings of another problem. Pain and problems; what absurd things to waste one's life over; I've long ago cast such matters adrift, and am much happier for having done so. Thus you find me. If coming to visit me is to cause pain + inconvenience, and fill you with apprehensive thoughts of a 'stranger,' why then perish the whole idea. Things don't seem the same; when you were in Pasadena and

I in Honolulu I did not pause a moment, but came without the least thought for inconvenience. I wouldn't do it now, and so can perhaps sympathize with your unwillingness to do so.

The reason I suggested it be soon, was due to the fact that I have not any definite plans for the summer. I can go North on the Holmes, or I can get a job ashore (at least I was offered one). I rather fancy taking a trip in the cutter this summer, but I'm a little bit afraid to play truant too much, gets to be a habit, and besides I'll have all next fall and winter even if I do go North. Anyway it's time for me to decide, and in all probability I'll go North. I can use the money. Were I able to talk to you I know it would all seem very simple, but writing letters hasn't ever gotten us anywhere. Of patience, I've a very small store; in fact it's a virtue entirely lost when practiced with women, as you once convinced me. Patience seems to spell insincerity in a woman's eyes. In fact I think women may even spell it as impotence.

So you see how I feel Bar. I wonder if you'll understand. Friendship and love are not mere words, yet that is about all we've been to each other; just words and ideas, and I'm a bit tired of just that. That is the reason I am not going to commence a long protracted correspondence with you. Nothing has yet been 'clarified' that way. All it ever did was to impose restrictions on me, I was so in love with you, that I forgot there were other women. How very quaint and old-fashioned Bar.

So let's be friends if that's what you think best, and if you want to come out here, then please come, and if you don't want to, don't, but for heaven's sake don't use me for psychic experimentation, and try studying my reactions to one impulse rather than another.

About my "ridiculous prejudice, about women wearing pants." That's the trouble with a lot of women, confound it. They want to wear the pants. But really! my prejudice is purely aesthetic. Most women are a bit knock-kneed, which is quite as it should be I suppose. Most women also have broad hips, and that's perfectly alright too. Now let's pause and reflect, what an incongruous sight, an otherwise perfect woman broad-hipped, a narrow head, etc., garbed in a pair of trousers designed for men; with the cunningest little pair of high-heeled shoes pecking timidly from the bottoms of the self-conscious pants. I cannot repress a groan. When women wear pants the hands are embarrassed, they never find their way into the pockets, as hands should do when idle. Pants on women usually fit too tight for that anyway; I've seen women in trousers carrying a purse; that would seem to solve the matter of the hands, but what good are the pockets in that case. Perhaps a pair of pants without the pockets and buttoned down the sides would seem more appropriate.

LIFE WITH NICK (1932–1939)

A Mrs. K. wife of the captain of the Commodore came aboard once, resplendent in starchy, well pressed ill-fitting white ducks. Captain B. was away, so I invited her to wait in the cabin. She glanced at the proffered chair with suspicion. My sympathetic glance must have reassured her. She managed to be seated without any mortifying sound of fabric parting. Even the most genial of hosts could hardly have suggested removing the offending strides for the sake of the visitor's comfort.

Soon, it will be spring. I must then start to work in earnest. I've had a shockingly idle, lazy, pleasant winter. Now I'm sort of rubbing the sleep from my eyes. It seems hardly true that I'm awake and writing to you. This letter is rather long, isn't it? I think Bar that we are making a mistake in writing these letters. I know I can't help feeling a little helpless before you, even in a letter. How you really feel, I am not sure. I think I'll steer my own course, and if you think the future may hold something for you & I together, then please don't hesitate. I'd do anything for you, yet I'm not going to press the point in the face of any reluctance, at least not by letter.

One little word of your last letter offends me dreadfully: "Experimental"!! it has a vivisectional sound and a grubby research odor. Makes me think of guinea-pigs and pathologists. Shocking of you to use it. I know what you meant, and I say come or do as you wish; let it be a visit, a reunion, an adventure, or whatever you please, but please don't call it an experiment. I'm very far from perfect and if you seek faults, they're mighty easy to find. If you haven't found the perfect or at least ideal mate these past years, don't be deluded that I may be that nonexistent specimen. I'm not. So here we are, right where we started, and until you make up your mind, I shall bid you a cordial adieu.

  E. A.

In 1932 the Appalachian Trail was in its infancy. It hadn't been cut nor marked for most of its 2000+ miles between Katahdin and Mount Oglethorpe in Georgia. (The first documented "thru-hike" was in 1948 by Earl Schaffer, although there's an unconfirmed report of a party of Boy Scouts from the Bronx who may have finished it in 1936.)

It surprises me that Barbara hadn't already told Alice about the three new friends she'd made the previous summer in Vermont. One of them—Nickerson Rogers (1908-1980), the "amiable lad with occasional unsuspected depths"—had just graduated from Dartmouth. Occasionally Nick traveled down from his parents' home in Brookline, Massachusetts, to visit Barbara over the winter and spring of 1931-32.

Eugene F. Saxton was editor-in-chief at Harper & Brothers.

Saturday
March 1932

Dear A.D.R.:

You really needn't feel so ashamed of yourself in the matter of correspondence, since you surely didn't owe me *much* of a letter, judging by my last two or three!

You are right when you surmise that I have been rushed and busy—more so than ever, since the beginning of 1932. My life is getting almost crowded, in fact. The job, of course, takes eight hours a day straight out, and everything else has to be jammed into the fringes. Since I can't satisfy mind, soul, or body with the job, I have to jam into the fringes almost as much as another person would put into an entire day.

You want TALK. Well, I'll try my best, and as there are a few more news items now than usual, maybe I can fill the bill a bit.

First, Helen's book is getting to that thrilling point. She has received proof of the illustrations—great illustrations they are, looking like very clever woodcuts—and Macmillan has done a surprisingly good job of the reproductions. But since she will doubtless tell you all about this herself, maybe I'd better concentrate on other things.

The more important thing I have to contribute is that *Lost Island* creepeth onward, in spite of God and the Devil (represented by various personages, of course!). In fact, I've gotten to that delectable point where there remains only about a chapter and a half—or *possibly* two chapters and a half—to be written. That will complete the first draft. Then to sail into a good thorough revision, editing, chopping, piecing, cross-hatching, weaving, repairing, tearing, rending, boiling, steaming, and general subjection to energy. I think I can have it in Mr. Saxton's hands—willing or unwilling hands—by June 1 at the latest. That's what I'm aiming for, anyhow. And I still have faith in the old thing, which is quite a point, you know.

When all this energy is accomplished, I'm going to bat out about three copies, of which two will be passed around among a few individuals. You are going to be one of the fortunate (?) recipients. I shall want your criticism—I mean, if you *are* willing, and want to give it—rigorous and stern and unsparing. There will be four or five other people, who will probably all contradict each other. Then it will fall to my lot to Think It Over, and do some more pounding. Among these selected critics, I'm going to pick out at least two entirely impersonal ones. For instance, a Professor of English at Dartmouth whom I encountered last summer.

After that job is all completely finished, and the black spring binder reposes under Mr. Saxton's nose, I'm going to sail into another job I have in mind—not such a lovely job, but an even more important one, because my entire existence rests upon it. It will be the introductory material for another book—a book about an adventure I think I shall have this summer. Woods and mountains. A. D. R., I'm going to tell you about it, and you must rise to the occasion, because I'm terrifically excited over the whole thing.

I've gotten together a party of four congenial brave souls—of which I am one (I hope)—and we may add two more members. Then, starting about the middle of July, we're going to Maine—Ktaadn—Thoreau's country—and from there we're going down the Appalachian trail, two thousand miles, Maine to Georgia, camping out, and carrying upon our sturdy backs the necessities of life. It will take between three and four months, and be the greatest release imaginable.

Well, I've even higher ambitions than that. I'm not just going to take money out of the bank, leaving a hole, to indulge my pleasure. I'm going to struggle to make the thing pay for itself, and the only way I know how to do that is to write about it. And as I said I've some ideas for the introductory materials which can be put into words before ever the adventure takes place. And that's what I'm going to do after *Lost Island* is carefully finished. All four of us are very much together on this. We're going to cooperate to the nth degree, and I think that among us all we'll succeed. You couldn't imagine a more congenial party. We are getting together this spring for house-parties at intervals, during which we paw over hundreds of maps, draw up provision lists, talk, laugh, anticipate, and in general have a grand time.

The party consists of an amiable lad with occasional unsuspected depths whom I met last summer when H. and I were living in the Vermont cabin; a pal of his, who has a remarkably good head on young shoulders; and a girl who is really a grand scout, with whom I get along quite beautifully. In fact, we all get along with each other beautifully. No friction anywhere, as far as we have been able to discover. There may be two others added to the Grand Expedition, as I said; and we would like of course to have an elderly leader, than whom no finer could be imagined than Meservey of Hanover—only I'm afraid Meservey of Hanover is tied up.

Well, that's the general idea. It may crash completely. Nothing is certain about it. But we're all hoping, and pulling together. We're all slightly rebels against civilization, and we want to go out into the woods and sweat honestly and shiver honestly and satisfy our souls by looking at mountains, smelling pine trees, and feeling the sky and the earth.

We went up to Bear Mountain this last week-end, for the Appalachian Trail strikes through there, and we explored ten or fifteen miles of that section of it. It gave us a tremendous thrill. I can't tell you what it meant to our world-weary souls to have our feet on that narrow, bumpy, winding footpath that goes clear from Maine to Georgia, marked out by little silver monograms on the trees, which change to yellow-painted arrows over rocks and ledges. Over Easter we're all gathering the clan again, for another expedition somewhere. These short trips help us to get personally adjusted and strengthen the congeniality still more. It also helps to give us an idea of what we need by way of food and clothes, and also puts us in training, more or less.

It will be a terrific trip, of course. There will be times when we'll probably be cold and wet and uncomfortable and grumpy. But we're ready for that—almost covet it in fact. Pitting one's strength and personality against the wilds—the greatest sort of opportunity on earth.... Well, there it is. My room is plastered with trail maps even now!

All this time I haven't so much as mentioned A., have I? Well, I've had him in the back of my mind—in reserve, so to speak. Luckily, the *C. S. Holmes* job holds. I guess he'll be going north again next summer—the third time. There really isn't anything else to do, with conditions as they are all over the world, especially along the waterfront. His life is odd and stern—verging on tragic, at times. He feels that now and then, and has down-spells, during which I am hard put to it to be cheerful and cheering. I am pretty sure, though, that next fall we shall actually be together, and discuss everything from moths to meteors, including money and mice and merriment and misery and—but that almost exhausts the m's I can think of at this Moment. That discussion will doubtless decide a good many points about this universe and the nature thereof. Right now he is a little sad, and alternates between letters about the futility of life with humorous epistles about politics in Seattle and other things.

As for being eighteen—well, I don't think there is anything especially momentous about that. It doesn't thrill me a bit.

Your mention of spring makes my mouth water. There hasn't been much around these parts. In fact, Bear Mountain was covered with snow last week-end, and there was driving mist and it was pretty dern cold. However, one can't stop the seasons, so I have hopes.

I'm so glad to hear the good news about Elizabeth. What an ordeal—or rather, what a series of ordeals—she has plowed through. Phoebe is apparently still toeing the mark, with her nose much to the grindstone. Darn these grindstones—I mean, damn them. And so B. R. is actually going west in the summer—actually, this time?

He west, A. north, I Appalachian Trail. Funny world, isn't it?

You know, I'm ashamed of myself, but it took me several seconds of puzzle to figure out "Miller." Then I remembered. Wonderful creature that he was! Supercilious, spruce, disdainful creature!

Thanks for letting me see the two pictures of you and P. in the desert. I return them herewith. They are sweet.

TALK? Will these pages do at all? If it's egocentric talk you were looking for, I should think maybe this would be a slight over-dose! On the other hand, you are so devoted and the lapse has been so long, that maybe it will be endurable this time. You know, I'm still hoping to see you sometime. I have a philosophy of life—one which has been evolving for many years, but which has suffered interruptions and repressions and smashes. Now it has taken root again— or, rather, I realize that its roots are not dead, but just beginning to be powerful. If it grows and thrives and survives the vile climate of trouble and difficulty and set-back, it may take me to almost any part of the old earth where I want to go. What is this philosophy, you ask? Well, I'm testing it warily, leaning on it cautiously, exploring it tenderly, thinking about it profoundly; and if I come to the conclusion that it's any good, I'll tell you sometime. Not until it has proved itself a little, though. I've lost faith in a number of things—or, rather, I've withdrawn from them the crushing weight of my faith. My philosophy aims now to stand upright. Tree-like....

I expect the next year to decide a number of important points. Beginning this summer. I think this summer will tell me a good deal. Being in the woods, standing on mountain-peaks—time to meditate and dream and get a perspective on life. There is nothing more soul-cleansing than to stand on a mountain, when you are inclined to feel hopelessly sure that the world is 99 100ths mankind, and see that vast tracts of it are blankets of forest and trees, after all! Mountains affect inward matters in the same way—reassure one about inward things in the same way as they do the visible things. So I expect to find out several things during the Appalachian Trail expedition—assuming and praying that it works.

Then, coming back from that to this—the complete contrast, the need for instantaneous adaption, and the fresh perspective on this— these things are also going to tell me a good deal. I mean, I shall be ready then to make certain decisions, about philosophy and about life.

Then I'll remedy the inner workings of the universe!

My love to you and all the Russell clan.

    Yours,
    B.

150 Claremont Avenue
New York
May 23, 1932

Dear A.D.R.:

There has been a terrific long gulf, hasn't there? It *is* hard, when all's said and done, to keep in touch with people who live thousands of miles away, no matter how much you love them. I do want ever so much to know the news—whether anything is wrong, or anything right, or whatever there is and has been.

Spring! That means leaves and fragrances and warm winds and—an Arctic-bound schooner.

The only *really* exciting piece of news is that this summer I and three very good genial friends are going to tramp down the Appalachian Trail, which runs over mountains clear from Maine to Georgia, a matter of twelve or fifteen hundred miles. Maybe I told you about that before, though. I can't seem to remember—it's all been so deathly long, anyhow.

Helen's book comes out on June 7; mine is in second draft form at last, and I hope to thrust it bodily under Mr. Saxton's nose sometime in June. It will be interesting to watch the reaction. It may turn straight up in the air—the nose, I mean.

I have decided that there are a good many big and fundamental things wrong with the world, and that nothing can be done about it; furthermore, that one *must* revolve quietly along with the world instead of trying vainly to buck it. If you compromise enough—to outward appearances, at least—and if you fully realize what a messy world it is, and are reconciled to certain facts, such as continual change and permanence in nothing—why, then you can have a surprisingly good time. That's what I've discovered anyway. I'm having a better time of it these days than I've had for ages—almost approaching gaiety sometimes, in fact.

But I confess to being a bit worried about you and yours. Things seemed so rather shaky and precarious for you anyway—always have, in fact. Do let me know if there's anything wrong. Not that I could do anything. I may be seeing you before the year is up. Quien sabe? It's a mysterious life.

I'm going to Delaware Water Gap over this coming Memorial Day week-end—at least, I think I am. In which event I'll convey your greetings to the general countryside. Oh, the beauty of that country in spring! How is spring out your way now?

My love to everyone, but specially to you.

Your Barbara

150 Claremont Avenue
New York
May 31, 1932

Dear ADR:

I'm relieved about You, at least, through your last grand letter, although the news about B.R. is anything but good, certainly. I don't know what to say about that, so I won't say anything.

And there WAS some good news, wasn't there? It sounds to me as if the little gods were smiling for a change on the desert. I'm quite thrilled over that. Also, it's good—damn good—to hear that P. is nearly through. What happens after that? "And Life Goes On," I suppose. Funny old life, isn't it? A very devil of a complex circular affair.

The book—this time I mean mine—has suddenly sprung a disconsolate discovery. I find, much to my disgust and up-noseishness, that I shall have to write another chapter to round out the thing properly. My nose is still so much turned up that I can't get after the chapter yet. Of all exasperating things to find out after you've written a book—to think it's All Done, and then to see some untucked frazzles hanging out the tail end! However, that's but a temporary set-back. I expect to have the whole thing done before I go away for the summer. In fact, I MUST. I'll try to get a copy to you, and I want your opinion including all the hard slams you like.

As for the AT (Appalachian Trail) we considered taking along "a second-hand burro," as one of the boys put it. But after all, there will not be any very long stretches of total wilderness, and we can easily carry enough on our own sturdy backs to eke out during those stretches. After all, the east coast—even its mountains—are pretty well civilized in spots—too much so, in fact. The best parts will be the extreme north and extreme south—that is, the Maine and New Hampshire woods, and the North Carolina country to Mount Oglethorpe in Georgia. We were discussing plans just this weekend, when three of the party got together "Beside an Open Fireplace," to talk.

Yes, Anderson went north again. He is now first mate of the schooner, and rather happy about that, of course. He is doing awfully well, considering everything. I MAY see him next fall—but don't you breathe a syllable about that, even to yourself! I'm keeping it a very strict secret from myself. If you know what I mean. I mean there are some things in this world that don't happen if you so much as admit that they're possible. Perhaps they sometimes happen if you keep your eyes tight shut and don't think at all.

Oh, I *was* in the woods yesterday. I'm sure of it, because I've a sunburn. It was beautiful. Light green leaves with gold light breaking through them; wild geraniums, birds singing, a lake to swim in, grand companionship—the wild open spaces—but principally sunlight. I know from that taste of it that I couldn't by any hook or crook stay here very much longer.

Next month I'm going to spend a short week-end in Hanover with some old friends—that will mean another taste of the out-of-doors. And it won't be so very long after that before we're off on the grand old trail! One of the boys sent me a couple of the AT trail markers the other day. I keep one of them on top of my office typewriter, where I can see it all the time. It cheers my soul.

Well, now I've got to turn to and tuck the shirt-tails of my story into its pants. Do you see what I mean?

GOOD luck to you—oh, Lord, good luck to everybody! God help us—not whelp us any more!

       Yours for sunshine,
       B.

The following is from the June 1932 issue of Young Wings: The Magazine of the Boys' and Girls' Own Book Club, *published by the Junior Literary Guild.*

"I've Got to Go to Sea Again!"
by Barbara Follett

Everyone who has ever gone off on an adventure knows that friends and acquaintances, especially aunts, have a way of firing difficult questions at you. "What made you want to go in the first place?" "Yes, but where did the *idea* come from?" (As if anybody knows where an idea comes from!) They want to understand the secret workings of your mind. They are interested in the "psychology" of the thing, and you feel like a rather small beetle under the microscope. If the adventure happens to be a nautical one, you say something about "the call of the deep, you know," and they appear to be satisfied.

But I did not go to sea the first time because of the call of the deep. That call is very real, and very potent, but in my case it came later. I went to sea for what I considered a simple and logical reason: *I wanted to be a pirate.* (These matters can't be explained to elderly aunts, so please keep it a secret!)

That idea quickly smashed, of course. I saw that evil-looking knives were no longer clenched between teeth, and that large gold earrings and red bandannas had gone out of style. Mutiny did not seem to be brewing. It was after this peaceful discovery that something else crept into the picture, much harder to explain or describe. I shan't try to do so. I shall be content with merely calling it the glamor of the sea. Joseph Conrad is the only writer I know who was ever able to put this into words, as you know if you have read any of his books.

Magic Portholes is the tale of my second sea adventure. It was an adventure of islands and ships and stars and laughter; of tropic winds, sleepy island harbors, pathways of moonlight over the waves, vibrant dolphins in the wake, and . . . *you know, I've got to go to sea again—oh, any day now!* Perhaps I'll meet some of you there.

Frederic Taber Cooper (1864-1937) was a writer, editor, and teacher of Latin at Columbia and New York Universities. His books include The Craftsmanship of Writing *(Dodd, Mead & Company, 1911).*

Old Lyme, Connecticut
June 29th, 1932

Dear Miss Follett,

Alas, for all my fine promises about returning the MS of your experimental final chapter within forty-eight hours! I am really feeling very contrite. But the simple truth is that after reading the chapter I mistrusted my own judgment and wanted the whole thing to simmer in my subconscious for a while. And then, after a few days I went down and compared notes with Ethel Kelley—as I dare say she has told you before now—and after that I just serenely and definitely knew that my first instinctive reaction had been the right one. Over the week-end I was camping out in the wilds of New Jersey, where apparently there were no post offices, any more than there were on your LOST ISLAND. Up here in Lyme, it is simpler—just a walk of a mile and a quarter, through blistering heat—and luckily I thrive on heat.

No, whatever you do, don't use that new final chapter. It is written in a wholly different mood, and even the tone of it, even Jane's attitude towards her specific problem and toward life in general is altered. It seemed to me as I read that some one else, and not Barbara Follett, had been taking a hand in things and giving her version and not yours. What it all means, if I am at all correct, is that you have already, in these weeks or months since you first drafted *Lost Island*, grown away from your former attitude and can't quite get back. We agreed the other day that there is no such thing as finality in human stories; but your original ending was as near a definite, logical rounding out as you can hope for. And at least the work was all of one piece. It had a unity in structure and in style. And my advice is to keep it that way.

Now, if some publisher wants a supplemental chapter, I don't say it would be a mistake to show the new chapter to him. The book as a whole would remain the refreshingly lovely thing that it is, either with or without the addition. Only I shall always feel that it is more artistic just as it stands.

I shall be down in the city again probably some time in July, and shall let you know. Perhaps you would give me a chance to see you again and talk further about what you have done in the way of a final revision. I have enjoyed our various brief contacts—and if I am likely to be of any service, you will please me very much by freely telling me just how I could aid.

                Cordially yours,
                Frederic Taber Cooper

Magic Portholes *was published in June and reviews were good. Here are excerpts from three.*

New York Times Book Review, July 3, 1932
"Mother and Daughter Go A-Voyaging," by Anne T. Eaton

[...] Here, however, is a travel book of a novel kind, for the author and her daughter, the two "shipmates" who are responsible for "Magic Portholes," have put into its pages so much of their personality, so much of their own zest for adventure, so much of their love for the sea and for strange new sights, that readers from 12 on will have a delighted feeling of making the voyage with them.

Barbara Follett was the author of "The House Without Windows" between the ages of 9 and 12; when she was 13 she wrote "The Voyage of the Norman D." an account of her first trip in a schooner. Though Mrs Follett is the chronicler of "Magic Portholes," the book is Barbara's as much as it is hers. Reading it, one feels that it is Barbara's thoughts and Barbara's feelings that the writer expresses, even more than her own. It is a young person's book, the older of the two shipmates giving the opportunity of self-expression to the younger one in its pages, just as she did when she made possible the voyage itself. *[...]*

New York Herald Tribune Books, Sunday, July 10, 1932.
"Girls and Boys With an Adventurous Spirit," by May Lamberton Becker

If alternative titles were still in vogue the one for Mrs. Follett's book might truthfully read: "Or, Bringing Up Mother." This being an enterprise forever in fashion, however fashions of doing it may change, it will be seen that the book has two chances in its favor for an audience larger than usual: it may be read, with entertainment and enlightenment, by daughters and by mothers—I don't know which will enjoy it more—and it may last over into the future long enough to let the next rising generation of girls know how this one met the age-old urge to run away to sea.

For on its first page fourteen-year-old Barbara—who had already, in her comparatively distant past, sailed with the Norman D and written a book about it—comes down with another attack of salt-water fever. Running away to sea, however, has always meant more than ships or salt water. It was once the great American gesture of the youth movement. Boys could do it—and in New England so many did that not to have a seafaring uncle in the family was to be noticeably out of step—but with girls it was only one of those serio-comic threats whose very unlikelihood shows the hopelessness of revolt. But in those days it never occurred to a girl to take her mother along. It did so to Barbara. It is a wonderful thing for a mother to find that her daughter really wants her to go along—anywhere.

[...] The pictures are striking black-and-whites by Amstrong Sperry, who made the brilliant color end-papers and jacket; altogether a work to catch the eye of any age.

The New York Amsterdam News, *founded in 1909 and still in operation, is a newspaper with a largely African-American readership.*

New York Amsterdam News, July 27, 1932.

An interesting and vivid account of a year's adventure by a mother who is persuaded by her 14-year-old daughter to pack up and go to the sea. These two shipmates, as they like to be known, leave New York for the West Indies with very little luggage, a slim purse and a desire to see and go as much and as far as possible. In the words of Jerry, the amiable Barbadian bell boy, the idea was "travel light— an' go far!" The Folletts do just that before their year of wandering comes to an end.

[...] Their first stop out of New York harbor was Barbados, with its tall native women, carrying on erect heads huge wicker baskets containing everything from crimson colored fish to brown and white chickens, still alive. In a rhythmic voice they advertise the wares for sale, in much the same manner, we imagine, as the Crabman in "Porgy."

These shipmates in adventuring mood trek to North Point, the land's end of the island, where the Caribbean and the Atlantic come together. The journey from St. Andrews, the last stop of the train to the sea, is a hot, tiresome one, through a miniature desert. On their way back to the railroad they stop at a little shop and to their utter amazement find that it is run by one Mrs. Lucas, who had lived in Harlem some years before.

[...] "Magic Portholes" may be read with rare pleasure. The style is so simple that the book should prove enjoyable to youngsters with a yen for seagoing and exploring and delight even mother and dad.

While the reviews appeared, Barbara and Nick began their Appalachian Trail adventure (their two friends didn't join them after all). After camping for two weeks on an island in Squam Lake, New Hampshire—letting Barbara strengthen her city muscles by swimming and paddling—they began their journey on top of Katahdin in mid-July, walked and canoed through Maine, hiked over the White Mountains of New Hampshire, and ended their approximately 600-mile journey down Vermont's Long Trail, reaching the Massachusetts border sometime around Hallowe'en.

"Howie" is Howard Dillistin Crosse (1911-1982), a friend of Nick's. He would go on to become president of the New York Bankers Association.

Harper & Brothers passed on Lost Island, *which would remain unpublished until I transcribed and posted it on my website, Farksolia, in March 2012. I've also posted* Travels without a Donkey, *Barbara's long account of the Maine section of their journey.*

Despite Barbara's offer, Helen didn't join them over the Presidential Range.

Oquossoc, Maine
Maine State Fish Hatchery No. 7
(on the grounds of!)
Date (God knows) [August 1932]

Dear H:

You are a brick; you took it like a grand sport, and I sure appreciate it. Thanks from the heart.

I am convinced that it was not a mistake. How long it will last I've no way of knowing, but I know that for the time being I'm healthier, browner, stronger, and happier than for years; it is the swellest kind of a life: all out of doors, warm and cold, wet and dry, sunshine and moonlight, fir boughs and sleep from sunset till dawn; lakes and rivers and hills, trails and wild country and long white roads; the feeling of utter independence—all one's belongings on one's back, and not too heavy at that—God! what a lot of junk civilization involves!

N. is swell—a grand out-of-doors person. We get along quite beautifully in our—what shall I say?—semi-Platonic way. It's the best thing one could imagine, and I frankly don't know of another male creature who could do as well. We intend more or less to stick together as long as it's good. We haven't any but the vaguest plans as to how a "living" is to be wrested from the world, but we're going to try various things, including maybe housekeeping in a cave in Tennessee this winter!

The AT is not marked out at all across Maine; consequently we've been having a swell time plunging across the countryside more or less on our own—following rivers via old tote roads, etc. Quite exciting and wild. If you are interested in details of the trip to date (geographically) Howie has maps which N. has been sending to him. These are marked up, and in some detail, including places where we had lunch or stopped for a swim or panned for gold without finding any, etc.

Our home is N.'s little 6-pound tent, but we don't set it up every night by any means. Sometimes, when it looks as if the weather could be counted on, we just spread out on our fir boughs under the open sky.

I wish you could see N. these days. He tells me that he too is healthier and happier than ever. When on the march he wears only a pair of shorts, and is brown as an Indian—maybe a picturesque-looking red kerchief around his neck. He has about a month of beard, which would look like the devil on anybody else; and I cut his hair, but you can't kill his looks, that's all there is to it! He's getting in pretty good training now, too—a bit thinner and more muscle and stands straighter. Eyes sparkle as ever. Always good natured.

Your letter reached me at Rangeley today. The old canoe we bought for twenty bucks at Moosehead Lake should be waiting for us here—we're going to paddle across these big lakes. Moosehead Lake, by the way, is about the finest looking big stretch of water I've ever seen. We hung about it for a week, camping on grand little islands, etc. Then we took our canoe, the *Skeleton*, down the Kennebec about ten miles—real white water, and we knowing nothing of river canoeing! Judging by the rocks we hit, you'd think that canoe would be matchwood! Well, she was a battered old veteran Oldtown—we broke a few more of her ribs, but otherwise she's O.K.! A marvellous craft!

I had a letter from Saxton. Oh, hell! Does anything ever satisfy him? Well, here's the letter. I don't see what I can do about it *now*, except suggest that if you feel like it you might trundle the MS to Alfred K. Also, old man Cooper had a lead or two. He could be looked up via Ethel. But don't go to wearing yourself out over it, because I doubt if it's worth it.

Barbara at camp, 1932

Now listen here, old girl—I've a real honest-to-God proposition. You were saying a while back that you were hankering for some mountains in September. N. and I both want you very much to join us at Pinkham Notch and go over the Presidentials with us—a matter of five or six days over glorious mountains during the best time of year. How does that sound? We'll hit Pinkham *about* September 12—of course there's no knowing for sure, but if we depart radically from that schedule I'll let you know. We want you to be waiting for us at the A.M.C. hut there, where you could stay cheap (something like $2.85 per day, bunk and meals). The procedure is as follows. You carry a light pack (not more than 15 or 20 pounds) including your bedding, clothes, and perhaps a little food. The only expense outside of carfare and board at the hut would be a very small amount for your share of the food going over. As for a pack: if you can't borrow one from Harley or somebody, don't worry: we'll rig you up. As for bedding: three of our* *[in margin: *This means your—we have only our own sleeping bags]* army blankets would be good—with some blanket pins to make yourself snug. As for clothes: you can have my pants, or you could doubtless get by with an old skirt (how about your yellow jersey one, and mine added to it?) and a sweater, I should think; and my green leather jacket would be good. You want quite a bit of warmth, of course, but also something light to wear while on the go—an old silk blouse, or an ordinary workman's blue shirt (59 cents!) would be good. I suggest a pair of shorts. They are simply grand for climbing—freedom of action, you know! Having once worn 'em, I wouldn't wear anything else. You can doubtless get 'em at L and T, although theirs are a little too stylish.

My costume now consists (except when I wear shorts) of ordinary dungaree pants ($1.00) and a blue shirt. As I said before, many people take me for a boy. N. cut my hair off quite short. You'd think it would look like hell, but it's really an improvement. It stands fluffily on ends, and curls all over the place. It too is having a taste of freedom! And it is wonderfully comfortable. It hardly ever needs to be combed.

But back to the main issue. As regards your footgear: high sneakers would be O.K. if they're good heavy ones. You can wear mine (they might fit you with plenty of socks). They're in my bureau drawer.

We'll take care of all the food question, etc.

Let us know—and do come. It would be grand. We'll take it all at comfortable speed and have a great time—some good talks, some good laughs, some great old hills. Write me Care of General Delivery, Gorham, New Hampshire. I'm looking forward to it, and so is N. I should think it could all be settled in that one letter. Then I'll write you again, just to report on progress, schedule, etc., because by the time we get to Gorham we shall know quite definitely when we shall hit Pinkham. N. says that it would be still better to wire you from Gorham, because you should start for Pinkham promptly then.

Here is the procedure getting to Pinkham Notch. The station you want is Gorham, N. H., which N. *thinks* you hit in White River and Littleton—but check that. Write to Joe Dodge, Pinkham Notch, Gorham, N. H., the hour of arriving, and someone from the hut will meet you. Simple enough, n'est-ce pas? *Do come!*

As I said before, it is very grand of you to take it all so well. I realize that it messes things up for you terribly, and am sad about that; still, we all have to follow the best thing that we know. Wouldn't some mountains help a little?

    Love always,
    B.

Barbara wrote a second letter to her mother from the same mountaintop that she and her father stayed on for several nights in 1925—where she saw frost feathers for the first time. Once again Helen declined Barbara's offer to join them.

The "letter from the far West" was probably from her father. She enclosed a letter to him when she wrote to Alice on October 4th.

Moosilauke Summit Camp
Dartmouth Outing Club
October 2, 1932

Dear H:

We've been up here several days in the Winter Cabin, nursing a bum toe which I acquired. Yesterday—believe it or not—all the little scrub trees were encased in snow, and there were frost feathers everywhere, some six inches long. Washington and the Franconias gleamed like Alps in the sun. There has been all sorts of weather—from specklessly clear days to mist so thick that you could cut it with a knife—we had to take axes and chop holes in it when we went outdoors!

There have been a few interesting people up here, too. Yesterday, for instance, we had a delightful little Englishman (cartographer for the American Geographic). He knows the West Indies, and the Canadian National boats, and he says "Jolly old boat"—it was good to hear, that phrase! We spent most of the time shouting duets and choruses out of Gilbert and Sullivan.

In a few days now we shall proceed to Hanover, and then to the so-called "Long Trail" in Vermont, which should be lovely, though probably not exciting, country. It should be fairly easy going, and there are shelters at convenient intervals. We're going to stick to this game until it gets too damnably cold—then we may beat it (hitch-hiking) to Tennessee or somewhere. We don't know for sure when the weather will get too much for us, but I expect not until late October or November. Anyway, the point is: how would you like to join us along the Vermont trail? We'd like to have you ever so, if you won't mind the cold—it *will* be cold, of course, some of the time. You will want to take plenty of warm clothes and blankets. One trouble is, we wouldn't be able to equip you with a pack on this stretch. That would have been possible if you had joined us at Pinkham, but not here. Either borrow, buy, or steal one.

Here are the practical details: write me Care of General Delivery ("hold until called for") at Hanover (address envelope to Nick, *not me*: that's the way we're handling the mail now). In that letter let me know definitely whether you can get away sometime after the middle of October for about a week or ten days. When I have your answer I'll write you from Hanover just where, and when, and how, you're to meet us—probably at East Clarendon, Vt. How does this sound? It won't be so utterly thrilling as the Whites would have been, but it ought to be fun; we can have some talks and laughs and stories. You can imagine that we've got some stories by now!

Did I tell you that I had a letter from the far West? The unrealest thing I ever saw. It simply doesn't exist.

N. wears well. I don't know anybody else in the world (at least, of the male sex) whom I would want to be thrown together with so closely for so long through so many variegated adventures. We haven't even scrapped at all, which is rather remarkable, considering how constantly and intimately we've been together since July. I've never had such an enjoyable and satisfactory relation with anyone. We're going to chuck it, clean, when we feel like it, but now it promises to hold out ad infinitum, and it's grand.

Don't lose your head or get scared when you see N: the beard is now three months old. The effect is a combination of prophet, Russian, pirate, and genius. Howie reports that friend Casseres has a mustache now—one that "would do credit to a Polish street-sweeper." I should like to see it.

How's everything down your way? Sabra, radio, etc.? Did the Sperry brat arrive O.K.? My love to them. Had an awfully nice note from Miss Carney—but Christ! am I glad I'm not there.

N. sends his best. We really hope a get-together can be worked out, though we thought it swell that you stuck to the job so heroically. More power to ye!

      Love,
      B.

Moosilauke Summit Camp
Dartmouth Outing Club
October 4, 1932

Dearest ADR:

I have so much catching up to do that I'm not even going to try! Someday, though, I'll *tell* you the things that have been happening—the curious, joyous upheavals my life has undergone, and the gipsylike ways I've been living, and so on.

Right now my object is the transmissal of the enclosed letter to W. F. (which I should be glad to have you read if you care to). It may be that you have no idea whatever of his whereabouts. In that case, merely destroy it, as circumstances are not opportune for writing to him through Helen. If you can get the letter to him in any way, and if he answers it, I want the answer to come through you, as I don't want just yet to give him the address which I'll give you at the end of this.

All this sounds terribly complicated and mysterious, doesn't it? But you see, I've jumped many hurdles of late, and want to be cautious. I've jumped the whole structure of what life was before: I've jumped the job, jumped my love, jumped parental dependence, jumped civilization—made a pretty clean break—and am happier than for years and years. I've a new, and I think a better, structure of life, though time alone can tell that!

How are you and yours? I long to know, fear to ask. It has been so long since we've been in touch! Write me a word at this address, and then I'll tell more about everything.

      Love as ever,
      Barbara

Address mail to:
Mr. Nick Rogers
℅ H. D. Crosse
834 DeGraw Avenue
Newark, N. J.
(*not me*—this will nevertheless be quite private)

Barbara must also have written to Anderson while on Moosilauke: his reply follows.

Richard Charnock's Prænomina, or, The Etymology of the Principal Christian Names of Great Britain and Ireland *(1882) gives the following definition for Auna: "... this female name is thought to be the same as Aine (pronounced nearly 'awna'), still given, or given till very recently, by Irish-speaking people to female children in the south and west of Ireland, and which he thinks is connected with the old Irish moon-goddess, commonly Anglicised to Anna or Anne ... the Erse word 'aine' signifies 'music, melody, harmony'."*

Box 65
Oct 21 1932

Bar, you wonderful woman, you can't imagine how I feel today. You think I am pained, or unhappy, then know that I feel quite the opposite. Now I know that everything is real that you are not after all, an ordinary person. Now I know that, had I but dared tell it to you, you would not have laughed at my own ambition, a 'madder' one than yours.

I *must* tell you now. I hate domesticity. I'm afraid of domestic people. I hate daily routine, and dollars and cents calculations; I wanted, *more than I want you*, to escape all that; the idea was breeding when I met you first. Perhaps you can guess what form my escape would take. I am going to have my own ship and go in my own way to do the things I choose. That is why I am working, for that, and not for the grubby comforts of domestic security. Before I met you, the idea was in a singular tense, then I had wild fancies that you might be a kindred spirit, and understand, but yet I was afraid to put words to it, and when you became efficient and psychological and, as I feared, ordinary, it was still harder to bring it to light. I then hoped that I could convert you to my faith after we came together. Yet it seems that you are as strong an advocate as myself, so therefore I feel as happy as if you had really known, and understood. We shall never grow old now Bar. This talk of love, that word love, what do *we* mean by it, not what you thought I meant. Poor abused word, with the weight of the whole world bearing down upon it. Happiness, contentment, security, bah, give me freedom. Why do you think I wanted to be definite and frank; because I wanted to feel free, and feel I was myself. Now I do, and I am happier than I've ever been before. You terrified me with talk of clothes, and dinners, and responsibilities, that is why I failed to make you love me. We two should have been more careful with that word love. It meant more than either of us realized. Now I know why I loved you, and why I still do, and even if you never see me again, I shall not cease to love you. I do not feel *jealous* towards your new companion, though I don't deny that my greatest wish is to have you myself. He can probably take better care of you than I. Yet you are my woman even if you try to deny it. You are life, and adventure itself, and you're completely wasted on anything else. Perhaps I shall meet you someday, maybe you'll come for a cruise.

There'll be no need for talking it over. (In fact what has talk done so far.) Would you come, or would [you] *discuss* it. Eepersip tired of the forest, and went to the sea, you know. So you must write to me, so that I may find you. Now you really are worthwhile, and to think I grieved over your *changing*.

Listen Bar, this is terrifically important to me. I want you. A year ago I was doubtful. Do you dare or care to take a real chance, on a real adventure. Think Bar, roll the words on your tongue. Marquesas, San Lucia, or what sounds best. Dolphins under the bow, flying fish, and the changing sky and water. Better than a cave perhaps. There'll be books to read too, when the mood takes you. Dungarees, and bare-feet, or shoes and skirts, whatever the mood asks. High latitudes or low, wooded shores or coral reefs, nature smiling warm, or nature riant, fearful. This has been my dream, this is why I have wanted you. This is why my woman was so treasured. I do not say 'please,' or 'do.' If you're the one, you'll know, if not, then solitude has no fears for me. The best years of life together. The end painless. No 'thou shalls.' Away from the pale ledger-minds; only the task of living to face.

You see, Auna, I'm myself now, you've lifted a tremendous load from my mind, now we need not be self-conscious or fearful of painfulness. You think a lot of 'Dartmouth' don't you? Are you sure? Come Bar, tell me, is he everything. Does he deserve all of such a one as you, can I not lay a fair claim to you. Do you think I'm working for its own sake, and saving for its own sake. Open your eyes. Life is not as transparent as you think, nor perhaps as obscure as you may have fancied. Let me rescue you now, from that *cave*. Step back a few steps, and let's start afresh, the way we should have started. Let not the dream be too easy of accomplishment, let it be not only today's but also tomorrow's. I do not say you may tire, but what of him, may he not. With me it might be harder, but more lasting, I know. Dungarees or skirts. You're the woman. You're my woman, but woman-like you're wondering about happiness, and so you deny me, thinking of the 'best happiness.' Put on your cap and coat and come West. Have a talk with me. If D's real, he'll understand, if he won't have it, then be a rebel and come on general principles, and if you don't like our prospects I'll see you safely returned, even to him. Surely you can take a month off.

I'll wire you the fare; the cave won't disappear in the meantime, nor will he. Try it. Try him, try me. Don't you think it would be a good adventure. Just to see, and know.

   I want you,
   A.

[undated, but early-mid November 1932]
℅ Howard Crosse
834 DeGraw Avenue
Newark, New Jersey

Dearest ADR:

You wanted to hear from me *promptly*—right away, return air mail and all that. But, you see, in the rather odd kind of life I'm living right now, such things can't be done. When your letter was forwarded to me, I was—well, where was I, anyway? Williamstown Mass., I guess—just in from a week's stretch of Green Mountains. The next day we pulled out, hitch-hiking. I'm in New York now, at the apartment, but only till about tomorrow. Then I light out again.

Now I'm in Brookline, Mass., clearing up a few earthly details before sailing for a little island off the coast of Spain—if you can believe that! No wonder you are puzzled. The reason I didn't try to go into any sort of detail in my first letter was that I wanted—well, to sort of feel around first, if you see what I mean.

However, before I go any further with this, I want to tell you how tremendously I was pleased with *your* news, which is at least as exciting as mine, only in a different way. That is, the good heart sings for you. Oh, how I hope nothing will go wrong this time! And then to hear that E. and M. have had no more devastating catastrophes, and that Phoebe is fairly happy, and that you yourself are surviving so well, head above water and all.

I don't enjoy going into terrific detail about myself, by mail. It seems so rather brazen and cold-blooded. And I've been writing fewer letters than ever. But to put it briefly, New York irked me past endurance, and I had an opportunity to quit it all. I thought about it pretty hard for a while, and then decided that in spite of certain complications, "obligations," and whatnot, I would chase them to the four winds and *take* my chance. So I did. I and a comrade escaped to the Maine woods (Katahdin, in fact) and then started off tramping south down the footpath that runs intermittently all the way from Maine to Georgia—the Appalachian Trail. It was a tremendous summer. There were mountains and forests, rivers and fields, sunlight and starlight, fir boughs and birds singing. But it was not only a summer. It will go on.

Those are the brief facts—which, of course, are not a satisfactory offering. You see how hopeless it is to give you a good idea of what it's all about, and why. Besides, it's all based on such subtle intangible things—except the boat to Spain, which is fairly tangible. I've tossed a lot of things to the winds, of course. I mean, I'm gradually getting to be a fairly "shady" character, but it's worth it. When it isn't worth it any more, I'll change it some how. There's always a way out, if you have courage—there was even a way out of New York!

Sometime my devious paths will lead me to you. I know that. Then there can be a real discussion, and real understanding. Right now I'm living in kind of a golden ethereal mist, and I haven't typewritten for a long time, either! So I'm handicapped, more or less. Besides, the things I want to say are too new. They are still seething and surging around in my heart, but they haven't been able yet to take their shape and wings and fly into the sun. It's all pretty experimental, anyway. This I know—life is better than I thought. It can continue being good, if one only knows how. I'm trying to learn. I am learning, a little.

Helen has both backed me up and condemned me. Of course, it's hard on her. A very subtle and complex question of ethics is involved—whether 'twere better etc. I've found this out—you *can't* arrange your life so that everyone is satisfied, including yourself—unless you are a very uninteresting person. And the break had to come. I'm not claiming I'm right (how foolish it is for anyone ever to claim that he's right about anything!), and God knows I may end up in an awful mess. Still, all I can do is follow the best I know—take the greenest and most verdurous trail that I can see. If it ends in a desert or a swamp, maybe I can go back and try another one. And that makes a cosmic adventure of if all.

We sail within a couple of weeks, probably. This was quite unexpected and out of the blue—we meant to go to Florida for the winter! I think you would like this person who has been constantly with me since the first of July, and intermittently for about a year before that.

Anyway, maybe I'll drop you a few lines from Majorca or Minorca or somewhere!

With much love, and the best of luck to you.

>Yours,
>Barbara

Thanks for transmitting that letter. I'm glad I wrote it, whether he answers or not. Above address holds good.

Nov. 23 1932

Dearest Barbara:

I could not help, a prayer. I love you. I love you. Write, please write to me. The long storm has hurt too much.

Forgive the way I wrote it, it was much earlier; want can exist on hope, for me awhile; if you'll but say a little "That it doesn't make you unhappy because I want you" "That it doesn't spoil a new something" If I would but really know, I would rest, no matter what. But this dreadful thought that we hurt for no reason other than lack of understanding is unbearable. Don't you see, Dear. I love you, therefore you may trust me.

A word of hope, please, or a word of reason why there's none; you didn't go from me, you drifted away. If no one took you, drift back; if someone did. Tell me. You've been so vague. You hurt. There's something of you within me that you left behind. A true word would remove it, and leave me in peace, content that you were happier. If there's a ray of your affection left, don't try to kill it, for I love you.

>A.

Anderson included a poem with his letter:

    A Prayer to Virodine
    Oh Virodine from you I pray a miracle
    Teach her please a want expressed in me
    Send back Auna of the darksome moody eyes
    She was not flame, but spread, cool and warm,
        a russet charm
    To match her autumn tinted hair
    It seems not fair that I should lose her now
    For I have learned of much to give
    Sympathy, and knowing wisdom besides just love
    Dear Virodine if I may humbly bow before Auna's shrine
    Will you not bid her stir and murmur,
    "I only left and had strange dreams awhile."
    She needs so little, yet so much.
    We should have a rare exchange
    A sort which does not take to keep a captive to oneself
    But roams in freedom, seeing, feeling, understanding,
        understood.
    If I'm a spirit, twas her creation, she must not push her
        work aside.
    The cry is need; To recognize, that here as
        well an earthly glamour has been too long denied,
        and threats to turn on spirit and devour.
    The counter-point of detail all around, dins in my ears.
    Drowns out a grander symphony that yet too
        softly murmurs.
    She must return; Don't let her say a "coward" plea
    There's nothing now we could not face, no nothing
    She must come to me.
    If she was sad, so was I.
    If she lost something, so did I.
    If something died, twas in us both.
    Twas only sorry tact kept us apart.
    She says she does not want a nest on ground: And nor do I.
    All cluttered round with routine.
    Perhaps it was your wish that we should learn thus so
    That when together we'd evade more lacerating hurt
    The petty gods now strewn away, in absurd posture, facing
        bolstered up.
    From which I turn to gaze at One
    I turn to you and ask Auna back.

It is not time for her to go to poppy isle.
Till I am ready too
Oh! place a word of hope, and promise on her reluctant lips.
Some little thing to live upon, or I shall starve.
Bring her to life for me, by sacrificing 'all' the wrong
   in 'past.'

In late November or early December, Barbara and Nick sailed from New York to Gibraltar aboard the S. S. Rex, an Italian luxury steamer. Also on board was Nick's aunt, who had her own stateroom in first class, while Barbara and Nick were in third. After exploring Gibraltar and Morocco, the couple took a bus up the eastern Spanish coast to Malaga, where they looked for good walking opportunities. They decided on the island of Mallorca instead, arriving there shortly before Christmas.

Unfortunately, the following letter to Helen is I think the earliest European correspondence from Barbara that survives in the archive.

Farksolia has two of the three stories Barbara was working on while on Mallorca: Mothballs in the Moon, *which takes place near Lakes of the Clouds on the Presidential Range, and* Rocks, *"about me going all over Ktaadn alone."*

Palma, March 20, 1933

Dear H:

You sound as if you were having a terrific whirl, what with radio, articles, lectures, etc. It must have its moment of being fun, even if it is built on air, so to speak. In fact, isn't it sometimes still more fun *because* it's air—about me, I mean. If people knew how thoroughly lousy—but let that pass!

Sorry you misunderstood me about coming over here. I didn't mean I didn't want to see you—hell, no—I only meant that I thought you'd be disappointed in this place. It isn't much, really. And it's overrun with the wrong sort of tourists. That stuff about it's being "native," "unspoiled," etc., is the sheerest balogney. When such reports are circulated about a place, it's a sure indication that the place *is* spoiled, I guess.

Do come across this summer, if you can. It would be swell. What would you do with S.? Our plans are uncertain as ever, but right now it looks as though we'd be getting out of here inside of a month. The Meserveys are in the Alps—we're considering paying them a brief visit, spending a month crossing France, partly afoot; then we want to get into Germany and tramp about nomadically through all the best parts of the country. That sort of thing is done there—*our* sort of thing—whereas in Spain they look at you a little askance if you walk a mile.

However, we've had a good time here. Met some odd people, had some amusing adventures. You have no idea how much fun it is to be married. I mean, when you really aren't. You get let into a great deal more. There's a lot of scandal and intrigue here. *We* pose as symbolizing solid respectability in the middle of a whirlpool of intrigue! We have agreed that the first requisite of a happy marriage is not to be married. N. introduces me as Mrs. R. with uncanny naturalness. Thoroughly delightful. We get along better now even than when we were over there, as we get to know each other more and more. N. still can make me laugh before breakfast, and he still labors under the pleasant illusion that I am beautiful.

For a week we worked—earned our meals and twenty-five pesetas besides. It was in a pension run (or limped, rather) by two English females—really the dumbest and most frightful people I ever ran across. I swept rooms, peeled potatoes, washed thousands of plates, N. polished shoes, lit fires, chopped wood, mopped floors, waited on table. It was thoroughly a scream. We laughed ourselves ill.

I can speak tolerable Spanish now, when the conversation is about simple little things. I'm reading Don Quijote in the original, and getting a great kick out of it. I had no idea what an amusing tale of woe it is. I'm also studying German grammar—although not very hard yet. I have read some good books, such as *Of Human Bondage* and Jacob Wasserman's two-volume thing called *The World's Illusion*—a strange, gruesome, spectacular work. Ever hear of it?

We made an excellent arrangement with a young Mallorquin which allows us the use of his grand new business typewriter in exchange for English conversation. So I have got two stories typed. They don't look bad, especially *Mothballs in the Moon*. I also dictated to N. one day a fairly complete outline for a story about me going all over Ktaadn alone. I'll try to get at that soon.

That's about the sum total of my intellectual activities—except, of course, a prodigious amount of pondering and philosophizing. There's a lot to ponder about. Life, and the best way or ways of living it. We'll probably never agree about that, you and I; and I, for all my wondering, arrive nowhere definite; and yet I think I have evolved a curious kind of wisdom that seems to *serve*. No code of morals, no rules of conduct, nothing whatever—no definite faith in anything—sheer black atheism—and yet I get along swimmingly. Instead of trying to pin myself to something, and sinking when it sinks, I have preferred to swim. When I'm tired, I float on my back and stare at the sky. I'll be all right that way until sometime an octopus devours me!

As for physical activities. I have swum once—very hastily—sea's *damn* cold still; I have danced a little, walked quite a bit. Presently, for the weather is getting good now, we're going to strike out and tramp round about this island—and then we're leaving it. There is getting to be lots of sun now. I strip to it when I can, and am raising a gorgeous crop of freckles—honeys, they are—the biggest and blackest yet. Old Nick remains true as steel—says they're swell and he likes 'em and I'm very beautiful. A man like that is about the best thing a feller can have.

We have moved from the Mallorquin pension where we were. We're now sharing a little house a few miles outside of Palma, with a rather interesting young chap, a Southerner, with a delicious drawl, boatfuls of nigger yarns and stories from the Kentucky mountains. He has good black eyes and an expressive face. Has been leading a rather dissipated life here, with several women and too much drink. The doctor told him to quit it, so he's on the water-wagon now and living alone in the house, until we come along.

Regards to "Bug" Clarke. Amusing chap. By the way, he promised to write to me, and hasn't a bit. Ask him if he's shocked at me, or what? Tell him I *might* even answer.

Howie Crosse's mother died—did you know? Heart. Good for him, in a way; he is free to grow up now and be a man.

No, I don't expect I shall be popping in on you unexpectedly. We don't expect to come back till fall anyway, and maybe not then, if we can get a job—in Germany, for instance. I've noticed that the feller who publishes the Tauchnitz Editions (English and American classics—very cheap and good paper editions) badly needs a proof reader, and shall look into possibilities.

Do try to work it so you can join me in Germany this summer. Keep me in touch with your plans, and I'll do the same. When do you think you could get away? There would be one or two conditions, of course. About the details of living, etc. But I'm quite sure there'd be no difficulty over that.

We would go roughing it, but not too rough, with our knapsacks and in pants, visiting the mountain huts, which sound altogether too good to be true. We'll sun ourselves, and swim, and pick berries, and sing songs, and forget woes and worries.

I guess that about exhausts the things to be said. From now on, I shall try to write a little oftener and fuller. I kind of think there's going to be more to say from now on. For so many weeks we did little but enjoy café life with our books and friends. The only excitement was when we would get just slightly lit up by a few glasses of excellent sherry or Moscatel, and go dancing.

>I adore wine, anyway!
>Love,
>B.

Sabra's accident at school resulted in a broken leg.
The "Ktaadn thing" was Rocks, *mentioned above.*
The "Herald article" refers to the Boston Sunday Herald *of March 5, 1933. Helen was interviewed on the radio program* Herald Headliners *on February 28, and a week later the* Herald *printed a photo of the cast and a story:* Mrs. Follett and Barbara Run off to Sea.
I don't think the photo of Barbara running on the beach with a wolfhound has survived, sadly.

Grand Hotel Alhambra
Palma de Mallorca
3 April 1933

Dearest H:

We are both terribly sorry to hear about S. Poor little kid—what will she do for two months? It seems quite cataclysmic. I do hope the school will help you out with the expense. How about that brick floor, for instance—should a gym have a floor like that?

Of *course* bring her over this summer. You *mustn't* think we don't want to see you; I never meant to convey that. Bring her over; we'll all get together somewhere, and we'll both do anything we can to be helpful. If I thought I could be of any real help at home, I'd consider coming; but seems to me that would only complicate matters.

The weather here is much better now. I am getting color all over me, and have been swimming quite a bit. N. is helping me learn the "Crawl." As you know, I am as at home in the water as any fish; yet I have never learned to swim *properly*. I am also developing wind and endurance and muscle; and *straightening my shoulders*. I am trying pretty hard, and they're almost all right now. All this is N.'s doing.

This morning your letter came. Today we are leaving, with our pack and a rented blanket, for a walking and swimming trip round the island. Sun and sea and open country. Muscles hardening. Moonlight. Good flowers everywhere. Will tell you about it when we get back.

I have actually started the Ktaadn thing. Semi-humorous in places, partly philosophical, adventurous, with characters in it and quite a bit of discussion about Ktaadn and New England in general. Fairly long, but doubtless cuttable to any desired length. By the way, it would be amusing to have a copy of the Horn Book, if you can conveniently send it, also the *Herald* article sounds amusing. I'd like a copy; but don't send the whole newspaper, for we are trying to cut out bulk!

Good for "Bug" Clarke! Sounds like a brick. A humorous brick, too, which is the best kind imaginable.

Did I tell you N. and I *worked* for a week? Earned two dollars (Spanish wages) plus our meals. In a *pension* which two foolish English women are trying to run. We swept floors, washed dishes, shined shoes, made beds, peeled potatoes, chopped wood, mopped, dusted, lit fires; and at meal-times N. put on a white coat and waited on table, with an incomparable calm, gentleness, and smiling efficiency. He is a wonder. It was a perfect scream.

My Spanish is pretty good now. I can discuss all the *ordinary* things with a fluency that fairly ripples at times. When it comes to the theory of relativity, however, I prefer to talk English. I love the Sp. language. It has a good sound. The verbs are conjugated very much as in Latin—surprisingly alike. Latin—my little knowledge of it has been an invaluable help. I get along much better in all languages than persons who haven't studied Latin. The trouble is, here in Mallorca they don't speak real Sp., although they understand it a little. They speak a lousy-sounding dialect.

Now do, for goodness sake, get this idea out of your head that we don't want to see you. We do, and we'll do all we can to be useful to you. For instance, if you keep us well posted in advance, we'll try to find places to live cheap wherever you're going. Our next stop, when we leave here, will be Grenoble, I think, so we can climb an Alp. Or even two Alps.

I have a picture I'm going to send you later—of me in a bathing suit running hard along the very edge of sand by the sea, with good waves in the background, and a marvellous jet-black wolfhound, who belongs to a Spanish soldier, running beside me. One of N.'s best, so far.

Well, I guess that's all. I'm really awfully sorry about this mishap. You're spunky, a good sport, a thorough brick. Come on over!

        Yours,   *[in Nick's hand]*
        Bar   Love, Nick

Had a good letter from *Normy*.

Have met some awfully good people over here.

As Barbara promised, she typed up her shorthand notes about the walking trip on Mallorca and sent them to Helen. They total about 11,500 words. The trip report was not published; nor was No Cobwebs or Ghosts, *Barbara's essay about traveling by sea. I will post both on Farksolia soon.*

℅ Am. Express Co.
Conquistador 44
Palma de Mallorca
April 13, 1933

Dear Helen:
　Your rather depressed-sounding letter was waiting for me when I got back, just yesterday, from ten days' walking trip around part of the island. And first let me tell you just a little about that, and then I'll talk about your problems, and possibilities of getting together, and so forth.
　I have about thirty pages of pencilled shorthand notes about this walking trip, which I wrote to you as we went along just because I felt like it, with no ulterior motives. But all of a sudden it occurred to me that it might be pretty useful material. Within two or three days I shall have it typed, and it shall go to you, and you will see what you think.
　It occurred to me that a long, entertaining letter from me to you might just fill the bill for you at this time. I mean, it would be an answer to all the questions about what I am doing, and why, and what I am getting out of it, and all that. You know: "Dear Mother:" —a letter to her mommy from the good little daughter, and all that. And there really is some pretty amusing stuff in it, as you will see. Would that sort of thing have any commercial possibilities, in connection with your lectures, radio, or a possible article in a newspaper, or something? Can you use it for anything at all? Could there be any money in it? Of course I realize you can't answer this much till you see the thing itself, but I just want you to be thinking it over a bit, so you'll be ready for the thing when it comes through presently.
　The personnel of the thing could be easily fixed up. This trip could hardly have been taken by me alone. Two girls, or me and Aunt Edith, could by a far stretch of the imagination have taken it. Nick graciously says that he is willing to be a girl for a while in the good cause. But I think the best solution is to make the companion an old and trusted family friend in the late forties or fifties—perhaps an uncle, or something. That would fit in perfectly.
　Anyway, you have full editorial powers over the material. Cut it

wherever you like, modify it (remember I wrote it simply as a letter to you!), add to it, arrange the personnel any way you please. I feel almost sure you can make something out of it.

If there is a chance of selling it, there will be pictures forth-coming, too, if you say the word. Nick doesn't know whether he wants to sell any negatives outright, unless he could get a fairly decent price for them, but he would sell the right to reproduce. And, although we haven't yet seen the pictures from this particular expedition, I feel confident that there will be some pretty good stuff among them.

Anyway, think it over, won't you?

If you like the material, and the idea seems to go over, I could think about keeping it up—a sort of series of "Dear Mother" letters from foreign countries.

As to Cobwebs and Ghosts, I'll try to get at that, too. Thanks for the tip.

And now about *you*.

We've got your problems in mind, and we're going to continue to have them in mind as we go places—thinking a little about cheapness, good places to live in various respects, schools, etc. And I don't see why, if we keep our heads and act sensibly, we can't dope out some very good scheme of life for the summer and through next winter. It is certain that you can live almost anywhere in Europe cheaper than in America. France is said to be more expensive than Spain, and Germany more expensive than France, but on the other hand I imagine you can live ridiculously cheap in Germany if you know how. We propose to learn how. I don't think I'd recommend Spain. What I've seen of it isn't so hot. France or Germany would be better. What I specially yearn for is to spend the winter in the ski country, and learn to ski. An accomplishment I'm ashamed of not having acquired already.

Of course you understand that Nick sticks to me and I stick to Nick. It couldn't possibly be any other way. The thing would be, for us to keep house for you. We're awfully good at that, and at marketing economically, and cooking on charcoal stoves, and things like that. Nick would manage a lot of that in his quiet efficient way, and I the rest; you'd never have to put your hand to a dish, or take up a knife to peel a carrot. We'd take care of Sabra, too, of course—at least, I imagine he would do most of that, and I'd help you with your stuff. We'd take it all quite seriously, as a definite, regular job, to be done every day. I'm glad you're thinking of another book, and I'd be glad to help all I can with it. I know you may say: "It sounds good, but it won't go through like that." Well, there is always the possibility that it won't, but I think there's a damn good chance if we all go at it cooperatively in the right frame of mind. Let's try, anyhow. We've talked it over a lot in the watches of the night since your letter came, and we think it's a good scheme, and advantageous to everybody concerned. If you have any alternative scheme, let's hear it; only don't try to get me alone because that *won't* work. I have to have him, to keep me good.

Well, I guess that's about all of that. You asked me about my plans. We shall probably be in Palma about a week more, in order to get some typing done—a lot of typing, in fact, while I have this very excellent opportunity. I want to get this Mallorca material off to you (by the by, Mallorca material is said to be more or less in demand), and the Ktaadn thing, too. Cobwebs and Ghosts, maybe. And Nick has some material to be typed, too. After all that is done, we may retire to a sweet place we know up the coast a way, and rest and swim for another week. Or we may not. But in any event, we shan't be on the island much longer. After that we plan to go up to Barcelona, across the Pyrenees, and maybe drop in on Ellen at Grenoble. Then Germany. But it's all a little vague as yet, and if you could tell us anything concrete about your plans it would influence ours. I mean, we can still mould our plans any way you like. We really do want to help you out. And we'll be thinking about it.

Keep your chin up, and don't let all the questions bother you. This material that's coming to you ought to serve as a pretty good answer to questions about *me*.

> How's the busted leg?
> Love, as ever,
> Bar

Grand Hotel Alhambra
Palma de Mallorca
28 April 1933

Dear H:

It's quite definite that we're leaving here May 3 for Grenoble, where the Meserveys are. If it's *good* there, we'll stay a little while. Our transit visas only allow us a month in France. After that expect to go to Germany. Will keep in touch with you frequently. You'd better not plan to come to Mallorca, though. Try Germany.

Please bring me (I know it's a nuisance, and I'm sorry, but please do):

(a) Large jar of peanut butter.

(b) A "bra" from Lerner's—one of those little lacy ones. Size 34.

(c) My Farksoo. It is in a large green box marked "Farksoo." I don't need all of it; I think all the important stuff is in one notebook at the top of the box. Look carefully and see if that notebook has the vocabulary in it—a bulky thing, incomplete, partly handwritten. I *need* Farksoo.

(d) My brown fountain pen, which is—or was—in that old pocket-book.

(e) I'm out of clothes. Bring a couple of things like that green and brown Jersey dress—old things to be worn up.

You're bringing a trunk, I suppose, especially if you're bringing Sabra. I think the Maine idea is good for this summer for her—but after that, what?

By the way, there could be a couple of photographs with *Rocks*. It would be a little clumsy to get hold of them, since Howie Crosse has all the negatives, but I imagine it could be done, if you like. Let me know.

See you sometime, somewhere!

   As ever,
   B.

Barcelona
May 4, 1933

Dearest ADR:

Your good letter came yesterday, and needless to say I'm tickled to hear that you aren't sitting in the fig-tree, that you are all alive and well, and that the Wolf is house broken (Oh, most admirable phrase!)

I am sitting at a little table on the sidewalk, waiting for a train to France, which leaves in an hour and a half. Beside me sit a knapsack and a small suitcase—our total luggage.

You are absolutely right, my dear, in resenting my not having taken you more into confidence. Try to believe that it wasn't so much that I didn't want to tell you all about it, as that I was all up in the air myself, not sure just what *was* happening and not knowing where to start or what to say in any event. It is bewildering to completely change one's life all in a minute. Do forgive me.

In brief, here is the story: I met this "mysterious figure N. Rogers" summer before last, when H. and I were living in that little cabin in Vermont. Then he showed up again that winter in New York, and we became good friends. He helped me through some trying times. We liked mountains—laid plans for getting away together the following summer. It was with him that I took that trip down the Appalachian Trail through Maine, New Hampshire, and Vermont. It was all so good that I decided to stick to it. In August I wrote Bingham, giving up my job. This—all this—is a continuation of that adventure.

That is very brief. It doesn't tell you anything about the delicious little island in the middle of a New Hampshire lake that we camped out on for two weeks in a tiny brown tent. It doesn't say anything about the things we have been doing in Mallorca (which we just left last night), such as living in a cave out on the coast and swimming in magic blue-green water. And it doesn't say a word about the mysterious figure himself. Well, that's difficult. A picture may help a little. I just know that I have never "hit it off" so well with anyone or known a more congenial comrade. We've been together day and night for upwards of a year now, and no prospects of splitting up. Sometime we're going out to explore the great North-West; and we'll come to see you, if you'll have us.

It all happened like a shot, you see. I was sorry to do this to E. A., but when crises arise things change. Besides, I think that was drawing to a close; and this was obviously right because it was so damn *natural*. I believe in nature. We have to follow the best thing we know—the thing that is at the time best.

Helen writes that she expects to come over, with Sabra, in June. We shall join up with her somewhere, and I shall help her with another book. As for my book, *Lost Island*, I haven't ditched it at all. I finished it about a year ago, and I suppose it is now wearily going the rounds of publishers' desks under Helen's guidance. I still think it's a pretty good book. I haven't written much since—a little short stuff.

But, writing or no writing, I've been living pretty hard, which is what I want to do. Last summer, that tremendous succession of mountains down the backbone of New England. Then, the business of sailing from New York. A rather dull winter in Mallorca, when it rained all the time, and we sat around Spanishly in cafés and read. Then, a good walking trip around part of the island, with a borrowed blanket. Living in a cave, making friends with carabineros (the coast guards—good fellows, all of them), eating with them in their huts, warming ourselves at night around their little fires and learning Spanish from them; swimming along great sweeps of beach, exploring Moorish watch towers about a thousand years old, sailing on several exciting cruises on a small sloop owned by an interesting chap. Now we are bound for France and Germany to tramp some more this summer. We are poor as church mice, of course, but progressively browner and happier as time goes on.

Grenoble, May 7

The train arrived. We took about five different ones before we were through, and eventually landed here, under a line of mountains—sharp white peaks, with blue shadows. I imagine we shall be here about a week, then go on afoot over Switzerland and part of Germany.

That's about all of it.

Thanks for the news about W. F.—not that there is much one could dignify by the name of news! I do want to look him up again sometime—be it Maine or California. That is another of the thousand-odd things we'll do when we get back. We shall probably establish ourselves in a shack in the woods somewhere and explore from it. I like Civilization less and less.

Your letter was *good* to have. Do it again when you feel like it! (The same address holds good—we have no other yet.)

Much love to the "family." I think they're grand, all of them!

    Love,
    Bar

Grenoble, France
May 7 (or 9?), 1933

Dear H:

We arrived here day before yesterday, after having taken five different trains from Barcelona. I can't talk French worth a damn. I say "Quiero" instead of "je veux," and "cuanto vale?" instead of "combien." Sometimes I mix both languages in one sentence; and N. still can't say "oui" to save his neck—invariably "si."

Otherwise it's all right, and especially the row of Alps above us is all right. They are not high ones, but they still have some snow on them, and good blue shadows in their bristling ravines.

The Meserveys have welcomed us, although of course N. was something of a surprise. Ellen whole-heartedly approves; Anne has lived in Hanover so long that respectability is a deeply ingrained habit, but she is too big a person to mind. She always introduces me as "Mrs. Nick Rogers." That makes her feel better. She looks older, by the way. Ellen is studying hard, and is pale; Bob is 12 and a corking kid. News from Edward states that he must shortly begin shaving!

I think we'll stay here about a week. Then we shall walk across Switzerland and part of Germany. We'll meet you in Freiburg, Germany (Baden). It is a little university town in the Black Forest. I imagine you can get there easily enough from Strasbourg. We'll be there around June 5 or so—you come right there from France.

They say you can live dirt-cheap in Austria, and I do want to ski next winter. This more northern country with mountains in it, is so much better than Spain that there's no use even comparing them.

I can't tell you how good it was to see an honest-to-God fir tree. If firs grew in India, I know Buddha would have picked one instead of a banyan.

Hasta la vista,

>Yours,
>B.

If you want to communicate again, write to American Express Co., Zurich, Switzerland. We shall pass through there.

And that, as far as the Columbia archive goes, was the last letter to or from Barbara in 1933—except for one from her old Carnegie friend, Gordon Campbell.

At Sea
S.S. Ad. Gove
Nov 12th [1933]

Dear Barbara

[...] I hope you enjoyed your trip to Spain last winter I made an interesting trip this summer myself (can you gess) Well I joined the C. S. Holmes with Ed Anderson Mate and Johnnie Oryzo Second and made the trip to Point Barrow 71° 30' N we were fighting the Ice for 2 month and eighty miles south of Barrow we were frozen in for eighteen days and were being pushed closer and closer to the beach we had only 2 ft of water under us and Captain Buckland told us to get ready to abandon the ship but the ice eventually broke up and a Government ship gave us a tow to Point Barrow.

Well Barbara I am sorry to say I did not get along very well with Mr. Anderson but the trouble lay with the enexperienced crew they had on board. She was so different as night and day compared to the old "Carnegie"

[...] Oh by the way Barbara I just thought of it you must be about twenty years old now (or young I mean) and I heard you were married is that true? You see I know with some people after a man gets married he dose not care to see his wife getting letters from strangers. But I hope you wont mind and answer this as soon as you can and give me some news of yourself.

>And oblig your shipmate
>Gordon Campbell

After staying for two or three months in a Black Forest hut where Barbara helped Helen with Stars to Steer By, *the couple continued their explorations before sailing from Hamburg back to New York, arriving on November 18th. (Helen and Sabra had returned in September.) Five years later Helen would publish a book about her time in Germany—* Third Class Ticket to Heaven. *Neither Barbara, Nick, nor Sabra are mentioned in it.*

Barbara didn't stay long at all in New York. Instead she accompanied Nick to Boston, where she rented a room while he stayed with his parents on Perrin Road, a quiet cul-de-sac near the Brookline Reservoir. I don't know where Barbara's first room was, but the one on Cumberland Street was near Symphony Hall in the Back Bay.

Despite Barbara's enthusiasm for it, Travels Without a Donkey *was not published until Farksolia.*

February 1, 1934
26 Cumberland Street
Boston, Mass.

Dear H.:

Have moved again, to a still cheaper room—$3.25 a week, which includes an electric grill to cook on, and is more fun, being downtown where things go on.

Thanks ever so for the check. It will keep me a good while.

I'm sorry things seem to be so mean with you.

I went to see Ding yesterday; she is getting better, Mrs. Deckard says, but was still too sick to talk to me, so I had to go away. Gallstones, apparently.

I have finished the story of the summer in Maine. It is my pride and joy. I adore it, and think it's by all odds the best thing I've ever done. But you won't like it. And I don't know what to do with it anyway, because it's too long for an article—sixty pages. Would divide nicely in the middle. I could get it out anonymous. I haven't any other title for it than Travels Without a Donkey, which suits it perfectly, once you've read it.

Have rehashed about half of the novel. The other half is harder, though.

Sure, I'll go to Mallorca with you sometime. But not this summer. Furthermore, you wouldn't want to be there in the summer. You'd die off.

Hope things break for you somewhere.

       Love,
       Bar

Barbara called her skiing skit Ski Heil!

26 Cumberland Street
Boston, Mass.
February 3, 1934

Dear H:

Of course I would work with you if you came to Boston for a week-end. I don't have much distraction any more in the form of Nick, as he is busy as hell and just drops around for lunch sometimes or in the evening. We do try to get in some skiing every week-end, but don't always manage it. By the way, could you use a short humorous skit about learning to ski? I've done one.

Anderson's post office box used to be 65—Box 65, Seattle. The schooner he was on last I knew of him was called *C. S. Holmes*. Of course I have no way of knowing whether he is still in her.

I telephoned Mrs. Deckard again on Saturday, thinking I would go over to see Ding if she were able to see me. Mrs. Deckard sounded rather worried, and Ding still can't talk to anyone, it seems. Deckard has another sick woman in the house, and hasn't been out of her clothes for days. But I imagine that Ding has had good care, and I doubt if there's anything you can do. I would leave it on the knees of the gods. Mrs. D. doesn't think there's any *danger* now.

Had a letter this morning from Effie Cummings, who just got married! Heigh-ho!

If you come to Boston, you might be able to stay in my room (if you don't mind sleeping with me), which would cost you very little if anything. Convenient, too. I have fairly good working facilities—light, table, good heat, etc. And a little electric grill on which I brew myself tea now and then. Have an enormous closet with a pantry in it consisting of two orange crates, which Nick brought up to me. Peanut butter, graham crackers, fruit, etc. Quite fun. No domesticity.

Don't worry too much about anything, and keep on pluggin'. When are your galleys ready?

      Love,
      Bar

26 Cumberland Street
Boston, Mass.
Tuesday [ca. February, 1934]

Dear H:

Sorry to hear you're laid up. What seems to be the trouble?

I have been keeping in touch with Deckard, and Sunday night

went over. Ding looks pretty bad—is only semi-conscious, and never comfortable, and extremely weak. Can't so much as lift her head. I don't know, and neither does anybody else, but it sort of looks as if she wasn't going to make the trip. I suppose it sounds heartless, but I can't help philosophizing about it, and thinking that she's getting on anyway, and has to die sometime. Deckard is carrying on splendidly. She's an awful bore, and long-winded as hell about all the tawdry details, but has a heart of gold. I can't help any. The only thing I tried to do, which was to give Ding a spoonful of water (which she wants all the time), was an utter failure. She choked. Ironical, what?

It's snowing cats and dogs this minute—has been all night, I guess. Boston's all tied up in knots again. I hope there'll be some skiing again. I'm getting so I can do Christies and jump turns. Marvellous!

Still struggling with the book, and still on the ninth and tenth chapters. Progress slow.

   Yours,
   Bar

Ding was living at 20 Wyoming Street in Dorchester when she died. She was 84.

Anthony Adverse was a 1933 novel by Hervey Allen. A film version won four Academy Awards in 1936.

26 Cumberland Street
Boston, Mass.
March 4 [1934]

Dear H:

I haven't written, because there has been nothing to say. I didn't think you wanted a "formal courtesy note." I was sorry about Ding—but what could I do? Death is one of those things that leave me with a sensation of abysmal impotence, as well as an instinctive sense that I'd better keep away.

What has laid *you* up?

As for your questions: I am living in a very respectable rooming-house in Back Bay, alone, and writing by fits and starts. What more do you want to know? Sometimes I go on a week-end ski trip, but not often.

Nick is still doing his job. Business has fallen off lately, and it's pretty discouraging. He is taking what appears to be a pretty good correspondence course in journalistic photography, which I think an excellent idea.

I have finished *Anthony Adverse*—grand; now I have reverted to the age of ten, and am reading with great glee Howard Pyle's King Arthur stories!

>Love,
>Bar

Stars to Steer By *was published by Macmillan in late spring. And from this snippet in the* Turns with a Bookworm *column by IMP (Isabel M. Paterson), we learn about another Follett house fire.*

New York Herald Tribune, May 27, 1934
Turns With a Bookworm
While writing "Stars to Steer By," in a cottage in the Black Forest, Mrs. Helen Follett and her daughter Barbara were burned out and the manuscript barely escaped the flames and was blown all over the village... The kindly villagers collected the pages, so Mrs. Follett sent the fist copy of the book to the local policeman, who took charge of the rescue.

Excerpts from the New York Herald Tribune, *June 10, 1934.*

Books for Young People
Edited by May Lamberton Becker
[...] Decidedly, this is no book for a New England conscience. Yet—how about this "new leisure" for which we are now so conscientiously preparing? Can it be that in Papeete they know about it already? At any rate, they know how to laugh. The Folletts sail away to the sound of girls laughing and calling, on the *Andromede*, a finer French steamer than the old *Louqsor* that brought them there. It has even a comedy pair of English on their honeymoon, whose chief interest in the South Seas is that they will get good stories to tell at home at tea. [...] The rest of the book tells how Barbara had a chance to become a Tongan princess, how her mother set up Leofi as a great doctor in his village by the gift of a spare thermometer and a bottle of soda mints, what life is like in Samoa and how Tusitala's grave looks at sunrise. Little things like that, told in continual amazement and delight that they are happening and that the travellers are actually there to see, Barbara even has the climax for which she longed. The last ship they take, the one that brings them back to the smell of pine trees and the solid Western shore of their own country, is a real sailing vessel at last, and they can hear the wind in the rigging. [...]

And from the Saturday Review of Literature, *June 23, 1934.*

Rare is the gift for attracting instantly, and for holding, the friendship and trust of a stranger. Rare, too, is the buoyant vitality which refuses to recognize discomfort. Scholarship and morbid sophistication would have been excess baggage to Mrs. Follett and her daughter on their Polynesian cruise. They travel light, bearing with them only alert sympathies, stout hearts, and—as a good-humored concession to the inevitable—two typewriters.

You will do well to put this book by when the mood of ruthless inquiry is on and when you are seeking life as you doubtless know it, light and shadow, storm and calm. There is no storm here, and the seas are shadowless. For all its title, this story is of life experienced at high noon. Its philosophy runs no deeper than the waves murmuring over the beaches at Tahiti, Tonga, Samoa.

News of Anderson from Gordon Campbell, who was recovering from tuberculosis in the high desert air of New Mexico.

Fort Stanton
New Mexico
June 27th, 34

Dear Shipmate

[...] I wonder if you noticed in my last letter it had a kind of discouraged background don't you think? I notice it myself now, I was feeling kind of blue for a couple of months before that and two weeks after I wrote you I went to the Hospital with a high fever and they discouvered my right lung plural fall of Fluid so they put a needle between my ribs and drew it off (16 hundred cc) and have done the same eight times now. [...] I am feeling first rate I am ten lbs more weight than I ever was.

[...] Well I have not been able to get "Magic Port Holes" yet but pleas give me the name of your Mothers new book and I will get them both I sure will like to read them. I wish you would take up writting again wont you?

From what Ed Anderson told me I think he plans about two trips more and I think he is going to build a yawl and go up to Alaska hunting and fishing and make his home there.

He and the Captain are the only two that went North on the Holmes this year Johny as Second Mate could not get along with me or Ed so he quit and is A. B. on the Schr. "Commordore" a week out from Honolulu to Seattle. I am sorry things turned out that way but I suppose it cant be helped.

[...] I will close now wishing you the best of luck and hope you enjoyed your trip to Spain.

> Your Old Shipmate
> *Mr* Gordon Campbell

P. S. So you are not Married eh. Well you have the right Idea, take a good look around first and pick a good one if you do. Ed told me you were Married and I thought you had probaly settled down and would miss those trips you have been used to.

Barbara and Nick were married on Saturday, July 7, 1934 in Brookline, Massachusetts.

Mrs. Nickerson Rogers, circa 1934

Along with marriage came a dearth of letters—at least judging by the contents of the Columbia archive.

In 1934 we have glowing words for Travels without a Donkey *by Barbara's "adopted uncle," Frederic Taber Cooper, who you'll remember advised Barbara about* Lost Island.

In 1935 there's a welcome letter from Anderson replying to Barbara's news that she had gotten married.

From 1936 there is nothing.

Happily, things pick up in 1937 when Barbara and Alice resume their correspondence. We learn that in the summer of 1935 Barbara and Nick worked at the new Putney School in Vermont, which, like Sabra's school in New York, was part of the progressive education movement. It opened for business that September, so Barbara and Nick must have joined the faculty and staff who actually built the school on the 500-acre farm that Carmelita Hinton had purchased for its home. ("Lots of good hard physical work that sweats the poison out of you!")

Back to Cooper's letter. Holderness is on Squam Lake in New Hampshire, and a particular island was one of Barbara's favorite places. It was probably the one she and Nick camped on before their long walk in 1932. If it happened to be Moon or Bowman Island, campsites are available from the Squam Lake Association for $60 per night ($50 for members).

Old Lyme, Connecticut
October 15, 1934

Dear long-absent Niece,

At sufficiently long intervals a not too grudging Fate still vouchsafes me unhoped-for gleams of sheer gladness. One such was the arrival a few days ago of your inspired little masterpiece, "Travels without a Donkey."

I gave it a first reading night before last. Unless you are in a great hurry to have the MS back, I want to wait a few days, to let my impressions sink in, before returning it. Also, I was a little in doubt about your address, "General Delivery, Holderness." It sounds so transient and migratory, that I hesitate entrusting a precious document to it until you assure me that you will still be there.

Now, here are some of the things that I am even now ready to say: In its way this very personal record seems to me one of those rarest achievements in writing, a successful attempt to do precisely what you were trying to do. Perhaps it is a little bit arrogant for me—a complete outsider in this particular episode—to state so assertively my sureness of your success. But I have always believed that certain kinds of work bear their own credentials with them. And, while they differ widely in their quality and their purpose, they always have one thing in common: they are the product of an inward urge that refuses to be denied.

Glancing back at this point to your letter, I notice that your specific questions are a more than usual blend of those two separate and often contradictory problems: what changes if any will help artistically, from the outside point of view; and secondly, what sheer practical concessions may be considered, to fit in with what some editor may want, for what he guesses will meet the widest range of his own special public. (And, mind you, no editor half the times knows what his public really does want!) And with the wholesale percent of magazines going to smash in the last eighteen months, they haven't learned even yet how far they are guessing wrong.

You are "not exactly sure whether the proportion of personal and impersonal is all right." Thank God, that you are not. I would gamble all I own that when you wrote your first draft you were not thinking for a moment of personal and impersonal proportions. Of course not—any more than Sterne was thinking of any such fol-de-rol when he wrote *A Sentimental Journey*, or Thoreau wrote the bulk of his books, or the French novelist Stendhal, when he wrote *Rome, Naples et Florence* (which got as far as Milan and, as I remember it, never got any further!) I believe firmly that, whether you are writing a travel book or a novel or a geological thesis or a Walton's *Compleat Angler*, the best guide is your own instinct. If you choose to interweave the personal equation, then only you can judge to what extent it is vital from your point of view. A second-rate painter told me that he had been trying for years to paint a bit of woods here in Lyme, just behind his home. "I love it," he said, "but it didn't make a picture. But suddenly I realized that all I had to do was to cut down mentally a line of trees, leaving a path and a glimpse of sunlight at the end." So that was what he did; and it was probably the worst picture he ever painted. You see, when you leave out elements from your own familiar, intimate picture—from the way you instinctively conceive it, you are leaving out essentials, whether you know it or not.

Now, the problem of making concessions to the editor is something else again. In your type of work, my guess is that any editor who has the right understanding and the right sympathy would feel as I do: he would feel that here was something that either wasn't right at all, or it was precisely right just as it stood. I will tell you more in detail just what I think, in my next letter. But for the moment let me say that if I had been fortunate enough to come across the counterpart of your little Appalachian journey when I was having a joyous free hand editing the *Forum* for three happy years, I would have snapped it up as eagerly as any hungry trout ever rose to a specially succulent fly.

Well, after having a most contented hour, reading your MS, I took a liberty with it: I read certain parts aloud to my grandson, Taber de Polo. To make you understand my motive, I must digress a moment and tell you something about him. He is eighteen; he entered Wesleyan in 1933; he has twice broken the half-mile record for Connecticut; and he has a hopelessly one-track mind. He has a natural gift for mathematics, a spongelike ability to absorb chemistry and geology, and a hopelessly blind spot for languages. I think he is the only student who ever succeeded in failing in five special German examinations—failing each time by barely five per cent—and that is why his is no longer a student at Wesleyan. But Taber is a natural born woodsman. He knows and loves the forests of Maine and of Canada, New Hampshire and Vermont, has shot game in all their woods and caught fish in all their waters. I have seen him single-handedly fell a tree and split it up into something over a cord of fire wood, in a day and a half. Lastly, he got a job last summer after his own heart: he was a member of the crew who finished up the last 71 miles of Appalachian trail from Katahdin south—or rather, I think he said, part of it was a northern extension. Anyway, he personally took a considerable part in breaking a virgin trail through forty miles of it and setting up those little metal markers you speak of.

So you can see now why I wanted to get Taber's reaction to your MS. I wanted to see just how far you had let yourself embroider your scenic background, and whether the personal element that you yourself distrusted had intruded upon the actual geography, and taken liberties with it. You see, I knew you and your personal relations with that whole little northern Odyssey; but I don't know an inch of the territory or the fauna and flora. But I got my answer from Taber. He knew nothing and cared less than nothing about the human story; but I wish you could have seen him come to life and thrill, as one name after another evoked nostalgic memories: Katahdin ... Moosehead Lake ... Ripogenus Dam ... "climbing Kineo by moonlight"—these were just a few of the points where he interrupted me to tell of his own memories that you had so poignantly evoked. I was almost sorry I had tried the experiment of reading it to him at all. Because we are trying to keep him to his German, so that he can enter the North Carolina University, which accepts students in January, carries them on through a summer session, and gets them back into Wesleyan, or wherever they belong, in October. But it looked for a time as though Taber would bolt, and obey the call of the wild.

Barbara, my dear, you are always something of an unknown quantity. Perhaps that is one of the reasons why I care so deeply for you and for your happiness. So you have been getting yourself married? As you must have realized from things I have said, I am in some ways ultra-modern about all those matters. I believe in marriage as an ideal goal for young people to hope and strive for—but not for the sake of any of the conventional reasons that most worldly minded families hold us up to. When Ethel and I discuss young people's problems, either personally or abstractly, I suspect that I mildly shock her sometimes; because, with all her rare intuitions and liberalities, she has a persistent soupçon of the old fashioned; while I verge perhaps on what I define in contrast as the young-fashioned. Do you remember the last luncheon you and I had together one day late in June? If you had known me better then, I like to think that you would have told me of this Appalachian trip and what it really meant. I think you would have found me rather comforting.

What I am rather clumsily leading up to is a most sincere wish for your happiness. I have never had a chance to meet Mr. Rogers, never had even the slightest verbal portrait of him drawn for me. But if your portrayal of him as "Nick," in your travelogue, is anything near the original, then his is very much a person after my own heart. But throughout my life my instinct has always been to convey my felicitations to the husband, rather than to the wife. Because I have an incurable belief that the best of men are not quite deserving of any worth-while woman. At my age I have one advantage: I can have intimate and fairly platonic friendships with women, without fear of foolish misunderstandings. But now and then, in the lapse of decades, I meet some one who makes me admit to myself: "If I were forty years younger, I would put up a pretty good fight for her." Do you mind, dear adopted niece, if I admit that I had some such line of thought, that June day when we last lunched together? And since that thought was accompanied with all due homage and loyalty, I think that I have a special reason for gladness, now that you have solved your problems and found tranquility and contentment.

But the artist in me is always getting the upper hand of the human being. So it logically follows that I cling especially to your concluding paragraph, wherein you tell me that "Lost Island may reasonably be expected to be hauled out almost any evening and be pored over by lamp-light." Please don't look at it through too critical eyes. Paradoxically, its greatest charm and its outstanding flaws came from the relatively naive attitude of the writer. And that is why I have been so anxious to have you get back to it before the old point of view had too far faded. Because there is nothing so hard to recapture as a mood that is past and gone.

Do send me just a brief line to say whether I shall return your MS to the Holderness General Delivery address or not.

With all best greetings in the world, I remain as always

        Your most faithful of adoptive uncles,
        F. T. C.

[undated, but about March 1935]
℅ C. S. Holmes – Foss Co
660 W. Ewing St
Seattle

Dear Bar:

I've just had a very strange dream, I dreamed I received a letter from you; Of course it can't be really so, and yet; Oh Bar! I'm afraid I've forgotten how to write letters. There just seems to be nothing quite appropriate to say.

You say nothing of yourself, and I want to ask a thousand questions about you. You don't even tell me your name; I've always thought of you as Barbara Hardy these last two years. A girl by that name wrote to a magazine about a sea-sick remedy some time ago, I read it, and as I recall, there was something hauntingly familiar about the way it was written. It may just have been a fancy of mine, yet it was real enough to prevent my trying to correspond with B. F.

Now that I look back, I can hardly understand how little I have changed. I still work on the C. S. Holmes. Times are tough as ever, I'm still a pessimist, and an independent ass. But you, how are you; about the only thing I can consider with surety is that you're about 21. If apologies are in order, let me extend mine. I think I'm the biggest fool in creation. Whatever it was went wrong, I know I was almost entirely to blame; No amount of verbal heroics could ever be worth the misery they put me in; Nothing that could happen, could have been worse than what did happen.

Bar! I cannot write coherently about myself just now, so I won't answer your queries about me, except that I have been getting by pretty much the same as ever. I'm not a captain, and I've no prospects of being one. I'm not married, and I've no money. As for escape, I've learned a lot about that too. There is no escape for those who think they need it: — More of this later if you wish.

(Hours later)

I've been reading your letter over and over, and I've been wondering. I'm really afraid of you. The reason is not far to search for, I'm still in love with you. Perhaps I shouldn't say this, yet why not; you may then understand me if I say that I don't think I'd accept just being friends the way you might expect or want us to be. I'd just be pretending and I don't think I could put up a very convincing pretense. I think you understand enough about me to accept this in the spirit it is meant, however funny it sounds.

However, I'm eternally grateful to you for writing, I wondered an awful lot about you; It's good to know you're alive and think enough of me to write; Although you say nothing of yourself, your picture conveys eloquent testimony of health and spirit. It would perhaps amuse you, could you but know the chaotic disarray of my thoughts when I read your letter; I may have said much too much in this letter Bar. If I have it's because of that one little word with which you concluded your letter. "Yours Bar" is how it reads; No doubt I'm a presumptuous reader.

Please write again Shipmate, even if you think you ought not to at least you once loved me, I think, and you can trust me enough to know I'll understand.

      As ever
      E. A.

Barbara and Nick liked to ski, and on one of their trips up to the mountains, on or about February 9, 1937, they visited my grandparents—now married for four years—at their home in Bradford, Vermont. The occasion was my mother's second birthday and, to my delight, Nick took a photograph of the family seated around the dining room table. The slide's colors may have faded, but Barbara's smile certainly hasn't.

Three generations of Folletts: Wilson, Margaret, Jane, Grace (Wilson's daughter from his first marriage), Barbara.

As I mentioned earlier, I don't think there are any letters from 1936 at Columbia.

In 1937 Barbara and Nick were living on Charles Street in Beacon Hill, between the Charles River and Boston Common. Nick had a technical job at the new Polaroid Corporation, where his brother, Howard, also worked. (Howard would become a key figure in the invention of instant photography.) Barbara worked as a secretary for the American Board of Commissioners for Foreign Missions, which operated in the Congregational Library at 14 Beacon Street, a short walk from their apartment. (The Congregational Library and Archives are operating today in the same building.)

Helen's manuscript was Third Class Ticket to Heaven. Despite the work Barbara put into it, her mother didn't credit her in the book (as was also the case with Magic Portholes and Stars to Steer By).

125 Charles Street
Boston, Massachusetts
April 5, 1937

Dearest A.D.R.:

Your grand long letter of mid-January has sat in my top desk drawer ever since it came, and every day, opening that drawer to get stamps, etc., I have promised it an immediate answer. However, a mere lapse of nearly three months at least isn't as bad as I have sometimes committed — (omitted?)

By this time, certainly, the iritis should be cleared up—or is it even longer than I think? At least that ski trip sounded grand, and I suppose there have been others since then. Little old New England has certainly fallen down badly on the job this winter. I think I have been skiing four times, and none of them was particularly good. Just last week-end we were at Moosilauke, and, though the snow conditions were none too good, the weather was perfect, and the snow-capped mountain gleaming in the sun more than made up for the slushiness underfoot. To cap it all, we were in the company of some of our very best and most congenial friends.

The South American affair continues to rile me thoroughly every time I think of it. There seems so little high adventure in life, that to have one come so near and then escape is practically intolerable. I've had one or two fairly high adventures, and am convinced that they are worth all kinds of sweat and pain and other troubles; in fact, they are the only things really worth suffering for. My greatest worry now, when I have time to stop and think about it, is that I am in a rather difficult position as far as Adventure is concerned, where that evasive spirit may have trouble locating me! Life right now is a very *quiet* adventure, though pleasant, at that.

I have been tangled up with thoroughly unsuccessful people in a world sense (i.e., the various members of my family!) so long that I guess I have developed a consistent pessimism on the subject. Anyhow, it is a welcome and happy relief to watch Nick's progress. A few weeks ago they gave him another raise; and now he is almost earning what can be called a "living wage"; though it is not yet so alive but that I must keep my own job, if we are to continue our present standard of living (car, occasional beer, week-end trips, and such rather fundamental pleasures). But anyway, he is making "progress," and he is still thoroughly absorbed and interested in the various aspects of his job. That is pretty thrilling, and compensates to some extent for the fact that I am thoroughly bored at present with my own.

Did I mention that I have been rather going in for "interpretative dancing" this winter? I started at it just for fun and exercise, taking one class a week with a very interesting girl who has studied abroad, and got so absorbed in the thing that I started another class in another studio. Some of the time I practice very regularly, although last week I hit what I hope is a temporary "low" in interest. Anyway, this dancing has been another thing to help me bear up under what is a pretty dull job most of the time.

I'm afraid there has been nothing but bad news on your MS., and I'm sorrier than I can say. Helen's own MS is now in the toils, I believe. I put a great deal of my very best effort into it practically all winter, when I didn't have any time; and to tell the truth, I'm very much relieved to have finished my part. I'm anxious to hear what comes of it.

It has often seemed to me rather a paradox that the people who really have the most to say, the most to contribute, are the ones whose manuscripts do juggling acts from one publisher to another without finding their resting places. I suppose the answer is that the people who read books don't really want to hear anything; they just want their own little pet romanticisms to be confirmed, over and over again, by the movies they see and the books they read. And so the real authors struggle along quietly.

That is swell news, about the house in Maine. One of our regrets this winter is that we haven't been able to get up there, since both of us work nearly every Saturday morning. We may be able to revise this schedule later on, which means that we could get a start on Friday night. Otherwise, such a long trip is practically out of the question. Summer vacation may offer possibilities. Neither of us yet knows how much time we can get, or what part of the summer, but we're determined optimists, and keep hoping for a lucky break in this direction.

I hope that by now Phoebe's eyes are all right enough so that she can start in on the textile work. It sounded fascinating, and I know she was impatient to get going on it. Please give her my very best. It gave me all kinds of strange and thrilling emotions to see her again, so changed and yet not changed.

Well, best of luck to you all. I'll write again when and if anything happens, outwardly or inwardly!

    Love,
    Bar

Barbara was of course referring to the Folletts when discussing Josephine Johnson's poem Postscript *(published in the* Saturday Review of Literature *on February 6, 1937). Its last verse:*

> And if the outraged tissues of the heart
> (Being made of flesh, not law,
> And subject to acid and the acid's fire)
> Burn down and blacken into ash,
> We may console ourselves with this:
> All the proprieties were kept,
> And no one pained.

125 Charles Street
Boston, Massachusetts
July 20, 1937

Dear A.D.R.:

I've been holding on to answer your letter—or at least your invitation to Maine—until I could find out something about my summer—how much time off I shall have, and all that. Well, I seem to be making very poor progress at that. I do know now that I shall have the last two weeks of August for my regular vacation (with pay), and I am going to try to wring two more weeks (probably the first of August) out of these people, without pay. It seems as if I *must* have more than just the two!

We do think very seriously of your proposition. As a matter of fact, it looks as if Nick and I may get some time off at the same time, which would make it ideal for the Maine jaunt. If I get only two weeks, though, I shall probably go to my Squam island and stay there. Sabra will be able to spend some time with me there, delightfully enough; and it happens that my other sister, Grace, gets her vacation at the same time, too. So I am definitely tied up with them for those last two weeks. But if I also get the first two weeks of August, I am free, and could very well go to Maine for a while. Of course the island is terribly, terribly dear to me. I think I am happier there than anywhere else in the world. I am selfish and greedy about it; but if my time is to be limited, I want to spend almost every minute of it right there. That's how I feel about the place, and I know you can understand that.

I'm glad of Phoebe's job in Yosemite, even if it does leave you alone for the summer. It must be very swell for her. It sounds just a little like the job N. and I were doing at Putney school two summers ago. Lots of good hard physical work that sweats the poison out of you! There's nothing else so good, unless it's good hard sport, like skiing or swimming or mountain-climbing. I'm glad she is having good young companionship, too. Not that *you* yourself aren't good young companionship—heaven knows there's none better. But it's surely true one has to go out and be on one's own some of the time.

I liked J. Johnson's poem. Of course in this particular case, those last lines are not true, for, although "all the proprieties were kept," it seems to me that *everyone* was considerably "pained"—denying us even *that* doubtful, dismal consolation. In fact, I see the whole thing as nothing but one of those irrevocable, unmitigated messes—and a mess with a bad barb in it, too.

It certainly would be a joke if N. turned out to be a money-maker, even on a moderate scale. Whether the joke would be on *me*, I don't know. I think the real joke would be on the rest of my family. My family has so long been associated in my mind with financial failure. It is hard for me to conceive that one member of it—me—could even be associated with, let alone married to, somebody who is going to be able to make a normal living! That sounds absurd, but it really isn't an exaggeration, as I think you will understand, who have seen so much of my family!

However, W.F. seems to be making out rather well, now. I think you will be pleased to hear that. How long it will last, I don't know, but he is selling articles, and they have rented a house in Bradford, Vermont, for two years. It is a grand place—"with not an ugly thing in sight," as he says. It overlooks the Connecticut River, and has a view north and south of the hills surrounding Hanover. He has a garden out of which they get a great deal to eat—and you know how he loves to tend a garden! They seem to be eating, buying dishes, towels, and what-not—in other words, having what they need. And they have just had another child. Did I tell you that one was on the way? Well, it has turned out to be a boy—the first male in the whole three batches of kids! Its name is Wilson Tingley Follett—"Ting," for short. (The Tingley was W.F.'s grandfather's middle name, I believe.)

We helped them move up there in early June, and since then have spent one week-end with them. I am very fond of them both. They are mellowing down somewhat, too, I think, what with a little less strain and worry. Of course I can never really be myself with them, they are so sort of formal, without at all meaning to be. Nick is completely at sea with them. He doesn't get the point at all. He is a simple person, and his family is simple, and all this much ado about nothing, these mannerisms, this literary pomposity, gets him down. He subsides into himself, and says nothing at all. I guess you have to be brought up with it to be used to it! And heaven knows I have a hard enough time myself!

So much for them. I haven't much news about Helen, because she doesn't tell me much. She doesn't like to go into things in detail, unless she has *good* news. So I take it she hasn't. They have moved into a friend's apartment for the summer, and what they will do next winter I have no idea. She says she has "a little work." I don't know what. I may be able to get to see her this summer; and I am trying to have her come up to my island for a few days. If any of these things work out, I'll have more to tell on that.

I haven't told you yet about the Possibility for next winter. Only a nebulous one so far, mind, but something to think and plan about. As you know, N. is very much interested in photography, and wants to do some work in color. I am interested in it, too, especially the darkroom end of things. We have met up with a very swell woman who has a portrait studio outfitted with several thousand dollars worth of equipment, and who seems pretty interested in some sort of semi-partnership with us. That means that I would do darkroom work for her. Probably I would drop half of this job at first, and do photography the other half of the time; then, if the thing worked out well and we made some money, I might drop all of this job. Nick and she would do the color experimenting, etc., together. However, this is all one of those things that I wouldn't mention at all to most people, because of the bother of having to explain it if it doesn't work out. You know how that is!

Well, does this wandering epistle serve as some sort of answer to yours? It's about the best I can do now, anyway. I certainly hope you aren't having too bad a summer. I wish I could come out and stay with you a while myself, for both our sakes. Maybe I shall, yet—not this summer, but some time!

      Love,
      Bar

LIFE WITH NICK (1932–1939)

Sarah Allen Medlicott (1887-1984) was the minister Barbara worked for on Beacon Street.

125 Charles Street
Boston, Mass.
December 21, 1937

Dear A.D.R.:

So now it's time for Christmas cards and bells and all that. Well, you know me. Anyway, the Happy New Year is the only important part of that story; and you know I wish one for you and yours.

I hope you did receive my letter from the island, in which I returned the pictures of the boys in South America. Not that I minded your not writing—for heaven knows I'm the worst possible offender in that respect—but I've wondered once or twice whether the pictures got home safely. I do hope so.

I'm back to the grind now, of course; have been since September—and am enjoying it more than I did last winter, you will be glad to know. My job has grown up a little in the year I've had it. I'm doing more interesting work, and more of it. Besides working for the minister, whom I like very much but whose work is rather meager for anyone as intelligent and speedy as I (Hurrumph!??) I'm now doing "manuscript work," as she calls it, for the most dynamic and meteoric lady who dictates everything she writes. As she happens now to be writing a book about India, my typewriter flies most of the time. So I find my job quite bearable.

Then there's another most interesting development. Way back in October we were prowling around the region near Squam Lake in New Hampshire when our eyes lit covetously upon an old farmhouse on a hill—a farmhouse that was in quite reputable condition compared with most of the abandoned houses thereabouts. To make a very short story of it, we rounded up the prosperous farmer on whose land the house is sitting idle, and persuaded him to rent it to us on the incredible and absurd basis of $2.50 a month—the altogether delightful basis, I should add!* We were quick to cart up some old furniture from Nick's family attic, and place same upon the floor of the farmhouse. Follett, over in Bradford Vermont, crashed through with the very important item of one kitchen range he was not using. So we set up house-keeping—week-ends. And, as easily as that, we had our much-longed-for, often-discussed Place in the Country.

We were up there faithfully every week-end for quite a while, fixing the place up, repairing a bit of floor here, slice of wall there; getting a little wood into the woodshed, to keep us warm and to keep the woodshed from falling down. Of course the main idea in the back of our minds is a skiing headquarters. We haven't yet been able to try it out as such, so far; but we shall be doing that soon now. For the last several weeks, as a matter of fact, we haven't been able to get away.

I crave Russell news. What is Phoebe doing this winter? Did she get a job at that school where she was camping last summer? What are *you* doing?

> Love as always,
> Bar

* Don't mention this around—it's a secret (the amount, I mean).

Alice's novel Strangers in the Desert *was accepted by* Harper & Brothers *and published in October 1938.*

125 Charles Street
Boston, Mass.
March 12 *[1938]*

Dear A.D.R.:

That big little postscript to your letter arrived last night, and I must take time in the middle of an office morning to give three rousing cheers. How tickled I am! How thoroughly sweet such a taste of success can be, after so much disappointment! And Harper at that. You see how it pays to fly high in the first place. In fact, I'm rather surprised you hadn't tried them before. I'm not up much on the publishers any more, but I'm inclined to think you couldn't do better. Oh, that is surely fine news. How I wish you and I could drink a quart of champagne on it together!

It is also fine—perhaps fine in an even more fundamental way—that you weren't swept out in the flood. That is indeed a relief. You say you lost two trees. Not the fig-tree!?? That would be a blow.

That sounded like a truly terrible accident to Phoebe's "rump." The dimensions you give are quite horrifying to me. It is a gay poem she wrote, however, and I gather the thing wasn't terribly serious, although it certainly sounded serious enough. I'm so pleased she's getting out with new friends and having herself something of a fling. I have been doing that to some extent for the last three or four years (although not enough) and find it really makes life worth while as nothing else can.

Did I tell you (this is probably another of those items so important I wouldn't mention it) that Helen's book was accepted, too? I guess I must have, as the good news came on Christmas Eve, just about the time I arrived for my visit. Pleasant all around! Winston is the publisher, down in Philadelphia. The book is due to come out some time this spring, soon. They are sort of rushing it through. Is yours scheduled yet?

I don't think the Folletts hold any bitterness toward you. I am quite sure you needn't have that on your mind. They always inquire for you, and are glad to hear any news of you. They do hold great bitterness toward the whole California episode, but the bitterness is directed toward Helen and her machinations, and I am sure it does not include you at all. I think I would know if it did, because they are pretty outspoken. In fact they were darned outspoken with me recently about one or two little errors in tactical judgment which I made in all innocence and good faith—about which I will tell you some other time if you think it worth while.

Well, this was intended to be just a cheer letter, with hurrays and hurrahs in great quantity.

      Much love,
      Bar

The building on Huntington Avenue is still there and now houses Wentworth Institute of Technology students.

The Great Hurricane of 1938 happened on September 21st. Sudetenland was ceded to Nazi Germany three days before Barbara wrote this letter.

It's good news that Barbara was still getting along with her father and even spent a week with her Vermont family. And that she and my grandmother were correspondents. I wish I could share those letters but my grandmother didn't keep them.

Apt. 43
574 Huntington Avenue
Boston, Mass.
October 4, 1938

Dear A.D.R.:

First, please note change of address. About a week ago we moved into this present apartment, which is very much brighter, cleaner (now), and cheerier than the old one.

The last news I had from South Pasadena was your excited note about Harper's taking the book. Tell me, is it out yet? I ought to know, of course, but I have just gone through one of those spells when I never glance at a newspaper and keep in no sort of touch with any bookshop. The only way I can ever keep up at all with books is by working in a bookshop, I guess! I hope I am through that stage for a while *[footnote: "I mean, not reading any news."]*. I am going to buy the Sunday New York Times every week and read it faithfully!

The world has certainly not been barren of news lately, anyhow, both abroad and home. Some of that has filtered through even to me. You will be glad to know that the hurricane didn't do anything to us personally, except we are sorry to see two thirds of the trees in Boston Garden lying low, and whole groves of trees up north swept down together as if they were no more than fields of corn. Our old rented farm house lost only a few shingles, settled a wee bit more, and one pane of glass was broken! When we went up there a few days after the storm we fully expected to see it rolled end over end, or else in smithereens.

I am at the same job, doing much the same things as before, and liking it just well enough to hang on; or, rather, not disliking it quite enough to leave. If I had any bright ideas about what to leave it *for* I might actually leave. Nick, on the other hand, is coming up in the world a little. They have made him a sort of special salesman for Polaroid. That isn't really what it sounds. His job is to go about to various companies who are already interested or have inquired by mail, and give little informal lectures and demonstrations; or suggestions to people who are already using it and want to know more about it. It means he will skip around a good deal over the country—often by airplane, which he loves—will meet lots of people and sort of see the country a bit. I think it's fine, and so far he hasn't been away from home enough to make me object—much! By the way, did you see his comely mug in Life, Sept. 12, in connection with an article on Polaroid? And did you recognize him? (The young man whose rear view shows in the picture above is Nick's brother Howard.)

I had a pretty good summer, the only hitch being that N. and I had no vacation time which coincided at all. I had a month off, part of which I used in a very exciting and wonderful canoe trip with two friends in the wilds of Canada—when I say "wilds," I mean it, too; there was one stretch of four days when we didn't see or hear another human being, though we were on the move all the time. We fished, swam, sunned, and paddled and paddled and PADDLED from one lake to another, one river to the next, each one being lovelier and wilder than the one before. We camped on idyllic little islands and beaches.

Part of my vacation—almost a week, in fact—I spent with Follett and Margaret at Bradford. I had one heavenly day there, during which I helped F. get caught up on his gardening. We worked together till we dropped, and it was lovely. After that things kind of petered out. They were having a financial crisis at the time (just for a change!) and that was weighing them down. There was a bad spell when they thought they were going to be thrown out of the house for non-payment of rent; but that passed, and there seem to be articles coming in the Atlantic now. Margaret goes through occasional very bitter spells, and then recovers. The children seem to thrive. I hear that their house survived the storm all right, although the yard and garden are a tangled mess of fallen trees so that they don't know how to begin to clean it up. When M. wrote a few days ago, they had no light or water.

I have no news from Helen since the beginning of the summer, which is my fault, because I hardly ever write. I am going to tonight. In fact, I have long been saving out this night (with Nick in the vicinity of Philadelphia) to write a few letters to deserving and long-suffering friends, and this is the first of the series, but if I'm to get any others done I must stop this some time.

Well, let's have some bulletins from out your way. I think I'm the world's worst letter-writer but I think of you all a lot. Love to everyone, please.

   As ever,
   Bar

Merry Christmas, in case I don't get around to writing again this winter.

574 Huntington Ave.
Boston, Mass.
November 1, 1938

Dear A.D.R.:

The book arrived very promptly, containing a business-like little card which said "With compliments of the author." I happened to have a comparatively clear evening that day, or maybe the next, so I curled up and read the book through. It certainly was entertaining. I found that the excitement carried over so well from one chapter to the next that I simply couldn't put it down. It is certainly a very "different" story, too, and full of deserty flavor. Thanks so much for sending it. And may it sell, dear Lord!

What a thrilling trip of Phoebe's up Mt. Lyell! It must have been, just as she said, the most wonderful experience of her life. I have wandered around alone a good deal, and climbed a few New England mountains on my own, but nothing comparable with that; but I can well understand what it must have meant, both from the angle of tremendous excitement and adventure, and that of the overwhelming peace and satisfaction of it. I admire and envy her no end.

I think I have a few extra copies of that issue of Life—the one with Nick's beaming countenance in it. If I can find one I'll endeavor to ship it off to you. He is now well launched in the new aspects of his job, and loves it, as far as I can see. Nothing could please me more; and it really doesn't matter what sort of a job I have in the mean time. I don't really want *any* job; as soon as we can afford it I shall certainly cut down at least to part time. I haven't the slightest intentions of being any kind of a career woman. The place I'm at is dull, but the particular people I work for are very nice, both of them; I couldn't do better on that score. In fact, they really are more than "nice"; they are pretty special.

Last week-end I was in New York and saw Helen and Sabra. (Helen, too, has received your book, by the way; and I imagine you will be hearing from her soon, if you haven't already.) Well, I'm afraid I haven't anything very cheering to report from that quarter. Helen's health is none too good; she is having trouble with her eyes and her teeth, and occasional touches of arthritis (did you know that?—I don't think she's telling people anything about it). Added to that is the rather overwhelming fact that the Jewish book-sellers of New York City have boycotted her book. You see, although it hasn't a mention of politics in it, it does happen to be about the pleasanter aspects of life in the German countryside! I don't know what her plans are; I don't know what she's living on, but it is certainly disheartening to her and to all of us, after so many years of desperate struggle, to be no better off. She has lots of friends, though, and her book has made her more friends—among the few people who have seen it, that is.

Sabra—to present the brighter aspects of the picture—gets to be more and more of a corker every day. She is fifteen now, and getting a kick out of being just in between, neither a child nor an adult, so that she can, as she says, get away with anything at all. When I contrast her with myself at fifteen, I am likely to weep and gnash my teeth with envy. She is happy, well poised, gets along well with everybody, a good sport, and a grand person. Added to all that, she is a marvellous-looking kid. She has got her hair done with a permanent in the ends of it, so that it falls softly around her face and turns up at the ends—lovely. She gets invited everywhere, goes to lots of parties, and gets fun out of every situation; and I guess all in all she is a principal reason why H. still feels that life is worth living.

Needless to say I am worried about H., but that is a situation of such long standing that I seem to have gone a bit numb on it. You know how it is—you can't just remain at a high pitch of worry for years on end! The same with W. F. and Margaret. What odd and tragic parents I have! And how I enjoy Nick's calm poise, and his "success" in general, by way of contrast and variety!

There were things in your book over which I chuckled a good deal, which made me think very definitely indeed of a certain situation in California some years ago; especially when everybody got flurried and flustered, etc. I think that consciously or unconsciously you must have been harking back to that!

I have been writing this in the office between other things, but I imagine I should get some work done some time today, so will call this off. How I wish you could do as you suggested, and drop in on us in the new apartment. Is there any chance at all of your coming east again in the reasonably near future? Do try! I am still hoping that Nick will some time be allowed to take the weeks and weeks of vacation he is owed, and that we can have a grand long leisurely vacation *together*. Maybe then we could drive leisurely across the continent. How grand that would be! However, the wildest of pipe dreams could be no wilder, as far as prospects look right at the moment.

Well, best of luck and love to you all, and thanks again for sending the book.

As ever,
Bar

Mary Starks Whitehouse (1911-1979) was a student of Martha Graham and Mary Wigman. As a dance therapist she founded the "Authentic Movement" in the 1950s.

Linwood, Utah
June 27 (approx.) [1939]

Dearest ADR:

Have been waiting for a quiet hour or so in which to write to you for some time now, and I guess I have it. You will be puzzled at the place from which this letter comes, unless I told you about Bennington—which I don't think I did.

Well, in the first place, I hope and fully expect that I shall be seeing you not too long hence! I am to be in Oakland (to which I am now en route) from July 1 to Aug. 11, and after that driving home by a devious southern route which includes South Pasadena—or which I shall arrange so that it *does*. That means that we shall be bursting in upon you—if you are to be there and are as keen about the idea as I am—around Aug. 13 or 14 or so. Details later of course.

Now I'll explain a bit. I guess I told you in one of my rare letters that I was getting very much interested in modern dancing? That is the kind that grew out of the old "interpretive" dancing—the barefoot kind, varying all the way from the sublime to the ridiculous. I studied quite hard this winter with a marvellous young woman, Mary Starks, who has a studio of her own and who this winter started a small lay group called "The Dance Workshop Group," to which she asked me to belong. With this group Mary put on several demonstrations at clubs and colleges, which consisted of a short lecture by her, a couple of group dances, and two or three solos by herself. It all was such fun and so exciting and satisfying to me that I decided to study some more of it this summer. In fact I decided to take the summer courses at Mills College in Oakland, which is where we're now headed.

"We" in this case consists of Marjorie Houser, her young brother, age 16, and me. Marjorie is a wonderful girl, whom I adore, and who plays the piano for all Mary's dance classes, and writes the music for the dances. She is a marvellously talented kid, and a delightful personality as well. You will love her, and she you. I won't try to describe her any more, as I am hoping you will see her yourself. Enough to say that she is a real genius, with music in every bone and every nerve. She is not planning to study this summer, but is just going out for the ride. We are camping out, and she and her brother will continue to do that while I am in school.

Now about Linwood, Utah, and why we are here. It is a real honest-to-goodness sheep ranch, a marvellous place, in a sort of high valley, desert on one side, snow-capped mountains on the other. It belongs to the father of one of the girls in the dance group, Frances Smith. Frances Smith is going to Mills, too; and Marjorie and I had an invitation to stop at the ranch on the way out. We are staying through tomorrow. It is weird and fascinating country. We have been out on horseback once and are going again—God, I'm a lousy rider! Haven't done *any* of it since I was twelve, and then not much, and on an eastern saddle!

We have had a swell trip—have been up through the Tetons—the most beautiful country I've ever seen anywhere, have seen the sights of Yellowstone with all the other tourists, and, as I said, have camped out every night, except one when it was stormy and we took a cabin. It has been such fun that I almost hate to buckle down to business out at Mills—and dancing is hard work, too!

But the high point of this summer will be seeing you, and I hope you are around. You can write to me in care of Bennington School of the Dance, Mills College, Oakland, Cal. up to Aug 10 or thereabouts. Where is PAR this summer? If she is up in Yosemite Marjorie might look her up. And how are the Max-and-Elizabeth outfit? Tell me, do they still have any ties at all up in the desert, or is that completely severed since they were burnt out?

Speaking of desert, we have certainly seen a lot of it while driving through Wyoming. It affects me in various ways. Sometimes I love the wide-open sweep of it, like the sea. Sometimes the thought of so much barren waste fills me with horror. I can easily imagine going mad in it. The desert near here is the most interesting I have seen, with extraordinary rock formations of all shapes and colors, gnarled and twisted old cedar trees, thousands of little scuttling sand-colored animals, and incredible brilliant flowers—strangers to me, all of them. I remember Elizabeth's desert vaguely, as in a dream, and remember that it was very beautiful and high.

Write to me at Oakland and tell me how you are doing. I am so looking forward to seeing you. I still can't quite believe I'm on my way, but I'm going to act and plan as if it were all perfectly real!

As ever, with love,
Bar

Merce Cunningham was one of the 170 dance students at Mills College in 1939. He was spotted by one of the instructors, Martha Graham, who asked him to join her company in New York. John Cage, a former Mills faculty member, accompanied at least one recital on piano.

Mills College
Oakland, Calif.
July 9, 1939

Dearest ADR:

It was a joy to receive your lovely long letter. Now that I have had this answer from you, the whole project seems infinitely more real, more plausible. I am so glad you are going to be at home, and that there is room for us. As far as beds go, Marjorie and her brother are used to sleeping double—also M. and I. They also have friends in L. A. too, whom they may be looking up. We shan't be able to stay long, I'm afraid; but oh, the time we do stay will be very full!

I'm so glad P. is up in Yosemite. I don't know yet whether I shall be able to get there, though I certainly hope so; but M. will certainly look her up. So far M. and Lee have found Calif. distinctly an *expensive* place to camp. First they had to buy a tremendous ax (we had only a small one) and a whopping shovel in order to get a fire permit at all. Then, up at Lake Tahoe this week, they had to pay 50¢ a night just to pitch a tent in the State campground—they said the public ones were unspeakably overrun!

It would certainly be an unexpected turn, wouldn't it, if P turned out to be a nurse? Or a doctor? It's a shame though that such a pitiful accident had to occur. My half-sister Grace Follett, you know, is a nurse—graduated now and working at Mass. General Hospital. An odd direction for a Follett to turn in; but she is good at it and loves it and I think it is fine.

I am loving Mills College. The campus is perfectly beautiful, more like a rich man's estate than like any institution I ever saw. And we, being summer students—and pretty special at that!—are subject to no rules or regulations that even I could object to. The work is thrilling, as we have courses with several of the "big shots" of the modern dance. My "major" is with Hanya Holm, whom I have long admired.

Also it makes life pleasant for me because another girl from our little Boston group is out here too, with her room next to mine; on Sat. and Sun., when we have no classes, we practice technique together amid much hilarity. Also we are still hoping that our own Mary Starks, with whom we studied all winter, will come next week. We heard that she hurt her back slightly, which has postponed her coming. I am hoping to do such a lot of dancing next winter. I know it is the thing for me to be doing right now. There are all kinds of satisfaction in it for me. Of course in this outfit some of the ideas are crazy to me—such as building composition out of nothing or abstract movement with no feeling—but you can't hope to agree with everything, and I know I'm getting a wealth of valuable material.

I am sorry to hear that M. and E. are still going through a "stringent period." I think they have had far more than their share of stringency. And you? How are you making out? Pot still boiling? My whole family is still in its perpetually stringent state, of course. Nick is about the only one I know who has a job, likes it, expects to keep it, and is earning a modest living wage! If I can just hang on to him I ought to be O.K. Whether or not I can remains to be seen! This winter I had a bad spell, made a mess of things, and have some ground to recover!

I'll let you know later just when we'll be coming. School finishes the 11th of Aug., and I imagine we'll waste no time. I'm terrifically excited! I've a power of hard work, real sweat and blood, to get through first, however. In fact, I must get down to business and practice right now.

        Much love,
        Bar

Young America Dances, an eleven-minute film of 1939's Bennington School of Dance session, was produced and directed by Ralph Jester.

Bennington
Sun. Aug. 6 [1939]

Dear ADR:

Good news and bad news all in the same breath! I'm arriving *sooner* than I had thought and staying *longer*! The reason: I've acquired a beautiful charleyhorse which will keep me out of the running—out of the leaping, anyway, for this last week. So rather than hobble about and watch classes, I'm coming down to see you. We are taking off some time today, going to Sequoia for a couple of days, then to S. P. Should probably arrive Wed. evening, though there's nothing cut and dried about it.

If it's OK with you, we're planning to stay over the week-end. Marjorie and Lee have some good friends in L. A. with whom they want to spend some of their time, but I hope and intend to spend my time with you. So they will probably stay Wed. night and then move on Thur. or Fri. which will suit them and make less of a strain on you.

When we arrive, Marjorie will relate the details of how she tried to look up Phoebe when they were in Yosemite, but without success.

Yes, I know Opal Sneed slightly—a nice kid. Wish I'd known about her sooner, I'd have gone more out of my way to become acquainted. We work so hard around here that my own reaction is to withdraw from people between times. I guess I'm still sort of peculiar!

One of Nick's acquaintances—business acquaintances—lives in L. A., and I shall probably look him up some time. He has connections at one of the studios, so we might get taken through. For that matter, we are a good deal of a movie studio right here now. They are filming a "short" on life at Bennington! This has kept the campus in an uproar and classes very much disorganized for several days. I would have been in some of the large group dance things except for my charleyhorse! To put it mildly, I am quite annoyed!

However, it does mean I'll see Sequoia, and more of you than would have been possible, and that is certainly a bright side—a positively scintillating side!

        Much love,
        Bar

Till Wednesday!

And now another dramatic turn. While visiting Alice, Barbara received a letter from Nick saying he was unhappy with the marriage and wanted out. That letter has not survived. Barbara left for Boston by bus the next morning and sent Alice a postcard from Kansas City.

Sun. [August 13, 1939]
Kansas City

Dearest ADR:

    Well, here I am—about half way now and holding out very well. The busses are fine and I manage to get some sleep now and then. Am really feeling O. K. and well under control! Hang on to your thumbs for me. I can never thank you for your moral support, etc.

        Love,
        B.

Will write as soon as there is any news.

*   I don't know what happened in the spring, but Barbara did mention some trouble in her July letter to Alice: "This winter I had a bad spell, made a mess of things, and have some ground to recover!"*
*   Charles E. Dunlap was a young doctor living with his family on Longwood Avenue, not too far from Barbara's apartment.*

Thursday, Aug. 17 [1939]
574 Huntington Ave.
Boston

Dearest A.D.R.:

    Well, this is the day on which I promised a bulletin; so here it is, but it won't be satisfactory because there simply ain't no news! I haven't even SEEN the guy yet! Because he's in New York!

    I got home on schedule Tuesday night, after a trip which was of course pretty strenuous, and even horrible at times, but not as bad as I had expected, really. I managed to get some sleep, though not much; and I kept pretty well relaxed and calm and controlled, and busied myself with imaginary conversations which wouldn't have worked out, etc., etc. The last day was the tensest of all; I think that one day was longer than all the other four days and nights. It was so terrifically tense that I thought I would simply fly apart. But I'm pretty well put together, and I remained in one palpitating piece! When I got home I was shaking like a leaf, of course.

    There wasn't anybody home. At first that was a relief; I thought, well, I'll have time to take a bath and rest before he comes. Then I noticed, on investigating, that one of his bags was gone, and toothbrushes, etc. So then I really lost my head. After all that tension, not to see him, was just too much. So I got on the telephone, and telephoned everybody I could think of who might know. Everybody seemed to be out, but finally I located a Polaroid man, to whom I said I had just come home unexpectedly and had to get in touch with Nick at once. He said Nick was in New York, and would probably be back the next day (that was yesterday). I then tried to get him in New York at the hotel where this fellow said he might be staying; but no soap.

I was really a wreck by that time. Of course sleep was out of the question, in spite of not having had any to speak of for so long. Finally I got a very good friend, Charlie Dunlap, on the telephone. Besides being a friend, who already knew a little of the situation from last spring, he is a doctor. He came right over to me, bringing (a) three large, juicy and delectable hamburgers; (b) a bottle of whiskey; (c) some sleeping dope. Well, the combination of those things, plus a good talk with him, just fixed me up. I slept well, and woke up yesterday quite relaxed and almost confident and hopeful—a little scared still, of course, a little strained, but hopeful. I spent the day very slowly and quietly doing domestic things, and time passed fairly quickly. I read and listened to the radio, and got to sleep last night under my own power without benefit of dope.

Today someone from the office called up and left a message for Nick with me. Shortly thereafter Nick's brother called me up, having heard I was here. He is coming out to have supper with me tonight. He says Nick will *probably* be back tonight! So you see I won't have any real news for another couple of days, but I'll let you know of course just as soon as I do.

You were wonderful to me; you certainly did a lot to pull me through what was, and is, the worst thing that ever happened to me. I'm sorry it had to be you to suffer again with my troubles; but I'm also confoundedly grateful from a selfish point of view that you were around. The time we had together B.C. (Before Crisis) was the happiest of the entire summer; and it was delightful to see E. and M. again and that marvellous magic house, which I do so much hope they can keep.

I shan't write any more now, but don't worry too much about me, because I think the patient is doing rather nicely, thank you. Of course the real show-down will tell the story, and then I'll tell it to you.

       Yours with love,
       Bar

Charlie said I was *lucky* that he wasn't home that night. Though I realized the importance of keeping under control, I doubt if I could have done it then. Now I feel pretty sure I can. I guess on the whole it *was* lucky.

574 Huntington Ave.
Boston, Mass.
August 22, 1939

Dear A.D.R.:

This is going to be a hard letter to write, and a confused-sounding one, full of ups and downs. Well, that's the way things are, like a giant roller-coaster. However, I must send some sort of report, with a promise of more later—and, I hope, more definite.

Nick got home from New York finally on Friday morning (I arrived, you will remember, Tuesday night). During that interval I did nothing at all except a little house-cleaning and some reading. I don't know where that piece of time went. It just disappeared.

The first thing we did was go away for the week-end in Vermont, where Nick had had a previous invitation. Well, Alice, all I can say is that what we conjectured was truer than true—I mean, that about the hell only beginning when I got home—not ending. I am glad I had thought it over so hard. I am glad I realized the importance of self-control. You see, the thing is really worse than I had thought possible. There IS somebody else. Just how serious I don't know, and I'm not asking any questions. That's part of the self-control. I haven't uttered one single reproach, or anything that could be construed as one. I've just dug my nails into my palms and held on, and held on, till now I think I'm getting to be quite a woman of iron and steel.

Well, I think there is hope for my side—some hope. I know it will be a long, patient process that will take all my strength and all my intelligence for a great many months. I think it is worth it, and I am going to make the fight. I don't blame him in the least. He really thought I didn't care; only, instead of saying anything about it so that I could have done something about it before, he just kept quiet and everything slid and slid. But it's really my fault; I had it coming to me, I know.

I think I've persuaded him to give me my chance. He is a very kind person, really, and hates to hurt people. He hated to write that letter; that's why it sounded so awful. I think that, if I can really prove that I'm different, why maybe things will work out. He still doesn't quite believe, as he says, that a leopard can change its spots! He thinks that in a month things will be all wrong again. So I say, at least let me have that month! I think I'll get it, and I think I can win if I've got the strength. I think he is a steady enough person, and a kind enough person, and also enough of an easy-going person, so that he won't go making drastic plunges if he doesn't have to; and if I can make a pleasant sort of life for him, I think he'll hang on. That's what I'm banking on, and I'm putting heart and soul into all the little things.

Here's one thing that's pretty hopeful—although there's an out to it, too. He has turned me loose to find an apartment. Of course we don't move till October, and he has plenty of time to say "nix" later on and cancel everything; still, he has started me looking, and I take what encouragement I can out of that. In lots of ways he is being terribly difficult, of course; but you see he's going through hell, too. I know that and can understand.

So that's the situation. My young doctor friend, Charlie Dunlap who came over to see me that awful first night, has stood by and encouraged me. I don't know whether I told you he gave me some sleeping stuff. Ever since Nick got back I've had to take it every night. The days I can stand, because they are sort of full of little things; but the nights I could never stand without some kind of help in achieving oblivion! My appetite has picked up a bit, though, I'm glad to say. For several days I ate almost nothing at all. But nature will win on these things; eventually you get hungry.

I'm glad you saw something of Marjorie. She is a grand person. She should be home soon, if she arrives according to schedule. Today, I reckon, or tomorrow. I haven't even called up Mary Starks yet, but shall do so soon.

Thinking it all over, I believe I have slightly more than an even chance, and I think that the scales are tipping in my favor, slightly, slowly, ever so slowly. I've got to believe that, so I do! So I can't say to you "Don't worry about me" because I know you will. If I can honestly send any really good news I'll do so just as soon as I can, you can bank on that!

I had a letter from Grace waiting for me. She has found herself a good job for the winter, teaching practically everything at a small hospital in Arlington. *And* she writes that the Folletts have now acquired a place of their own in Bradford, Vermont, near where they were living before; which sounds perfectly entrancing, and as though their affairs were, for the moment, on the up-beat. Also they are "expecting" again!!!!!

That letter you forwarded to me, Alice, was an identical copy of That Letter. He sent one to Bennington, too, you see—making quite sure I'd get it! He said "Tear it up" which I took as another slightly hopeful sign.

You'll be glad to know that the trouble in my leg seems to be completely gone now, so that I expect to get back to my dancing very soon. That will be a joy and a relief.

I'll be out there again, you can bet your life, and under happier circumstances, and I'll find Phoebe if it's the last thing I do!

       Yours with much love,
       Bar

P. S. Ha, ha!

574 Huntington Avenue
Boston, Mass.
August 28, 1939

Dear A.D.R.:

Thanks so much for copying for me part of Phoebe's letter. In regard to that horrible accident—well, since they are all here, and relatively in one piece, there isn't much to be said, I suppose. It certainly gave me some shudders to read about it, though. One doesn't known whether to be absolutely horrified that such a thing happened, or just plain damn glad it wasn't worse. I find myself a mixture of the two feelings. The climb sounded wonderful. I suppose the moral to be derived, if any, is that you just *mustn't* drive when you are so bushed. These machines that man has made will conquer him yet. Some people I know, when they are as tired as that, make it a rule to pull up by the side of the road and snatch a little sleep; even a few minutes sometimes does the trick.

I will hastily make a progress report on my situation—or, rather, my Situation. Right now I'm on an up-beat, so to speak, so I shall quickly write and mail this letter before the next down! We are just back this morning from a week-end that really was very pleasant, considering. We sailed, swam, had a party with some friends, and explored quite a lot of Cape Cod, alone together, *looking for some nice country in which some time to have a summer place.* Of course, whether I am included in that pleasant picture, or somebody else, is an unknown quantity; but I was at least there for the exploration!

We talked a good deal about things, and at one point the conversation got to a point where it was logical for me to ask right out whether he *wanted* to make a go of things. I had had the feeling up till then that he definitely did not want to. So imagine my amazement, my almost hysterical delight, when he said yes, he wanted to make a go of it. Right away he qualified it, of course. He said: "Don't get too excited about that; I'm not sure that I *can.*" I said if he *wanted* to that was more than half the battle; with both of us wanting it so much, and pulling as hard as possible, I don't see how there can be any failure, really. Well, Alice, what he said gave me enough heart to keep up the struggle. I had hit a very low point just before that—a point at which it just seemed impossible to keep it up any longer. Now I feel that I can; and I feel that if I handle it right for the next difficult few weeks, or maybe months, I can still win this game.

Things are far from fixed, you understand, but they are improving a little. This morning, when he left to go to work, he gave me a sort of rough pat, which is absolutely the first gesture of affection of any kind that has come my way! I still don't know how much of a situation I have to cope with in regard to this other person. I still have no idea who it is, how much he has seen of her, how far the affair has really gone, whether he is still seeing her at all, or how it stands. I know absolutely nothing, and I still refuse to ask any questions. Marjorie (she is now home, after a terrific trip, and has talked with Nick once about the thing) has an idea that the other person may be trumped up—that he might have simply set his heart on our separating, and thought that telling me that might send me hurtling off in disgust or rage. He apparently talked to her a little about this situation, and she claims he didn't sound a bit convincing when it came to this mysterious person. It would be lovely to believe something like that; it is a great temptation. But I have resolutely made up my mind that I have something pretty desperate to face in that respect; I am sort of disciplining myself to believe just about the worst possible, so that if ever I find out it *wasn't* that bad, the discovery will just be a relief. Well, I just don't know, and I have no way of knowing. Nick is the kind of person who may very well *never* tell me just what it was all about; and if he will only come back to me I don't much care anyway. That again is absolutely proof—to me at least—that I am a radically changed person. I used to be full to overflowing with silly little petty jealousies. Now that the *real* thing has come up, while of course I feel terribly hurt, nevertheless any feeling of jealousy I might have seems to be completely lost in the bigger thing—which is simply that I want him back!

I think maybe I could teach Helen a thing or two or three at this point! I wonder if maybe she could not have won her game, if she had played it cautiously and quietly. She had fourteen years and two children to back up her side; I have only five years and no children, and even those five years seem to be exerting a certain pull right now! (Don't mind me—I know it's too much too soon to crow, and I'm not really a bit confident, yet—just a little more hopeful.)

You ask if Nick was surprised to find me home. I don't think he was. He first heard about it, as luck would have it, at the office. You see he came home from New York on the sleeper, and went straight to the office. There of course he heard it from his brother, whom I had seen, and from other people whom I had called when I had tried to locate Nick before. He came home that day at lunch time. (That was when I first heard about what I was up against.) No, I don't think he was surprised. He even acted as though he thought I'd been a little dumb not to wire him when I was coming! I think he realized that letter would affect me rather like a stick of dynamite!

I'll keep you posted, of course. Don't be surprised if the next bulletin sounds down-hearted. I know this is going to be a long, slow job—almost intolerably so, I fancy; and it will not be a steady climb, either; it will have ups and downs. I'm due for a good down pretty soon, I guess!

The other day, for the first time, I did a little practicing. I'm a little worried about my physical condition; I get tired terribly easily, and am afraid I've lost a lot of what I gained this summer in strength and ability; however, I shall try patiently to build myself up again, and I don't imagine Mary Starks will be calling on me much before October, so I have a little time.

I'm glad Max thinks I'm somebody now. I guess if I live through this I might be!

There's another encouraging thing that I haven't told you, because it's so intangible. A change has come over Nick, a little, in the last day or two. He *looks* a little different, more natural, less strained. He *moves* more in the old easy manner—not harshly, abruptly, angrily, as at first. And he *sounds* different—whether he's talking to me or to somebody else when I'm around, his voice sounds more natural. He's obviously suffering, obviously puzzled, and looks pretty downcast a good deal of the time; but the tortured note, and the tortured look, the terrible strain, the angry glowering, have pretty much disappeared. I think that means a lot, and it bolsters me up, too.

We have talked quite a lot about *my* future. This can be interpreted either favorably or unfavorably. Nick is very anxious for me to drop the Board job and get myself something in its place that I really like and that is interesting. In other words, he wants me to do the job with Mary, and another part-time one as well, if I can find one I like. Whether that is just his way of easing me gradually on to my own feet, I don't really know. It might be, but it sounds more like genuine concern for my own interests and happiness. He wants to see me live about as fully as possible. I say: "But how about meals, house-keeping, etc." Well, he says he'd rather see me doing an interesting job, in which we could afford to have somebody in to do house-work. It apparently doesn't mean as much to him as I thought it did, to have me personally doing it. I had thought that it was in that, among other things, that I had gone wrong, but apparently not. This leaves me with mixed feelings. I would be perfectly happy to do as he suggests on that; on the other hand, that makes it a little less clear to me where I went wrong before; I'm a little less sure of my ground. I feel that maybe the holes into which I fell are still uncharted after all!

All this remains to be seen. I'm spreading out the whole confused picture before you as it unrolls. It doubtless will go through many fluctuations and perhaps complete changes. This is just how it stands as of today!

My best love to Phoebe, and congratulations to both you and her on a nastily narrow escape which I don't like to think about.

   Much love,
   Bar

In October, Barbara and Nick moved to a new apartment on a quiet street in Brookline. Barbara says that she wrote to Alice on September 11th; if so, I think that letter may be lost. (Speaking of lost letters, I've been told that the next one has gone astray from the Columbia archive. It was there when I visited in 2012.)

48 Kent Street, Brookline

48 Kent Street
Brookline, Mass.
November 4, 1939

Dear ADR:

I'm sorry you should have been caused to worry by me, when heaven knows you've had enough to worry about right at home! I'm glad E is coming along all right—but what a shocking experience—just as shocking as Phoebe's automobile crash. I *do* agree with you that the Russell family seem prone to accidents. I guess it's because they live so fully and have no fear and no caution! And I think they are right. And they take the consequences gallantly.

As for me. Have I really not written to you since September 11? That is shocking. Well, the above is the new address. It's a very big, old-fashioned apartment, with two fireplaces and a full-sized kitchen. Nick's brother is rooming with us now, until he gets married, in January some time. Yes, I'm working, sometimes half-time, sometimes full time; and I'm dancing too; the dancing will go on until Christmas. After that I don't know what I'm going to do in a dancing line. I must get some additional training somewhere, and so far I don't know where.

But that isn't what you really want to know, of course. In my last letter I told you things were going well, and I thought they were. They continued to go well for a time—at least I thought so, and I was happy, and decided that the worst part of the ordeal was over. But that was too easy. No such luck! I don't know what to say now. On the surface things are terribly, terribly calm, and wrong—just as wrong as they can be. I am trying—we are both trying. I still think there is a chance that the outcome will be a happy one; but I would have to think that anyway, in order to live; so you can draw any conclusions you like from that!

Marjorie said the other day that she was thinking of you and had owed you a letter for a long time and would be writing one of these days. I don't see much of her these days. She is very busy, and having a lot more dates, etc., than last winter. She dashes in town to play for the dance group, and then dashes away again, usually before I am even dressed! She is having a fine fling for herself, and I'm very glad. I'd like one too, but don't quite know how to go at it, under the circumstances!

Best love to you. The reason I haven't written so long is that I hate to write when things are just up in the air—loose, kind of. I keep thinking Something will happen—must! But anyway, I'll try to do better from now on.

       As ever,
       Bar

LIFE WITH NICK (1932–1939)

And that was the last letter Barbara wrote to Alice, and the last letter she wrote to anyone—as far as the archive at Columbia goes, at least.

According to Nick, Barbara walked out of the apartment in the early evening of Thursday, December 7th, and no one seems to know where she went or what happened to her next. According to Harold McCurdy, she left with about thirty dollars and the shorthand notes she had taken that day at the Missions Council on Beacon Street. He almost certainly obtained that information from Helen, who would have gotten it from Nick.

The last known photograph of Barbara

6

GONE

On December 21st, Nick informed the Brookline police department that his wife was missing. Waiting two weeks doesn't surprise me—Barbara was a free spirit. He asked that there be no publicity. After the California episode of 1929 that doesn't surprise me either, but it won't have made finding his wife any easier. Had the local newspapers been notified I'm sure they would have published an article about the former child prodigy, probably on the front page with a photograph.

Nineteen weeks after Barbara's disappearance, on April 18, 1940, Nick again contacted the Brookline police, this time requesting publicity. On April 22nd, Officer McCracken sent out a teletype to eight states:

> Brookline. 139 4-22-40 3:38PM McCracken Missing from Brookline since Dec. 7, 1939, Barbara Rogers, married, Age 26, 5-7, 125, fair complexion, black eyebrows, brown eyes, dark auburn hair worn in a long bob, left shoulder slightly higher than right. Occasionally wears horn rimmed glasses.

Mentioning that it was Barbara Newhall Follett who was missing—not the unknown Barbara Rogers—might have helped. Any follow-up the police may have made turned up no result.

A year later my grandfather wrote To a Daughter, One Year Lost, an anonymous letter published in the May 1941 issue of the Atlantic (you can read it on Farksolia—it's an extraordinary thing). His version of December 7th differs to McCurdy's, suggesting that she disappeared after work instead of leaving the apartment in the evening. (Was that actually what happened, or did he misremember what he'd been told? I would guess the latter.)

> She disappeared one afternoon between the office in which she worked and her apartment, and not even her husband has heard from her for ten whole nights and days. It is preposterous that such a one should just drop out of existence for that length of time, as if she were one of the indistinguishable crowd. Could Helen Hayes be lost for ten days without a trace? Could Thomas Mann? Could

Churchill? And now it is getting on toward forty times ten days, and the thing four thousand times as preposterous, as ever after a twelvemonth.

According to his letter in the Atlantic, *my grandfather believed Barbara was alive and had once again chucked her current life (as in Los Angeles in 1929 and New York in 1932). He spends a good part of the letter lecturing Barbara about her decision.*

[...] I know what you will say: that you have asked only to be yourself, and that being yourself demanded release from a set of conditions that thwarted and wasted and compromised you until they had become unendurable. Well, every creature has to be his own judge of what is endurable, his own discoverer of what he was meant to be. But let me remind you of this: You were a great person before, whether or no. You were born one. It is pretty safe to say that no one ever questioned that who has known you, or read those still radiant early books of yours, or received your letters, or followed you through much of either the work that you treated as play or the play that you sometimes made such hard work of. Confined, repressed, and stultified as you may have come to seem to yourself, you were to all others a very synonym of generous freedom, the ardent spirit, the courage to be oneself. Can you, in whatever your new surroundings and relations may be, remake yourself into a being more satisfactory to yourself than you used to be to the rest of us? If you can, you are indeed struck by the lightning of creative genius, and all the moral probabilities, the natural law of conduct, are suspended in your behalf.

He goes on to tell his daughter what it takes to be a good partner in marriage...

And here I must say some candid words about the marriage that you have yourself slipped away from — words that I could never have said unasked if you had not by your own act made the extreme, the ultimate comment on your five years with X.

You will hardly have come to the age of twenty-six without discovering at least some important aspects of the fundamental paradox that a normal woman cannot be herself without giving herself. Whatever she holds back, on some theory of saving her independence, her freedom of initiative, her selfhood, she holds back first of all from herself. There are two-person relationships — parenthood, marriage, all friendship worth the name — that by their very nature constantly ask you to throw yourself wholeheartedly into serving the other person's necessities, just because they seem to be his necessities. It becomes your prime necessity to see that his are served. If you fail, you do not merely cheat him of the service: you dam your own deliberately chosen outlet of self-expression and so cheat yourself. To carry into wedlock the premarital valuation of oneself is to be no more than nominally wife or husband.

The Columbia archive is silent regarding any further effort made by Nick to find Barbara, and it appears that Helen left the matter entirely in his hands—despite his filing for divorce on December 14, 1943 (it was granted three weeks later) and marrying Anne Bradley (1912-2008) soon after. Paragraph 3 of that Libel for Divorce states:

(3) That during said intermarriage, the Libelant has always conducted himself as a dutiful and faithful husband, yet the said Libelee, wholly regardless of her marital duties and obligations, has for a period of more than three years together been absent and not been heard of, in that said Libelee disappeared from Brookline, Massachusetts on December 7, 1939, and the Libelant has had no word or information concerning her existence or whereabouts since that date despite frequent inquiries directed to the parents of the Libelee and persons who would naturally be expected to know of her whereabouts or existence.

Those inquiries weren't exactly frequent, according to Helen. At almost seventy and with heart trouble, she wrote to the Boston police department late in 1952.

11 November 1952
Edward W. Fallon
Superintendent, Police
Boston, Massachusetts

Dear Sir:
    The New York Police, through the Bureau of Missing Persons, have suggested my writing to you for information that may be in your files concerning the disappearance on December 7, 1939 of my daughter Barbara Follett Rogers. The case remains unsolved.
    At that time, my daughter was married to Nickerson Rogers, their address being, I believe, Charles Street, Boston, or, possibly, 48 Kent Street, Brookline.
    The problem of Barbara Rogers' disappearance from the Boston area was left to her husband. I, myself, was living in New York where I was working and supporting my younger daughter of High School age. Therefore, I trusted Mr. Rogers to keep me informed of any

developments that transpired through his own personal efforts and through those of the police. I was led to believe that the police of both Boston and Brookline had been informed of the circumstances.

Only rarely, perhaps two or three times did I receive any word from Mr. Rogers, always to the same effect—that my daughter was still missing. No details concerning his efforts or those of the police were mentioned.

In 1943, Mr. Rogers divorced my daughter. He remarried and for several years now he has been teaching in the Loomis School at Windsor, Connecticut. I still trusted him to keep me informed of any news concerning my daughter's disappearance, especially because, over the last five years my own activities, due to a cardiac condition, have been rigidly curtailed.

On August 20, 1952 I wrote to Mr. Rogers asking that he give me a complete summary of what he himself had done and what the police had done to locate my daughter. Still no reply.

Because of the long silences without news of any sort, my trust in Mr. Rogers has been changing, by degrees, into doubt and uncertainty. Did he ever report the case to the police, I wonder, and what definite efforts have been made to find my daughter?

Consequently, I am turning directly to you and asking that you, if you will be so kind, search your files and report to me any information found there. Perhaps, if your files contain nothing, you will be good enough to get in touch with the Brookline police and ask that their files be looked into for this particular case.

Your cooperation will be very much appreciated.

       Very truly yours,
       Helen Follett

Acting Superintendent James Daley replied to the above, providing the April 22, 1940 teletype and saying that he would forward Helen's letter to Chief Tonra in Brookline.

Department of Police
Town of Brookline
Massachusetts
November 19, 1952

Dear Mrs. Follett:

Relative to your request for information regarding your daughter, Barbara Follett Rogers, who disappeared on December 7, 1939, I have checked the records and find that on December 21, 1939 Nickerson Rogers, 48 Kent Street, Brookline, officially reported his wife missing.

At that time Mr. Rogers did not desire publicity. However, on April 18, 1940 Mr. Rogers, in a letter to the Department, requested publicity and on April 22, 1940 a teletype notice #139 was sent out. The teletype is carried through the system to 8 different states.

In addition to the contacts with the husband we received a letter from Ruth Isabel Seabury, Secretary of Education, American Board of Commissioners for Foreign Missions located at that time at 14 Beacon Street, Boston. Miss Seabury enclosed a 2-page letter giving a description, habits, and characteristics of your daughter, of whom she spoke very highly.

Notwithstanding the information which went out to 8 states, nothing has been heard regarding your daughter.

>Sincerely,
>James W. Tonra
>Chief of Police

404 West 116th St. Apt. 21
New York City
November 23, 1952

Dear Chief Tonra:

Please accept my sincere thanks for your letter concerning the disappearance of my daughter, Barbara Follett Rogers.

Being entirely unfamiliar with the processes of law and police routine, may I ask you personally to suggest what means can be taken to uncover some of the details that I feel must have been going on during these twelve years. In other words, it seems incredible to me that my daughter's husband failed to turn the country upside down to find his wife. Certainly, over the years, I have taken it for granted that such a course was being pursued.

Recently, however, I have begun to have some misgivings. From your record, it would seem that no report since April 1940 has reached your office. That makes me wonder what effort Mr. Rogers ever made.

As my letter to Superintendent Fallon in Boston explained, I myself am unable to get any report from Mr. Rogers. As late as August, 1952 I wrote to Mr. Rogers asking him to please send me a résumé of his search from the beginning. I appealed to him as a father who might imagine his own grief were he to lose one of his children, and of the intolerable burden of not knowing whether that child were dead or alive.

Since three months have now elapsed without any answer, I am wondering if your department can get this information both for your police record and for me, either through writing or through direct contact with the Windsor police who might interview Mr. Rogers. Such information is necessary, it seems to me, before anything further can be done in solving this mysterious case.

Thank you for sending me word of Miss Seabury. She is at present in Africa. I am in touch with her office in the hope of locating some young woman who worked there with my daughter. Barbara was an excellent editorial secretary (as well as author of two books) and I feel sure she could find work to support herself.

However, there is always foul play to be considered, the chance of a young girl's being shanghaied to South America, perhaps, or the chance of a mental breakdown and hospitalization. Such things, you will agree, are bound to occur to a mother left in this state of doubt and fear.

Consequently, whatever you can suggest that may help in a renewed attempt to find out what happened to my daughter, will be deeply appreciated.

    Very truly yours,
    Helen Follett

Department of Police
Town of Brookline
Massachusetts
December 12, 1952

Dear Mrs. Follett:

I'm sorry that I am unable to furnish any additional information regarding your daughter. At the time of her disappearance Miss Seabury forwarded a letter to the Boston Police Department, a copy of which was forwarded to this Department, and I quote a paragraph in that confidential letter:

"He and Barbara are to the best of my knowledge and belief very happily married, but for some time had had a very sharp difference of opinion on a matter which both regarded as of fundamental importance. Barbara had seemed very unhappy about it especially in her last day at home. She evidently decided to go her own way but her husband, hopeful of her return, has hesitated to do anything to distress her, especially if publicity were involved, for fear she might not return at all. He did, however, on December 22, report her absence to the Brookline police and at their request, I believe, went to the Morgue on Charles Street in Boston. No clues were raised there, however."

Apparently, at that time Mr. Rogers was cooperative, but no clues were discovered as to the whereabouts of your daughter.

>Sincerely,
>James W. Tonra
>Chief of Police

Next Helen tried the Department of Social Security, who were unhelpful in their letter of December 15, 1952:

We regret we cannot grant your request. The records of the Social Security Administration are confidential and have been designed solely to insure proper identification of an individual's account and to assist in adjudicating a claim. However, these records do not show whether an individual is deceased unless a claim for survivors' benefits has been filed and her death established.

Helen also wrote to Sarah Medlicott at the American Board of Commissioners for Foreign Missions and was visited by her colleague, Hugh Vernon White, who had also worked with Barbara. After the visit she thanked Mrs. Medlicott on December 11th.

How can I ever thank you for sending on a copy of my letter to Mr. White! My pleasure in seeing him—especially cherished since he was so busy with committees—was unbounded. Just our little talk gave me an assurance that he had a friendly feeling toward Barbara and that he would assist me in every way possible in my search (almost hopeless, I realize) for information about her disappearance.

A week after Barbara's 39th birthday—fourteen years after her disappearance—Helen wrote to Nick. I don't know whether or not he replied. My guess is not.

404 West 116th Street
New York 27, N.Y.
11 March, 1953

Dear Nick:
  I can't understand why you didn't stop in to see me on Saturday last. I was here all day, and Sabra says you not only telephoned her but also stopped in at her house at eleven P.M. before she had returned. Why, I ask again, did you not take the trouble to see me? Especially, I might add, since you have owed me an answer to my letter of August 20, 1952.
  All this silence on your part almost looks as if you had something to hide concerning Barbara's disappearance. I hope not since I have

always trusted you to the point of believing you were doing all you could to solve the mystery. Such a mystery is not something you nor anyone else among Bar's friends, can ever forget. That you can forget the grief of a mother in these circumstances adds, I must say, to the mystery.

In the meantime, since I received no word from you, I've been in touch with the Brookline Police, and with Bar's office on Beacon Hill, and have received friendly cooperation from both sources. You cannot believe I shall sit idle during my last few years and not make whatever effort I can to find out whether Bar is alive or dead, whether, perhaps, she is in some institution suffering from amnesia or nervous breakdown.

The letters you promised Sabra we would both like to have. I've been urged to write Barbara's tragic story, and if I am able, I shall do so.

I hope you will get around to answering my letter of last August. Kindness to others is often a rewarding experience to ourselves.

  Sincerely,
  Helen

By this time Helen must have felt that her daughter was lost forever. Was she dead? If not, could she really have been so cruel as to leave her family and friends unaware that she was still living? Or was she alive but incapacitated in a psychiatric institution, as Helen seemed to fear?

Alice Russell thought Barbara, if living, could not be so cruel. Helen had sent her a poem for Christmas 1948, which she had written while visiting St. Croix in May 1947:

> Where are you, child of the mountains and of the sea?
> Did you climb the heights
> To reach for the sun?
> Did you sail over the horizon
> To touch a lonely star?
> You who created for all of us a shining world
> of freedom and of radiance in words of
> startling beauty,
> Did you try to find that land?
> Did you yearn for its beauty, its freedom?
>
> 'Tis well for you, my precious one. But for me,
> your mother?
> You left me chained to fear and awful imaginings,
> To a constant searching on

Busses, street cars, subways, trains, ships, planes — for
    Your face among the millions,
The deep brown eyes, the hair, copper-tinted in
    the sun,
  the puckish nose and laughing mouth,
You left me chained to despair and to a fading hope.

Come back, child of the mountains and of the sea!
    My eyes are tired, my heart weary with all the
      searching,
Come back, and let me look into your face again, and
    stroke your hair,
    Let me hear your laughter once more — before
I must heed the wanderer's call and be on my way —
    forever.

(Dictated to Elizabeth)
2001 Marengo Avenue
Pasadena, Cal.
January 5, 1949

Dearest Helen,

    I was so happy to receive your letter which came to me straight a few days before Christmas. It was too late then to write you the letter I wanted to, so I postponed it until the furore of Christmas should be over. But the furore proved to be greater than anticipated, I adding to it myself by breaking my right arm on the morning before Christmas—if you will believe it, by *slipping on the ice [...]*

    So any letter-writing has to be postponed for some six weeks. But I cannot bear you to think I did not receive your letter, or that I am not thinking of you! All you say about yourself and Bar goes to my heart, and I could hardly read your lines of poetry (they *were* poetry!) without tears.

    I will write more about Bar when I can write myself. But I want you to know that I do not believe, and have not believed for years, that she is still alive. It is impossible that she would have treated you, and Sabra, and all whom she loved, with cruelty deliberate, for so long a time. She had no quarrel with anybody but Nick, and what she did I believe she did out of an impulse against him. That seems to me possible; anything else does not. And Nick lost the chance of finding out what happened by his long long delay in reporting her disappearance. It is true that I wrote to Anderson, but the letter came back. I have really no idea she went to him. And by this time, all trails must be lost, and I see nothing that could be done.

I am glad that Sabra is near you, and that you have the joy of sharing in her life, and seeing her little son.

Phoebe has two little boys, and she and they live with me. I will tell you more about us all when I write. In the meantime, I think of you with great love and great sympathy, and hope you will grow stronger, and as you grow stronger, find your load lighter.

   Love always, from
   ADR

Around the same time, Helen wrote to Barbara's old Chief, Andrew Burt.

February 8, 1949.

Dear Mrs. Follett,

I received your letter all right last week, but was very sorry to get the news that it contained. It is so many years since I saw Barbara or yourself, and I had imagined that you would all be settled down somewhere living happily.

It must be around fifteen years if not more, since I saw Barbara. She came on board the "Lady Nelson" one day in Boston, there was a young man along with her, and asked to be shown around. We all had tea together, and she was talking about a walking tour through Spain. It seemed to me at the time that that was one of the things that they might talk about but never do. I cannot remember the name of the young man who was along with her, but it may have been the man she married.

That was the only time I saw her after the trip to Tahiti, and it is so long ago that I cannot remember whether it was before or after that that you visited the ship. That must have been before Magic Portholes was published.

I am very sorry that I am unable to help you in any way, as I can well understand how much of a worry it must be, just not knowing what can have happened. And there are some aches that time does not seem to ease. But I think you will know that I would have been the last person in the world to have advised Barbara to leave her home, or to sever her connections with her mother, even if she had come to me for advice. But since that time she visited the ship, I have had no news about her at all, she made no attempt to communicate with me and I didn't even know that she had got married. [...]

   With best wishes,
   Yours sincerely,
   Andrew Burt

The Columbia archive doesn't have any of the letters that Helen wrote to Alice, but there are several from Alice to Helen—a second from 1949 and others from 1956-59.

I'm not so sure that Anderson and Barbara parted on bad terms: see Anderson's friendly letter of ca. March 1935.

2001 Marengo Ave.
South Pasadena, Calif.
Dec. 22, 1949

[...] What I am enclosing in this will be a sad Christmas remembrance, but I think you will want to have it just the same. It is Barbara's last letter to me—you see in it she was definitely thinking of the future. And it was written, as you will see, not many days before her disappearance, when for some reason, she was suddenly overtaken by despair. You know, Helen, I have always felt that Nick *could*, if he had wanted to, have told us more about his last talk with her and given us perhaps some clue. But it is no use to think of that—now. The dark waters closed over her long ago. I *know* it is an everlasting pain to you—I know from what is in my own heart—and there seems no way to ameliorate, only to live with it. It will only be by the grace of Heaven—and I don't believe much in the grace of Heaven—or some turn of sheer luck, that we will learn more. Of course you have thought of Anderson, but as Barbara told me and you probably know, he and she parted on bad terms, and I can't believe that under the circumstances she would go to him. Also, Anderson was a friend of yours and not likely to be a party of such lasting intolerable wrong to you. [...]

2001 Marengo Ave.
South Pasadena, Calif.
Feb. 26, 1956

[...] I know—who better—the grief that underlies your life, and always will. Do you know, Helen, this last year, after such a long time of thinking otherwise, I have had the conviction that Barbara *is* alive. Not long ago, on a bus, I saw from the back a head of glorious red hair on a girl. A thrill ran through me and when she turned I realized with a shock that I really expected it to be Bar. I don't believe I can again believe she is dead, no matter what my mind tells me. She may so easily be living a satisfying life somewhere, the circles of which would seem best to her not to break. We may never know, but, Helen dear, let us not believe that her life was broken off, that she still goes on. [...]

In 1956, Helen was thinking about publishing Lost Island *with Alice's help. Alice thought it better to let the next generation decide. (I would love to see it published, along with Barbara's other prose and her two long-out-of-print books, and maybe one day they will. As of this writing there are two self-published editions of* Lost Island *for sale online—the second one copy and pasted from Farksolia. Whether or not the story is in the public domain is questionable, since we don't know when Barbara died, or even if she's dead at all—she could still be living at 101. Stranger things have happened!)*

2001 Marengo Ave.
South Pasadena, Calif.
June 30, 1956

[...] I never saw any parts of Bar's "Lost Island." It was, of course, her last piece of writing; but I know she was working on it even while she was with me. It makes me *ache* to think of it, and I believe it would be almost impossible for me to judge it dispassionately. The image of Bar would get between me and it—as I am sure happens with you. That is just our personal side of any attempt to deal with it, and it might be overcome all other things being equal. But they are *not*. Here to me is the really important angle—that work belongs to Bar. If she is alive it would be a piece of impertinence to print it, with, as would have to happen, mention of her tragedy, however delicately done. If she is dead, it would seem an exploitation of that tragedy for commercial purposes, and I could not bear to do that. (Incidentally and less importantly I am not sure I am fit or able to the task.) I would be hamstrung at the start—as I believe you, too, Helen, really are, or you would not want my help. Put the manuscript away—in a safe deposit box?—and wait. If she lives, Bar may yet come back to us, and we will be glad, then, that we safeguarded her secret and her tragedy. If she never does, then let the next generation decide, if it's worth revealing, in itself, on its own merits.

Oh, my dear, I hope I have not hurt you, that you will understand how I feel! If you do not, I cannot make myself clearer. But I bank on your understanding.

It's a lovely, tempting picture of our working together on a manuscript of Bar's, but everything within me tells me that it *just won't do*.

[...] It is the last ironic touch if the W.F.s have separated. Did you have that from a reliable source? Certainly they must have had hard sledding for years and perhaps W. F. went off to find paying work elsewhere. I wish them no hard luck. I am only sorry for the children. [...]

My grandparents separated in 1947, but never divorced. As Alice supposed, my grandfather had left his family to look for work. He returned to New York, the city he had hated so in the 1920s, and remained there until dying alone in his boarding house room on January 7, 1963, where he was trying to finish Modern American Usage *for Arthur Wang.*

2001 Marengo Ave.
South Pasadena, Calif.
July 25, 1956

[...] Helen, if you were not so far away and if trips were not so expensive, how I would love to see you! I will always love Bar—she was one of the highlights of my life. And you were there, too. I can't think of Bar without thinking of you—hoping, hoping for both of you—oh, if there were only a way to reach her (if she lives) and tell her how we want her back. If I could believe that the publication of her manuscript would be the gesture I'd be all for it. I hope I'm right in what I told you I felt. I still feel it. I still feel that if she comes to know it, she would think: "How could they!" and that I could not bear.

I *wish* I had seen it. If there ever is an opportunity for you to come out, bring it with you. She would not mind your sending it to me.

Helen, would you like Bar's letters to see? I kept everything she ever wrote to me and always thought I'd have them to read—and read again. But I know I'll never be able to do it now. And I cannot bear to destroy them. Would they hurt you too much? I'll send them to you if you say the word. I *must* make decisions like that now. This summer, naturally, has not been very good for me. [...]

2001 Marengo Ave.
South Pasadena, Calif.
Sept. 18, 1956

My dearest Helen:

You must forgive me being so slow in regard to Bar's letters. I had little time to myself all this summer, and after Phoebe and the boys left, a little over a week ago, I have indulged myself in feeling let down (also straightening the house!) I knew too, that I could not let the letters go without glancing over them and that meant a sadness I dreaded.

Well. I had the box out this morning. I picked the enclosed letter out at random and read it through. (I *can* do that, you know, as much as that, though my eyes suffer afterwards.) What a wonderful person she was, I thought. *How* she could write, *how* she describes her own emotions and those of others! I knew at once that you should have this letter, without delay. It may give you a lift to know what she thought of your writing and the delightful way she describes a writer's temperament and the agonies one goes through during the process of creative work.

Almost every line of hers makes you feel this vivid creature she was. She comes alive again, you *see* her.

Ah, Helen, two of the loveliest young girls I have ever known—brilliant, exceptional, creative, promising, beckoning, as it were, to the best things *life* had to offer, how cruelly life has treated them! I mean Bar and Phoebe. Bar sunk without a trace—all her gifts, her brilliant promise gone. Phoebe still rides the waters, stronger perhaps, but with her fairy-like quality and spirit quenched, the poetry in her unable to lift its voice.

I won't go on with this. But it shows you what even a limited sort of excursion into Bar's letters will do to me. Perhaps I should destroy them. But I won't. It is a precious thing to have this sense again of her presence.

Hot weather here. Be thankful you have brisk autumns in New York.

Love ever,
Alice

I wish Alice hadn't destroyed any of Barbara's letters.

2001 Marengo Ave.
South Pasadena, Calif.
Oct. 1, 1956

Dearest Helen:

Here they are—or most of them. A few I destroyed; a very few I kept, just to have *something* of Barbara. I feel as if I were sending away a piece of myself; but you should have them.

I read bits here and there. Her "Lost Island" was early written, was it not? Probably during the time when she was romantic about Anderson. Bar *had* to be romantic, didn't she? That was the root of her characters—it explains so much.

I remember that when discussing Bar's disappearance with Max that he said she may well have got herself into a situation which she did not want to tell anyone in her former life about. As time went on, it would have grown harder and harder to do so. There *was* a streak of hardness in her—"cruelty," as Sabra said—that would have acted as an iron deterrent. I refuse to believe that anyone with so rich and deep a vitality would have ended her own life. Helen, I believe—

let us believe—that she lives somewhere, still enjoying sunsets and mountains and water.

Let me hear that these have reached you safely.

> With love,
> Alice

I agree that Barbara may have felt her marriage was "crucifying her," and also that she was perfectly capable of starting a brand new life alone. (Or did she have an accomplice, sworn to secrecy?) She'd tried it in 1929 and succeeded in 1932. She lived for adventure, and what an adventure it would've been in 1939!

Was Barbara also capable of starting over without letting anyone know she was still alive? By 1956 (contrary to 1949), Alice had come to think so. I agree, but of course it's also what I want to have happened.

2001 Marengo Ave.
South Pasadena, Calif.
Oct. 6, 1956

My dearest Helen:

Your letter brought the tears somehow—and they come hard now. There is so little to say to heal the grief you bear. I know, for I bear my share, too. To handle Bar's letters, to feel her presence again, has brought it all to life. I read more than I thought I could, or should. My eyes suffered, but it was worth it. I have done some intense thinking on the subject. Helen, now these many years after, I tell you it seems to me impossible that anyone with Bar's rich endowments, with her capacity for joy, her delight in new experiences, should have thrown it all away—thrown her very life away—for a man. With all my heart and mind I do not believe she did it. I think she meant to hurt Nick, I think she meant to get away from a situation that was crucifying her, even if it meant cutting herself off from everything and everybody she loved and knew. She had "jumped hurdles" before—I believe that is what she did and she may well have got herself into a situation (Max suggested this once) which it would have humiliated her to reveal, and as time went on, the barrier between her past life and her new might well have grown more impassable. With you I believe we will not now ever see her again; but I think she lives. Marjorie Houser Susie told me once that Bar boasted to her that she could disappear if she wanted to, and never "leave a single trace"; that she'd dye her hair, pull out her eyebrows, completely change her personality, and that she could always take care of herself. Marjorie believes she did just that and still lives, really becoming by now a completely different Barbara.

It is natural for the young to judge what she did more harshly than the old. It is natural for Sabra to feel that Bar deserted her. Well, she did; and I do not belittle the selfishness and cruelty of her act. But I do not think it was because she "lacked the fortitude to face life in its unpleasantness." It was an act of egoism. Bar was a supreme egoist—perhaps it was partly her genius that made her that. She was completely centered in self and blind to the needs of others. I'd seen that, of course, but hoped that with maturity, awareness might develop, awareness that one cannot live to oneself alone. If it did, she cannot know what other factors have intervened.

I must not go on writing like this; but I felt the need of communicating some of my thoughts to you. As you say, time is getting short. Others may forget, bury it all, but you and I, Helen, never will. And let us keep a spark alive that the miracle may some day happen.

I sent her letters to you on October 1st by insured parcel post. I hope they reached you safely. I had expected to send them first class registered; but the gruff postmaster (I told him the package contained letters) said it wasn't sealed tight enough for that! I couldn't walk home and then walk back again and he said it could be insured and sent parcel post if I just wrote "Can be Opened for Inspection" on it. (I wonder if they ever do open anything for inspection!)

    Ever loving and hoping for you,
    Alice

Unfortunately there is nothing to nor from Marjorie Houser Susie at Columbia. She died in 2004.

2001 Marengo Ave.
South Pasadena, Calif.
Oct. 18, 1956

My dearest Helen:

Thank you, but I don't want your stamps. Take them back. Sending Barbara's letters to you was my own project. I know what you mean by waiting for the time and mood. Through all these years I had often looked at the box containing the letters and thought: "No, not now. I can't bear it." It was only the feeling that you have, too, that time is short that finally drove me to it. I tried to put them in order by years, so that if you liked you could begin with the period when you and Bar were struggling together to gain a foot-hold in New York. The time when I heard the least from her was after her marriage to Nick. But I saw her in 1936 (so vivid, so beautiful) and she seemed fond of me in the same old way.

Marjorie Houser (Mrs. Alfred Susie, as you know probably) has been moving around the country quite a bit the last few years. She is now living in Texas (of all places for a N. E. girl!); has four children and I judge leads an active, busy and happy life. Her address is: 1702 Woodlawn Dr, Baytown, Texas. She thinks Bar is still alive, and I believe she was as close a friend as Bar had and certainly knew as much as anyone of those last few weeks. She has your address and has told me that if she ever heard anything of Bar she would let you know immediately. [...]

I hope Alice won't mind that I wanted to continue Barbara's story after the California episode. Her childhood may have ended there (or the year before, I'd say), but her story didn't.

Did Barbara really write to Alice only a few days before disappearing? Barbara's letter of November 4, 1939, is the last one at Columbia (or was—I've been told it's now missing). I hope any later letter(s) weren't among the ones Alice destroyed.

2001 Marengo Ave.
South Pasadena, Calif.
Nov. 2, 1958

Dear, dearest Helen:

Every day since your dear beautiful letter came I have thought I would surely get an answer written—and still, although it has been on my mind and in my heart constantly, it is not written. I am sorry and ashamed, but perhaps you will understand, for there have been many interruptions and I, like you, get "depleted" very easily...

[...] This house holds so many memories. How many times has the image flashed through my mind of Bar, so happy and vivid, as she bounded through the door on the evening of her last visit to me. We planned to have such a wonderful time together, and then, then, the very next day came Nick's brief letter, so final, so cruel; and she said at once that she would return east the next day. Marjorie, who was with her, as you may remember, and I saw her off the next day, subdued and sad, a different girl than the one who had come bounding through my door. I suppose Nick did not know what he was doing. I have tried to tell myself that. I have tried to excuse him. I have found it a little harder to excuse him—although I can understand why he acted as he did—for not immediately reporting Bar's disappearance. Of course the delay meant that all trace of her was lost.... Helen, I am faced, as of course you are, too, with two beliefs that are equally incredible. I could not bring myself at the time, and for years I could not, that anyone full of such vitality and gifts as Bar, who could enjoy life so much, would throw that life away. But, on the other hand, I have found it incredible to believe, just thinking of myself alone, incredible that she would live *anywhere* all these years and never, never send me one word. She wrote to me, you know, up to the last two or three days before she vanished. We had always been in touch. She could always come to me—she knew that. Then, why, *why?* For so long I have refused to believe that that question would never be answered; but I have given up hope now. I think we shall never know.

Of course, the above goes for you and Sabra, too. She did love, she did value Sabra—Sabra must know that. And between you and Bar, although at times she might seem to flout it, there was an unbreakable tie. You must remember it. She really couldn't do without you. Again, then *why?* You told me once that Sabra said there was a cruel streak in Bar. I think she was right, although it was never really deliberate—only the undisciplined impulse or expression of a strong, egotistic nature. Bar was Bar!

Well, all this is pointless, really. Only I go over it so many times in my own mind. I've thought so many, many times that I would someday see Bar at my door again. And I've thought of the joyful wire I would send you.

Those early letters of hers must be exquisite. I long to see such a memorial of her, as they would be, in print. I long to feel that you are strong enough to put them together. "Autobiography of a Young Girl," or perhaps "Of a Child." It would be my feeling that they should stop upon reaching the California episodes. Too much tragedy begins there; too much involvement with others than herself. Her childhood really did end then, and so had the story better end. My heart and mind shrink from what came after. Oh, let it be a happy, peaceful book! All the tragedy we will keep to ourselves.

Have the W.F.s really parted? That makes me a little sad somehow—sad, I suppose, that there should be a little less love, a little less fidelity in the world. Their children must be pretty well grown by now—the older ones, at least, of college age. [...]

These are the last lines of what might be the last letter Alice wrote to Helen. She died five years later, aged 83.

2001 Marengo Ave.
South Pasadena, Calif.
Jan. 19, 1959

[...] Thirty years since the winter you and Bar spent together in this house—can you make it seem possible? If she lives, does she ever think of us? I cannot believe now that she does still live. My dear, how cruel, cruel, it has been for you.

My remembrance—bitter and sweet—and love always,

    Alice

Early in 1960 Helen read an article in the New York Times—Childhood Path of Genius Traced—and saw an opportunity for help with a book she wanted to write about Barbara. After consulting Sabra and Norman Donaldson, she wrote to the article's author, Harold Grier McCurdy (1909-1999), a poet and professor of psychology at the University of North Carolina.

Speaking of Sabra, she also had quite a life. After graduating from Barnard College in 1945 (summa cum laude, Phi Beta Kappa) and earning a master's in modern European history from Columbia University, she taught English for three years in Istanbul before joining Douglass College in New Brunswick, New Jersey, as an assistant professor in history. In 1961 she was the first woman to be admitted by Princeton University as a full-time degree candidate, enrolling in the Oriental Studies graduate program and earning a master's in 1964 and a PhD in 1966. She remained in academia for the rest of her career and died on March 29, 1994.

404 West 116th St., Apt. 21
New York 27, NY
14 March 1960

Dear Professor McCurdy:

Your study of childhood patterns of genius as summarized in the N. Y. Times of Jan. 6, 1960 attracted my attention for a special reason that I think may interest you. To state it simply, I have in my possession what I believe is a case study (possibly a unique one), voluminously documented, that seems to fulfill the high points of your thesis.

This documentation consists of a child's own writings from about the age of four through a ten or twelve year period. Mostly, it is in typewritten form, the child having appropriated the small typewriter at an early age as a useful tool for avid desire to express herself in words.

There is in this collection a vast amount of prose and poetry (fact, fiction, fantasy), whichever mode of expression suited the demands of her ever-expanding imagination. And—what may be of the greatest importance—are the hundred or more personal letters the child wrote to friends (three adults in particular over an extended period of years). These letters were returned at a later date, the recipients believing them to be of documentary value.

If anyone is interested in tracing the development of one child's imagination as it went joyously, restlessly, often discontentedly on its way, a perusal of this child's own writings would reveal some of the hundreds of details that fed and stimulated her questing, creative spirit. There came a moment of satisfaction, I believe, when the child's fancy came to fruition, taking form and pattern in a small book, called "The House Without Windows" published in 1926 by Knopf.

Howard Mumford Jones (Professor Jones was, I believe, at Chapel Hill at the time), in his review of "The House Without Windows" spoke of the author as a child genius. He wrote in part: the book was "the profoundest revelation of a child's fondness for beauty yet in American prose ... a lyric artist. She writes as though she were living in that serene abode where the eternal are ... that is where she lives and where she takes us ..." Professor Jones adds: "The author has never been to school. There seems to be no sane reason why she should ever go to one, unless she wants to."

Whether this child-author would have come under your classification "genius," I don't know. A costly gift, if so, as you pointed out. Whether this young writer should have gone to school is something to ponder about (as you suggest) in terms of gains or losses. But that she had literary talent can hardly be doubted, although one wonders whether it should have been curbed or allowed to run riot. A happy medium, perhaps?

Your article re-awakened my interest in the whole matter of creativity and the child, together, I must admit, with the many current essays on the subject and the complaints of educators against too much "conformity." And I am wondering if a selection of those documents, accompanied by an editorial comment from a competent person in this field of education would be of any help to parents, teachers, and psychologists, would even serve, perhaps, as a warning.

As for myself, I am neither a psychologist nor a teacher. I am a more or less retired writer, who, as a parent has retained a lively interest in today's children and their education. I live in the neighborhood of Columbia University and am accessible to anyone (and with pleasure); and to anyone concerned with the matter referred to, I would add a special welcome.

My gratitude goes to you for any comments you wish to make. If, in your busy life, there is no time for such details—that, also, is understandable.

>Very truly yours,
>Mrs. Helen Follett

McCurdy wrote back saying that he would track down a copy of The House Without Windows, *which he eventually did through an interlibrary loan. He was enthusiastic about it, as he wrote to Helen on May 20, 1960:*

Both my wife and I were fascinated by the book. The style and content are both remarkable. I felt especially the urgent rush of the later sections, where it seemed to me the visionary world had claimed the author for its own. The musical rain of colors is dazzling, the power in Nature and in the girl herself (Eepersip) is more than hypnotic, the conclusion inevitable. The joy is profound. It is only from the human, housekeeping point of view that the story threatens us. For us who are more domestically attached to earthly life, however, it does have its threatening aspects—the flight from all human contact, the absorption in non-human beauty, the ecstasy. We earth-keepers, hearth-keepers, feel loss.

On June 1st, the McCurdy family visited Helen before sailing to Europe for the summer. Afterward he reiterated his enthusiasm for Helen's project to organize Barbara's papers and make notes. He wanted her to send him the material as she worked her way through it, and they were already thinking along the lines of a co-authored book.

Regarding Helen's reference to "two little girls (yours and mine)": Ann, the McCurdys' fourteen-year-old daughter, had died in 1958 following "a brief but dramatic and mysterious illness."

404 West 116th Street, Apt. 21
New York 27, N. Y.
25 Sept. 1960

Dear Professor McCurdy:

I presume you are back now and I can thank you for your kind and thoughtful shipboard letter. And, I hope you're back after the loveliest of summers, the most restful, and the most inspiring, which means that I hope you and your family had a lot of fun in your unplanned wanderings.

My own summer was more exciting than I had anticipated. And that means that I found my roaming about in the beautiful, fantastic, sad and questioning world of a child's imagination an enlightening and often joyous experience.

It has been a difficult and confusing task—the sorting out, the reading and the attempt (not very successful, I'm afraid) to analyze a vast number of writings in terms of a developing personality.

The greater part of this material I had never read. The letters to Mr. Oberg and to Mr. St. John (strangers to each other) were sent to me quite voluntarily, and I simply added them to the collection of Barbara's writings, where they remained until you, yourself, via the N. Y. Times, induced me to take a long look at the entire collection and ponder about it.

So I have much to thank you for, and when I consider your kindness in stopping here with your family on the very evening of your departure, I feel an inexpressible gratitude.

I am planning to send this collection of writings with all my notes (that I found necessary to put down in order to keep straight for my own purpose a few hundred of the details which you, by the way, are very welcome to disregard entirely) in early October.

I do hope with all my heart that, among these writings you and Mrs. McCurdy may be touched now and again, as I have been, by that delicate light of faraway beauty and mystery that two little girls (yours and mine) would, I feel sure, like us to feel and understand.

With kindest regards and with warm feeling for you both.

I won't delve deeply into the back-and-forth between Helen and McCurdy. They discussed whether Helen wanted a dramatic biography or a more limited "psychobiography," to use McCurdy's word. Since Helen was concerned about the privacy of just about all of the characters who would appear in a thorough biography, and was also averse to including "grim details" such as Barbara's breakdown in Tahiti and her detention in California, they settled on the latter.

Not surprisingly, the two major publishers who saw what McCurdy had come up with by late 1964 (Harcourt, Brace & World and Random House/Knopf) rejected it, suggesting that such a book wouldn't appeal to a general audience. Fortunately, in October 1965, the University of North Carolina Press accepted the manuscript—now distilled into a "relatively brief psychological monograph." Moreover, the book would receive top billing as their chief trade book in the spring of 1966. McCurdy and Helen signed the contract as co-authors, splitting royalties 50:50, and review copies were sent out in March.

Barbara: The Unconscious Autobiography of a Child Genius *was published over a quarter century after December 7, 1939. It must have been quite a shock to anyone who remembered the young girl and her books to learn that she had disappeared. As far as I'm aware, Barbara's vanishing was not once mentioned in the media after the Brookline police's 1940 teletype for the missing Barbara Rogers.*

The book received good reviews. In the June 12, 1966 edition of the Hartford Courant Magazine, Paula Clark wrote:

A strange little lyric hybrid, this book is a cross between a biography and a case history [...] The story is told through her own writings—fiction and letters—interlaced with comments by Harold Grier McCurdy, poet and expert on the psychology of personality, in collaboration with Barbara's mother, also a writer [...] Nobody knows what fate finally overtook the lovely girl whose first novel was published when she was 13 years old. But readers interested in personality development and the growth of literary genius will find this sensitive, "unconscious autobiography" most compelling.

Aurora W. Gardner wrote in the June 1, 1966 issue of Library Journal:

[...] This book is a selection of these materials, bound together by a running commentary. Having learned to type at four, the child poured out a stream of fact, fiction and fantasy for the next 10 or 12 years. Unfortunately there will be scant appreciation today for the flight-of-fancy writing at which Barbara was so adept. Her heroine, crowned queen of the fairies high among the mountain snows and then rapt away by butterflies, leaves us cold. What does interest us is the maturing girl adjusting to her father's desertion, to the necessity for self-support, and to her difficult marriage. And since we need Act Five to clarify Act One, her disappearance at the crux of the story is keenly disappointing.

With Barbara back in the news, Robert B. Wyatt of Avon Books (then part of the Hearst Corporation) secured the rights from Knopf to reprint The House Without Windows *as a mass market paperback in 1968. (Priced at 60 cents, copies now fetch at least a hundred times that amount.) Wyatt received a blurb for the book from McCurdy, which concluded with these lines:*

It is a legend for our times even more than for 1927 when it was first published. The magic, the mysticism, the intoxication with color and violence, the loneliness and childishness of it, put it in tune with the psychedelic adventures of today. I often felt as I examined her life that Barbara Follett was the forerunner of many another restless spirit of the present decade. In its way, this book testifies to the same tensions and visions.

The Avon Books edition of The House Without Windows *led to* Barbara *being reprinted as a paperback in 1971 by Ballantine Books. Helen did not live long enough to see it, however. She died in St. Luke's Hospital in New York on April 21, 1970, aged 86.*

And that—unless one counts the two editions of Lost Island *on Amazon and other online retailers, and three pages in Malcolm Forbes'* What Happened to Their Kids: Children of the Rich and Famous *(Simon and Schuster, 1990)—was the last book by or about Barbara.*

Well over half a century after her disappearance, and thanks to the Internet, Barbara's story resurfaced. First came an intriguing series of posts in 2007 by the mysterious JKel on his Astral Aviary *blog. JKel had become enchanted with Barbara after reading* Barbara.

Three years later she received a lot of attention when Paul Collins published Vanishing Act *in the Winter 2010/2011 issue of* Lapham's Quarterly, *and was interviewed about his essay on National Public Radio on December 18, 2010.* Vanishing Act *was republished in* Utne Reader *and in Mariner Books'* Best American Essays *of 2012, kindling the interest of a new generation of readers. I've since heard from many who are working on their own Barbara Newhall Follett projects—books, plays, films, even an opera—and I hope this book will help.*

Sometimes I'm asked what I think happened to Barbara. My mother, perhaps taking her cue from the end of Barbara, *thought that she headed up to the White Mountains and died of hypothermia or was buried by an avalanche, sort of like Eepersip's final act:*

And, when the sun again tinged the sky with colour, a flock of those butterflies, of purple and gold and green, came swooping and alighted on her head in a circle, the largest in front. Others came in myriads and covered her dress with delicate wing-touches. Eepersip held out her arms a moment. A gold-and-black one aligned on each wrist. And then—she rose into the air, and, hovering an instant over a great laurel bush—vanished.

She was a fairy—a wood-nymph. She would be invisible for ever to all mortals, save those few who have minds to believe, eyes to see. To these she is ever present, the spirit of Nature—a sprite of the meadow, a naiad of lakes, a nymph of the woods.

But my mother never read anything by or about Barbara that hadn't been in a book (nor, alas, will she: she died in 2010). She didn't know about the archive at Columbia, and probably wouldn't have wanted to visit it anyway. The printouts I gave her from Astral Aviary left her distraught. She couldn't finish them because it was too painful to think about the loss of her half-sister.

After spending a lot of time absorbing Barbara's words, the idea of her tramping about alone in the White Mountains and dying from hypothermia or an avalanche seems very unlikely to me. Barbara loved and valued life far too much to let a failing marriage want her to end it all, no matter how bitter things may have become. (Having said that, it's a fact that depression is common in the Follett family, although I don't know of anyone who has gone so far as to commit suicide. I can't entirely rule it out for Barbara, however. If depression grabbed her and wouldn't let go, suicide may have felt like the only option.)

If Barbara didn't kill herself, and I really doubt that she did, I think that leaves accidental death, foul play, insanity, or escape as the other possibilities.

Accidental death: An imaginative person could come up with any number of scenarios. Barbara was a very strong and capable woman, and an accidental death doesn't seem particularly likely, but it's of course possible. Wouldn't a body have been found? Maybe one was, somewhere far from Boston's morgue, but there was no way to identify it.

Foul play: "Her husband killed her"—or so I've read on the Internet. I don't for a second think that Nick killed Barbara. I briefly entertained the notion that she died at home by accident or from an overdose of Charlie Dunlap's tranquilizers, and that a panicking Nick disposed of her body to avoid another scandal. But that seems very unlikely to me now.

Again, one could come up with any number of scenarios in which Barbara was murdered by a stranger, perhaps on the night of December 7th, perhaps days, weeks, or months later in a place near Boston or miles away. It's possible, I suppose. Helen mentioned in a letter to the police that her daughter could have been "shanghaied to South America"—kidnapped. In that unlikely event, wouldn't she have found a way to escape?

Insanity: Did Barbara really lose her mind and get locked up in a sanitarium? It seems unlikely.

Escape: Of course, this is the one I keep returning to—the one I want to believe—and the one I think most likely. If I've learned anything about Barbara, it's that she was supremely self-reliant, capable, independent, and unwilling to sacrifice her freedom or her values or her life to please her husband or her family. Her entire life involved escaping from circumstances that had become untenable to her, and it makes complete sense to me that that's what she did in 1939. Once again she "chucked everything" and escaped, this time for good—to where? Squam Lake or Ktaadn? The West Indies? The Teton Range in Wyoming? The Pacific Northwest? Anderson and his sloop? Were Barbara and Anderson shipwrecked and drowned together at sea? Stranded together on a lost island? That would be a good ending.

If she escaped and lived for any length of time, we are left wondering: could Barbara have been so cruel that she never let anyone who loved her know that she lived? I think yes. If you're going to escape properly and start anew, you have to be committed to the cause. It would be best for everyone back home to believe you're dead. That way everyone can get on with their lives.

But surely Barbara knew how much her family and friends loved her? Maybe not, after the lesson her father taught her in 1928. My grandfather wasn't the only Follett to sever ties to his home and family, but he might have been the best at it. Barbara couldn't have asked for a better teacher.

My grandfather left his first daughter in the care of his parents in 1911. He rarely visited them in Attleboro, and as far as I know they never came to New Haven. He deserted Helen and their children in 1928, and if Sabra ever saw her father again, it was when she was very young—no older than six. And in 1947 he abandoned my grandmother and their three children. Here's a letter my mother, then twelve, wrote to him a few months later.

Bradford, Vermont
August 28, 1947

Dear Father,

I wish very much that you would come home as soon as possible. That means soon. I thought that you might be able to help us if no one else can. When a person is in trouble and needs help and the person she appeals to just asks a lot of questions, but doesn't make any effort to help, what is one to do? I don't know, and I don't think anyone else does. I sometimes think that I am on the way to being grown up, but now I just don't know what to do. Someone has to do something for Mother; you are the only person I know of to appeal to. Mother is afraid that she is losing her mind. I don't think so, but she acts not at all like herself sometimes. Especially when the boys aren't nice to her. They yell at her because they don't know what else to do. Then they are afraid and run from her. I am sometimes afraid. I understand a little better what is the trouble. She needs someone to take care of her so she can feel that she is taking care of her children properly. She does not feel that she is now. She thinks that what is partly the trouble with us and with her is that we are not getting enough to eat. At least of the right things. We are eating; lots of bread and spreads. That is about all. Some meat, some apples, some tomatoes. Not enough for growing children's minds and bodies.

We are underclothed. We do not have a good school. Our father is not with us. Growing children and a mother need their father. They can live without him, but something important is missing. They are different; they are not as nice. It would be different if their father were dead. They would be different. I do not like it, and neither does anyone else. Doctors and other prominent people who know know that children need someone besides their mother. I feel it. You should. I don't care for myself. I am young. I am strong. It is for someone else that I am making this appeal. She needs someone. You know that. No one comes. Someone should. Won't you? The boys need you, you are their father, and you are not there, seeing through their difficulty. Why? There is nothing wrong with them except that they need you, why not be there. Give them a feeling of security. I care but I do not need you. I am older. They do. Come.

Jane

Happily, my mother and grandfather kept up a correspondence until his death, but is it any wonder that Follett children may not be convinced that their parents love them, or even want them? It's something my mother struggled with her whole life. She never felt that she measured up to her parents' standards and always believed she was a disappointment. I've struggled with the same beliefs. Barbara was wiser and stronger than I am, but she also had her Follett blood to contend with. I think it likely that she felt her family just didn't care all that much about her—maybe even that they were better off without her—sad as that may sound.

If I'm right and Barbara escaped to start over, I hope that she had a long and happy rest of her life. Perhaps she left behind a sealed envelope—"Not to be opened until fifty years after my death" or some such. Barbara liked puzzles and she left us with a classic. Maybe she buried a clue in the Pine Grove near the Cottage in the Woods or under a rock on her Squam Lake island or on Ktaadn—waiting for another young treasure hunter to find it?

My sincere thanks to you for reading my big book for Barbara. I hope that her life and letters have touched you even remotely as much as they have me. And I hope this book will lead to hers getting back in print, preferably with a companion volume for Lost Island *and* Travels Without a Donkey, *as well as her short stories such as* Rocks *and* Mothballs in the Moon.

Stefan Cooke
Somerville, Massachusetts
August 2015

Made in the USA
Lexington, KY
16 April 2017